REPRESE

The four fundamental forms of sociality structure our relationships. By comparing hundreds of cultures across more than 5,000 years, this book builds on relational models theory to reveal how each of the four basic types of relationship is conceived in their own distinctive cognitive medium. The text demonstrates how people use their food and bodies to foster affiliation, spatial dimensions to form hierarchy, concrete operations of one-to-one matching to create equality, and employ arbitrary, conventional symbols for proportion-based relationships. Originating from the author's ethnographic fieldwork in a West African village, this innovative social theory integrates findings from social, cognitive, and developmental psychology, linguistics and semiotics, anthropology, archeology, art history, religious studies, and ancient texts. The chapters offer compelling insights into readers' everyday social relations by showing what humans think their social relationships actually are.

ALAN PAGE FISKE is a professor in the Department of Anthropology at the University of California, Los Angeles, and known for creating the relational models theory. His notable publications include *Structures of Social Life* (1991), *Virtuous Violence* (2014, with Tage Shakti Rai), and *Kama Muta: Discovering the Connecting Emotion* (2020).

REPRESENTING RELATIONSHIPS

Modes of Cognition and Connection

ALAN PAGE FISKE

University of California

CAMBRIDGE
UNIVERSITY PRESS

CAMBRIDGE
UNIVERSITY PRESS

Shaftesbury Road, Cambridge CB2 8EA, United Kingdom

One Liberty Plaza, 20th Floor, New York, NY 10006, USA

477 Williamstown Road, Port Melbourne, VIC 3207, Australia

314–321, 3rd Floor, Plot 3, Splendor Forum, Jasola District Centre,
New Delhi – 110025, India

103 Penang Road, #05–06/07, Visioncrest Commercial, Singapore 238467

Cambridge University Press is part of Cambridge University Press & Assessment,
a department of the University of Cambridge.

We share the University's mission to contribute to society through the pursuit of
education, learning and research at the highest international levels of excellence.

www.cambridge.org
Information on this title: www.cambridge.org/9781108837729

DOI: 10.1017/9781108942645

When citing this work, please include a reference to the DOI 10.1017/9781108942645

First published 2026

Cover image: trendmakers/DigitalVision Vectors/Getty Images

A catalogue record for this publication is available from the British Library

A Cataloging-in-Publication data record for this book is available from the Library of Congress

ISBN 978-1-108-83772-9 Hardback
ISBN 978-1-108-93162-5 Paperback

For my mom, my dad, Susan, Gwendolyn, Colin, Zoé, Kai, Wyatt, Benjamin, Elliott, Kathy, and Siri.

All that is social consists of representations and consequently it is a product of representations.

Durkheim 1897: 69

To explain culture is to answer the following question: why are some representations more successful in a human population, more contagious, more "catching" than others?

Sperber 1985: 74

A psychology without mental representations is no more possible than a physics without masses and energies. Thus, from the standpoint of a cognitivist, psychology is the science of mental representations. The essential questions in psychology are: What representations does the mind compute? From what data does it compute them? How does it compute them? How does a given representation get translated into observable behavior?

Gallistel 2001: 9692

The most important explanatory posit today in cognitive research is the concept of representation. ... there has been no single theoretical construct that has played such a central role in the scientific disciplines of cognitive psychology, social psychology, linguistics, artificial intelligence, and the cognitive neurosciences.

Ramsey 2007: xi

We are trying to probe what underlies ... cultural construction, what makes cultures get off the ground so to speak-what makes them learnable, and what provides the framework within which the cultural can do its work. The positive reward for speculating about common human potentialities is that we may understand much better what generates the diversity itself.

Levinson 2006: 55

Contents

Acknowledgments

This book's taproot was my participant observation in a small Moosé (pronounced **MOH**-say) village in Burkina Faso (at the time, La Haute Volta – Upper Volta) from 1979 to 1982, doing research for my PhD. I am extremely grateful to the Moosé for their hospitality, tolerance, and friendship. They did not know what "research" was, let alone a "university" or a "dissertation," so they had no idea what my wife and I were up to. Nonetheless, they not only tolerated our research, they were uniformly patient and kind to us, and wonderfully caring with our baby daughter.

I also appreciate the perceptive feedback I have received when giving talks based on earlier versions of these ideas: I presented preliminary versions of these ideas at the Philadelphia Anthropological Society in 1988; a symposium on Methods in Psychological Anthropology, sponsored by the Society for Psychological Anthropology at the 1988 meetings of the American Anthropological Association, Phoenix; the Sloan Cognitive Science Seminar at the University of Pennsylvania in 1989; the Social Psychology Brown Bag of the University of Massachusetts at Amherst in 1989; the Michigan Conference on Culture and Cognition in 1991; the UCLA Developmental Forum in 1997; a Cotsen Institute of Archeology Pizza Talk at UCLA in 2003; the UCLA Close Relationships Interest Group in 2003; Harvard Psychology and Rebecca Saxe's lab at MIT in 2021. As I've lectured and taught seminars since 1997 about these phenomena and ideas in my undergraduate and graduate psychological anthropology courses at UCLA, innumerable students have raised insightful questions that have deepened my own understanding.

The Commissioning Editor for Cambridge University Press, Emily Watton, kindly got me in the door, and found two excellent reviewers who made invaluable comments and recommendations. Thank you for making this book possible, Emily and the two wise reviewers. I am really grateful to Helen B. Cooper for copyediting the manuscript with precision, patience, and perspicacity. With care and alacrity, Laura Simmons, the Content Manager for the book, shepherded the manuscript into and through production. Thank you for that. Many others behind the scenes at Cambridge University Press have capably contributed to making this book a reality, for which I am grateful.

Some of the time I initially devoted to thinking and reading about all this was supported by National Institute of Mental Health (NIMH) grant MH43857, which I am grateful for.

Many people have provided invaluable intellectual help along the way. I am indebted to Michael Sean Smith for persistent, insightful searches in the ethnographic literature, and Cathy Lee for energetic and intelligent pilot work with diverse informants around UCLA. I thank Henning Brinckman for recommending and Lotte Thomsen for translating several Danish sources on land distribution. Nick Haslam, Roy D'Andrade, Barbara Fiske, Kevin Haley, Lotte Thomsen, Sam Cumming, and Denis Tatone carefully read early or partial drafts of the manuscript and made many helpful suggestions. Thomas Schubert read the nearly final draft and made extraordinarily incisive and valuable comments. Kathryn Mason was my wife and my coresearcher in Burkina Faso; my heartfelt thanks to her. I am extremely grateful for all this help.

PART I

Modes of Minding Social Action: Bodily Indices of Unity, Dimensional Icons of Rank, Concrete Matching Operations of Equality, Arbitrary Symbols of Proportions

CHAPTER 1

Meaning to Relate

In Burkina Faso, West Africa, I am going to meet the chief of a Moosé village, seeking permission to live and do participant observation in his village. Knowing that I should accord him a large area of personal space, I stop about thirty feet away. Then I *kudi kantιsse*: I prostrate myself, forehead against the dusty earth, my arms on the ground in front of me with my forearms rising and falling together. Only men show deference this way; women crouch on their knees, head down and arms folded against their torso, making themselves as small as possible, while speaking in a quiet, extremely high-pitched voice which evidently acknowledges their "smallness" and "weakness" vis-à-vis the chief.

The chief, wearing a conical hat, sits up on a hassock, looking down at me; he verbally acknowledges my greeting. Remaining prone throughout, I try to explain who I am and request his permission to do research on social relations for my PhD. To be formally and fully respectful, and because I do not yet speak Mooré very well, I speak to my temporary assistant in French, who corrects and improves what I said and says it in Mooré to the chief. When the chief speaks to me, he actually addresses my assistant in Mooré, who translates to French when he tells me what the chief said. The chief is courteous and wishes to accommodate me, though he is not familiar with the concepts of research or university.

I have been told by my assistant that I must scrupulously follow the proper temporal sequence of paying my respects to the authorities. So, when I came to the village once before this and found that the chief was absent, I understood that no one else in the village would speak with me until I met the chief. And now, as soon as the chief and I have exchanged formal greetings, he indeed checks to confirm that, before coming to greet him, I have already been to greet the paramount chief. Likewise, when I had gone to visit the paramount chief, his first question had been whether I had already paid my respects to the subregional administrator; he will only receive my visit when I tell him that I have done so. Before going to pay my respects to the subregional administrator, of course I had made a formal visit to the regional administrator, seeking his permission to work here. And, before that, I had sought the permission of his superiors at the Ministry of the Interior. I absolutely had to observe the correct temporal order of precedence, thereby acknowledging the hierarchy of authority.

Once we had paid our respects to the village chief we next went to the religious leader of the village, who belongs to the same ethnic subgroup as my assistant. The next several times we returned to the village, we also went to see the chief before doing anything else. My assistant took great pains to ensure that we observed this rule, even when it meant him postponing greeting personal friends and members of his own clan.

Over the following months, on ritual occasions where a chief appears, I hear drummers loudly beat out that chief's praise proverbs, using the tones and cadence of the drums to reproduce the verbal declaration of their "war names," such as "hippopotamus" and "elephant." Metaphorically, chiefs are huge and powerful animals. Consonant with this, when villagers speak of their relationship to a chief or a village elder, they say *Eb yiida maam*, "They exceed me, they are greater than I" – always speaking of higher-ranking persons in the plural. And to respect a chief or village elder, others refer to him as *taorendamba*, "in-front people, leaders," and refer to themselves as *porendamba*, "behind people, followers." People also speak of a chief or village elder as *paeseramba*, "the strong ones." On ceremonial occasions the chief and others of his clan also differentiate themselves with a light–dark contrast: they wear white robes, while others wear robes heavily dyed with indigo to a dark blue.

Do you see what is going on here? All of these practices make sense if we recognize that they are based on an underlying representation of relative ranks as relative positions on dimensions and magnitudes.

Some features of these practices, such as the tonal drum beating to imitate speech, are more or less unique to the region. Yet there are obviously deep resonances between these twentieth-century West African practices and the practices and speech of innumerable other societies. In this book I show that, around the world and throughout history, people tend to represent hierarchical social relationships as BIGGER–SMALLER, MORE NUMEROUS–FEWER, PLURAL–SINGULAR pronouns of address and reference, ABOVE–BELOW, TEMPORALLY PRECEDING–FOLLOWING, IN FRONT–BEHIND, MORE FORCE ("POWER," STRENGTH) – LESS FORCE, LOUDER–QUIETER, and BRIGHTER–DARKER. That is, people represent social ranks as relative positions on physical dimensions.

A great number of studies of infants' core knowledge of physics show that when preverbal infants watch events, they look longer at unexpected events than they look at events that are consistent with their intuitive expectations. So infant researchers use relative looking time to assess what infants intuitively expect, versus what surprises them (Margoni, Surian, & Baillargeon 2024). Nine-month-old American infants presumably have never seen a person prostrate themself in deference, and have never encountered a situation where, on a narrow path, one person had to step aside to let the other pass first. But already they have expectations about such interactions. Consider what happens when infants watch animations of two blocks with simple faces. When the larger block prostrates itself in front of the smaller block, and then moves out of the way, ceding precedence to the smaller one, infants continue to look at the scene for a while. They look at this scene longer than when the smaller block prostrates itself and moves out of the way to let the larger one go first (Thomsen et al. 2011).

This shows that infants who have never seen interactions of this sort expect that BIGGER, ABOVE, and TEMPORALLY PRECEDING should go together in social interactions. Why would they expect that? We can presume that the infants in this study had never seen anyone bow to someone, and few (if any) of them had seen two persons attempt and fail to pass each other on any sort of path. The only explanation that makes sense of their evident expectations is that these infants perceive all three of these dimensions as representations of social rank. That is, American infants understand how to show respect for social rank in the ways that deference is performed in West Africa – and, with variations, performed everywhere else. Infants don't start with a blank slate for enacting social hierarchy; they don't have to learn from scratch, by observation, reward, or punishment. They are born with core knowledge of these fundamental modes of showing deference and authority that all cultures use (Thomsen & Carey 2013).[1]

Of course, this is not to say that any culture uses only dimensions to represent social hierarchy. Prostrate in front of a Moosé chief, the complete *kudi kantııse* postural-gestural greeting includes repeatedly raising and lowering one's forearms. The verbal greeting to a chief, whether one is prostrate or not, is *Y ziig be neere*, "May your place be beautiful." Most

[1] In fact, Lotte Thomsen designed this study specifically to test the theory (originally set out in Fiske 1991, 1992, 2004) that infants have innate core knowledge of the fundamental types of social relations, together with core knowledge of the distinctive manner by which people characteristically represent each type of relationship. Many subsequent studies, reviewed in later chapters, have confirmed this for the three types of social relationship that infant researchers have investigated so far.

Moosé live in round houses; only the chief may build a rectangular house, and only the chief may place ostrich eggs at the corners of his roof. These are culture-specific representations of a chief's status that have nothing to do with dimensions or magnitudes (so far as I know). Every culture has its own particular ancillary means to represent hierarchy; infants and ethnographers must learn those ancillary codes by building on the innate, core, universal representations of rank as relative positions on physical dimensions.

This book is devoted to exploring the representations of social relations evident in ethnographies, historical accounts and religious texts, art history, archeology, and linguistic typology of lexemes. It begins with a fairly condensed account of the systems of representation of social relationships in the lives of the Moosé villagers with whom I lived for two years. Then we proceed to ethnological comparison across hundreds of cultures, where we will see that each of the four fundamental types of social relations consistently operates in its own specific mode of representation. We will see these patterns in Sumerian epics, the archeology of complex societies, art history, the etymologies of Chinese characters, modern English, Proto-Indo-European lexical roots, contemporary and past architecture, and many other domains of social life. We will consider some corresponding patterns of representation in animal behavior, suggesting phylogenetic roots for the modes of representation of at least two of the fundamental types of social relations.

The Fundamental Forms of Social Relationships

The core thesis of this book is that people use a distinctive mode of representation for each of the four fundamental forms of social relationships. So, the first thing to do is to explain what the fundamental types of social relationships are. I use the term "relationship" in a broad but conceptually precise sense to mean coordination in which each person's actions complement the others' actions; by "action" here I mean to include emotions, motivation, commitment, and moral sentiments. In a social relationship the actions of each participant do not "make sense" in isolation, but fit together to compose a dynamically emergent structure. This definition of "relationship" is meant to encompass not only personal and enduring interactions, but also anonymous and one-time interactions, as well as structured interactions between people who do not feel "close" to each other.

What kinds of social relationships does one find in every culture? What are the basic building blocks with which people construct a society? My research and my relational models theory, which built on that research, followed by the work of hundreds of other scholars, has established that people use four fundamental relational models for nearly all social coordination. The relational models are communal sharing, authority ranking, equality matching, and market pricing.

The first relational model, communal sharing, is a relation in which two or more people feel that they are the same – equivalent – in some essential respect. They may share property, share responsibility, share a common task or goal; they may pool their labor or seek to make a decision on the basis of consensus. Communal sharing relationships motivate kindness and compassion based on mutual identification. The second model, authority ranking, is a hierarchical relation of inequality. Superiors are entitled to deference, respect, and sometimes obedience from their subordinates, and, by virtue of their superior rank, are responsible for providing leadership, wisdom, guidance, and protection. Authority ranking is not interaction based on pure power or force; rather, participants perceive the relationship as natural, legitimate, and morally necessary. The third model, equality matching, is a relation of being separate and distinct, but equal. Equal, but not equivalent: each person is distinct and their portions are distinct, but their portions correspond one-to-one with each other person's portions. Likewise, when equality matching governs responsibilities, each person's responsibilities are distinct, and are connected to that specific person, but their responsibilities match the other person's responsibilities: they are even, one-to-one. For example, participants may receive even shares, or make evenly balanced contributions, or reciprocate in kind, tit-for-tat. Turn-taking is equality matching when turns are evenly balanced so they truly match, or the difference incurs a debt or credit. Merely alternating, as in speaking in a conversation, is not equality matching. In the dynamics of equality matching the participants may not always be even, but the imbalances are supposed to be temporary: they know whose turn it is or who needs to make a matching return gift to even things out. The fourth relational model is market pricing, in which participants coordinate with reference to socially meaningful proportions, ratios, or rates, such as prices, wages, rents, interest rates, cost–benefit analyses, points in a course-grading scheme, or moral standards of rewards and penalties justly proportional to what each person does. Another example of market pricing is a university granting faculty a year's sabbatical after every seven years of teaching. None of the four models inherently involves selfishness, utility maximizing, competitiveness, or individualistic orientation. That is important to keep in mind; market pricing need not involve selfishness, utility maximizing, competitiveness, or interactions among individuals. Market pricing is decidedly different from interaction among the "rational actors" posited by economics.

Every domain of sociality can be organized by one relational model or a series of them in sequence. People build complex practices and institutions by assembling multiple relational models to coordinate the myriad aspects of that social system. People use them singly or in combination to coordinate work, consumption, material transactions, the use of land and objects (on all of these, see Fiske 1991), violence (Fiske & Rai 2014), and morality (Rai & Fiske 2011). Each relational model can generate social identities and be the basis for the formation of groups. Those are the four fundamental structures through which people generate, understand, motivate, and morally evaluate most social relations.

I posit that relational models are innate (Fiske 1991: 199, 400–407; 2000, 2004a). Reviewing the literature, Lotte Thomsen and Susan Carey (2013) and Ashley Thomas (2024) show that preverbal infants have core knowledge of communal sharing, authority ranking, and equality matching. (Researchers have not yet designed studies to find out whether preverbal infants know market pricing.) Infants recognize, understand, and respond to the social interactions they observe.

Hundreds of experiments, scores of interpretive analyses, and a number of theoretical advances have established the plausibility and explanatory power of relational models theory (Haslam 2004). Furthermore, it is pretty much the only recent comprehensive theory of human sociality, and certainly the only one that fully integrates innate, developmental, cultural, cognitive, emotional, motivational, and moral aspects of social relations, as well as explaining most punishment and most violence.

What was not yet established before the present book is the mode of representation distinctive to each model: the mode in which it is encoded in the mind, communicated, and by which it constitutes emotion-imbued, motivated, and morally evaluated social relationships. That's what this book is about. I show that each relational model has a distinctive mode of representation that is universally intuitive and especially evocative of the emotions, motives, and moral sentiments supporting that specific type of relationship. Moreover, I argue that social relationships are not just products of these mode-specific, directive representations. Social relationships exist only by virtue of their affect-imbued representations – that is, by virtue of their "conformations," a concept I introduce in a few pages.

Consider the example we began with. Imagine that I am prostrate in the dirt in front of the chief because I'm observing an intriguing small beetle. In this hypothetical event, I'm not flat on the ground in order to be BELOW the chief; although in purely spatial coordinates, I am lower than the chief. But my intention in lying there is not guided by any mental representation of him as ABOVE me. In such a case, lying there is not a social relational act because it is not meant to modulate any relationship between us. Conversely, even when I intend to affirm my subordination by prostrating, if the chief knows that I'm enthralled by beetles and interprets my position on the ground as intended to enable me to closely observe a beetle, then from his perspective, too, my position is not constitutive or communicative of a social relationship between us. For the chief to perceive my position as a social relational act, he has to infer that I have taken my position as a vertical spatial representation and affirmation of our authority ranking relationship. If he infers that I am acting with reference to such a representation, thereby showing deferential respect to him, he perceives us to be engaged in a social relationship. And only in that case.

Likewise, suppose that the chief, not expecting any visitors, is seated on his hassock purely in order to rest his sore knee, which hurts when he sits cross-legged on the ground. Since he has not adopted his seat to accord with a representation of his social rank, he is not engaged in an intentionally social relational act. A social relationship exists only when a person acts with reference to a representation of a social relationship. So, if I recognize that the chief is seated up there purely to rest his knee, I do not perceive him to be asserting, by being above me, his "superior" position in an authority ranking relationship with me. (It would be wise, nevertheless, for me to act as if the chief were asserting his rank, in case I am wrong about his intention, and to demonstrate my deference even when it is not strictly necessary for me to do so.)

When interacting, people act with reference to a representation of the social relationship, and are motivated by that representation, but typically without noticing that they are doing so. For the most part, people use implicit representations of their social relationships without reflective awareness of the underlying cognitive or affective processes. That obliviousness is analogous to the fact that when people are speaking they rarely (if ever) stop to note that they are using the present perfect progressive aspect. Indeed, few speakers have an explicit representation of the present perfect progressive aspect; their implicit procedural representation of it can only be inferred from their speech. More or less the same thing is true of many representations of social relations.

When a set of persons' actions and thoughts about their actions, along with their motives, emotions, and moral sentiments, are organized by a representation of their relationship, that social relationship exists for them, whether or not they consciously reflect on the matter. In the absence of such a representation with its affective aspects, there is no social relationship.

Coordination with Generativity Requires a Shared Template, and Common Knowledge of Participants' Commitment to that Template

Scholars have extensively studied "cooperation," greatly illuminating what was once a major puzzle of evolution and a mystery for economic theory. The formal analyses of cooperation in economic games have elegantly demonstrated the conditions under which cooperation can be adaptive-rational for a selfish actor aiming to maximize fitness or some other utility. That is a huge (and ongoing) scientific advance. This book considers a new explanation of cooperation, while focusing on another aspect of human sociality: coordination.

Humans coordinate innumerable activities, in innumerable ways. Among nonhuman animals there is far, far less frequent coordination; coordination of far, far fewer activities; and relatively little coordination among nonkin. Furthermore, human coordination is extraordinarily generative. Encountering or inventing a promising new possibility, humans quickly come up with ways to coordinate effectively. Like everyone else, we scientists are so used to social coordination, so engaged and embedded in coordination, we take it for granted. But how do we do it?

Coordination does not just arise automatically whenever animals or artificial agents encounter a situation where their respective actions affect each other. Anarchy is the default – and, indeed, the only – possibility for most animals: they do not coordinate much beyond obeying the laws of physics so as not to occupy the same space at the same time. For the most part, nonhuman animals coordinate with conspecifics about as much, and in about the same ways, as they "coordinate" with rocks and trees.

Imagine a set of humans – say, six of them. Suppose that they all have some vague, inchoate idea that there are tasks they can accomplish better together than they could separately, as well as tasks that they can only accomplish by acting in concert. But they do not have any definite idea of what "acting in concert" would mean. What they implicitly imagine is that acting in concert would consist of "coordination," such that all of their actions would somehow "fit together," enabling something to be done, or done better (in some sense or another) than if each person acted without regard for what each other person did, and without regard to what each other person was intending to do next. And they know there are some worthwhile tasks that no person can do alone, such as carry a heavy canoe, but that a larger set of people can readily do, if they coordinate appropriately.

Without language, it would seem that the six have no hope at all of devising a coordination scheme; so, let us suppose they do have a human language. Even with language, though, it seems that their problem of coming up with a coordination scheme is insuperable. First, because there are an infinitude of possible coordination schemes, they cannot possibly consider them all. It is also insuperable because they have to find ways of specifying what counts as an "action" of each relevant kind, for the purpose of coordinating. And they have to specify how each person's actions are congruent with, and contingent on, other persons' actions. Can they come to any agreement on the coordination scheme they will use, and, if so, how much time and energy will go into the joint decision process? Will there be any time or energy left over to actually do the task? After discussing options, will they all feel well disposed to cooperate, and, indeed, committed to doing so? Or, in the discussion, will they have offended or threatened each other, creating anger, ill-disposition, and distrust toward one other? Once they start to try to coordinate, a scheme that seemed good in prospect may not feel acceptable to all in practice. Moreover, whatever coordination scheme they come up with, surely it will soon fail, breaking down into confusion and anarchic chaos, because all six of them will not have quite the same understandings of the scheme. To coordinate effectively, efficiently, reliably, amicably, and to everyone's satisfaction, the six persons have to have precise common knowledge of the coordination scheme. They must all have the same understanding of the scheme. How could they possibly achieve that?

Getting everyone on the same page, with common knowledge that they are all on the same page, is necessary, but it is not sufficient. Beyond the difficulty of aligning participants' dispassionate cognitive representations, there is the difficulty of aligning their affective engagement. To amicably sustain a coordination scheme, to fully engage participants for the duration of the activity, and for the coordinated activity to be satisfying and meaningful, the respective participants' emotions, motives, and moral sentiments must be congruent with the affects of the other participants: either isomorphic, or suitably complementary. That is to say, coordination depends on affective commitment, with common knowledge of everyone's commitment, together with common sentiment that everyone ought to be committed, and ought to judge that others ought to be committed. Of the infinite number of conceivable coordination schemes, how many have intrinsic commitment "glue" to bind them?

There are four. Four coordination schemes have that necessary intrinsic affective glue, such that participants make trustworthy commitments. Those four coordination schemes are evolved adaptations whose specific functions are to afford smooth, reliable coordination. They are intuitively known to all neurotypical humans, and humans have common knowledge of them. They are the four fundamental relational models: communal sharing, authority ranking, equality matching, and market pricing. Everyone knows all four, and, with the exception of highly psychopathic persons and a few others, everyone has the requisite emotions, motives, and moral sentiments that support each of the four. For a moment, let's call having the requisite emotions, motives, and moral sentiments "feeling the relational model." Everyone knows and feels the four relational models. Everyone_1 knows that everyone_2 knows and feels them, and feels that it is natural, right, and necessary that everyone_2 know and feel them. And everyone_1 knows and feels that everyone_2 knows and feels that everyone_3 knows and feels the four relational models, and feels that it is natural, right, and necessary that everyone_3 know and feel them and feel that it is natural, right, and necessary that everyone_4 know and feel that it is natural, right, and necessary that everyone_5 know and feel all four relational models and that everyone feel that it is natural, right, and necessary that everyone_5 know and feel them ... More concisely, there is common knowledge of all four relational models, along with common feeling of the relational models. For example, I would be horrified to discover someone who did not feel that everyone should feel that everyone should feel that that it is morally wrong to kidnap and torture people for amusement. In other words, I feel that it is wrong to be tolerant of people who are tolerant of people who are tolerant of others' kidnapping and torturing for amusement. Surely everyone agrees about that.

In sum the four fundamental relational models make social coordination possible – in any domain of human activity. To do something jointly, people do not have to devise and agree upon a coordination scheme, ad hoc. Simply "choosing" any one of the four, people can readily coordinate any aspect of any interaction – they are exceptionally good ways of coordinating. The four relational models have the same respective structures as the four fundamental types of measurement, and the qualities that make these structures uniquely suited to measurement also make them uniquely suited to social coordination (Fiske 1991: 229–230). They provide the structure essential to social coordination, with just the right degree of flexibility. There are no other coordination structures as good as these four. Which is surely why the capacities to use them evolved: capacities to use them generatively to create culturally informed, task-specific cooperation schemas anywhere they are beneficial.

Going beyond the Concept of "Representation": Introducing Conformation Systems

As sampled in the epigraphs, the concept of "representation" – or, rather, the set of intersecting, theoretically evolving constructs sharing that name – has been central to the social and cognitive sciences, as well as to the philosophy of mind. The prototypical concept of "representation" designates something that refers: something in the mind, or presented to the senses, to "stand for" some pre-existing entity. The typical usage of the term takes for granted that whatever is represented exists prior to its representation and regardless of whether or not it is represented. Of course, scholars acknowledge that a person can mentally or tangibly represent a hypothetical, or even represent the idea of something that could not exist. But in those cases, too, "representation" connotes something passive and inert with respect to the represented entity. This book is about "representations" that do not merely refer to social relations that exist apart from their representation, but representations that generate, inform, and guide social relations, while motivating them and serving as moral standards.

That is, the "representations" of social relations that concern us are ontologically crucial to the social relations. To reiterate: a "relationship" exists only when the parties to a social relationship are acting, understanding each other, judging, having emotions, being committed, and being motivated by their shared "representation" of and for their social relationship. That is, an essential function of these "representations" is to catalyze the coordination of action, affect, and judgment.

So, notwithstanding all the aggravations entailed by coining a term, I must do so. I regret having to impose on you, the reader, the burden of learning a novel lexeme, but as you read on, it will free you of the various confusing preconceptions you would invariably have if I were to continue to use the term "representation." A new scientific construct needs a new name. So here we have it: this book concerns conformation systems. My collaborators and I published earlier versions of conformation systems theory in several works, especially Fiske 1991, Fiske and Haslam 1998, Fiske 2004, and Fiske and Schubert 2012. This book further develops the theory, and more rigorously specifies it. Here you will also find quite a number of prevalent phenomena that the theory encompasses, but had not previously been recognized. And here you will find more than a thousand new descriptions of conformation practices, around the world and deep into history. Consideration of these practices fills out the theory, and in some cases reshapes it a bit.

A conformation system of a relational model has at least seven tightly integrated facets:

- The conformation system of a relational model is the primary mode[2] of constructing social relationships, including their creation, modulation, resistance, transformation, and termination. "Primary" mode means the mode that is most culturally and historically widespread, and that is most emotionally, motivationally, and morally efficacious. A crucial aspect of this is that the conformation system of a social relationship is the standard for what the relationship should be: it is the template that guides the joint generation of the relationship, and its ongoing evaluation. So, it is the basis for morally judging social relationships. It also functions as a potential goal: a person or set of persons may aim to form a relationship corresponding to the conformation system.

  For example, the Moosé lower themselves BELOW the chief on ceremonial occasions, visitors to the village come to pay their respects to him BEFORE anyone else, and so forth. Observing proper precedence is obligatory – it is what one should do. Paying respects to someone else before paying respects to the chief is an offense, an insult, a challenge to the chief's authority, and potentially an act of resistance to and rejection of that authority.
- Inseparable from the first facet, the conformation system of a relational model is the mode of affirming and committing to that type of relationship. A conformation is an unmistakable declaration of engagement in the relationship, an acknowledgment of the moral responsibilities the relationship entails. In the medium of language, it can be a promise, a pledge, a vow. One symbolic example in the modern world

[2] For a long time I mulled over whether to use "means," "medium," or "manner" for this. I finally chose "mode," but the other words would have been about equally apt.

is signing articles of incorporation, bringing into effect a charter that forms the constitution of an organization.

- The conformation system of a relational model is the preponderant mode of communication about that type of social relationship. This includes the social relationship's depiction in "art" (in the broadest sense); architecture, furniture, fabrics, accoutrements, and other artifacts; speech; gesture, action, and other sorts of nonverbal communication; myth and all sorts of narrative; puppetry and animation; and other signal systems such as, for example, lighting, sounds, spatial arrangements of persons. The conformation system of a type of social relationship is the mode of communication or display that is most readily produced, most readily understood and remembered, most proper, and most impactful.

  To illustrate: A Moosé person says that the chief "exceeds" him, and addresses the chief and refers to him with plural pronouns. They say of an elder, he "precedes me, came first."

  These first two facets of conformation systems, their function in constituting and communicating the relational model, are the two facets that are most patently manifest to observers, so they are the facets that this book most often considers.

- Additionally, I posit that the conformation system of a relational model is the predominant mode of mental models of perceived, remembered, desired, aversive, planned, and imagined social relationships, including types of social relationship that a person or person judges to be bad and wishes to avoid or suppress. "Predominant" means operating early in life and throughout ontogeny, and most frequently used within and across persons, cultures, and contexts. If people in a great many cultures and across millennia, including contemporary preverbal infants in the West, intuitively understand and commonly use a particular mode of representation for constructing and communicating a relational model, the most plausible explanation is that they are using that mode of mentally representing it.

  For example, the thesis is that Moosé think of their relationship to a chief as relative positions on physical magnitudes and dimensions such as ABOVE versus BELOW, PRECEDING versus FOLLOWING, IN FRONT versus BEHIND, STRONGER FORCE versus WEAKER force, and so on.

- Given the first four facets, a fifth emerges: The conformation system of a relational model is the mode through which infants and children discover their community's implementations of the relational model and, simultaneously, that conformation system is infants' and children's "blueprint" for initiating social relationships they want to form. Likewise, the conformation system is the principal bridge for adult immigrants, anthropological participant observers, and other newcomers to join the social relations of communities they come to. It is how we recognize what is going on in a culture we are not yet familiar with.

The infant and toddler, the spouse marrying in, and the ethnographer all intuitively and clearly recognize the authority ranking relations in the village by attending to villagers making themselves low and small when they greet the chief, by attending to statements that the chief "exceeds" the speaker, by the use of plural pronouns to address and refer to the chief, and so on. These signs of the relationship are intuitively clear to newcomers because they too mentally and communicatively represent authority ranking, and constitute and commit to authority ranking, by relative positions on dimensions.

- By the same token, I posit that the conformation system of a relational model is the proximate mode of cultural reproduction of, diffusion of, transformation of, or resistance to the community's present implementations of the relational model. This follows from the conformation system being the mode for children's discovery of how the relational model is implemented in their community.

  Authority ranking structures are sustained in the village by children's and in-marrying spouses' recognition and imitative reproduction of villagers' use of physical dimensions to construct and communicate village hierarchies. For example, observing his mother bringing food to the lineage head before she eats, then observing the lineage head toss a bit of food on the ground for the ancestors before he starts to eat, the toddler sees who ranks "above" whom. Then, in play and in his initial, minimal participation in social relations, the toddler enacts her own social relations with reference to the dimensions that she has observed.
- Conformations are emotionally evocative and motivating, at least to some degree. Moreover, people judge their own and others' actions by comparing them with the relevant conformations; this comparison produces "positive" or "negative" moral sentiments and judgments. The emotions, motives, and moral sentiments that conformations evoke are essential to sustaining and regulating social relationships. Dispassionate cognition is not enough (Fiske 2002, 2010).

  A person hoping to be named chief of the village is motivated, in part, by his desire to be the one whom visitors greet before they greet anyone else. And when a visitor comes first to the chief and prostrates

> before the chief, the chief feels "pride" in the honor he is being accorded. Furthermore, observing proper precedence is obligatory – it is what one should do. Paying respects to someone else before paying respects to the chief is an offense, an insult, a challenge to the chief's authority, and potentially an act of resistance to and rejection of that authority.

In all, the conformation system of a relational model is the predominant, intuitive mode of creating, affirming, and modulating that relational model. Furthermore, the conformation system of a relational model is the means through which even preverbal infants recognize the relational model that people are engaged in and committed to.

To illustrate what a conformation system is, consider the proposition that people around the world cognize social ranks as relative positions on the vertical dimension – that is, as being ABOVE versus BELOW. Concordantly, people use postures, architecture, and depictions of ABOVE versus BELOW to construct hierarchical relations: for example, by prostrating themselves in front of a chief, or by constructing organizational diagrams that place high-ranking persons higher on the page than their subordinates. Visitors to the headquarters of an organization find that personnel have offices on different floors, indicative of their ranks. Infants and toddlers discover people's social ranks by observing their postures and positions: for example, in Myanmar, by seeing school children crouch as they pass by their teacher. And when children and immigrants observe, learn from, and imitate these practices, they thereby reproduce the existing social hierarchies. Or they could resist the hierarchy by refusing to crouch as they pass in front of their teachers.

Keep in mind that conformations concern social relations, not traits of persons. In a given context person B may be BELOW A, but inferiority is not thereby a property of individual B, who, though BELOW A, may be ABOVE C (Fiske & Haslam 1996). Indeed, B may be BELOW A in certain contexts, but ABOVE A on other occasions where they relate according to distinct authority ranking hierarchies. For example, an undergraduate who is a terrific soccer player may be the coach of a team whose players include graduate students and postdocs.

The conformation system of a relational model is the mode of constituting, communicating, and mentally encoding that relational model. For example, physical dimensions are the conformation system of authority ranking. A conformation is a specific instance of a conformation system. My prostrating myself in front of the chief was a conformation. Another conformation was the chief tossing a bit of food on the ground for his ancestors, before beginning to eat a meal. Another conformation, I presume, was the villagers' thinking of the chief as temporally preceding them.

Concomitant with this usage, I adopt "conform" as the verb denoting what a conformation does. So I would say that my prostrating in front of the chief conforms his rank relative to mine: it communicates this ranking, it meets my moral obligation to respect him, and it commits me to deference, while more or less motivating deference and tending to evoke relationship-sustaining emotions such as "awe." By virtue of all that, my prostration to the chief on his hassock partially constitutes our authority ranking relationship.

In conjunction with mental models and communications as such, many kinds of material things conform social relationships. A gigantic statue of the Buddha displays, resonates with, reifies, and reinforces the mental and communicative conformation of "superiority" as "great size" and "above." Currency is an integral component of the symbolic conformation of the most prominent implementation of market pricing. Cardboard ballots used in voting reify and therefore conform equality matching in that practice. When taken seriously as kin, totems and mascots are material conformations of communal sharing.

To sum up, a "conformation" is a mental model together with corresponding substantial realizations: it is both internal-mental and out there objectively in the perceptible world. It may be materially realized in artifacts, architecture, places, or landforms. It guides the construction of social relationships, and is the primary mode of communicating about those relationships. Conformations are motivating, evoke emotions, and are the essential standards from which moral sentiments arise. Conformation systems are innate, and they are understood and used by all infants, children, and adults. Conformation systems are the mode-specific means – the necessary means – for infants to recognize how relational models are implemented in their community. Concomitantly, conformations mediate the reproduction and diffusion of the social systems of any community, as well as the transformation of social systems or resistance to them. Each system consists of a distinctive mode of interpreting actions and representing existing social relations, of guiding coordinated construction of new or imagined relations, and of motivating and evaluating relations. There are four conformation systems; each of the four fundamental forms of sociality relies primarily on a distinctive conformation system, operating in a particular mode, that is specific to that one relational model.

Psychologically, a conformation consists of a mode of representation of and for the social relationship, together with the enabling and more or less constraining emotions, motives, moral sentiments, and commitment to the relationship. In addition, a conformation often also comprises all sorts of bodily and material things that complement these psychological aspects. Operating as a conformation system, representations, emotions, motives, moral sentiments, and commitments are not functionally separable.

Having said that, I need to issue a humdinger of a caveat: I do not know what a "motive" is, despite considerable pondering about that. Again, I have been studying "emotions" for more than twenty-five years, and have published several articles on emotions, as well as a book on one. But I still cannot figure out what an emotion is. And I wonder all the time whether "emotion" is a useful scientific category, or just a vernacular English word. After studying moral psychology for fifty years, I have some provisional, heuristic, incomplete conceptions of what moral psychology might be, and have published those ideas in a couple of books and several articles. But I cannot adequately delineate what, if anything, is special about the moral "domain," if there is one. I am intrigued by the idea of social relational commitment (which "solves" difficult social coordination challenges, such as the Prisoner's Dilemma). But I have no intellectual commitment to any definite conceptualization of "commitment." I have no confidence that "motivation" exists as a distinct biopsychological or functional entity, and I distrust the scientific validity of the concepts of "morality" and "moral psychology." One sufficient reason for all of those doubts is that each of these concepts fallaciously takes for granted that vernacular lexemes in one language – English – fortuitously identify real and definite psychological entities (Fiske 2020a). I also have lots of other, quite sufficient reasons for being dubious about the scientific usefulness of each of those concepts. But I use them in this book because I have to use them, in order to say what I (sort of) mean. I am trying to communicate with you, dear reader, who doubtless perceives persons as having emotions, motives, moral sentiments, and social commitments – as I do, too, when I remove my scholar's hat. I'll keep using these words because they get us "in the right ballpark," or at least in the same neighborhood.

The Respective Conformation Systems of the Four Relational Models

Precisely what are the four conformation systems? For authority ranking relationships, people use magnitudes or dimensions, treating some people as ABOVE, GREATER than, having MORE FORCE than, temporally PRECEDING others, etcetera. This use of dimensions and magnitudes is iconic, in the Peircean sense. Iconicity of dimensions and magnitudes to constitute authority ranking is the conformation system specific to authority ranking. For equality matching relationships, people perform concrete actions of one-to-one correspondence that operationally define being even: one-person, one-vote ballots; shares that match one-to-one; taking turns; flipping a coin; or assuring that the distribution of work is even. The concrete one-to-one correspondence operations create the emotions, motives, and moral commitments that sustain and modulate, resist or transform the equality matching relationship. In other words, equality matching's conformation system is concrete operations of one-to-one correspondence. Imagine that your platoon is isolated in a battle, and one person needs to scout an escape route, but whoever scouts it stands a good chance of being killed. The platoon draws straws to decide who will reconnoiter, and you draw the short straw. You are now morally committed to scouting the escape route, and motivated to do so in a way that you were not before drawing straws. Needless to say, you feel some strong social relational and other emotions as a result.

For communal sharing relationships, people use relations between their bodies to indexically conform relations among their social selves: caressing; snuggling; affectionate sex; nursing the baby; commensally drinking from the same vessel; moving in rhythmic synchrony in dance, ritual, or military drill; circumcising or otherwise modifying their bodies in a common distinctive manner. These all connect participants' bodies and thereby connect them socially. Because people create or recognize communal sharing by the equivalence or contiguity of their bodies, especially the body substances that make them who they are, this conformation system is called consubstantial assimilation. The sign system is: equivalence or continuity of bodies means equivalence of social selves. The conformation system is indexical in the sense that that the use of bodies to represent social persons is based on the typical and salient co-occurrence of body and social person. In the modern era, this co-occurrence has been vastly attenuated with writing and printing; visual, audio, and video recording; telephonic and digital communication. But the link between body and person remains evocatively salient. When a woman suckles a child, when one person cooks for or feeds another, when people eat from the same dish and drink from the same vessel, or smoke marijuana from the same joint, or share another drug, the equivalence of the ingested substance makes the social persons in some respects socially equivalent. There are many kinds of indexicality; conformations of communal sharing rely on the contiguity, co-occurrence, and causal connections between bodies and social persons.

For market pricing relationships, people use things such as money, PIN codes, stock ticker codes, and numeric bids and prices. Grades are market pricing in the valuation of student performance. For currency, some regions of the world have used cowrie shells during certain periods of history, other regions have used iron rings, others printed certificates of deposit, and others have used digits in the cloud. In this system, signing a check or presenting a credit card and entering the PIN are legal commitments. If someone writes and signs a check without the funds to pay it, people get angry because, in this system, one's signature on a check constitutes an obligation to pay. These are all arbitrary symbols whose meaning and value entirely depend on the community's use of them and people's expectation that the community will continue to use them as such. The arbitrary conventional symbols that are market pricing's conformation system are most salient in the numerals (८, 捌, 八, И, VIII, 8) and currency signs (֏, ௹, ريال, ₪, £) used to indicate prices, payments, contract terms, and so forth, as well as in the coins, bills, checks, pin codes, and digital representations of money. In digital, internet-linked systems, the string of 0s and 1s that indicate a payment from a particular agent to another agent have value only because people use them to denote the given values, and actually do accept them in payment. There are an unlimited number of possible symbols, but conformations of market pricing rely especially on symbols that indicate proportions.

The symbols conforming market pricing may indicate proportions directly, as in a retail sign indicating X units of currency per unit of Y. Often, however, the signs conforming market pricing indicate rates, ratios, or proportions indirectly, often by declaring a price without explicit mention of the denominator, which, in the situation, is common knowledge by conventional usage: X dollars (for this one house), or "$1.50" (per pineapple). In their text and in the signatures that make them binding, contracts use symbolism to conform market pricing. Peirce noted that in ancient Greek the verb *συμβάλλιν*, "symbolize," was used "very frequently to signify the making of a contract or convention," while the noun *σύμβολον*, "symbol" was "early and often used to mean a convention or contract" (Peirce 1903, V. 2, chapter 2, paragraph 297). So the conformation system of market pricing is symbolism, in the strict, specific, Peircean sense that a symbol has meaning only by virtue of its conventional use in a community of symbol users – and, I would add, common knowledge of its conventional use and moral entailments.

To posit, for example, that (all or most) conformations of authority ranking are iconic uses of dimensions obviously does not imply the converse – that all iconic uses of dimensions are conformations of authority ranking – let alone that that all iconicity, or all uses of dimensions, are conformations of anything. A person who builds a scale model airplane, an icon of the real airplane, relies on dimensions, but does not thereby conform a social relationship. Similarly, hung over a door, a signboard with a depiction of a mug full of a light brown liquid is iconic (the depiction represents by virtue of resembling a mug of beer) and indexical (the placement of the signboard indicates where such drinks can be had). That signboard facilitates the market pricing relationship of selling of beer, but it does not conform that relationship, or any other relationship. Merely observing the sign does not constitute a social relationship. Humans have many social relational uses for indexes, icons, concrete operations, and arbitrary symbols. Conformation of social relationships is just one of the relational uses of each of these four kinds of signs. If one person says to another "Come here, please," the meaning of that request is indexical: "here" is wherever the speaker is, and the target of the request is the person to whom the utterance is directed, discernable by the location and gaze of the speaker. Likewise, the midwife weighing and measuring a newborn is using magnitudes and dimensions, but not thereby iconically conforming an authority ranking relationship with the newborn, or with anyone else.

Consider some examples of the four conformation systems. Imagine that five people raise their hands to vote on the game they will play, and then draw cards to see who deals. The dealer shuffles the cards, another player cuts the deck, and the dealer deals one card in turn to each player. They take turns betting. Then there are more rounds of betting after each player gets another card, until one player wins the pot. On successive hands, they take turns dealing the cards. These procedures make the game "fair," in the specific sense that each person is treated equally. All of these actions are operational definitions of equality, because they operationally put the players' turns, their cards (their "hands"), or their chances in one-to-one correspondence with the others' turns, cards, or chances. Participants and anyone else watching can see that the operation has evenly matched the participants.

Now think of a person who comes into a grocery store. On each product she sees tags that indicate a ratio of currency to quantity, where the currency and quantity are communicated with arbitrary symbols (e.g., "$6.50/pound"). She chooses several items and goes up to the front, where the proprietor uses a machine to multiply quantities times prices and add them up (calculations based on the distributive law), showing a total indicated again by numerals (e.g., $48.20). The shopper pays with currency, or with a check that she writes out and signs, or with a numbered card and PIN. The funds in the shopper's account and the account of the proprietor, as well as the funds that are transferred in payment, have no material existence and no definite location; they consist of digitally encoded numeric symbols in a database "in the cloud." Consider also the numerals used to communicate prices and that commit the proprietor to sell at those prices. Those numerals are uninterpretable to anyone outside the particular linguistic community, and all of the means of payment have value only so long as people use them to make payments and keep accounts, and expect this to continue. There is no way to know what a string of symbols means without knowing how the symbols are actually used in the community. This symbolic mode is distinctive of market pricing relationships.

Now imagine that a man removes his hat, and is given permission to enter an enormous, high-ceilinged chamber. He crosses the room and bows in front of a woman seated on a dais. She wears a crown and is dressed in glittering robes, wearing sparkling jewels; he is dressed in plain dark cloth that does not reflect the light. The woman gets up and proceeds to another room; the man follows her, with others coming behind. The woman sits, then the man and the others sit; the woman is served a drink, then the man is served, then the others. She addresses him in the singular, he addresses her in the plural and calls her by a title such as *your majesty*, derived from a word meaning "huge," and *your highness*. What all these actions have in common is that they use relative positions on physical dimensions to represent and constitute authority ranking. HIGHER rank versus LOWER rank is constituted by the presence or absence of stature-augmenting headgear (TALL versus SHORT), occupying a large chamber (GREAT VOLUME), ELEVATING oneself to go ABOVE or LOWERING oneself to go BELOW, clothing and accoutrements that are reflectively BRIGHT versus DIM), GOING AHEAD or COMING AFTER, positioning IN FRONT versus BEHIND, the temporal precedence of receiving something EARLIER or LATER, being addressed as MANY or ONE (numerical magnitude), as GREAT or not (large magnitude), and as HIGH or not.

Now imagine a fourth example. Two people meet; they hug and kiss, and walk to a restaurant holding hands. They dance, then at dinner they drink out of each other's glasses and feed each other tidbits of food, including morsels they have already eaten part of. Then they go home, caress, kiss, have affectionate sex, cuddle, and sleep snuggled up against each other. What all these actions have in common is that people use the contiguity and sharing of substances between their bodies to represent their social selves: by connecting their bodies they indexically "connect" socially, affirming their communal sharing relationship.

Conformation Systems Enable Humans to Jointly Use and Rely on the Relational Models

In the second section of this chapter, we considered the essentially insuperable obstacles to social coordination relying on ad hoc schemas. Coordination looks more feasible when people have their pick of four prespecified relational models that are common knowledge, and commonly felt. However, to coordinate, everyone must be using the same relational model, implemented in the same way – especially as regards who is engaged, and in what role. For secure coordination that participants can count on, participants also must be disposed to the necessary emotions, motives, and moral sentiments. An aspect of this is that participants must commit to the relationship, be confident that the other(s) are committed, and be confident that the other(s) are confident that all of the others are confident in everyone's commitment. That is, there must be common knowledge of mutual commitment. Participants' and observers' common knowledge of mutual commitments and the legitimacy-validity of those commitments is especially important because that tends to dissuade participants from defecting, brings knowers' persuasive pressure to bear on participants who are on the cusp of defection, and helps to assure that third-person knowers will punish defection.

Those commitments involve belief in the importance and legitimacy of the relationship, along with emotions of devotion to it, motivational dedication to engage, and moral sentiments of responsibility to uphold it or punish those who defect. Dispassionate knowledge of the relational model is not sufficient to sustain it (Fiske 2002, 2010).

What creates common knowledge of the relational model that participants are engaged with, in association with common knowledge of how participants are implementing the relational model in this instance? What evokes the emotions, motives, and moral sentiments that support the particular relational model, as implemented in this instance? What assures common knowledge of those affects, along with metamoral sentiments that everyone ought to have those affects and ought to feel that everyone else feels the same? Conformations do all that. Not perfectly, but adequately, and indeed often beautifully.

The conformation systems of the respective relational models are universal, but in each context in each culture at each point in history people implement each conformation system in ways that are more or less particular. That is, cultural evolution results in more or less unique ways of implementing each conformation system in each context in each culture in a given era. To mark relative rank, a person may incline their head, bow, courtesy, kneel with their head to the ground, prostrate himself, wait for the other to begin speaking at a meeting, and so on. Faculty may be seated at high table above the students, be served first, and have the privilege of leaving the room in order of academic precedence before any of the students may leave. All of these are variant uses of dimensions such that relative positions or amounts map social ranks iconically. At any point in history, each culture "selects" among those and other iconic dimensions, conforming authority ranking more or less uniquely within this mode.

Similarly, while people everywhere connect in solidarity and love by assimilating each other's bodies, kissing is limited to some cultures, while mixing one's blood with another's and drinking the combined substance is limited to cultures that practice blood brotherhood. Classical Athenian democracy consisted of allocating people to juries by lottery; they also chose most officials by lottery, taking turns at each office for a year at a time. To choose the treasurer and the generals in the Athenian democracy, adult male citizens cast ballots into an urn. Modern democracies vote by marking cards or pressing buttons or touch screens. The specific concrete operations of one-to-one correspondence used for equality matching vary across time and place, but they all constitute social relationships as egalitarian, by putting persons in one-to-one correspondence.

Grounded, Situated, Extended, Embodied, and Enactive Cognition

Conformation systems theory is more or less consistent with, and intersects with, several of the theories of grounded, situated, extended, embodied, and enactive cognition, especially the versions of those theories that encompass socially shared cognition, and versions that encompass cognition about social relations (for an overview of this field of theories, see Robbins & Aydede 2008). In the broadest sense, all conformation systems can be construed as situated cognition, I suppose. I think it probably makes sense to treat consubstantial assimilation, iconic dimensions and magnitudes, and probably concrete operations of one-to-one matching as perceptual symbol systems, more or less. Consubstantial assimilation is surely embodied cognition – and a whole lot more. Concrete operations of one-to-one correspondence can be conceptualized as extended and enactive cognition – but they also go way beyond the sorts of cognition that are usually considered under those rubrics, so far as I know. The conventional symbols conforming market pricing are instantiated in currency, academic grades, and other entities and systems, including digital records, computations, and transfers; all of that qualifies as extended cognition, I believe. But it is crucial to conformation systems theory that such symbolism creates, coordinates, and modulates market pricing relationships, not cognition regarding individuals. Iconic dimension and magnitude conformations include meaningful bodily actions, hence embodiment. Iconic dimension and magnitude conformations of authority ranking prominently include artifacts, architecture, and topographical elevation, so they certainly can be construed as extended cognition, involving situated cognition. But theorizing these conformations as "embodied," "extended," or "situated" cognition ignores their function: aligning the cognitive representations of participants in a relationship, while evoking emotions, motives, and moral sentiment that inform the relationship.

There is another, rather crucial difference between conformation systems theory and many of these "outside the brain" theories. Conformation systems theory posits that external conformational acts and artifacts do not substitute for neurocognitive conformations, but coexist with them, resonating and strengthening each other. External conformations are effective because, and to the extent that, they are products of and "awaken" their internal counterparts, with which they are isomorphic.

Likewise, people invent new external conformations by externalizing their internal conformations. External conformations are realizations of internal ones. Conversely, people implicitly and explicitly learn from each encounter with an external conformation, discovering and internalizing the specific local cultural complements that realize specific conformations in specific roles and contexts. By observing and participating in these specific implementations of each conformation system, children and newcomers learn with whom they should relate according to which of the four relational models. So do other people who are transitioning between social relationships or, for any other reason, are uncertain what type of relationship they should have with whom. Furthermore, from seeing and engaging in conformations, everyone learns or is reminded of everyone's relationships with everyone else, and learns that those relationships are common knowledge. Also, it is possible that observation and engagement in conformations somehow consolidates innate a priori knowledge of the conformation systems and the relational models. However, if people's innate a priori knowledge of the conformation systems and the relational models is solid and well formed in the first place, I wonder to what extent and in what respects learning could further consolidate that knowledge.

In important respects, conformation systems theory goes far beyond the theories of grounded, embodied, extended, situated, and enactive cognition. Like other forms of grounded, situated, extended, and embodied cognition, the four conformation systems are, among other things, ways for individuals to offload cognitive functions and thereby transcend what individual minds can do. But conformation systems are much, much more than that. Conformations support attentive awareness, memory, personal knowledge, and common knowledge of social relationships. Conformation systems enable interacting persons to announce and affirm what they are up to, while recognizing and acknowledging what the other persons are up to. Conformation systems also enable third parties to see what the interactants are up to. By engaging in a conformation, people commit themselves to one of the four fundamental kinds of social relationships (as implemented in a particular way, with particular persons) while demonstrating to everyone their commitment. The resultant common knowledge of the participants' social relationship, along with common knowledge of the participants' commitment to that relationship, makes that commitment all the more binding, and makes defection all the more costly. All of these processes align participants' mental social relational conformations. That alignment function is the key to conformation systems, but, so far as I know, is ignored by theories of embodied, extended, and situated cognition.

Unfortunately, I formulated conformation systems theory long before I knew anything about theories of grounded, embodied, extended, or situated cognition. I hope that theorists of these sorts of cognition will formulate ideas about how to integrate these theories with conformation systems theory. It seems that a promising first step may be to incorporate into those theories the proposition that a frequent function of these forms of cognition that extend beyond individual minds is aligning the cognition of participants in a social relationship. Without proper alignment, there really is no social relationship, in the technical sense of participants' coordination by means of their each/all being guided, motivated, and morally directed by the same conformation, through which they each generate their own actions and make sense of each other's actions (Fiske 2004, Haslam, Reichert, & Fiske 2002). So, we need to further investigate when and how participants externalize conformations of social relationships beyond their individual minds. And then, how do externalized conformations become common knowledge, common motives, common emotions, and common moral sentiments?

Complementarity Theory

The foundation of each of the four conformation systems is an evolved psychosocial adaptation that predisposes a person to recognize and affectively respond to conformations that operate in one specific mode. One of these psychosocial adaptations is prepared for and attentive to indexical consubstantial assimilation; it responds by creating or solidifying a mental representation of being "one" with the other participant(s), while generating the emotions, motives, and moral sentiments that, informed by the representation, constitute a communal sharing relationship. But that psychosocial adaptation does not – cannot – know what specific realizations of consubstantial assimilation people in the community use (see Fiske 2000). Kissing? Coloring bodies blue? Forming a circle holding hands and dancing certain steps to a certain rhythm? The psychosocial adaptation is set up to represent and devote themselves to sets of persons who are socially equivalent to each other. But the adaptation cannot foresee what equivalence groups it will find, cannot foresee who will belong to which equivalence groups, nor, most crucially, cannot innately know which groups the person herself will belong to. The psychosocial adaptation includes the motivation to discover these groups, and will find them, because it is attuned to consubstantial assimilation. As a function, the adaptation takes as input the consubstantial assimilation conformations the person encounters or engages in; its output is specific communal sharing dyads and groups, including the communal sharing dyads and groups to which the person herself belongs.

The indeterminacy of these psychosocial adaptations is what makes them flexible, so they can, and do, coordinate any activity, and allows them to be adapted to coordinate newly invented activities, as well as new constraints and opportunities (Fiske 2000). When the worldwide web was invented, people quickly applied the four relational models to organize social activities on the web. Using them for coordination on the worldwide web provided definite common knowledge structures with moral legitimacy, simultaneously requiring the adoption of many cultural practices to complete each relational model so that it functioned to coordinate well in this part of the new electronic medium.

In short, the infant's innate psychosocial adaptation that is evolutionarily prepared for consubstantial assimilation, and hence responsive to it, cannot function to coordinate social relations until it encounters the particular consubstantial assimilation conformations of the community into which the infant is born. The adaptation needs those particulars; it is "lost" without them. Conversely, the particular consubstantial assimilation conformations of any community would never have arisen, would never have been culturally reproduced, and would have no effects without the psychosocial adaptation. Communal sharing relationships are formed by the conjunction of the evolved system with particular cultural conformation practices. Under the rubric of "complementarity theory," I have theorized this sort of system, composed of mutually presupposing innate and cultural components, neither of which can be realized without the other (Fiske 2000). The innate and the cultural complement each other; neither would exist without the other. The innate component is the "mod," the cultural complements are "preos." Mods and preos depend on each other; each has no function without the other.

In this framework, the evolved psychosocial disposition to create and reaffirm authority ranking relations by engaging in iconic dimensional and magnitudinal conformations is a mod; the cultural practice of building giant, gilded statues of the gods is a preo, and the cultural practice of women curtseying to show respect is another preo.

Another mod is the evolved psychosocial disposition to create and affirm equality matching relations by engaging in conformations consisting of concrete operations of one-to-one correspondence. Complementing that adaptation, one cultural preo is the pan balance; another, in classical Athenian trials, is the water clock used to allot equal time to the accuser's speech and the defendant's rebuttal. In the absence of the concrete operations mod, neither pan balances nor water clocks would have any effect on social relationships. In the absence of any preos such as pan balances and water clocks, the concrete operations mod could not be realized; it would not function.

A fourth mod is the evolved psychosocial disposition to create and affirm market pricing relations with symbolic conformations. One cultural preo complementing that disposition is a course-grading system composed of point values of assignments and tests, assessments to assign points, and then computation of final grades. Another preo consists of laws specifying prison sentences according to the lawmakers' sense of the proportionality of offenses.

In complementarity theory (Fiske 2000), the complementarity of preos to their mods, along with the mutual presupposition of mods and their preos, is theorized atemporally, without regard to dynamics: the theory says nothing about how preos come into existence, nor anything about how people adopt, reproduce, transform, or reject preos. In Chapter 3 and thereafter, we will consider a theory that extends complementarity theory to illuminate those processes: the theory that a mod, such as these four adaptations, provides a fertile niche for the cultural evolution of congruent social practices, along with the artifacts and architecture that people use in those practices.

Metaphorically, we can say that a conformation system is like a restaurant menu; it provides the options. In most cases, one cannot go into a restaurant and simply eat dinner. One has to choose what dinner, and select among the available side-dishes (French fries or salad? Honey vinaigrette salad dressing, or oil and vinegar?). When one wants to conform an authority ranking relationship, one cannot just do iconic dimensions in general. One must choose one or more specific dimension(s). And one must then select ways to realize that dimension. There are at least ten iconic dimensions that cultural evolution somehow "chooses" among, for each type of authority ranking in that culture, and there are innumerable ways of using each dimension. The king chooses ABOVE–BELOW, implemented by his sitting on a high throne, while others bow to him, and their authority ranking relationship is also implemented by placing his palace at the top of the hill, looking down on his subjects in the valley.

This generativity gives each of the four relational models, with their respective conformation systems, the amazing potential to coordinate anything that humans need to coordinate, and gives humans innumerable ways of coordinating each aspect of any coordinated activity. Suppose nations get together to send a thirty-seven-person team to Mars, and say the mission, from launch to return, will take four years. How should the team organize their responsibilities and decisions, so as to survive and return, while also collecting a satisfactory amount of good scientific data? The options known to coordinate well are communal sharing, authority ranking, equality matching, and market pricing. That's the core repertoire. For each aspect of each thing to coordinate, pick a relational model or two – or more. Now, how should the selected relational model(s) be implemented to govern each aspect of each coordinated task? If need be, we can invent entirely new implementations especially suited to this mission.

I do not have any theory of how persons and societies make those "choices." Choosing may sometimes consist, in part, of conscious, reflective, explicit thinking. But I believe that choosing often occurs mostly through other cognitive modes. And often no conscious or actual choice is involved. Whatever the mental processes involved, society-level processes are usually the main determinants of choices from the menu of each conformation system. If all known kings conform their rulership by wearing crowns, among other conformations, and especially if a king's predecessors wore crowns, the new king has little choice if he is to foster the representations, emotions, motives, and moral sentiments necessary for sustaining his kingship. We will return to consider this issue in regard to each conformation system as a niche in which conformation practices culturally evolve. The gist of the idea is that a conformation practice thrives to the extent that the practice is isomorphic with the niche in which it functions: indexical, iconic, concrete operational, or symbolic.

What this all comes down to is that a social relationship is constituted, modulated, transformed, morally assessed, resisted or rejected through its conformations. If I think of you as, communicate about you as, or position myself such that you are ABOVE me, GREATER THAN me, AHEAD OF me, and MORE POWERFUL than me, then I am relating to you as my "superior," my "leader" in an authority ranking relationship. Indeed, the POWER dimension and the ABOVE–BELOW, VERTICAL dimension are so fundamental to human conformation of authority ranking that even social scientists constantly write about "POWER," and the "VERTICAL dimension of social relations" as if, well, social hierarchy literally consisted of relative altitude and force.

But, on the other hand, suppose I think of you and I as having an essential essence such as genes in common; then, I am relating to you as socially equivalent in a communal sharing relationship. Likewise, if I communicate that we have the same bodily substance such as "blood," if I make my body contiguous with yours as we cuddle, or constitute us as a single being by marching or dancing in rhythmic synchrony, then we have a communal sharing with each other.

Alternatively, if you or I perform concrete operations that ostensively make you and me evenly balanced, matching each other in one-to-one correspondence, then I am relating to you as my peer in an equality matching relationship. Likewise, when I think of us as distinct but evenly matched and seek to make us even, evaluating our relationship according to whether we are striving to be even with each other, then again we are conducting equality matching.

Fourthly, if we conceptualize and conduct our relationship according to a rate, ratio, or proportion, then I am relating to you in a market pricing relationship. For example, suppose that eight completed homework assignments together with a 20/20 on the final combine to be worth a course grade of A. Likewise, if I am motivated by the prospect of publishing many papers, each cited many times, and we construe our respective academic worth as proportional to such a metric, we are structuring our relationship as market pricing. This is implemented in some universities that score their faculty's publications according to a system that awards points based on the impact factors of the journals in which articles are published.

In each case, a relationship exists by virtue of being generated and coordinated by a conformation in the sign mode specific to the relational model. The social relational actions, emotions, motives, and most moral evaluations that we engage in are manifestations of the mode of coordination, so we interpret each other's actions in term of the conformation system of the relationship we are engaging in.

Conformation systems theory was pretty well developed (Fiske 1991, 1992, 2004) before I encountered conceptual metaphor theory (Lakoff & Johnson 1980, Lakoff 1993, Fauconnier & Turner 2002, Kövecses 2010). The theories share a number of the most general features, though conformation systems theory does not focus on concepts, as such, and does fully incorporate relationship-sustaining emotions, motives, and moral sentiments. The basic difference between conceptual metaphor theory and conformation systems theory is that conformations are not metaphors for a truer, more literal, more basic, more accurate, or more detailed level of cognition. Conformations are the fundamental cognitions of the four relational models. There is nothing beneath them; they are the foundations.

Likewise, in its essentials, conformation systems theory was also solidly formulated (Fiske 1991, 1992, 2004) before I encountered and became intrigued by commitment theory (Hirshleifer 1987, Schelling 2006, Frank 1988, Nesse 2001). Since then, commitment theory has helped to guide the further development of conformation systems theory.

Overview of the Book

Chapter 2 dives into a West African culture to describe how one traditional community constitutes and conducts everyday social relations. I worked in

Burkina Faso for two years as Peace Corps Country Director, then did two years of ethnographic fieldwork in a very small village, along with my wife and baby daughter. You will see that the ways that the Moosé construct their social relationships are at once fascinating, strange, and intuitively familiar.

Chapter 3 explores the phylogenetic roots of consubstantial assimilation, the conformation system of communal sharing. I describe how nonhuman animals suckle their young and the few mammals that bring food to close kin and initiate food sharing; we will look in particular detail at primates. Then I discuss licking, grooming, and affiliative touch among primates and other mammals. Chapter 4 describes how humans use nursing, feeding, and sharing food, drink, and drugs to create and reinforce communal sharing relationships. Humans also use spit and blood to form bonds, and they perceive the closest relationships to be based on shared physical substance. Conversely, observing taboos against eating a specific type of food, or against eating with or having sexual relations with a specific type of person, is also constitutive of important communal sharing relationships.

Chapter 5 assesses how people use the surface of the body to connect and separate themselves. Skin color and applied pigmentation, hair type and coiffure, scarification, distinctive piercings and genital operations define people as belonging to distinctive groups. Synchronous rhythmic movement of the body, often to percussive music, also bonds people, whether in military drill, ritual dance, or even raves. These are all ways of making bodies alike and different, thereby marking persons as socially alike or different.

At this point, the reader will have had an ethnographic close-up of all four conformation systems in one tiny West African community, then conceptual expositions of each of the four formation systems, followed by a broad survey of consubstantial assimilation across a wide range of contexts and cultures. At that point, it will be fruitful to search even more broadly, and to dig even more deeply into another conformation system: the iconic dimension and magnitude conformation of authority ranking. That exceptionally detailed investigation will enable us to figure out whether conformations – at least this one – truly are the fundamental conformations of their respective relational models, or whether, for example, they are conceptual metaphors for "deeper," more fundamental conformations. The extensive investigation will also enable us to see whether there are any basic differences between iconic dimension and magnitude conformations in radically different societies, in very different contexts, or across millennia. By investigating a great many iconic dimension and magnitude conformations, we can see whether different subtypes conform different kinds of social relationships, or all conform the same relational model: authority ranking.

Part III does all that.

Chapter 6 looks at the "Your Highness" phenomenon of ABOVE–BELOW conformations: that is, depicting rulers and elites as taller, or thinking of them as taller, or their wearing high headdresses that make them appear taller. That's the "UP" side; there are also "DOWN" positions: In a great many societies, subordinates conform authority ranking by prostrating, stooping, bowing, or, at a minimum, tilting their head DOWN to superiors, who may be RAISED on a dais or throne.

In Chapter 7, we look at palaces and temples, mounds, monoliths, and monuments that iconically conform authority ranking with a number of dimensions and magnitudes, especially SURFACE AREA, GREATER MASS–LESSER MASS, and GREATER VOLUME–LESSER VOLUME. Watching the construction of such grand edifices, or looking at the great blocks of stone that compose them, and thinking about how such constructions must have been built, conforms through FORCE–STRENGTH, and/or NUMBER of workers. Animal dominance hierarchies are commonly mediated by the postures and displays of the animals: subordinates lower themselves and make themselves appear small, while animals asserting dominance make themselves tall and large. After reviewing this animal behavior literature, Chapter 8 looks at the myriad ways that humans use physical dimensions to assert status and to defer. The rise of institutionally stratified "complex" societies is closely associated with the construction of imposing mounds, tombs, pyramids, and palaces that rise ABOVE the approaching viewer and whose MASS is awe inspiring. Elites have always tended to build residences and temples on high ground, with inferiors occupying topographically lower grounds. Wearing robes and crowns that make them majestic, elites occupy large dwellings and hold audiences in grand halls. The immensity of their halls and reception rooms make subjects feel small, and high-ranking persons control large personal spaces that their inferiors may only access with permission. Linguistically, superiors are often treated as many, while subordinates are singular. In short, social status is displayed and in part created by the "greatness" of persons and the objects and spaces associated with them.

Chapter 8 discusses two more dimensions ubiquitously used to conform authority ranking: IN FRONT–BEHIND and temporally PRECEDING–FOLLOWING. "High" rank is also conceived and communicated by vertical differentiation. Chapter 9 shows that subordinates bow or prostrate themselves to superiors, who may be raised on a dais or throne. Along with elevation goes the horizontal differentiation of being in front: "Leaders" stand BEFORE their "followers" or "backers" BEHIND THEM; no one may turn their back on the monarch, which would be to place the monarch BEHIND them. Status is also marked in TEMPORAL PRECEDENCE when people receive greetings and gifts or are served in order of rank, process in rank order, and begin to eat or speak according to their rank. Conversely, seniority often confers status: people are TEMPORALLY ORDERED according to when they entered the role, position, or rank.

Chapter 9 also presents evidence supporting a conclusion that I drew some years ago about the neurocognitive system that humans and other mammals are known to use to make nonsocial assessments of the dimensions and magnitudes discussed in Chapters 6–8. That system is called the analog magnitude system (or, sometimes, the approximate magnitude system). Its focal neural substrate is in the intraparietal sulcus. This neurocognitive system also processes stimulus intensity, such as BRIGHTER – DIMMER luminosity (lumens), and LOUDER – QUIETER sound (decibels). At the point when I realized that, I had not looked for the use of either of these dimensions to conform authority ranking, and indeed could not think of any conformational uses of luminosity or sound levels. But when I went into the various literatures I had been exploring for the other conformational dimensions, I immediately discovered that the use of BRIGHTER – DIMMER and LOUDER – QUIETER is, indeed, ubiquitous. So, Chapter 9 presents many instances of the iconic conformation of authority ranking by means of luminance and sound.

Chapter 10 summarizes this use of the dimensions of physics to constitute, communicate, and mentally represent authority ranking: above, in front, greater in magnitude (size or number), preceding in time. We even use force: we think of some leaders as having "power" or being "strong." These physical conformations of authority ranking are iconic: real or putative or imagined relations on physical dimensions are congruent with social relations. That is, when we think about authority ranking we map social "position" onto space, magnitude, and time. Conversely, to communicatively represent authority ranking, and to evoke the emotions, motives, and moral sentiments that authority ranking depends on, we marshal space, magnitude, and time. This iconic physics is so pervasive in English and other languages that the majority of words for authority ranking are terms whose basic sense concerns the physical relations among objects.

We construct and conduct equality matching relations using concrete operations such as taking a turn or aligning objects or actions in one-to-one correspondence. Chapter 11 shows that these procedures function as operational definitions of equality matching: they are ostensive demonstrations of even balance. Thus, flipping a coin or lining up on the starting line, taking off simultaneously, and running to the finish line constitute equally matched opportunities for victory. If the procedures are followed, the race is demonstrably fair. Throughout all of history most of the rules of most games and sports, together with most procedures of gambling, consist of concrete operations that define and demonstrate equality of opportunity. Cognitive experiments with adults provide another kind of evidence for iconic conformations of authority ranking, as do cognitive experiments with preverbal infants. Chapter 12 reviews those adult and infant cognition experiments. Then, Chapter 13 describes the approximate magnitude system (also called the analog magnitude system) in humans and nonhuman animals. The functions and features of this neurocognitive system strongly suggest that humans rely on it for iconically representing and computing authority ranking. Brain-imaging studies confirm that.

Chapter 14 peruses the multitude of concrete operations of one-to-one correspondence that people use to conform equality matching. Infant studies are consistent with the hypothesis that infants expect concrete operations of one-to-one correspondence among peers. These experiments further suggest that infants prefer concrete operations of one-to-one correspondence among peers, and perhaps even judge that it is "good" in some proto-moral sense.

The history of the development of large-scale social coordination is the subject of Chapter 15. Coordination in cities and states requires calendars, weights and measures, and bookkeeping, all of which are systems of abstract symbols for ratio-based calculations. "Symbolism," meaning representation based purely on conventional use, is absolutely essential to making the calculations for coordinating time and quantities and transactions of goods and labor. Combining calendars with metrology, arithmetic planning, and bookkeeping permits the regulation of labor and tax collection for large-scale enterprises. Money, an extremely abstract symbol system, developed as an offshoot of weights and measures. Writing initially developed as a refinement of bookkeeping and a mode of coordinating transactions across removes of time and space. In short, the use of market pricing to coordinate many interactions involving many entities among a large number of people required a specific psychocultural development: the invention and use of symbolic systems.

Finally, Chapter 16 draws attention to some features apparently shared by all four conformation systems, and then addresses the generative potentials unique to symbolism. It concludes by explicating some final issues to consider about conformation systems.

In the aggregate, this book presents the thesis that each conformation system consists of a mode of cognition; a mode of communication; a mode of getting everyone "on the same page" concerning which relational model they are to use and how it is to be implemented; a mode of constituting and committing to relationships; a mode of coordination; a mode of morally evaluating relationships; a mode of emotion, motivation, and other social relational affects; and a mode of reification and communication in art, artifacts, architecture, locations, clothing and accoutrements, sounds, narratives, and so forth. Above all, in conjunction with their corresponding relational models, conformations make social relationships possible. Without relational models and their respective conformation systems, there would be no social relationships, and, hence, hardly any social coordination of consequence.

Is that conceivable? What does it even mean? Read on.

* * * * *

Building on the orientation the first chapter provides, let us take a close look at the operation of the conformation systems in everyday life in a tiny West African village in 1980–1982. Looking closely at the conformation systems in one community at one point in time allows us to compare the four conformation systems, while holding nearly everything else constant. The observations and experiences I describe in Chapter 2 were the inspiration for the ideas that developed into conformation systems theory, motivating me to write this book. Let's see if you see what I saw and experienced among the Moosé.

CHAPTER 2

The Moosé of Burkina Faso, in One Village, 1980–1982

I'm talking with a very, very old man, our wonderful neighbor, in whose maize garden we built our mud huts. I hear four ten-year-old boys chattering, and I turn to see them returning with our baby daughter, whom the villagers, hearing us call her "Gwen," have named Gũwende, "wait for God" (i.e., a name marking the fact that when the mother hoped to get pregnant, she patiently waited until God gave her a baby). As always, one of the boys is carrying her on his hip. They never put her down except to seat her together with others for a meal, or to play with her. Gũwende is happy in the arms of the boys all day, and we're happy to have her up off the ground where she's safe from the ubiquitous scorpions and poisonous snakes. The boys, whom we pay to take care of her while we are working, have our permission to take her anywhere in the village, so she knows every compound in the neighborhood. And she takes it for granted that wherever she is in the village, if she's hungry, anyone will feed her. Perhaps it is this experience of being constantly held and compassionately fed that gives her what is evidently a confident sense of belonging. When we go to the market, though she knows just a few of the scores of vendors sitting on the ground, and knows hardly any of the hundreds of buyers circulating around, she happily roams all over, chatting with everyone. (Of course, we watch her constantly, but she can't see that we are doing so.) When we go to town to a restaurant, the waitresses (most of whom she does not know), invariably ask to pick her up, and they carry her into the back out of sight, holding her until our food is ready, and we ask to have her back. She's extraordinarily comfortable with everyone and has absolutely no fear of strangers.

Moosé infants are in body-to-body contact with caretakers twenty-four hours per day. Moosé don't put toddlers down to walk because, they say, "They'll just stumble and fall." When the baby's mother is walking, hoeing a field, grinding grain with a stone quern, pounding foods with a huge pestle, or stirring a pot on the fire, her baby, wrapped against her back, moves in rhythmic synchrony with her. When the mother dances, the baby is always there against her back, moving with every step and turn the mother takes.

My favorite photo from fieldwork shows Gũwende, around fifteen months old and still learning to walk on the irregular surfaces of the village. In fact, until she was almost two, she refused to walk at all unless she held someone's hand. She's with the old man, whom she visits from time to time when she is not with the boys. Virtually or completely blind, he almost never leaves his hut. On the rare occasions when he does go out briefly, he walks cautiously with a staff. The photo shows the two of them walking together holding hands as he walks her home.

And all that is a picture of consubstantial assimilation in the village, creating and sustaining communal sharing relationships between Gũwende and the boys, and between Gũwende and the old man.

Starting Off

From 1968 to 1972, I was a Peace Corps volunteer: first, in a tuberculosis control program in Malawi, then in the World Health Organization's smallpox eradication campaign in the Congo. Both jobs consisted of daily interactions with rural populations of multiple cultures; in Malawi I managed in two local languages, while in the Congo I used French, with interpreters. From 1977 to 1980, I was Country Director of the Peace Corps in Upper Volta, based in the capital, Ouagadougou, working closely with my staff, Moosé officials, and those from other several other groups. French was the language of administration, so that's what I spoke. I travelled extensively to the small communities where Peace Corps volunteers worked, and began to study the Mooré language. After my two-year term as Country Director ended, I located a field site, Habra, a village of about 400 people in what was then the Mané Subprefecture of the Kaya Prefecture. After obtaining all permissions and choosing a site for our compound, I followed local practice, inviting my neighbors to build mud huts with me, after which we drank lots of village beer, passing around the hemispherical calabash. Later I purchased thatch; a few neighbors built conical roof frames and attached the thatch for us, and then lots more assembled to lift the roofs onto the huts and drink beer with me. And then I moved into the village with my wife, Kathryn Mason, and our infant daughter Gwendolyn. Kathy was also an ethnographer and, like me, a PhD student in the Committee on Human Development at the University of

Chicago. We did participant observation there for twenty-four months, from the summer of 1980 to the summer of 1982.

Once we moved in, we worked without interpreters or assistants, using only the Mooré language; very few villagers spoke any French and none spoke any English. Having already done two and a half years of fieldwork with monolingual Moosé women in Ouagadougou, Kathy was quite fluent when we moved to the village. Gwen soon became a native speaker of Mooré. After completing my term as Peace Corps Country Director and before moving to the village, I had had roughly 1,200 hours of one-on-one tutoring by excellent Peace Corps-trained native-speaking language instructors. Still, at the time we moved into the village I hadn't yet mastered the language. But before long I, too, became fully fluent. To be polite, Kathy and I always spoke Mooré to each other when anyone else was around, so Gwen spoke no English until we returned to Chicago.

It is estimated that more than 11,000,000 Moosé live in West Africa, most of them in Burkina Faso, which was at one time a French colony and formerly called La Haute Volta (Upper Volta). The Moosé have been well described by a Moosé ethnographer, Dim Delobsom (1932), and subsequently by Skinner (1964), Hammond (1966), Izard (1985), and Izard-Heritier and Izard (1959). Culturally, the Moosé are closely related to the Tallensi to the south, in Ghana (Fortes 1945, 1949), and to the Dogon to the north, in Mali (Van Beek 1991). They live in small villages, each typically composed of several patrilineages. Moosé grow millet, sorghum, maize, and beans; they raise some goats and sheep. A few Moosé own horses or mules. A very few own a cow, which they entrust to a Fulani herdsman until they need it. Moosé also forage for wild plants to eat, while exploiting baobab trees for leaves to eat and bark to make rope. For generations they used to be involved in long-distance trade in salt from the north and kola nuts from the south, carrying heavy loads of these commodities on their heads. In recent generations the majority of young, unmarried Moosé men have left the village and worked for a few years as wage laborers in Ghana, and later, during the time of my fieldwork, in the Ivory Coast.

All of the inhabitants of our village were Moosé, belonging to four distinct subgroups. About a fifth of the inhabitants were Sãaba, who, like other villagers, are farmers, but among whom the women also are potters and the men blacksmiths and wood workers. The Sãaba refuse to give women in marriage to any other caste, though the men are pleased to marry women from other castes, on the rare occasions when the opportunity arises. The other three subgroups of Moosé freely intermarry. Around one-sixth of the villagers were Nakomse, whose ancestors, fighting on horseback, are said to have come up from the south and conquered the Indigenous Yîyôose. The Nakomse (literally, "chiefs' children") identify themselves as descendants of chiefs. When the village chief dies and the paramount chief names a successor, he must be Nakomse. About a third of the villagers were Yîyôose, the people who claim to be the original inhabitants of the region, who have an especially close ritual connection with *Tenga*, the Earth, and hence responsibility for rainfall and the health of the crops. Approximately a quarter of the people in the village were Yarse, who are Moslem. Many others, including virtually all who had worked in the Ivory Coast, had Muslim names in addition to their Mooré names, and prayed toward Mecca on important occasions on the Islamic calendar. Only a tiny fraction were Roman Catholics; none in the area where I worked were Protestant. Aside from the Yarse, and regardless of taking Muslim names and occasionally praying in the Muslim manner, all villagers practiced their traditional religion, based on animal sacrifice to the earth (Tenga) and to the ancestors. I'll describe the key rituals later in this chapter. Many people practiced more than one religion, especially women who marry into or out of the Yarse. Everyone used magic for many purposes, especially to protect their children and themselves.[1]

My fieldwork began where the book began: with me prostrated in the dust some yards in front of the paramount chief, my forehead against the ground, raising and lowering my forearms. As I mentioned earlier, when we moved into the village, I found that women coming to visit me would typically kneel and curl up in ball, while uttering a quiet, very high-pitched *eeee, eeee; eeee, eeee.* This is *yigmsigi*, and can be exhibited in an infinite series of gradations, including simply stooping and placing the curled closed hands and forearms along the chest. It was clear to me that visiting women were visually and acoustically making themselves small, to accord me respect.

Before starting my fieldwork I had never seen either the Moosé male or female respect postures or sounds, yet they somehow make intuitive sense. But why should that be? Coming into an unfamiliar culture, why would

[1] In many sources, the people are called "Mossi," but that spelling distorts native speakers' pronunciation of the term. When they adopted their own official orthography they spelled their name "Moose," which makes orthographic sense in French. However, spelled like that, English-speaking readers will tend to pronounce it like the name of the large, broad-antlered animal in the deer family. So I take the liberty of adding an acute accent on the final é, to indicate a pronunciation closer to that of native speakers. The *o* is long; English speakers will get it approximately right if they pronounce it with the stress on the first syllable, like **MOH**-say.

you and I and everyone else immediately recognize the social relational meaning of making oneself LOW or small before a person, and according to that person a very large personal space? As I wondered about this at the time, I was struck by the fact that I not only perceived the social relations constituted in this manner, but when performing or receiving these postures, I felt the social positioning. It affirmed an authority ranking relationship between us.

Learning the Mooré language, I had found that Moosé address social superiors with *yâmba*, plural "you," and address inferiors and intimates with *fo*, singular "you." For third person pronouns, the singular *a* or *yê*, "he, she, it," is used to refer to an individual of equal or lower rank, or an intimate, like a son or daughter. Moosé use the plural *bamba*, "they, them" to refer to someone of higher rank, particularly a paramount chief. Curious about these Moosé uses of physical dimensions to represent rank, over the next couple of years I looked into it carefully. Here's what I found.

Magnitudes and Dimensions of Moosé Social Rank

The number of wives that a Moosé man has depends to a considerable degree on his age, except that village chiefs seem to have more wives than their age alone would warrant. When a patrilineage receives a bride, generally she goes to the eldest unmarried men; the next bride ordinarily goes to the next oldest, and so. As a result, men under age thirty or thirty-five are often unmarried. But the head of a minor lineage often has three or four wives; a village chief often has four or five; a paramount chief or king often has scores of wives.

After a ceremony or after receiving a gift, when Moosé distribute kola nuts, tobacco, beer, meat, food, money, or other goods, it all goes initially to the senior person of the relevant group, who passes it on to the second-ranking person to distribute. The share that each person receives is determined by rank: any socially meaningful difference in rank among people is signaled by a difference in the QUANTITY allocated to them. To divide according to rank is *pui natende*, "divide by rank." The distributor hands over the shares to recipients in temporal order of their rank. The distributor typically does not indicate the number of items given to each, and perhaps does not even count them, although he would be able to do so; the language has lexemes for numbers all the way into the millions. The distributor simply assures that the amounts patently differ. That is all that seems to matter. They do not seem to be concerned with the quantitative difference between greater and lesser shares.

Paramount chiefs are expected to be men of great girth, and some of the Moogo Nanamse, who deem themselves Kings of the Moosé, have been enormous men, according to photos and descriptions. On ceremonial occasions, chiefs and other nobility wear great billowing robes and large conical leather hats with knobs on top, amplifying the apparent SIZE of their bodies, and their overall height. The Nakomse (the chiefly clan) also mount on horseback for some ceremonial displays, which further enhances their stature and bulk. Indeed, only Nakomse and the Islamic Yarse (who in some ways are associated with Nakomse) may own or ride horses at all, my informants said. (Anyone may own or ride a donkey or mule.)

The eldest male of a patrilineage is the *kaasma*, a word that in nonsocial contexts literally means "big." Moosé consistently speak of elders and chiefs as *nim beda*, "big people," or *beda bedarâmba*, "big, big ones," while a subordinate shows his/her own inferiority by calling him/herself *bi bilifu*, "SMALL child" (plural, *koom baanego)*. Even a man in his fifties or sixties may refer to himself thus, for example when deferring a question or the authority to make a decision to *ninkeemba*, the "old men." When they lack sufficient age and rank to qualify for something, Moosé will say *m pa ta woto ye*, "I am not up to that, I don't reach that." The term that specifically conveys social superiority is *yɩɩde*, whose literal nonsocial meaning is "to be greater than, to exceed, be more than, to have great magnitude." So a man says of an elder *Eb yɩɩda maam*, "They are greater than I." Moosé also say of someone of higher rank *a keema maam*, "he is senior to me." In nonsocial contexts this root, *keem*, refers to LARGE size or magnitude, as in *tus-keemde*, literally, "a great thousand = one million." Two key verbs that can be either transitive or intransitive further illustrate ranking in magnitude: To show respect, deference, and courteous obeisance to someone is *waooge*, "to make much of" – literally, "to be BIG, ample"; while to disrespect is *paoge*, "belittle" – literally, "to be small, meager, insufficient." Mooré is a Gur-Voltaic language in the Atlantic-Congo family, with no evident links to the Indo-European family. I don't recall any English words that had been adopted by Mooré, and most of the few French words adopted into the language referred to introduced artifacts such as bicycles. So, I was struck by the similarity of meanings of these terms with the English lexicon of rank: GREATER, SENIOR, LEADER versus FOLLOWERS or BACKERS; BIG PERSON, HIGHER or LOWER STATUS, SUPERIOR versus SUBORDINATE, and so on.

In other deferential forms of behavior, Moosé also reveal that the PERSONAL SPACE, the social VOLUME, occupied by very high-ranking people is greater than that of their social inferiors. When someone of higher rank approaches, lesser people get out of the way, leaving the path, and, to show still more respect, turning to face slightly away. The Moosé proverb is *Pâng sâ n tûd sore, bumb buta moogo*, "When FORCE goes along the path, moral right goes through the grass [alongside the path]." When the village chief came to my compound, unlike anyone else, he often declared his presence at the entrance and then simply strode in. Conversely, when approaching the compound of a person of higher rank, visitors announce themselves vocally and approach slowly, in increments, waiting for permission to enter, and, ideally, greeting at a distance before approaching. Other than the village chief's wives, when coming to our compound women of any age announced their presence, waited to be invited to enter, then knelt on the ground some yards away to greet me before approaching more closely. In general Moosé do not come near the person of a paramount chief (*kombere*) or other person to whom they are showing extreme respect, unless and until they are called to approach. The "personage" of a great chief encompasses a volume vastly greater than his physical body.

People of very high rank, particularly chiefs, are often described as having *pânga*, "force, strength, or power." Moosé usually refer to the *Kombere*, Paramount Chief, as *Pâesrâmba*, "the strong ones"; note the plural suffix.

Magnitude, number, and force combine in aggrandizing praise names: *zab yüüya* (singular *zab yüüre*), literally "war names." At ceremonial occasions drummers with tonal drums, and with tonal positioning of their beating hands on other drums, beat out the pitch, rhythm, and cadence of these individual praise proverbs of the chiefs and linage heads who are present. The drummers also beat out the praise proverbs of the clans present. One element of this is simply the loudness of the drums; the drumming is a high-decibel announcement of a chief's presence. The declaration of the war names is the other element of the drumming. The *zab yüüya* of most men are rarely used and not widely known. However, when a chief takes office, he (or his sister; Mangin 1916: 20) chooses or makes up three proverbs as the basis for his war names (Delobsom 1932: 130–134, 142). From one of these he picks his chiefly name, commonly the animal or thing which is favorably compared to lesser things. Once a man become a chief, no one may ever again address him or refer to him by his former personal names, and in fact no one else may use his personal name any longer either. If they happen to have the same personal name as the man who becomes chief, they have to adopt a new name. Anyone under the new chief's jurisdiction who had the name the chief formerly bore is now euphemistically called *Naaba*, "Chief," or else is called by one of his (or her) alternative names. (In addition to their primary, initially given name, Moosé often have one or more other names).

Proverb-based war names often express defiance, or have to do with the often conflictual circumstances under which the chief came to power. They express the protective capabilities of the chief over his vassals, or simply vaunt his strength and ferocity. Chiefly names invoke the fearlessness of lions or crocodiles faced with lesser animals. Or, conversely, the names of subordinate chiefs may refer to their reliance on a paramount chief. For example, Naaba Yemde, "Chief Hippopotamus," gets his name from the proverb *Yemd dêng külga tı zim bi dat n dem yaare*, "Once the hippopotamus is in the river, the little fish can play without a care [under his protection]." Another war name is based on the proverb *Baning sora yoabga n tilig kyêse la wâamse*, "White millet hides in the [poisonous] strophantus bush and escapes from the parrots and monkeys." Thueuex (n.d.: 409–416) records that the late king at Ouagadougou was Naaba Wobgo, "Chief Elephant," based on the phrase *Kıım misri lagem koabga kô n bugs wobgo*, "One hundred bloody ancestor spirits do not frighten an elephant." The previous king was Naaba Koom, "Chief Water," based on the proverb *Koom suu tapo tı bag-bi lad moagna*, "Rain has been mobilized for war [amassed in great quantity], so the small ponds laugh with joy." Another of his proverbs was *Saan dib lagem koabga tı piig paam yôore*, "[Though] one hundred visitors' sticks get together, granite withstands." There is also Naaba Tâaga, "Chief Mountain," from the proverb *Kata lagem koabga kô n sirig tâaga*, "[Even if] one hundred hyenas get together, they will not make a mountain crumble." Another is *Adga yegda ne kiuugu, adg gus a menga t'a pelem ka yiid kiuugu*, "[If] a star goes along with the moon, the star better watch out since it will not outshine the moon" (Mangin 1916: 20). These *zab yüüya* are intended as taunts and insults to defeated rivals, threats to potential usurpers, expressions of thanks and obeisance to higher chiefs, or promises of rewards to loyal supporters and dependents.

As I reported, to show great respect, Moosé men lie down on the ground with their elbows on the ground, a posture called *wôgmse*, and move their raised, closed hands back and forth in the air, *kudi kantıse*. This is a display given when commoners approach a paramount chief, or suitors pay formal respects to elders of lineages whom they hope will eventually give them a wife. The earliest books by European visitors to the Moosé include illustrations of this posture, and it is still very much in use. A related traditional gesture, *tom yugri*, is "to press one's forehead to the dust," as Moslems do in prayer.

People adopt similar postures in other West African cultures; in parts of Nigeria, for example, when people prostrate before a chief, they place the right and then the left cheek against the ground (see Walker 1969). A more moderate and more common posture of Moosé respect is an attenuated version of this, in which a man lies on his left side on the ground in a slightly curled posture, again with head down and elbows to the ground. Men adopt this posture when greeting a village chief with the elders at a ceremonial event like a funeral or courtship ritual, or any time they intend to exhibit great deference. As long as they remain there, the greeting men tend to remain on their side in this semi-prone, semi-curled position, called *küümbe a menga*, "bend oneself." Alexandre's (1953: 200, 451) wonderful Mooré–French dictionary translates *küümbe a menga* as "to make oneself SMALL."

Less elaborately, a man may adopt a slightly less recumbent posture, seated while leaning over on his side supporting himself on his outstretched arm (the verb is *kɩlle*). If a man is walking and encounters a superior, short of these postures he may stoop, *robende*. A man may convey moderate but still polite deference in the less salient display of bowing, *pomse*, or merely bending slightly at the waist, *zoonde*, though I did not see this often.

The verbal greeting to a chief is distinctive: *Y ziig be neere*, "May your place be beautiful." (I could never find any explanation for that greeting.) Also, Moosé often snap their fingers, *wê nug pɩrse*, when approaching a paramount chief, *kombere*, and in formal events do the same to applaud his actions or statements. They may also make appreciative, respectful noises to acknowledge his pronouncements. Traditionally, at least in principle, only a chief (at any level) or other member of the Nakomse clan was permitted to have a rectangular house, although now others sometimes do, especially Yarse. Nonchiefs who build rectangular homes today do so, I imagine, because they are using modern construction techniques: Walls built with lumber framing are flat, resulting in rectangular floor plans, and large rectangular galvanized steel roofing sheets lend themselves to rectangular roofs. Anyway, until recently all non-Nakomse lived in circular houses; village chiefs often did, and many still do. Ideally, a chief should display ostrich eggs on the corners of his roof, but there are no longer any ostriches in the region.

Chairs are modern introductions, but on any occasion when chairs are available they always go to the highest-ranking people present, while lower-ranking people sit on the ground. When people are all seated, the person sitting in a chair is above those on the ground. My wife and I had the only chairs in our neighborhood, and probably the only chairs in the whole village. When the village chief had important visitors, he sent a boy to get our chairs – and did not return them. He was entitled to do so because, in principle, the chief "owns" or "rules over" (the verb is *so*) all persons and things in the village (though not the land itself).

Men of high rank, chiefs, and elders increase their apparent stature – especially on ceremonial occasions when their rank is conformed – by donning a conical straw hat decorated with leather and surmounted by a leather knob. Other men never wear such a hat. Coming in to the presence of a superior, if men are wearing any sort of hat they remove it, and remove their shoes if they are wearing any.[2] On formal occasions, paramount chiefs wear distinctive billowing robes and leather slippers. The significance of this garb is demonstrated by the fact that in the funeral ceremonies of high-ranking Nakomse, when daughters temporarily assume the mantle of their deceased father, the daughters put on these conical hats and dress in these robes and sandals, sitting on mats at the head of a small retinue. This makes them look much larger (greater in volume or mass) and taller than they appear in ordinary clothes. Otherwise, women never wear hats, slippers, or robes of this kind.

The Moosé idiom for disapproving of someone who is who is excessively self-important (in English we might say, "too big for his britches"), is to say that he is a *zek m menga*, literally "raise myself."

In all these ways Moosé display differences in rank along a VERTICAL DIMENSION.

When a village chief dies, the paramount chief picks his successor from among the descendants of past chiefs – that is, from the *Nakomse* clan. Many men want to be chief, so they make presents to the paramount chief and do whatever else they can to promote their case. As in other pursuits, Moosé use magic (*tɪɪm*) to augment their prospects. Magic can be purchased by the dose, ready-made, or, for a much higher price, one can purchase the secret formula, with which comes the right to make the magic for one's own use or to sell doses to others. Before I left the village, I went to a couple of different purveyors, from each of whom I purchased the right to make magic to rise ABOVE others in social rank, saying that, on returning home to the US, I hoped to raise my status. Both of the purveyors gave me similar recipes, which I cannot disclose. But I can reveal a couple of the ingredients. Moosé magic operates by amalgamating instances of the

[2] Moslems are accorded a dispensation from removing their distinctive hats, as their religion forbids them to remove them before any authority, I was told.

property one seeks, and transferring the property to the person by eating the magic, wiping it on the body, or wearing it enclosed in a leather amulet on a leather necklace. (Tylor [1871] called this manner of action "similarity" or "resemblance"; Frazer [1890] developed Tylor's ideas, variously characterizing this kind of action as "sympathetic magic," "imitation," or "homeopathy.") So it will not surprise you, or any Moosé, if I tell you that the ingredients of both of the recipes for magic to rise above others included a rock from the top of the tallest mountain, an epiphyte growing at the top of the tallest tree, and other items that likewise have the principle of "superiority" – of being ABOVE everything else. When Moosé grind up the ingredients with this property of HIGHNESS–SUPERIORITY, mix them, and ingest them, they intend to acquire the property of HIGHNESS in an authority ranking relationship. This magic is a clear and direct window into the ABOVE–BELOW conformation dimension.

Moosé also conform hierarchy along a dimension of FRONT to BACK. When a Moosé social group arrays itself for ceremonial purposes, "leaders" station themselves ahead of "followers." For example, at a funeral the elders sit on mats in the shade of a sun shelter, while their social inferiors sit fanned out behind them, in the hot sun. As a courtesy, elders will invite a highly respected visitor to join them at the head of the group (in the shade). Conversely, the small groups of people coming to greet the elders are literally "lead" by their "highest" ranking member of their delegation, although a local host may also be at their head, serving as an intermediary. This spatial arrangement is clearly conformed in the Mooré language by the fact that people of high rank are called *taordamba*, "in front people," and their subordinate followers are *poorêdamba*, "behind people." (A tilde over a vowel, e.g., *ê*, indicates nasalization.) Moosé also conform rank by order of march in ceremonial processions, PROCEEDING FIRST–GOING LATER, though ceremonial processions are infrequent. However, PROCEEDING FIRST–GOING LATER is complicated by a number of factors, including the practice of setting a youth or other subordinate at the head of the procession to absorb and bear the ill effects of any malicious magic the processors might encounter on the trail. The logic of this resembles the old European custom that, while the king or highest nobleman drinks "first," his young taster drinks before him, in case the drink is poisoned.

Moosé also consistently use the temporal dimension to conform social rank. When any group offers gifts to another, they present them in strict TEMPORAL ORDER according to the rank of the recipients. People dividing up sacrificial or other ritual meat or beer carefully observe the same procedure, allotting shares in temporal order of rank. Likewise, consumption is temporally ordered. When beer or food is served, no one may partake until the senior person present has poured a libation of the beer or tossed an offering bite of the food on the floor for the ancestors, and then taken the first sip or bite.[3] And when a woman brews beer, she always sends a pot to the chief BEFORE selling any or giving any away. On a much longer timescale, no one may begin to plant their field at the beginning of the rainy season until the chief begins to plant his. And at the end of the growing season, no one may begin to harvest before the chief does. Furthermore, the heads of each compound will not eat any of the new millet or sorghum until they have performed a first fruits ceremony at the ancestor altar, offering the first meal of the harvest to the ancestors. This ceremony is called *M bara renga ma*, "My fathers precede me."

Among the dead, precedence must also be observed. Moosé address their ancestors in sacrifices and libations when presenting each offering. When doing so, Moosé told me, it is crucial to address the ancestors in the proper order of succession; it could be fatal for the sacrificer to insult the senior ancestors by mistakenly addressing a more recent, "junior" ancestor before having addressed each of the senior ones.

Within gender, Moosé rank themselves very strictly by seniority in age, and they almost always know the precise relative order of births of all their lineage-mates, neighbors, and associates, although no one knows anyone's birth date or year, nor is anyone sure about their absolute age in years. In any lineage, the eldest living male (excluding descendants of sister's sons) is the *buud kasma* or *sak kasma*, "lineage elder," who has authority over all the members of the lineage, officiates at sacrifices and other ceremonies, and is the official giver and receiver of all brides. The next oldest man is the *kasm pugedga*, "elder follower," who is next in line of succession. He has important roles, including being the official divider who apportions gifts received, as well as apportioning sacrificial and ceremonial beer and food.

On ceremonial occasions, I observed that Nakomse and Yarse wear robes that are *peelega*, "white" (a color term which, in the Mooré three-color lexicon, semantically includes what I perceived as pale blue), in contrast to the indigo-saturated deep blue robes of Yîyôose and Sãaba.

3 However, to show that beer is not poisoned, the woman bringing the beer immediately takes a sip, and then the host takes a sip before presenting it to the senior guest. This raises the intriguing question of why neither the taster's nor the beer-brewer's sip represents either of them as socially "first." We return to this issue in Chapter 16.

This contrast between undyed white cotton and dark indigo-dyed cotton is one of the few means by which Moosé traditionally could create differences in LUMINANCE, since they had neither bright lamps nor reflective fabrics. In ceremonies, Nakomse and Yarse carry spears, while Yîyôose and Sãaba carry ritual axes.

****

This is what I observed and participated in. Reflecting on these practices and trying to distill them, I eventually recognized that nearly all Moosé representations of authority ranking consisted of relative positions on physical dimensions: BIGGER–SMALLER, MORE NUMEROUS–FEWER, ABOVE–BELOW, TEMPORALLY PRECEDING–FOLLOWING, IN FRONT–BEHIND, MORE FORCE ("POWER," STRENGTH)–LESS FORCE, LOUDER–QUIETER, MORE LUMINOUS–LESS LUMINOUS. Eight dimensions. No one dimension seems to have definite primacy – they are all comparably prevalent and meaningful. For the six dimensions that have inherent MORE and LESS poles, MORE always represents "higher" status.

In sum, Moosé do authority ranking by positioning themselves along temporal and spatial dimensions, representing authority ranking iconically, as RELATIVE ELEVATION, IN-FRONT VS. BEHIND, TEMPORALLY PRECEDING VS. FOLLOWING, STRONG FORCE VS. WEAKNESS, PLURAL VS. SINGULAR, and so forth. Correct relative positioning likely evokes emotions that support the authority ranking relationship. Moreover, properly positioning oneself and others on these dimensions is morally obligatory, and it invokes participants' commitment to sustain the authority ranking relationship. The iconic actions and postures are affirmations of the authority ranking relationship. Conversely, misplacement on any dimension, reversing the relative positions, is a grave transgression, evoking strong moral emotions. Moreover, the means for resisting or rejecting authority ranking in a given domain of social life, or resisting or rejecting the placement of persons in the authority ranking, is refusal to adopt proper positions on physical dimensions. Furthermore, iconic dimensions are the mode of imagining, prospectively evaluating, and planning authority ranking relations, as well as constructing authority ranking proverbs, narratives, and such.

Seeing how the Moosé use physical dimensions to represent social rank, what jumps out is that other cultures also use physical dimensions to represent relative statuses in authority ranking relationships in similar ways. Chapters 6 through 11 explore that.

Concrete One-to-One Correspondence Operations of Moosé Equality Matching

Recall that equality matching relationships are not simply the absence of hierarchy – they are organized by a distinctive relational model with its own structure. Concomitantly, Moosé do equality matching in a different mode. Moosé engage in equality matching relations far less frequently than in authority ranking relations, but equality matching is salient in certain contexts.

During courtship prestations and on other occasions, a group of Moosé peers (*redẽtaase;* usually men of nearly the same age) often receives a pile of kola nuts. They will *pui ti zemse*, "divide equally," but not by doing arithmetic division. No one counts the kola nuts or does any math. Rather, the divider uses a CONCRETE OPERATION to make an even distribution. Their procedure is a particular form of ONE-TO-ONE MATCHING. One person will put the kola nuts out one by one, round after round: one in the first pile, one in the second pile, one in the third pile, etc., where the number of piles equals the number of people. Each round should consist of evenly matched kolas, so far as possible. If there are kolas remaining at the end of the last round, the divider breaks them into equal-sized pieces and repeats the operation of one here, one there, etc. At this point, the piles have not been allocated to persons. If there is currency, tobacco, or something else to divide, the divider repeats the procedure separately with each coin denomination or each substance. That is, the division of each substance is independent of the division of each other substance.

Typically the person who divides gets the last pick among the piles he has created. Cowives use this concrete operation to divide salt they purchase with money they get as a gift from a lineage seeking one of their girls in marriage (Mason 1988).

Moosé use a variant of this CONCRETE ONE-TO-ONE MATCHING OPERATION to make even distributions of substances that do not consist of discrete natural units. For the annual *Kiuugu* rituals, heads of households often purchase a cow to eat; it is simply butchered, not sacrificed. Few villagers can afford a whole cow, and few have families large enough to eat one before the meat spoils. So two or more men will go even shares to purchase an animal together. Then they have to divide up the meat. First they separate each kind of meat: intestines, ribs, legs, neck, etc. Then they meticulously set out even piles of one kind of meat. They do this visually and by weighing the meat in their hands; they do not have access to pan balances or scales. When the participants all agree that all are indifferent as to which pile they get, they each take possession of one pile, and go on to divide the next type of meat in the same manner.

Moosé villagers buy and sell all kinds of local products in the markets held every three days, although they sell only a very small percentage of what they produce. Villagers may go to the market when they need something no one in their family produces. Commonly they have no cash. They may not want to wait for the next market day, they may not want to make the long walk to the market, or for any other reason a person seeking agricultural products may propose to a neighbor a *tekre*, "even trade." For example, if a woman has peanuts but needs cotton, she will fill a basket with peanuts and find a neighbor who is willing to trade. The first woman empties her basket of peanuts onto the neighbor's mat, and then the neighbor fills that same basket with cotton, which the woman who came with peanuts takes home. Of course, they are aware that the monetary value of the two commodities differs in the market, but that is irrelevant to their *tekre*. What happens in a *tekre* is that the substances exchanged are evenly matched in quantity, by virtue of the CONCRETE OPERATION of filling up the same basket first with one product, then with the other.

Moosé also use CONCRETE ONE-TO-ONE MATCHING OPERATIONS to evenly match their labor. For example, if they get along well, cowives may take turns, with one wife cooking the meal for the entire household each evening (Mason 1988). In many families, the woman who cooks is the one who sleeps with the husband that night.

Equality matching also organizes certain Moosé agricultural activities. Each family stores unthreshed millet in their granaries beside their homes, threshing the millet in batches as they use it. But they thresh all of their sorghum in one day, on threshing grounds near their fields, and then bring the threshed and winnowed grain to their granary in the village. Threshing sorghum is a group activity. The owner of the sorghum invites his neighbors, friends, kin, and in-laws to come on a fixed day, arranged so as not to conflict with the scheduled threshing days of anyone else. The event is called a *zaiiga*. Men show up, spread the sorghum across the threshing ground, and line up with wooden flails. They beat the sorghum in strokes, in rhythm with drums played by men walking behind them. Each thresher synchronizes with one of the two sets, each of which occupies alternate positions in the line (i.e., person 1, 3, 5, etc. synchronize on one beat, alternating with person 2, 4, 6, etc., who beat the alternate beat). Since there are usually more men than flails, men regularly move into the line at the left end, with each person in turn moving one position to the right, while passing his flail to the left, until the last man on the right drops out for a rest, to return to the line later. Soon another man likewise enters the line of threshers. They do this passing on of flails without missing a beat, staying in synchrony according to their position in line. When all the grain is threshed, the host serves food and beer. I participated in many of these threshing bees. It was hard work in the hot sun, but the synchronous rhythmic work to the drum beat was emotionally meaningful, the camaraderie was great, and it was satisfying to see the work we had jointly accomplished. In each rotation through the line, at least, each man strikes the grain with a flail the same number of times as each other man in the line. That is patently evident, though no one knows or cares how many strikes on the grain anyone made. They just see that they are "even."

The host keeps track of who attends, and subsequently attends the *zaiiga* of each man who came to his. But he skips the *zaiiga* of anyone who failed to come to his *zaiiga*, unless they have a good excuse.

Thus, sorghum threshing consists of ONE-TO-ONE MATCHING OPERATIONS at four levels: matching each beat of the flail to the set of threshers in your alternation, matching one's strokes with the threshers in the alternate positions, matching rotations though the entire line, and matching attendance at each other's *zause*.

Likewise, during the growing season, when the weeds get ahead of a farmer, he may invite his neighbors, friends, kin, and in-laws to come on a scheduled day to hoe his field together; that is a *sisoaaga*. With or without drums, the participants line up at one edge of the field, and at the same moment they all begin to hoe the weeds. They work in parallel, side by side, in a line across the field, with the strip each person cultivates roughly matching the strip each other person cultivates. When the line reaches the far side of the field they all move down the field together, turn around, and, still side by side but facing in the opposite direction, they again cultivate matching strips of land. At the end, the host normally provides millet beer for everyone to drink together. If a man comes to the host's *sisoaaga*, the host will, in return, come to that man's next *sisoaaga*.

Moosé organize some other types of group work with many of the same procedures, such as the work of women beating flat the clay surface of their patios in rhythmic unison to their singing, or men digging catchment ponds side by side in unison to the beat of drums. Women pound grain or other materials in a large mortar, using a pestle nearly two meters long. Often a pair or a trio of women sing as they pound in the same mortar, taking precisely timed turns so their pestles do not strike the others' pestles.

Sometimes each woman in turn tosses her pestle high, claps her hands, and then regains control of the descending pestle.

A dramatic form of ONE-TO-ONE MATCHING occurs on festivals, and ad hoc near the market during the dry season, on fallow fields. A pair of horsemen gallops across the field, starting simultaneously and going all out, then abruptly pulling up, often very nearly galloping through the spectators. To a naïve Western observer, from a distance, these resemble horse races, or else a cavalry charge – except that the two horsemen have an arm around each other, and stay precisely side by side. They make sure to be aligned throughout the course.

ONE-TO-ONE MATCHING and TURN-TAKING procedures constitute the framework for a pan-African game that Moosé play. This game uses four rows of holes in the ground or in a wooden board, together with counters (pebbles or large seeds). There are several variants, but, basically, play consists of choosing one hole on the player's own side, picking up all of the counters in that hole, concealing them in the hand, and dropping them very rapidly, one into each successive hole along the board, going around and around along the two rows of holes on the player's side. If the last counter falls in a hole that contains counters and is opposite an opponent's hole that contains counters, the player takes his opponent's counters from that hole, adds them to the counters in his hand, and continues play. If the player's last counter falls in an empty hole, he stops and the other player's turn begins. The last player with counters remaining on the board wins. Experts play very fast, which makes it possible to cheat if the opponent is not watching very closely and counting carefully. My understanding is that, in many communities, anyway, it is "legitimate" to "cheat," but you have to stop and redo the play if the other player detects your cheating. What makes this a fair game is that the two sets of holes match, the initial number of counters match, and the players take turns. Most games in most cultures have similar equality matching structures (Murray 1952, Bell 1979, Bell & Cornelious 1988; for further discussion of games and sports, see Chapter 14).

As the structure of these coordinating practices demonstrates, in Moosé equality matching relations, concrete operations of one-to-one correspondence are the mode of coordination, and simultaneously the moral standard for equality matching: to do equality matching properly is to perform the concrete operations of one-to-one correspondence. Hence, these concrete operation conformations create commitments that motivate participants to do what they are supposed to do. Concomitantly, participating in these concrete operations of one-to-one matching is meaningful, satisfying, fulfilling. That is, these concrete operations evoke emotions, and violations of these operations evoke other emotions, as well as moral judgments. Furthermore, imagining concrete operations of one-to-one matching is the mode of conceiving of possible or impossible equality matching relations, before they exist, or without the relations ever being realized.

****

Long before deciding to do my dissertation fieldwork in Burkina Faso with the Moosé, over several years, I had constructed a proto-theory built on my integration of aspects of the concepts of legitimacy in Max Weber's *Economy and Society*, together with the successive historical forms of Christian theodicy posited in Paul Ricoeur's *The Symbolism of Evil*, and with the stages of moral development formulated in Jean Piaget's *The Moral Judgment of the Child.* My theory posited the existence of three fundamental structures of social relations – the ones that, with further theoretical development, eventually became communal sharing, authority ranking, and market pricing. I intended my fieldwork to determine whether these three forms of social relations were apparent in Moosé society, and, indeed, doing my fieldwork in the village I found that they were each clearly evident in Moosé social relations. But in addition to those three forms, I kept encountering other social relations consisting of what I have reported above: concrete procedures of one-to-one matching, making things even by alignment, taking turns, and precise, in-kind reciprocity. I tried to shoehorn these social relations into the three categories I expected, but they just didn't fit – they patently did not correspond to any of those relational structures. So I had to add to my typology a fourth type of fundamental social relational structure: the one that, with further refinement, eventually became equality matching. In order to characterize the mode of its construction, coordination, and communication, I drew from three of Piaget's other books: *The Language and Thought of the Child*, *Play, Dreams and Imitation in Childhood*, and *The Child's Conception of Number.* In these works Piaget elegantly described how, at a certain stage of cognitive development, children judge whether two quantities are equal. Piaget observed that, whether the experimenter asks the child to compare liquids, compare solids, or compare discrete items, children at the stage of "concrete operations" performed an operation of aligning the two things, making it easy to compare them to see if they are even, albeit by only one criterion. Or, in some other concrete manipulation, they put the sets they were comparing in one-to-one correspondence. But Piaget showed that at this stage of cognitive development, children judged equality by any one concrete operation that matched the two sets one-to-one. Thus, children would say that there was the same amount of water in two beakers when the level of the top of the column of water was the same, though the diameter of the two beakers differed substantially. But they understood that another concrete operation also established equal quantities: pouring one liquid into a vessel, noting how high it comes on the vessel, pouring it out, then pouring the other liquid into the same vessel, looking to see whether the second liquid came to the same height as the first. The children Piaget studied whom he identified as at the "stage" of concrete operations apparently did not observe, or if they observed, did not reconcile, the fact that while one concrete operation showed equality, another concrete operation could show inequality. For example, the liquids in two glass vessels could be level, making them the same by that operation. But if one poured the liquid out of the thinner vessel, and then poured into it the liquid from the vessel with greater diameter, the liquid would overflow the thinner vessel, concretely manifesting inequality.

In these works, Piaget was concerned with the psychology of the individual child comparing two quantities. But what I saw among the Moosé was adults' use of concrete operations to make things equal in social relationships – that is, to make the work that each person contributes equal the work that each other person contributes; to divide things up into equal shares; or to make an even trade, and so forth. In each case the Moosé employ a procedure that is, pragmatically speaking, the operational definition of social relational equality. No doubt, when cultivating a field side by side, the strips that each person cultivated differ in hardness and stoniness, and have somewhat different widths. But Moosé disregarded that, treating the work of cultivating side by side, from one edge of the field to the opposite edge, as constitutive of social relational equality. A surveyor would have found that the two edges of the field were not parallel, but the cultivators ignored the consequent differences in the lengths of the strips cultivated by different participants. Likewise, in modern sports, if, at halftime, the wind gets stronger, blowing from one goal line toward the other, and snow starts falling rapidly, well, nonetheless, each team defends each end of the pitch for the same length of time. And that is judged to be fair, by virtue of the concrete operation of one-to-one matching.

Let us take stock. Authority ranking conforms inequality of social rank by relative positions on continuous dimensions that simply represent the direction of the inequality; the amount of inequality is neither well defined nor definitely represented. This is the structure mathematically known as a *linear ordering*. That is also the structure of ordinal measurement. Equality matching conforms equality by concrete operations such as aligning, placing in one-to-one correspondence, or cycles of taking turns. These operations instantiate the structure of an *ordered Abelian group* (i.e., a mathematical group in which addition and its inverse are defined and that is closed under both operations, but no zero is defined, nor is there a definition of multiplication or its inverse). This is exactly the structure of an interval measurement scale.

What, then, are the respective conformation systems of communal sharing and market pricing?

Constitution of Communal Sharing by Consubstantial Assimilation

The tie between mother and child is the strongest communal sharing bond in Moosé society, I believe. Moosé conform this bond as based on suckling, and Moosé denote the strong communal sharing relationships among uterine siblings are as *ma biiri,* "mother's children"). *Biiri* is presumably derived from *biisum*, "milk." They say of a full sibling, *tônd yaa ma a ye, ba a ye*, "we are one mother, one father." Half siblings say that they are *ba a ye*, "one father." Members of the same lineage, *buudu*, say *tônd yaa bûmb a ye*, "we are one thing," or *tônd fãa yaa a yembre*, "we are all one." A Moosé women often nurses her child until she is pregnant again, which does not happen soon when the infant, held in a cloth on the mother's back or side, is suckling on demand, off and on all day, and lying beside her, suckling ad lib all night. (Married woman totally flatten their breasts because they're not supposed to look like unmarried girls. This incidentally elongates the breasts considerably, enabling infants in the supporting cloth to reach the nipple easily.)

After they are weaned, girls join the group of women and girls eating directly out of a common pot of the staple dough-like *sagbo*, together with a common pot of boiled leaves or other vegetables. Boys and men gather in another place around their shared pot of *sagbo* and their shared pot of vegetables. Men and boys never ever eat or drink with women or girls, nor vice versa, no matter what their relationship and no matter what the occasion. (This gender separation at meals is virtually universal in traditional Africa.) However, sometimes men are fed with the understanding that when the men stop eating, a women will take the leftovers to the women; in that case the men know that what they leave uneaten is the only food the women will have.

A Moosé person does not eat alone, with two exceptions: if he or she is very old, then, out of respect, he or she is served an individual bowl of *sagbo* and an individual bowl of vegetables to eat alone, out of sight. An honored guest is also fed separately and eats alone, out of sight, so that without embarrassment they can eat the choice vegetables, or even meat, that others may not have been served. When there is beer, each pot is served to a group, which pours some into a fairly large hemispherical calabash that they pass around and around. When the women bring out the pots of food for the main daily meal for all of the men of a compound (or a set of adjacent small compounds), the women from each household all put all of the pots they bring out in one spot and all the men eat together, sharing the food cooked by everyone's wives. Also, when women prepare some special food they very often take a portion of it and give it to each of the neighboring compounds.

I never heard Moosé talk about this commensalism, but it seems to play an important role in constituting, affirming, and communicating the communal sharing relationship among a group of kinsmen, and, interestingly enough, among their wives (who belong to different natal patrilines). Likewise, the separation of men's commensalism from women's commensalism strikingly constitutes and communicates the social distinction between genders.

The profound moral implications of commensalism for the Moosé are evident in two intriguing metarelationships. Moosé believe that it is fatal to link commensalism in certain configurations with certain other relationships. Here is the most salient example.

Funerals of senior men are the occasion for the largest sets of persons to eat and drink beer commensally. Every person in the patrilineage attends such a funeral, along with their wives. Also attending are members of patrilineages who have given or received a wife from the patrilineage of the deceased. Friends and neighbors attend so there may be several hundred people at a funeral. None of the people attending knows everyone else; some know hardly anyone, I imagine. As far as I could see, they rarely (if ever) introduce themselves to people they do not know. When the women bring out pots of beer or food, men sort themselves into groups of roughly eight to fifteen men who are of similar age. I believe that often some of the men in such an ad hoc group do not know some (or any) of the others. Each group passes around a calabash of beer, refilling it from the pot when necessary. Or the group gathers around the bowl of *sagbo* and the bowl of cooked leaves. Then they disperse, joining the set of people they came with, or wandering around. This assembling into commensal groups occurs a few times every day, as more food or beer appears. After the three-day funeral ends, everyone departs. I assume that many of the people attending probably will never see, and certainly will never interact with, many of those with whom they were commensal in one or more of these drinking or eating groups.

Hence, this is a social practice in which the consubstantial assimilation conforming the relationship comprises the entire relationship; there is nothing more to it. I doubt that participating in one such commensal event with strangers ordinarily has any lasting representational, emotional, motivational, or moral effect – with one remarkable exception that evidently is a salient concern of Moosé men. If one of the men who drank or ate commensally on such an occasion, or any other occasion, has had sex with the wife of one of the others eating or drinking commensally with him, Moosé are certain that the woman's husband will die. Virtually all men have long-term lovers who are married (essentially all women of child-bearing age are married), and, additionally, men sometimes (perhaps frequently) have sexual relations with other married women. But men do not know their lovers' husbands, nor do husbands know their wives' lovers. So far as I know, Moosé do not worry or even imagine that a man would knowingly eat or drink with the husband of his lover, let alone do so intentionally, in order to kill him. But occasionally men accidentally drink or eat with a wife's lover, without either of them knowing it when they did so. From time to time, people see this revealed. That is, at a funeral, the deceased, when asked what moral transgression led to his death, occasionally indicates that his death is the moral result of some man's having sex with his wife. Moosé are certain that the deceased's testimony is infallible. We can analyze this in conformations systems theory thusly: Moosé believe that, among men in a certain configuration of relationships, commensalism on a single occasion has an immanent fatal moral effect. Observing or hearing of such testimony has representational, emotional, motivational, and moral effects on the living.

There is another configuration in which commensalism is fatal, again showing its moral significance. Suppose Noraoogo finds that someone has stolen his goats or run off with his young wife. Noraoogo does not know who the thief is, and the thief may be some stranger. Noraoogo can swear an oath like this, addressing a *Têese* ("Earths," always pluralized) with its proper name, "[Name], my goats were stolen. I do not know who stole them. Whoever it is, kill them. I will thank you with a goat." There are a number of *Têese*, any of which anyone may invoke with such an oath.

Moosé with whom I discussed *Têese* readily explained what it did, but could not say how a *Têese* came to have such power and insight, how it identified the culprit, nor how it killed him. What a *Têese* does is to respond justly to such an oath: in the coming weeks or months, it will kill the transgressor. Especially if there is a *ku miuugu*, "red death" – that is, someone dies by lightning, by snakebite, by a wild animal, or a fall from a tree – everyone immediately recognizes that there is a moral reason for the death, and if a death occurs within a few weeks of such an oath, it must be the *Têese*'s verdict. In that case the person who has died the "red death" would be immediately buried, without a funeral, in a shallow rectangular grave a little ways into the bush, *weoogo*, rather than in the grave chamber of their kin. If someone dies in some other way, some people will assume that the *Têese* has rendered its verdict, but the deceased's husband or a senior kinsman might go ask a diviner to see whether that is, indeed, the moral explanation for the death.

Once the *Têese* has killed the culprit, Noraoogo absolutely must sacrifice a goat to the *Têese* he invoked, thanking it for rendering its verdict. To do this, Noraoogo slits the goat's throat and holds it so that its blood flows over the "altar" – that is, into and onto an ordinary -looking pot covered in dried blood from the sacrifices of thanks that it has previously received. Noraoogo pours libations of beer, and then his boys butcher and roast the goat. Noraoogo and his close kin commensally eat the goat and drink the beer. So, making the sacrifice, Noraoogo is performing consubstantial assimilation to and with the being to whom he makes the sacrifice. Noraoogo has an absolute moral obligation to do this sacrifice. If a person whose oath the *Têese* has enforced fails to give sacrificial thanks to the *Têese*, the *Têese* will kill the ingrate. This, I believe, shows the moral impact of consubstantial assimilation. And there is further evidence of the moral impact of commensalism. Suppose that the *Têese* has not yet executed the culprit and, one day, Noraoogo joins a group of men sharing a pot of beer in the market or at a funeral. It may happen that, among the men with whom Noraoogo drinks commensally, unbeknownst to him, one of them is the culprit. Then, sooner or later, the *Têese* will kill Noraoogo, leaving the culprit untouched. I interpret this as meaning that it is morally wrong for Noraoogo to implicitly promise consubstantial assimilation with the *Têese*, and then, however unknowingly, engage in consubstantial assimilation with the person whom Noraoogo has asked the *Têese* to execute. Though I could never get any informant to explain the moral-relational logic, that seems to be it. In any case, this definitely shows, again, that, for the Moosé, commensalism is a conformational act with profound moral entailments, regardless of the participants' knowledge or intentions (see Fiske 2023).

The Moosé are just one of many cultures with salient metarelational models in which consubstantial assimilation in one relationship, linked in a certain configuration to sexual relations in another relationship, has profound moral consequences, especially death. For other examples, see Fiske (2011)

As mentioned earlier, Moosé invariably share their food and drink with their ancestors. Whenever men eat, the senior man tosses the first bite of food on the ground, feeling the *kɩmse*, "ancestors." Whenever they drink beer, the senior man first pours a little on the ground, giving the ancestors the first sip. So, for example, our neighbor and host, the very old man, may appear to be eating or drinking alone, as there is no one visibly sharing his meal. Perhaps he feels that he is not alone because he is eating and drinking commensally with his ancestors; I don't know. But he knows that when he dies and becomes an ancestor himself, he will continue to share every meal and every pot of beer with his descendants, who will always give him and his co-ancestors the first bite and the first sip.

Beyond the daily commensalism among women, among men, and between men and the ancestors, there is one day of the year, *Kiiugu*, when each lineage, and the village as a village, engage in especially vital commensalism connecting them with their ancestors, and with the Earth itself, through blood sacrifice, with libations. Of all the acts of consubstantial assimilation that I participated in or observed, this somehow seemed to me the most emotionally intense, the most strongly motivated, the most constitutive. On behalf of the lineage, its oldest man in each lineage, the *buud kasma*, goes to the lineage's ancestor altar and sacrifices chickens to *Naaba Wenaam*, "Chief God"; to *Tenga*, "Earth"; and to the individually, sequentially named *kɩmse*, "ancestors." (I never heard anyone ever mention *Wenaam* except in such sacrificial invocations.) On the same day, the *Têngsoba*, "Owner/proprietor of the earth," also performs a ritual seeking well-being, good crops, and fertility for the village as a whole. As he does so, members of each of the Yîyôose lineages of the village look on. The *Têngsoba* sits facing a *têkugri*, located in the *weoogo*, some hundreds of meters from the village. Physically, a *têkugri*, "earth stone," is an "altar" simply consisting of a very old tree stump, or a set of half-buried smooth granite stones in the earth, in no particular arrangement. I do not know where these stones come from, as I have never seen any granite in the region. For many years, beyond memory, the *Têngsoba* and his predecessors have performed the *Kiiugu* ritual at this *têkugri*, as well as at other *têkuga* (plural of *têkugri*) where he will repeat the ritual during the course of the day. At each one, he places his ritual axe, which is thickly encrusted with the blood, feathers, and bits of flesh of many previous *Kiiugu* rituals. The *Têngsoba* addresses *Naaba Wenaam* and *Tenga*, asking them to protect the village, as he pours plain water from a hemispherical calabash over the axe and *têkugri*. He then address his *kumse* – specifically, his predecessors who were *Têngsoba* before him. Then he takes a calabash of water mixed with flavored millet flour, pouring it over the axe and *têkugri* as he invokes *Wenaam* and *Tenga* again, and then the *kumse*, invoked in exact order of their precedence. Next, he takes a calabash of millet beer and does the same thing. Then someone hands him a chicken, which he holds by the legs above the axe and *têkugri*; he takes his knife and cuts the jugular vein of the chicken and holds it while the blood pours over the axe and *têkugri*. After a couple of minutes he tosses the chicken to the ground, where it flops around. In principle, if the chicken stops moving when lying on its breast, the beings whom he is addressing – *Wenaam*, *Tenga*, and his *kumse* – have accepted the sacrifice. But if the chicken ceases moving while lying on its back, they have rejected the sacrifice: something is wrong, someone has committed some transgression, so the ritual must stop until that transgression can be identified by a diviner, and accordingly rectified. All sacrifices are tentative in this way, to be accepted or refused. But, as in most sacrifices where the sacrificers anticipate no problems, at the Kiuugu sacrifices on behalf of the village as a whole, the young man who is stooped over the chicken knows that he should grab it and pick it up the first time it flops onto its breast; there is no point in waiting for the chicken to signal anything but its acceptance by the beings to whom the sacrifice is addressed.

After sacrificing a chicken, the *Têngsoba* pours more libations of water, flour water, and beer, as he again asks *Wenaam*, *Tenga*, and the *kumse* for the well-being of the village. He plucks a few feathers and pastes them onto the bloody axe and *têkugri*. Then he takes another chicken, cuts its jugular, bleeds it over the axe and *têkugri*, and tosses it on the ground to flop and be picked up by the young man the moment it is on its breast, signaling acceptance of the offering. The *Têngsoba* plucks a few feathers and pastes them onto the bloody axe and *têkugri*. He may go through this cycle a couple more times, then he stops and takes a sip of the liquids he has been offering, from the calabashes he has been pouring the libations. The boys who are in attendance soon pluck the chickens, butcher them, build a fire, and roast them. They then bring the roasted chickens in a basket to the *Têngsoba*, who pours more libations as he again asks for the well-being of the village. He takes bits of the beak, a few claws, bits of a thigh, and pieces of the liver of the chicken, tossing them on the axe and *têkugri* while again asking *Wenaam*, *Tenga*, and his *kumse* for their protection; he does the same with each chicken, then sets them all aside.

The attendants then bring the *Têngsoba* a goat. Two men hold it by the rear legs, head down, while the *Têngsoba* cuts its jugular so the blood gushes over the axe and *têkugri*. They hold it firmly as it continues to bleed and dies. The *Têngsoba* cuts off bits of the ear, bits of the tongue, bits of the tail, and a bit of the cord used to restrain the goat; he tosses all of them on the axe and *têkugri*, asking for village well. The boys then skin, butcher, and roast the goat. They bring it back to the *Têngsoba*, who tosses onto the axe and *têkugri* pieces of the liver and pieces of the stomach, pouring more libations as he again asks *Wenaam*, *Tenga*, and his *kumse* to protect the village.

Finally, the *Têngsoba* and the assembled senior Yîyôose drink the remaining beer, flour water, and plain water, and share the roasted chickens and goat. Then they move on to the next *têkugri* and repeat the whole cycle of sacrifices. They save some of the meat to bring home to share with Yîyôose men with who were not in attendance, with all of their wives, and with their children. All Yîyôose of the village get at least a little of this meat, I believe. It is a "treat," a "luxury," because Moosé often go weeks or months without meat. Indeed, most of the meat that most Moosé ever eat is the meat of sacrifices. There are hardly any wild animals left to hunt, and most villagers can only rarely afford to buy meat in the market. The few goats, sheep, and chickens that Moosé raise are almost all saved for ritual sacrifice, unless they need to be sold for emergency expenses. For the *Têngsoba's Kiuugu* sacrifices that I've just described, the goats are purchased with contributions collected from all over the village, including the Nakomse, Sãaba, and perhaps (I don't know) also the Yarse. The head of each lineage neighborhood also sends representatives with beer and a chicken, but only the Yîyôose and their wives share in the sacrificial meat and liquids.

While the *Têngsoba* is sacrificing on behalf of the village as a whole, back in the village the head of each lineage is sacrificing on behalf of his lineage, speaking to his *kiĩmse*, to *Tenga* the earth, to the *têese* if he has one, and to the *tubo*, another altar force that protects the compound. Most lineages most years cannot afford a goat; they pour libations and sacrifice only chickens. They perform these and other sacrifices over a set of clay pots along the outside wall of the hut of the lineage head. The pots, which to begin with were ordinary pots indistinguishable from those used for everyday purposes, are encrusted with the dried black blood, feathers, and bits of chicken of previous sacrifices.

When anyone is seriously or chronically ill, or suffers a misfortune, or is planning a major undertaking and wants to assure that *Wenaam*, *Tenga*, and his *kɩɩmse* are well disposed to have it go smoothly, the lineage head consults a diviner, who almost invariably prescribes a sacrifice implicitly directed primarily at a particular though unnamed being, performed on a specified day at a specified location, with a certain color chicken or chickens. (The Yarse, as Muslims, do not perform blood sacrifices, so diviners prescribe for them analogous nonbloody offerings.[4])

I found these sacrifices emotionally evocative, and memorable. Perhaps they have less impact on people who have grown up hunting and raising animals for sacrifice. On the other hand, presumably sacrifices have more impact on people who, unlike me, believe in the beings to whom they are addressed, believe that those beings are somehow partaking in the sacrificial meat and libations, believe that these beings are pleased when people offer them sacrifices, and believe that the sacrificer's welfare, and his family's welfare, depends on the dispositions of *Wenaam*, *Tenga*, and their *kɩɩmse*, "ancestors." In any case, the people gathered at the sacrifice see *Wenaam*, *Tenga*, and their *kɩɩmse* being fed the blood and bits of the flesh of the animals, the bulk of whose meat the people then join them in eating. People see beer, flour water, and plain water given to *Wenaam*, *Tenga*, and their *kɩɩmse*, and then themselves drink the rest of the beer. So they do not simply observe, they experience the commensal sharing of the meat and beer with these beings, and among their lineage-mates. This commensalism is especially salient because apart from such rituals they infrequently have meat, and relatively infrequently have beer to drink. They see and hear that their welfare depends on the benevolence of *Wenaam*, *Tenga*, and their *kɩɩmse*, whom they are feeding with the libations and sacrifices. And they are notably reminded of the ancestry they share. Perhaps during these rituals, and certainly at funerals, they are reminded that when they die, their bodies will be placed in the earth in the lineage

[4] In most of the sacrifices that I attended, the sacrificer spoke very quietly and did not clearly articulate all of his words. So, although I was typically only a meter or two away, I couldn't hear much of what he said, and even on the occasions when, with permission, I used a tape recorder with a microphone on the ground next to the altar, I couldn't capture everything. Hence, my account of the invocations may be incomplete or even inaccurate in some respects. Note, however, that at sacrifices by the lineage head, I found that few if any others typically were present while the lineage head was addressing his ancestors, and at the *Têngsoba's Kiuugu* sacrifices, the only person who might have been close enough sometimes to hear his words was the young man standing there to pick up the chicken.

tomb chamber near their compound, alongside the bones of their *kumse*. That postmortem body-to-bone contact may add another aspect to the consubstantial assimilation in rituals that evoke and renew the communal sharing relations among lineage members, *Wenaam*, *Tenga*, and their *kumse*.

Moosé use additional means of making their bodies alike. Recall the cultivating and threshing bees, respectively *sısoose* and *zaııse*. Earlier in this chapter, I emphasized the concrete operation of one-to-one matching of strokes each person performs, but note now that the men threshing in rhythmic synchrony with each other are also thereby making their bodies equivalent in their motions, thereby indexically performing consubstantial assimilation. Women do the same when they gather to pound the mud to renew a courtyard, beating it hard with their mallets, in rhythmic synchrony.

As the reader may have noted, another ubiquitous example of two separate conformation systems operating in the same event occurs at all commensal eating and drinking where, before anyone eats or drinks, the senior man tosses a morsel of food or beer on the ground for the ancestors, and then himself takes the next bite or drink, before anyone else may begin. This temporal precedence is iconic conformation, while the commensal consumption is indexical consubstantial assimilation.

A factor in women's identity as "Moosé," it seems, is that women are made equivalent by all having their incisors filed to a point. Men are bodily connected through the equivalence of their circumcised penises, in contrast to some of the surrounding societies that do not circumcise. Likewise, Moosé women all have had a clitoridectomy, which makes their genitalia morphologically equivalent to those of all other adult Moosé women. Without a clitoridectomy a woman is not really a proper woman, Moosé women say. Without that, the women said, no one would ever marry Gũwende or take her as a lover. They laughed that though we might be squeamish about it, not to worry, they would take care of it when the time came. We knew that it would not be done on a young child, and we were long gone before she was old enough that we needed to protect her from that.

Ineffability

Since sacrifices appeared dramatic to me, and were certainly salient, significant rituals, I assumed that the Moosé obviously must have extensive and well-formulated concepts of them, and, if they wanted to, could surely tell me a lot about them. That is, I took for granted that they could tell me what had happened, or was going to happen, and why. What was their intention in doing them? In memory systems terms, I assumed that they must have both articulable semantic knowledge of these rituals, and episodic memories of them as well. Yet I repeatedly struggled to get any sort of exegesis for sacrifices. I simply never could elicit reflections on sacrificial rituals, let alone explicit verbal conceptualizations or commentary. When I spoke to Moosé after we returned from a sacrifice, they had almost nothing to say about the event. At most, they would simply tell me the kind of event it was, naming it: "We sacrificed" or "We made a rain sacrifice," but that was about all. That is, in practice, they never mentioned any beliefs at all. This perplexed me, and increasingly frustrated me. It was a long time before I began to appreciate what it indicated about the conformation of sacrifice.

During the first months of our fieldwork, I knew that the villagers were concerned about how I judged their rituals, and their culture in general. This concern, I imagine, is based on their colonial experience, as well as, more recently, the attitudes and actions of some missionaries and Indigenous church leaders who have been or are today quite hostile to traditional religion. Villagers initially wondered whether I would be hostile toward their religious traditions, or mock them, and they were somewhat concerned, and even fearful and potentially embarrassed, at the prospect of my discovering what they were doing in these matters.

Still, after it became obvious that I respected their rituals, very little changed. By all indications, they seemed to be quite comfortable having me closely observe their sacrifices and even tape-record their invocations. Some villagers retained the lingering suspicion that my true intention was to take away or destroy the *al haali*, the ritual efficacy or soul of their altars, when we left at the end of our sojourn. (Note the borrowing of an Arabic term for this.) However, many people, especially those near my own age, came to trust us. Several disclosed other kinds of semantic and episodic information to me that made them very vulnerable to others, were I to disclose it to anyone. People who were interested in helping me and informing me about other matters, or who felt they needed to return a favor I had done for them, still apparently could not explain or even just <u>say</u> much about religion and ritual. I hoped I could identify the steps – the meaningful units of action – in Moosé rituals, by hearing their narration of their episodic memories of the rituals, or their scripts, expectations, and plans for rituals. But I never could elicit <u>any</u> narratives or scripts. Of course, I wanted to learn how they conceptualized their religion, and

I assumed that they surely must conceptualize it. I assumed that their conceptualizations would explain a lot about why they did sacrifices, and perhaps how and when sacrifices fulfill, or do not fulfill, the sacrificers' intentions.

For a while I assumed that this paucity of verbal description must be due to reticence about revealing secrets. But Moosé were no more forthcoming in their accounts of these events when they got to know me better, and when they had welcomed me to attend these and other rituals. Even when I was invited to attend sacrifices and other such rituals, if I asked what would take place, people would just say "Come and see." Or they would simply say "You know, it's a sacrifice." Some of the people saying this had trusted me with important secrets, but they would not interpret their rituals, nor analyze or simply explain them in any way, nor even describe them. I could elicit no narrative accounts of particular sacrifices, or of sacrifices in general. At these events themselves there was little commentary about the actions people were performing, and usually such talk as there was amounted to no more than labeling segments of action, and consultations or reminders about their proper sequence, when performing a ritual that the sacrificer did not know well. Overall, as far as I was able to hear or discover, among themselves Moosé engaged in hardly any interpretive, explanatory, analytic, or reflective commentary on their rituals. Furthermore, after the event, when I asked for an exegesis of the events I had observed, participants had virtually nothing to say in explanation of the ceremonies in which they had been participants, or which they themselves had conducted. They simply said "You were there! You saw it!" Or they laughed at my curiosity and said what the sacrificer says right at the beginning of the event: "*Yaa tônd rog m miki. Ed barâmba maaname, ti tônd me maandame* (It's what we were born and found. Our fathers/ancestors did it, so we too do it)." This is akin to what most Americans would say if you asked them why they put candles on a birthday cake, and then blow them out again, or why they carve faces in pumpkins. I never detected any irritation or discomfort at my questions about sacrifice; no one every showed any sign of taking offense. They just had nothing to say in answer to my inquiries.

In the first several months of my fieldwork I observed everything I could about all aspects of Moosé life, and participated in most activities. But for a while I held back from participating in sacrifices because I had compunctions about engaging in practices that I did not believe in. I am an atheist, so it seemed to me to be disingenuous to make sacrifices to a god, an agentic Earth, and ancestors watching over their descendants. Since I do not believe in their existence, I judged that it was dishonest to act as if I did. I do not see any way that pouring libations and sacrificing animals, then partaking of those offerings, could affect rainfall, epidemics, locust plagues, the success of projects, or anything else. How could I engage in practices whose premises I rejected?

As I got to know the culture better, and I got to know my best informants better, it slowly dawned on me that, from the Moosé point of view, conceptual premises – if they had any – were irrelevant to the performance or efficacy of the rituals. My Moosé friends and neighbors were curious about me, asking me many questions, but they had no interest at all in my religious beliefs (or lack thereof). Indeed, they did not concern themselves with anyone's religious convictions. It was essential to perform sacrifices correctly, but that was a matter of practice, not ideas.

So I became a participant in many of these rituals, assisting in burying corpses, making my own offerings to the deceased, partaking of sacrificial beer and meat, and so on. Eventually I myself became the principal in quite a number of rituals, as people did divination and made sacrifices on my behalf. In appreciation for my help and services to people, several villagers transferred to me, in the traditional manner, a substantial number of magical and ritual forces, entities, and powers of great value, some of which are rarely passed on to others. But even when these magical and ritual forces, entities, and powers were passed on to me, when I myself became the duly qualified proprietor of these entities and the chief officiant responsible for sacrificing to them and conducting the other relevant rituals, their donors told me nothing of their "meaning." They offered no explanations, no conceptualizations – let alone theories – about how these things operated. For two years I actively sought semantic "explanations" of Moosé sacrifice and other rituals, or at least some conceptual exegeses. I never got any.

Although I was attentive to the matter, and became fluent enough to understand most of the speech I overheard, I never heard commentary on these sacrifices, before, during, or after the event. Talking to each other, the villagers simply did not conceptualize their rituals, at least not in my hearing. Each year, several people told me that *Kiuugu* was coming up, and reminded me the day before. But they merely named it, without any descriptors, evaluations, explanations of what it was, or, indeed, any adjectives. The *Kiuugu* sacrifices that the *Têngsoba* performed on behalf of the village, together with the *Kiuugu* sacrifices that each lineage head makes that day on behalf of his own lineage, comprise the most salient, most crucial ritual of *Moosé* religion. But I heard no exegetical discourse whatsoever on *Kiuugu.*

The most perceptive, deep-digging, and insightful ethnographer I have ever read is Edward E. Evans-Pritchard, so in this connection I was reminded of his comments about another set of practices in an African society in Southern Sudan:

> I have frequently been struck when discussing witchcraft with Azande by the doubt they express about the subject, not only in what they say, but even more in their manner of saying it, both of which contrast with their ready knowledge, fluently imparted, about social events and economic techniques. They feel out of their depth in trying to describe the ways in which witchcraft accomplishes its ends … In truth Azande experience feelings about witchcraft rather than ideas, for their intellectual concepts of it are weak and they know better what to do when attacked by it than how to explain it. Their response is action and not analysis … My impression in discussing magical rites with Azande was the same as that received in discussions about witchcraft … [Both kill people but Azande do not know how they kill.] We find the same difficulty in seeking to translate their ideas about oracles, for though in action and speech they appear to personify them and to treat them as though they possessed minds, yet there is no pattern of thought which the observer can evoke in which such a belief is enunciated … It is we who question them about their beliefs and by our innovations challenge them; they enact them and feel little urge to explain them … Above all, we have to be careful to avoid, in the absence of native doctrine, constructing a dogma which we would formulate were we to act as Azande do … The Zande actualizes these beliefs rather than intellectualizes them, and their tenets are expressed in socially controlled behavior rather than in doctrines. Hence the difficulty of discussing the subject of witchcraft, for their ideas are imprisoned in action and cannot be cited to explain and justify action. (Evans-Pritchard 1937: 81–82)

Studying rituals among the Ndembu of south central Africa, Victor Turner encountered this as well; he only ever found one oddball informant, Muchona, who could formulate a semantic account of any aspect of the pivotal rituals that Turner observed (Turner 1967, 1969). Listening to Muchona explaining things to Turner, other Ndembu ridiculed Muchona's explanations, saying that Muchona should be ignored, because he was not making sense.

Similarly, objects like the *têese* and *tɪɪbo* are meaningful because of their material metonymy: They contain substance drawn from a predecessor entity, a "parent" [my way of putting it, not theirs] *têese* or *tɪɪbo* which has always been the object of sacrifices and the focus of lineage solidarity and

Box 2.1

With respect to this issue, let us reflect on the learning of these ritual practices – their cultural transmission. When his predecessor dies and the next eldest man in the lineage becomes Moosé *buud kasma*, "biggest [eldest] of the lineage," he is responsible for making sacrifices on behalf of the lineage. No one else could conceivably do so. I believe that he has never received any instruction, any explanation, any initiation, or any indoctrination in the secrets or underlying meanings of the rituals he is to carry out. He simply has to perform them as he has seen them performed for as long as he can remember. His enactments are imitative replications of the many past enactments he has attended. If his actions and his recitation of the invocation formulas duplicate previous performances, thereby carrying on the tradition unchanged, then he has correctly done what he should do. From the time they are eight or ten years old, Moosé boys attend many sacrifices, watching up close, butchering the sacrificed animals, and partaking of the sacrificial libations and meat. They know just how to do sacrifices. But they evidently grow up without acquiring or needing any articulable semantic representation of sacrifice, or even any narrative representation of what happens. They have what memory researchers call procedural representations of sacrifice, which is just what they need to *enact* sacrifices. They have no need of a propositional theology.

commitment since time immemorial. These are powerful because of their continuity of substance with predecessor *têese* and *tɩɩbo*. In other words, *têese*, *tɩɩbo*, *têkuga*, and the like are indexically meaningful. Indeed, one could argue that the *Têngsoba* himself is an indexical conformation of the Yîyôose clan, and, by extension, the entire population of the village. Likewise, as an officiant, the head of each lineage, sacrificing to the ancestors, in his very person indexically conforms the lineage. And the *têkuga* where the *Têngsoba* sacrifices are correct and evocative because of their indexicality; *Têngsobas* have sacrificed at exactly these places since time immemorial. Likewise, one of the sources of validity and imagined efficacy of a lineage head's sacrifices at the lineage's ancestor shrine is the indexicality of that shrine, where generations of preceding lineage heads have sacrificed. In both kinds of sacrifices, the sacrificer and his audience of lineage-mates see the blood that flows over the altar and the bits of the bodies of the sacrificial animals tossed on it. They merge with the blood and body bits of the many previous sacrifices there.

To summarize, while Moosé have many religious and other rituals, they have virtually no theology. Though they address sacrifices to them, they have virtually nothing to say about who *Wenaam*, "God," is; nothing to say about the sentiments or thought of *Tenga*, the "earth"; no conceptions of where the *kuimse*, the "ancestors," dwell or what they think or do. There is a definite belief that these beings are somehow behind the misfortunes that occur (to guilty or innocent parties) when people commit major transgressions. But they have no theory at all of how *Wenaam*, *Tenga*, or the *kuimse* bring about these misfortunes. They do not even concern themselves with whether these beings, who are moral agents of the misfortunes, are causes of the misfortunes, in terms of the Moosé conceptualizations of causality in farming, construction, food preparation, smithing, or making pots (see Fiske 2023).

Of course, this is not to say that no traditional Moosé ever conceptualize their religion. Surely some do, though I never encountered them. But the occasional conceptualizations of religion by individuals, if and when they do occur, are not the bases for the religious practices of most Moosé. The primary, default Moosé representation of their communal sharing and their consubstantial assimilation is not semantic, not conceptual, and certainly does not consist of language-like propositions. Nor do they have salient narrative representations of communal sharing or consubstantial assimilation, based on their episodic declarative memory system. Sacrifice respects powerful beings while sharing food and drink with them – indexical acts of bodily connection. In religion, as in daily life, the basic representation of communal sharing is procedural: consubstantial assimilation – making bodies equivalent, to make the persons socially equivalent. Ingesting food and drink from the same vessels socially connects the persons with each other and with whatever beings are sharing that food and drink. The Moosé procedural representation of consubstantial assimilation incorporates feeding the earth and ancestors and sharing commensally with them and each other: ingesting food from the same vessels and meat from the same sacrificial animals.

I imagine that, performing these sacrifices, the *Têngsoba* and the lineage heads, along with the other participants who expect to succeed them, may have an implicit but profound sense of belonging to a timeless community. Procedurally, without articulating it semantically, they "know" that just as they are now sharing the sacrificial meat and beer with the ancestors, with the Earth, and with their lineage-mates, when they die and become ancestors, their successors will continue to share the sacrificial meat and beer with them. Their names will be added to the sequence of ancestors to whom future sacrificers will address the sacrifices. And as they have been cared for by the ancestors during their lifetime, when they themselves become ancestors, they will join in caring for the lineage. Consubstantial assimilation evidently does not require or depend on explicit, declarative conformation in any semantic or episodic narrative mode.

Had I known the history of Western religions, I would not have been surprised at any of this: "Greek literature and documentary texts abound with references to rites but have little to say by way of explanation for them . . . Theoretical support for animal sacrifice comes only in . . . the fourth century AD when paganism was in retreat before Christianity" (Jameson 1988: 959–960); "For many rites the naming of the gods involved was relatively unimportant or even omitted. The action itself, engaging the supernatural in human concerns, was paramount" (Jameson 1988: 962).

Constitution of Market Pricing with Arbitrary Symbols

In contrast with the representations and mode of constitution of the other three types of social relationships, Moosé conform market pricing with arbitrary convention-based symbols (whose meaning is purely derived from usage), articulable concepts, and linguistic propositions.

A Moosé market is full of talk. One hears lots of propositional language in any setting where the interaction is structured in terms of prices, in which Moosé are comparison shopping among substitutable commodities and negotiating agreements about ratios of exchange. Here is an example, in translation which, for lack of relevant fieldnotes on making purchases, I have made up. But it is typical. Imagine that we are in the market that is held every third day, several kilometers from the village. A man is sitting in one of the rows of vendors, holding a rooster and two hens.

FISKE: How much do you want for that rooster?

VENDOR: 750 francs.

FISKE: 750! I just saw a bigger one sold for 600. I'll pay 400 francs.

VENDOR: You saw that black one? It has avian cholera. But this one is healthy. There's no cholera in our village.

FISKE: But yours is smaller. I'll give you 450.

VENDOR: I wouldn't sell it at all, but I need to buy kola nuts for a marriage. It's worth 800. I won't take less than 700.

FISKE: No. it's red – who wants a red rooster?! I'll pay 450.

VENDOR: It's not really red, it's mostly black. If I went into town I could sell this for 800 easily; I know people who have sold roosters this size for 1,000 francs. But you can have it for 600.

FISKE: For 600 francs I could buy two chickens. But how do I know there's no avian cholera in your village?

VENDOR: Look at it – does it look sick? Anyway, we vaccinated this rooster, which cost me 50 francs. I bought it in the rainy season from my brother for 500 francs before it reached full size. I need to get my money back and make a little profit; 600 is my final price.

FISKE: 500.

VENDOR: 550.

FISKE: It's a deal. Here's the money.

In such a bargaining session, the two sides negotiate in language, asserting symbolically formulated propositions about the relevant attributes of the commodity. They make statements about similar transactions by others, systematically assessing alternative opportunities for purchase and sale. They make formal, abstract comparisons among the monetary values, positive and negative, of a variety of features of the commodity. Whenever my wife or I returned from the market, made a major purchase anywhere, or showed up with any interesting new commodity, people would always inquire how much we had paid for it – and they expected an answer. When the commodity was familiar, they usually gave an evaluative commentary on the price. They also asked each other the same questions, and were generally forthcoming when I asked them how much they had paid for their purchases. There could not have been a greater contrast between the explicit verbal commentary on everyone's market purchases and the total lack of the same in regard to sacrificial rituals.

Without symbolism, it is hard to imagine how it would be feasible to make choices between bundles of commodities. Furthermore, without a numerical symbolism system, it would be difficult to bargain about the value-relevance of qualities of items, or generate a market consisting of ratios of prices of every pair of commodities. Until recently the Moosé did not have written language or written numerals, but for centuries they engaged in long-distance trade and held regular markets where they sold hundreds of commodities. That would not have been feasible without the lexemes they have for numbers (going up to very large numbers), or without cowry shell currency that was accepted in payment for any commodity, and hence made possible comparison of the values of all commodities. That is, cowry shell money symbolically represented commodity value. All commodities were compared, evaluated, bought, and sold at prices specified with these arbitrary words and shells.

****

Within any one conformation system, Moosé use some possibilities but not others. They speak of higher-ranking persons as EXCEEDING or being

GREATER than subordinates, they accord chiefs especially EXTENDED PERSONAL SPACE, the ideal for paramount chiefs is to be HUGELY CORPULENT, and chiefs adopt LARGE and POWERFUL ANIMALS as honorific war names. This is all iconic. But perhaps due to economic and technical constraints, the Moosé do not build massive pyramids, palaces, statues, tombs, or other monuments: They do not use mass, volume, or area architecturally. The Moosé with whom I worked conformed equality matching relationships by TURN-TAKING; by ONE-TO-ONE ALIGNMENT of allocations; by STARTING A TASK SIMULTANEOUSLY, WORKING SIDE-BY-SIDE AND STOPPING SIMULTANEOUSLY; by exchanging commodities ONE-BASKETFUL FOR ONE-BASKETFUL; and so forth. But, so far as I could see, they did not use other concrete one-to-one matching operations, such as MATCHING THE PAN LEVELS of pan balances. They did not use LOTTERIES, and in the village they did not CAST BALLOTS. In communal sharing they engage in all sorts of commensalism, including SACRIFICIAL FEEDING OF THE ANCESTORS AND THE EARTH. But they do not SHAKE HANDS, HUG, or KISS. They thresh, pound in mortars, pound hard their courtyards in synchrony, but they do not do SYNCHRONOUS RHYTHMIC MARCHING IN STEP. In market pricing they did not do BOOKKEEPING, make WRITTEN CONTRACTS, WRITE IOUS, or SIGN THEIR NAMES TO FINANCIAL AGREEMENTS. When I was there, neither they nor anyone else in the world had ACCOUNTS DIGITALLY REPRESENTED IN THE CLOUD. There are indefinitely many ways of realizing any conformation system, only some of which are utilized in any given type of coordination, or in any given community at any given historical moment.

Conversely, it is interesting to note from the Moosé ethnography that within each conformation system there is a lot of redundancy. The Moosé I lived with use multiple forms of consubstantial assimilation within any given communal sharing relationship – for example, making family members' bodies equivalent by CARRYING THE INFANT AGAINST THE BODY ALL DAY and SLEEPING BESIDE IT ALL NIGHT, by SUCKLING, by COMMENSALISM later in life, by GENITAL SURGERY, by speaking of close kin as *tond yaa bumb a ye*, "WE ARE ONE THING," by BURIAL IN A COMMON TOMB CHAMBER WITH KIN, by making BLOOD SACRIFICES AND POURING LIBATIONS TO SHARED ANCESTORS, FOLLOWED BY CONSUMPTION OF THE SACRIFICIAL MEAT AND BEER. Their COMMENSALISM also consisted of SHARING DAILY MEALS, BEER, KOLA NUTS, and TOBACCO. But, so far as I know, they did not perform the BLOOD BROTHERHOOD RITUALS that are fairly common in Sub-Saharan Africa.

Redundancies are common in the deployment of conformation systems, but people utilize different combinations in different relationships and different communities in different historical periods. Moosé represent authority ranking relations with many dimensions, but they do not employ all of the dimensions that can be used. Each of the dimensions they use for authority ranking represent the same thing: the differences between persons in a linear ordering. PROSTRATING IN FRONT OF THE CHIEF is putting oneself BELOW, which is taking a position subordinate to the chief in a linear ordering. Prostrating affirms and motivates the same authority ranking relation as does according the chief TEMPORAL PRECEDENCE in greeting and in serving beer, taking a position seated BEHIND him on formal occasions, addressing him with the plural pronoun, and so forth.

But there are innumerable occasions when being objectively BELOW, TEMPORALLY FOLLOWING, BEHIND, and so forth do not matter, simply because, on those occasions, people have common knowledge that the people in these positions do not intend positions on dimensions to constitute, represent, communicate, motivate, or affirm authority ranking relationships. It just does not matter if the chief sets off for his field LATER than others, walks along a path that passes BELOW others on a hillside, and then joins the others' path such that the chief is hundreds of meters BEHIND them.

I do not have an account of when Moosé use magnitudes and dimensions to conform authority ranking relationships, and when positions on magnitudes and dimensions have no social meaning. Nor do I have good accounts of when the other three modes generate social relationships versus when the Moosé ignore any potential conformational implications of same actions. In Chapter 16, the section on Felicity addresses and explores this issue.

CHAPTER 3

The Modalities of the Four Conformation System

The major root of conformation theory was my ethnographic research with the Moosé, which led me to realize what I have depicted above: that each relational model utilizes a distinct conformation system. To characterize these systems and distinguish among them, I turned to C. S. Peirce, who formulated a number of taxonomies of representation. By far the most influential, and the most relevant to conformation systems, is his typology of indices, icons, and arbitrary conventional symbols (Peirce 1903, V. 2, chapter 2, §5, paragraphs 247–249; and V. 2, chapter 3, §1, paragraphs 275–308). In this typology, an **index** represents an entity because the index is caused by or consistently co-occurs with the entity that it represents. Footprints, deer scat (poop), the tapping sound of woodpeckers, and the reading on a thermometer are indices because they are caused by the thing they represent. Similarly, smoke indexes fire, lava indexes volcanoes, a fever indexes an infection, a burrow indexes a burrowing animal. Co-occurrence indices include a hammer and saw indexing carpenters, because they are commonly found with carpenters, who use them to do carpentry. Likewise, a leash indexes dogs; a knife and fork together indexes eating, cattle egrets index large grazing animals, and monarch butterflies index milkweed, because milkweed is the only thing that monarch caterpillars eat. A honeybee indexes a hive, a meerkat indexes a pack, and an orca indexes a pod – because these are eusocial animals whose behavioral ecology is based on group living.

In much the same manner, a living human body **indexes** a social person. Consequently, connecting human bodies through consubstantial assimilation indexes social relational "equivalence" – communal sharing. A prototype, perhaps, is that giving birth indexes a mother–child bond. In the modern world, when people identify with each other based on belief in having ties of "blood" or DNA, the believed common bodily essence creates and reflects their common social essence. When essential substances are one, social selves are one. Eating and drinking commensally from the same vessel indexes social equivalence, as does formation-marching in synchrony, or rowing an eight-oared racing shell together.

In the realm of communal sharing, the co-occurrence that makes consubstantial assimilation indexical results from, reveals, and evokes emotions, motives, and moral commitments. So, in consubstantial assimilation bodies may be made equivalent partly in order to foster increased social equivalence, while at the same time social equivalence motivates making bodies equivalent. Moving in rhythmic synchrony makes people feel connected, and, conversely, in apt circumstances, people who feel connected are disposed to move in rhythmic synchrony together. When people hold hands, "high five," pile on top of each other after a sports victory, hug, cozily lean on each other, cuddle, caress, or have affectionate sex, the contact and contiguity of their bodies results from and in turn reinforces communal sharing. These are instances of what Peirce calls "real connections" that comprise indexicality (1903, V. 2, chapter 2, paragraphs 286, 287).

The conformation systems represent relations, not entities, categories, or concepts, so we are going beyond the phenomena that concerned Peirce. We are also going far beyond Peirce's purview when we analyze conformation systems as modes of evoking emotions, eliciting motives, creating evaluative standards, instilling and declaring moral commitments. Moreover, we are going beyond Peirce in another respect: conformation systems are not merely representations of pre-existing entities. A tree exists whether or not it is represented, but communal sharing exists only when is it is conformed in consubstantial assimilation, mentally and usually in action. Without the cognitive and performative conformation of communal sharing, there is no communal sharing relationship. Furthermore, conformation systems are not simply representations of pre-existing relationships, they are also models for relating. They are "blueprints" for planned, imagined, or mandated action, as well as for modulation or repudiation of relationships. And conformation systems are standards for morally evaluating actual or possible actions. (Some of the roots of my thinking on some of these issues are in Geertz 1966, D'Andrade 1984, and D'Andrade and Strauss 1992, particularly D'Andrade's concept of the "directive force" of cultural models).

Nevertheless, consideration of Peirce's concept of indexicality illuminates consubstantial assimilation. Conformational acts are indices of communal sharing because they co-occur with communal sharing, since they are motivated by that relationship and in turn motivate it. Acts of consubstantial assimilation also co-occur with communal sharing because they enact the moral commitments of communal sharing. Furthermore, some of the acts of conformation systems are tokens of what they conform. For example, commensal eating and drinking is an instance – a focal instance – of communal sharing: one feeds or shares drinks with those with whom one is engaging in communal sharing. Similarly, commensalism, cuddling, dancing together, or modifying bodies to be like other bodies are all indications of intent to be socially equivalent, and at the same time tend to evoke the perceptions, affects, intentions, and commitments that constitute social equivalence. In a positive feedback loop, those tend to generate further consubstantial assimilation, intensifying the perceptions, affects, intentions, and commitments that constitute communal sharing. This makes them especially effective indices of communal sharing.

Peirce's second mechanism of representation is **iconicity**, where the sign represents something by isomorphism: similarity of configuration. Iconicity is the conformation system of authority ranking. A portrait is an icon, and so is a map. Dolls, scale models, and many sculptures are icons. A wiring diagram is a kind of icon because it displays what is connected to what, showing the paths for electricity. Unlike many other visual icons, the wiring diagram is not to scale and does not have the geometric shapes of the paths of the wires in the machine. Rather, it topologically corresponds to the configuration of the actual or intended wires and components of the circuits.

There are also auditory icons, such as kettle drums representing a thunder storm, or Ferde Grofe's representation of the sounds of donkey hooves on a rocky trail in *The Grand Canyon Suite*. For a blind person, a three-dimensional topographic map serves as a tactile icon of the terrain. When you bounce a toddler on your knee so she can pretend she's riding a horse, you are providing a vestibular and kinesthetic icon of horseback riding.

At one limit of iconicity are representations whose function is to be mistaken for the "original": counterfeit money, or benign species that escape predation by Batesian mimicry of noxious and toxic species (e.g., robber flies mimic bumble bees). Iconicity is also the basis for realistic movie backdrops that lend verisimilitude to fictional experience.

At the other extreme of iconicity are griffin gargoyles, dragons on tapestries, cinema depictions of students playing quidditch, and the virtual worlds of video games and virtual realities – instances where icons represent something that never has existed and is not expected to ever exist. Icons readily represent such imaginary things, regardless of whether people have ever encountered those things or believe in them. An animation of the fire coming out of a dragon's mouth is an icon, though the viewer has never seen a dragon, and never will.

Military and sports planning uses diagrams that iconically depict prototypical, planned, desired, or threatening actions of persons in certain roles. Whiteboard diagrams of plays in American football or basketball are icons directing the players: they are representations of what the players are being told to do, indicated by their positions relative to each other, relative to diagrammed opponents, and relative to the field or court.

What these examples demonstrate is that an icon represents by resemblance of form, in the particular sense that the configuration of the elements in the icon is congruent with the configuration of the elements in the thing represented. An icon represents by its isomorphism with what it represents – whether that isomorphism exists independently of the icon, or is purely imagined, or is a prescriptive guide, a preparation for opponents' possible tactics, or a standard for evaluating what it represents. For example, a blueprint iconically specifies how to put components together to construct something, and may be used as a standard for the goodness of the thing constructed. The blueprint is iconic regardless of whether the building is ever built, and, for that matter, regardless of whether the principles of physics make it possible to build it.

The kinds of isomorphism that are crucial to iconic representation depend on the icon's purpose and use. A wiring diagram does not need to show what the electrical system actually looks like in, say, an actual automobile. What matters is that the lines correspond to electrical circuits, and that the components be in the correct relative positions on the correct circuits. Indeed, we do not want the wiring diagram to look like the actual wiring because the actual wires installed in the automobile have curves, crossings, and tangles, sections concealed by parts of other systems, and paths hidden in grease and mud. If the wiring diagram showed all that as it actually appears in real life, it would be very difficult to understand the circuits. Indeed, that is one of the main uses of wiring diagrams: they make essential information apparent when the information is not clear looking at the real thing.

Likewise, a map does not much resemble what you actually see when you are in a place that the map depicts. The map might show your path to be blue and the land green, though the path itself is actually brownish and the land mostly yellow. The map might show the width of the path equal to the width of the river, though actually the river is hundreds of times wider than the path. On the two-dimensional map a waterfall is visible to the viewer beyond the mountain, though on the three-dimensional earth you cannot see through the mountain. But it is a good map if it shows, for example, that along the path you are taking there is a pond on the right, then a path on the left intersecting at right angles, with a church to the right of the main path just on the other side of that intersecting path. A dress pattern iconically maps the shapes, sizes, and positions of the pieces to be cut and sewn, but it is not intended to resemble the colors, textures, or feel of fabric of the intended dress (though colors and fabric may be represented by words, cross-hatching, or other symbols on the pattern).

At the limit, icons can be useful without corresponding with anything directly perceptible, though the depicted entity is real. Illustrations of the human circulatory system are especially informative because one will never see an actual, complete human circulatory system. A subway map shows what one cannot see in the dark tunnels and anyway could not see from any one place; instead, it shows what one wants to know in order to get from one place to another: what stations are on what lines in what order, and where there are places to change from one subway line to another.

The conformation of authority ranking relations by a dimension or a magnitude is the distillation of iconicity to its one-dimensional limit. It is iconicity refined to the geometric essence of a line with directionality, such as ABOVE or BELOW. Iconicity is representation by depiction of relations among elements; here the relations are reduced to >, "greater than." This reduction to one iconic relation makes that one relation sharply salient, and helpfully ignores other relations that are not so relevant or especially meaningful.

In this regard, note that iconic conformations of authority ranking have the mathematical structure of a linear ordering, which is also the structure of an ordinal scale of measurement. These systems represent asymmetrical differentiation, but not the magnitudes of differences. It is clear to all concerned that a colonel outranks a lieutenant, but it is impossible to specify by how much, in any metrical sense that is commonly agreed on.

Peirce's third type of representation is **symbolism**, which can be used to represent anything simply by convention or fiat. Market pricing cannot function effectively without such symbols. For example, suppose I come to the market with two chickens, and want to return from the market with forty kola nuts in place of the chickens. But suppose there is no one in the market today who has kola nuts and wants chickens. The problem is easy to solve with a type of symbols that is extraordinarily important in modern life: currency. I find someone in the market who wants chickens, who will pay me with currency – for example, cowry shells. I take the currency and purchase kola nuts. The seller of the kola nuts then takes the currency and purchases rice, which she can do, even though no one in the market today who had rice wanted to exchange rice for kola nuts. That is how markets work, using symbols for storing wealth and making payments. Most kinds of currency have no value beyond what commodities people will exchange for it, and what work people will perform for it or – exchanges and work they will perform because they assume that other people value the currency, in the sense that they in turn will do a certain amount of work or exchange some sorts of things for it. Currency is simply a convention, existing so long as people use it in such ways and assume that everyone will continue to use it in those ways. It depends on common knowledge, combined with common moral sentiments about what it is worth. Another symbol system consists of letter grades assigned to students. Grades matter to the person graded because grades matter to parents, to people selecting students for admission or employment.

The most ubiquitous symbolism in human life is language. Language functions alongside other forms of representation, including the indexical, iconic, and concrete operational representations of social relations. Indeed, social relations are probably the major topics of discourse in most communities. And certainly language is a major mode of conducting and modulating some social relationships in some domains of some cultures. Thus, we would not expect indexical consubstantial assimilation to be the sole mode of representing communal sharing. We would not expect iconic dimensions to be the sole mode of representing authority ranking. We would not expect concrete operations of one-to-one correspondence to be the sole mode of representing equality matching. Rather, the thesis is that consubstantial assimilation, for example, is especially pervasive, especially evocative, especially motivating and committing, and especially morally meaningful in communal sharing relationships. In sum, my contention is that, while people speak in and about nearly every kind of relationship, the motivational, emotional, moral, and constitutive effects of language tend to be subsidiary to the proper conformation system of the particular type of relationship.

A crucial aspect of the primacy of the conformation system that is proper to each relational model is that infants innately know it. As well will see, before they can speak, and before they can ever have possibly seen a given conformation, infants recognize conformations as conforming specific relational models (reviewed in Thomas 2024). Furthermore, when infants want to initiate or modulate a social relationship, they spontaneously use the proper conformation system to do so. For example, preverbal infants, as well as toddlers, feed people with whom they want to form, affirm, intensify, or signal a communal sharing relationship.

Moreover, while language itself is symbolic, the language that people use to characterize social relationships is itself often based on the mode of representation of the nonsymbolic conformation system. For example, in Europe and North America, people speak of *blood kin*, referencing familial communal sharing, as based on having an essential substance in common (Schneider 1980). When people speak about equality matching relationships, they may characterize those relationships by referencing a concrete operation that establishes one-to-one symmetry, as when English speakers say someone intends to *get even* or *balance the score* with someone who has harmed them, *get square* with someone, or exact vengeance: *an eye for an eye, a tooth for a tooth, a hand for a hand, a foot for a foot*. Likewise, we saw that when speaking about authority ranking relations, Moosé identity relative rank as positions on dimensions and magnitudes: for example, *eb yiida maam*, "he [respectful plural "they"] exceed me." Similarly, an English speaker would talk of *her superiors* and *the people below her; powerful, forceful leaders* and their *followers;* the *great* and *the small*, the *high and mighty*, and so on. So, even when using the symbolism of language meta-conformationally, people evidently are often thinking, and making their symbolic speech understood, in terms, respectively, of the consubstantial assimilation of communal sharing, or the dimensions of authority ranking, or the concrete operations of equality matching.[1] Chapter 11 digs deeply into English and Chinese linguistic metaconformation of iconic dimensions and magnitudes conforming authority ranking.

Why Conformation Systems Theory Matters

Knowing the conformation systems of the four fundamental structures of social relations is crucial to understanding infants' innate knowledge about social relations, and to understanding how infants discover how to participate in the particular social relationships of their specific community. If infants innately recognize the respective conformation systems,

[1] For semioticians, I should note that I use "icon" in the particular sense of a Peircean "hypoicon," specifically a "diagram"; and I use "index" in the sense of the kind of index that Peirce calls a "reagent." What I call a "concrete operation" Peirce also apparently would sometimes have classified as a reagent, but I have adopted the Piagetian concept of concrete operations because, so far as I know, Peirce did not definitively conceptualize this mode of representation. Ayer (1968: 138–147) clearly and cogently discusses Peirce's sometimes obscure, changing, and inconsistent uses of "index," "icon," and "symbol," and in any case Ayer is an excellent place to start exploring Peirce.

Box 3.1

There is a lot of variation in the frequency of conformations within an enduring relationship. People may perform a conformation just once, or repeatedly, or incessantly over the course of a relationship. I imagine that people conform a relationship frequently when they perceive a relationship to be vulnerable or threatened, but one or more of the participants wants to sustain the relationship because it is very important to them. A person or persons wanting to transform a relationship uses conformations to try to reshape it; that, too, may affect the frequency of conformations. Discovering what factors affect the frequency of conforming would illuminate all sorts of aspects of human sociality.

innately use them to try to create their social relationships, are innately motivated by them, and innately perceive them as morally binding, that explains the crux of social development. This is a transformative paradigm for the ontogeny of sociality, not least because it solves the learnability problem in social development (a close analog to the learnability problem in language acquisition).

Likewise, we need to know about conformation systems so as to guide phylogenetic explorations into the antecedents of human social relations in order to formulate valid conceptualizations of how natural selection provided the foundations for human social relations, and to illuminate the processes of cultural evolution that shape human social relationships. Understanding how humans conform social relationships is also crucial to discovering the functional neuroanatomy and neurochemistry of human sociality, as well as social relational attention and memory. Without a valid conceptualization of the human conformations of social relationships, we cannot correctly identify the biological mechanisms of human sociality in the brain, in sensory systems, in motor systems, or in endocrine systems. To understand social development, to understand social motivation and emotions, to understand trust and commitment – together with their limitations, failures, and psychopathologies – we need to understand conformation systems. To enable social psychologists, sociologists, and other social scientists to understand how social relationships work, how relationships are sustained and modulated, and how social relationships do not work or break down, we need to understand conformation systems. Likewise, understanding conformation systems provides a new tool for historians, archeologists, epigraphers, philologists, and art historians.

Some scholars have posited that human sociality is largely based on mind reading. They posit that to function in a social world, a person must be able to know what others are thinking. (Theory-of-mind theorists focus on knowing what others believe, tending to ignore inferences about others' emotions, motives, and moral sentiments.) The focus of theory-of-mind theories and research has been whether and when children understand others' false knowledge of the location of objects. Research in this stream hardly ever concerns what children know about others' thoughts and sentiments about social relationships.

As I see it, the challenge to a theory-of-mind conceptualization of social relations is that people think about anything and everything; the possibilities are endless. Faces reveal very little about this. So the task of reading a mind's social relational thoughts is impossible – unless there are very strong, very clearly apparent constraints on the other's likely thoughts, and/or unless something else potentiates cooperative social relationships in such a manner that there is no need to know exactly what the other is thinking. Something else like conformations systems. Conformations are salient, unmistakable indications of what the relationship is and how that model is being implemented. In routine social relations, that's about all one needs to know. Take work, for example. One needs to know whether one is working communally, working according to authority ranking, working in the equality matching framework, or working so as to adhere to the proportions of market pricing. And, for each relational model, one needs to know the cultural implementations for the context one is in. Suppose that in a given interaction, person A knows which relational model is to be used and how, and knows that the other person(s) B knows that, and knows that the other person(s) B know that A knows that. Then, for routine interaction, neither A nor B needs to know anything else about each other's minds (Haslam & Fiske 2004, Bohl 2015). Mind reading is needed only when a person aims to change to a different implementation of the current relational model, aims to resist the current relational models and switch to another relational model, or cannot make sense of the other's action. In such cases what a person needs to know about the other's mind is the relational model the other intends to use, or wants, and the implementation of that model the other is using (Fiske & Haslam 1996). Reading that in another person's mind is feasible, because the other's aims are typically apparent in the manner of the other's engagement in conformations, their perfunctory engagement, or their refusal to engage in conformations.

So far as I am aware, theory-of-mind conceptualizations rarely, if ever, explicitly address what a person needs to know about others' minds in order to coordinate with them – specifically, in order to cooperate to form and modulate a social relationship. In the absence of any conformation systems, there would constantly be confused failures to coordinate. In complex social activities, it might be virtually impossible to smoothly coordinate, especially when unforeseen issues arise. Interactions would be anarchic. But coordination can be quickly arranged and set in motion if the participants all know the four relational models, and know their conformation systems – that is, know how to propose–initiate–commit to using a specific relational model and how to recognize others' proposal–initiation–commitments. That puts the interacting persons all "on the same page."

Moreover, conformations infuse emotions, motives, and moral sentiments. Consequently, a person who has engaged in a conformation with others knows more than just the others' dispassionate cognitive representation of what is going on. The person knows the others' probable emotions, motives, and moral sentiments. Furthermore, engaging in a conformation is an affirmation and a commitment. Common knowledge of the effects of conformation systems enables people to greatly increase their benefits in various cooperation dilemmas by enabling mutually trustable commitment (for more on commitment, see especially Chapter 4).

By the same token, conformation systems theory explains how people can socially coordinate across cultures, even without having a common language. In-marrying spouses, immigrants, trading partners, and others coordinate through the conformation systems that every human recognizes and cognizes, and that emotionally, motivationally, and morally affect every human (or at least every "neurotypical" human).

Also, conformation systems theory may ultimately illuminate aspects of various psychological disorders of social relations.

Furthermore, we need to understand conformation systems because understanding them integrates innumerable particular ethnographic accounts, and data of all sorts from all across the social sciences. Incorporating innumerable particular phenomena into a parsimonious description is, I believe, the point of science. Science seeks patterns. It seeks regularities across observations that otherwise seem chaotic. Physicists and associated mathematicians call such patterns "symmetries," defined as invariance across specified transformations. Theorizing, identifying, and verifying symmetries is what modern physics is all about (Zee 1986). Finding social relational symmetries should be a foundational goal across the social sciences (for a symmetry-breaking account of relational models, see Bolender 2010).

For example, prostrating to a chief seems to have nothing to do with addressing him with plural pronouns, and neither seems to have anything to do with giant pyramids, blaring trumpets, and drum rolls when a head of state is received, the necessity for junior officers departing from a ship to wait for senior officers to leave first, the importance of not turning your back to a king, the depiction of the king as illuminated in a bright nimbus, or the perception of him as "powerful." Conformation systems theory says that all of that, and a great deal more, consists of iconic conformations of relative rank by positions on physical dimensions or magnitudes. Across innumerable transformations among dimensions, what is invariant is the linear ordering in the conformation. Recognizing this symmetry provides insights about specific, perhaps seemingly unique events: we understand cultural particulars of affirming hierarchy when we recognize that they are instances of iconic conformation of relative rank by positions on physical dimensions. Furthermore, what makes a conformation system a "system" is that each of the conformations is a transformation of each other the others, such that the relations remain the same. That is, each of the conformations in a conformation system is symmetrical with each of the others. For example, if the chief is ABOVE me, he also temporally PRECEDES me, and he is construed as having GREATER MASS, as well as GREATER FORCE. Relative positions on every dimension and magnitude are symmetry-maintaining transformations of every other transformation that leave the ordinal relations unchanged.

At the same time, one understands more clearly what something is when one contrasts it with what it is not. We better understand prostrating before a chief when we recognize that it is not an arbitrary symbol. Prostrating contrasts with, say, the symbolic character ȝ, or ostrich eggs on the corners of the roof. Likewise, it is illuminating that while composed of phonetically arbitrary phonemes, and in that respect symbolic, *waooge*, "to respect," literally means "to increase, to make more of, to aggrandize, to increase in magnitude." The lexeme is an instance of linguistic symbolic metarepresentation of the iconic conformation of relative rank by relative positions on physical dimensions.

Beyond all of that, awareness of the conformation systems alerts us to what matters in social relations – it illuminates why people care about certain aspects of social life. Personally, I always wondered why each of my children, when they were aged around three to five, wanted to be first doing all sorts of things, or wanted to sit in the front seat of the car, and I wondered why they cared about how tall they were relative to others. Now I think I know why. Furthermore, awareness of the conformation systems provides insight into not just others' motives, emotions, and evaluative standards, but also our own. Do I actually want to board the airplane first, or would I be more comfortable walking around near the gate for a few more minutes? Concomitantly, appreciation of the conformation systems may help immunize us from their unwanted, untoward effects. Like any human, I find myself motivated by the iconicity of GREATER POWER, LOUDER, IN FRONT, and TEMPORALLY PRECEDENT. But does it really make sense to drive a LOUDER car with GREATER POWER that readily gets me IN FRONT of any car ahead of me on the highway, and gets me to my destination FIRST? No, it does not "make sense"; but now I understand why I might want to, and why it is satisfying to drive such a car.

Above all, conformation systems theory helps to account for *Homo sapiens'* phenomenal success with social relationships. Evolutionary theory, game theory, economics, and political science have shown that there are dismaying impediments to cooperation. Yet humans everywhere generally do cooperate; indeed, our lives depend on cooperative social relationships. Conformation systems theory shows something about how we do it.

Most of the rest of this book consists of concise accounts of exemplars of the respective conformation systems, drawn from ethnographies, histories, classic documents and narratives, art, lexicons, and cognitive experiments with adults or infants. In their own right, these exemplars are intriguing and illuminating instances of human life, serving the core anthropological purpose of enlarging our understanding of humankind. And this compilation of social relational practices serves at least fourteen more purposes:

- The descriptions comprise an ostensive definition of the respective conformation systems.
- They comprise the inductive evidence for conformation systems theory.
- The exemplars show something of the range of forms that the conformations in each conformation system can take.
- They offer the equivalent of type specimens and holotypes in biological taxonomy: they are protypes that typify and thereby define each of the conformation systems.
- They provide provisional prototypes to guide further investigations by ethnographers, archeologists, and art historians. As such, these exemplars can be used to orient searches for corresponding conformations in

other communities and at other points in time, which researchers then can compare and contrast with the exemplars in this book.

- They provide bridges linking research across many fields of social science, humanities, and life sciences. Researchers in one field can now realize the relevance of findings in other fields, and develop new research programs inspired by findings in other fields.
- They illustrate the materials that enable children to become proficient participants in their particular cultural community.
- They are models for constructing stimuli (including real or virtual experiences) to use in experimental designs; models for coding schemes in qualitative and quantitative research; and models for training machine-learning algorithms.
- The exemplars train readers to recognize conformations encountered in daily life, media, ethnographies, history, mythology and folk tales, archeology, epigraphy, and art history.
- They give some indication of how widespread the respective conformations are across diverse cultures and across human history.
- Likewise, they provide a foundation for future research on how and why, within each conformation system, specific conformations operate in specific contexts, change over time, compete with, and replace each other.
- They indicate the many spheres of human life and social systems that are shaped by the respective conformation systems – and the many rituals and practices that consist of conformations.
- They comprise a framework for investigating what, when, and how technologies have emerged and developed as humans sought to construct more effective conformations.
- At the same time, they are materials for development and criticism of conformation systems theory. They are invitations to elaboration or correction by colleagues who know far more than I do about particular exemplars and their history, their connections to other aspects of the cultures in which they operate, and the phenomenological experiences of participants.

Cultural Evolution of Conformations Adapting to Their Niches

There are extensive cultural consequences of the psychological dispositions to initiate, and to strongly and specifically respond to, each of the four conformation systems. We considered this synchronically, in the framework of complementarity theory (Fiske 2000). Now consider complementarity dynamically. Each of these four dispositions is a niche for the cultural evolution of congruent practices. That is, people are likely to invent, attend to, remember, be affected by, and reproduce practices that fit one of these four dispositions. For example, the mind's cognitive–emotional–motivational–moral system for cognizing communal sharing provides a niche that specifically fosters the cultural evolution of indexical actions of consubstantial assimilation. The mind's system for cognizing authority ranking comprises a niche that specifically fosters the cultural evolution of iconic dimensional and magnitudinal actions and artifacts. The cognitive system for equality matching offers a rich niche that specifically fosters the cultural evolution of acts and artifacts of concrete operations of one-to-one correspondence. The mental system for market pricing comprises a niche for the cultural evolution of symbolism, especially symbolism that facilitates market pricing.

The cultural-evolutionary process here consists of differential cultural reproductions of different practices. People are more likely to invent practices congruent with the niche in which people perform them. Practices congruent with the niche in which they occur attract more attention, make a greater impression, and are more memorable – and more correctly remembered – than incongruent practices. Above all, people are more likely to reproduce practices congruent with any one of the four psychological dispositions.

Practices congruent with the niche in which they occur make the social relationship salient and clear, facilitating social coordination. All this is due in large part to the simplicity and directness in which mental conformations are properly transduced into actions and artifacts, and, conversely, actions and artifacts are properly transduced into mental conformations. Likewise, practices congruent with the niche in which they occur are more readily computable: congruent practices facilitate the essential calculations enabling people to interconnect, understand, explain, and predict the social relationships of that relational model. Equally important, compared to less congruent practices, practices that are more congruent with the niche in which they occur are better at evoking the specific emotions, motives, and moral commitments necessary to the relational model of that niche. For all of these reasons, the cultural evolution of conformations is subject to strong selection for congruence to their specific niche.

In part directly because of all these processes of social cognition, but partly separate from them, practices congruent with the niche in which they occur have another result: they generate and sustain better coordinated, more motivated, and more committed social relationships. The better the functioning of dyads, groups, and networks, the more the social relations endure. The longer a social system endures, the longer it tends to carry with it the culturally evolving practices that constitute it, the longer a social system "lives." Living longer, it is more likely to bud off similar social systems, carrying with them the cultural practices that constitute it. Also, the better it functions and the longer it lives, the greater the chances that other social systems will copy the practices that constitute it. In these ways, cultural group selection may possibly promote the endurance and diffusion of niche-congruent practices.

Through all of these processes, the crux is that people more frequently reproduce practices that are highly congruent with the niche in which they occur, while people less frequently reproduce practices that are less congruent. For example, chiefs may build rectangular houses, contrasting with everyone else's round houses. Chiefs may place ostrich eggs at the corners of their roofs. But since neither of these conformations of rank are congruent with the iconicity of dimensions, all else equal, neither rectangular houses nor ostrich eggs at their roof corners is likely to endure as long, nor reproduce as frequently and reliably, as conformations of rank such as prostrating in front of chiefs, putting oneself BELOW, or, according to TEMPORAL PRECEDENCE, waiting to eat until the senior person makes an offering to the ancestors and then begins to eat. (For detailed analyses of other social practices culturally evolving to adapt to another innate psychological niche, see Fiske 2019, 2023, Fiske, Schubert, & Seibt 2025, Fiske, Seibt, & Schubert 2019.)

As a terminological note: I call the four conformation niches "niches" because each of them is an amalgam of selective factors co-shaping the cultural practices that conform one of the relational models. The selective forces of a conformational niche consistently co-occur, so a cultural conformation practice must culturally adapt to the selective forces all together. One or two of the selective forces, without the others, do not constitute a niche. A cultural adaptation might be beneficial with respect to one of these forces in an environment in which no other conformational selective forces existed, yet that adaptation might be deleterious in the presence of the amalgam of selective forces that, all together, form the niche. Thus, to understand how cultural conformation practices adapt to conformational niches, we need to figure out how the practices adapt to the combined effects of the selective forces that, in conjunction with each other, constitute the niche. That is, we should not expect that the combined effects of these selective forces is a simple sum of their effects alone. Operating as an amalgam in a niche, their selective effects likely interact. If so, studying the effects of these selective forces separately, holding the others constant, will not predict how they operate all together. In short, these conformational niches are "niches" for the cultural evolution of conformation practices not simply because, in such a niche, there are several selective forces. Each conformational niche is a niche because the selective forces in it, when combined in that niche, create unique adaptive opportunities for the cultural evolution of conformation practices, and unique obstacles that those practices must culturally adapt to. That is what makes a niche a niche.

What are the selective forces that, in combination, compose a niche for the cultural evolution of conformational practices? I described them above as components of a conformation system, when I defined what a "conformation" is. But it is useful to list the components here, where we can also recognize them as selective forces. Each selective force is labelled according to the aspect of a conformation that it favors: in the niche, social practices with the feature survive and reproduce well, and often diffuse to other communities. More exactly, the more effective the feature, the better it survives in the niche, the more it reproduces within the niche, and the higher its rate of diffusion. That is, cultural evolution selects for conformation systems with the following features:

- Attracts the "attention" of the psychological disposition for this conformation.
- Is readily and reliably recognized (implicitly) as pointing to the particular relational model, such that the person perceives and represents this as an instance of the relational model.
- Is readily encoded, stored, and retrieved in the sign mode of the specific relational model.
- Lends itself to mental computations in the sign mode specific to the relational model.
- Evokes one or more emotions that attract the persons to the relationship, making it "feel good."
- Evokes emotion(s) that make the persons feel morally committed to the relationship.
- Evokes relationship emotion(s) that others judge to be morally laudatory.
- Evokes moral emotion(s) like shame or guilt when the persons violates the relationship

- Motivates the persons to engage in the relationship and make it work.
- Motivates the persons to punish partners' transgressions of the relationship.

The more such features a conformation system has, and the greater the efficacy of each, the greater the possibility for people to form culturally advantageous and fitness enhancing social relationships coordinated by the particular relational model.

PART II

Consubstantial Assimilation: The Conformation System of Communal Sharing

Prepared by Part I, we are ready to explore conformation systems around the world, from prehistory through history to the present. We begin with the indexical consubstantial assimilation of communal sharing, to which the next four chapters are devoted. But first, we need to note that when communal sharing suddenly emerges or intensifies, that moment evokes a distinctive, very positive emotion: kama muta (Fiske 2019, Zickfeld et al. 2019, for an up to date bibliography, see www.kamamutalab.org). Kama muta results from the sudden creation or renewal or the sudden salience of communal sharing between the person and another or others, and also when the person observes or hears of the sudden creation or the sudden salience of communal sharing between others. Kama muta does not emerge from unchanging or slowly strengthening communal sharing, no matter how intense the relationship; it arises only from sudden emergence or attention to communal sharing. The emotion often, though not invariably, is felt as a warm or pleasant "fuzzy" feeling experienced as in the heart, often with tears, goosebumps, chills, and/or feeling "choked up." Experiencing kama muta, people often put the palm of the hand on their chest, and may utter something like awww! The emotion itself is brief, but it is followed by a more enduring motivation to be affectionate, kind, and compassionate – that is, to foster further communal sharing.

Hence, when consubstantial assimilation suddenly creates or intensifies communal sharing, we can be fairly confident that participants, and often observers, feel kama muta. However, when there is no sudden change, kama muta does not emerge, no matter how strong the steady communal sharing relationship is.

Ethnographers have not known about kama muta until recently (and most still do not know the concept), and if an observer is not on the lookout for kama muta it is easy to miss it or misinterpret it. So, the sources I draw on here do not identify it, nor, for that matter, do many of them have much to say about any other emotions. But, as we consider accounts of consubstantial assimilation practices, we may wonder whether kama muta does accompany the practices.

CHAPTER 4

Indexically Conforming Communal Sharing by Substance-Sharing

> In Chinese literature, the metaphor of two lotus flowers growing off the same stalk evokes a married couple who passionately love each other.
>
> (Zhengyu 1997: 26)

Communal sharing is operative when people are socially equivalent with respect to whatever they are coordinating: whatever they are coordinating in this manner is theirs together, not divided or apportioned to the individual persons. The same persons may coordinate other aspects of their interaction according to other relational models. The relational models are a menu from which people select a coordination scheme for doing something together on a particular occasion, or as an habitual default for coordinating many things across many occasions. As indicated in Chapter 1, the conformation system of communal sharing is consubstantial assimilation, which means "assimilating bodies together as one." That is, when a set of people perceive their bodies to be the same, they are disposed to engage in communal sharing relations. Conversely, when people are engaged in communal sharing relations, they are disposed to make their bodies alike.

The perception of equivalence of bodies follows the same principles that operate to generate the perception of entitativity of any and all objects. A constellation of features is perceived – though any sensory system – as a single entity if it

- appears continuous, such that there is contiguity from one element or region to another;
- there are no discontinuities;
- the surfaces of all regions are the same;
- appears to have the same composition – be the same substance throughout;

- the motion of all regions is the same, such that the entirety moves together.

Anthropologists have long recognized the role of consubstantial assimilation in creating communal sharing relationships (though, of course, without using either construct, as such). William Robertson Smith (1889) theorized that kinship is a "common life" represented as entailed by a physical unity "as one living whole, a single animated mass of blood, flesh and bones, of which no member could be touched without all the members suffering" (p. 274). This connection is formed through birth from the mother's body, then by suckling, then by feeding, "so that commensality can be thought of (1) as confirming or even (2) constituting kinship in every real sense" (p. 274). Robertson Smith saw the representation of a physical connection in blood and nourishment as the source of the binding moral force of parenthood (p. 41). Ritual commensalism then has the potential to constitute bonds between nonkin such as blood brothers, because "any food which two men partake of together, so that the same substance enters into their flesh and blood, is enough to establish some sacred unity of life between them" (p. 313). Rites of mixing and ingesting blood have the same effect, but stronger. Less frequently, and often less emotively, transfer or contact with other bodily substances, such as tears or hair, can create connections (pp. 323–335).

Robertson Smith (1889) concludes that one of the most culturally pervasive, historically enduring, and morally powerful acts of connection among humans is the communion act of partaking in the flesh and libations of sacrifice, cementing bonds among the humans, along with the union they form with their god. (He argued that this was the origin of Christian communion rites.) Hartland (1895) had previously made the same point about ritual sacrifices: "Their great aim is union with the deity. It is attained by placing in contact with him something already part of ourselves, as our blood, hair, clothing, or other property; or else the blood of a victim of which we are about to consume the remainder" (p. 243).

Crawley (1902) also emphasized the importance of bodily contact in creating social relationships: skin-to-skin touching, ingestion of one's another's blood or saliva, commensal eating, and sexual union. Conversely, he pointed out, taboos on contact correspond to social differentiation. Concurring with Crawley, van Gennep (1908/1960: 29) emphasized that "eating and drinking together ... is clearly a rite of incorporation, of physical union" (see also Hartland 1895). Van Gennep emphasized that rites of incorporation typically join a person to a group through actual contact (e.g., a slap, a handclasp); through exchanging gifts of food or valuables; eating, drinking, or smoking a pipe together; sacrificing animals; sprinkling water or blood; anointing; being attached to each other; being covered together; or sitting on the same seat (p. 28).

Birth, Nursing, and "Blood" Kinship

The phylogenetic and ontogenetic roots of consubstantial assimilation consist of giving birth, nursing, feeding, and commensalism (see the end of Chapter 5). This reflects, and is reflected in, the perception of people in a communal sharing relationship having some fundamental bodily essence in common. People may be unable to articulate the exact nature of this shared substance, or, in contrast, in some cultures this intuitive sensibility is elaborated into a salient discourse on the substances of sociality and the processes of their transmission. For example, cultural articulation of consubstantiation is particularly notable among many of the cultures of New Guinea, where the stuff of kinship is FEMALE BLOOD, which makes the infant's flesh, and male SEMEN, which becomes the bones of the child (e.g., Herdt 1982, Poole 1985). Elsewhere, this conformation also has deep Western roots going back to the Proto-Indo-European cultures, who represented lineage and clan membership as shared blood (Linke 1999). Etymologically, this is reflected in the Proto-Indo-European root **gene-* or **'ken-(th-)*, "to give birth, beget," and also "clan, tribe, collectivity." The derivatives of this root have to do with kinship and ethnicity. In English, for example, these include: *gonad*, *gene*, *genealogy*, *genesis*, *genitor*, *genus*, *homogeneous*, *genre*, *gender*, *genocide*, *genial*, *congenial*, *congenital*, *agnate*, *cognate*, *nascent*, *innate*, *nation*, *nature*, *benign*, and *kin*. In addition, **gene-* or **k'en-* is the root of Old English *cynd*, *gecynd*, "origin, birth, race, family, kin," which gave rise to modern English *kind* – in both senses (Gamkrelidze & Ianov 1995: 652, Watkins 2000: 26, Harper 2025). Latin derivatives include *gens*, *race*, *clan*, *tribe*, and *nation*, as well as *genus*, "innate quality." From ancient Germanic through medieval society, Europeans continued to define group membership as COMMON BLOOD: "The unity of relatives, understood as a merging of power, was symbolized through organic metaphors, that is, the single human body, and the actual mingling of blood" (Linke 1999: 55). For this conformation in the ancient Arab world, see Smith 1885; on modern American cultural conformations of kinship, see Schneider 1980.

This conformation of communal sharing is not limited to Europe and Western Asia. Malays on Langkawi Island define kinship in terms of blood and milk (Carsten 1992). Kinship is formed in large part by SUCKLING MOTHER'S MILK, which is thought to come from her blood. This links not only mother and child and siblings, but also any two people who have suckled at the same breast: "You become one blood, one flesh," they say (Carsten 1992: 37). Like Moslems elsewhere, Malays regard those who have suckled the same milk as "milk kin," entailing communal sentiments and obligations, as well as absolute incest taboos. Rice consumed is believed to produce blood, so that consuming rice from the same hearth creates kinship, too. Thus, through their rice meals, milk, and blood, Malays perceive that women link kin; indeed, they say that nursing is the necessary source of the infant's love for its mother, and that it is how it recognizes its mother.

Other pervasive, powerful forms of consubstantial assimilation include sharing comestible substances such as tobacco, and taking drugs together. In addition, under appropriate circumstances, merging bodies through SEXUAL INTERCOURSE creates powerful bonds of consubstantiality (see Pitt-Rivers 1973: 92–93). CONCEIVING A CHILD TOGETHER, followed by the woman's gestating and bearing the child, may also create powerful bonds between a man and woman (e.g., see Evans-Pritchard 1951).

Some cultures have communed with their gods through human blood; Mayans, Incans, Aztecs, Yorubas, ancient Mesopotamians, Hawaiians, Shang Chinese, and other early civilizations sacrificed humans to feed and bond with their gods (Sharer 1996: 168, Trigger 2003). And the core of a great many religions consists of sacrificing animals and pouring libations to feed the gods, or placing vegetable foods on an altar, after which the sacrificers or offerors consume the food and drink they have offered. Thus, sacrifice is at the same time feeding the gods, commensalism with the gods, and commensalism among the congregants. This much social scientists and scholars in the history of religion mostly agree on, but they have long struggled to come up with a convincing explanation for the prevalence and endurance of BLOOD SACRIFICE (for some of the many attempts, see Fortes 1945, chapter VII; and Barth 1975, chapter 21). Furthermore, SHARING IN THE BEER LIBATIONS and the MEAT of the animals offered up at these SACRIFICES cognitively defines the group and instills a sense of membership in a collectivity (Durkheim 1893).

Feeding and commensalism can be done with any comestible substance, so why kill an animal to entreat the gods, ancestors, or spirits? Observing quite a number of Moosé sacrifices, I was struck that the crucial act is not killing, as such. Sacrifice is not about the death of the animal sacrificed. Rather, the essential act is, after cutting the animal's throat, having its blood flow over the altar, and then, completing the consubstantial assimilation, the participants commensally eating the sacrificed animal. At a sacrifice, one's attention is strongly drawn to the blood flowing from the throat of the dying goat or chicken and onto the altar: The observer cannot miss the sanguinous contiguity from animal to altar. This substantial connection is reiterated when the officiant tosses onto the altar feathers, bits of the cord that held the goat, and, a little later, pieces of cooked meat. Then the participants partake of the meat together. While they eat it, they cannot fail to remember what they saw: the blood flowing over the altar came from the animals they are eating. Thus, the participants vividly experience their bodily contiguity with the altar, and hence with the beings indexically worshipped through it.

Participants may SHED THEIR OWN BLOOD to make their bodies equivalent to the bodies of others who shed their own blood. Medieval Christians scourged themselves as a bloody penitential act of identification with Christ (Eller 2010). Similarly, during Muharram, Shias commemorate the bloody death of Muhammad's grandson Husayn ibn Ali in the 680 CE succession battle at Karbala. In India, Pakistan, Afghanistan, Iraq, and Bahrain, Shia men do *zanier kea matam*: they flagellate themselves with chains, some of which incorporate knives or razors. The pain and bloodshed they inflict on themselves conforms their love for Husayn (Pinault 1992, Schubel 1993, Chelkowski 2010). This self-inflicted painful bloodshed has also now become an act of consubstantiation marking Shia identity in contrast to Sunnis, and at the same time marking Pakistani Punjabis and others who perform it as "true" Muslims – more Muslim, the Punjabis assert, than Arab Muslims (Chelkowski 2010). Covered in the blood that all can see, feeling the pain that they all feel, their bodies become all one, and become one with the bodies of Husayn and his followers. Correspondingly, in renaissance Florence, religious brotherhoods of laymen formed confraternities whose focal act of solidarity was members' collective rituals of self-flagellation (Weissman 1982).

With new technologies, new forms of consubstantial assimilation arise. To contemporary persons, it is self-evidently motivating, emotionally evocative, and constitutive of moral commitments when people discover that they share GENES with someone – especially when they share DNA indicative of paternity, maternity, or siblingship. To have this social relational effect on people, they do not have to have a scientific understanding of what a gene is, or what DNA is molecularly, or what proteins a DNA segment codes for. In most modern cultures, *genes* and *DNA* are popularly construed as the essential substances that determine who a person is, and therefore determine who is the same as whom.

Commensalism

> To eat together signifies amity; to refuse, or to be prohibited from doing so, signifies its absence
>
> (for the Tallensi of northern Ghana; Fortes 1969: 236)

> The one point upon which every theorist of food taboos seems to agree is that the taboos will among other things mark out social identities . . . In turn, commensality is deeply involved in "we" feeling and group affiliation. The point is so obvious as to be considered boring in most academic discussions of the subject
>
> (Whitehead 2000: 59)

The sense of equivalence of persons is conformed through their acceptance of, or active desire for, CONTACT WITH CERTAIN SUBSTANCES COMING FROM OTHER PERSONS' BODIES, while the sense of difference is conformed by avoidance of contact with the substances coming from the others' bodies (Douglas 1966, Goffman 1971: 46–58, Rozin et al. 1989). Social scientists often use the term *taboo* as the specific label for the strictest avoidances of intermixing of bodily substances.

In an influential review, Sahlins (1965) analyzes patterns of exchange in traditional societies, noting that "food dealings are a delicate barometer, a ritual statement, as it were, of social relations, and food is thus employed instrumentally as a starting, a sustaining, or a destroying mechanism of sociability" (p. 215). Compared to other substances, Sahlins finds that food is more likely to be shared than exchanged in balanced reciprocity (equality matching), distributed up and down a hierarchy (authority ranking), or transacted in antagonistic or selfish economic interactions (asocial and market pricing relationships). Sahlins cites numerous ethnographies that describe food sharing as constitutive of what he calls "generalized reciprocity" (a construct more or less similar to "communal sharing") among kin or other intimates, or as a way of cementing friendly relations with others. Thirty-five years after Sahlins' influential essay, in another review of the literature on eating together, Sobal (2000) noted that "Commensality is widely recognized as an important component of initiating, building, confirming, deepening, and reaffirming social connections" (p. 124). More specifically, "commensal circles demarcate 'us' versus 'them' by consumption of 'our foods' and not 'their foods'" (p. 123). Mere simultaneity of eating or drinking or smoking have little effect: what evokes the emotional bonds is ingesting the same substance from the same vessel, or feeding someone. Schieffelin (1976) offers a particularly clear and detailed example. He shows that, among the Kaluli of central New Guinea, giving and sharing food is the most important mode for establishing or adjusting the relationships that relational models theory conceptualizes as "communal sharing." As in many other cultures, ritual sharing of cooked meat, in particular, expresses affection and creates a special bond of identification and solidarity; after ritual meat sharing, Kaluli participants subsequently address each other by the name of the animal whose meat they ate together: for example, "my bandicoot" (p. 50).

The communicative meaning, emotional evocativeness, and inclusivity of different ways of transferring food compose a spectrum of conformative effects on food sharing (Miller, Rozin, & Fiske 1998). Mere transfer of cooked food, as such, does not create a communal sharing relationship: theft of food, or the purchase of a meal at a restaurant, has no effect. A gift of uncooked food may be weakly conformative. Consuming the same food from distinct sources sometimes has a modest effect: choosing to drink Guinness along with everyone else is a way of belonging, compared to drinking Merlot while everyone else drinks Guinness. Consuming something provided by another person is generally a bit stronger: "What will you have? Try some of this single malt I just discovered." Depending on the context, consuming food or drink prepared by a person may be distinctly more meaningful, especially if the person prepared it especially for the recipient (e.g., a batch of cookies, a birthday meal). Eating the same food divided into distinct portions and eaten off of separate plates has a moderate effect, but true commensalism generally marks and makes a stronger bond (Miller, Rozin, & Fiske 1998; Woolley & Fishbach 2019). Consider drinking out of the same glass or passing a joint around; the Norman Rockwell print of an adolescent boy and girl sipping one soda through two straws captures the feeling.

Explicitly testing whether consubstantial assimilation evokes communal sharing relations among strangers, Brito et al. (2023) did an experiment in which Western European student participants in the experimental condition were asked to eat a dessert – yellow mango mousse – that they served themselves from a common bowl onto individual bowls. The experimenters intended this to be an experience of commensalism; in my view, it was weak commensalism, because participants did not eat directly from the common bowl, but the experimenters recognized that Portuguese strangers would often be unwilling to eat directly from a common bowl. In one control condition, participants were asked to move yellow paint from a common bowl onto individual bowls, and then each participant was to use it to color a sheet of paper. In another control condition, participants did not share any substance. One outcome measure assessed any consequent communal sharing among the participants, based on their individual responses on Likert scales to a series of written items. Another outcome measure for communal sharing was a graphic showing nonlapping circles and a series of sets of circles that overlapped to varying degrees. A third graphic measure was a thermometer image on which participants rated how "warm" they felt toward the other participants in their group. On the verbal and on both graphic measures, participants who had shared the mango mousse reported feeling stronger communal sharing than participants who merely distributed paint or those who did not share anything. In another experiment by Brito et al. (2023), in the experimental condition, participants were asked to serve themselves from a common 1.5 L bottle of water onto individual plastic cups. This, again, was intended to be a consubstantial assimilation conformation, which I judge that it was – albeit, again, a weak instantiation of commensalism, because participants did not drink directly from the same bottle. Participants in one control condition were asked to drink out of separate bottles of the same brand and, in another control condition, to drink from separate bottles of different brands. The experimenters measured consequent communal sharing with the same measures used in the mango mousse experiment, and the results were the same: drinking water distributed from the same bottle evoked perceptions of communal sharing, while the control conditions did not.

In many parts of the world, families and other close associates eat commensally, reaching their hands into the common food bowls or passing a calabash of beer around. Putting food into another's mouth is an index of greater intimacy (see Goffman 1976: 35), but Americans, at least, perceive still greater intimacy when the feeder has already partaken of the proffered food (e.g., a woman bites a French fry and feeds a man the second half; Miller, Rozin, & Fiske 1998, Erwin, Burke & Purves 2002, Alley 2012, Alley, Brubaker, & Fox 2013). Analyzing data from a restaurant-based reality show in which British couples meeting for the first time eat a meal together, Hendrie and Shirley (2019) found that fifty-four of fifty-eight couples in which one fed another during the meal subsequently indicated they would like to go on a second date, in contrast to twenty-one of forty-nine couples in which neither fed the other.

In many traditional societies, mothers and other adults chew food and then give it to infants and toddlers, in some practices transferring the food directly, mouth to mouth. This can become a meaningful practice among adults. When an Oglala Sioux man was dancing in the Sun Dance, tethered by thongs attached to pegs through his flesh, "sometimes a young woman who liked one of the dancers would put a herb which she had been chewing into the mouth of the dancer in order to give him strength and ease his thirst" (Black Elk 1971: 95). Still more intimate than this is ingesting the substance of the other's body, especially by suckling at the breast. In a few New Guinea societies, the ultimate expression of affection and desire for unity with deceased close kin is to eat their bodies (Gillison 1983, Lindenbaum 1979; note Freud's strangely conceptualized but strangely apt theories, 1913, 1939).

In a number of polygynous patrilineal cultures of Africa, as we noted among the Moosé, the closest kinship relations – other than the mother–child relationship – are those among children of the same mother, and such people often characterize their relationship as having "SHARED THE SAME BREAST." Indeed, nursing a baby has the potential to create very strong bonds even when a woman has not given birth to the child she is suckling. Notably, in many African and Mediterranean cultures, women may suckle each other's children, which creates an important permanent communal sharing bond between the children who have shared milk from the same breast (e.g., Smith 1889: 274, 1903: 57, 176 ff.; Davis 1977, Altorki 1980, Dettwyler 1988, Fildes 1988). In nearly every such culture, this "milk-kinship" entails prohibitions against sexual relations and against marriage between the woman and her nursling, and, more practically significant, between people who nursed at the same breast. In many of these societies, when two groups have been fighting, a woman from one group suckling an infant from the other, even briefly, creates milk kinship that entails indissoluble peace and commits both sides to mutual aid (Hollis 1905: 321–322, Beidelman 1963: 334, Thompson 1989: 313, Khatib-Chahidi 1992). Classically, in at least a few societies near the Mediterranean, a man could assure himself of safety and protection from a threatening person or group if he managed to suckle momentarily from his enemy's wife (Westermarck 1926: 522, Lindblom 1920: 141, Pitt-Rivers 1968, Jaymous 1981: 213).

Similar practices appear far from the Mediterranean. Of the Malays on the island of Langkawi, (Carsten 1995: 224) writes:

> It is through living and consuming together in houses that people become complete persons-that is, kin. The core substance of kinship in local

> perceptions is blood, and the major contribution to blood is food. Blood is always mutable and fluid–as is kinship itself . . . Food creates both persons in a physical sense and the substance-blood-by which they are related to each other.

For Langkawi Malays, commensality begins in the womb, where the mother's blood feeds the fetus, and continues through breastfeeding. Diverse fostering practices are common on Langkawi, and nursing a baby is a common part of these practices. The nursing mother and all the children she ever suckles become kin: "Co-feeding can create shared blood, shared substance, and kinship. People in Langkawi say, 'If you drink the same milk you become kin . . . you become one blood, one flesh'" (Carsten 1995: 228). Indeed, they say that the child's love for its mother and the child's very ability to recognize her are based on nursing. And since blood and flesh come from cooked rice, eating their staple food (rice) commensally connects people in shared flesh. Likewise, Mayans identify themselves as maize eaters, which they declare gives them a truly different flesh than other people (Christenson 2005). According to their origin myth, the creators formed the original four Maya out of maize, using water to make their blood. Since then, Maya have bled themselves and given their blood back to the gods.

In contrast, in a number of societies at various points in history, elite families have employed wet-nurses to breastfeed their infants. I do not know of any societies in which wet-nursing conforms culturally recognized moral obligations, nor in which the pair become socially equivalent in other respects. That is a reminder that behaviors as such do not constitute a conformation. To function as conformations, the potentially conformational acts have to occur in felicitous circumstances, and, usually, their conformational effects must be intentional (see Chapter 16).

There are innumerable clear and definite examples of commensalism conforming the most intense communal sharing relationships; there is no point in summarizing more of them. For some of the best descriptions of commensalism conforming the most intense communal sharing relationships, see Richards 1948 for southern Africa; Watson 1987 for Hong Kong; Walker 2012 for the Comoros; Barth 1975: 197 for the Baktaman of Papua New Guinea; Feeley-Harnik 1994: 10–11 and Fajens 1985: 379–381 on New Britain in Papua New Guinea; Lutz 1988: 129 on Ifaluk in Micronesia; Rabain 1979 and Zemplini-Rabain 1973 for the Wolof of Senegal; Heath 1991a & b for the Camba of Bolivia; and Fischler 2011 for the historical French, and ancient Greece and Rome.

In many cultures, marriage ceremonies join the bride and groom in part by FEEDING EACH OTHER (e.g., Hartland 1895 on ancient Greece, Whiting 1941 on the Kwoma of Papua New Guinea). An American bride and groom feed each other the first bites of the wedding cake, each taking a piece in the hand and putting it directly into the other's mouth (for a similar practice among the Nyanga of the north-eastern Democratic Republic of the Congo, see Biebuyck & Mateene 1969: 50–51).

People in many cultures drink alcohol together in practices that form and sustain networks of mutual aid, enhance integration and corporate identity, and alleviate social tensions (e.g., Gordon 1984, Maida 1984). Moreover, drinking alcohol together has been the way for men (but generally not women) to conform binding, trusted commitments in medieval Germany (Tlusty 2001, Bloch 1989), seventeenth-century North American colonial practices (Conroy 1995, Rice 1983, Kross 1997), eighteenth-century Paris, nineteenth- through early-twentieth-century American saloons, late nineteenth- to mid-twentieth-century working-class pubs in England (Adler 1991, Brennan 1991, Powers 1991), nineteenth-century Ireland and the Irish diaspora in North America (Lender & Martin 1982, Thompson 1989), and in nineteenth-century Poland (Freund 1985). These practices had antecedents in early northwestern European practices of drinking together out of a shared vessel (Hackwood 1909). Alcohol commensalism continued to conform communal sharing relations in Mexico City (Lomnitz 1977) and among Mexican-American men in recent times (Gilbert 1985), as well as in San Francisco bars in the 1960s (Cavan 1966). In many of these places, drinking alcohol together was the only way to conform binding commitments (other than marriage). In all or most of these practices, it appears that the communal sharing relationship conformed by commensal drinking often guaranteed mutual commitment and ensured mutual trust in one or more market pricing transactions. That is, the market pricing relationship was intentionally and explicitly nested within the communal sharing relationship. Such nesting merits further research.

Feasting and Group-Conforming Foods

In most agricultural societies, at one or more times in the year, people gather together to FEAST, expressing and reinforcing their communal sharing by commensal eating and drinking (e.g., see Wiessner 2001 on the Enga of Papua New Guinea). In Africa, for example, feasts

> are extremely important in establishing sentiments of friendship, kinship, and community solidarity, as well as cementing bonds between affine groups and political links between leaders of various kinds. In this sense, they may be seen to perform, at a variety of scales, the classic integrative function of creating *communitas* (Dietler 2001: 69).

> Commensality is a powerfully expressive trope of intimacy (Dietler 2001: 73).

Feasting, or even commensalism in a smaller group, is possible only when there is sufficient food for all. Consequently, behavioral ecology and political economy impose constraints. To amass enough food for a feast, people have to store food, and may have to transport it to the feasting site. The hosts must be organized so that they coordinate to have a large food surplus on hand at the same time; this may be difficult without some sort of chiefs or at least a council with sufficient authority. Agriculturalists who can preserve, store, and guard their harvest may often be able to host feasts on a scale that is challenging or impossible for most hunter-gatherers, except those who can store large surpluses of food (e.g., dried fish). Over the past 10,000 years or so, it seems likely that communities have sometimes been motivated to intensify production in order to hold feasts.

When early humans invented cooking, they may have thereby enhanced the conformational effects of commensalism. Raw food is readily eaten as it is collected away from camp, or, in camp, eaten separately by individuals whenever they are hungry. But when a large piece of meat is roasted, or food is boiled in a pot, people are more likely to eat together when the cooking is complete. And, compared to eating raw food from separate sources, it is more intimately commensal to tear food from a shared roast or dip hands into a shared pot.

Very often, CONSUMPTION OF A PARTICULAR FOOD or set of foods is uniquely important in conforming ethnic identity (Brown & Mussell 1984, Fischler 1988). Eating crawfish is a core conformation of being Cajun (Gutierrez 1984). Commensal consumption of the identity-defining food, such as *kimchi* in Korean culture, incorporates and sustains ethnic membership, often more effectively than language or legal citizenship (Lee 2000). In western Kenya, the Luo love of fish and the Kisii disdain for fish is a component of their sense of ethnic difference. Similarly, the Luo believe that their revulsion at the thought of eating caterpillars separates them from ethnic groups to the north (Dietler 2001: 89). Fischler (1988: 287) suggests that in India, Europe, and elsewhere, combinations of spices and other flavoring ingredients constitute local "dialects," family practices, and self-defining "maternal" identity. This conformation can be taken one step further. Strathern (1973: 29 ff.) shows, based on New Guinean ethnographies, that EATING THE FOOD GROWN ON THE SAME LAND can link people in kinship by creating common substance – just like solidarity based on a culturally defined common substance derived from descent.

In the early modern period in Augsburg, the primary mode of inclusivity was drinking beer, wine, or other beverages together (Tlusty 2001: 125). The elite drank in the marble and gold Lords Drinking Room Society. Wealthy non-nobles belonged to the prestigious second-tier Merchants' Drinking Room Society next door. Members of the Lords' Drinking Room Society had free access to the Merchants' Drinking Room, but this privilege was not reciprocal. A wider circle of noble and wealthy men met to drink in the six taverns of the Wine Market neighborhood. In all of these places, DRINKING ALCOHOL TOGETHER conformed something like brotherhood. Moreover, both citizens and visitors to Augsburg sealed virtually all important voluntary social commitments by drinking alcohol together; breaking a pact sealed by a drink was "virtually unthinkable" (Tlusty 2001: 104): "The basic contract drink (*Leikauf* or *Weinkauf*), which was shared by seller, buyer, and witnesses to the transaction, marked the point at which a contract became binding . . . Following through on the deal then became a matter of personal honor between the parties to the contract" (Tlusty 2001: 107–108). One may wonder exactly why drinking alcoholic drinks together evidently augments the moral commitments and the motivations to cooperate, compared to nonalcoholic drinks.

In such practices of bonding and binding by drinking alcohol, three aspects stand out that I think are quite general. The first is that while commensal drinking binds and bonds, exclusion from commensal drinking separates, as we saw was the case for commensal inclusion or exclusion of solid foods. That is, the men (in these cases) who are not welcomed, and in some cases are explicitly and even legally denied participation, are thereby negatively conformed as outsiders who are not in the communal sharing relationship conformed by commensal drinking. Furthermore, the exclusion conforms them as lower ranking than those who (may) join in the commensalism. In this respect, these practices of exclusion from commensal drinking are homologous with the South Asian demarcation of caste by exclusion of commensalism with persons of lower caste. Third, in certain social circumstances, at least, people evidently count on the motives and commitments emerging from consubstantial assimilation, far more than they trust the motives and commitments emerging from the symbolism of market pricing. Consequently, they use commensal drinking to bind and bond participants to market pricing contracts. In this case, that is surely in part because many or most of the people making the contracts are illiterate, so they cannot create, retain, and make recourse to written documents specifying the terms and signed by the parties. In part, it is also because there is no reliable court system to impartially and effectively enforce symbolically conformed contracts. So when they make a market pricing contract, they drink together in the expectation (or, at least, the hope) that this consubstantial assimilation will afford motives and moral sentiments of communal sharing solidarity that will tend to augment the motives and moral sentiments of their symbolic verbal conformation of the market pricing relationship.

I believe that it is quite common to deploy commensalism to backstop the commitment arising from pure market pricing symbolism. Who would cheat a drinking buddy? At any rate, in early modern Germany, and subsequently elsewhere in Europe and America, these practices of drinking alcohol together functioned along these lines to conform communal sharing by commensal consubstantiation, in the hope and expectation that the consequent communal sharing would assure mutual commitment to the market pricing relationships between the drinkers. This is not unique; it would be fruitful to research where and when people use communal sharing bonds to assure commitment to market pricing relations. Perhaps there are other practices in which people mobilize the bonds of one relational model to assure commitment to another relational model.

Smoking the Sacred Pipe

> The pipe should be filled and lighted and then it would be passed from one to another, each smoking a whiff or two . . . The spirit in the smoke will soothe the spirits of all who thus smoke together and all will be as friends and all think alike. When the Lakotas smoke in this manner, it is like when the Christians take communion. It is smoking in communion.
>
> (Sword 1896: 83; see also Paper 1988)

> When a [Lakota] person wishes Hunkapi with another, the taking of the bond closer than kinship, the two involved see the pipe as the power binding them together. When joining as relatives, these two signifying the bond between man and Wakan Tanka, they know the

> pipe holds them always, reminding them to walk gently with this bond, nurturing it through all their days.
>
> (Kaiser 1984: 22)

To become one through commensalism, the substances jointly ingested need not be liquids or solids. In widespread Native North American rituals, participants SMOKE A SACRED PIPE, offering smoke to Sky and Earth, joining themselves to each other and to all living beings, as well as to the ubiquitous spirits: "When you pray with this pipe, you pray for and with everything" (Black Elk 1971: 7).

Sacred pipe ceremonies involved unwrapping the sacred pipe bundle, filling the bowl with tobacco and lighting it, offering the smoke to six directions – East, West, North, South, Sky, and Earth – to encompass the universe, and passing it around the circle so that each participant smoked a few puffs. Ceremonies commonly involved dancing to drums, group singing, feasting, exchange of gifts, and sometimes animal sacrifice and face painting (Hall 1997). In late-seventeenth-century Apache, Illinois, and Cahinnio (Arkansas) calumet rituals, the hosts HELD THE GUEST and ROCKED HIM BACK AND FORTH during the dance (Blakeslee 1981, Springer 1981).

Many sacred pipe rituals were described as acts of adoption. Indians smoked the pipe together in friendly reception of strangers; to end a battle; to forgive and pardon an injury and restore amity; as a pledge of peace; to request and commit to help; to unite as allies and commit to a joint decision such as making war together; to enhance trust and sociability as a preliminary to trade; to come together as a family member is dying; to connect with all their kin, living and dead; to join a military fraternity bound to mutual support; or to form the bond between mentor and participant in the excruciatingly painful Sun Dance (McGuire 1899, Walker 1917, West 1934, Black Elk 1971, Dempsey 1972, Neihardt 1979, Kaiser 1984, Steinmetz 1984, Voget 1984, Fletcher 1996, Williams 1997, Hall 1997, von Gernet 2000, Paper 1988, 2005). Among the Omaha and others, smoking the calumet pipe together created ties closer than kinship (LaFleche 1884). Indians also carried the calumet for safe passage through hostile territory. Conversely, refusing to smoke together was a refusal of connection (Walter 1917: 63).

> In a Natchez marriage when the parties of both the bride and the groom agreed [on the marriage], the future husband went on a hunt and brought back sufficient food for the feast. The two families contracted the alliance. They all assembled at the house of the girl's parents. They served the parents

> who ate from the same dish. After the meal the bridegroom smoked the pipe with the parents of the bride and then with his own parents. (Steinmetz 1984: 65)

Among the Oglala Teton Dakota Sioux, the *Hunka* ceremony consisted of pipe-smoking, feasting, beating drums, shaking rattles, PAINTING THE PARTICIPANTS WITH A RED STRIPE, and waving horse-tails over them; it "binds each to his Hunka by ties of fidelity stronger than friendship, brotherhood, or family" (Walker 1917: 122). During the ritual, the Hunka participants likewise bound themselves to the spirit of the buffalo and their grandmother earth by sharing smoke with them and painting a red stripe on a buffalo skull (130–138). The participant often chewed a bit of meat and then gave it to the established Hunka conducting the ceremony, and then stripped off his clothes and gave them to him, showing that he would behave as a Hunka should, giving all that he has to a Hunka in need (138). Then the Hunka conducting the ritual bound the two new participants together with thongs, arm to arm, side to side, and leg to leg. Then they gave away numerous presents and feasted together (138–139). Black Elk also describes putting smoked buffalo MEAT INTO EACH OTHER'S MOUTHS in this peace-making, kinship-forming rite (Black Elk 1971: 113). In Black Elk's account of a prototypical ceremony, the Chief of the Ree said to the Chief of the Oglala Sioux:

> "I am to be your father. . . . We are here at the center, and the four Powers of the universe join in us. This meat I shall put in your mouth, and from this day forth you shall never fear my home, for my home is your home, and you are my son!" . . . For by this act the two people had been made one.

The Oglala Chief then made a corresponding speech and put food into the mouth of the Ree Chief. Then they smoked the sacred pipe in turn and passed it around among their followers. Black Elk (1971: 115) concludes by noting that through this ceremony, the participants "realize their relationship, their oneness, with the universe and all its Powers, and when they realize that at the center of the universe dwells *Wakan-Tanka*, and that this center is really everywhere, it is within each of us."

Early pipe-smoking rituals sometimes also connected the participants through the substance of their tears (Hall 1997). From 1658 to 1660, the French explorers Groseilliers and Radisson came to a village of Ottawa refugees, guests of the Santee (Eastern Dakotas). They gave the Ottawa a number of presents, and the Ottawas brought the Frenchmen to a council of welcome, a FEAST of friendship, and a welcoming DANCE. Then a delegation of the Dakota hosts arrived, stripped Groseilliers and

Radisson naked and redressed them in buffalo and beaver garments: "After this the Dakotas honored the Frenchmen with a weeping greeting, CRYING OVER THEIR HEADS UNTIL THEY WERE WET, then offering them their PIPES TO SMOKE, and finally "PERFUMING" the French and their weapons with smoke from their pipes" (Hall 1997: 1–2).

The first French trapper to follow Groseilliers and Radisson was Perrot, who built a fort on the Mississippi in Wisconsin, where a delegation of Iowas treated him to a weeping greeting, coming to Perrot and his party "weeping hot tears, which they let fall into their hands along with saliva, and with other filth which issued from their noses, with which they rubbed the heads, faces, and garments of the French" (Hall 1997: 3).

Besides tobacco, many other comestibles and drugs mediate communal sharing relationships in many cultures, including kola nuts in West Africa and areca nuts with betel leaves in South and Southeast Asia and the south western Pacific, as well as alcohol, tea, and coffee in many cultures. Are there any intrinsic biological affordances that make commensal consumption of some substances more efficacious than commensal consumption of other substances?

For interesting early accounts of the widely used conformation of communal sharing relationships between North American tribes as "eating from a dish with one spoon," see Lytwyn 1997, Brooks 2008, and Simpson 2007.

Host–Guest Bonds and Blood Brotherhood

Commensal conformation of communal sharing may become a well-delineated ritual, establishing other sorts of broad, strong, and enduring moral commitments. Notably, the sacred duty of hospitality (ξενιη) is a pivot of the *Odyssey* and *Iliad* (Kakridis 1963: 86–108; Reece 1993, Yamagata 1994: 28–39, 40–41, 135–136, 163–164). In Homeric Greece, it was a sacred duty to provide hospitality to supplicants; a host had to receive any stranger without asking his identity. Once a host received a guest, the host was bound to give him aid and protection – even if they were otherwise enemies – and then to send or take him safely to his next destination. Homer's representation of this indicates that the HOST FEASTS the ANONYMOUS GUEST with meat and wine and other foods. After the stranger reveals his identity and exchanges information with the host, the host may provide entertainment, and later the guest may pronounce a blessing on the host, who then may invite his guest to share in a libation or sacrifice. The host provides a bed and has the guest bathed by women of his household; the guest is offered clothing. When the guest subsequently departs, the host may initiate an enduring bond of guest-friendship (ξειvoζ) by giving his guest a special gift. The host may provide a departure meal before they pour a libation and exchange farewell blessings. Zeus himself was the god of hospitality and guest-friendship, avenging violations of the obligations entailed by such bonds.

The Greeks were not the only people who engaged in such practices. Texts from other cultures indicate that host–guest bond friendship was important in many European and Mediterranean Bronze Age and early Iron Age societies (Kristiansen & Larsson 2005: 238). The bond was often attested on small inscribed bronze or silver tablets, *tesserae hosptialis*, which took the form of animals, a hand, or a pair of clasped hands (Sánchez-Moreno 2001). The reconstruction of the Proto-Indo-European root, *ghos-ti*, the source of the English *host*, is taken to indicate that such ritualized host–guest relations existed on the southern Ukrainian–Russian steppes in the fourth millennium BCE (Gamkrelidze & Ivanov 1995: 657, Anthony 2007: 303, 342).

In Judaic, Islamic, and some South Asian traditions, people bind themselves to covenants of loyalty and friendship by CONSUMING SALT TOGETHER (Thompson 1989). In early Arabian culture

> every stranger whom one meets in the desert is a natural enemy, and has no protection against violence except his own strong hand or the fear that his tribe will avenge him if his blood be spilt. But if I have eaten the smallest morsel of food with a man, I have nothing further to fear from him; "there has been salt between us," and he is bound not only to do me no harm, but to help and defend me as if I were his brother. (Smith 1889: 269–270)

In a large number of societies across history there have been practices in which two men cut themselves and bleed into a vessel, mix their blood, and both ingest their mixed blood. This creates indissoluble BLOOD BROTHERHOOD communal sharing relationships. Evans-Pritchard (1933) description of Azande rituals in Southern Sudan provides the classic ethnographic account of blood brotherhood; de Dampierre (1967) later described similar practices among the neighboring and very closely related Nzakara. Azande men, as well as Nzakara men, form an extremely strong bond by making incisions and consuming each other's blood while speaking to the blood, invoking its power to destroy a blood brother who harms his partner, and spelling out benefits that each will provide. They then toss down gifts, usually large knives, that begin the relationship. Blood brothers should be hospitable, feeding each other and offering beer, giving gifts, never refusing any practicable request from a blood brother, and providing refuge for him if he is pursued. Blood brothers should warn each other of danger (including impending action by chiefs), stand up for each other in quarrels, never speak ill of each other to a chief, pay fines to save each other from vengeance or execution, and give each other scarce ritual goods. In particular, Azande blood brothers and Nzakara blood brothers should not refuse a partner's request to give his daughter in marriage. "A man constantly eats meals at his blood brother's homestead and is invited there to beer parties. When a man kills a large beast his blood brothers come to ask him for a share of the meat" (Evans-Pritchard 1933: 389). A man has free access to his blood brother's homestead and is treated as a special guest there; he may even take up residence there. However, blood brothers refrain from making immoderate, unreasonable, or unnecessary demands on each other. Men also form these pacts with men from other, potentially hostile tribes to assure safe passage when traveling in dangerous territories or to facilitate material exchanges. Blood brotherhood was the closest, most trusting, intensive, and extensive relationship in Azande or Nzakara society. Violations of this commitment were thought to destroy an entire kin group. Though I never encountered blood brotherhood among Moosé, it has been important in numerous African societies and on other continents (see the early comprehensive review by Tegnaeus 1952; also Eisenstadt 1956, Beidelman 1963, Brain 1976, Smith 1885: 56–62, Thompson 1989: 312; for ancient China, see Lewis 1990: 43–50). These bonds are often the closest, most trusting relationships in the society.

Bloch (1989) cites mutual bloodletting and co-drinking rituals to bind participants to oaths, alliances, or bond friendship in antiquity and the Middle Ages among Scythians, Iberians, Hungarians, Armenians, Montenegrins, Southern Slavs, Medes (NW Iran), Lydians, Mongols, Greeks, and Romans (see also Róheim 1945: 9–10). Trumbell (1885) argues that the Christian communion ritual is historically derived from this kind of blood-sharing covenant.

In medieval European chivalry, a bond of brotherhood in arms was often created by swearing an oath or signing a written contract, but was ideally conceived as based on corporeal connection – for example, by eating together or sleeping in the same bed. Mixing of the partners' blood (and sometimes consuming the mixture) was salient in representations of these bonds (Keen 1962, Oschema 2006). Sometimes the blood mutually shed in combat also bonded men (Kaeuper 1999: 215–219). After fighting fiercely for several hours, two knights might each tear his own shirt to bind the other's wounds, then express their undying love for each other, kiss, and swear to always stay together. This blood ritual made them BROTHERS-IN-ARMS, committing themselves to helping each other in combat, in legal proceedings, and in all other material and social ways. They might ask to be buried in the other's tomb.

So far as I know, wherever any form of blood brotherhood exists, it is always precisely two men who form this bond; I have not seen accounts of three or more men making themselves blood brothers, nor have I read any ethnographic explanation of why this does not occur. I have seen no reports of practices in which women form comparable blood-sisterhood bonds, nor practices in which a woman and a man create such bonds. Nevertheless, the moral commitment and affiliative emotions conformed by mixing blood is evidently intuitive to English-speaking writers and readers, without such limitations. In the United States, at least, it is construed as emotionally evocative and morally committing. Mark Twain has Huck and Tom do this to bind themselves to secrecy (2004 [originally published 1876]), and Rebecca Wells (1996) has the Ya-Ya Sisterhood do it, marking the origin of their lifelong communal sharing relationship. (In these two novels, participants mix their blood, but do not drink the mixture.)

All of these covenants conformed morally binding, trusting bonds with persons outside one's kinship networks and community. These covenants were essential in stateless societies. In the absence of states, a stranger was likely to be robbed or killed if he lacked such guest-hospitality bonds in the regions where he travelled.

Conforming Communal Sharing Through Other Sorts of Bloodshed

There are other practices of communal sharing conformed by shedding blood together. During Muharram, Muslims fast for one or more days, and Shias in particular commemorate the death of Muhammad's grandson Husayn ibn Ali in the 680 CE succession battle at Karbala (Pinault 1992, Chelkowski 2010). Shia identify themselves with Hussain as the legitimate heir of the Prophet, while Sunnis identify themselves with the lineage of Yazid, the ruler who ordered the killing of Hussain and his followers. Shia men and women share Hussain's suffering and exhibit their devotion to him and his people by *matam* (beating their chests). In India, Pakistan, Afghanistan, Iraq, and Bahrain, men flagellate themselves by *zanier kea matam* with chains, some of which incorporate knives or razors. In some Shia communities, men – and a few women and children – make razor incisions on their foreheads (Chelkowski 2010). Along with the flagellants, they experience and display the pain and bloodshed they inflict on themselves as the consubstantial reinforcing and displaying communal sharing empathy and compassion for Hussain and his followers, and an act of consubstantiation marking of Shia identity. In Pakistan, at the same time, it marks Pakistani Punjabis and others who perform it as "true" Muslims, "more Muslim" than Arab Muslims (Chelkowski 2010). Beyond the bleeding wounds they flaunt for a day, the flagellants bear lifelong SCARS that identify them as dedicated Shi'ites.

CHAPTER 5

Shared Surfaces, Motion, and Fear

Body Marking: Genital Modification, Scarification, Tattooing, Piercing, Hair, Clothing, and Adornment

Beyond the commensalism characterized in the preceding chapter, we noted cases in which people also conform communal sharing by making their body surfaces the same through body modification, body marking, dress, hair, adornment, or "uniforms." Synchronized rhythmic motion, as in rowing or marching together, also conforms communal sharing when, for participants, their bodies become one.

Military units and forces, police, teams, schools, universities, marching bands, choirs, and the like fabricate their social equivalence through their UNIFORMITY OF GARB AND INSIGNIA . Monks and nuns of different religions and distinct orders wear identifying robes, as do priests, pastors, rabbis, Krishna devotees, and other religious adepts. Adolescent fashions, team uniforms, school dress codes, or hats, sweatshirts, tee shirts, and class rings are surface signs of equivalence groups: bodies covered in the same garb constitute the wearers as to some degree socially equivalent for some purposes. Matching wedding bands are conformations of marriage. All of these mechanisms join people by making their body surfaces the same. Amish men and women wear clothing that sets them apart from their non-Amish neighbors, and Amish men wear beards without mustaches. When they originally established this practice, not having a mustache made them stand out from non-Amish men. And still today, in southeast Pennsylvania at least, a beard with no mustache conforms a man as Amish. Living in and near Philadelphia in the mid to late 1980s, I had a beard with no mustache (because I didn't like the appearance of my mustache when allowed to grow), and was quite often mistaken for Amish, even though I did not have the black hat that Amishmen typically wore. Sikh men wear white turbans and do not cut their hair or beards; observant Jewish men wear yarmulkes; Hassidic Jews and their subgroups wear distinctive clothes and headgear.

Many Muslim women declare their identity by donning the *hijab/chador/burqa* veil and hair-covering. Many Catholics wear a cross. Urban gang members index their membership by the specific colors or items they wear (and by tattoos). In response, school and prison authorities often ban the display of these emblems. In conjunction with the national independence movements of the 1950s and 1960s, many Africans and American Blacks expressed their solidarity with those movements by sporting dashiki shirts and Afro hair. And there are numerous other clothing practices that conform racial, ethnic or national identity (e.g., Eicher 1995, Hansen 2004).

For example, in Guatemala, *traje* Mayan dress is a core component of Mayan identity (Hendrickson 1995). The Incas were distinguished by their short haircut, braided headdress, and pierced and extended ear lobes whose specific style conformed subgroups whom the Inca had conquered (de la Vega 1961: 12–13). Each of the "nations" in the Inca empire also dressed their hair in a distinctive manner (de la Vega 1961: 216). Revolutionary regimes often implicitly or explicitly specify the clothing required of party members or true nationalists (e.g., in China: Wilson 1999, Chen 2003; for Africa: Allman 2004). In some modern communities, people are especially moved to don ethnic or religiously identifying COSTUMES on ritual occasions in which marking their identity is one focus of the performance of a tradition. For example, on Norwegian national day, many Norwegians of all ages wear traditional clothing that conforms them as Norwegian, while at the same time the specifics of the style conform specific regional identities within Norway.

In much of Latin America, a *pollera* (full, pleated skirt) indexes Indian identity, while a *vestido* (factory-made dress) indexes mestiza or white (Hansen 2004: 373). By changing clothes, a person may switch the collective identity they conform. For example, Peruvians in Caylloma change their clothes to transform their situational identities as Indian, mestizo, or white (Femenìas 2004). Clothing style conformations of "ethnicity" are mutable; as fashions change, the out-of-date clothing that signifies "indigenous" may change (Meisch 2002).

In some societies, at a certain stage of life, PIGMENTING THE WHOLE SURFACE OF THE SKIN with ochre or other dyes functions to conform ethnic/tribal/community identity and/or the emerging identity of initiates (Turner 1980, Duarte 2014). For example, among the Maasai of East Africa, the moran, an age-grade of warriors who share everything and risk their lives for each other in battle, wear their hair in long ringlets and are always red from head to toe – both skin and robes (Amin, Willetts,

& Eames 1987). Initiates in the rites of many cultures color their bodies with distinctive white clay or dyes (Cohen 1991, Dulaney & Fiske 1994, Newman 2001). When the Romans arrived in the northern part of Britain, they were struck by the blue-tinted Picts, who colored their skin with woad (from the woad plant; Carr 2005).

Women among the Ovahimba of Angola and Namibia cover their skin, hair, and personal attire with *otjise*, a red substance consisting of red ochre powder and butterfat:

> Upon inquiring about the reasons behind this customary cultural feature, Nakara from Otjongoro answered, "It is our culture and our tradition. It makes us look and feel beautiful. And all can see that we are real Himba women ... There are no Himba women who are not red. They do not exist." Otjise also features prominently in male and female initiation ceremonies and is applied by men when they are to be wed or undertake extensive journeys. Otjise is also applied to human corpses prior to interment. (Rifikin 2015: 8–9; ellipses in original)

Although very little is known with confidence about the conformational significance of prehistoric pigments applied to the skin, hominins have used mineral pigments such as ochre (mostly red, also yellow or purple), specular hematite (red and bluish, sparkling), and manganese dioxide (black) for about 500,000 years. For example, South African Middle Stone Age sites typically contain hundreds or even thousands of pieces of ochre (Hodgskiss 2018). Sometimes the pigment minerals were transported tens of kilometers. A subterranean ochre mine in Swaziland dates about 43,000 years before the present. Paleoanthropologists posit that the most likely use of these pigments was to color the skin (D'Errico 2008, Hodgskiss 2018, Watts 2018, Wolf et al. 2018). Over the millennia, the use of ochre and also other pigments generally became even more prevalent and more intensive, notably in mortuary practices, where it may have been used to color the bodies of some deceased persons.

More permanent modifications of the body surface show irreversible identity commitment. Most evocatively, people mark their identities on their bodies with CIRCUMCISION or subincision, CLITORIDECTOMY or infibulation, FACIAL AND BODY SCARRING, PIERCING and stretching holes in the nose, lips, or ears. Modification of the foreskin or head of the penis occurs in many regions of the world and dates at least as far back as ancient Egypt (Pritchard 1954, fig. 629, Gollaher 2000, Hodges 2001). For Hindus and Muslims of Barabanki and Mumbai, to be Muslim is to be circumcised (Mehta 1986). Many Moosé traditionally exhibited a diagonal

SCAR from the bridge of the nose across the cheek, together with a circle (or two) around the face. In some Pacific cultures, such as groups of Dyak in Borneo and Chin in Burma, people have distinctive TATTOOS that conform their social identity. Some Dyaks, some African societies, and other groups wear distinctive ear plugs or distended holes in their earlobes. A number of societies in New Guinea and elsewhere pierce the nasal septum and wear ornaments through them that are striking conformations of their community or tribe. Likewise, men or women in some cultures wear plugs and plates in the lower lip.

In Bali, and in certain cultures of Africa and elsewhere, people FILE THEIR INCISORS into a point, conforming their collective identity. Around the world, over several millennia, to conform persons as members of their particular society, a number of cultures in Europe (especially France, until recent times), North Africa, Australia and insular Southeast Asia, northern South America, Mexico, and other regions DEFORMED THE CRANIUM by confining the heads of infants so as to produce a distinctive shape as the child's head grew (Gerszten & Gerszten 1995, FitzSimmons, Prost, & Peniston 1998).

By seven or eight months of age, US infants observing three animated entities (shapes with eyes) infer that similarities in the appearance of the animated entities will be associated with individual entities' later moving in synchrony with their "social group" members (Powell & Spelke 2013). By thirteen months, watching human actors, US infants expect a bystander not to help a person who had taken a toy away from a victim if the bystander and victim were both dressed in the same distinctive clothing (tiger ears, a black turtleneck, and a tiger-fur collar; or an orange hoodie and purple eyeglasses). But the infants were not surprised if the bystander did help a transgressor if the bystander and victim were dressed differently (Ting, He, & Baillargeon 2019). That is, the infants expected agents to intervene on behalf of someone dressed in the same distinctive manner, but not on behalf of an agent dressed differently.

Initiation: Shared Uncertainty, Fear, Pain, Bloodshed, and Body Modification

In his fieldwork among the Ndembu of Central Africa, Victor Turner (1969, 1973, 1975), drawing on Durkheim's theory of ritual, showed that participants in a ritual experience an emotionally intense communal sharing that he called "communitas." In focusing on initiation rites, one find that they combine several forms of consubstantial assimilation. Traditional initiation rituals commonly involve commensal consumption of special foods, and often dancing, especially to percussion (Dulaney & Fiske 1994, Fiske & Haslam 1997, Morinis 1985). The initiators often beat the initiates and cut their bodies (e.g., Herdt 1982; see Girard 1977 on violence in ritual). Shaving or dressing of hair, applying pigments or other substances to the body, and special clothing or adornments are very common components of initiation. Moreover, many initiation rites center on modifications of the body, especially genital operations, but also other kinds of scarring. For example, all of these features are prevalent in the seven-stage series of initiation rites that Barth (1975) describes in central Papua New Guinea. Elimination of polluting "female substance" by bleeding, extrusion of pus, and vomiting are core activities in the initiation rites of many New Guinea cultures (Herdt 1982). In several Papua New Guinea cultures, people say that boys are born with little or no semen, although semen is the substance from which bones are made and is necessary for procreation. So, in order to complete their development or acquire the supply of semen they will need as adults, boys must repeatedly ingest semen. They do this in and around initiation rites, by fellating young men. Given such beliefs, participants perceive this particular consubstantial assimilation practice to be absolutely essential.

"Initiated together, emotional and social bonding may occur that lasts for a lifetime and that involves social cooperation and respect" (Ottenberg 1994: 354). Young (1965) coded ethnographies from fifty-four cultures; he found that male solidarity is greater in societies with more elaborate male initiation rites, and female solidarity is greater in societies with more elaborate female initiations. In a number of societies, in addition to their bonds with fellow initiates, initiates form lifelong ritual bonds with the person who holds them during circumcision.

It is not clear how the initiates' fear of the anticipated ordeals interacts with other aspects of initiation conformations. In initiations that culminate in genital or other surgery, fear of that surgery beforehand, the effort to control and hide the fear, observations of fellow initiates in pain when each knows that it will soon be their turn, the pain of the surgery, and the memory of that pain must sharply focus the initiates' attention on their newly enhanced bodily equivalence.

Male initiations are more prevalent and often more intense than female initiation rites. Male initiations can be extraordinarily severe in cultures where warfare or raiding is frequent, so men must be courageously loyal to each other in their raiding, and in their defense against raids (e.g., Herdt 1982). In many pastoralist societies of East Africa, where warfare and raiding was constant, men formed their strongest communal sharing bonds with their age-mates who were initiated during the same span of years (e.g., Spring 2005 to Spring 2009). Age-mates share food, pay each other's cattle fines, and, in cattle raiding, risk their lives for each other. A man is initiated together with only a few others from families that happen to be nearby. These pastoralists are widely dispersed, so a man does not know most of the others who belong to his age set. Thus, it is striking how strong their moral commitments to each other are, and their evident affiliative sentiments as well. When a male stranger shows up in a community, if he turns out to belong to the age set of some man of the community, that man becomes his host. The host provides food and bedding, and will graciously encourage the visitor and the host's wife to have sex and sleep together, if they wish to (Baxter & Almagor 1978, Spencer 1985).

People in cultures that do not perform female genital surgery often find it difficult to understand why, in cultures where it is done, girls, their mothers, and other kin generally feel that it is morally right and necessary to do it, and the girls, fearful as they are, want it done and are proud to have had it (Atiya 1982, Ahlberg et al. 2000, Abusharaf 2001, Shweder 2002). It may be easier to understand why they want it done if it is recognized to be an extremely emotive and irreversible act of consubstantial assimilation, transforming a girl into a woman – a woman whose genitalia are just like her mother's and grandmother's, her sisters', her aunts', and every woman in the community.

Touching

People conform communal sharing with body contact, such as when a caretaker carries an infant, caresses or bathes an infant, or when people sleep together. HUGGING, CARESSING, SHAKING HANDS, or KISSING, NUZZLING or TOUCHING THE OTHER'S BODY WITH ONE'S NOSE, GROOMING, HUGGING or CARESSING, CARRYING A BABY, HOLDING HANDS, or WALKING ARM-IN-ARM or ARMS AROUND SHOULDERS potentially conform communal sharing (Darwin 1872: 213–214; Tylor 1878: 51; Goffman 1971: 226–237, 1976: 54–56, 75–81, Casson 1975: 31 & 44, Morris 1977: 92–101, Montagu 1979, Mehrabian 1981: 23, Thayer 1982, Eibl-Eibesfeldt 1989: 138–139, 209–234).

Affiliative touch conforms communal sharing in myriad cultures. For example, to express affiliative sentiments, Indians on the coast of northern California HUGGED European sailors visiting in 1775 (Camp 1964). Old

Babylonian versions of the Epic of Gilgamesh conform Gilgamesh and Enkidu's bond of friendship in their "KISSING" and TAKING EACH OTHER BY THE HAND, though we do not know exactly what sort of kissing this was (George 2003: 197, 201). Middle Babylonian versions only represent their friendship by their taking each other by the hand (George 2003: 319, 331). The comforting protection of the sun god Shamash when Gilgamesh is in peril is repeatedly represented in art as Shamash taking his hand (George 2003: 235, 251). Kissing and hugging also marked affection among seventh- to tenth-century Anglo-Saxons. In the Epic of Beowulf, when Beowulf takes leave of King Hrothgar, who has become very fond of him, the king embraces Beowulf's neck and kisses him (Heaney 2000: 129; Gummere 1910).

There are a great many representations of the CLASPING OF RIGHT HANDS on classical Greek and other grave stelae, bronzes, amphoras, Roman coins and sarcophagi reliefs, and Christian mosaics and sarcophagi reliefs (Tylor 1878: 45–46, Ricks 2006, Herman 1987: 51, 64, fig. 9, Prudhommeau 1965: plate 835, British Museum London B 226). This gesture evidently conformed relations of allegiance, mutual faithfulness, and loyalty. It was also the act which incorporated initiates into the secret cult mystery religions, and there are numerous representations of husbands and wives holding hands. This conformation has been significant in Europe ever since then (Roodenburg 1991, Saffire 2008, Stephey 2008, Schiffrin 1974).

Perhaps historically independent of these European conformations, the Ashanti of Ghana greeted with mutual hand clasping (Firth 1973: 319). The Bambara of Mali touched hands in greeting, marking relative status by placing their palm DOWN to an inferior, UP to a superior, or PERPENDICULAR to an equal (Firth 1973: 321). (The Moosé did not touch hands in greeting, nor touch any part of the other's body.) Also perhaps independent of European conformations, the Chinese character 友, *yǒu*, "friend, companion; fraternity," is derived from a pictograph of two clasped hands (originally, two right hands side by side; YellowBridge, Zhengyu 1997: 86, Peng 2005: 20, Schuessler 2007, Xie 1997: 123).

The Indo-Europeans had several words for love, affection, and friendship – words whose verbal root is *kus- or *kwas-, "to kiss," although again we don't know just how they kissed (Watkins 2000, Mallory & Adams 2006: 343). In various modern European cultures, kissing conforms communal sharing, with different kinds and intensities of kissing conforming differences in the communal sharing (Nyrop 1901, Garnier

1989, Frijhoff 1991). Apparently, Europeans and Americans returning home safely after long or harrowing travels may kiss the ground, though I have never seen this.

In medieval stained glass and in manuscripts, pairs or groups of persons who are socially equivalent are represented by double or multiple SUPERIMPOSED SILHOUETTES, nearly completely overlapping – just slightly offset, like a double or multiple image; indeed, sometimes the image shows a single, shared right or left arm or leg (Garnier 1989: 68–70). Some images depict one figure completely superposed on another as if inside, often with the interior figure surrounded by two or more concentric circles; this indicates identification or adhesion (Garnier 1982: 92–95 & fig. 37). For example, Jesus is shown on/in God the Father, or in/on Mary; John the Baptist is depicted on/in his father Zechariah. Similarly, the figure of Moses is shown within the figure of the Pharaoh's daughter, who is presenting Moses to the Pharaoh, evidently indicating her adopting and protecting Moses (Garnier 1982: 95 & fig. 203F). Conversely, medieval art placing the image of a person against a distinct field – for example, against a contrasting color in a bounded frame – indicates a social separation (Garnier 1982: 101 & figs. 15 & 44; 1989: 60–61).

In American sports at all levels, at the end of practice or before going into the field, team members often join hands. Players on a team touch hands to mark their solidarity when one of them scores for the team; football and soccer players hug (Smith, Willis, & Gier 1980). The winning team may mob each other, piling on top of each other, forming a single collective body. Players may jump into each other's arms, and be held there for a few moments. In American Sign Language *friend* is INTERTWINED INDEX FINGERS, while for *close friend* the finger grasp is stronger and longer (Taub 2001: 118–122). LOVE IS THE CROSSED FOREARMS PRESSED TIGHTLY AGAINST THE CHEST; MARRIAGE IS CLASPED HANDS.

Neolithic burials at sites in Europe and one in central Africa include pairs or trios of skeletons whose faces are adjacent and/or whose arms are around each other or whose legs are intertwined (Leclerc & Masset 2006, Urbanus 2008, Meyer et al. 2008, Sereno et al. 2008, Hettwer 2008). This suggests that, for thousands of years, "hugging" or "cuddling" may have been an important conformation of communal sharing – a conformation that people intended to preserve after death.

Of course, there are different meanings to touching different parts of another's body, and touch in a medical examination or procedure does not mean what a similar touch would otherwise mean. Touching a person while guarding them in basketball or playing football is another thing, again. There is hardly any meaning to being involuntarily pressed against another person in a crowded trolley.

Synchronized Rhythmic Motion

Many of the earliest preserved representations of human figures depict lines of virtually identical people apparently dancing, often hand in hand (e.g., Olivova 1984: 41, 118–119, Scarpari 2000: 152, Prudhommeau 1965, plates 536, 229, and 303, Lonsdale 1993: 216, 253, Linduff & Yan 2004: 41). Beyond the image itself, there is nothing to tell us what relationship among the dancers the artist meant to conform, but it is difficult to imagine that the dancers' relationship was anything but communal sharing. That such images are often the only images in a given place, from a given time, strongly suggests that their ancient artists perceived the depicted interactions to be especially significant, probably because of their function as consubstantial assimilation. The artists, or the persons requesting the images, likely intended the images themselves to be conformations of a communal sharing relationship among a number of persons. More speculatively, Carl Schuster (1986, Schuster & Carpenter 1996) collected many examples of many centuries of art around the world consisting of identical elements joined together in an indefinitely repeated, tessellated pattern. He interprets the elements as geometrically stylized human motifs.

From the fact that, in several regions, the oldest surviving representations of humans evidently depict identical figures dancing in synchrony, holding hands, we can tentatively infer the widespread importance of communal sharing, and the evocativeness of this conformation of consubstantial assimilation, thousands of years ago. The capacity to synchronize vocalizations and other behaviors has a very deep phylogenetic history (Greenfield & Merker 2023), although its function in bonding participating nonhuman animals is less well understood.

McNeill (1995) investigated the history of close-order MILITARY DRILL, concluding that the synchronized rhythmic movement of military drill effectively bonds recruits who are initially strangers to each other. McNeill's research found that each time and in every place where military drill was invented, the resulting communal solidarity among the soldiers was a major determinant of success in warfare. McNeill argues that prolonged movement in unison heightens positive emotions, which "binds the community more firmly together and makes cooperative efforts of every kind easier to carry through" (39). Soldiers today, especially in basic training, are still ordered to drill and march in rhythmic synchrony. This is a nice example of a social practice culturally evolving in the niche constituted by the innate psychological mechanism of consubstantial assimilation. The practice of military drill and marching was originally intended to organize battlefield maneuvers and control the soldiers' loading and discharge of muskets, but evidently it established itself, endured, and spread precisely because it created and sustained strong communal sharing relations.

It seems plausible to suppose that the practice of great masses of soldiers synchronously marching in military parades was fostered by linking this consubstantial assimilation niche with another set of conformational niches. Chapters 7, 8, and 9 describe ten iconic conformations of authority ranking based on magnitudes such as mass, volume, multiplicity, force, and loudness. These magnitudes iconically conform authority ranking, thereby constituting niches for the cultural evolution of practices that reinforce the legitimacy of the authority of superiors. Dictators in Russia, China, and elsewhere stage enormous military parades whose MASS, VOLUME, MULTIPLICITY, FORCE, and LOUDNESS were intended to iconically conform the dictators' authority.

McNeill describes the history of the bonding effects of rhythmic movement in community dances, work gangs, religious rituals, calisthenics, synchronized collective exercise in East Asian businesses, and political rallies and marches. He concludes that MOVEMENT IN RHYTHMIC UNISON produces "a blurring of self-awareness and the heightening of fellow-feeling" (McNeill 1995: 8), meeting the human need to define identity and orient loyalties, answering the question "To what, and with whom do we belong?" (156). A well-described instance of this emerges in Brown's (2013) interviews with oarsmen from the 1936 University of Washington crew who won the Olympics eight-oar competition. Seventy years after the experience, their memories were vivid and their sentiments about rowing together were still intense. Although they were competing in the Olympics, seven decades later their memories and sentiments were not focused on their victory, but rather on the wonderful brief experiences they had of being one with each other in the short intervals when they were perfectly in synch.

Box 5.1

To remove any ambiguity, let me make clear that conformations create and modulate social relationships, but people relating to each other ordinarily do lots more than conforming their relationship. If the family commensally shares a meal, that is consubstantial assimilation. But when Zena washes the dishes, that is an act of communal sharing, not a conformation of communal sharing. If Zena is outside, talking to a neighbor, turns to see that the house is on fire, and runs into the house to save her family, at great risk to herself, that is communal sharing at its most consequential, but is not consubstantial assimilation.

However, in the limiting case, the conformation and the relationship may coincide. Suppose Patrice is attending the wedding of her cousin. Patrice's mother comes up and introduces Patrice to her great aunt Matilda, whom Patrice has never seen before and cannot recall ever hearing about. Matilda gives Patrice a big hug and offers her the rest of the cake she was eating; Patrice accepts, and finishes off the cake. Because of these acts of consubstantial assimilation, at that moment, Patrice and Matilda have warm communal feelings toward each other. But then they hear that they should take their seats, the groom walks to the front, and the wedding ceremony absorbs all of their attention, and then each of them is occupied with the reception. Consequently, perhaps, their meeting never gets from short-term memory into long-term memory, so they both forget meeting each other, and forget the affect of the moment. In that event, their relationship does not extend beyond its conformation.

This may be rare. But perhaps in the present day of digital lives and innumerable short interactions with strangers on social media, conformation and relationship coincide from time to time when a person watches a video, or has a brief encounter with someone who, the day after the event, does not matter to them or they do not even remember encountering.

Cultural Differences and Historical Changes in Consubstantial Assimilation Practices

Within the scope of consubstantial assimilation, there are innumerable intriguing cultural differences in the ways that people conform communal sharing and, in principle, people can form communal sharing relationships with reference to anything that they have in common (Tajfel 1978). But the pattern across cultures shows that people are strongly disposed to conforming communal sharing by making their bodies the same in some way, and perceive communal sharing when they implicitly think and feel that their bodies are the same in some essential respect.

There is great cultural diversity in specific conformational practices and great variety in individual actions, and each culture has important unique features. For example, in most societies, neither milk kinship nor bond friendship through mutual ingestion of blood are culturally recognized and elaborated. But they are intuitive and emotive to everyone, which leads to repeated independent invention of such practices. And, once invented, this psychosocial affordance constitutes a niche that results in general susceptibility to cultural reproduction and diffusion of consubstantial assimilation conformations.

Consubstantial assimilation is often more or less inaccessible to conscious reflection or articulate expression. It is not based on semantics, reasoning, concepts, propositions, or language. This may be a reason why, in contrast to organizations based primarily on authority ranking, equality matching, or, especially, market pricing, communal sharing organizations articulate few explicit rules, often eschewing written codes or manuals (Rothschild-Whitt 1979, Henry 1988). It is characteristic of communal sharing relationships that people often feel that such relationships simply are, without being able to articulate precisely why they are as they are. However, when communal sharing, authority ranking, or equality matching relations are contested or otherwise problematic, a discourse usually develops that entails translation of the primary conformation system into ideology. Then people do tend to develop declarative semantic, conceptual, propositional accounts of communal sharing. But it appears that articulable accounts are derivative of the fundamental conformations: communal sharing, authority ranking, and equality matching relationships do not require conceptual formulation or explicit declarative expression. People "do" consubstantial assimilation and communal relationships without needing to analyze them abstractly, although they can find semantic ways to approximately articulate them, if need be.

Formed by natural selection, consubstantial assimilation is an adaptation whose function is to coordinate communal sharing relationships. The human genome, neurophysiology, neuroanatomy, ontogeny, and life history mediate the conformational effects of consubstantial assimilation on communal sharing. Conversely, the genome, neurophysiology, neuroanatomy, ontogeny, and life history mediate the expression of communal sharing through consubstantial assimilation. More simply, consubstantial assimilation is a biological cause and consequence of communal sharing, integrating participants' psychologies so they jointly create this mutually adaptive social relationship.

The conformations of consubstantial assimilation form an integrated set, functioning as potential substitutes of differing intensities, while also capable of being added together. In England during the seventeenth and eighteenth centuries, men publicly hugged, and kissed on the cheek, to signal a commitment to a semi-ritual friendship (Bray & Rey 1999). Among these people in this era, EATING AT THE SAME TABLE in the great hall of the English great houses, or even serving at the table when the server was of noble status, entailed similar obligations of ritual friendship (the servers presumably sat together to eat the leftovers). SLEEPING IN THE SAME BED or pallet, or even in the same room, was a sign and a commitment of the same kind in noble houses as well as universities, as was being alone in the coach with the king (Bray & Rey 1999). Likewise, men formed connections by EMPTYING ANOTHER'S CHAMBER POT: "For someone to dispose of someone else's bodily wastes could carry the same implication of intimacy as sleeping or eating together, to which it was of course an adjunct" (Bray & Rey 1999: 72). I imagine that bathing and dressing another had similar meanings in medieval England, giving rise to Knights of the Bath and the Order of the Garter. The bond of the body continued into death, such that there are at least two instances of pairs of English knights entombed together, depicted on the monuments as embracing each other (Bray & Rey 1999: 82). "Gestures of this kind did more than indicate bonds of friendship, as a signpost might indicate a town: they created [bonds of friendship]. This ... is a way of thinking ... in which representation is constitutive and not merely mimetic" (Bray & Rey 1999: 70). These acts "gestured towards a place of comforting safety in an insecure world" (76), conveying a formal commitment of "love."

Conformation systems change. KISSING was prevalent in medieval Europe, then waned, then waxed again; representations in art and literature also varied, though possibly not in proportion to the prevalence of kissing in everyday practice (Frijhoff 1991). Around the end of the seventeenth century in England, male kissing began to suggest that the men were "sodomites," and service at table or in the bedchamber began to be regarded as servile rather than merely intimate (Bray & Rey 1999: 79–84). Bodily intimacy became more restricted to immediate family members. In England, first, then in Holland and in various continental nations (at different times in each nation) there was a partial or complete transition from kissing non-family associates to handshaking (Frijhoff 1991, Bray & Rey 1999). However, in France people continue to greet and take leave, at least on some occasions, by kissing on alternate cheeks (three kisses is warmer than two). And in Eastern Europe and European Russia today, even male politicians from different nations may greet with a kiss on the mouth.

In Guinea, Camara Laye (1966) describes his mother lovingly SPITTING ON him when he left for boarding school, and Leakey (1966) reports that the Kikuyu of Kenya spat on him in blessing. Leakey also describes the Kikuyu practice of spitting in the hand before shaking hands to demonstrate your friendly trust. Spitting is an act of bonding and blessing practiced in some other societies as well, including Greece, and among English school boys at some times (see Hartland's [1895: 259] citation of Henderson 1891). I do not recall ever seeing kissing during the eight years I lived in East, Central, and West Africa. In contrast, many African and Asian societies traditionally regarded mouth kissing as disgusting and immoral (at least in public; Firth 1973: 315). However, many younger urban Africans have increasingly adopted the practice in recent years. In China, there are detailed descriptions of kissing in some novels, some of which date back 300–400 years, and the oldest sex manual that described kissing skill is nearly 1,800 years old (Yan, personal communication, November 23 & 28, 2005). Apparently kissing was quite common among the Chinese urban elite for quite a long time, but it was absolutely private until the 1980s, when it began to become increasingly common. Now it is not unusual to see youths of the opposite sex kissing in both public and quasi-public settings, although hugging and touching is still more prevalent in public than kissing. Only lovers kiss each other on the mouth in China (Yan, personal communication, November 23 & 28, 2005).

Summary of Kinds of Consubstantial Assimilation

To get our bearings, let us consider a simple list of the most common forms of consubstantial assimilation:

- Perception of common person-defining substance, such as "blood," "bones," staple foods, "DNA," "genes."
- Giving birth to
- Suckling
- Feeding or giving drink to (especially directly to the mouth)
- Commensalism (eating or drinking directly from the same vessel), especially sacrificial substances; including drugs from the same source, and passing a ceremonial pipe
- Consuming the same food substance produced from the "same land," or prepared in a distinctive manner.
- Affectionate sex
- Mixing blood (usually then consumed by participants)

- Spitting on, wiping spit on (when affiliative)
- Eating deceased kin
- Body-surface sameness
- Scarification or tattoos (when intended to mark shared identity)
- Hair type or distinctive coiffure
- Genital modification (e.g., circumcision, clitoridectomy)
- Uniform clothing and accoutrements
- Gentle body contact, such as caressing, hugging, or cuddling
- Hand shaking, fist bumping, and the like
- Carrying an infant or toddler against the body
- Kissing
- Wearing clothes worn by another
- Rhythmic synchronous motion:
  - Rocking an infant or carrying an infant on the body while walking, pounding, hoeing
  - Dance, especially in "ritual"
  - Military drill, or similar calisthenics
  - Marching
  - Rowing in synchrony
  - Rhythmic laboring in time to drumming or shanty

Typically, the performance and the cognitive representation of these conformations are symmetrical vis-à-vis the persons, at least to some degree. When people shake hands or move in rhythmic synchrony, each person is doing what each other person is doing. Kissing, caressing, and cuddling may be anywhere on a continuum from symmetrical to entirely one-sided. In contrast, giving birth, suckling, and preparing food for others are asymmetrical. An intriguing question is: Does conformation symmetry matter? If so, how?[1]

Some of these conformations, such as kissing, snuggling, breastfeeding, and commensalism, are limited to face-to-face interaction. However, oral and sign language, art, writing, and especially digital communication often metarepresent such conformations, and there are symbols for many of them, such as "XOXO" and various emojis. Some, such as synchronous rhythmic movement, required copresence before electronic sound and images became available, but are feasible, and perhaps more evocative, with large numbers of participants and, especially, electronically amplified music.

[1] Thomas Schubert raised this important issue in some wonderful conversations.

Tattoos, scar patterns, excision, and circumcision each scale up to make the bodies of any number of persons equivalent, and, once inscribed on the body, are more or less permanent, though they may be hidden by clothing, although tattoos can be removed and scarification can be hidden with plastic surgery, I imagine. Other conformations, such as hugging, can be enacted in the moment, or withheld, depending on the immediate circumstances, but leave no tangible trace unless represented in language or images. Some of these consubstantiations, such as blood brotherhood rites, are more or less voluntary, though there may be strong social pressures for or against them. In contrast, some human features that many societies use to conform social relationships, such as skin color and physiognomy, are not choices, nor easy for individuals to modify, except at the margins. But it certainly is not inevitable that a community use skin color or physiognomy to constitute social categories; there is variation on this from culture to culture.

That brings us to the question of why a given community, in a given context, uses specific types of consubstantial assimilation but not others, or gives more importance to some than to others, or combines certain subsets in certain contexts. Part of the answer is in the "economy," in the broad sense, including the technology, the skills, and the environment, including available materials. Moosé men make their bodies equivalent by the equivalence of their motion when they thresh grain in synchrony, while Moosé women make their bodies equivalent by their synchronous rhythmic motion when pounding the grounds of a compound, or when they stand at the earthen platform in front of their compound, grinding grain or karite in synchrony, using saddle querns (shaped stones similar to metates). Men without grain to thresh, or who use mechanical threshers, do not use these specific conformations. Nor do women without querns and without mud patios to pound have those specific opportunities to make their bodies equivalent with synchronous rhythmic movement. In ancient Greece, to row a trireme, the crew of roughly 170 men had to row in perfect synchrony. Triremes were not widely available, so only a small proportion of men engaged in this conformation, and only during one historical era.

People often employ more than one conformation for a social relationship, but what happens then? We do not know much about how the effects of various forms of consubstantial assimilations combine. Does the motivation to sustain a relationship endure long after a hug and a kiss, compared to how long the motivation persists after a kiss without a hug, or a hug without a kiss? What about the strength of the moral sense of commitment? Are conformations of communal sharing that make bodies equivalent in different ways equally good at satisfying the need for communal sharing? Does a person feel a greater sense of belonging to a group when they have eaten commensally, when they have synchronously rowed together, or when they get a tattoo matching the tattoo that everyone in the group exhibits? Connected to this, is trust in the relationship fostered equally by different conformations? And how do different conformations affect moral commitment to it, such as willingness to make sacrifices for it, or adhering to the communal sharing relationship when one could secretly defect? For restoring a communal sharing relationship after a breach, are all of the forms of consubstantiation equally effective? We need research on all of those questions, especially research in the field, participating in and observing conformations in action.

Suppose some of the women at a gathering have had identity-conforming genital surgery, while others there have not had such surgery. That is a conformation that differentiates the bodies of the two sets of women, thereby socially separating them. In the event, they all dance for hours in rhythmic synchrony, holding hands, and, let us suppose, at the end of the dance piling on each other. (This is entirely hypothetical; I have never observed nor read about any such thing.) Then they sit down to eat with their hands, out of one shared pot of food. Those are three bodily equivalence consubstantial assimilation conformations, fostering a communal sharing relationship in which they are all socially equivalent. What is the mathematical function that maps their combined effect? That is, what is the net effect of adding synchronous rhythmic movement, plus body contact, plus commensal eating, minus genital differentiation? Emotionally, do they feel that they are all one, or do they still feel divided by their contrasting genitalia? The answer is likely to depend on the details and duration of the dance, the way they hold hands, the manner of their piling onto each other, the experience of commensal eating (does it feel cozily homey, or does it feel germy and disgusting?). Surely, for those who have had the surgery, what they finally feel depends to a considerable degree on their social experience of the initiation, and the cultural meanings of it.

An important aspect of conformations is apparent in these descriptions of consubstantial assimilation, though it is easy to miss: An individual does not, and cannot, conform communal sharing by doing just anything she likes to make her body equivalent to a certain set of others. If she seeks to create or strengthen a communal sharing relationship, she does not have freedom to choose any random act that "should" consist of consubstantial assimilation, simply because in some way it makes her body the same as the bodies of some others, and in fact may be effectively used in other cultures. Rather, she must adopt what we can call a legitimate conformation. By definition, a conformation is legitimate if (and only if):

- Participants implicitly or explicitly construe it as a conformation.
- Participants trust that the other participants implicitly or explicitly construe it as a conformation. That is, trust that other participants understand it as a guide and moral standard for action, are committed to it, and are motivated to sanction deviations from it.
- Consequently, participants trust that other participants will engage in complementary actions. You cannot eat commensally by yourself; it takes two or more who are intending to eat commensally: My dipping my hand into the pot and eating from it does not make my body equivalent to your body unless you also dip your hand in and eat from it, with the intention to be commensal. Likewise, genital surgery makes your body the same as others who have the same surgery with the intention of making their bodies equivalent with the relevant set of persons. If you are the only one who has such surgery, it makes you different, rather than what you intended, which is that your body becomes equivalent with a certain set of participants.
- Participants implicitly trust that the other participants trust that all participants implicitly or explicitly construe it as a conformation, and feel committed to the communal sharing relationship that it conforms.
- Participants trust that observers (including those who later learn about it) implicitly or explicitly construe it as a conformation; that is, observers understand it as a guide for action and a moral standard for action, and are committed to sanctioning deviations from it.

Box 5.2

Consubstantial assimilation is embodied social cognition, so it would be interesting to see how embodied cognition theorists can incorporate consubstantial assimilation into their metatheories. If researchers acknowledged consubstantial assimilation as a form of embodiment, how would that shape the general conception of what embodiment consists of? Surprisingly, the function of conforming social relationships is not often considered by embodiment theorists, if it ever is. (See Goldman and de Vignemont 2009 for a clear review of the concept of embodied cognition.)

Linguistic Metaconformation

People do consubstantial assimilation in actions and artifacts, but people also speak consubstantial assimilation. Consider this example that I've made up, of a mother speaking to her daughter:

> You were created from your father's body and mine, growing in my womb, forming yourself from my nurturing blood. Emerging from my body, I held you close against me, and for many months nourished you with the milk from my breasts, as you continued to form yourself from the genes we gave you. You are our daughter.

The phonemes of, say, *blood*, /blʌd/, are purely conventional: Each phoneme is a phoneme only because people in a speech community in a given time period use them as phonemes. There are constraints and pressures on the phonology – some sounds are not pronounceable by the human vocal system, some phonemes are transformed in predictable ways by adjacency to other phonemes, and, in the long run, phonemes change in predictable ways. But within such constraints and transformations, any ordered set of phonemes functions as well as any other, so across languages there is an essential randomness in the sets of phonemes that arbitrarily mean "blood." Concatenated, the ordered set of phonemes, /blʌd/, compose a lexeme that is symbolic, in this respect, representing what it represents – meaning what it means – entirely by virtue of its use in a speech community.

But sometimes the speaker intends to use the lexeme in an illocutionary manner, as a social relational performative, and listeners perceive and are affected by that intention (Austin 1961, 1962). That is, the utterance does something social relational. It conforms a communal sharing relationship in a decidedly nonarbitrary respect – not merely as a result of people's use of its lexemes in a particular speech community. Quite the reverse: people in all or most speech communities speak performatively of "blood" and other bodily substances because of their innate indexical psychological conformation system. That is, an innate, universal neurocognitive system enables and effectuates illocutionary uses of phonetically and lexically arbitrary conventional signs for "blood," rather than, say, "lemonade." Because of this, instead of the mother saying "forming yourself from my nurturing blood," if she said "perceiving me knitting a cover for the teapot," that utterance would have little or no conformational effect.

Innate conformational psychology is also operating in utterances concerning blood that, on the surface, are mostly (or entirely, if that is possible) locutionary and constative, in Austin's (1961, 1962) terms. So, if someone says "They are blood kin," the foundation of the cognitive and moral-evaluative conformational effect of "blood" is not fundamentally grounded in symbolism – that is, not based on conventional use. The phonology is symbolic, but deeper than the phonology, an essential aspect of the semantics is not symbolic. The mother's utterance and the third party's utterance are metaconformations solidly rooted in a particular, decidedly nonarbitrary conformation system: consubstantial assimilation.

Another, perhaps clearer way to think about this is to recognize that an utterance such as "forming yourself from my nurturing blood" conforms the mother's communal sharing relationship with her daughter by symbolically representing the indexical conformation of consubstantial assimilation. The conformational efficacy of consubstantial assimilation from the act (nursing the infant) is "passed through" to the verbal symbolism, so that it is "contained in" the utterance. The conformational effects are likely to be attenuated by this transmission through speech or text, but are available where the actual act of indexical consubstantial assimilation itself is not – say, the daughter is an adult, weaned many years ago, and the mother, who has had a double mastectomy, is speaking to her on the telephone.

Likewise, an utterance symbolically representing consubstantial assimilation may have effects as a reminder of past interactions, or as a revelation of them – for example, if the daughter never knew her mother had nursed her. Further, the utterance, or text, can convey a wish, intention, or imagination of consubstantial assimilation: for example, "I want to kiss you," or "When we grow up and get married, we'll kiss," or "XOXO" at the end of a letter or message.

We will return to the discussion of linguistic metaconformation in Chapter 11, where we will examine the semantics of authority ranking in four languages.

Mammalian Precursors to Consubstantial Assimilation

The unique adaptation of the class Mammalia is the suckling of infants. This adaptation may have emerged when the clade became distinct 300 million years ago, or soon after. The suckling infant, tight against the mother, immediately recognizes, in some sense or other, that its sustenance comes out of the mother's body, while the mother appreciates this in another way, and, to some degree in some respects, observers do as well. Of course, mammalian mothers and observers cannot help but recognize that the infant emerged from her body. Humans, at least, also recognize the prior growth of the fetus inside the mother.

Because of their small size and, hence, compared to adults of the same species, high surface-to-volume ratio, infant mammals lose heat relatively rapidly. Because they are homeotherms, in cool or cold environments infant mammals' rapid heat loss can be deadly, so in many environments they must initially maintain a compact aggregation with litter-mates, or be in close contact with their mother or other kin. Most mammalian infants can locomote sufficiently to reach the mother's teats. In all living primate species except humans, before long, infants capably cling to the fur of their mother or other caretaker. In the vast majority of human cultures, infants and toddlers are carried much of the day by the mother or close kin, sleep next to their mother, and, later, sleep next to another close kinsperson (Whiting 1961). As the infant grows, the human mother and other close kin supplement the mother's milk with soft food. That may include prechewed morsels passed directly from the chewer's mouth to the infant's mouth. As the infant grows, in most cultures the infant's siblings and older kin frequently hold, carry, and feed it, and often sleep with the toddler after it is weaned. With the infant or toddler wrapped against skin of the mother or other caretaker, whenever the mother or other caretaker walks, digs, pounds, grinds, or dances, the infant passively experiences rhythmic movement in synchrony with the carrier.

Nearly all mammal mothers lick their newborns immediately; sometimes this is necessary to stimulate the newborn to begin breathing. Mammalian mothers of most species continue to lick their offspring as they grow, and adult mammals of many species lick kin or others with whom they are fostering affiliative relationships. Mammals have specialized sensory nerves, unmyelinated cutaneous afferents, that are tuned to gentle stroking at speeds probably corresponding to a licking tongue (Olausson et al. 2010, Morrison 2012, Ackerley 2022, Schirmer, Croy & Ackerley 2023). These nerves project to the anterior granular insulae where, we may imagine, they signal, in effect, "this animal loves me."

However, primates rarely, if ever, lick newborns or adults. What they do instead is "groom": run their fingers (or, in a few species, teeth) through the fur of the other, removing whatever is in the fur, and eating parasites they remove. This gentle combing presumably activates the unmyelinated cutaneous afferents, just as licking does – or even better, because fingers reach more deeply into the fur than a tongue. Primates groom infants, close kin, "friends," and others with whom the groomer evidently intends to form, sustain, or restore affiliative relationships. And such grooming is a common practice in humans who have ectoparasites, especially in head hair. Human caretakers obviously bathe infants and children, comb their hair, and remove ectoparasites. Moreover, grooming is the crucial mechanism for creating, sustaining, and repairing relationships in most nonhuman primates, and most primate species devote considerable time to grooming (Goosen 1987, Estes 1991: 534, Dunbar 1996, Dugatkin 1997: 116–124). In particular, our closest relatives – chimpanzees, bonobos, and other apes – frequently run their fingers through the hair of those whom they affiliate with, removing and eating the parasites they find (Badrian & Badrian 1984, Muroyama & Sugiyama 1994). In addition to their fingers, chimpanzees frequently use their lips to groom others (Goosen 1987). Chimpanzees also pat and touch each other affiliatively (Montagu 1986: 45, Fossey 1983). Chimpanzees are especially prone to touch, pat, embrace, "kiss," or groom when they greet kin or friends after a separation, reconcile after aggression, or when they are apparently seeking reassurance or providing reassurance when they are afraid or highly excited (Goodall 1986: 124ff). Bonobos engage in some of those behaviors in such situations, but their predominate affiliative action is massaging each other's genitals, within or between sexes (Goodall 1986: 127, 130; Montagu 1986: 45; Estes 1991: 434, de Waal 2001, Arnold & Aureli 2007).

For many millions of years, these forms of affiliative contact among nonhuman primates must have created and sustained the proto-communal sharing bonds essential to infant, toddler, child, and adult survival. That is, these behaviors were likely present in a species ancestral to human, so these behaviors (or ancestral forms of them) were phylogenetic precursors to human consubstantial assimilation. This means that there must have been very strong selection to make this conformation system cognitively robust, and to make it affectively, motivationally, and morally compelling.

Few mammal species bring food back to their kin or other animals in their group and offer to share it. However, when they get something bigger than a bite, a few species regularly do actively bring food to kin or others in their group, especially to infants. Most canids, such as wolves, supply food to infants in the den, and also to the animal(s) who stayed behind in the den to guard the infants or keep them warm. The species of orcas who hunt mammals, when they catch one, regularly bring it to share with other members of the pod. Callitrichids (New World monkeys such as tamarins and marmosets) bring back even small food items such as berries, actively offering the food to infants but also to other kin.

Bonobos, chimpanzees, gorillas, and orangutans are the primates most closely related to *Homo sapiens.* In these four species, animals very rarely, if ever, transport food to conspecifics or initiate sharing, though bonobos and chimpanzees may more or less passively give up bits of food to conspecifics who come to them and beg insistently. Both species beg by reaching a hand toward the food, and bonobos often touch the mouth of the animal that is eating the desired food (Kuroda 1984). Bonobos fairly often permit others to take food, and chimpanzees sometimes do. Compared to other dyads, mothers are most likely to give food to their offspring; on rare occasions, a mother bonobo actually puts food into its infant's mouth (Kuroda 1984). Bonobo females fairly often permit unrelated animals to take food, as well. In both species, males are often relatively tolerant of females who attempt to take food that the male controls, especially if the female is in her sexually receptive phase. Chimpanzee males also sometimes permit other males to take some of a prey they have captured. Most chimpanzee begging and acquiescent transfer involves meat, but bonobos also beg and acquiesce in the taking of vegetable food, including large fruit and sometimes even common food that is readily available nearby (Kuroda 1984, Badrian & Badrian 1984).

Homo sapiens are only very distantly related to callitrichids; orcas and canids are even more phylogenetically distant from *Homo sapiens*; orcas and canids are phylogenetically very distant from each other. None (or very few) of the clades that are phylogenetically close to any of these food-sharing taxa bring food back to kin and actively initiate sharing the food with them. So, the active initiation of food-sharing adaptation must have evolved independently in each of these four taxa. There is a dearth of solid evidence about most aspects of the social behavior of fossil Hominoidea (apes and closer relatives of *Homo sapiens*), but, given the absence of observations of active initiation of food sharing in living Hominoidea other than *Homo sapiens*, it is very unlikely that humans inherited the food-sharing disposition from an ancestral species that lived before the separation of the genus *Homo* from the genus *Pan* (chimpanzees and bonobos).

In virtually all contemporary human hunter-gatherer societies, hunters who kill a large animal share the meat with the entire band; indeed, in a number of such societies the hunter turns over the animal he has killed to someone else to divide, and, in the end, may himself get a very modest share (Testart 1987, Hawkes, O'Connell, & Blurton Jones 2001). In every human community, coresident kin commensally share at least the major meal of the day – except that, as I have indicated, traditional African men and women absolutely always eat separately.

Presumably, the efficacy of consubstantial assimilation is mediated by the powerful hormone oxytocin (and perhaps vasopressin), likely in conjunction with mu-opioids, dopamine, and serotonin. Researchers are identifying the gene expressions involved. Once these cognitive, hormonal, and gene-expression mechanisms are well worked out, we will see how, at the levels and time spans of ontogeny and psychology, these mechanisms mediate the effects of consubstantial assimilation, and mediate motivation to engage in consubstantial assimilation. But psychological and cultural anthropologists and cognitive social psychologists need not, and should not, wait for the biology of communal sharing to be well worked out. We already know enough about consubstantial assimilation to enable us to shed light on how cultural practices, artifacts, and narratives culturally evolve in the niche that the human psychological disposition for consubstantial assimilation offers.

In the mammals investigated, maternal bonding to their newborns depends on oxytocin. Most mammals do not form pair bonds, but in the pair-bonding mammals that have been investigated, pair bonding depends on oxytocin in females, and, in males, oxytocin and/or its close cousin, arginine vasopressin.

In short, the human disposition to initiate consubstantial assimilation, together with kama muta and other emotional, motivational, and moral commitment responses to it, compose an adaptation that evolved in humans because of its facilitation and support of communal sharing relationships, which generally are beneficial to human fitness. This adaptation does not generate fixed, invariant behavior. The consubstantial assimilation adaptation cannot function without cultural complements that specify, for example, whether and whom to kiss, and in what manner; and who to spit on, where on the body, when, and whether to mix the spit with nasal mucus. The consubstantial assimilation adaptation produces no emotional bonds, no compassionate motivation, no moral commitments, and no cognitive representations of communal sharing except in conjunction with cultural specification of the specific practices that operationalize it in a given community in a given era. The culture determines whether people realize the conformational potential of consubstantial assimilation by filing their incisors to sharp points, deforming young children's skulls in a particular manner, fellating youths to acquire the semen that boys need, smoking a sacred pipe together, or determining whether they share DNA indicative of common ancestry. The culture shapes the proclivities comprising the adaptation, providing local precedents for whether and when, with whom, and just how to commensally consume food, alcohol, tobacco, sacrificial meat, and so forth, or eat your deceased kin.

The adaptation does not specify that two men mix their blood and drink the mixture, committing themselves to blood brotherhood. What the adaptation does is to make this ritual likely to be invented, make drinking their mixed blood memorable and evocative, and dispose the participants to adopt the cultural model that blood brotherhood is the deepest of all moral commitments to communal sharing.

Infant monkeys and apes "pout" when something touches their mouth, and also pout spontaneously (Maestripieri & Call 1996: 628). Pouting consists of "a slightly opened mouth with mouth corners brought forward and lips protruded," with raised eyebrows (Maestripieri & Call 1996: 627). De Waal (1988: 195) describes the expression in bonobos: "the lips are pursed forward and curled outward in front, resulting in a circular opening" with the lips pressed somewhat forward at the corners of the mouth. It closely resembles the position of the mouth in nursing. Ape infants pout when they want to nurse, and later when they want solid food that their mother is eating (de Waal 1988: 195; Maestripieri & Call 1996: 629). Bonobos and chimpanzees also pout when seeking body contact or sex. Bonobos (but not chimpanzees) display a very similar expression, which de Waal calls "duck face," when grooming or being groomed. Perhaps this pout–duck face is related to the fact that bonobos and chimpanzees fairly frequently kiss mouth-to-mouth, often actively involving their tongues (de Waal 1988: 238). In many human societies, mothers and other caretakers chew food and then transfer the masticated food directly from their own mouth to the mouth of an infant (Morris 1973, Eibl-Eibesfeldt 1996).

The vast majority of mammals avoid conspecifics, except briefly when courting or mating, and when a mother cares for offspring for some time. However, a few mammals and species of many other vertebrates form groups, often of matrilineal kin. Animals within the same group seek some degree of amicable proximity to other group members and may tolerate relatively close approach by other group members.

Toothed cetaceans such as dolphins touch each other affiliatively, even stroking each other or swimming with a flipper in contact with the other. Dolphin "friends" also swim side by side, repeatedly leaping out of the water in synchrony with each other (Bateson 1974, Samuels et al. 1989, Rose 1992, Stacy 1997, Johnson 1987, 1988, Wilson 1998, Gordon 1998, Ford & Ellis 1999, Mann & Smuts 1999, Connor et al. 2000, Whitehead & Weilgart 2000, Whitehead 2003). Some but not all of these cetacean affiliative behaviors may be homologies to certain primate affiliative behaviors, inherited from a very distant common mammalian ancestor. Porpoise and dolphin friends' swimming and jumping out of the water in synchrony is curiously analogous to human rhythmic synchronous whole-body movement, but the disposition for this surely evolved separately in the two lineages. Looking closely into this approximately convergent evolution might illuminate how synchronous rhythmic motion functions in humans, at least, as a conformation of communal sharing. Is it effective because synchronous matching motion makes each participant's proprioception of their own movements match their visual perception of the others' movements, creating the illusion of all being one and the same body?

At least some of these nonhuman behaviors are probably homologous to human consubstantial assimilation or communal sharing. That is, the behaviors are likely precursors by descent. Other nonhuman grouping behaviors may not be phylogenetically continuous with similar-seeming human consubstantial assimilation conformations or communal sharing relations; rather, they may be analogs that occurred by convergent evolution. In the latter case – analogy – it is intriguing to consider how evolutionary convergence came about, forming analogues to consubstantial assimilation or communal sharing. In the former case – homology – it is equally intriguing to consider how evolution preserved the homologues for millions of years.

Preverbal Human Infants Recognize Consubstantial Assimilation

At ten months, American infants understand that an agent gently resting in contact with another agent has a social intention in doing so; and the effort the agent makes to be in contact indicates the intensity of their motivation (Liuet al 2017). Recent studies indicate that infants aged 8.5–10-months old expect especially intimate commensalism to be a sign of communal sharing, or some precursor to communal sharing. In several experiments, Thomas and colleagues (2022) found that infants and toddlers perceive "saliva sharing" as a conformation of a relationship in which one sharer would come to the aid of another in distress. In one saliva-sharing condition, the infants and toddlers watched an actress and a puppet alternately eat from the same orange slice; in the other saliva-sharing experiment, an actress "put her finger in her own mouth, rotated it, put her finger in the puppet's mouth, rotated it, and finally returned her finger to her own mouth" (Thomas et al. 2022: 2). In both saliva-sharing experiments, the toddlers (aged 16.5–18.5 months) and the infants (aged 8.5–10 months) expected the actress who had "shared saliva" with the puppet to come to the aid of the puppet when the puppet expressed distress. In contrast, simply watching the actress play ball with the puppet, or share units of divisible food (i.e., shown as a set of separate items, like, say, popcorn) did not lead to the expectation that the actress would come to the aid of the puppet when the puppet expressed distress.

Steele et al. (2024) did an experiment in which 8–10-month old infants observed a large agent and a small central agent moving in rhythmic synchrony, and then observed the small central agent moving in rhythmic synchrony with another small agent. Then the infants saw either the small or the large agent overlapping slightly with the central small agent; the experimenters' aim was to represent them as touching. Then the infants observed a scene in which "the central character made a sad face (i.e., closed eyes and frowning) and shook, while the sound of a human baby crying played" (Steele et al. 2024: 1624). By the standard looking-time measure of expectancy, the researchers found that infants expected that, if the two had previously overlapped ("touched") the large character would do something in response to the crying – presumably, comfort the crying small agent. The infants exhibited no differential expectation if neither agent had previously touched the central character. In short, 8–10-month-old infants expect a large agent to provide some sort of comforting to a small agent if the two previously moved in rhythmic synchrony, and, if and only if, in another scene the two have touched.

However, in another study, infants understood conformations consisting only of synchronous rhythmic movement. Pun, Birch, and Baron (2021) performed a revealing study with infants aged 17–19 months old, then replicated their results in a second sample of infants aged 9–13 months old. The methods were identical in the two studies. Infants observed a video in which a group of three blue agents were gathered on one side of the screen, and a group of three green agents were gathered on the other side. The green agents bounced in synchrony for three seconds and stopped, then the blue agents bounced in synchrony for three seconds. In a subsequent scene, the infants watched two green agents and two blue agents evidently observing an event that occurred three times in succession: a blue agent moved across a platform from one side, heading toward the other side, while a green agent came from the other side. The two bumped into each other, which the experimenters intended to indicate a conflict such that only one of them at a time could proceed. The infants saw this video three times. Then, infants saw a final video in which an agent from one of the two groups of "observing" agents came to the center of the platform, between the two travelers who had tried to cross it, and pushed one of them off the platform, allowing the other traveler to achieve its goal. Infants looked longer, indicating a violation of their expectations, when a blue intervener pushed the blue traveler off, clearing the way for the green traveler. Infants looked for a shorter timer time when the blue intervener pushed the green traveler off platform, making way for a blue traveler to proceed. Every infant observed both variants; order of viewing was counterbalanced.

In short, infants expect an agent to help another member of their own group, a traveler, by pushing out of the way another traveler who is a member of another group. It does not make sense to infants when an agent pushes an agent of their own group out of the way to help the other group's traveler. This strongly implies that the infants recognize that a communal sharing group is conformed when a set of agents are the same color and jump in rhythmic synchrony. Moreover, infants expect that in a communal sharing group, members help each other.

For some of the other studies showing that infants understand that synchronous rhythmic movement conforms communal sharing, see Cirelli, Einarson, & Trainor 2014, Cirelli, Wan, & Trainor 2014, 2016, Cirelli, Wan, Spinelli, & Trainor 2017, Tunçgenç, Cohen & Fawcett 2015, Tunçgenç & Cohen 2016, Fawcet & Tunçgenç 2017, and Spokes & Spelke 2017.

Of course, some of these infants may have been rocked frequently, and learned from their experiences. They may well have extrapolated from their own experiences to interpret what they observe others doing and experiencing in these experiments. So, we cannot infer that their understandings of observed synchronous rhythmic movement conformations are innate. Still, every parent knows that holding and rocking a baby, or simply rocking it in a cradle, tends to be one of the most effective ways to calm and comfort them. This implies that whatever preverbal infants know about agents whom they observe, even newborn infants feel comforted and reassured by synchronous rhythmic movement. It may be that, in some sense, what comforts the rocking infant is the caring social relationship that rocking conforms: "She's rocking with me, so she loves me."

In a remarkable result, Bian and Baillargeon (2022) found that at twelve months, infants expect a human confederate dressed in distinctive clothing to preferentially interact with a second confederate dressed in the same clothing. But the infants do not expect the confederate to prefer to interact with the similarly dressed confederate if the infants have observed the second confederate using a feature of the clothing instrumentally, putting it to practical use (in one experiment, wiping something clean; in another experiment, putting several things away in a big pocket on the clothing). This seems to indicate a metacognitive appraisal of whether the confederates are wearing distinctive clothing conformationally, as consubstantial assimilation to make their bodies appear the same, or whether the confederates are employing the clothing as a nonsocial tool. The infants' default appraisal is that same-appearance conforms communal sharing.

Taken together, all of these results, replicated in multiple labs, imply that infants recognize at least three variants of consubstantial assimilation and know what consubstantial assimilation conforms. They recognize that "saliva sharing," synchronous rhythmic movement, and sameness of dress or special pigmentation conforms communal sharing relationships among persons or animate figures (on these signs of communal sharing, see Fiske 2004). Furthermore, infants know that agents who form a communal sharing relationship will be kind and caring to each other, and will come to aid a communal sharing partner who expresses distress.

In most of these studies, together with all of the infant studies of iconic dimensional conformations that I have seen (reviewed in Chapter 12), and the studies of concrete operational conformations (reviewed in Chapter 14), infants observe interactions among animated agents on a screen, puppets, or stuffed toy animals – not human beings. My reaction is, "Wow! Even though these agents do not remotely resemble humans, infants nevertheless recognize conformations from three conformation systems, know which relational model is conformed, and know how agents will interact in each of the three relational models. Infants must be so avidly seeking to identify relational models, they even perceive social relationships between circles with eyes!"

But other scholars might be dubious about the external validity of studies using agents that do not look anything like humans. Kominsky and colleagues (2022) analyze this issue in infant studies, showing why researchers use artificial agents, and why results from such designs are likely to have <u>fewer</u> confounds than there would be if infants observed interactions among humans. Kominsky and colleagues offer convincing reasons for having considerable confidence in the external validity of studies using nonhuman agents. Revencu and Csibra (2024) suggest that, in addition to understanding the social interactions among such agents, infants in these studies recognize puppets and animated agents as "pretend," in the same manner as toddlers engaged in pretend play use objects to symbolically represent beings and other objects. If so, that suggests the capacity to symbolize, at least in this manner, is either innate or very quickly grasped by infants. But, with an interesting twist, I would add: using objects that are ready to hand, infants do not require conventions in order to create symbols, but can <u>symbolize by fiat</u>. For example, the infant can nonlinguistically think "This [banana] is my pretend baby, this [piece of wood] is my pretend dog." An infant can pretend that without having seen anyone else pretend that, and without anyone knowing that she is pretending that. No convention needed.

So, in sum, these studies show that when infants watch other persons, puppets, or animated agents, they understand that consubstantial assimilation conforms communal sharing relationships, and that beings engaging in communal sharing take care of each other. That concerns observation of third parties. What is far more important to infants is who is relating communally with them. But that is much more difficult to study with preverbal infants; I have not yet found any studies on that. When infant researchers do find a way to study preverbal infants' own social relationships, I hope we will find out how infants affectively respond to conformations. In the meanwhile, for a thorough review of the research on infants' core understanding of communal sharing relationships, authority ranking, and equality matching relationships, see Thomas's (2024) outstanding review, as well as Thomsen and Carey's (2013) earlier review. Thomas discusses many more studies than I have room to consider here.

Finally, let me prevent one misconstrual that might be made by a casual browser of this book. Obviously, smoking the sacred pipe is not innate, nor are host–guest bonds, nor is modification of the genitals, as such. Conforming communal sharing by smoking the sacred pipe, bathing a guest and proving a bed for him, or modifications of the genitals, are cultural customs that have thrived in the niche provided by this particular evolved neuropsychological adaptation. Without this innate neuropsychological adaptation, none of these practices would have been invented, perpetuated, or diffused to new communities. They would not work, so they would not long endure, nor reproduce. These social practices arise, are culturally shaped, and reproduce themselves because of this specific adaptation. The adaptation does not strictly determine any particular cultural practice, but it powerfully potentiates an indefinite number of culturally and historically particular practices that are concordant with it. This adaptation is the principal cultural selection factor enabling, pruning, orienting, and transforming practices of consubstantial assimilation that are concordant with the adaptation.

Conversely, complementarity theory (Fiske 2000) reminds us about the incompleteness of the psychosocial adaptation consisting of the proclivity to form communal sharing relations through consubstantial assimilation conformations. That adaptation cannot function without cultural preos that complement it, specifying specific forms of consubstantial assimilation for particular communal sharing relationships in particular contexts. If, somehow, there were no such preos, and something prevented anyone from inventing them, the adaptation would not "work," so it would not enhance the fitness of carriers of the enabling genes. The adaptation "presupposes" cultural complements, and the cultural complements presuppose the adaptation. Neither would exist without the other.

PART III

Iconic Dimensions and Magnitudes: The Conformation System of Authority Ranking

At this point, I hope that it is becoming clear what a conformation system is, and what each of the four conformation systems are, distinctively. So, it will be fruitful now to roam wide and dig especially deep into one of the conformation systems: the iconic dimensions and magnitudes of authority ranking. (Hereafter, to abbreviate "dimensions and magnitudes," I usually write "dimensions," though still meaning to include FORCE, MASS, VOLUME, SURFACE AREA, NUMEROSITY, and the other parameters that in English are called "magnitudes.")

This part of the book collates far more examples, from far more contexts, cultures, and historical periods, than the parts on the other three conformation systems. This will enable us to better understand what differs and what is the same across the manifestations of a conformation system in different communities and contexts and across epochs of prehistory and history. At the same time, this compendium of cases shows how iconic dimensions influence architecture, landscapes, sculpture and figurative art, clothing and accoutrements, narratives, rituals, postures and positioning of bodies, temporal sequences and processions, sensory intensity, etymology, and iconic language. I think that it is a rather astonishing, revealing discovery that one conformation system encompasses all of these spheres of human action, manifesting the same linear authority ranking relations in each. Insofar as theory consists of parsimonious, simple, and clear description encompassing myriad, otherwise disparate phenomena, the iconicity of dimensions conforming authority ranking is, I think, a rather elegant theory.

This especially deep, broad, and thorough exploration of iconic dimension conformations enables us to see more clearly whether these conformations definitely are the fundamental and primary conformations (and, ipso facto, representations) of their respective relational models, or are nonfundamental, derivative conceptual metaphors (Lakoff & Johnson 1980, Lakoff 1993, Fauconnier & Turner 2002, Kövecses 2010). Is there a truer, more accurate primary representation "beneath" conformations, or not?

Part III looks especially deeply and especially broadly into iconic dimensions, across more contexts and cultures, to find answers to some other crucial questions. Do specific dimensions each conform a distinctive sort of authority ranking relationship, or do the all dimensions conform exactly the same authority ranking relations? For example, does being HIGHER conform representations that differ from relationships conformed by being BIGGER? Does each culture have its own distinctive conformations that differ from the conformations found in other cultures, or in other time periods? If there are differences in conformations across cultures and eras, how are those differences linked to technology, economy, and/or social structure?

To try to answer questions like these – and simply to see whatever we can discover – in principle, one could, and eventually should, do extensive and intensive research on all four conformation systems. But this book does not have enough space to do that, and I doubt that most readers have enough time and patience for all that. So, extensive and intensive examination of just one conformation system will have to suffice for the time being. The clear choice for that exceptionally thorough study of one conformation system is the iconic dimension and magnitude conformation of authority ranking. It is the clear choice because this conformation system has the most direct, definite congruity with the linear ordering that is the defining structure of authority ranking (Fiske 1991, 1992, 2004). And it is also the right choice because, at this point at least, its conceptualization is the clearest and simplest. The iconicity is as direct and definite as it could be: relative positions in a linear ordering. And it is the right choice because its subtypes, the iconicity of different dimensions and magnitudes, are clear, simple, and definitely isomorphic with each other. Furthermore, the psychophysics and the cognitive neuroscience of non–social relational dimensions and magnitudes are well understood, enabling straightforward comparison with the psychophysics of iconic dimension and magnitude conformations of authority ranking. At this point in the empirical exploration and the conceptualization of the other three conformation systems, they are not quite as well delineated or conceptually tractable as iconic dimension and magnitude conformations. So, this is the most promising conformation system for a super-wide and super-deep investigation.

Each of the following chapters focuses on one or a few dimensions. But it is neither possible nor necessary to make that categorizations rigidly distinct, since the laws of physics tend to connect any one dimension or magnitude to other dimensions or magnitudes. For example, a temple that is VOLUMETRICALLY HUGE has a large SURFACE AREA, is likely to have a HIGH roof, and may be constructed of MASSIVE stone blocks. It may contain a HUGE statue, like Athena in the Parthenon. Such a temple may have extensive grounds covering a great SURFACE AREA, through which it must be approached. As time passes, the humans encountering the temple will increasingly know that the temple is ancient – its construction PRECEDES their births. All of these dimensions may contribute to some or all of the aspects of the conformation, and without well-controlled experiments, perhaps in virtual realities, the individual dimension-magnitudes' effects cannot be separated. Quite possibly, the effects of the temple's multiple dimension-magnitudes may be synergistic, not merely additive. Or their respective effects may be redundant, such that the HEIGHT of the temple and the MASSIVENESS of its stone blocks add very little to the conformational effect of its VOLUMETRIC HUGENESS.

We must leave those questions to later experimentation. In this book, I simply describe the dimensions that people use, apparently everywhere, to conform authority ranking, and have used for millennia. Chapter 6 focuses on relative ELEVATION. Chapter 7 focuses on architectural MASS, VOLUME, and SURFACE AREA, which, of course, are highly correlated. Chapter 8 concerns being IN FRONT of, MULTIPLICITY, TEMPORAL PRECEDENCE, and FORCE–STRENGTH. Chapter 9 shows the ubiquity of two magnitudes whose conformational use escaped me for many years, until considering a well-known cognitive system, the analog magnitude system, impelled me to go look for them: BRIGHTNESS (reflected sunlight) and LOUDNESS.

Within the confines of a readable book and the limits of available sources, for each magnitude I offer many instances from cultures that vary greatly in location, technological development, economic system, and subsistence basis. This enables us to see whether the conformations that people use vary as a function of any of these factors or remain pretty much the same. I also go as far back in time as archeological evidence permits, because doing so allows us to see whether the conformations we find in the modern world differ from those in nonmodern societies. The modern world is unique and peculiar in so many respects, including technology, literacy, and communications, that we have to find out whether the conformations we see around us today differ from the conformations people have used throughout history and prehistory, or are much the same as they were long ago. Also, going back millennia to the earliest known instances of these conformations sometimes gives hints about whether the same conformation has been independently invented multiple times in different societies, or invented just one or a few times and then diffused widely.

Unlike my expositions of the three other conformation systems, for iconic dimension conformations I present lexical metaconformations. As we saw in the brief ethnographic sketch of life in a Moosé village, the linguistic metaconformations of authority ranking shed a lot of light on the conformations themselves. To see what linguistic metaconformations reveal, I present in Chapter 11 the lexicons of authority ranking in English and in Chinese, with cursory looks at Turkish and a couple of other languages. Linguistic metaconformations are wonderful cross-checks on our interpretations and classifications of nonlinguistic conformations. In measurement theory terms, comparing data of one kind with data from a second kind of evidence provides convergent validation of our construct: iconic dimension conformations.

Serendipitously, the compilations of Mooré, English, and Chinese bring to light something extraordinary. Linguistic theory is founded on the axiom that language is truly symbolic, in the sense that the words in all languages have a purely conventional connection to the entities and ideas that they represent. With the tiny exception of a few words based on onomatopoeia, any word could mean anything. But what we will see is that in three languages from entirely different families, spoken on different continents, the lexicons of authority ranking relations almost entirely consist of lexemes that also denote physical dimensions and magnitudes. The lexical semantics of authority ranking in Mooré, English, and Chinese are not at all arbitrary; on the contrary, in all three languages, the words used to conform social superiority also quite literally mean ABOVE, BIG, STRONG, IN-FRONT, TEMPORALLY PRECEDENT, LUMINOUS, MULTIPLICITY, or some other physical dimension or magnitude; the words used to represent social inferiority-subordination mean exactly the opposite position on the same dimension or magnitude: BELOW, SMALL, WEAK, etcetera.

This convergent linguistic evidence is extremely strong evidence for conformation systems theory, or at least for the component of that theory concerning iconic dimension and magnitude conformation of authority ranking. That is why there are so many chapters on this, including a very long one (Chapter 11).

I enjoyed discovering and writing about all these dimension and magnitude conformations; I hope you enjoy reading and mulling over them. After this intensive and extensive exploration of the iconic dimension and magnitude conformation system of authority ranking, we can suitably scout out the remaining two conformation systems much more briefly in Chapters 14 and 15.

CHAPTER 6

Your Highness

Stature

> For Tom Sawyer, "the greatest man in the world (as Tom supposed), Mr. Benton, an actual United States Senator, proved an overwhelming disappointment – for he was not twenty-five feet high, nor even anywhere in the neighborhood of it."
>
> (Twain 1876: 120)

Mark Twain's fictional account of Tom Sawyer's conformation of status corresponds to the earliest depictions of authority ranking that have been preserved: Sumerian, Assyrian, Babylonian, Hittite, and Old, Middle, and New Kingdom Egypt depictions conform social status by the RELATIVE SIZES of the figures (Pritchard 1954, Gombrich 1972, Schäfer 1974, Winter 1987, Saggs 1995, Black et al. 1998–2007). Medieval European paintings also exhibit this "hierarchic scaling" (Bunim 1940, Travis 1999), as do late Roman and early Christian art, as well as twelfth-century Romanesque painting (Thompson 1989). Sinha (1980) describes ancient Hindu conformations of Shiva and Visnu's great size.

Statues of the Buddha also meet Tom Sawyer's expectations. Chinese Buddhists built TALL pagodas and GIANT statues of Buddha and the bodhisattvas; some wood statues are more than 20 meters high (see images in Chan 1982, and Liu 1989). In the Chinese caves, several statues of the Buddha carved in native rock are over 50 feet long, and one is 90 feet tall; a reclining Buddha in a Dunhuang cave is 100 feet long (Juliano 1981). The Buddha carved in the rock of the bluff at Leshan is 71 meters tall. In Bamiyan, Afghanistan, sixth- to early-seventh-century Buddhas carved out of the cliff face were 125 and 120 feet tall (Leidy 2008: 67 & fig. 3.9). A seventh-century Chinese monk reported that a few kilometers away there was a reclining Buddha about 1,000 feet long, although that sculpture can no longer be located. (See also Howard et al. 2006, pl. 339, 3.40, 3.60 [515], 3.71 [523], 3.73 [545], 3.103 [593], 4.17 [936], 4.18 [1038].)

Many conformations of the Buddha consist of a large central Buddha statue in front of or surrounded by scores or hundreds of smaller Buddhas, often carved in relief (e.g., the sculptures of Guyang Cave, Longmen, Hénán Province, Northern Wei, started in 495–498 AD). This conforms the Buddha to be both GREAT and MANY.

People may also understand landforms to be signs of gigantic divinities:

> The flat summit of Samdanhela or Adam's Peak, in Sri Lanka, bears what appears to be a giant footprint, which has been interpreted by Muslims as Adam's footprint, Christians as the footprint of St. Thomas the Apostle, and, before them, Buddhists considered it to be the footprint of the Buddha and Hindus believed it was the imprint of Shiva. (Locke 2006: 29)

To commemorate his victory over Napolean in 1834, Emperor Alexander erected in Saint Petersburg a granite monolith 47.5 meters tall, surmounted by an angel carved to resemble Alexander. This is an instance of a general sculptural practice in the European sphere, where creators of statues of superior political and religious beings often position the STATUES ON PLINTHS or on mounds above the viewer, and/or above lesser figures (see, e.g., Michalski 1998). Garnier's (1982) analysis of medieval manuscripts, reliefs, and stained glass systematically demonstrates that the SUPERIOR SIZE and SUPERIOR VERTICAL POSITION of figures consistently represent their social and evaluative superiority – their hierarchical grandeur (see also Michalski 1998: 67–78). Lesser persons may be represented so that their surface is only 8 percent of the AREA of the socially supreme figure, although the more typical range is 17–75 percent. Christ is shown larger than all other figures (Michalski 1998). The figures of masters are LARGER, HIGHER, on the right of, head tilted down toward, and wearing some kind of HEADDRESS; their disciples are smaller, lower, on the left, LOOKING UP AT, and bereft of head gear (Garnier 1982: 77–79, 1989: 60). God is above humans, angels are above saints or monks, political authorities above subjects (Garnier 1982: 82–88). God, popes, and kings are seated on THRONES with their feet on footstools, while their courtiers stand on the ground (Garnier 1982: 103, 112–113). In this art, KNEELING OR PROSTRATING before a person represents social inferiority or humility (Garnier 1982: 113–117). A superior figure often points his index finger up, indicating authority or commandment (Garnier 1982: 167–196 & associated figures; 1989: 41). Figures of equal area and elevation indicate equal social and moral status (Garnier 1982: 68, 87, and associated figures). Likewise, Icelandic mythology incorporates the motif of choosing as king the man who fills a certain wide seat (Thompson 1989: P11.5).

The great gods have great MASS, reflected in WEIGHT. In the Iliad (5.838 f.), the appearance of Athena makes a chariot axle groan from the load, and in a Norse epic the Swedish King Eric detects the presence of the god Lýtir when his great weight bears down on Lýtir's ritual wagon (West 2007: 133). An Indo-European reflex of rank as mass is the Sanskrit *guru-s*, meaning "one to be honored, teacher, venerable person of authority," literally "heavy, weighty"; texts often refer to the three *guru-s*: teacher, mother, and father. *Guru* is derived from the PIE $*g^{w}reh_{x}\text{-}u\text{-}$, "heavy" (Watkins 2000, Barnhart 1988, Mallory & Adams 2006: 345–346).

The earliest preserved representations of kings and religious leaders depict them as LARGER than their associates. The votive slate palate of Narmer, possibly the first king of unified Egypt, shows the king wearing the tall White Crown of Upper Egypt, holding a mace high above a helpless keeling captive; in the register below are two similarly small, naked, sprawled captives (Kemp 2006: 85, fig. 27). Behind the kind is a high-ranking attendant about one-third the size of the king. On the other side, in the top register, King Narmer is shown wearing the tall Red Crown of Lower Egypt, with attendants one-third to half his size; five of them precede the king, holding four standards emblematic of his kingship. They are all looking at half-sized bound and beheaded captives. In the bottom register the king is depicted as a bull whose horns menace a fortified enclosure; the bull STANDS ON a sprawling naked man. In the time of Thutmose IV, a painting of a nobleman from Thebes in his tomb shows the him more than a third taller than his wife and the tallest of his children (Casson 1975: 43). Indeed, the representation of status by size was quite general in ancient Egyptian art (Brewer & Teeter 1999: 181):

> By a process which is common in primitive art there is a gradation of scale according to the importance of the persons. The king is the dominating figure. The "hierarchic scaling" has nothing to do with the peculiar non-perspective method of representation of pre-Greek art. It derives from an emotional attitude toward the king. We also find it in drawings which use perspective. (Frankfort 1948: 7)

Ancient Chinese art also often represented rank iconically, by SIZE, ELEVATION, AND FRONT–BACK position. For example, a painted silk from Han Dynasty China (first century BCE) shows servants crouching before their somewhat larger mistress, who stands in front of three other (slightly smaller) members of her household (Watson 1975: fig. 5). A Chinese stone relief from second-century CE Shantung shows figures with headdresses and VOLUMINOUS robes (Watson 1975: fig. 7). An eighth-century cave wall painting from Kansu shows the king larger than the other figures, two of whom stand behind him (Watson 1975: fig. 13). Around the world and over millennia, the vast majority of dominant gods have been construed to be spatially above humans (Laponce 1981: 69–92).

Modernity has not changed this iconic conformation of rank by relative vertical position; it is omnipresent in the modern world. Goffman (1976) used magazine advertisements to show that relative elevation in space indicates high social position (43–45), and "social weight – power, authority, rank, office, renown" is also conveyed by size, especially height (28). Paintings and banners of Mao show him the leading others, standing IN FRONT and ABOVE others, standing ON A MOUNTAIN TOP OR IN THE CLOUDS, or looming above landscapes and buildings, while imaging him as TALLER and somewhat BROADER than others, sometimes with an arm raised expansively (Cotter 2008).[1]

Children understand this and, like Tom Sawyer, expect height to be associated with rank. For example, US New England children aged 4–6, looking at images of two people, rate the taller person, male or female, as the one who is "the leader of the trip and tells the other person what to do," and the person who "will be the one in charge and make up the rules of the game" (Montpare 1995). Indeed, a meta-analysis of twelve study results from Western populations found that a person's height correlates 0.36 with social esteem, which is measured differently in different studies, but can be summarized as "perceived status, potential, esteem, or social stature" (Judge & Cable 2004). This HEIGHT effect remains after controlling for the gender of the person depicted. Taller people are more likely to be selected for corporate leadership, and to be elected president (Hensley & Cooper 1987, Melamed & Bozionelos 1992). Reviews by Schwartz (1981: 60) and Roberts and Herman (1986) show that this finding is commonly replicated, as does Ellis's (1994) review, which also found this effect in studies of nonindustrial societies.

Moreover, the "personal space" of high-ranking persons is greater than the personal space of lower-ranking persons: high-ranking persons have more social relational VOLUME. Subordinates must not intrude on the personal space of superiors. That is, subordinates – other than regular retainers – must await permission before deferentially approaching. The

[1] Additional images at Asia Society Exhibition web site: https://asiasociety.org/new-york/exhibitions/art-and-chinas-revolution.

higher a person's rank, the further away others are kept; one must stop before entering the superior's space (Firth 1973: 308). For example, when US naval personnel interact during duty hours in nonwork settings on a naval base, a subordinate initiating contact approaches more closely as the rank differences between the interactants decreases to zero; when superiors initiate approach, however, there is no effect of the differences in rank – superiors are free to approach as close as they like (Dean, Willis, & Hewitt 1975). Similarly, undergraduates taking a seat in an experiment position their chairs farther from a thirty-six- or fifty-year-old person than from a peer their own age (Latta 1978). A meta-analysis of nonverbal behavior studies found that people *perceive* "higher verticality" (operationalized as social rank or personality dominance) to be associated with "smaller interpersonal spaces," and, indeed, other studies show empirically that "higher verticality" is associated with "smaller interpersonal spaces" (Hall, Coats, & Smith LeBeau 2005). Presumably these are smaller interpersonal spaces for a person *approached* by a person of higher status, while a person of lower relative status accords a superior greater space, but the authors do not make this distinction because they treat "verticality" as an aspect of individuals rather than an aspect of relationship.

Male passersby are less likely to stop and drink at a water fountain in a university administration building when a high-status person is standing nearby compared to when no one is there, while there is no effect of a low-status person near the fountain (Rosenfeld, Giacalone, & Kennedy 1987). When it became evident that John F. Kennedy was to be the Democratic candidate, his associates abruptly began to accord him a large personal space, which they entered only when invited (White 1961: 171).

During the seventeenth and early eighteenth centuries, elite European men wore high-heeled shoes to conform their superior status, raising them ABOVE men who wore ordinary shoes (Bata Shoe Museum Foundation 2015, Bass-Krueger n.d.).

Postural and Positional Elevation and Abasement

> Viewed as a power structure, every political system incorporates elements of hierarchy, i.e., relations of "superiority–inferiority." The very words we use in English indicate how deeply ingrained is the idea that this kind of social relationship can be represented in "the logic of the concrete" by differences of relative level, above–below. This idea certainly comes fairly close to being a human universal. The

> political leader is "above" and "in front of" those whom he "leads" just as the head is above the feet and in front of the tail. This applies equally to the priest at his altar, the king on his throne or the college don at his "high table," all of whom are *raised on a dais above* the commonality. The anthropologist on his travels would be very surprised to find such spatial valuations systematically reversed. On the other hand it is by no means always the case that "leaders" are expected to walk in front of their "followers"; if hierarchy is transferred into sequence the rank order can just as easily run "early to late" as "late to early" [this is doubtful] . . . .
>
> In the case of kneeling and prostration the above–below criterion nearly always applies. Both attitudes are almost invariably deferential, and prostration then denotes a greater degree of submissiveness than kneeling.
>
> (Leach 1972: 335–356, 337)

As Leach points out, conforming authority ranking by ABOVE versus BELOW is not limited to "art"; it is ubiquitous in human action. In the Olympics and many other such sports contests, winners stand on a podium to receive their medals, the victor on the highest level of the podium, above the athlete who came in second, who in turn is above the one who finished in third place, who stands on the lowest level, yet still above those standing on the ground.

In late Ming China (around the sixteenth century), every town in China was required to hold monthly ceremonies of obeisance to the emperor, the focus of which was to *kowtow*: to kneel and bend down so that one's head rests on one's hands, which are on the ground (McDermott 1999: 299, 306–307).

In Paris in 1537, Francis I conformed his superiority over Parliament by arranging it so that he sat on a dais at the highest level, surrounded by other nobles and officials arrayed at lower levels on steps or seats at levels indicative of their rank (Hanley 1985: 79–80). That was serious, but the motivation to be ABOVE can be represented as an absurdity. As Spiegel and Machotka (1974) point out, in the movie *The Great Dictator* Charlie Chaplin caricatured Hitler's and Mussolini's concerns about their short stature and their relative political superiority by representing them in a barber shop, successively raising their chairs to stay above the other, until they reach the ceiling. The motivation to conform hierarchical rank by superior vertical position is ubiquitous (see Spencer 1896: 116–143, Firth 1970, Leach 1972, Goffman 1976: 40–41, Morris 1977: 142–147).

The vertical differentiation conformation is salient in the oldest existing sources. Ancient Egyptian images show this by depicting figures of outsiders (such as Syrians, Libyans, Black Africans) kneeling and sometimes putting their faces to the ground or prostrating themselves in submission, often with their hands raised in supplication (Pritchard 1954, Kemp 1989, fig. 92, 279; see also fig. 93; Kemp 2006, fig. 104). To show their deference to the high gods, pharaohs also occasionally had themselves represented kneeling as they made offerings to the gods (Pritchard 1954, fig. 391, 392). "In ancient Egyptian art from the Old Kingdom through the New, higher social rank was represented as placement in a higher vs. lower register in the depiction, larger vs. small size, and in-front vs. behind" (Robins 1993; see also Davies 1908). In practice, when they received visitors, the rulers of ancient Egypt sat on a throne on a raised dais under a canopy (Brewer & Teeter 1999: 137, 139).

For similar ABOVE–BELOW iconicity in Hittite society and religion, see Singer 2002: 51; in Indo-European religion and Zoroastrian worship see Burkert 1996: 210, and West 2007: 129–130. For texts exalting Sumerian gods as TALL, ABOVE, and BROAD, see ETCSL, lines 123–124: Black et al. 1998–2007; see also Kramer 1963: 56); for Sumerian kings, see Pritchard 1954, fig. 355, 371, 549. In ancient South Asia, see Proferes 2007: 20, 50–51, 85–91; Sengupta 1951: 50, 82; Singh 1981: 211, Ashok 2000, Sinha 1980. For Tang Dynasty China, see Scarpari 2000: 172, 174–175. For deferential abasement in ancient Mayan society, see Sharer 1996: 124. For abasement in prayer in early Hebrew and Akkadian society, see Burkert 1996 :87–88.

In twentieth-century Bali, ABOVE–BELOW conformations of authority ranking were pervasive (Bateson & Mead 1942: 6–7, 10, 12, 74–77). In the Solomon Islands, see White (1985: 345); in the Trobriand Islands, Malinowski (1935: 34). In a classic paper, Firth (1970) describes the use of space to constitute authority ranking in Tikopia. At public events, being seated IN FRONT of someone indicates higher rank: "The general Tikopia proposition is, 'My front to the rear of a person indicates he is of higher status than I. My rear to his front indicates that I am of higher status than he'" (195). Relative ELEVATION is even more important: In Tikopia, standing up indicates superiority over those seated. Sitting up conveys superiority over those crouching, squatting, kneeling, or crawling at a lower level. On ceremonial occasions, only chiefs sit on stools, raising them above those sitting on the ground. The gods are thought to be above humans and vertically differentiated among themselves. This comes out in the Tikopian lexicon, as it does in many languages from diverse families: the term *mau runga* indicates higher in either physical or social position.

Likewise, in Pohnpei (Micronesia), as well as in Samoa, VERTICAL DIFFERENTIATION to conform authority ranking is pervasive, while TEMPORAL PRECEDENCE and MAGNITUDE are also used (Garvin & Riesenberg 1952, Keating 1995, 2000, Keating & Duranti 2006). A conformational combination of elevation, temporal precedence, and magnitude operates in Fiji (Toren 1990).

In some circumstances in some cultures, subordinates may conform status by LIFTING a high-status person. In contemporary Euro-American culture an admiring crowd may occasionally lift a victor or hero onto their shoulders or arms. Likewise, among the Nyanga (north-eastern Democratic Republic of Congo) lifting a person up into the air on the lifters' finger tips is a traditional gesture of honor (Biebuyck & Mateene 1969: 114–115, 117).

Height-Exaggerating Headdresses and Diameter-Exaggerating Robes

In life, or in depictions, a person's height can be extended by a TALL HEADDRESS, and all over the world, rulers have worn such headdresses for thousands of years. A Mochica image (between 100 BCE and 700 CE) shows two elaborately costumed figures hunting with javelins; each wears an enormous headdress, and their heights are about three times that of four smaller figures who seem to be driving the game to them (Cordoza 1990: 77; pl. 45). Mayan rulers wore huge headdresses with iridescent feathers, mosaics, and jade (Sharer 1996: 124–125). Aztec deities and rulers are depicted in very elaborate tall headdresses (Stierlin 1984, Quinones Kebber 1985), as are Mayan rulers and gods (Berjonneau & Sonnery 1985, Solís Olguin et al. 2002, Guernsey & Love 2005; there are many depictions in the Boturini Codex and the Dresden Codex). Nazca deities and rulers wore tall feathered headdresses (Quilter 2005). Chimu and Moche gods and rulers wore large but simpler headdresses, often of gold plate (Ubbelohde-Doering 1954, Rowe 1984, Sterlin 1984, Quilter 2005).

There are no permanent chiefs on Mount Hagen, Papua New Guinea, but at dance displays men wear huge wigs and very tall and elaborate feather headdresses to celebrate and assert the superiority they have achieved in a bout of exchanges (Strathern & Strathern 1971).

Headdresses marked rulership in ancient Mesopotamia (Strommenger 1964). Seated on a throne on a high dais, Sumerian, Assyrian, Babylonian, Hittite, and Persian kings wore crowns when they received visitors (Pritchard 1954, figs. 446, 447, 450, 458, 460, 463, 529, 609, 626; Joannès

2007: 38; Black et al. 1998–2007, Halloran 2006, Cooper 1984: 51, 53; lines 9, 68–69, Michalowski 1989: 43, 49, 65; lines 100, 193–194, 439–440). In the eleventh century, Mongolian rulers wore gold crowns (Watson 2000: 22–23). The goddesses of archaic Greece and the Near East were depicted in a tall headdress, the *polos* (Burkert 1996: 91). Egyptian pharaohs are depicted with the tall crowns of either Upper or Lower Egypt (e.g., Pritchard 1954, figs. 296, 297, 349, 378, 379, 383, 401, 404, 408, 409, 415, 420, 425). Egyptians and Hittites depicted their gods with tall crowns (Pritchard 1954, figs. 539–541, 551–553, 556–573, 611).

In sixteenth- to eighteenth-century Poland, men doffed their hat in the presence of a higher-ranking person; "The hat would also be doffed while reading a letter from a person of high social standing or even when a well-respected name – of the King or the Pope – was mentioned in the letter" (Bogucka 1991: 193–194). Congruently, some paintings of this period depict the comparative status of men by representing the higher-status person(s) with hats and the lower-status men without (Roodenburg 1991: 165, 167).

In many cases, the constitution of a person as ruler or king centers on a coronation ceremony in which the person initially puts on a crown. (For ancient Egypt, see Frankfort 1948; for Sumer, see Klein 1981: 83, 87, 89, 90, 127, 139, 145, 197, 201; Kristiansen & Larsson 2005: 63; for fifteenth-century Chimor in North Peru, see Rowe, 1984; for Aztecs, Rowe 1984, Quiones Kebber 1985; for pre-Columbian rulers and gods in the southern central highlands of Mexico, see Díaz & Rogers 1993; for ancient Mayans, specifically, see Schele 1997).

Along with crowns, elites have worn coiffures or headgear that make them appear taller and enlarge the visual impression of their heads; rulers and elites can also augment their apparent VOLUME or MASS by wearing great robes (e.g., for medieval rulers, divine figures, saints, and other high-status figures, see Garnier 1982: 51, 77, and associated images; for renaissance European monarchs, see images in Strong 1973, and depictions of Louis IV in Giesey 1985: 61, including Thackeray's satirical drawing showing the small man beneath the grand attire that is his monarchical conformation).

Actual body MASS and VOLUME may be important conformations. In Hawai'i, people of the chiefly class were distinctly corpulent, embodying "the widespread Polynesian cultural logic that chiefs should naturally be bigger than their subjects" (Kirch 2001: 178). As mentioned in Chapter 2, this was also the ideal for the Moosé Moghonaaba, the paramount chief in Ouagadougou who claimed to surpass all other Moosé chiefs.

There is, however, one widespread positional conformation of rank that seems to be based on something other than the iconicity of physical dimensions. In a great many, widely distributed societies, it has been the case for thousands of years that the very highest-ranking persons are privileged to sit on a throne, chair, stool, or ottoman – while everyone else stands (e.g., in ancient Egypt: see Kemp 1989: 295 & fig. 99, 297). This results in the heads and torsos of the seated persons being at a lower level than the heads and torsos of those who are standing.

CHAPTER 7

Architectural Mass, Volume, Surface Area, and Elevation

The iconic conformation of authority ranking by positioning bodies ABOVE and BELOW is part of a much larger conformation system. People iconically conform authority ranking though the VOLUME, MASS, SURFACE AREA, ELEVATION, and construction FORCE necessary to build monuments, mounds, palaces, temples, and such. At times, a king uses some constructions to position him HIGH above his people. However, most of the time, the king is nowhere to be seen, yet the monumental construction itself conforms his rulership. Let us look at instances of this.

Tongan chiefs commonly sat on large raised platforms with commanding views. On special mounds, they engaged in the chiefly sport of pigeon snaring, and they were buried in mounds; the particular type of mound in which the paramount chief was buried was called *langi*, "sky/heaven" (Kirch 1990: 210). Kirch studied mounds used for burial and kava-drinking rituals on Niuatoputapu Island: "Relative status of lineages was expressed in the size and elaborateness of these monuments, with the largest mounds belonging to the paramount line" (213). Similarly, in Hawaii, temples vary in volume and area as a function of the rank of the officiating paramount chief, regional chief, or individual household (Kirch 1990: 218–219).

Archeologists take it for granted that elites occupy topographically higher ground than persons of lower status (personal oral communications, October 2005, from Joyce Markus, Charles Stanish, Monica Smith, Richard Lesure, and Geoffrey Brantingham; see Tuan 1977, and Wason 1994: 137–142). With this topographic stratification, elites look down on lower-status persons, who look up at elite residences on hillsides above them, and must proceed up-slope to interact with the elite. For example, in ancient Rome, "The Capitol looming over the forum was the hallowed seat of Roman domination ... It was up there that the gods of city life dwelt" (Dupont 1992: 140). The elevation of home sites around the forum reflected Roman social hierarchy (Dupont 1992: 146). Aristocrats dwelt in the hills, above the plebians who occupied the low-lying areas on either side of the forum. However, the Roman populace actively resisted the residential expression of excessively "lofty" ambitions and "grandeur" (Wallace-Hadrill 2003).

Medieval British lords frequently built castles on elevated ground or high on artificially raised earth mottes, giving the castle a wide panoramic view across the landscape, while also making the castle a prominent, impressive fixture of that landscape (Creighton 2002). The raised site and high walls and towers had direct military functions, but at the same time – indeed, most of the time, when there was no battle in the offing – the castle's position, looking down on those who looked up to it, signified the seigniorial power of the lord. Within a castle or manor house, there was further vertical conformation of rank. Before the end of the fourteenth century, in the great houses of England those of high social standing ate in the great hall on a table raised on a dais above other diners; by the end of the fourteenth century, the high-status diners had moved up to the great chamber above (Bray & Rey 1999). Both before and after this architectural transition, the dishes were served to them first, and then to those below them to eat what remained. In nineteenth- and early twentieth-century England, masters and servants' living quarters were vertically differentiated, as so effectively depicted in the TV series *Upstairs, Downstairs* (produced by London Weekly Television, 1971–1975) (Lichtenberger 2001).

Earlier, in eighth-century Andalusia, the Moors forbade Christians and Jews to build houses taller than Muslims' homes (Lewis 2008: 203). In medieval Italian cities, feudal lords competed to build ever-higher towers, the tallest being up to 100 meters high, until the republican governments imposed height limits (Lichtenberger 2001). Cathedrals, reaching up to God, were the only tall buildings allowed for many centuries thereafter.

Studies of New England cities find remarkable correlations of 0.57 to 0.74 between elevation and census tract income, rent, or social class (Meyer 1994, 2005). For this phenomenon in 146 cities in the US South, see Ueland and Warf 2006; for Montreal, Debarbieux 1998. Within buildings, upper floors formerly commanded lower rents because people had to walk up, but once elevators were introduced, the pattern reversed (see sources cited in Meyer 1994). In Cape Town, apartheid planners designated elevated regions of the city as white zones, in order to give white residents "(a) strategic physical defensibility, (b) psychological domination from an overlooking height, and (c) residential amenity"; coloreds, Malays, Indians, and Blacks were segregated into low-lying zones (Western 1996: 92; Chapter 4).

The conformation of authority ranking by topographic elevation of residences evidently does not depend on face-to-face interaction among the persons concerned, nor even the visual perception of the relative spatial elevations of the persons themselves: they do not have to see each other, only to see each other's residences.

Approaches: The Grounds

Coming into ancient Babylon, the visitor passed between high walls 200 meters long, under a high gate arch, another 800 meters or so through the streets, and finally up to Nebuchadnezzar's 52 by 17 meter throne room (van de Mieroop 2003). The palace of the Assyrian King Sargon II (722–705 BCE) at Dur-Sharrukin was 290 meters long; visitors climbed two flights of stairs and passed through a high wall into a large courtyard, then passed through additional gates and rooms to reach the hall of the throne (Ascalone 2005: 321). Similarly, in Egypt from the Early Dynastic period through the New Kingdom, Egyptians created dramatic settings for the appearance of the pharaohs, including a huge open plaza that separated viewers from the pharaoh and had to be crossed to approach him, and a throne on an elevated dais (Kemp 1989: 57–62). Likewise, to approach their gods ancient Egyptians often had to traverse long passages flanked by large statues and pass through numerous awe-inspiring gates with colossal statues beside them, arriving finally at grand temples with high walls and towers (e.g., Kemp 1989: fig. 65, pp. 185–190).

Rulers around the world have built imposing palaces approached from below; the visitor must mount steps that ascend to grand, high reception halls. Dramatic examples include the palace of Darius and Xerxes at Persopolis in the late sixth century BCE (Pritchard 1954, figs. 766 & 767), and the Caliph of Córdoba Abd ar-Rahman III's overwhelming palace, Madina Azahara (Lewis 2008). In fourth-century China, the Zhongshan royal palace was entered by two large gates passing through concentric walls; guests then ascended stairs mounting a terrace, then more ascending the central palace (Scarpari 2000: 109). In pre-conquest Peru, the citadels of the rulers in Chimor were also raised spaces surrounded by high perimeter walls, enclosing vast courtyards, often approached through long passageways (Quilter 2005: 158).

Perhaps the most impressive instance of conforming supremacy by the surface area of courtyards and distance from the exterior to the ruler, together with great walls and great gates, is the Forbidden City in Beijing, the abode of the emperors of China. Surrounded by a moat and successive walls, the largest more than 10 meters high, the Forbidden City is approached by a walled road:

> When foreign dignitaries came to present their credentials or important embassies were received by the emperor, they proceeded along this 3-mile road, sometimes strewn with golden sand, through one impressive gate after another. Varying in scale from the merely large to the gargantuan, most of the gates have brick or stone bases pierced with arched tunnel-like entrances and single- or double-story wooden towers rising above. ... [After being admitted through a series of these,] foreign embassies, awed and intimidated by the orchestrated theatrical and architectural experience, had been appropriately humbled to meet the Son of Heaven, or, at least, made acutely aware of his immense power.
>
> To today's visitor approaching from the south, the first glimpse of the Forbidden City comes from the incredible 98 acres of the famous public square, which easily holds several hundred thousand people, just in front of Tien-na Men. The sweeping horizontal panorama is broken only by this monumental gate rising 80 feet from the cobbled pavement [reached by mounting a flight of stairs, guarded by giant bronze lions on daises] ... Beyond [the gate] spreads the first vast stone-flagged courtyard and the winding Golden Water River spanned by five marble bridges ... through the red-lacquered pillars of the Gate of Supreme Harmony opens a breathtaking courtyard with the Tien-he Dian, the Hall of Supreme Harmony, the first and largest of the ceremonial halls, 87 feet high, 210 feet long, and 115 feet wide ... Twenty four columns hold up the roof ... [The light] flickers across the carved, lacquered, and gilded surfaces of the emperor's throne and dais, the focal point of this vast space. Rising 6 feet off the polished black stone floor, the dais supports a seven-panel screen shielding the back of the throne and also framing it. (Juliano 1981: 48–50)

Within the inner city walls of Beijing, before 1911, no residential building of more than one storey was permitted. It was considered unthinkable that ordinary beings should have houses taller than the walls of the Forbidden City (Alexander et al. n.d.; see also Watson 2000: 99). The current government imposes height restrictions of three storeys on buildings around the Forbidden City (Gaubatz 1995).

The Chinese emperor encountered his ancestors and the gods in a temple situated within two concentric perimeter walls, the outer one enclosing nearly 4 square miles and the inner 2.5 square miles. Approaching up a long set of stairs, the emperor prayed in the Hall of Prayer for Good Harvests, an imposing three-tiered temple rising 160 feet (Juliano 1981: 100–101).

These monumental constructions must have been impressive – conforming the greatness of the persons who directed their elevation. These magnificent, lengthy approaches, this crossing of wide spaces, this passage through multiple gateways and doors, can be construed as iconically conforming extensive PERSONAL SPACE. That is, the dimension is SURFACE AREA. The expanse of the palace grounds and the breadth of the courtyards a person must cross to reach the monarch, together with the formidable walls whose gates must be traversed, demarcate a zone as the dominion of the ruler, or, in a sense, the ruler's EXTENT. Whatever we call this planar dimension, it is also observable on smaller scales when there is asymmetry in who may enter the other's domain without permission, versus having to be summoned or ask permission. The captain of a warship my freely enter any compartment, while ordinary seamen must receive permission to enter the officers' wardroom, let alone the captain's cabin. If the president is out in a park, she may go right up to anyone she chooses, but not anyone can closely approach the president without permission or summons.

AREA conforms rank in a completely different manner in maps. In a funny episode of *The West Wing*, the fictional television series about the White House, "Cartographers for Social Equality" try to persuade the president's staff to mandate that schools use the Peters World Map, based on the Gall-Peters projection (Redford & Sorkin 2001). The White House staff initially are derisive and incredulous about the group and its critiques of the Mercator projection, but slowly get the idea. The cartographers object to the Mercator projection because it makes Europe and North America look larger, and most of the developing countries (nearer the equator) appear smaller than they really are. In contrast, the Peters projection is an equal area projection, so it doesn't make this distortion. The cartographers argue that making poorer countries appear smaller makes them seem inferior in relation to the rich countries, which appear disproportionately large. And, in the real world, some institutions that care about how people think about rich and poor nations have in fact adopted the Gall-Peters projection.

In the *West Wing* episode, the cartographers go on to argue that placing Europe and North America at the top of a map compounds the perception of these regions as politically superior to developing countries cartographically below them, and they suggest reversing the map, placing the south pole at the top! They then show a Peters map with the south at the top, totally flummoxing the White House staffers.

Monumental Architecture

Beyond the topographically elevated location of much monumental architecture, and their surface area, perhaps the most prominent and prevalent material conformations of authority ranking are the height and the mass of the structures themselves. These have been salient conformations for several thousand years. In prehistory, the emergence of institutionalized rulership and social classes is closely contemporaneous with the construction of massive earthen mounds, including tombs, as well as large palaces and temples for the elites, often build on raised platforms (Trigger 2003: 564). Indeed, archeologists have found "monumental architecture universally associated with all early civilizations and, indeed, all class-based societies" (Trigger 1990: 122); "In the early civilizations monumental architecture becomes still more ubiquitous, elaborate, and differentiated. Monumental constructions ... correlated with increasing stratification within the upper classes" (Trigger 1990: 120). Trigger quotes Peter J. Wilson (1988: 148), voicing what archeologists hold as a truism: "It was by and through their association with these monuments that men in the office of kings, and their agents, had access to power." Impressive monuments also were often erected for worship of high gods, or as tombs for deified rulers (Trigger 1990: 121).

For China during the Warring States Period (350–207 BCE), see Chan (1982: 33). The first emperor of China, Qin Shihung, died in 210 BCE. He was buried at Lishan (Mount Li) in a tomb landscaped to look like a mountain. Emperor Qin reputedly commanded 700,000 laborers to build a vast, elaborate underground mortuary palace. It has not been excavated, but the artificial mound today is still 76 meters high, 485 meters wide and 515 meters long (Chan 1982: 38). Associated pits have revealed an entire army of life-size, incredibly detailed terracotta soldiers, with real weapons, as well as life-size terracotta horses, along with real and half-scale bronze chariots. Based on the sample excavated, it is estimated that the entire army consisted of 7,000 warriors, each with individualized facial features and a great variety of armor and clothing. Notably, the officers are a few centimeters taller than the soldiers, while the generals are taller than the other officers (personal oral communications of local guides, March 2008).

Subsequently, other Chinese dignitaries were sometimes buried in "mountain" tombs, referencing their "status and achievement" (Howard et al. 2006: 2). In China, Korea, and Japan during the third through seventh centuries, mound tombs became larger and more complex when rulers were competing for domination, then declined when one paramount ruler consolidated control (Wasson 1994: 83).

Often Chinese imperial tombs were surrounded by huge stone sculptures of elephants, tigers, and horses (see Juliano 1981: 149–158). Leading to such tombs was a Spirit Path, lined with long rows of "massive sculpted human and animal figures ... meant to convey the solemnity and majesty of the emperors" (Howard et al. 2006: 2; see pls 2.80–2.98). The animals lining this and other spirit paths were large and imposing, such as rhinoceroses, lions, and fierce mythical beasts (see Howard et al. 2006: figs. 1.12, 1.56, 1.13, 1.57).

Rulers and elites of societies in the Pacific and the Mediterranean also built monuments of great volume and mass, such as huge statues, imposing tombs, large temples, and impressive palaces whose function seems to have been to enhance and sustain authority (Kolb 2011). Likewise, in the empire of the Inka of Peru, "Major state settlements were dominated by a large, often trapezoidal plaza in which stood a ceremonial platform. Because the emperor stood upon this platform to address his subjects, it was a symbol, acting even in his frequent absences as a physical reminder of his central role in the proceedings" (DeMarrais, Castillo, & Earle 1996: 30).

Inca, Egyptian, and other rulers had monuments built of huge stones. It seems that the MASS of each great stone and the MASS of the whole monument conform the supremacy of the ruler.

Enormous Palaces

Dimensions iconically conform authority ranking not only in structures, but in narratives as well. In the Norse Edda myth in which King Gylfi of Sweden goes in disguise to visit the supernatural realm of the Æsir (gods), he enters the town and sees a hall so high he can barely make out the top. It is the hall of the king of the gods (Sturlson 1916).

In medieval Italian towns including Verona, Padua, and Brescia, among others, powerful leading families competed to build the highest towers as conformations of their relative status; in some cases the authorities regulated these contests of elevation to prevent "upstarts" exceeding their "superiors" (Dean 2000). Similarly, the nobility of medieval France built castles with massive, tall towers, partly as a safe retreat from attack, but, more immediately and saliently, as a tangible iconic sign of authority, domination, and superiority (Panouillé 2003: 33, 80). Medieval epics exulted in the enormous size of the great hall or the reception chamber of elites, often raised above ground level (Panouillé 2003: 81, 103).

Mounds and Pyramids

In the Old World, Uruk, perhaps the world's first city, was remarkable for its massive monuments (Cooper 2004). A temple there, built around 3000 BCE, was raised on a mound about 40 feet high, but subsequent temples grew larger and larger (Kramer 1963: 136): "Without counterparts in contemporary peripheral societies were the scale and extent of the public structures at the very center of Uruk at this time – the 8–9 ha of walled-off ceremonial and administrative buildings in the Eanna precinct and, in a separate part of the city, the massive Anu Ziggurat and associated temple, which towered over the site and the surrounding plain" (Algaze 2001: 214). The Eanna temple complex incorporated several buildings ranging up to 80 × 50 meters (Nissen 1988: 96). In Uruk and elsewhere in Sumer, at different times, a number of successively larger ziggurats and temples were built over earlier ones, suggesting the builders' intention to "overtop" their predecessors. Toward the end of the Uruk period (in the late fourth millennium BCE), Mesopotamians began building enormous city walls, as Shang rulers also did (Trigger 2003: 568). The brick wall around Abu Sibikh was more than 15 meters wide: "Monuments are meant to impress, as the passage quoted earlier from Gilgamesh epic makes clear. A massive wall such as the one encircling the Uruk town of Abu Salabikh did not just protect the inhabitants against enemies; it was a visual statement of power" (Pollock 1999: 178).

******

The first complex society in Mesoamerica was the Olmec. The development of social stratification during the Olmec Early Preclassic period (1200–900 BCE) coincided with the construction of mounds; the building of sets of buildings on platforms; the construction of pyramids; the erection of stelae; and the sculpting of large statues, including the gigantic Olmec stone heads (Love 1999, Cyphers 1999, Pool 2007: 10). Early mounds were only a few meters high; later preclassic mounds reached 25 meters in height and 14,000 square meters in base area. From 1400 to 1000 BCE at San Lorenzo, at least 10 rulers had themselves represented with colossal heads from 1.5 to nearly 3.5 meters in height and weighing 6 to 50 tons (Pool 2007: 1). Olmec rulers had stone thrones; one such throne weighs about 28 tons (Cyphers 1999). At both San Lorenzo and La Venta, the architecture of Olmec rulership also included massive stone daises now called "table-top thrones" (which may also have functioned as altars), weighing from about 5 to 40 tons. On the sides of these are carved figures with elaborate headdresses, indicative of high status (Pool 2007: 116). Another Olmec site, Tres Zapotes, included a massive 5-meter high stela with a carved figure wearing a tall headdress (see also Love 1999: 146).

The archeology of the Preclassic Mayans during the Middle- to Late-Formative transition reveals this same association between the emergence of social differentiation and the construction of large buildings and tall pyramids (Hendon 1999, Ringle 1999). The rise of elites among the Mayans and in the Oaxaca Valley also coincides with the first building of large open areas surrounded by walls (Hendon 1999, Love 1999). The mid-fifteenth-century Aztec ruler Moctezuma also used dimensional conformations (Durán 1994: 210, quoted in Smith 2003: 49; see also 175).

In the archeological record of both the Old World and the New World, the development of legitimated and heritable political, religious, and social hierarchies – which define what archeologists call "complex" societies – is commonly associated with the appearance of megaliths, vast chiefly tombs, grand temples, and other large edifices. In the North American Southeast, the rise of complex societies in the Woodland (100 BCE–700 CE) and subsequent Mississippian periods is associated with the construction of great platform mounds (Knight 2001, Blitz & Livingood 2004: 291, Fagan 2005: 487, Pauketat & Alt 2003, Lindauer & Blitz 1997, Blitz & Livingood 2004, Wallis 2008). There are indications that when a new chief succeeded to office, he often rebuilt and raised existing mounds on top of his predecessor's level.

On the Peruvian Coast, even before ceramics were in use, rulers began organizing vast amounts of labor to construct huge temple mounds; built beginning around 2150 BCE, the mound complex of Huaca La Florida had a total volume estimated at 400,000 cubic meters (Wason 1994: 147–149; see also Ravines 1990). During the Middle Preclassic period (ca. 1000–400 BCE), the Maya began to build stone or adobe platforms up to 135 feet high, supporting temples (some enclosing tombs) and large elite homes, and some communities erected stone monuments (Sharer 1996: 37). In the Late Preclassic (400 BCE–252 CE), Mayans built many more and larger temples, including an enormous complex at El Mirador, where La Denta temple rose about 72 meters, with a volume of 2,800,000 cubic meters, built atop an 18,000 square meter platform (Sharer 1996: 47–48). Similar conformations are visible in the mountains near Lake Titicaca (Kolata 2004).

In sum, to conform their authority ranking superiority, rulers everywhere built MASSIVE, HIGH mounds, bearing palaces of great VOLUME, with access routes through MASSIVE walls and enormous, STRONG gates, as well as palace grounds of great SURFACE AREA. Somehow visitors' responses to this architecture transferred to conformation of the ruler's position at the pinnacle of the polity's authority ranking.

Costly Signals, Conspicuous Consumption of Energy, or Dimensions Iconically Conforming Authority Ranking?

Alongside the conformation of rank by the MASS of monumental architecture and statues, by the HEIGHT of monumental structures and statues, and by the SURFACE AREA of mounds and palace grounds, there is a second system that may operate. That is the unfakable costly signaling, also known as self-handicapping (Maynard Smith 1991, Zahavi & Zahavi 1999). The costly signaling theory of monument construction explains that constructing a monument demonstrates the capacity to mobilize labor and obtain materials. What costly signaling theory does not quite explain is why, noting and believing those capacities, observers would feel the emotions, motives, and moral commitments that support an authority ranking relationship. Why should people follow the leadership of a person who is capable of building big things?

Apparently independently of concurrent evolutionary theorizing on costly signaling, Trigger proposed a similar theory:

> In human societies, the control of energy constitutes the most fundamental and universally recognized measure of political power. The most basic way in which power can be symbolically reinforced is through the conspicuous consumption of energy. Monumental architecture, as a highly visible and enduring form of such consumption, plays an important role in shaping the political and economic behaviour of human beings. (Trigger 1990: 128)

Joye and Verpooten (2013) point out that costly signaling theory doesn't explain why leaders aiming to consolidate their authority would universally emphasize the construction of massive monuments. There are innumerable costly ways to signal power that do not involve construction of massive, high edifices composed of heavy blocks requiring great force to put in place. A ruler could dig enormous holes, scattering the excavated earth. Or the ruler could mobilize laborers to clean the town every day, carrying out night soil and washing down the streets. Signaling theories do not quite explain why rulers' and elites' costly displays universally consist of the construction of monumental structures. Conformation systems theory does explain why, showing that the construction of monumental structures is congruent with the iconicity of conformations employing several other physical dimensions, In contrast, signaling theories do not predict that rulers also ubiquitously use the other dimensions to conform – use even when such conformations are cheap or free for the ruler. There is no cost in positioning the ruler in front, with followers behind. There is no cost to the ruler in being greeted first, in his subjects' addressing him with plural pronouns and the honorific *your highness*. There is no cost to anyone in subjects' doffing their hats to the ruler, bowing to him, or according him extensive personal space. Neither costly signaling theory nor conspicuous energy consumption can explain the ubiquity of use of those dimensions in conforming superiority in authority ranking relationships. Conformation systems theory explains all that and much more. In short, only conformation systems theory's explanation of monument building is congruent with the ubiquitous use of MASS, VOLUME, SURFACE AREA, and FORCE in cheap conformations as well as costly, energy-consuming conformations.

Still, the question remains: How do the cognitive and affective effects of monumental architecture transfer to the rulers who ordered and organized the construction, so that the effects become conformations of authority ranking? There would be no point at all in Khufu's ordering and organizing the construction of the Great Pyramid 5,000 years ago, unless, based on people's responses to earlier pharaohs' pyramids, he was confident of the conformational results. He must have been certain that this pyramid would assure his rule over Egypt. But *how* would it? What are the psychosocial processes by which perceivers' thoughts and feelings about the pyramid become thoughts and feelings about Khufu?

CHAPTER 8

In Front, More Numerous, Earlier, and Greater Force

The ethnographic, historical, and epigraphic evidence discussed in the two preceding chapters shows how people use ELEVATION and/or HEIGHT, MASS and/or VOLUME, and SURFACE AREA to conform authority ranking. People sometimes use these four dimensions separately, but more often use them in conjunction with each other. In this chapter, we examine four more dimensions : IN FRONT–BEHIND, TEMPORAL PRECEDENCE, NUMEROSITY, and FORCE.

Leaders in Front and Followers Behind

In one of the oldest preserved folktales, recorded in cuneiform on a clay table, an ancient Sumerian tale tells of The Debate Between the Hoe and the Plough, in which the two are competitively boasting and "putting each other down" (to use an English idiom; Vanstiphout 1984). At one point the Hoe says, "Plough, what does my being SMALL matter to me, what does my being exalted matter to me, what does my being POWERFUL matter to me? At Enlil's palace I take PRECEDENCE over you, in Enlil's temple I stand AHEAD of you." In another Sumerian tale, The Debate between Sheep and Grain, Sheep taunts Grain: "When you are put on the table I am BEFORE you – you are BEHIND me." At the end of the debate, the god Enki passes judgment: "Grain shall be the GREATER. Let Sheep fall ON HER KNEES before Grain, Let her kiss the feet of . . . . [lost segment]." The concluding words of the tale are, "Sheep is left BEHIND and Grain comes FORWARD – praise be to Father Enki!" A similar concern with who is IN FRONT is apparent in the *Rig Veda*, apparently arranged around 1000 BCE from older poems. There we find that an epithet often used for the sun god Agni is *puró-hita*, "placed IN FRONT" (Thomson & Slocum, 2011).

In 1911, to conform King George V and Queen Mary as Emperor and Empress of India, the British invited all of the governors and rulers of Indian princely states to a durbar in Delhi. When the British authorities and Indian princes came up to their majesties' thrones to pay homage, they did so in strictly choreographed TEMPORAL ORDER of precedence (Nuckolls 1990: 536–537). But one prince, the Gaekwar of Baroda, caused a scandal by paying homage cavalierly, walking perhaps a bit too fast, swinging his cane, BOWING ONLY ONCE or perhaps a slight second time, and, worst of all, after backing up a few steps, apparently TURNING HIS BACK on their majesties as he left the carpet – perhaps because he had backed into a pole holding up the canopy. The *Manchester Guardian* proposed that the Viceroy punish him by reducing the NUMBER of guns in his salute, "and if the Gaekwar's salute had been cut down on the spot a real impression would have been made on Indian opinion" (Nuckolls 1990: 544). There were discussions of his action that framed it as sedition. He wrote an apology, and retold the incident in an exculpatory manner in three biographies he commissioned. The Viceroy emphasized the offense in his own memoires thirty-seven years later. Indeed, in European court etiquette, one must always face the ruler; to TURN ONE'S BACK to the ruler is to place oneself IN FRONT, the ruler BEHIND. In seventeenth- and eighteenth-century France, this conformation extended so that the subjects of Louis XIV of France, the Sun King, could not even turn their backs on his portrait (Muir 2005: 281).

In the modern world, occupying positions in front versus behind others is still an important conformation of authority ranking. For example, the seats at a fashion show are RANKED FRONT TO BACK: At a Jil Sander menswear show in Milan, "We watched the personages discover their seats, and thus their status. Prominent bloggers, who had to stand in the back only a few years ago, enjoyed favorable placement." The CEO of Jil Sander's online distributor sat IN FRONT, where "his prime seating suggested that he was a person of some importance to Sander" (note the adjective PRIME; Seabrook 2012: 50).

Note that conformations are conformations, establishing or reaffirming a type of social relationship – say, authority ranking – to coordinate a given set of activities. In the conduct of that relationship, the persons necessarily occupy spatial, temporal, magnitude, and other dimensional positions relative to each other. But *those* positions are not conformations. The emperor who is having his palace renovated may occupy a SMALLER dwelling while the work is being done; indeed, if the palace is the BIGGEST edifice in the realm, all dwellings are smaller than the palace. If the emperor wants to keep a close eye on the renovation work, he may choose a relatively modest dwelling near the palace, rather than going to a duke's far away palace, the second biggest palace in the realms. Likewise, for tactical reasons, a general may locate her headquarters far behind the front line, and hence BEHIND most of the soldiers.

Common knowledge of the conformation systems creates opportunities to invert them, actually or rhetorically, to strikingly make a point. The pope may KNEEL and wash a poor person's feet. An English speaker may advocate "LEADING FROM BEHIND." That phrase sticks in the mind. It means listening to UNDERLINGS, and involving them in planning and policy, at least nominally. It does not mean positioning people on the ground so that subordinates are IN FRONT and the leader BEHIND. If a leader ever actually did that, it would be precisely in order to violate subordinates' expectations, perhaps dramatizing the precept that each subordinate should "LEAD" within their domain, and not passively wait for directions from the leader.

Temporal Precedence

As among the Moosé, birth ORDER is a determinant of status in Bali, such that "the exclusive distinction between those born in the village and those who came later is never forgotten" (Bateson & Mead 1942: 10). In many cultures, the ELDEST son inherits his father's estate. Nearly everywhere, succession to kingship or other hereditary office is by birth order.

Rank is also conformationally displayed and affirmed by TEMPORAL PRECEDENCE, for example in being served food or in others' waiting for a superior to begin to eat. We noted this among the Moosé. In northern India in the tenth century, the gods were offered food BEFORE humans began a meal, and food was set aside for birds and cattle. The chief guest started to eat FIRST, followed by other guests, and then their hosts, beginning with the most senior member of the family (Singh 1981: 108–109).

As I mentioned earlier, in late Ming China (around the sixteenth century), every town in China was required to hold monthly ceremonies of obeisance to the emperor, the focus of which was to *kowtow*: KNEEL AND BEND DOWN so that one's head rests on one's hands, which are on the ground. At these ceremonies, the ORDER OF ENTRANCE, seating POSITIONS, and the exit SEQUENCE of participants conformed their ranks (McDermott 1999: 299, 306–307). Participants also performed a prescribed set of five bows and three kowtows (307). In early-twentieth-century India, there were similar temporal precedence conformations of authority ranking (D. Haynes 1990: 506, 510; E. Haynes 1990: 468;

Nuckolls 1990: 532, Allen & Dwivedi 1984: 210–211). In virtually every society where people are ranked, OLDER siblings are superior to younger siblings, and, other attributes aside, seniority in age denotes relative social status (e.g., Toren 1990).

Contemporary diplomatic protocol continues to conform rank by TEMPORAL PRECEDENCE in addressing or introducing guests (Foreign Service Institute 2013: 3). Among ambassadors, precedence is conformed by the ORDER OF THE DATES on which they first presented their credentials (Vienna Convention 1961, Article 16). Within any given military rank, officers are ranked in ORDER OF THEIR DATE OF COMMISSION; even a day's difference is sufficient to give the senior officer command over others of the same rank.

Note that people use conformations to modulate relationships, so that by rejecting use of a dimension, people resist or reject the social relationship it conforms. For example the Quakers have an antiauthority ranking ideology, refusing to give deference to anyone; they believe that deference should be given only to God. They enact this refusal by addressing everyone with the familiar, SINGULAR "thou" – never the deferential PLURAL "you." They refuse to LOWER themselves by bow or curtsey, or to remove their hats (Roodenburg 1991). Instead, they shake hands to indicate brotherhood and friendship by mutual TOUCH: consubstantial assimilation.

Occasionally, DURATION IN OFFICE conforms authority ranking. In the US Civil Service, military services, universities and colleges, and some other bureaucracies, duration of service – seniority – may be the major factor in promotions. In another context in the modern world, rank may be partially conformed by possession of an OLD family house or estate, heirloom family jewelry, or even an ancient family name.

Order in Processions

When a set of people process, or otherwise move together in the same direction or through the same door, the order in which they proceed often conforms their rank – for example, in colonial India (see Allen & Dwivedi 1984: 249). Renaissance Venice had no written constitution, so the ORDER of persons during the annual processions reflected and defined the ranks of the offices in the political hierarchy (Muir 1981: 185–211): "In effect, the ducal procession was the constitution. Changes in processional order were, hence, grave matters . . . In the procession, position was everything" (Muir 1981: 190).

When a set of people proceed according to rank, this potentially comprises two different dimensions: in FRONT versus BEHIND, and EARLIER DEPARTURE and ARRIVAL versus LATER DEPARTURE and ARRIVAL at their destination, and at any given point along their route. It is not clear whether one of these dimensions typically is determinative, or whether the effects of each augment the effects of the other.

Note that in the conformation of rank by ORDER OF PROCESSION, the order of certain persons may not be conformational but have some other function. In Renaissance Venice, the procession may be headed by bearers of flags or insignia. Or, the safety of the leaders may require that guards go ahead of them. We noted that in a Moosé procession, a boy precedes the chief so that, if someone has put poison on the path to kill the chief, the boy will step on it and die, instead of the chief.

There is another, more widespread exception to the conformation of superior rank by going FIRST. Military personnel (at least in the Western world) DEPART from a ship or from an event IN ORDER of rank, beginning with the highest ranking and then on down. However, military officers arrive in inverse order of their ranks, beginning with the most junior (Dutton 1893: 11). Diplomatic protocol also observes these TEMPORAL ORDERINGS, at least when leaving:

> Departures from events are according to rank and precedence: You should remain at any dinner party (US or foreign) until all persons of all nationalities who outrank you have departed . . .
>
> It is best not to leave prior to the departure of the senior official of any nationality. Do not leave before the guest of honor or the senior representative of your mission leaves. (Foreign Service Institute 2013: 11 & 14)

In part, no doubt, they observe these two sequences because the result is senior personnel never having to wait for their subordinates.

Another practice of subordinate-before-superior is that, for centuries right up to the present day in Europe and North America, at least, when military personnel in uniform encounter each other, subordinates must salute FIRST and hold the salute until the higher-ranking person returns the salute. Similarly, when naval ships pass, the ship commanded by the junior officer renders passing honors first.

Multiplicity: More Numerous Is Superior

Another variant of the iconic physics of authority ranking is the conformation of superior status by MULTIPLICITY. This is manifest in a number of ancient Greek, Roman, Akkadian, Neo-Babylonian, Egyptian, Iranian, and Biblical deities who are represented as having MULTIPLE heads, arms, eyes, or bodies (Srinivasan 1997: 9). For example, more than 3,000 years ago, the Vedas and subsequent Hindu texts stressed the multiplicity of body parts of their highest deities. The Rigveda (whose core was composed around 1400 BCE) includes more than seventy references to divinities with multiple body parts and forms (Srinivasan 1997: 5, 27–28, 182). Deities are said to have "multiple heads, faces, mouths, arms, feet, bellies, backs, bodies, or testicles" (Srinivasan 1997: 182). The somewhat later Atharva Veda contains about fifty-five verses representing multiplicity in deities (Srinivasan 1997: 33). In the Bhagavad Veda, when Krishna manifests himself to the human prince Arjuna, he appears in "HUNDREDS AND THOUSANDS of multifarious divine forms of different colors and shapes" (11.05), "with many mouths and eyes, and many visions of marvel" (11.10), a "LIMITLESS God with faces on all sides" (11.11). Awed, Arjuna says, "O Lord of the universe, I see You everywhere with INFINITE FORM, with many arms, stomachs, faces, and eyes." Shiva's consort Kali is represented either with four arms or, in her Mahakalid avatar, with ten arms, ten faces, ten feet, and three eyes. Dated to the second and first century BCE, some of the earliest preserved Indian sculptures, seemingly conforming deities, are multiheaded or multiarmed (Srinivasan 1997: 185ff. & pls. 14.1, 14.3, 15.1, 15.2). Indeed, this multiplicity of heads, eyes, and arms is perhaps the most pervasive feature of the art of this region. A gilt watercolor of Visnu from Bilaspur in the Panjab Hills has twelve legs, sixty-eight heads, and about thirty-six arms (www.columbia.edu/itc/mealac/pritchett/00rou tesdata/0100_0199/gita/vishvapaint/vishvapaint.html).

In the Purusha Sukta, hymn 10.90 of the Rigveda, Perusha, a primeval giant cosmic being, is represented as having 1,000 heads and 1,000 legs (see also Linrothe et al. 2004). The Indian Buddhist goddess Avalokiteśvara or Sitātapartrā, often referred to as a Buddha or Bodhisattva, is usually said to have 1,000 heads, 1,000 eyes, and 1,000 hands. When Avalokiteśvara describes herself in the Sūraṅgama Sūtra tradition she says that she may manifest herself with 2 to 84,000 hands, 2 to 84,000 eyes, and 1 to 84,000 heads (Yü 2001: 47, Hua 2003: 178, de la Valléea Poussin 1910, Chandra 1988, Wen & Shuming 2002: 104, Shaw 2006). A recent sculpture in Wu-tun Temple, and a new painting, both from Tongren County (Rebkong), each appear to actually have 1,000 arms, with an eye on each palm – but only 11 heads, as far as I can make out.

Sanskrit texts of the *Divyāvadāna* from the early centuries of the common era recount stories of the Buddha which diffused widely among lay

Buddhists and greatly influenced monastic Buddhism (Rotman 2008). A famous tale tells of the Buddha performing miracles at Śrāvastī to prove his supremacy over heretics who challenged him; one of these miracles was that he MULTIPLIED himself into innumerable Buddhas, each seated on a lotus, beside and above each other "RISING up to the abode of the gods" (Rotman 2008: 279; in the section on Luminance, we will consider other miracles he performed then). Beginning during the Gupta period (fourth–sixth centuries CE), relief sculptures in Sārnāth and paintings in the Ajaṇṭā caves depict this miracle, which developed into a pervasive artistic tradition of 1,000 Buddhas (Brown 1984, Scarpari 2000: 283). Textiles apparently from Tibet and adjacent regions of China, probably dating from the seventh to ninth centuries CE, depict myriad embroidered Buddhas in rectilinear arrays, each with a halo or surrounding aureole (Reynolds 1990). As Chapter 9 shows, halos, aureoles, and mandorlas are conforming by LUMINOSITY. Many old Chinese temples and sculpted caves from a wide range of dates have a large central Buddha sculpture and two or more smaller and lower bodhisattvas, with the walls behind and beside them covered with HUNDREDS OR THOUSANDS of usually identical small images of the Buddha carved in relief (personal observations; also Howard et al. 2006, especially pl. 42., p. 362). The Longmen caves near Luoyang, in Hénán Province started in 494 CE, include 97,300 statues of Buddhas, bodhisattvas, and Arhat celestial guardians, distributed among 2,345 niches and caves (www.china.org.cn/english/kuaixun/75219.htm; Howard et al. 2006, Scarpari 2000: 278). In Nara, Japan, a gold-leaf sculpture of the Buddha Vairocana from the second half of the eighth century shows him backed by a sort of mandorla composed of hundreds of small Buddhas (Leidy 2008: 116 & fig. 5.16). HIGH on a mountain in Sha Tin, Hong Kong, is the Ten Thousand Buddhas Monastery, which actually displays 12,800 GOLD-colored statues of the Buddha (http://en.wikipedia.org/wiki/Ten_Thousand_Buddhas_Monastery). (As we shall see in Chapter 9, because gold reflects sunlight and does not tarnish, gold surfaces conform by LUMINOSITY.) An eleventh-century Japanese temple to Kannon exhibited 1,000 life-size wooden images of the Buddha. In Java, the MASSIVE Borodubur monument displays more than 400 statues of the Buddha on nine levels, together with 2,500 linear meters of relief carvings of the Buddha and other deities (Fisher 1993: 197–200). Currently, in Mendocino County, California, the walls of the Jeweled Hall of 10,000 Buddhas apparently display 10,000 Buddhas that "SHINE Their Light Upon the Sagely City" (www.cttbusa.org/cttb/history&background.asp).

The Egyptian high gods Amun, Re, Osiris, and Isis each had MANY names. Sometimes, it was written, they had so many names that humans could not specify any finite number; each these deities often received the epithet "of many names" (Hornung 1982: 86). The central deity of Zoroastrianism, Ahura Mazdā, has 101 names – a number of which are epithets of great luminosity – or, later Parsis said, 1,001 (Panaino 2002: 20). Allah has 99 names – or sometimes 1,000.

At smaller scales, the NUMBER of certain items that a person owns conforms the person's rank. For example, Western Zhou nobility were divided into four ranked classes, according to the number of *ding* (鼎, sacrificial tripods) and *gui'* (𣪘, tureens) they were allowed: 9 *ding* and 8 *gui* conformed the highest rank, followed by 7 *ding* and 6 *gui*, then 5 and 4, and, for the lowest-ranking nobility, 3 and 2 (von Falkenhausen 1993: table 2, pp. 34–35).

In the sources that I have consulted, there is no suggestion that any number that conforms a deity has any meaning on a ratio or interval scale. In numeric conformations of authority ranking, the scale is ordinal, not interval or ratio. What seems to matter in the multiplicity conformations of deities, at least, is their being or having many MORE heads, arms, or bodies than humans do.

"Strength–Force" and Identification with Large and Powerful Animals, or Killing Them

Some of the earliest representations created by humans and preserved in large quantity for contemporary analysis are paintings, reliefs, and sculptures in caves. Those that are currently recognizable are predominantly LARGE, POWERFUL animals: mammoths, bison, horses, aurochs, deer, caribou, ibex, boars, bears, rhinoceroses, and large felines. Some of these representations could be related to hunting magic connected to the great risks of hunting large and powerful animals, or these representations could be celebrations of hunting achievements or evocations of myths. However, the late Paleolithic representational preoccupation with the biggest animals, including groups of big animals, could also correspond to the most widespread and consistent meaning of such representations in early historical representations, where LARGE and POWERFUL animals are iconic conformations of elite men. Prehistoric leaders may have sought to identify themselves with these animals, invoking their impressive size, strength, and aggressiveness in cave representations to evoke the awe and respect of potential or actual followers (for some outstanding examples, see Leroi-Gourhan 1967).

Recall how Moosé chiefs choose proverbial war names that represent them as an elephant, a hippopotamus, or an impervious mountain. Similarly, in Sumerian poetry dating to around 2500 BCE, (*a_2-ĝal$_2$*), "STRENGTH" and "might" are used as synonyms of authority and aristocracy (Alster 1974: 17, 47). For example, the divinity Ninurta is conformed thus:

> Sovereign of all the lands, in your massive might, warrior of Enlil, in your great might, fierce warrior, you have taken up the divine powers which are like heaven, son of Enlil, you have taken up the divine powers which are like the earth, you have taken up the divine powers of the mountains, which are HEAVY as heaven, you have taken up the divine powers of Eridug, which are HUGE as the earth. You have make the gods PROSTRATE(?) themselves before you. You have made the Anuna salute(?) you. Ninurta, you are made complete by heroic STRENGTH. . . . Horned wild bull . . . Wild ram and stag . . . The great wild bull of the mountains . . . (ETCSL; Ninurta's return to Nibru: a *sir-gida* to Ninurta)

The poem also contrast his "lion's body and lion's muscles" with the gods who flee before him like SMALL birds and who hide like mice (ETCSL; Ninurta's return to Nibru: a *sir-gida* to Ninurta). Like other gods, he is repeatedly praised as a terrible storm and as a deluge. Other texts in praise of the supreme sky god, Enlil, "the great mountain" (i.e., MASSIVE), describe him on a "LOFTY dais" in a "lofty dwelling," receiving the earth-gods bowing DOWN in fear (Kramer 1963: 120).

From 2400 BCE through 700 BCE, Sumerian and Assyrian kings were often depicted hunting, battling, subduing, or having killed one or more lions, spotted panthers, or bulls (Ascalone 2005: 8, 15–21, 80–81, 122; Sefati 1998: 76). King Šulgi is addressed as a "great bull," "great ox," "raging lion," "dragon," "strong like an *ildag* tree," "mighty," and "endowed with STRENGTH" (Klein 1981: 73, 75, 141). He is a "fierce panther, who feeds on rich milk, [a] rampant bull, who was born to be a great beast" (73). On the "royal stand" he is "clad in terror like a lion" (Klein 1981: 195).

In another hymn, Šulgi boasts of his wisdom, his piety, his wonderful constructions, and, above all, his strength:

> I Šulgi, from my birth I am a MIGHTY man,
> I am a fierce-faced lion, begotten by a dragon,
> . . .
> I am the powerful king of Nanna,
> I am the growling lion of Utu,
> . . .
> I am a mule, most suitable for the road,

I am a horse, waving its tail on the highway,
I am a stallion of Sarkan, eager? to race,
...

I, Šulgi, the mighty king, superior to all,
Because I am a powerful man who rejoices in the STRENGTH of his loins,
...

I, the lion, never failing in his vigor, standing firm in his strength,
...

An placed the legitimate (and) LOFTY CROWN on my head,
In the LUSTROUS Ekur I seized the holy scepter,
On a SHINING DAIS, a throne of firm foundation, I lifted (my) head toward heaven;
...

May they glorify my majesty!
(The king) who is provided with LOFTY royal power,
Whom Suen, from the Ekisnugal,
Grants heroism, power and a good life,
Whom Nunamnir endows with superior strength.

(Klein 1981: 189–193)

The Lion Hunt Stele from around 3000 BCE depicts lion hunting, as do seals and sculptures in the round. "Hunting dangerous wild animals is a motif that is closely associated with high political office in Mesopotamia" (Pollock 1999: 184) and in Assyria (Pritchard 1954: fig. 626).

In Mesopotamia, beginning at least 5,000 years ago, lions or bulls are often represented adjacent to kings (Strommenger 1964). There were sculptures of dragons, "awe-inspiring lions," and other wild animals in front of Mesopotamian temples (Michalowski 1989: 63; lines 421–424).

Anyone entering the portals of Assyrian palaces passed GIANT winged bull or lion figures with bearded human heads, wearing elongated headgear (Pritchard 1954, figs. 646, 647). Assyrian gods and goddesses are represented STANDING ON a lion, a bull, or similar mythical composite animals (Pritchard 1954, figs. 470–474, 486, 500, 501, 522, 526, 534, 537). A grave from the Maikop culture, just northeast of the Black Sea, dated 3700–3400 BCE, contains silver cups impressed with images of a bull, a horse, a panther, a lion, and other animals; the buried "chief" wore a tunic covered with nineteen [SHINING] gold bulls and sixty-eight gold lions – although lions seem not to have been native to this region (Anthony 2007: 287–290).

The Emperor Ashoka of the third-century BCE Maurya Dynasty of northern India and the Achaemenid Persians of the same period erected

15-meter HIGH stone pillars topped by lions or bulls (Adams 2004: pls. 3.8, 3.9; Leidy 2008, fig. 1.1).

Similarly, ancient Egyptian kings were conceived as endowed by their very office with "overwhelming physical STRENGTH" manifest in "mighty athletic feats" and the defeat of all enemies (Decker 1987: 20). During the Middle Kingdom (ca. 2040–1730 BCE) "the LARGE statues picture the kings as warrior-heroes with great strength and physical power" (Kristiansen & Larsson 2005: 70). Tuthmosis III (reigned 1479–1425 BCE) had it reported that he killed 120 elephants, then 120 wild bulls in one hour, and 7 lions in the blink of an eye (Decker 1987: 59; note the LARGE NUMBERS conforming the pharaoh's supremacy).[1] He also claimed to have shot arrows through a copper target three fingers thick, but his son, Amenophis II, claimed that, shooting from a moving chariot, his arrows penetrated four copper targets in succession, each a hand's breadth thick. He is described as "MIGHTY in his strength . . . whose strong arms have no equal" (Decker 1987: 41, see also 57; Casson 1975: 48). Amenhotep III boasted of killing 102 lions in the first 10 years of his kingship, as well as 56 bulls in one day, with 40 more later, and had inscriptions carved with his boast that he was a "lord of strength" and a "fierce-eyed lion" (Casson 1975: 100; Decker 1987: 152).

From the predynastic period on throughout the history of ancient Egypt, rulers were depicted as bulls or lions, or with bulls or lions, often with defeated enemies underfoot (Pritchard 1954, Schäfer 1974: pl. 2, 4, 9). Egyptian pharaohs had sculptors create sphinxes with the body of a lion and their own heads; the most famous is the Great Sphinx at Giza, whose head is thought to represent the pharaoh Khafra (see Pritchard 1954: fig. 763). Several New Kingdom kings evidently kept a tame lion beside the throne and brought it along to battles (Decker 1987: 157).

Using the same conformation, Jewish mythology depicts a king keeping lions at his palace (Thompson 1989: pl. 14.22). In the Old Testament, Samson, David, and other distinguished men were renowned for killing lions, and Solomon's throne was configured with twelve lions (Stallman 1997). Moreover, Yahweh sent lions to kill people who were disobedient or disrespectful, and is often linked to a lion, or portrayed as one, yet said to be superior to one. When he is angry, he ROARS like a lion (Proverbs 19:12, 20:2, 28:15; see Stallman 1997).

[1] This is a rare premodern instance in which the rate of accomplishing something conforms authority ranking.

The first emperor of China, Qin Shihung, died in 210 BCE. He was buried at Lishan (mount Li) in a tomb landscaped to look like a MASSIVE mountain; subsequently, other Chinese dignitaries were sometimes buried in "mountain" tombs, references to their "status and achievement" (Howard et al. 2006: 2). Often, the paths to tombs or the tombs themselves were surrounded by huge stone sculptures of elephants, tigers, and horses (Howard et al. 2006). Likewise, in Mohenjo-Daro (in what is now Sindh, Pakistan), an elephant, rhinoceros, bull, or tiger is the principal figure on seals that may be signs of royal ownership or control (Sengupta 1951: 122).

Indo-European mythology evidently referred to gods and kings as bulls standing forth conspicuously; the image appears in the Rigveda and in Homer (West 2007: 97–98). Vedic mantras for overcoming rivals, and proclamations of sovereignty, ask to be a bull, a tiger, a lion, the sea that rules over the streams, or the moon that dominates the stars (i.e., the moon is much BRIGHTER than any star; Proferes 2007: 92–93).

In the fourth century BCE, the Indian King Chandragupta made some of his state appearances on an elephant, hunted on one, and is said to have gone to war with 9,000 war elephants (Sengupta 1951: 61, 64). Indian princes often rode on elephants or in carriages pulled by elephants, while in major processions an important prince would be accompanied by a number of additional elephants, some carrying big BOOMING DRUMS (Allen & Dwivedi 1984: 59, 155, 169, 177, 185, 255, 263, 278, 279, 282, inter alia). In colonial India, shooting tigers was a conformation of royalty and high colonial office (Allen & Dwivedi 1984). Princes displayed the heads and skins of tigers, leopards, and other large game they or their ancestors had killed, had pictures painted or photographs taken of themselves with tigers or leopards they had shot, and, in their palaces, sometimes sat on tiger skins. Princes vied to have any distinguished guest shoot a tiger BIGGER than the guest was able to kill when hosted by another prince (Allen & Dwivedi 1984: 140).

The Buddha's mother dreamed of a WHITE elephant before he was born, and statues of the Buddha often depict him on or with an elephant. In one of his lives, he himself was the elephant king Chaddanta (Liedy 2008: 17–18 & fig. 1.8). Also, the Buddha was the "Lion" of his Sakya clan, and he is often shown seated on a throne guarded by lions (Adams 2004: 26, pl. 4.15).

Texts in several Indo-European cultures, including Hittite, Sanskrit, and ancient Greek, praise their ancient deities as having great "POWER" (West 2007: 309). Greek gods are the "strong ones," and Zeus has the greatest κάρτος/*kartos*, "strength, vigor, force, courage" (Burkert 1996: 81). Odin and Krishna are declared to be mighty, and the Christian God is the Almighty. In

Irish and Spanish folklore one finds the motif of choosing a king on the basis of his strength and physical exploits (Thompson 1989: pl. 11.4).

In the New World, there apparently is a corresponding pattern of conforming rulers with powerful beasts, as well as with impressive celestial phenomena. The most common titles of the pre-Columbian rulers of the Mixtec of southern Mexico, recorded in their pictographic writing were names such as "Stone Jaguar, Jaguar Who Carries an Alligator in His Breast, Blood Jaguar, Blood Eagle, Eagle that Came Down from Heaven, Rain Sun, Venus Sun, or Plumed Serpent" (Jansen & Jiménez 2005: 47–48).

****

There are an indefinite number of possible conformations that could utilize any particular dimension. It is a process of cultural evolution that leads to any given community's use of any given iconic conformation of authority ranking in any given manner in a given kind of event in any given era. But an innate neuropsychosocial adaptation is the principal section force in that process of cultural evolution. The adaptation is always there, exerting its relentless selective force on the cultural evolution of conformations of authority ranking.

People can try any conformation of authority ranking, and any community at any time is likely to employ a few conformations, or embellishments of conformations, that are not iconic or are not based on dimensions. If a conformation has no such basis, no resonance with iconic dimensions, then the conformation is symbolic, based purely on commonly being used to conform authority ranking. For example, some European courts used the color purple and ermine fur as conformations of royal or noble rank. Those conformations can be established by edict and enforcement, so that they become informative – they can become established by fiat as symbolic cues to rank. But because neither purple nor ermine fur inherently resonates with the iconic dimensional and magnitude system for conforming authority ranking, the consequence is that neither purple nor ermine fur significantly affects subordinates' authority ranking representations of the relationship, nor their emotions, motives, moral sentiments, or commitments to the persons wearing purple or ermine. Nor will purple or ermine be as salient or as memorable as would an iconic dimensional conformation of authority ranking. So neither purple nor ermine will thrive in the iconic dimensional conformation niche; they will be ineffective conformations. Neither purple nor ermine is likely to endure for many human generations, nor is either likely to diffuse to many cultures.

From Disappointment to Deduction to Discovery

Ever since I lay prostrate before the Moosé village chief in 1979, I have been ruminating, off and on, about what I came to call conformation systems, especially mulling over what I came to conceptualize as the iconic dimensions that conform authority ranking. At some point, I encountered a cognitive science phenomenon that has long been extensively researched and is increasingly well understood: the analog magnitude system, also known as the approximate magnitude system. That system is pivotal in the perception, computation, mnemonic storage, and retrieval of relative numerical and nonnumerical magnitudes and dimensions, but without enumeration as such. It is the cognitive system that is concerned with what is more than what. A great deal is known about how the analog magnitude system (AMS) cognizes dimensions, knowledge which I do not review in this book (for good reviews, see Cohen, Lammertyn & Izard 2008, Beck 2015). When I first learned about the AMS, I was tremendously excited to find that one specific neurocognitive system deals with all of the dimensions that I knew to conform authority ranking!

But reading more and more research on the AMS, I came up against findings that disheartened me. I was disappointed, deflated, and discouraged to discover that the dimensions cognized in the AMS quite prominently and definitely include stimulus intensity. In particular, the AMS is the primary system for cognizing luminosity (brightness) and loudness (sound pressure). "There goes the fit of the AMS with the iconic conformations of authority ranking," I disconsolately thought, because, so far as I knew, neither luminosity nor loudness conforms authority ranking. After moping a bit, I decided I had a scientific obligation to return to the ethnographic, historical, and textual sources in order to establish that neither brightness nor loudness commonly conforms authority ranking. So I went back to take another look at the literature. Chapter 9 reports what I found, to my surprise.

CHAPTER 9

Luminosity and Loudness

Luminance

> "He's like a lighthouse."
>
> A man's comment on seeing Winston Churchill when Churchill visited Plymouth during the blitz.
>
> (Gardiner 2010: 315)

> The common association of celestial and solar light with power and elevation in particular seems often to issue in the emergence of symbolic codes that are remarkably similar even in altogether different cultural and historical settings . . . [There is a] persistent connection between religiously charged light symbolism and monarchical power – if saints have their halos, so do emperors and kings. (Kapstein 2004c: 275)

King Louis XIV of France (ruled 1643 to 1715) was *Louis le Grand*, "Louis the GREAT/BIG." Moreover, he officially identified himself with the sun, and so was universally known as *le Roi Soleil*, "the sun king' – and still today is so identified.

Sumerians represented high rank as luminous (Waldman 1984), and sometimes likened the radiance of their kings to that of the sun (Cassin 1968: 67–69). Many Mesopotamian texts describe gods as covered in fire or light, and narratives say that it is through overpowering radiant light that gods, temples, kings, and heroes "establish control over space or authority over the enemy" (Emelianov 2010: 1118; see also Cassin 1968). Furthermore, in ancient Mesopotamian texts, the more awesomely "powerful" the god, the "stronger" his influence, and the more "strength" he has – enabling him to overcome and dominate others – the brighter his brilliant luminance (Cassin 1968). Texts boast of the brilliance of the gigantic ziggurats dedicated to different gods, whose shining surfaces of glazed tile on the lower levels were surmounted on higher levels by even more brilliantly reflective sheathing in bronze, silver, and gold (Langdon 1916, Peters 1921: 157, James & van der Sluijs 2008).

To similar effect, Egyptian pyramids were faced with polished limestone that must have been designed to reflect the tropical sun, making them dazzlingly brilliant (Lehner 1998: 6). Indeed, the names of a number of Egyptian pyramids from the fourth to the twelfth dynasties denote them as *xai*, "shining," ( Bennett 1966). The pharaohs associated themselves with the sun, and the Pyramid Texts write of "the sun's rays as a ramp by which the king MOUNTS to the sun" where his glorious shining *akh* lives on (Lehner 1998: 35, 18).

Shining Robes

In both the Old World and the New, people seem to have initially developed technologies of mining, smelting, alloying, and shaping metals not so much, if at all, for tools and weapons. Their primary purpose was to create polished, shiny, noncorroding surfaces that BRILLIANTLY REFLECTED SUNLIGHT, thereby conforming the supreme authority of rulers and other high elites, as well as conforming the greatness of the highest-ranking deities: "The evidence suggests that in early civilizations copper was used first to manufacture [shiny] ornaments and ritual objects and only later to fashion weapons, craft tools, and finally agricultural implements" (Trigger 2003: 341). Before the discovery of technologies for working gold, in the region around the Black Sea and the Mediterranean, elites in the first stratified societies conformed their rank with whatever WHITE AND SHINY materials they could obtain. For example, around 5200–5000 BCE in the Pontic-Caspian region north of the Black Sea and north and west of the Caspian sea, elites wore "belts and strings of polished shell beads, bone beads, beaver-tooth and horse-tooth beads, boars tusk pendants, boars-tusk caps, boars-tusk plates sewn to their clothing, pendants of [imported] crystal and porphyry, polished stone bracelets, and gleaming copper rings" (Anthony 2007: 160; see also 181). In Assyria and Babylon, and elsewhere in the region, from around the twelfth to the eighth century BCE, first gods and later kings were conformed as dressed in one or more garments to which were affixed gold rosettes and other shimmering gold ornaments – sometimes several hundred of them (Anthony 2007, Renfrew 1978, Marx 1988, Rolle 1989). In the Aegean between 1650 and 1500 BCE, elite Mycenean men were buried in gold death masks and breast plates, while women were covered with incised gold rondels, belts, and leaves; even a buried infant was wrapped in gold foil (Marx 1988: 105). Later in the same region the Scythians buried elites so covered with gold that they were virtually gilded (Rolle 1989: 47–51). In some instances, as least, these glittering robes were the official conformations of their office (Oppenheim 1949). These flashing spangles later spread to other Near Eastern cultures, as well as Rome (Oppenheim 1949).

Many centuries later, Shakespeare's *Henry VIII*, first performed in 1623, begins with Buckingham describing the meeting of the kings of England and France. First Buckingham treats their mass as an icon of their authority:

> I was then present, saw them salute on horseback;
> Beheld them, when they are LIGHTED, how they CLUNG
> In their EMBRACEMENT, as they GREW TOGETHER [three conformations of communal sharing];
> Which had they, what four throned ones could have weigh'd [MASS]
> Such a compounded one?

Then Buckingham describes the brightness of their retinues:

> To-day the French,
> All CLINQUANT [glittering with gold or silver], all in gold, like heathen gods,
> SHONE down the English; and, to-morrow, they [the English]
> Made Britain India: every man that stood
> Show'd like a [gold] MINE [shining]. Their dwarfish pages [i.e. knights BIGGER than their pages]were
> As cherubins, all GILT: the madams too.
>
> (*Henry VIII*, Act 1, Sc. 1)

Then Buckingham calls the two kings "SUNS – for so they phrase 'em." "Few things expressed the majesty of kingship more vividly than the sight of hundreds of BRILLIANTLY dressed men and women, walking or riding with solemn dignity around an even more resplendent monarch" (Smuts 1989: 71).

Indeed, all around the world, chiefs, kings, and elites have conformed their rank by donning SHINING OR GLITTERING costumes (Rivers 1999). Ancient Egyptian elites wore clothing made with an opalescent and irides cent textile called *abu qualmun* or *buqalimun* (Rivers 1999: 26). In twelfth-century Egypt, under the Fatimid Caliphs, "Robes of honor marked ranks at all levels in Fatimid society, and their meaning was constructed within the framework of hierarchy" (Sanders 2001: 233). Fatimid robes of honor were woven of shimmering gold and silk: robes of fabrics containing GOLD invariably conferred higher rank than those made from silk alone (231), perhaps, we might speculate, because they shone brighter. From the ninth through the fourteenth centuries throughout the Islamic world, "the conferring of robes was an ubiquitous symbol of bonding between a superior and an inferior" (Hambly 2001: 215). These robes apparently glittered with jewels.

The Mongolian emperor Chinggis Qan (Genghis Khan, reigned 1206–1227) and his successors used glittering fabrics for their tents and robes (Allsen 2001: 305). Emperors distributed silk and gold brocade robes to everyone in their retinue; followers who received such robes were morally bound to serve the leader who bestowed them (Allsen 2001: 306).

In this tradition, a thirteenth-century Mughal Indian theologian wrote that "royalty is a LIGHT emanating from God, a RAY FROM THE SUN, the ILLUMINATOR of the universe (Asher 2004: 170). Subsequently, the early seventeenth-century Mughal emperor Nur al-Din Muhammad Jahangir Badshah Ghazi took the title of "Light of the Faith," giving his favorite wife the title of "Light of the Palace" and later "Light of the World" (Asher 2004: 179–180). Artists began to depict him and then his successor Shah Jahan with their heads surrounded by a BRILLIANT NIMBUS. Showing himself to his subjects below, Shah Jahan stood just below a steeply sloped gilded roof so that the REFLECTED SUN gave him a brilliant halo; inside the palace, he sat in a golden throne (Asher 2004: 184–185).

Safavid Persians imbued prestige fabrics with metallic gold and scorched them with a hot iron to make them SHIMMER (Rivers 1999: 28). For many centuries, the most widespread shimmering fabric was silk, produced in China and Persia, worn by Chinese and Persian elites, and exported to other elites around the world (Rivers 1999, Gordon 2001: 4). Indonesians, Thais, and Filipinos applied various plant-based materials to silk, or rubbed it to make it more SHINY (Gordon 2001: 30). Likewise, for at least seventeen centuries, Persians, Arabs, and Indians have applied starch, glue, or albumin to fabrics and rubbed them until the burnished fabric shone (Gordon 2001: 29). In Nigeria and Arabia, to make prestige clothing, even deep blue indigo is pounded or rubbed until it shines (Gordon 2001: 31–32). In China and surrounding regions, elite clothing was lacquered by applying sap from certain trees.

People have displayed high status by wearing GLIMMERING SHELLS in many cultures, including, for example, indigenous peoples of Taiwan, the Americas, and Melanesia (Strathern & Strathern 1971, Rivers 1999: 124–125). In northeast India, shiny, often IRIDESCENT BEETLE ELYTRA (wing covers) were affixed to clothing, often in association with gold or silver, to conform prestige among the Angami Naga, and in Mughal Jaipur (Rivers 1999: 134–135). In eighteenth- and nineteenth-century France and England the most elegant ball gowns, often of muslin, glittered with elytra (136).

In the New World, too, clothing and ornaments BRILLIANTLY REFLECTING SUNLIGHT conformed the highest ranks. Peoples of the New World invented and perfected this shiny conformation independently of this conformation in the Old World; "SHINY objects were definitive statements of prestige, centrally located in the symbolic representation of political power and elite status" (Saunders 1998: 244). Across the Americas, for their conformational uses, diverse cultures valued polished wood; gleaming shells; burnished ceramics; bright textiles; and glossy minerals such as gems, crystals, mica, obsidian, and mercury, or minerals that could be cut and highly polished, such greenstone, magnetite, and other iron ores (Saunders 2003). These brightly reflective materials were worn and displayed as "the ultimate symbols of power and influence" (Saunders 2003: 22). Pearls and IRIDESCENT, SHIMMERING shells conformed the prestige of their Incan and native North American wearers. Later, fifteenth- to seventeenth-century European royalty and nobility competed in their pearl displays – for example, studding royal crowns with them (Saunders 1999).

Aztecs paid iridescent minerals as tribute to elites. Mesoamerican elite burials included associated MERCURY, SHELLS, PEARLS, AND SHINY MINERALS. In North America, in the Mississippi flood plain east of St. Louis, at Cahokia. one elite man buried in the 7-meter-high mound #72 was interred wearing garments of shiny white beads imported from the Gulf of Mexico, and some elite burials in these mounds contain as many as 20,000 such beads (Iseminger 2010: 68). Another Cahokia burial contains an offering of about 70 LITERS of mica, along with rolls of copper sheet of the sort used to make shiny reflective garments (Iseminger 2010: 70).

Olmec rulers and other high-status persons in the Early Formative Period (1900–1000 BCE) wore POLISHED IRON-ORE MIRRORS on their chests or foreheads, and were buried with them (Carlson 1981, Tolstoy 1989, Heizer & Gullberg 1981). The manufacture and display of these mirrors appears soon after the appearance of the first monumental architecture across Mesoamerica: earthen platform mounds up to 25 meters high (conforming authority ranking by MASS, VOLUME, and HEIGHT) in which elites were often buried with polished jade and shell ornaments, and, before long, with these iron-ore mirrors (Joyce 2000: 71). These optically excellent concave (and sometimes convex) mirrors appear to have been important in conforming power and royal succession. It seems likely that they were manipulated or worn so as to reflect the sun to DAZZLE onlookers (Carlson 1981). More than a millennium later, Classic

Period (200–900 CE) high-status Mayans in Palenque also wore and were buried with mirrors, and indeed there is Mayan etymological evidence that "RELATES THE MIRROR ROOT [NEN/LEM] TO RULERSHIP, SUCCESSION in office, brilliance, lightning, contemplation, meditation, and imagination" (Carlson 1981: 127). Certain Mesoamerican deities were also associated with mirrors or the sun. The Mayan sun deity and other gods were often depicted with what Mayanists sometimes call the "god marker": the *nen* sign for "mirror, shiny reflective surface; EYE (REGARDED AS PROJECTING LIGHT)" (Houston & Taube 2000: 284). Mayan rulers and gods were conformed as bright and shiny, like obsidian or polished stone (Houston, personal communication, April 19, 2011). Altogether, mirrors were prominent in Mesoamerican costume, ritual, and iconography for more than 3,000 years (Taube 1992).

Also, in the Americas, for about 4,000 years, people have worked GOLD to use for display (Aldenerfer et al. 2008). The very sophisticated metallurgical technology of South and Central America was dedicated to fabricating conformational displays on the persons and residences of the elite, and in temples (Helms 1981). Among the Incas and their Andean neighbors, metallurgy was focused on gold-alloy sheet metal, or gold and/or silver finishes on bronze, designed to produce the shiniest possible surfaces (Lechtman 1984). The various chemical and physical technologies they developed MAXIMIZED THE REFLECTANCE OF THE METALS. "In the Andes, metals ... carried and displayed the content or message of status, wealth, and political power and reinforced the affective power of religious cult objects" (Lechtman 1984: 9).

Beginning around 1200, when the Incas established themselves, gold and silver production was monopolized by the high nobility, who displayed and sometimes redistributed shiny metals as icons of "charisma." Inca palace and temple walls were SHEATHED IN SHINY SILVER AND GOLD ALLOYS, and they created entire indoor miniature gardens of shimmering gold (Helms 1981, Lechtman 1984: 14, 36). From one palace, the Spaniards removed gold-alloy plates weighing 200,000 *pesos* (probably about 7,300 metric tons; Lechtman 2007: 320). (Compare Solomon's Temple in Jerusalem, whose whole interior, about 135 feet by 35 feet and 50 feet high, was likewise said to be sheathed with gold; Marx 1988: 118.) The Corichancha Temple on an outcrop in Cusco was dedicated to the Sun, ancestor of the Inca rulers; it was the center of Incan royal ritual. On the temple, a band of 700 gold-alloy plaques 450 paces long reflected the sun's light; each plate weighed 500 *pesos* (13.7 kilograms?) (Lechtman 2007: 320, MacCormick 1991: 63–64). The entire inside, including the ceilings and walls, was covered with gold sheets, and there were many statues of gold or silver (Cobo 1990: 50). A huge altar of gold occupied the temple patio:

> It was a solid piece, called Punchau, which means "the day," and it was entirely made of the finest gold with an exquisite display of JEWELS. It was shaped like a human face surrounded by SUNRAYS ... as the sun rose it would strike the image. Since it was a sheet of the finest metal, the sunrays reflected off it, SHINING WITH SUCH BRIGHTNESS THAT IT LOOKED LIKE THE SUN. The Indians said that along with its light the sun transmitted its power. (Cobo 1990: 26)

For celebrations or when they went to war, Inca elite men wore on their chest and on their heads gold or silver disks called *canipos*, the size of a European dinner plate, along with gold bracelets and small masks of gold or silver on their feet (Cobo 1990: 187). Chimu and Moche gods and rulers were conformed by LARGE HEADDRESSES, often of gold plate (Ubbelohde-Doering 1954, Rowe 1984, Sterlin 1984, Quilter 2005). The Inca and other nobility of the pre-Hispanic civilizations of the Americas also wore crowns, diadems, breast plates, earrings, necklaces, pendants, and other ornaments of SHINY gold alloys (for impressive examples, see Emmerich 1965, Grewenig 2004). After the Spanish had taken all their gold, the last Inca ruler, Atahualpa, had the walls and trim of his private rooms covered with "bright red bitumen which was extremely LUSTROUS AND FIERIER than ochre" (Stevenson 1959: 43, note 81, quoting in translation Franciso de Xérez).

On the north coast of Peru, between the second and ninth centuries of the current epoch, Moche elites dressed head to foot in shiny, shimmering gold and silver ornaments composed of a large high-rising headdress, large ear ornaments, a nose ornament that covered the mouth and cheeks, a necklace, a pectoral that covered the chest and shoulders, a flat curving tail flap, and garments covered with gilded metal platelets (Donnan 2011). The metal surfaces had MIRROR-LIKE SURFACES; beads and inlays were highly POLISHED. All over northwest South America and eastern Mesoamerica, "the emphasis in metallurgy lay in crafting ornaments that, as the Spaniards described it, seemed to cover warriors and chiefs from head to foot with GLITTERING metal" (Helms 1981: 226). Around the fourteenth century, Tarascans "considered golden and silvery objects divine, they associated them with the sun and with the moon deities, and nobility wore them to reify their status" (Hosler 2009: 207). Wearing these shimmering metal ornaments, produced by sophisticated technologies that made them brilliantly reflective, west and central Mexican political and religious elites literally DAZZLED their subjects (Hosler 1994: 227–233).

Early European interlopers sought American gold, silver, and pearls, while native Americans sought European glass beads, glazed pottery, mirrors, brass, and copper "power objects." Initial meetings between the leaders on the two sides consisted of honorific exchanges of their respective SHINY prestige objects (Saunders 1998).

As in early Mesoamerica, several Old World societies perfected MIRRORS to conform high rank. Bronze disks first appear around 3500–3000 BCE in Namazga, southern Turkmenistan, and later in Uzbekistan (Li 2011). The earliest sustained use of metals in China, in the Quijia culture of circa 2200–1700 BCE, included bronze mirror disks 6–9 centimeter in diameter, with attachment loops; evidently they were worn on the chests of elites (Li 2011: 34–51). From there, such mirrors spread across northwest China and then, by the late Shang period (ca. 1300–1046 BCE), to the central plains, where they appear in elite tombs.

These ancient Old World and New World technological advances are shining examples of the global, perpetual, vigorous development of all sorts of technologies that enable more effective conformations. Rulers and lesser elites recruited and motivated skilled craftspeople, constantly seeking to exceed the limits of existing means of iconically conforming high ranks. Surely there was intense technological competition between rulers in nearby polities, all seeking to outshine the others. Also, one imagines that elites in each court competed to discover new methods, new materials, or more accessible sources of crucial materials. Whoever succeeded at this could present the most DAZZLING gifts to the ruler, and, with the ruler's consent, wear these most dazzling robes and accoutrements, and dress their family in them. Similarly, one supposes that rulers searched widely for the engineers and builders who could construct the BIGGEST mounds, pyramids, ziggurats, temples, palaces, and monuments. Engineers and builders must have been greatly pressured and richly rewarded for devising techniques for making these icons of political supremacy bigger, TALLER, and more SHINY than ever. In such ways, elites' desire to conform superior status in authority ranking relationships was the impetus for advances in metallurgy and metal crafts, engineering of various sorts, architecture and construction, and means of transportation need to obtain HIGHLY REFLECTIVE materials for clothing, accoutrements, temples, and palaces.

Luminous Divinities and Kings

The *Rigveda*, one of the oldest texts in any Indo-European language, was probably composed a few centuries before 1000 BCE. It contains a great many hymns to the gods.[1] The root of "*rig*" is /*arc*, which means something like "praise" or "recite," and also "shine" (Jamison, personal communication; March 24, 2011). The *Rigveda* consists of *cha/ndas*, "praise songs" addressed to the gods; *cha/nda* means not only "singing" praise songs, but also "shining" (Karen Thomson, personal communication). And, indeed, one of the most recurrent themes in praise of the gods in the *Rigveda* is their BRILLIANT LUMINOSITY. The gods give off light, they make known the world by illuminating it, and their light shines on those who sacrifice to them, bringing them wealth, well-being, and power (Roessler 1997). The deity Agni notably transforms himself into SUN, LIGHTNING, and FIRE (Srinavasan 1997: 30). In the Vedas, Visnu, especially, but also Agni, Indra, and Soma, are described as *hari*, "pale, yellow, tawny"; it is an adjective also applied to the sun, to lightning, and to rays of light (Gonda 1954: 107). *Hari* is derived from the Proto-Indo-European **ghel*, "to shine." Combining all of the lexemes for brilliant light, by my rough count in the *Rigveda* luminosity is attributed to the gods at least 500 times.

Kings in the *Rigveda* also shine brilliantly, conforming their kingship. The early Vedic *dyumná*, derived from a word for brightness, was the epithet for a ruler's "glory" and "prowess" (Proferes 2007: 33). Political dominance is iconically represented in the *Rigveda* as INTENSE LIGHT SHINING DOWN on a ruler's domain: "May our glory [*dyumná*, radiant light] shine unsurpassably from above over the Five Peoples, like the sun" (*Rigveda* 2.2.10; Proferes 2007: 68). Beginning the ritual of assuming office, the new ruler utters the mantra, "I invoke you, all fires sitting within the waters; in me deposit strength, and might" (*Aitareya Brāhmanica* 8.6.10; Proferes 2007: 77). The ritual confers on him *várcas*, "SPLENDOR OF ALL THE FIRES in the universe, energy, might"; *dyumná*, "LUMINOUS glory"; and *téjas*, "BRILLIANCE" – thereby conforming his dominion (Proferes 2007: 81, Gippert 2002).

But, above all, it is *téjas* that makes a person a sovereign (Hocart 1927: 42, Gonda 1954: 165). *Téjas*, whose root meaning is "sharp," is a kind of divine energy that manifests in fire, lightning, sparkling jewels, shiny metals, and

[1] I am extremely grateful to Karen Thomson and Stephanie Jamison for their very generous super expert help with this text. I also appreciate Reinhard Kraus's generous diligence in perusing Roesler (1997) and explaining to me what he found in the German text.

the destructive power of divine weapons (Whitaker 2000). *Téjas* is the ferocious power to defeat and dominate others. Gods can confer *téjas* on subordinate gods and on kings, giving them authority over their subjects (Whitaker 2000). Many verses make the claim that, like the sun, the gods and kings shine down on the whole world (Proferes 2007: 82–91, 135). Verses in the *Atharva Veda* liturgy of assuming office make this clear, such as "Make me SPLENDOROUS today, O Fire, with that splendor through which the elephant originated, through which the king among men and among the waters (originated), through which the gods became gods in the beginning" (Proferes 2007: 83, 96). Thus, like the sun, the king becomes *svároci*, "SELF-ILLUMINATING" (Proferes 2007: 84). In various Sanskrit texts, *téjas* is frequently specified to be an important quality of the gods Visnu, Ṣiva, Kriṣna, and Sūrya; distinguished warriors and ascetics; and of the sun (Gonda 1954: 105, 123). Moreover, the king has *téjas*, "brilliant fiery energy, luster, might, dignity"; indeed, he has the *téjas* of all the gods (Proferes 2007: 40, 70). The sovereign makes himself ruler by possession of the physical burning FIRE that manifests *téjas* and demonstrates his assimilation of the qualities of the SUN. It is the king's *téjas* that "entitles him to respect and enables him to perform great exploits" (Proferes 2007: 71). A being can have more or less *téjas* energy compared to other beings, and this inequality determines victory in battle and, hence, rank (Whitaker 2000). The epithets of famous kings praise them as having GREAT OR BOUNDLESS *téjas* exceeding all other (Proferes 2007: 66, 71).

Likewise the *Rigveda* iconically represents the consolidation of political power as intensification of LIGHT (Proferes 2007: 101). By the time the earliest hymns of the Rigveda were composed, people conceived of legitimate authority as light shining on subjects (Proferes 2007: 136). The king's power comes from his assimilation of the light of the sun, but the sun's power is more than light: it is worshipped as *práthas*, *váras*, *vyácas*, and *loká* – respectively, "BREADTH, WIDTH, EXPANSE, and scope/expanse/open space/free motion' (Proferes 2007: 136; Monier-Willams 2003). Kings are also noted as having Indra's *varcas*, "brilliance, illuminating power" that is associated with fire, and *bhrājas*, "the power of shining radiantly" with the sun (Gonda 1954: 166). In the *Rigveda*, the gods, too, are often praised as ABOVE, and said to be MIGHTY, or compared to RAGING BULLS OR RIVERS. Furthermore, in a great many verses the gods are said to ROAR, BELLOW, OR THUNDER. Thus, intensity of LOUDNESS, LUMINOSITY, FORCE, SPATIAL EXTENT, and being ABOVE are all used together to conform the superiority of gods.

Luminant conformation of rank is also salient in the Bhagavad Gita, composed between about 200 BCE and 200 CE (see Chapter 11, especially). Krishna says, "Whatever being is glorious, splendid, or powerful, know it as originated by a particle of my own *téjas*" (Bhagavad Gita X, 41, quoted in Magnone 1992: 142–143; see also 145). Luminant conformations using other words are prominent in another text, the *Manusmṛti*, also composed between 200 BCE and 200 CE (Gonda 1956: 60–62). In Stella Kramrisch's (1981) retelling of the famous myth of Shiva, Brahma, and Visnu, the DAZZLING BRILLIANCE of Shiva is linked to his IMMENSE size. These qualities subordinate the two other high gods, who hence BOW to him.

Moving to Mesopotamia, we find that in Sumer, a core attribute of the gods and kings, as well as places and things associated with them, was *lem4*. This is an ancient root meaning "divine RADIANCE, NUMINOUS SPLENDOR, AWESOME LUMINOUS AURA"; it apparently derives from a word for "fire" or "burn," with an original core sense of "INCANDESCENT." This was combined with the root *me*, "divine power," to form the word *melammu*, "RADIANCE, SUPERNATURAL AWE-INSPIRING SHEEN," a quality inherent in all things divine and royal (Cassin 1968; for more on Akkadian derivatives, see also Roth 1977). Royal hymns of the late Sumerian period, as well as annals and inscriptions of Neo-Assyrian and Neo-Babylonian times, frequently attribute *melammu* to kings (Emelianov 2010). *Melammu* evidently evolved into the halo in Christian iconography.[2] Another root, *nmr*, also meaning "to be luminous, burn," is the basis for the Sumerian terms *namrirrû* and *namurratu*, "flashing luminous splendor," a characteristic frequently attributed to gods and kings (Cassin 1968). Again, the root *ní* (corresponding to Akkadian *palâhu*) means "terror, awe, respect," but also "brilliantly flash," giving *nígal*, which we could translate as "overwhelmingly radiant," another common epithet of deities and kings (Cassin 1968). Akkadian *raššubbatu* and *rašalummatu* have meanings and usage very similar to *ni*. The texts say that gods' and kings' luminous flashing splendor inspires fear, awe, and reverence. In particular, the heads of their gods and kings were described as SPARKLING with light, and there are indications that kings reified this with JEWELED crowns and turbans (Cassin 1968: 25–26, 50).

Around 100 CE the north Indian deity Avalokiteśvara, whose multiple heads and many arms we considered, appears in the *Sukhāvatīvyūha Sūtra*,

[2] I am greatly indebted here to Daniel A. Foxvog for his personally communicated, brilliant illumination of *me-lem4*.

which characterizes him and another bodhisattva, Mhāsthāmaprāta, as full of light (Yü 2001: 13–14). Likewise, third-century and later texts such as the *Lotus Sūtra* emphasize the "majestic light" emanating from Avalokiteśvara's whole body, that "issues forth great brilliance" and "shines universally" (Yü 2001: 34–40, 52 & fig. 6.8). When he manifests in nonhuman form, the form is "golden" (Yü 2001: 229). Over the centuries, as Avalokiteśvara-worship spread eastward into and across China, he transformed into the female bodhisattva of compassion, Guanyin (or Kuan-Yin). Chinese sculptures from 599 and 703 have both HALOS and MANDORLAS as luminance conformations of her greatness, while another sculpture from 703 has a halo and eleven heads (Yü 2001: figs. 2.4, 2.5, 2.7).

Congruently, in Old Iranian and Middle Persian, *xvarna*, "RADIANCE of the royal majesty" (Sasanian *farr*) conformed the entitlement to rule, and was perceived as radiant illumination of kings or on kings (Deignas & Winter 2007: 234; Jamison, personal communication, personal communication; March 24, 2011). In Zoroastrian texts, too, *xvarna* is a SHINING, miraculously strong property associated with the sun and fire, and of the supreme deity, Ahuramazdā (= Ohrmazd), who is "on high," "ever in the light," and in "endless light' (Boyce 1984: 45). More generally, *xvarna* is a crucial property of beneficial immortals, the Beings Worthy of Worship, of many heroes, and of the perhaps mythical great king Yima (Boyce 1984: 29–30, Stausberg 2008: 38–342). Indeed, *xvarna* or *hvarenō* is what people worship in them, as it is the very power and authority of Zarathustra. Persian kings also claimed to have Zarathustra's *xvarna*, the glowing power expressed in a ruler's victory and dominance over enemies (Jones 1916, Soudavar 2009). *Xvarna* is what makes a king a king, or a hero a hero (Eliade 1971: 15). But when a king loses his legitimacy through a major transgression, he loses *xvarna* (Boyce 1984: 30–31).

In an early Pyramid Text, the first god, Atum, creates the world and RISES as or on a hill, and the sun is addressed as "the high one" (Badawy 1956: 182). The king is associated with Atum and asks to be HIGH above the earth, shining. "Ascending" the throne is analogized to ASCENDING to join the gods after death, facilitated by his MASSIVE mastaba (tomb) rising toward the heavens. When he dies, the king ascends steps of LIGHT to the circumpolar stars where he will "lead," "in the FOREFRONT." Royal mummies and the caskets enclosing them were often gilded, so they still shine today.

In ancient Greece, luminance was a prominent conformation of being a hero, a king, or a deity. In the *Iliad*, Agamemnon, Menelaus, Paris, Odysseus, Achilles, Aeneas, and other heroes are said to wear GLEAMING/SHINING (λάμπετο) armor; carry shining shields, reins, and whips; and throw shining spears. King Nestor's chair is shining. Hector's epithet is "of the shining/gleaming/flashing helmet" (κορυθαίολος). Hera, sister and wife of Zeus, dons a headdress as bright as the sun; even her feet are shimmering.

Diomedes was a warrior hero at Troy, who was later worshipped as a god. To make Diomedes a hero, Athena

> made weariless FIRE BLAZE from his shield and helmet
> like that star of the waning summer who beyond all stars
> rises bathed in the ocean stream to GLITTER in BRILLIANCE (παμφαίνῃσι).
> Such was the fire she made blaze from his head and shoulders
> (*Iliad* 5, 2–7; Lattimore 1951 translation)

Hephaestus forges shining armor for Achilles, so his shield emits a light like that of a fire seen across the waters, a light that shoots high into the air (Lattimore 1951: 19, 373–380). His gold-fringed helmet shines like a star, his chariot driver takes up a shining whip, and Achilles stands behind him, "shining (παμφαίνων) in all his armour like the SUN when he crosses above us" (*Iliad* 19, 398; Lattimore 1951 translation). Later, Athena made Achilles' body emit blazing lights visible from afar, and then she and Achilles uttered war cries as LOUD AS WAR TRUMPETS. The blazing fires around Achilles's head and the terrifying war cries struck fear in the hearts of the Trojans, routing them (*Iliad* 18, 206–229). Hector is also conformed as brilliant (*Iliad* 11, 61–66).

Homeric Greek gods are BRILLIANT – and Zeus abides above them all in SHINING/RADIANT (αἰγλήεντος; 1, 532; 13, 243) Olympus. In the Odyssey, when brightness fills the hall where the suitors are gathered, Telemachus and Odysseus realize that a god must be present, for brilliant luminosity is a sign of the Olympians (*Odyssey* 19, 39–43). Athena comes down from Olympus like a shining, sparkling comet (4, 75–78). Brilliant light often marked the birth or epiphany of Greek gods (Dietrich 1983: 67–68).

It is not only Homer who highlights luminant conformations. Pindar (ca. 522–443 BCE), the great Greek lyric poet, does the same. Introducing his edition of Pindar, Gildersleeve (1885: xxxvii) describes the iconicity of Pindar's language.

> The word splendor and all its synonyms seem to be made for Pindar. He drains dry the Greek vocabulary of words for LIGHT and BRIGHT, SHINE and SHIMMER, GLITTER and GLISTEN, RAY and RADIANCE, FLAME and FLARE and FLASH, GLEAM and GLOW, BURN and BLAZE. The first

> Olympian begins with wealth and strength, with flaming FIRE OF GOLD, and SHINING STAR of the SUN. The fame of Hieron is resplendent, and the shoulder of Pelops gleams.

In the Acropolis of 460–430 BCE Athens, the high-crowned statue of Athena was made of IVORY, clothed and gilded in about 1,100 kilograms of GOLD. The statue of sitting Zeus in Olympia, 12 meters HIGH, was likewise of ivory clothed in gold-plated bronze (Marx 1988: 158).

We see the same iconic luminance in medieval Sufism. Sufi saints were said to be LUMINOUS, as were their tombs, often made of LUSTROUS WHITE marble, and some saints were named for their luminosity (Ferhat 2010: 458, Asher 2004: 167). Those Sufi saints who achieved their goal of *fana'* (annihilation in union with Allah) were said to have experienced visions of Allah's BRILLIANT LIGHT, in accord with the Koran's declaration that "God is the light of the heavens and the earth" (Asher 2004: 163).

For luminosity conformations of supremacy in twelfth-century Persia, see Asher (2004: 169). For that in the Byzantine empire, see Corripus *In Laudem Justini* (3.224–230, translated by Cameron 1876, quoted in Sidéris 2002: 166)

In Sumerian, Akkadian, and Hebrew, the terms for the majesty and glory of superior beings, sacred objects, and temples denote brilliant, radiant luminosity (Waldman 1984). In Hebrew, כָּבֵד *kabod*, which originally meant "HEAVY, WEIGHTY" in the sense of physical MASS, evolved into כָּבוֹד, *kabowd*, or כָּבֹד, *kabod*, "imposing, honor(able), dignity, high rank, respect, reverence" (Weinfeld 1995, Collins 1997b, Fossum 1999, http://lexiconcordance.com/hebrew/3513.html). The antonym of *kabod* was *qll*, "LIGHT" IN PHYSICAL WEIGHT, as well as social insignificance – not meriting respect or honor (Weinfeld 1995; compare with English contrast between *gravitas* and *lightweight*). Likewise in Aramaic, *yeqār* means both physically "HEAVY" and socially "respected, honored," and in both languages is an epithet of kings. Sometimes *kabod* referenced the multitude of a person's chattel, gold, and silver (hence, their wealth), especially the honor of receiving or amassing great wealth, but it came to be used more generally to indicate "high," honorable status (Collins 1997b). In the Hebrew Bible the term *kabo(w)d* appears about 200 times, usually in reference to the majesty or splendor of God but also declaring the greatness of kings, priests, or sages. *Kabod* also means "MASS, MULTITUDE, GREAT QUANTITY OR EXTENT," sometimes characterizing a gift or portion allocated to someone (Vermeulen 1956: 6, Weinfeld 1995). *Kabod* also meant physical "FORCE" or "strength," sometimes "war prowess," and sometimes social "might" (Weinfeld 1995). Likewise, *geḇûrâ* and *`ōz* both denote physical "power" and/or social "power"; both, but especially *`ōz*, are closely associated with God's *kabod* and with his will and commandment.

However, most of the time *kabod* takes on a visual meaning, signifying the brilliant, sometimes unbearably BRIGHT LUMINOSITY of a supreme being (Vermeulen 1956, Mettinger 1982: 122–123, Weinfeld 1995). In short, "kabod has weight, substance, brilliance and divine power" (Loerke 1981: 20). Adam, Abel, Michael, and Moses are all characterized by their *kabod*, and in the New Testament, so is Jesus (Fossum 1999). Likewise, early rabbinic literature portrayed Adam's body as incomparably luminous, using the term *kabod* (Gottstein 1994). The luminosity of God and the prophets is sometimes described in terms of blazing fire, a torch, gold, crystal, and the sun or many suns; see Weinfeld 1995, Mettinger 1982: 115, Collins 1997b. God's *kabod* is associated with his THUNDERING (Mettinger 1982: 118, 122) and with his *rwm*, "HEIGHT' (Collins 1997b). Sometimes God's *kabod* covers or FILLS the temple, whole regions, or the entire earth (conforming by surface area), and it is often said to be ABOVE, to protect, to be dangerous, and to evoke fear (Mettinger 1982, Collins 1997b). Throughout Jewish mysticism up to the present, "light is one of the most important symbols that has informed the texture of the experience of the divine" (Wolfson 2004: 106).

In the Hebrew Bible and Old Testament, many other terms also describe this iconic LUMINANCE conformation, including *`ôr*, "light"; *ngh* and *nōgah*, "shine" and "brightness, shining"; *zārah*, "brilliance"; *hôpîa`*, "shines forth"; *yp`*, "shine out"; *nhr* II, "be radiant"; *qrn*, "be radiant, send out rays"; and *`wr*, "be light, bright, shine" (Mettinger 1982: 36; Waldman 1984, Weinfeld 1995, Selman 1997a, b, c, d, e; for a number of others, see VanGemeren 1997: 119–120, 153, 172–173, 180). These terms all have a nonsocial, physical meaning referring to a kind of light or shining, and a social relational meaning of majesty, supremacy. Likewise, in the Hebrew Bible, *hod* and *dóxa* are closely associated with the luminously shining, often unbearably brilliant splendor of God and other greatly respected religious beings (Vermeulen 1956, Waldman 1984). *Kabod*, *hod*, and *dóxa* were usually translated into Latin as *gloria*, splendid power, renown, and kingship; and into English as *glory*, perhaps the most characteristic Biblical aspect of God and Jesus (Bromiley 1982). *Claritas*, which already meant both "light, transparent" and "fame," was another important early Christian Latin word for God's luminous splendor (Vermeulen 1956: 2). The Hebrew Bible also contains a great many references to God, Jesus, and angels as LIGHTS: for example, Ezekiel 1:4–10:

"And I looked, and, behold, a whirlwind came out of the north, a great cloud, and a fire infolding itself, and a brightness *was* about it, and out of the midst thereof as the colour of amber, out of the midst of the fire." And Ezekiel 1:13: " As for the likeness of the living creatures, their appearance *was* like burning coals of fire, *and* like the appearance of lamps: it went up and down among the living creatures; and the fire was bright, and out of the fire went forth lightning" (King James Bible 2017).

Similarly, the Neoplatonist mystical theurgists posited that divinity consisted of FIERY LIGHT (Johnston 2004). Again, in twelfth-century Persian philosophy, God is the light of lights: "A ruler's legitimacy is seem in his manifest 'luminosity,' . . . 'seen' in his manifest auralike luminous quality" (Johnston 2004: 28). In Middle and Late Byzantium churches the window-sills were angled and polished so that they reflected the light of the rising sun onto the icon of Jesus at the top of the dome, brightly illuminating him in the otherwise dim interior light (Louth 2004: 86).

In the texts of a number of other world religions, too, "the birth or illumination of the great saviors and sages is announced by a profusion of supernatural LIGHT" (Eliade 1971: 4). Such a light is said to have appeared at the birth of Mahāvira, one of the founders of Jainism, who is typically represented with a halo. Again, a fundamental aspect of the Buddha is his luminosity (Soper 1950, Yü 2001: 13–14). Statues and images of the Buddha commonly depict him with a halo or mandorla (Fisher 1993, Kapstein 2004a: pls. 1, 2, & 3). Texts focus on the Buddha's brilliant luminosity (Eliade 1971: 5, Yamamoto 2007: 153–154, Rotman 2008: 273–280). Images of the Buddha and bodhisattvas often were, or still are, made of SHINY bronze, or GILDED (Fisher 1993: 51, Leidy 2008: 67). Images and sculptures from India, Dvāravatī (Thailand), and other regions commonly depict a HALO around the Buddha's head or a MANDORLA around his entire body (Brown 1984). In fact, the earliest sculptures of Buddha, from the second and third centuries, from what is now India, Pakistan, and Afghanistan, show a circular halo behind his head (Adams 2004: figs. 3.15, 31.16, 3.18; Leidy 2008: figs. 2.2, 2.3). And sixth-century Chinese sculptures of Buddha show both a halo around his head and a flaming mandorla, indicating radiant luminance surrounding his whole body and rising above him (Adams 2004: 4.15; 6.2).

In ancient Tibetan texts, "it is clear that the equation among divinity, kingship, LIGHT, and ELEVATION in space is an ancient and compelling dimension of the autochthonous Tibetan religious system," as well as of ancient Chinese religious traditions (Kapstein 2004b: 138). Indigenous Chinese representations of the moral power of rulers also converges with

Mahāyāna Buddhist representations of bodhisattvas: "In both of these cultural complexes the appearance of bright light signifies appropriate power" (Birnbaum 2004: 196).

The 125-feet and 120-feet TALL sixth- to early-seventh-century Buddhas carved out of the cliff face at Bamiyan, Afghanistan were painted and GILDED; in 629 the Chinese Buddhist monk Xuanzang describes one of these Buddhas, reporting that "Its golden hues sparkle on every side, and its precious ornaments dazzle the eyes by their brightness" (Hiuen Tsiang 1908: 51). He writes that nearby there was another COLOSSAL free-standing Buddha covered in cast GOLDEN metal.

Chinese generally depicted goddesses and the Buddha as white-skinned (Li, et al. 2008), and by the second century BCE depicted the Buddha with a HALO (Hung 1995: figs. 2.56–8, pp. 139–140). In the fourth century CE, the Buddha is described as 16 feet TALL, gold colored, wearing the LIGHT FROM THE SUN AND MOON on his neck. Around the same time, another Chinese writer also represents the Buddha as brilliantly LUMINOUS, and various writers from this period and later centuries again represent the Buddha as golden (and therefore brilliantly reflecting sunlight; Hung 1995: 136–137).

Likewise, Mao Zedong had millions of HUGE posters prominently displayed, depicting him ABOVE masses of citizens or laborers of the world, IN FRONT of a SUN, often a rising sun, or with his head surrounded by a sort of radiant MANDORLA or HALO. The captions often declared that "Chairman Mao is the red sun in our hearts," linguistically emphasizing his loving warmth, while alluding to his role in RAISING China out of OBSCURITY – that is, the darkness of low rank among nations.

Of course, it is not just in Asia that people have depicted divinities and rulers with halos, aureoles, or mandorlas indicating brilliant luminosity. Mosaics created 540–47 CE in the Byzantine church of San Vitale in Ravenna depict HALOS not only on Christ and angels, but also on the Emperor Justinian and Empress Theodora (Adams 2008: 156–161). Subsequent images of many other Byzantine emperors also show them with halos (Grabar 1936, pls. vii, xvi, xvii, xviii, xix, xxi, xxiii, xxiv, xxvi, xxviii). A late-twelfth-century relief represents Constantine VII in front of a disk whose diameter slightly exceeds his height, apparently evoking RADIANT LIGHT, perhaps the sun Cameron 1987, fig. 19, p. 121). In arts from their respective reigns, halos conform the authority of Roman emperors beginning with Antoninus Pius and continuing thorough Constantius, Galerius, Theodosius and Theodosius II, Valentinian I and III, and beyond, as well as Emperor Constantine IV, Constanine IX, Alexius IV, Akbar II, Moghul Emperors Aureng-Zeb, Shah Jahan,

Bahdaur Shah II, Jahandar Shah, Muhammad Shah, and Emperor Louis I, the Pious (ca. 1170–1179). For example, an early-seventeenth-century gilt and paint image of Jahangir, the fourth Mughal Emperor of India, shows a large golden sun halo behind him, with the edge of a white moon halo behind that (Adams 2004: pl. 5.13). Other images of Jahangir on paintings and coins also depict him with various halos of radiant gold beams emanating from his head (http://en.wikipedia.org/wiki/Jahangir).

Black Clothing

There is no doubt that luminance conformations of authority ranking are widely distributed and prevalent across cultures over millennia – especially for high gods and rulers. This indicates strong cultural selection for luminance conformations, but of course it does not mean that luminance is always used everywhere. An interesting case is the European elite transition from brilliant clothing to black, beginning in the late sixteenth century (Schneider 1978):

> According to Renaissance ideology, black garments, such as those painted in fifteenth- and sixteenth-century portraits, were ideally reserved only for those who held power and authority in society . . . For example, the laws concerning the use of black in Siena, issued first in 1588, made it absolutely forbidden for men and women to wear black, as well as dark *pavonazzo*-purple, considered a kind of "sub-black," unless they were connected to the ruling classes through their birth or marriage. (Hohti 2022)

Among other factors, elites had previously been deterred from wearing black clothing by limitations in European dye technology that made it impossible to produce truly black, saturated, evenly dark cloth (Boulboullé & Dupré 2022). When this technology advanced to the point of enabling the production of such cloth, late sixteenth-century elites in some European courts adopted it, in many cases motivated in large part by Protestant ideologies disfavoring ostentation. As the technology developed to make it possible to produce evenly saturated, totally black fabrics at ever decreasing prices, this created the "potential of black garments to convey status and distinction across the lower social classes" (Hohti 2022).

Loudness

We have established that the conformation system of authority ranking is iconic on at least nine dimensions: ABOVE–BELOW, TALLER–SHORTER,

GREATER–LESSER (VOLUME and/or MASS), GREATER–LESSER SURFACE AREA, MORE NUMEROUS–FEWER, IN FRONT–BEHIND, EARLIER–LATER (temporal precedence, seniority), GREATER FORCE–LESSER FORCE (often as muscular strength, or strong animals), and now MORE LUMINOUS–LESS LUMINOUS. Do people also use the LOUD–SOFT dimension? Let us consider acoustic conformations of authority ranking.

Asia

In the Griffith translation of the *Rigveda*, the gods Agni, Indra, and others are said to "THUNDER" in 266 instances, "ROAR" in 127 instances, "SHOUT" in 34 passages, and "CRY" in 39 passages (e.g., battle cry, raise a cry, cry of glory). The gods' utterances are also described as "LOUD" 100 times. For congruent acoustics in Nepalese and Burmese worship, see Cooler 1986, Price 1983, and Tingey 1992. For the Norse, Thor was the god who conformed his supremacy with THUNDER; Zeus was the Greeks' thunderer.

Likewise, ancient Sumerian gods ROAR a lot. When the goddess Inana fought a monster mountain, she "roared like THUNDER" (ka gal gu3-an-ne2-si, literally "mouth big thunder" ETCSL Inana and Ebiḫ t.1.3.2 line 143, t.4.07.3 line 112, t.1.3.2 lines 152–9 n). The god Ninurta is described as "thundering" as well (t.1.6.2 line 112). Sumerian kings also thunder or roar. For example, King Šulgi is often said to roar (za-pa-aj$_2$, or gu$_3$, e.g., ETCSL, A praise poem of Šulgi [Šulgi D], t.2.4.2.04). In connection with kings, gods, and kings' prayers to gods, Sumerians beat several kinds of DRUMS, as well as using CLAPPERS, SISTRA, BELLS, and CYMBALS (Blades 1970: 152, 159, and figs. 50 & 51; Gudea, cylinders A and B, ETCSL t.2.1.7).

Tingey cites Farmer's (1939) account of the Moghul Emperors in Persia who had pairs of HUGE KETTLEDRUMS (*kurka*), conforming their rule; the drums were beaten in conjunction with issuing royal edicts. On the death of a sultan, after being played at the royal funeral, the drums were broken to pieces (Farmer 1939: 12–13). Moghul rulers in processions in late-seventeenth-century Surat City were accompanied by elephants and attendants wearing bells, while drummers BEAT LOUD KETTLE DRUMS and BLASTS OF LONG TRUMPETS sounded (Freyer 1909–1915: vol. 1, pp. 151, 242). In this era Persian Patriarchs were installed with LOUD MUSIC and the DISCHARGE OF CANONS (Freyer 1909–1915: vol. 2, p. 272), while Persian kings sometimes gave a SMALL KETTLEDRUM to high nobles as a mark of honor and favor (vol. 3, p. 62). A photograph from about 1905

Table 9.1 *Naval Honors: Salute Guns and Parade Guards*

Personage	Salute guns	Parade guard	Side boys
Rulers & exrulers of nations, & members of royal families	21	present	8
Vice-President of the US	19	present	6
Cabinet ministers, admirals, governors, justices of the supreme court, congressional committees	17	present	6
Vice-admirals, US or foreign ministers	15	present	6
Rear admiral	13	present	6
Commodore, chargé d'affaires	11	present	6
Consuls general	9	none	6
Consuls	7	none	4
Vice-consuls	5	none	4
Captains & commanders	0	none	4
Commissioned officers of lower grades	0	none	2
Officers & other officials in civilian dress	0	none	2 at foot of gangway to hand out man-ropes

shows trumpeters blowing and drummers beating ahead of a Moghul prince riding an elephant (Allen & Dwivedi 1984: 169).

In South Asia there were similar practices (Allen & Dwivedi 1984: 22, 23 quoting the Raja, 88). In 1784, when the British Resident of Hyderabad first arrived, he found that twenty-five emirs were entitled to be, and were, attended by a KETTLEDRUM, so the Resident felt that he was justified in having similar honors (Fisher 1990: 432).

Sound and Number Combine in Gun Salutes

For some centuries, ships and land batteries have fired CANNONS to salute each other, and especially to salute the arrival and the departure of high-ranking officers, dignitaries, and rulers. Dutton (1893) sets out the required naval salutes, along with the NUMBER of side boys who line up to honor a person coming on board a vessel (see Table 9.1).

In India, the salute for the Queen-Emperor was 101 guns, for the Viceroy of India 31 guns, for rulers of sovereign Indian states 21 guns, for lesser states 19 guns, and so on down to the minimum salute for minor princes: 9 guns (Allen & Dwivedi 1984: 17). Batteries fired salutes on the occasion of a

Salute-State ruler's installation, birthday, departure or arrival, his departure to visit another state, and major state functions (Koiiman 2006: 307). Below the 118 First Division Salute States were 117 Second Division Non-Salute States that were not entitled to any honorific gun salute (Koiiman 2006). Among Indian princes under British rule, "the prime arena for status rivalry was the salute table established by the paramount power," and, indeed, "gun salutes soon became the principal determinant of precedence" (Koiiman 2006: 303, 305; see also Allen & Dwivedi 1984: 211); "It became a matter of great prestige as to whether a ruler had one gun more than another" (Allen & Dwivedi 1984: 86, quoting the Maharao of Kutch).

European gun salutes combined with other acoustic conformations of status. When Philip II approached Seville in 1570, he was announced by drums and trumpets, then "a massive ARTILLERY AND HARQUEBUSES DISCHARGE filled the air with noise," and, as he reached the arches built for the event, sixty-two cannons saluted him (Ruiz 2009: 44).

People have used acoustic conformations of authority ranking for millennia. Beginning more than 3,000 years ago, both before and after Indian cultural influences affected the region, southeast Asian DRUMS seem to have been essential in the regalia of chiefs: to be legitimized as chief, it appears, one had to possess certain bronze drums (Pirazzoli-T'Serstevens 1979, Loofs-Wissowa 1991). Bronze drums appear in South China beginning in the late eighth century BCE; many of the designs on the tympanum (head) of these include a prominent sun motif, linking their deep, LOUD SOUND to brilliant LUMINOSITY (Shih 1990). In 43 CE, the Chinese general who put down a rebellion in northern Vietnam reified Chinese rulership over the region by confiscating and destroying the bronze drums of the local chiefs. In later centuries, the Chinese claimed to have invented bronze drums, and Chinese emperors were said to have bestowed such drums on local chiefs, thereby conferring local political authority (Pirazzoli-T'Serstevens 1979).

Oracle bone and bronze vessel inscriptions indicate that during the Shang and Western Zhou period (1046–771 BCE) in the Emperor's ritual Mingtang temple, it was customary to beat HUGE THUNDEROUS DRUMS (*lei-gu*, later *feng*) in rituals addressed to heavenly deities and the spirits of royal ancestors, inviting them to come down to the Mingtang (Hwang 1996: 285–318). During the Western Zhou (1122–771 BCE) and Eastern Zhou dynasties (770–249 BCE) "BELLS became status-defining objects" and were important tomb accoutrements (Price 1983: 4, Rossing 2000: 165–166). "Within the highest echelons of society . . . bell-chimes played a tremendously important role in defining and iteratively reaffirming relationships of power" (von Falkenhausen 1993: 32). When the king bestowed a fief on a prince or noble, he bestowed a bell set too, conforming their authority. Several thousand ancient bronze bells have been found in various Bronze Age sites around China, mostly from tombs, and always limited to elites (Price 1983: 4; von Falkenhausen 1993: 18, 25). Bells up to 1,000 KILOGRAMS rang in Chinese Confucian, Shinto, and Buddhist temple worship, from there diffusing into the practices of local religions by the Ming period (Price 1983, 2004, Rossing 2000).

These bell practices culturally diffused to Japan along with Buddhism in the late sixth century, and are still used, sometimes along with large drums. Heavy *shō* bells are said to be the voice of Buddha, and the still larger *bonshō* drums are perceived to be the actual essence of Buddha (Rossing 2000: 179, Price 2004). Furthermore, "as [a bell] vocalized, it reflected glory on its patron, the bellfounder, and the temple where it hung" (Price 2004: 51). Chinese, Korean, and Japanese rulers pushed the technology to build ever LARGER bells: late in the seventh-century ones of 115 and 130 centimeter diameter in Japan; then in 711 one of 20 metric TONS for the Chinese Emperor in Nanking; followed by one of 277 centimeter diameter and 26 metric tons ordered by Emperor Shōmu of Japan, built in 732. Korean King Gyeongdeok commissioned a bell of 19 metric tons, 3.3 meters high, to honor his father, King Seongdeok (Lee 1998). At the beginning of the fourteenth century, Ming Emperor Yung Lo ordered that several bells be cast that were supposed to weigh at least twice as much as the Nanking bell; one of those that survives still hangs in the Temple of the Great Bell outside Beijing. It is about 5 meters TALL with an additional 2 meter suspension loop; it weighs about 50 metric tons (Price 1983: 13). The Bell of Good Luck in Foquan Temple, Pingdingshan, Hénán, China, weighs 116 METRIC TONS, and is 8.1 METERS HIGH (https://en.wikipedia.org/wiki/Bell_of_Good_Luck). In 1484, King Dhammazedi of Hanthawaddy Pegu had a bell cast for the Shwedagon Pagoda (Burma) that was said to have weighed 290 tons (https://en.wikipedia.org/wiki/Shwedagon_Pagoda).

Casting such bells was a huge technological feat; another impressive feat was devising techniques for raising and hanging them in structures that withstood the swinging of their enormous weight. It is not clear whether rulers who commissioned these bells aimed to surpass their predecessors by the LOUDNESS of these bells, their MASS, their DIMENSIONS, or even their VOLUME. The aim of surpassing other rulers' bells is complicated by their each being so far from the others, it seems, that no one could directly compare their volume, and surely no one had any means of weighing them.

However, it does appear that the commissioning rulers intended one or more of these dimensions to conform their supremacy. In so doing, presumably the rulers pushed the bronze-casters, engineers, and architects to constantly advance their technologies. It would be worth researching whether, how, how quickly, and at what distances others learned and adopted the advancing technologies developed for casting ever more gigantic bells. The crucial question for conformation systems theory is the conformational efficacy of louder and larger bells to augment allegiance to the ruler. How much greater was the commitment to the ruler, or the perception of his legitimacy, for every additional decibel, kilogram, or centimeter? Or, whatever the ruler believed, was there any actual increase in conformational efficacy of bigger bells? Whatever the level of initial conformational efficacy of a bell of a given magnitude, did efficacy decline with successive ringing – say, every time the ruler left or returned to the palace? Or was the efficacy constant across many iterations?

Let us compare this with the history of bell-casting in one place – Moscow – by one dynasty – the Tsars. The details provide a neat illustration of the cultural evolution of social practices in the niche consisting of the iconic magnitude conformation of authority ranking : the metallurgical, engineering, and architectural developments that generation after generation of Russian tsars pushed to ever-farther limits. It is reasonable to suppose that each tsar in turn was emotionally affected by the MASS, SIZE, and SOUND of his predecessor's bell, in comparison with the MASS, SIZE, and SOUND he himself hoped to assert. Each in turn was motivated to top his predecessors' sonic and mass conformations of their superiority, thereby legitimating his superiority in rank. Each tsar in turn felt it was his moral right to make louder sounds with bells of greater mass. Each felt that the louder the sound, the more emotionally overwhelmed and overawed his subjects would feel; each tsar judged that the louder the bell's sound, the more moral respect his subjects would feel, and the greater would be their commitment to his rule.

This required advances in foundry technology; the casting of each successively greater bell pushed (and sometimes exceeded) the limits of existing casting technology. And the giant bells were extremely expensive to create. The raising, hanging, and support of massive loud bells imposed huge engineering challenges, which were surmounted – if they were surmounted – only because of the enormous wealth and political impetus expended on them. The motion of ever-greater bells ringing threatened the integrity of the ever stronger towers in which they were placed, requiring advances in architecture. When Boris Godunov became Tsar in 1598, he solidified his tenuous claim to legitimacy, and asserted his son's right to succession, by adding two segments to raise the Kremlin's Bono tower ABOVE the palaces and churches built by his predecessors (Williams 1985). He had the tower topped by a SHINING GOLDEN cupola and cross. Moreover, he had two great bells cast. The one which hung in the Kremlin weighed around 74,000–80,000 POUNDS, larger than any bell previously cast in Russia. To ring it, TWENTY-FOUR MEN pulled the ropes attached to the clapper. The Godunov bell was later destroyed by a fire, after which Tsar Alexis Mikhailovich ordered its remnants to be combined with additional metal to cast a bell of 289,000 pounds. However, this bell later broke while being rung, so in 1655 Tsar Alexsis had a bell cast that weighed somewhere around 361,000 pounds, perhaps more; it was around 19 feet in diameter, and required about 50 men to ring it (Williams 1985). It was so loud that before it rang for state and church rites, Muscovites had to be warned to remove crockery and glassware from their shelves. A 1701 fire sent it crashing to the ground, smashing it.

When Anna Ivanova was crowed Empress in 1730, she ordered an even larger bell to be cast. After a failed attempt, the world's largest bell was cast in 1735, weighing about 433,000 POUNDS; it was 19 FEET HIGH and 19 FEET IN DIAMETER (Williams 1985). The sides of the bell bore engravings of Empress Anna and Tsar Alexsis, beneath cartouches showing Jesus, Saint Peter, John the Baptist, and Saint Anne. However, before it could be raised and hung, it was cracked by water used to extinguish a fire that ignited the shed over the casting pit.

Along with the MASS of the Kremlin's imposing architecture, the booming of these bells were "aural acclimations of the city's new leadership in the Orthodox East. At the same time, they were symbols of the burgeoning political power and territorial aspirations of the rulers of Muscovy" (Williams 1985: 173). "Awesome and earth-shaking utterances from these enormous instruments were calculated to stun the foreign visitor and to convey an aural impression of the presence and power of the august ruler in whose residence they hung" (Williams 1985: 174). The largest of these bells rang at a pitch approaching the lower limits of human hearing; perhaps this low pitch contributed to their conformational effects. These giant bells made the ground tremble. And there you have the cultural evolution of the Russian practice of sonically and massively conforming tsars' authority. It was a sound strategy.

Vietnamese and other Buddhist temple worship now employs several distinct kinds of PERCUSSION INSTRUMENTS: large drum, small drum, gong, large bell, small bell, bowl bell, hand bell, bronze or stone plaque, and wooden plaque, together with blowing a pair of conchs called *pháp loa*, "the voice of Buddha's teaching" (Nguyễn 2008). Similar devices and practices are found in Borneo up to the present day (Matusky 2008: 409).

Processions of the Caliphs of tenth- to twelfth-century Fatimid Egypt included mounted TRUMPETERS blowing ten GOLD trumpets and thirty SILVER trumpets, along with an UNCOUNTED NUMBER of trumpeters on foot blowing brass trumpets (Gourlay 1982: 50). The iconic conformation of early medieval Islamic rulers included "the blowing of horns and trumpets, the beating of drums," a THRONE, and the enlargement of the PERSONAL SPACE (enclosures set aside for his prayer, tents, and, later, palaces) which separated the ruler from those not privileged to approach him (Hambly 2001: 194).

At ancient Dodona in northwest Greece, a GONG that was continuously beaten, perhaps by a wind-driven mechanism, was a central element in in oracular practices or the worship of the mother goddess Dione, and later Zeus (Cook 1902). Similarly, worshippers beat bronze gongs/cymbals and drums to invoke Demeter, and they applied the epithet "NOISY" to her (Cook 1902: 15). CYMBALS were also associated with her daughter Persephone/Kore, and cymbals were important in the Mycenaean and Greek Eleusinian Mysteries dedicated to Demeter and Persephone. Worshippers of the Phrygian (central Anatolia) Cybele and her consort Attis beat drums, CLASHED SHIELDS, rang bells, and SHOUTED. Likewise, the attendants of Dionysus beat kettledrums edged with bells, or clashed cymbals (Cook 1902: 17). At least some Roman temples, including ones dedicated to Jupiter, held multiple large bells or gongs. Medieval Venetians used similar acoustic conformations for the Doge (Kurtzman & Koladau 2002: 11.3, Muir 1981: 121, 281).

Long royal trumpets and drums were insignia of the founding ruler of the Nupe Kingdom (Nigeria), and of the Sultan of Karnak (Cameron 1876: 55). Long trumpets and drums, some described as kettledrums, were insignia of office in Yoruba and Hausa states, in the eastern Nigeria state of Ilorin, and in north Nigerian states (Gourlay 1982: 59, 67). British explorers of the early nineteenth century described trumpets of 10–14 FEET LONG, blown by mounted trumpeters accompanying Bornu, Mandara, and Sokoto (Nigeria) rulers; such trumpets were restricted to royalty (Gourlay 1982: 53, 63). In Sokoto, this mounted escort consisted of 150 DRUMMERS AND TRUMPETERS.

Nigerian royal trumpets, like the drums, often played praise epithets, recognizable by their tones, stress, duration, and phrasing. For example, they would blow three times *cika sarari*, "he has FILLED SPACE" (Gourlay

1982: 63). Big bells were prominent in the conformations of the kings of the Bushong (Kuba, West Kasai, Democratic Republic of the Congo; Vansina 1994: 20). Flanged FORGED clapperless iron BELLS 15–80 centimeters tall and 10–20 centimeters wide are emblems of chieftainship or the leadership of a senior clan in many communities over the very wide Bantu cultural region of Central and West Africa (Vansina 1969). The tones of the double bells seem to have been used like African tonal drums to sound the praise proverbs honoring political leaders (Vansina 1969).

Among the Ankole, Baganda, Ashanti, Akwapim, Igbo, Barotse, and Hausa, some Sudanese cultures, and many other African societies, the deep, loud sounds of DRUMS were important in royal courts. In various cultures of Zimbabwe, royal drums beat the praises of kings, preceded them in processions, and were pivotal to royal succession (von Sicard 1942). Indeed, over a vast region of Central and West Africa, drums, along with leopards or lions, the sun, and the anvil, have been the emblems of chieftainship (Vansina 1989: 341, 358). Yoruba worship, honor, please, and communicate with their *Òrìsà* ancestor deity by beating a variety of drums, as do a number of other African societies (Adegbite 1988). Each *Òrìsà* has its own drum ensemble, which beats out the tones and stresses of praise proverbs, just as each Yoruba chief has a drum ensemble that does the same (Lindon 1990).

The organs of Byzantine Constantinople (probably descendants of late imperial Roman organs) played at imperial coronations, processions, state arrivals, palace ceremonies, diplomatic receptions and banquets, imperial weddings, and when the emperor appeared at the politically framed horse races in the Hippodrome (Williams 1993: 146–147). Constantine VI (reigned 780–797) travelled with his organ; a half century later Theophilos himself built two organs of bejeweled gold.

Europe

In Europe, the technologies of noise-making were different, but their conformational functions the same. Driven by water or men working bellows, multipipe WIND ORGANS were important conformations of Byzantine and Carolingian emperorship beginning in the eighth century, and may have been sounded to acclaim Roman emperors in earlier centuries (Williams 1993: 15, 71, in many passages citing Schuberth 1968). Byzantine organs "were an integral element of imperial pomp; in certain respects their clamors symbolize majesty and power" (Perrot 1965: 21). Such organs were capable of playing extremely low notes, and playing very

LOUDLY – louder than any other artificial sound except, perhaps, great bells. (For more on this, see Perrot 1965: 271–276; Williams 1993: 81, 137–142). From the Renaissance through the present day in Western culture, it has often been said that the organ is "the king of instruments" (e.g., Perrot 1965: 369) and "the voice of god" (Menuhin 1984: 7, Yearsley 2002: 84. Sometimes it is specifically the lowest-pitched rank of pipes that receives this latter epithet.

In medieval Europe, carrying a HORN was the exclusive privilege of kings, princes, nobles, and knights (Bowles 1958). Elite men wore the horn constantly, and their horns, like their swords, often had proper names. In addition, along with DRUMMERS with drums that were often enormous, TRUMPETERS SOUNDED FANFARES to announce an elite person's arrival at a town, their meals, and their decrees. Trumpets, along with drums, marked "power, command, lay and military authority," "the felicity of duty accomplished and the glory of power," "the state, power, and domination" (Cartier 1984: 161; my translation; see also p. 168). In 1529, when the emperor Charles V made peace with Pope Clement VII in Bologna, their joint arrival at the piazza was marked with the blare of 2,000 TRUMPETS (Kertzer 1988: 77–78).

English monarchs displayed and legitimated royal authority by the NUMEROSITY OF THEIR RETINUE (sometimes 1,000 horsemen), together with the blasts of their trumpeters. In the procession, THE ORDER OF THE MARCH was magistrates first, "followed by the livery companies in an order reflecting the superiority of some crafts and the relative inferiority of others" (Smuts 1989: 72). The crowd received the royal procession "by making an enormous amount of noise. Especially during a monarch's first entry, spectators always cheered loudly, adding to the sound of artillery salutes and the pealing of the bells of London's 104 parish churches" (Smuts 1989: 74). When Queen Elizabeth II was crowned in 1953 with the glittering crown, clothed in golden cloth, sitting on a throne, the royal trumpeters sounded fanfares and the great guns at the Tower and at Hyde Park again fired salutes (*Sydney Morning Herald*, June 13, 1953, front page). Thus, in public ceremonies the conformation of British royalty was generated by the combined iconicity of MASS, NUMEROSITY, LOUDNESS, TEMPORAL PRIORITY, and POSITION IN FRONT.

In the US today, the Marine Band plays RUFFLES (ON DRUMS) AND FLOURISHES (ON TRUMPETS) for dignitaries at state ceremonies; regulations specify different NUMBERS OF RUFFLES AND FLOURISHES for different grades, titles, or offices, from a maximum of four sets for all those who receive seventeen-gun salutes, three for those entitled to fifteen-gun salutes, two for those who get thirteen guns, and one ruffle and flourish for those who rank only eleven guns (Wikipedia Ruffles and Flourishes). At John F. Kennedy's funeral, drums, trumpets, and cannon salutes conformed his greatness (Kertzer 1988: 59–61).

Indigenous Americas

The sounds of TRUMPETS, CONCH-SHELL AEROPHONES, AND DRUMS were essential in Aztec royal rituals and sacrifices to the gods, and two kinds of drums were themselves venerated as reified gods (Stevenson 1968: 90, 111–115). Aztec priests blew conch shells and wood or metal trumpets in religious rituals (Stevenson 1968: 73–79).

During the Classical period (ca. 200–900 CE), Mayan status rituals involved processions in which the beating of a tall *pax* drum and turtle shell drums, the blowing of conches and long trumpets, and the shaking of RATTLES conformed the supremacy of nobles, rulers, and gods (Sanchez 2007). The blare of trumpets and conches, together with the beat of drums and rattles, sounded for the proclamation of a royal heir (Miller 1986).

The Incas used trumpets, including long metal ones, and large conch shells. Conch shells were restricted to the nobility, and are found only in the graves of chiefs (Stevenson 1968: 266, 273). The royal trumpeter was the highest ranking of royal officers. Silver, bronze, and copper trumpets sounded, along with very large drums, in worship of Inca *huaca* deities (Stevenson 1968: 268–269). A particular LARGE DRUM, the *guiyyaya*, beat the rhythm of an important dance performed only by dancers of royal blood, while other drums beat at noble funerals (Stevenson 1968: 269–270). FOUR HUGE DRUMS, EACH BEATEN BY FOUR SENIOR CHIEFTAINS, sounded at the annual December solstice llama sacrifices. A widely attested Inca practice for conforming their supremacy and humiliating defeated enemies was to make drums from the enemies' skins, and then beat the drums with drumsticks made from their arm bones (Stevenson 1968: 271–272).

****

We do not know whether, in authority ranking, the conformational efficacy of sounds depends purely on the decibels, or also on duration, pitch, rhythm, or other factors. Does timbre (tone color) matter? Do drums have effects that differ from trumpets? Does a pipe organ playing in a cathedral where it reverberates have different conformational effects on worshippers' relationship with their god than an equally loud gong, struck in an open-sided pavilion?

Even if it were only decibel level that mattered, aspects of the conformational efficacy of sound are probably not linear functions of LOUDNESS. BUT what are the shapes of the efficacy functions? Likewise, what are the shapes of the functions mapping each of the other nine iconic dimensions onto their conformational effects? Well-designed experiments will give us answers, if we can develop valid, reliable measures of the representations, emotions, motives, and moral frameworks evoked by these conformations.

CHAPTER 10

The Dimensions and Magnitudes that Conform Authority Ranking

We need to keep in mind a defining aspect of the iconic dimensions discussed in this book: in conforming authority ranking, conformation systems theory posits that the dimensions are all used ordinally, simply conforming MORE than or LESS than. In other contexts, of course, people attend to interval differences between steps on some physical dimensions, and in still other contexts, on ratios of amounts. For example, in equality matching, imagine that some people have cast their votes, but not everyone, X has eight votes and Y has five. Now the last four voters arrive and all cast their votes for Y, giving Y a total of nine votes, thereby conforming Y's winning the election. Addition and subtraction of units or intervals are metrically meaningful in an interval scale, and socially meaningful in equality matching. In contrast, when conforming authority ranking, people do not perform addition or subtraction as such. Suppose Maharaja X is entitled to a nine-cannon salute by virtue of his rulership over one domain, and entitled to eleven cannons by virtue of his rulership over his other domain. He does not ever receive a twenty-cannon salute, just eleven. In short, physical dimensions and magnitudes can be employed for ratio measurement (e.g., this weighs 1/6 of the weight of that), or for interval measurement (e.g., your office is eight floors above his office). But in the conformation of authority ranking, dimensions and magnitudes are used ordinally, so that what is conformed is simply A > B, or else A < B, without clear, definite, or consistent representations of quantitative differences. There is common knowledge of the ordinal asymmetries of a linear ordering, but, the theory posits, little or no consensus beyond that, and low reliability of any individual's interval or ratio representations of differences in rank.

Do All Ten Dimensions Have the Same Conformational Effects?

Expanding on the five issues raised in Chapter 5, let us consider here a total of eleven issues that future research should explore with regard to the representational, emotional, motivational, and moral effects of the iconic dimensional conformations of authority ranking, and for each of the other three conformation systems.

The first concerns how iconic dimensional conformations operate with respect to the asymmetry of authority ranking. For example, the moral sentiments that a conformation evokes in a superior are distinct from and complementary to the moral sentiments evoked in a subordinate. But is there symmetry in the degree of the conformational impact of, say, the ABOVE–BELOW dimension? Did my prostrating to the chief affect my moral sentiments about our authority ranking relationship to the same degree that it affected the chief's moral sentiments? And exactly how would one measure the degree of the two distinct moral sentiments, in order to compare them?

Second, do some of the ten iconic dimensions generally have greater conformational effect than others? And do the relative conformational effects of each dimension depend on context or other moderators? Are the relative effects of any two dimensions the same across representations, emotions, motivations, and moral sentiments, or do conformations using some dimensions have more pronounced effect on, say, moral sentiments and commitment to authority ranking relationships, while conformations using other dimensions have more effect on, say, the memorability of representations of authority ranking relationships?

Third, consider the issue illustrated by this question: just how does the emotional impact of ringing a giant bell change as a function of the sound pressure of its ring? If one bell produces sound waves whose pressure is twice that of another bell, are listeners twice as impressed by it? Are listeners twice as motivated by it? If all aspects of the conformational efficacy of MASS are linear functions of the MASS, do all of the functions have the same slope and intercept? More generally, what are the mathematical functions connecting the physical properties of a conformation to each of the cognitive, affective, and moral responses to it? Are some of the mappings linear, while others are logarithmic or sigmoid ("S"-shaped)?

Following from that, how are the iconic conformational effects of the ten dimensions calibrated to each other? For example, does a doubling of MASS have the same social relational effects as the doubling of FORCE? And how do the representation, emotion, motivation, and moral mapping functions of different dimensions align? Does doubling mass increase the emotional effects to the same degree that it increases the representational, motivational, and moral effects? Or does each of these effects follow the shape of a different function?

Fifth, if a conformation is repeated, what effect does that have? For example, what is the effect on listeners' perception of the moral legitimacy of a tsar after his giant bell rings 8 times, compared to their perception of his moral legitimacy after the bell rings 80 times? What are the conformational effects of ringing 80 times today, 80 times next week, and 80 times the week after, compared to ringing 240 times today? And how do the effects of conformational events decay over time after a conformational experience? These are some of the principal parameters that learning theory addresses: Which findings of learning theory apply to conformation systems?

Sixth, how do different dimensions of conformations combine? For example, are the effects of ABOVE, together with the effects of IN-FRONT, additive, multiplicative, redundant, or what? For analytic and expository simplicity, so far as possible I have presented the iconic dimensions separately, one at a time. But in many iconic conformations of authority ranking, multiple dimensions vary together (e.g., HEIGHT, MASS, and SURFACE AREA), or people actively conjoin multiple dimensions. For example, young American men of some subcultures, regions, and social classes aspire to *lifted* pickup trucks raised ABOVE normal vehicles by modifying the suspension and fitting very LARGE tires. The ideal raised truck has a set of highly amplified speakers, including a powerful subwoofer; the driver plays this sound system very LOUDLY. Exhaust and tail pipe modifications often make these trucks' engines rumble deafeningly, and many of these trucks have extra driving LIGHTS. Ideally, such a vehicle should have a POWERFUL engine. The extreme vehicular conformation in this subculture is the *monster truck*; in exhibitions, it drives right over ordinary vehicles (placed there for the show), crushing them. What are the conformational effects of such combinations of iconic dimensions?

The seventh issue concerns felicity: the facilitating and inhibiting conditions for responsiveness to conformations. What developmental, cultural, motivational, and situational factors affect a person's disposition to respond to various conformations? When a conformation is unwanted, inappropriate, or illegitimate, its effect may be the opposite of the effect it has when it is wanted, appropriate, and legitimate (Fiske & Schubert 2012). So, a person who STANDS ON A PEDESTAL but has no right to claim high status may actually "lower" himself in the eyes of mocking observers. What sort of openness or desire make a kiss a welcome conformation of communal sharing, but in the absence of which, make being kissed disgusting? (We return to this issue in Chapter 16, in the section on Felicity.)

Eighth, when a massive pyramid shines brilliantly in the sun, how and when and why do the conformational effects it inspires transfer to its architects, to its construction supervisors, to the laborers, or to the king who directed its construction? If a person knows that the tsar commanded the casting and emplacement of a giant bell, and has now ordered that it ring, is that sufficient for the loud ringing to conform the tsar's supremacy? Or does the iconic conformational effect require an indexical co-occurrence of hearing the bell sound while seeing the tsar, or at least while having salient thoughts about him?

Ninth, in ontogeny, does sensitivity to all ten dimensions emerge simultaneously, or sequentially? Is that affected by aspects of the social environment of the neonate?

Tenth, in ontogeny, do representational, emotional, motivational, and moral sensitivity to a given dimension emerge simultaneously? If not, is their order of emergence the same for all ten dimensions?

Eleventh, what other social relational or nonsocial cognitive activities compete with responsivity to, and memory for, conformations using each of the ten dimensions psychologically? When one cognitive activity uses mental systems that another cognitive activity also uses, doing both simultaneously (or in close succession) results in more errors, and/or slower response times, and/or more memory errors in one or both activities. So, that effect is informative about whether the two activities both do use one or more of the same mental systems. Also informative is observing whether the same neurological lesions disrupt both or all of the neurocognitive processes. It will be illuminating to determine whether the same lesion tends to disrupt representational, and emotional, and motivational, and moral effects of iconic dimensional conformations. And/or whether lesions in a specific neurocognitive system disrupt one or all of those conformational effects, while also disrupting functioning in other social relational or nonsocial activities. Are there lesions that affect one of these conformational effects but not the others? What about autism? Likewise, is psychopathy correlated with diminution of emotional, motivational, and moral sensitivity to iconic dimensional conformations, but not correlated with diminished representational sensitivity?

We can ask very similar questions about each of the other three conformation systems. And these are interesting new questions that conformation systems theory raises, as a fruitful theory should.

Is It Mass that Matters?

Up to this point, I have been writing as if an observer could correctly identify the effective dimension of any iconic conformation of authority ranking. I believe that when directly observing in a well-known culture, usually one can make that inference with reasonable confidence – but not always. It seems to me that the greatest uncertainty concerns conformations that I have been identifying as based on "MASS." In the first place, by using the term "MASS" I do not mean to imply that people using that dimension as a conformation conceptualize or operationalize "MASS" in accord with Newtonian formulas for, say, momentum or kinetic energy. Nor do I posit that the users of MASS-based conformations think that, or act as if, MASS is conserved under all the transformations that physicists posit conservation. But I do think that, like mass in Newtonian physics, the authority ranking conformations based on MASS incorporate the sense that the greater the MASS, the more force is required to accelerate or decelerate it, and the more work (in the technical sense) is required to raise it a given distance. That is, on seeing a 5-ton stone block on rollers coming toward him on a horizontal surface, a monument builder would not expect to stop it with one hand. Nor would the builder worry about the wind blowing such a block across the desert. But if people conforming authority ranking are not Newtonian physicists, how do they construe the iconic magnitudes and dimensions?

Another issue is the standard problem of discerning causality based on observations of naturally occurring phenomena when two variables are correlated. MASS and VOLUME of monuments are highly correlated – so, are both magnitudes of monuments conforming authority ranking, or, if not, which one is? Additionally, MASS of monuments, palaces, temples, and the like is correlated with ELEVATION ABOVE and with SURFACE AREA. Without data from controlled experiments, we cannot determine the relative degree to which the conformational efficacy of a given sort of monument is a function of its MASS, its VOLUME, its ELEVATION, its SURFACE AREA, or some combination of these magnitudes and dimensions.

A further uncertainty concerns entanglements that occur with most dimensions. Consider the example of the HEIGHT of monuments. Do the conformational effects of HEIGHT depend on:

The difference between the elevation of the top of the monument and the elevation of the surface on which it is built (that is, the height of the monument itself)?

The difference between the elevation of the top of the monument and the elevation of the eyes of the observer, who could be in a valley below the surface on which the monument stands, or could be on a hill above the surface on which the monument stands?

In the eye of the viewer, the angle above level of the monument's peak (or its center), which depends on how close to the monument the viewer is?

The vertical angle and/or the horizontal angle visually subtended by the monument, which also depend on how close to the monument the viewer is? (The visual angles subtended by a monument are also likely to affect how massive it seems, and its apparent surface.)

There are virtually the same confounds among these four parameters when an observer perceives the tallness of persons; perceives the height of headdresses; perceives the voluminousness of gowns; and perceives postures of respect. For example, consider the feeling of respect conveyed by bowing. Is it a function of the absolute differences in the elevation of the heads of the person bowing and the person receiving the bow? Or is it a function of, say, the angle, in the monarch's perception, between a horizontal plane and the head of the bowing person? Or, more probably, of perceptions of the angle of the person's back relative to vertical? We will need experiments to find out.

I hazard a guess that while MASS is the principal conformational magnitude of a solid such as a solid mound, pyramid, ziggurat, or megalith, VOLUME is the principal conformational magnitude of a palace, temple, cathedral, or mosque that is "hollow" (perceived or known to consist of one or more vast chambers). Moreover, I imagine that when a person is inside a palace, cathedral, or vast mosque, VOLUME is the principal conformation, and HEIGHT of the ceiling also has effects, while MASS does not operate at all.

It is also plausible to suppose that part of the conformational efficacy of a monument may result from its perceived age, and/or its TEMPORAL DURATION into the future – its permanence.

If it is purely the relative VOLUMES or relative SURFACE AREAS of monuments that matter, conformationally, then tents of the same dimensions should work as well as stone monuments or earthen platforms. But surely they don't. Or suppose people are gazing at a 30-meter tall statue of the ruler, evidently carved from a single block of stone. Suddenly they see that the statue is actually a balloon. I imagine that the conformational efficacy of the sculpture would be greatly diminished, or even reversed. That is, I imagine that people would be more likely to mock, to resist, or to overthrow the ruler whose statue was a balloon, compared to the ruler whose statue was a granite monolith.

For further consideration of some of these and related issues, I refer the reader to an article by Thomas Schubert, Sven Waldzus, and Beate Seibt

(2011), along with Schubert (2019), in which they elegantly compare and illuminate various theories of the cognitive and experiential processes that may be involved in the conformation of authority ranking by the iconic physics of magnitudes and dimensions.

Finally, I should straighten out a potential muddle: iconic dimensions conform ranks: that is, ordinal positions in an authority ranking relationship. But in principle, the efficacy – the impact – of a conformation or set of conformations surely can be measured on a ratio scale, or any other scale. That is, we could sensibly try to develop ratio measures of the degree to which specific conformations evoke the emotions that support authority ranking, or come up with ratio measures of the degree to which specific conformations elicit the relationship-supporting motives, as well as ratio measures of the intensity of moral devotion and commitment to the authority ranking. It should be possible to develop ratio measures of specific conformations' impact on the certainty and stability of people's cognitive representations of the ranks of persons in authority ranking relations. That is, one could measure the Bayes factor or, in an information theory framework, the reduction of uncertainty about the relationship. For example, imagine that a prince, the second oldest child of the king, builds a palace in the heights above town, but at a lower topographic elevation than the palace of his older brother, the crown prince, the eldest child of the king, and of course at a lower elevation than the palace of the king himself. Ideally, we could use any kind of scale, including a ratio scale, to measure how much the relative elevation of the prince's palace increased others' confidence that he is, indeed, the third-highest ranked person in the kingdom. Likewise, in principle we could devise valid scales of any type to measure how much the relative elevation of the prince's palace emotionally awed the population. And in principle we could devise, say, a ratio scale of the average increase in peoples' motivation to respect the prince, loyally follow him, and defer to his will.

My point is that the prince would be solidly legitimated and secure in his position if, in response to his new palace, everyone was at the maximum on all four of these scales measuring aspects of the efficacy of the relative topographic elevation of the prince's palace. But even if everyone was at the maximum on all four of these factors, measured on ratio scales, that would not conform the prince as number two in the kingdom, nor conform him as number one, the king.

The same concept applies to consubstantial assimilation's effects on communal sharing. The concept likewise applies to the effects of concrete operations of one-to-one correspondence. For example, in a distribution, no degree of certainty about the relationship, no degree of impact on the social relational affects and sentiments, could make the distribution even (fair, balanced) if it was patently uneven.

Again, suppose a given symbolic conformation of market pricing leaves no ambiguity about the terms of the relationship. Consider a detailed signed contract, for example. Suppose, too, that the symbolism is maximally evocative of the motives and emotions crucial to the relationship, and suppose also that the symbolism maximally invokes participants' moral commitments to the relationship. None of that changes the ratio that participants use to coordinate their interactions.

It may be very difficult to develop reliable and valid measures of the four effects of a conformation, and especially hard to come up with measures that are demonstrably divergent (do not all measure the same thing). I do not mean to imply otherwise, nor do I mean to imply that scales of the effects of conformations need to be ratio scales. For many social science purposes, interval ordinal, or even nominal scales may suffice.

Before investing the wealth of the kingdom in gold garb, a palace or pyramid, the king and his councilors surely weigh their estimated cost against some sort of estimate of their efficacy. Evaluating the king's plans, the treasurer may estimate that a pyramid of half the mass would have 9/10 the conformational effect. The queen may argue that a temple costing ¼ as much as the proposed pyramid will be twice as effective. Even if no one explicitly raises issues about the costs and benefits, or no one even consciously formulates in their head the ratios of costs to benefits, the decision makers may do so implicitly, as a pigeon apportions its foraging time between two locations in proportion to the rate that it finds food in the respective locations. That is, behavioral researchers long ago showed that all sorts of animals readily compute the ratio of two rates, and act accordingly – presumably without consciously cognizing their computations. We need to do the research that will reveal whether or not elites engage in implicit or in explicit ratio cognition about the relative efficacy of individual conformations, or even, using the distributive law, combinations of different conformations. "Your highness, it would be cost-effective to super highly polish the marble facing of the pyramid, and have people gather where the sunlight will be reflected on them, while 1,000 drummers beat the great kettle drums."

It will be extremely illuminating if researchers are able to develop conformation measures with solid external validity, or, better yet, measures that work in naturally occurring social relations. Measuring the impact of different conformations on representations, emotions, motives, and moral sentiments will have myriad practical, clinical, and conceptual benefits. Can we devise such measures?

Box 10.1

Lest there by any doubt, let me note once again that while conformations create and modulate social relationships, typically, most everyday engagement in a relationship is not conformation, it is just relating. For example, students doing assignments that their teacher has told them to do are carrying out their relationship, but not conforming it. The teacher is carrying out the responsibilities of their authority ranking relationships with students when instructing them, answering questions, and grading assignments. But none of that conforms the authority ranking. Standing in front of the class, and students waiting for the teacher to speak first at the beginning of class, conforms the teacher's authority.

Unused Dimensions and Differential Prevalence of Dimensions

There are dimensions that seem logically capable of iconically conforming rank, but that are much less frequently employed, and generally less salient even when they are used. In an influential essay, Hertz (1909) used his reading of early ethnographic evidence from the Māori as the anchor for his comparative study of collective representations of the contrasting social values attributed to the left and right hands. Hertz examines this as a purely dichotomous contrast, not as a continuous dimension, but it is nonetheless intriguing that he concludes that there is a universal dualistic opposition:

> To the right hand go honours, flattering designations, prerogatives: it acts, orders, and takes. The left hand, on the contrary, is despised and reduced to the role of a humble auxiliary: by itself it can do nothing; it helps, it supports, it holds. The right hand is the symbol and model of all aristocracy, the left hand of all common people. (Hertz 1909: 335)

Hertz goes on to write about the "nobility" of the right hand and the "servitude" of the left, with the right hand regarded as "sacred" and the left as "profane" and impure – an attitude that is "half esthetic, half moral" (p. 338).

But the ethnographic evidence accumulated since 1909 shows that there are relatively few societies in which LEFT–RIGHT conforms authority ranking. In most of Africa and much of the Arab world the left hand is unclean; one would not touch someone with the left hand, nor give or receive a gift with the left hand alone, and it is inconceivable to eat with the left hand, which is used to clean oneself after defecating. However, in many such African cultures, I have experienced that it is respectful and polite to use both hands together, especially in receiving a gift, with the left hand positioned so it appears to be supporting the right wrist. Indeed, doing so often expresses the greatest appreciation. In any case, in my experience over eight years in Africa, I never saw any indication that people perceived the right hand to be "sacred," whatever that means. More generally, in my view, social science does not support the once-popular thesis that much of religion and social life around the world is based on the sense of the sacred, in contrast with the profane.

Hertz wrote about the hands, not spatial hemispheres or directions per se. Yet for the past 200 years, in French, English, and other languages, the LEFT–RIGHT DIMENSION has been widely used to represent political attitudes, dichotomously or as a continuum (Oxford English Dictionary 2022: "left," "right wing"). And there are some cultures where people sometimes do use laterality to conform authority ranking, though there seem to be far fewer cultures where people do so, compared to the ubiquitous use of the other dimensions we have considered. In ancient Egyptian art from the Old Kingdom through the New, higher-ranking gods or persons were depicted on the figures' left side, facing right (Robins 1993). In the modern West, when according seats in European or American formal meals or meetings, the position of greatest honor is to the host's right, although the guest of honor may be seated to the right of the hostess if the guest of honor is a man and the hosts judge that it is proper that men and women alternate around the table. Among the Kaguru of Tanzania, the right versus left opposition is linked to upper hand versus lower hand, ahead versus behind, above versus below, first versus second, strong versus weak, mountain/hill versus valley, dominant versus passive, center-pole versus hearth, male versus female, and many other contrasts (Beidelman 1973). For other instances of LEFT–RIGHT conformations of status, see Needham 1973, Tuan 1977, and Roodenburg 1991.

Another kind of dimension whose conformational use is comparatively infrequent consists of polar coordinates defined by compass directions, by points of intersection of the ecliptic with the horizon (i.e., where the sun rises), or by other absolute frames of reference such as "toward the sea" or "up slope." In some languages, such absolute frames of reference are the predominate locatives (indications of where things are), with corresponding salience in everyday cognition; for a wonderful analysis of absolute and other frames of reference, see Levinson 2003. Many early monuments were built to align with absolute directions, and hence, it is inferred, worship or other rituals were so oriented. Yet there seem to be comparatively few cultures where people commonly or saliently conform social rank itself on absolute dimensions. The only place where I know that this occurs is Bali, where "the superior person should sleep to the east or inland of the inferior, and his head should be inland or east of his [own] feet; for this system of orientation is a part of the code of respect as well as a frame of interpersonal reference" (Bateson & Mead 1942: 6; see also 75). Likewise, the Balinese village temple is in the inland-east quadrant of the village and the family shrines are on the inland or eastern side of the house yard.

I have not seen conformations based on dimensions derived from combinations of other dimensions or magnitudes, such as density (mass divided by volume), acceleration (change in velocity divided by time), momentum (mass times velocity), frequency (number of occurrences divided by time), or wavelength (distance between cycle peaks). It is conceivable that these are absent or rare simply because they are, in in one way or another, difficult to implement in conformations.

Temperature is rarely, if ever, used in authority ranking conformation. Yet in some cultures temperature is a salient dimension of illness, and of foods, metaphorically (regardless of the physical temperature of the substance in a given instance).

I imagine that we would learn a lot about conformation systems if we figured out why conformations constantly polarize dimensions in the same relation to social rank: On any dimension, MORE always conforms "higher" rank, never "lower" rank. Full explanations will have to integrate phylogeny, adaptation by natural selection, behavioral ecology, life history, ontogeny, perception, memory and motivation systems, the functions of emotions, the organization of brains, neurochemistry, cultural transmission and cultural selection, social systems, and more.

As we considered in Chapter 7, to reach an emperor, everyone may have to cross multiple VAST courtyards, separated by HIGH archways that one must pass under, going through MASSIVE gates, and traverse a LONG avenue lined with MASSIVE statues of POWERFUL beasts, then ASCEND many steps, and WAIT for attendants to open HIGH, MASSIVE doors. I described this as an extreme SURFACE AREA conformation, in conjunction with the other indicated dimensions, and noted that less imposing versions of this can be called PERSONAL SPACE conformations. This is PERSONAL SPACE because, while the subordinate hoping to approach the superior must cross spaces and pass barriers, in principle, and in some systems in practice, the superior is free to approach a subordinate without overcoming any of these obstacles. Whatever we call this dimension, it does involve DISTANCE, including the entitlement of the superior, whenever they wish, to keep subordinates at a DISTANCE. For a parochial, small-scale instance of this DISTANCE and PERSONAL SPACE ASYMMETRY conformation, imagine a student making an impromptu attempt to see the president of the university, in contrast to the president making an impromptu visit to a student.

In a completely different way, DISTANCE also conforms communal sharing, both in bodily proximity and in speech. Generally, the stronger the communal sharing relationship, the closer either person can position themself to the other(s), the closer they both (or all) wish their bodies to be, and the socially closer they want to be, in felicitous circumstances. Likewise, English speakers say, for example, "We're very close" or "He's acting very distant lately," and one speaks of "close" kin and "distant" relatives. English speakers, at least, can apply this distance conformation to abstract visualizations of varying degrees of social relational "closeness," rating a relationship on a scale consisting of pairs of circles at varying distances apart, from well-separated at one end to increasing overlap at the other end of the scale (Aaron et al. 1992).

I have not investigated how widespread this DISTANCE conformation of communal sharing is, but it seems to be an expression of the communal sharing motivation to be in close proximity with the other(s) to whom one is relating, and of course, is intrinsic to conformations based on consubstantial assimilation. Kisses, caresses, and cuddles require zero distance between bodies. This association between "affection" and physical proximity is virtually universal across nonhuman animals that engage in parental care, as well as nonhuman animals that sleep in contact with each other to say warm. Human motivation to be in physical proximity to persons with whom one engages in communal sharing is doubtless homologous to this system in other vertebrates.

CHAPTER 11

Iconic Metaconformations in Language

What Language Has to Say

People use language to do all sorts of things. In particular, people represent social relationships linguistically: "The professor gave the student a good grade"; "For them, the team always comes first" (on the language of "vertical relationships," see Wetzel 1993). People may use a role term to invoke the ideal representation of the role, along with the emotions, motives, and moral standards of the role. "You're the leader" refers to a role, and, by that reference, prods "the leader" to make a decision, by invoking the moral responsibilities and motives of authority ranking. People also use language explicitly to create, modulate, or terminate social relationships (Austin 1961, 1962, Searle 1989). The appropriate religious or civil authority saying "I hereby declare you man and wife" makes the couple married. On the battlefield, the commanding general saying "I'm promoting you to lieutenant" makes the addressee a lieutenant on the spot. "I accept your offer" constitutes a commitment by the speaker to sell to the target of the utterance, at the specified price. "You take the first turn" creates equality matching between the speaker and target.

Many utterances, as well as some texts, have the surface form of a representation, but use that representation to modulate a relationship. "We saw a lot of Monterey Pines." That sentence represents. At the same time, that sentence could also be intended as a display of arboreal knowledge, to imply that the speaker is smart or well informed. "There was a tree across the road; we had to take a detour" refers and represents, in order to explain and justify the speaker's late arrival. I say "This is my brilliant, distinguished little sister" to refer to her in a way that honors her, while teasing a little. People say or write statements such as "She ranks higher than Mvula," "The two of them are blood kin," or "That makes things even between us."

If any social relationship can be, and often is, linguistically denoted and, moreover, any social relationship can be conformed symbolically in language, just what is special about, for example, iconic dimensional conformations of authority ranking? Likewise, what does it mean to posit that consubstantial assimilation is the primary, natural, universal, and prevalent conformation of communal sharing, given the fact that, using symbols, a person can say or write "I love you" and that utterance generally has a conformational effect? A person can draw a heart in the sand, or put a heart in a text message. Such symbols can affect emotions, motives, moral sentiments, and representations of a communal sharing relationship between the sender and the recipient, so they can function as conformations.

There are two different issues here. First, as discussed in Chapter 10, language is capable of metarepresentation, and people often employ language for metarepresentation. In particular, innumerable linguistic symbols are symbolic metarepresentations of a primary conformation of consubstantial assimilation, iconic dimensions, or concrete operations of one-to-one correspondence. To say that a person "ranks higher' is to use linguistic symbolism to metarepresent a primary iconic dimensional conformation of authority ranking. To say "blood kin" is to use symbolism to metarepresent a primary indexical conformation of communal sharing. A sculpture such as Rodin's *The Kiss* is an iconic metarepresentation of the indexical consubstantial assimilation of communal sharing. In these last two cases it is clear that indexical consubstantial assimilation is the primary mode of representation of the social relationship, while symbolism and iconicity are metarepresentations of that. Likewise, linguistic symbols such as "make things even," "level playing field," and "one-person, one-vote" metarepresent concrete operations conforming equality matching.

Second, linguistic symbolism alone can directly conform communal sharing, authority ranking, and equality matching, but tends to conform them less effectively than their proper conformations. Rowing an eight-oared shell in perfect synchrony has greater conformational effect on the communal sharing among the rowers than saying "Wow! What a team we are!" Prostrating in the dirt in front of the chief affected my emotions, motives, and moral sentiments much more than using plural pronouns to address him, and more than my saying *A yiida mam*, "he exceeds me." Taking turns standing guard conforms the players' equality matching more effectively than simply saying "We're equal here."

Linguistic conformations of communal sharing do vary in their efficacy. Consubstantial assimilation conformations vary in their efficacy, too, but the mean and modal efficacies of consubstantial assimilation conformations are considerably greater than the mean and modal efficacies of linguistic conformations. Likewise, conforming equality matching with concrete operations of one-to-one correspondence has far greater mean and modal efficacies than linguistic conformations of equality matching. Similarly, most iconic dimensional conformations of authority ranking are more effective than most linguistic conformations of authority ranking.

People often combine linguistic conformations of a relational model with the relational model's proper nonlinguistic conformation. A person kisses someone, and then says "I love you." A person whose coffee was intentionally knocked into his lap may do the same thing back, tit-for-tat, and then say "Now we're even."

Language Is Symbolic in Some Respects, But Not Others

It is an established truism that language is phonetically and lexically symbolic, not only in the general sense that language carries meaning, but in the much narrower, precise Peircean sense: a word is purely arbitrary, determined entirely by the way that people in a particular speech community use the word, and common knowledge of that convention. One speech community uses *baga*, another uses *chien*, another uses *dog*, and so on – people in a speech community could equally well use any word that they can readily pronounce and listeners can reliably distinguish. There is nothing doggish about dog, nothing chien-ish about chien, nothing baga-ish about baga. Any word is just as good as any other, because there is no connection between the animal and the sound, other than people's use of the sound to refer to that animal, together with common knowledge of that usage. The only widely mentioned exception to the arbitrariness of words is onomatopoeia, such as *bow-wow*, *screech*, and *splash* (although the words for these sounds do vary appreciably across languages). Another exception to the arbitrary symbolism of lexemes are the short, informal words for mother and father, such as *ma* and *pa*, that are rather similar across language families. Apparently these or similar phonemes repeatedly arise in language after language because these are among the easiest phonemes for infants to utter intelligibly. So perhaps they are typically among the earliest infant utterances that caretakers "recognize," and therefore, one imagines, are among the first "words" that caretakers use when speaking to infants.

However, there is a huge exception to the general principle of lexical arbitrariness, at least in the few languages I have investigated. For authority ranking, not just any word will do. We considered the fact that in Mooré, virtually all of the words concerning authority ranking have something in common: their nonsocial and likely original meaning refers to dimensions. As we shall see in this chapter, the same is true in English, in Proto-Indo-European, and in ancient Chinese. To talk about authority ranking, speakers of all four languages rely on words whose original and often current nonsocial-relational meaning concerns dimensions or magnitudes. Indeed, in English and in Mooré, at least, it is hard to find words denoting authority ranking relations that do not also have a dimensional or magnitude meaning, or that are not derived from such words.

Why? The only plausible explanation is that in Mooré, English, Proto-Indo-European, and Chinese, at least, authority ranking words culturally evolved in the niche formed by the biologically evolved adaptation consisting of the psychosocial proclivity to use, understand, remember, and affectively and morally respond to iconic dimensional conformation. Evidently, in these languages, at least, when a coined or borrowed word for a manifestation of authority ranking also iconically referred to a dimension, people readily "got" it – it made sense, intuitively. It was easily stored in memory and retrieved. Furthermore, it was readily used to compute authority ranking relationships, for example, in figuring out unknown ranks based on transitivity. A word compatible with the iconic dimensions niche tended to intuitively lend itself to conforming authority ranking, at least weakly. Also, words that fit the iconic dimensions niche made it a little easier to report, gossip about, and keep track of other people's authority ranking relationships. When a coined or borrowed word for an aspect of authority ranking did not iconically refer to a dimension, it did not intuitively make sense, it obfuscated the representation of the relationship, it required transducing in order to use in cognitive computations, it was harder to store in memory and harder to retrieve, it was more often misremembered, and it did not lend itself to affectively and morally conforming authority ranking. So, using a word incompatible with the niche made it a bit harder to make the speaker's and listener's authority ranking relations work. And it made it a bit harder to monitor other people's authority ranking relationships and gossip about them. People often speak in or about authority ranking relationships; those relationships and that speech are often important to people. So, before long, words that are more niche-compatible replace words that are less niche-compatible.

Other than this cultural-evolutionary process, what else could account for the overwhelming prevalence of iconic dimensional words for every aspect of every sort of authority ranking, in multiple, unrelated, widely separated language families?

In English, at least, there are some words that once referred both to a physical dimension and to authority ranking, and that subsequently lost their strictly dimensional meaning, while retaining their authority ranking meaning. These cannot be maintained in the language as authority ranking words because of a dimensional meaning that speakers are no longer aware of, even implicitly. Once such words have lost their resonance with the iconic dimensional niche, will people gradually decrease their use of them, until the words become obsolete and disappear? Or, despite losing their iconicity, will such orphaned words continue to be maintained in their social relational uses purely by convention? The English word, *head*, used to conform authority ranking – as in *head of state*, *head waiter*, *head-up a committee* – resonates with the iconic dimensional conformation of authority ranking because a person's *head* is the top of their body. In contrast, *captain* originated and for many centuries iconically resonated with the dimensional conformation system in exactly the same way; in Latin and all the way back to Proto-Indo-European, *captain* referred to a person's head. Harper (2025) gives the etymology: "from Old French*capitaine* '*captain*, leader,' from Late Latin *capitaneus* 'chief,' noun use of adjective '*capitaneus*,' prominent, chief,' from Latin *caput* (genitive *capitis*) 'head' (from PIE root *kaput- 'head')." But for English speakers, this reference to the anatomical head has been lost, so English speakers say *captain* purely because of its conventional use and common knowledge of that usage.

In sum, words for conforming authority ranking are not arbitrary. Like other words, words conforming authority ranking are sustained by convention. But many such words are not sustained <u>only</u> by convention. They are sustained by their fit with the iconic dimensional niche for social practices that conform authority ranking. Furthermore, the invention and borrowing of authority ranking words, and their initial reception, must be afforded by their resonance with the iconic dimensional niche. So, in those respects, authority ranking words are not just symbolic, they are metaconformations of iconic dimensional conformations. Simply that, in some languages, at least, iconicity is a significant aspect of a great many words conforming authority ranking. And to repeat: in English and in Mooré, nearly all words that conform authority ranking also represent physical dimensions, or, in English at least, formerly represented physical dimensions.

That said, what can be learned from a compendium of the words in some languages that refer to aspects of authority ranking relations? I see seven learning opportunities. First, sometimes language is the only evidence that a researcher has about a population. Or, language is the principal source, in conjunction with, say, a little archaeological evidence from sites that may or may not be associated with the speakers of the language. For example, the inferred Proto-Indo-European language provides most of what is known about the speakers of that language.

Second, language offers the opportunity to convergently validate our conceptualization of the conformations, confirming or disconfirming conformation systems theory. So, when we observe the eldest man of a lineage seated IN-FRONT of the other men of his lineage, and only observe that once, it is possible that the dimension conforming the eldest's rank is, say, UP-WIND–DOWN-WIND, regardless of the direction in which anyone is facing. Or the conformational dimension could be EAST–WEST. Or it could be that there is no conformation at all; the person in front is simply functioning as interpreter, or is the most hungry, or got there first. We need many observations to make sure what the conformational dimensions is. And if we know the authority ranking metaconformations of the Mooré language, we can confirm that the men we see are conforming their social ranks as IN-FRONT–BEHIND. One of the ways that Moosé verbally conform ranks is by speaking of the *taorẽdamba* and their *poorêdamba*, respectively, which literally mean "in-front persons" (using the respectful plural in reference to the elder), and "behind-persons." Moosé use this verbal conformation regardless of whether or not the people referred to are at that moment spatially arrayed that way. Likewise, what could a naïve outsider infer from seeing an Englishman bend at the waist in front of a woman, addressing her as *Your highness.* Knowing the conformations of rank in the English language allows the naïve observer to infer that the man was not merely showing the woman his new haircut.

The neurocognitive pathways from the most basic mental conformations to speech are more or less independent of the neurocognitive pathways to action. Let us assume that both pathways "begin" in the same deep mental iconic conformation of authority ranking. Granted that, we do not know to what extent the pathways from mind to action are independent of the pathways from mind to speech. But to the extent that there are differences between the way the mind generates action and the way the mind generates speech, speech is an independent window for researchers to view their common starting place, the deep mental conformation of authority ranking. Likewise, language provides an independent window for researchers if perception of conformational language follows a pathway into mental conformation that differs from the pathway coming in from conformational actions or artifacts. This epistemology is analogous to Susan Goldin-Meadow's brilliant demonstration that the pathway though which ideas emerge in gesture differs from the pathway though which ideas emerge in vocal speech, and the pathway by which perceivers interpret gesture differs from the pathway by which perceivers interpret speech (Cartmill, Beilock, & Goldin-Meadow 2012, Goldin-Meadow & Alibali 2013, Jouravlev et al. 2019). Since the two renditions of the mental source have different biases, errors, and ambiguities, researchers can learn a lot from comparing them.

Third, beyond convergent validation of the characterizations of the dimensions that we have found in actions and things, there may also be conformational dimensions that we easily recognize in language, but that we have thus far failed to recognize in action and artifacts. Furthermore, there may be linguistic conformations that exist only in language. If so, we want to identify and characterize the conformations we discover in language, and then study why people restrict their use to language. It is certainly conceivable that language conforms with certain dimensions that cannot be well realized in actions, architecture, art, or other material things. But I don't know any.

Fourth, related to the third point, is the fact that compared to enacted or material conformations, linguistic conformations can more clearly designate abstract or indefinite dimensions. Moosé say of a superior *Eb yɩɩda mam*, "They [respectful plural] exceed me." The verb *yɩɩde*, like the English *exceed*, does not specify the magnitude or dimension of comparison. It encompasses any sort of MORE, any >. English speakers may say that God is *infinite*, which does not specify any particular dimension, but may imply "in all dimensions" or a more general sense of >. Likewise, in Arabic, the ninety-nine names of Allah include *Al-Mutakabbir*, اَلْمُتَكَبِّرُ, which means "the supreme one, the exalted," without specifying any one magnitude (so far as I understand it). These Mooré, English, and Arabic words hint at a level of conformation that transcends any one dimension or magnitude, and possibly, in some sense underlies all of them.

Fifth, language readily conforms relations among third persons, while enacted conformations may not lend themselves to that. One may say "She is the Mother Superior of the convent" or "She is their leader." To communicate such concepts, one cannot easily enact an iconic dimensional conformation about her. Sculpture and painting do readily conform third-person relations, but are much more cumbersome than language, much less adaptable to circumstances, much harder to do privately for a specific audience, much slower to deploy, and generally much more expensive. I cannot build a huge statue of the provost, and, even if I could, it would not be feasible to build a statue immediately and display it only to you, in order to conform the provost to you, and I certainly could not do so without anyone else knowing that I did so, if I wish my conformation to be private. But language permits instantaneous, costless conformation, private or public.

A sixth reason for scholars to attend to linguistic conformations is that enacted and material conformations are more difficult to integrate into complex ideas, judgments, emotions, and so forth. When you look at a pyramid, you look up to the Pharoah with much less nuanced reverence than you do when you hear his advisor say "He would be the greatest pharaoh of all time if he just listened to the provincial governors. He is so wise, and so smart, and he makes brilliant decisions when he does listen. But then, he cannot be a great pharaoh without the backing of the gods, and that plague apparently shows that the gods don't favor him. In any case, the people will lose faith in him if he fails to defeat the invaders this fall. But I am confident that he will defeat them, and remain Pharoah." A pyramid cannot so readily convey those complexities as language can.

Seventh, and finally, language offers the possibility of collecting enormous samples of conformations, because people frequently speak. For every palace that conforms the king's supremacy, there are millions of utterances metaconforming the relations between the king and subjects. Also, the cost of compiling linguistic conformations is far less than the cost of compiling conformational actions and artifacts. With appropriate and subtle coding, the corpuses in large language models offer new opportunities for studying conformations systems. More data afford more opportunities for discovering patterns and better chances of detecting rare types of conformation. Moreover, linguistic conformations are often the only way to compare different persons' authority ranking relations with the king.

Any of these seven opportunities make it worthwhile to study linguistic conformations in conjunction with the many other conformational phenomena we are exploring in this book.

****

Before we dig into linguistic conformations of authority ranking, we need to address one common misapprehension about language. That is the misapprehension that language consists of simply naming, referring, or conveying information: "This is a tree. Trees have leaves." As I mentioned earlier, linguists all recognize that language also does things. Linguists discuss these matters under the rubrics of *speech acts*, *performatives*, *illocution*, and *perlocution* (Rawls 1955, Austin 1961, 1962, Searle 1989).

This aspect of language is salient when, for example, during a battle, the admiral says "Turn the fleet to starboard and open fire" or "You're captain now, Roger! Take over." Moreover, in discourse, many utterances that, on the surface, appear to be merely locutions have illocutionary force, as Rawls, Austin, and Searle have noted. A women changes a relationship with a person when, for the first time, she introduces them by saying "This is my partner, Josephine."

Consider another example. Suppose that a visitor comes on board a ship and asks the Lieutenant "Are you the Captain?"; the Lieutenant responds "No, that is the Captain over there." Simply designating a person as "Captain" likely makes the visitor understand that the indicated person has the authority to make decisions about shipboard matters, makes the visitor feel respect for the person, perhaps feel a bit intimidated, and judge that the person should take responsibility for the ship's crew. Also, that verbal designation motivates the visitor to go to the Captain with a request concerning the ship. When the visitor addresses the person, asking "May I speak to you, Captain?," the visitor is implicitly invoking the Captain's command of the ship and his responsibility for its crew. The visitor's uttering the word "Captain" affords her own awe, affords the Captain's pride, invokes regulations and obligations, and potentiates moral sentiments on both sides – sometimes not very much, sometimes quite a lot.

I have already cited a number of dimension and magnitude words conforming the supremacy of gods and kings in Sanskrit, Greek, and a few other languages. We will now more extensively consider English, Mooré, Ancient Chinese, and, less fully, Sumerian, Turkish, and Burmese. The challenge for our present purposes is that we must be chary of bilingual dictionaries and circumspect when reading texts in translation. The aims of lexicographers and translators differ from our aims, so they may not tell us what we need to know in order to understand whether a word metaconforms through a dimension. When we read the translation of a Sumerian word into the English, *leader*, we have no idea whether the Sumerian word means both "person responsible for the group" and "person in front." The source word may or may not have a dimensional meaning; we cannot tell just from its translation into an English word that conforms IN-FRONT. Hence, I restrict this chapter to my own native language and the languages that I could explore in collaboration with perceptive and reflective native speakers, or, in the case of Sumerian and ancient Chinese, with the support of very kind, wonderfully expert scholars.

I was not able to devise an explicit, formal method for selecting authority ranking words in any of these languages. Each list surely leaves out many words that belong there. I did not use thesauri, because I could not come up with a systematic method for choosing the key words, nor for choosing which synonyms to select. Moreover, thesauri offer synonyms, broadly construed, but do not offer words that are nonsynonymous with the key term. If one looks up *superior* in a thesaurus, one does not find *precede*, *promote*, or *seniority*.

Consequently, the authority ranking word lists below are not complete, not methodologically replicable, nor usable for computing meaningful statistics. Nevertheless, the lists are sufficient to provisionally serve the seven scholarly functions indicated above.

English

The lists below are categorized by the dimension that they represent, but, as we have noted for conformational actions and artifacts, within a single domain of life, people draw on multiple dimensions to conform authority ranking. A study of medical discourse illustrates this. English patients speaking about doctors use vertical conformations such as "You go to the psychiatrist, who is, you know, UP there, BIG job," and speak of "doctors being UP there and we being DOWN here" (Rees et al. 2007). Physicians are conformed as "talking OVER" patients and talking "down to" nurses and others. Patients conform themselves as "ROCK BOTTOM" while their physicians are on their "HIGH HORSES" or up in their "IVORY TOWER." Doctors and medical students also talk about their relations in terms of going ahead and following behind: "there's a student sort of TAILING OR SHADOWING [the doctor]"; a medical student says "They [the doctors] just go in and do the operation and you FOLLOW them." Medical students conform themselves as "MINI-DOCTORS" (Rees et al. 2007, pp. 730–731).

Above–Below

above (e.g., "marry above her station"); ascend or mount the throne, ascendancy; come out on top; hand down (a court ruling); condescend; crush (an opponent, an uprising); elevate (promote to higher rank); haughty; head and shoulders above; highness ("Your Highness"), friends in high places, high and mighty; headman, head of the class; high vs. low rank/status, high-muck-a-muck; hold a high opinion of; look up to vs. look down upon; ladder of promotion/success; lord it over someone; overlord; oversee, overseer; overshadow; overween; prominent; rise to a position of authority, rise in the world, rise through the ranks, uprising; talk down to; think highly of vs. think little of; top ranking official/player, top dog, top brass; towering figure; under one's command/control/supervision; upper crust, upper vs. lower echelon; uppity; upper vs. lower class/school; belittle; beneath him/her [dignity]; bow to someone's wishes; bring someone down a notch; diminish; downtrodden; footman; grovel; inferior; lesser person; lowly, low man on the totem pole; oppress; overthrow; put down; step down [from a high office]; stoop to do something; submit, submissive, subordinate, subject, subaltern, support, supporter, suppress; under the command of someone, underling, undersecretary, under house-parlor maid (see also Tolaas 1991).

exalt (literally, "to raise high," from Latin *altus* "high," literally "grown tall,"

excel, eminent, eminence, preeminent, His Eminence, His Excellency, from Latin *excellere*, "rise, project, stand out, surpass, be eminent," from PIE *kel(hx), "lift, rise up" (nominal form *kel, "hill"; Mallory & Adams 2006, Watkins 2000); haughty (prideful sense of high status), derived from Old French *haut*, "high" (Barnhart 1988), paramount (from Old French *amont*, "up," "above").

superior, supervise, supervisor; supercilious; superintendent; supreme, surpass; sovereign from Latin *supremus*, "highest," the superlative of *superus*, "situated above," from *super*, "above, over" in a physical sense (Barnhart 1988); status (originally, "height" of a situation or condition: www.etymonline.com/word/superior); suzerain (from sus, "high, above").

hegemony is derived from the Greek, *hēgeisthai*, "to lead, to guide, to seek the way" (Partridge 1958).

Likewise, the English *haughty* and the French, *hauteur*, indicating prideful sense of one's own high status, derive from the Old French *haut*, "high" (Barnhart 1988; consider also the expression, "high and mighty"). Conversely, the English *humble*, *humility*, *humiliate* come from the Latin *humilis*, meaning low, lowly, or base, from *humus*, ground or soil (Morris 1969). *Supreme*, *superior*, and *superintendent* come from Latin *supremus*, "highest," the superlative of *superus*, "situated above"; like *sovereign*, they are derived from the Latin *super*, "above, over," which in turn came from the Indo-European root **uper*, "over" (Barnhart 1988, Watkins 2000).

vassal and valet derive from Celtic **wasso-*, "one who stands under," from the Indo-European root **upo*, "under, up from under, over" (Watkins 2000).

abase & debased are formed from de- "down" + base "low" (Harper 2025).
humble, humility, and humiliate derive from Latin *humilis*: low, lowly, or base, from humus, ground, or soil (Morris 1969).

Mass or Volume

(self-)aggrandize; big shot, big wig, big cheese, big name, big wig, big fish, big gun, big wheel, big man on campus, too big for his britches;
grand duke; grandee; grandiose; great president/scientist/student, etcetera;
heavy weight;
make much of;
belittle;
puffed up, puff oneself up;
swell headed;
majesty is from Latin *maiestatem* (nominative *maiestas*) "greatness, dignity, elevation, honor, excellence," from stem of *maior* (neuter *maius*), comparative of *magnus* "great, large, big" (of size), "abundant" (of quantity), "great, considerable" (of value), "strong, powerful" (of force); of persons, "elder, aged," also, figuratively, "great, mighty, grand, important," from suffixed form of PIE root *meg- "great."
authority and august descend from an Indo-European root, *aug-*, via Latin, meaning "increase" or "enlarge" (Partridge 1958, Watkins 2000).
lesser/least (person); lightweight; the little guy; small fry.

In Front–Behind

lead, leader; advance (in a business or field), advance placement; back bencher, take a back seat (to someone); come in first vs. come in behind; foreman, foremost; lead, leader vs. follower, backer; pass or surpass (someone), rear admiral.
promote (from Latin *promotus*, past participle of *promovere* "move forward, advance; cause to advance, push onward; bring to light, reveal");
demote.
duke (from Latin dūcere, to lead).
obsequious comes from the Latin, *sequentem*, to follow (sequence, sequel), which comes from the Indo-European *sekw-*, to follow (Onions et al. 1965: 621, Watkins 2000: 74).

Temporal Precedence

precedence; seniority.

first, second (lieutenant; lord of the Admiralty) [These words conform positions in TIME, and/or IN FRONT–BEHIND, and/or "generic" ordering.]

senior, sir, sire, and senate, as well as the French seigneur, Monseigneur, and monsieur, are descended from the Latin, *senior*, "older," from PIE root *sen- "old") (Morris 1969, Harper 2025).

obsequious (from PIE *sekw*, "to follow," via Latin, *sequi*, "to follow").

hierarchy from Greek *hierarkhia*, "rule of a high priest," from *hierarkhes* "high priest, leader of sacred rites." That Greek word is a combination of *ta hiera* "the sacred rites" (neuter plural of *hieros*, "sacred"), with *arkhon*, "ruler, commander, chief, captain," noun use of present participle of *arkhein*, "be the first," thence "to begin, begin from or with, make preparation for"; also "to rule, lead the way, govern, rule over, be leader of" (above paragraph is mostly direct quotation from Harper 2025).

Force

forceful ruler.

mighty, the Almighty.

powerful (politician).

Strongman.

In politics of all sorts where people seek authority ranking, they want *strong*, *forceful*, *tough* leadership. In recent decades, Minnesota elected Jesse Ventura, a professional wrestler, as governor, and California elected a former bodybuilder and actor who played violent avenger roles (Arnold Schwarzenegger). Neither had any political experience or credentials; apparently they were elected because they appeared, literally, powerful. Schwarzenegger's campaign unabashedly focused on his muscular strength to conform him as a potentially *powerful* governor.

Luminance

A *leading light* is an important, distinguished person – *she shines* or is a *shining example*. An intelligent person is *bright*, while a person who is extraordinarily talented, greatly excels, is eminent, or achieves distinction is *brilliant*, as are their achievements. Distinguished or famous people are *luminaries*. They *outshine lesser lights*, and they *overshadow* or *eclipse* others. A person who is extremely famous or outstanding is a *star*, while fashionable, wealthy, or famous people who attract attention at *A-list* events are *glitterati*. To *shine* at an activity, *be a shining example*, or *be a leading light* is to have very high status.

Describing imposing magnificence, distinction, or transcendence, we speak of a *splendid* achievement or the *splendor* of a court, using a word whose primary and root meaning is "brightness, brilliant light." *Splendor* derives from the Latin *splendēre*, "be bright," which in turn derives from the Proto-Indo-European **(s)plend*, "bright, shine, glow" (Barnhart 1988, Watkins 2000, Harper 2025). We regard an *illustrious* person with awe for their *luster*, "brightness, shine," that is, their glory and fame. The word comes from the Latin *illūstris*, "bright, distinguished, famous, high ranking," which derives from the Proto-Indo-European **leuk*, "light, brightness" (Onions et al. 1965, Chambers 1988, Watkins 2000). A person who distinguishes themselves by a brilliant achievement but fails to achieve continued success is a *flash in the pan*.

Around this luminous center there is a corona of English words that denote aspects of high rank or associated displays and signs. To conspicuously dress or display possessions so as to claim superiority and impress others is to be *flashy*. Similarly, Greek *klidē*, "flashily luxurious living, hence arrogance," derives from the PIE **ĝher-*, "to shine, glow" (Partridge 1958: 256; [Mallory and Adams 2006: 330 indicate that **ĝher-* is only attested from northwestern IE languages]). Several other status-declaring words come from this **ĝher-* root; for example, to *gloat* is to be prideful. An evaluation that describes someone as outstanding is a *glowing* recommendation. Also coming to us from **ĝher-* is the characterization of the look of an angry superior, *glower*, from Middle English "gleam, stare." To *glare* at a subordinate is to "look brightly and angrily," derived from "shine dazzlingly" (Partridge 1958: 256, Watkins 2000).[1] In addition to meaning "exalted honor" and "renown," *glory* is the medieval and sometimes modern English term for "halo, nimbus"; *glory* derives from Latin *gloria*, which was used to translate the Hebrew Bible term

[1] Some cultures treat vision as akin to light coming *out of* the eyes; these etymologies may reflect that conception, so to speak, of ocular luminance.

kabod (K-B-D), which originally meant physical "heaviness," and then evolved to mean "importance, honor, respect, majesty" (Botterweck et al. 1995 VII: 23; Harper 2025).

Loudness and Multiplicity: Missing?

I cannot find English lexemes that conform superior rank as LOUD, or subordinate rank as QUIET. Perhaps there are some that I have missed. But evidently there are not many of them, nor are there any in frequent use in the dialects of English that I know. MULTIPLICITY also seems rare or nonexistent as an English lexical conformation of authority ranking. That is intriguing, since in English, until the seventeenth century, *you* or *ye* was the plural pronoun and conformed an (individual) addressee's higher rank; *thou* was the singular. As mentioned in Chapter 7, speakers of many languages use plural pronouns of address and reference when speaking to superiors.

It is a mystery to me why both LOUDNESS and MULTIPLICITY are common and salient among enacted and material conformations of rank in many English-speaking communities, and have been for centuries, yet seem not to linguistically metaconform rank in English.

From these lists we can conclude that at least eight dimensions are manifest in the lexicon of contemporary English. There are more contemporary English words conforming authority ranking by ELEVATION than words conforming by any of the other dimensions.

I did not discover English lexical conformations of authority ranking based on dimensions other than the ten that people use for enacted and material conformations. If there are English lexemes conforming authority ranking with other dimensions, they might have escaped my notice because I failed to recognize that they were dimensional. In any case, there is an important implication of the absence or paucity of English lexemes metaconforming authority ranking with additional dimensions beyond the ten that we have seen in artifacts, architecture, and postures. The implication is that, at least among populations who speak English, there may not be any other dimensions used in conformation of authority ranking.

In English at least, most of the lexemes that speakers continue to use to conform authority ranking contemporaneously refer to physical dimensions. I found far fewer lexemes conforming authority ranking that are derived from lexemes that formerly denoted physical dimensions but which no longer have that meaning for English speakers today. I found those words systematically, by investigating the etymology of every English lexeme I could think of that conforms authority ranking but does not have a dimensional reference in modern English. All of them turned out to be derived from lexemes that formerly denoted a dimension.

It is significant that that the great preponderance of authority ranking-conforming words presently also have a dimensional meaning, often a physical meaning that seems to be the "primary" and initial use of the lexeme. This is significant because it supports the hypothesis that these dual meanings resonate with the iconic dimension niche constituted by the evolved psychological adaptation disposing people to use and respond to dimensions to conform authority ranking. This niche supports, informs, and orients the invention and cultural transmission of dimensional lexemes in linguistic metaconformations of authority ranking. Indeed, the reader may take it as a challenge to try to come up with even one authority ranking word in vernacular English that does not, and never did, also have a physical dimension meaning.

But English is just one language, atypical in some respects.

The Cultural Evolution of Some Proto-Indo-European Roots

In the section on English, working backward from contemporary words to their origins, we found a number of words that formerly denoted a dimension, then came to be used also to conform authority ranking. Some of them eventually lost their original dimensional sense while continuing to be used to conform authority ranking. In this section, we will go in the opposite temporal direction, starting at the earliest inferred Proto-Indo-European words denoting a dimension. Did people subsequently adopt such dimension words to confer authority ranking? That's a different question from the one considered in the section on the English language. Finding that most English authority ranking words are derived from ancient dimension words does not imply that most ancient dimension words turned into English authority ranking words. The following sample is intended as an initial foray into this issue.

The Proto-Indo-European **eug-*, colored to **aug-*, "to increase," is the root of the Greek *auxein* and the Old English *ēacan*, both of which continued to mean "to increase." It is also the root of the Latin *auct-*, "to increase, promote, originate," which gave rise to the modern English words *authority*, *august*, and *augment* (Onions et al. 1965: 63; Watkins 2000: 6, *aug-*). The early Greek word *arkhein* meant "to begin, rule, command"; the ten leaders of Athens were *archons;* rule by one is *monarchy* and rule by the few is *oligarchy*; see also *archbishop*, etcetera (Onions et al. 1965: 47, Watkins 2000: 5).

Likewise, the Indo-European root *meg-*, "great," is the source of many words in English and other languages denoting either social or physical greatness: *majesty, maestro, master, mister, mistress, magnate, magistrate, mayor, major, much, magnificence, magnanimous, magnify, magnum, magnitude, mega- (e.g., megalith, megafauna, megabyte), maximum, much, mickle* (a widely used archaic English word meaning "much, great"), as well as *maharaja, maharishi, and mahatma.*

In Proto-Indo-European, the word **sek^{w}-* meant "follow," from which was derived "follower," in the sense of a subordinate, giving rise to a Germanic word for one who follows into battle (Mallory & Adams 2006: 267). From Proto-Indo-European **prai-, *prei-*, "in front of, before (in time)," is derived the Latin root *pre- (prae-)*. From the Latin usage of *pre-* as "beyond or over all," come the English *preeminent, prevail, prefect* (Onions et al. 1965: 703–704; Mallory & Adams 2006: 288–289). In fourteenth-century English, the word *precede*, which originally meant "surpass, exceed," in the next century came to mean "go 'before' in place or rank" (Onions et al. 1965: 704). Only in the sixteenth century did it come to mean "go before in time." From Proto-Indo-European **per*, meaning "forward, in front of, before, early, first, chief," comes *pride*, and, through the Latin, *princeps*, "he who takes first place," and *primus*, "first, foremost, prince," gave rise to the English *prince, principal, premier, prime minister, primogeniture, primate* (the ecclesiastical high office) (Morris 1969, Watkins 2000). As a verbal root, **per* meant "to lead, pass over" (Gamkrelidze & Ivanov 1995: 741, Watkins 2000: 65–66, Onions et al. 1965: 703–704). From Latin *privus*, which came to mean standing apart or in front, comes *privilege*. In the *Rig Veda*, the god Agni is praised as *purohita*, "set/placed in front" (Thomson & Slocum 2011, Watkins, personal communication; December 8, 2009). Among the many English words with this root are *first, foremost, foreman, prior, prime, pride, premier, principal, prince, priest, prelate, prefect, precept, preeminent, prerogative, preside, prestige, preach, prescribe, predominate*, and *prevail.*

The Proto-Indo-European verb **wal-* initially meant "to be strong," but soon came to also mean "to rule or command" (Watkins 2000, Mallory & Adams 2006: 267–268, 284). It is the root of Old Germanic, Old Norse, Old English, Lithuanian, and Old Church Slavonic words meaning "to govern, to rule" (Watkins 2000, Mallory & Adams 2006: 267, 284).

Early Indo-European cultures used three color terms to refer to social strata (Sanskrit *varna*, Avestan *pištra*). They consistently associated white with priests, the highest stratum; red with the warrior stratum; and apparently black or blue with the lowest stratum (Dumézil 1958: 7–8, 25–26; 1983: 17–27; Watkins 2000: 133; Adams & Mallory 1997: 120). These three Indo-European strata are also respectively identified with the sky, the earth, and the subterranean (Adams & Mallory 1997: 120), and also with the head, upper body, and lower body (Lyle 1982). The Proto-Indo-European root **(s)kóitós*, "bright, clear," evolved into Old Norse, Old English, and Old High German words for "rank, status," while another Indo-European root, **gwhaidros*, "bright, shining," evolved into Greek, *φαίδιμος*, "bright, shining, glistening; famous, glorious" (Adams 1997a, b). The Proto-Indo-European root **dei or *dyeu*, "shine, gleam, be bright, bright sky" is the root of *Jove*, *Jupiter*, *Zeus*, *deity*, *divinity*, and is the source of words for god in many other Indo-European languages (Watkins 2000, Mallory & Adams 2006: 329, 408–409). Indeed, the core Proto-Indo-European word for god, *deiwós*, is derived from the word *dyeu*, "sky," and closely related to roots for "sun" and "shine" (Gamkrelidze & Ivanov 1995: 694–695, Mallory & Adams 2006: 408).

Another possible PIE, or else Celtic, word for god, *bhr̥⟨hn̥tih$_a$*, means "high one," which is the root of Indo-European words such as *fort*, *force*, *enforce*, *strong*, and *mighty* (Watkins 2000, Mallory & Adams 2006: 410; cf. Gamkrelidze & Ivanov 1995: 576, 683). According to Mallory & Adams (2006: 412–413), another PIE root, *h$_a$euges*, "strength," has early derivatives meaning both "mighty" and "spiritually potent."

The English words *majesty*, *major*, *mayor*, *majority*, *magistrate*, *master*, *mister*, *maharajah*, *mahatma*, *magnum*, *magnitude*, *magnify*, *maximum*, and *mega-* are all derived from an Indo-European root, **meg-*, "great," which has given rise to a family of words in many languages, from Latin to Sanskrit, with the meanings of "larger" and/or "socially superior" (Onions et al. 1965). The epithet "great" was given to Zeus and, in Persia, to the Zoroastrian deity Ahura Mazdā (West 2007: 130). Likewise, the Indo-European root **meg-*, "great," is also the source of words in English and other languages denoting either social or physical greatness: *majesty*, *maestro*, *master*, *mister*, *mistress*, *magnate*, *magistrate*, *mayor*, *major*, *much*, *magnificent*, *magnanimous*, *magnify*, *magnum*, *magnitude*, *mega- (e.g., megalith, megafauna, megabyte)*, *maximum*, *much*, *mickle* (a widely used archaic English word meaning "much, great"), as well as *maharaja*, *maharishi*, *and mahatma* (Morris 1969, Gamkrelidze & Ivanov 1995: 684).

In Sanskrit, the adverbs *ud*, "up," and *para* or *parma*, "beyond, extreme," are the roots of several words for superior social status (Hartmut Scharfe, personal communication, June 27, 2008).

Evidently the Proto-Indo-Europeans bent their bodies in deference to superiors. PIE _*h$_2$enk_, "bend," seems to be the root of a Hittite word meaning "bow or courtesy reverentially" (Mallory & Adams 2006: 382). Another PIE root, _*bhedh_, "bend (one's body)" gave rise to a Tocharian B word meaning "to honor (by bending one's knees)," and to Germanic cognates, including modern English "bow" (Partridge 1958, Watkins 2000, Mallory & Adams 2006: 382). Proto-Indo-Europeans also seem to have thought of political power or status as involving swelling or expanding the body: _*k̈eu(h$_1$)_, "swell (the body)," generated a Sanskrit word for "swell, become powerful," a Greek word for "lord," and words in Indo-Iranian languages for "(socially) powerful." The verb _*keuh$_1$_ is the basis for the adjective _*kouhr$_1$os_, "powerful," applied to human heroes, and is also the root for a PIE word meaning "holy," which was perpetuated in words for holy in Avestan, Lithuanian, and Old Church Slavonic (Mallory & Adams 2006: 385, 412). Perhaps this was based on the MASS or VOLUME iconic dimensions. Another PIE root also meaning "swell (the body)," _*teuha_, was the source of a Sanskrit term for "strong/powerful." Likewise _*h$_a$euges_, "strength," evidently meant both "the physical might of a warrior and the spiritual potential of a deity" (Mallory & Adams 2006: 412–413). Another PIE root, _*rāj_, probably meaning "strength, power," is the source for later words for king: Latin *rēx*, Sanskrit *rājan*, Old Irish *rī*, French *roi*, English *regal*, *royal* (Scharfe 1985). This root, _*rāj_, was probably also the basis for the Greek *arēgō*, "protect" – the action of a god or, occasionally, a high-status person, assuring that no harm come to a human of much lower status – in other words, carrying out the moral responsibilities of a superior in authority ranking relation.

From these examples it is clear that numerous Proto-Indo-European words for physical dimensions acquired a second meaning in one or more languages and became conformations of authority ranking. In a number of cases, the original physical dimension meaning of a word faded away, leaving the word to conform authority ranking by convention alone, without invigoration by iconic resonance to the niche. Some Proto-Indo-European dimension words culturally evolved into several distinct authority ranking-conforming words in one of more of the roughly 450 languages in this family. But I drew on only English etymological dictionaries, which infrequently mention words in other languages that evolved out of the same Proto-Indo-European source word. It would be illuminating to take a large random sample of Proto-Indo-European dimension words and roots and find out how many languages adopted each of them to conform authority ranking.

I am not especially concerned about what proportion of dimension words in how many languages were independently adopted to conform authority ranking, rather than being borrowed or calqued. (Calquing consists of a language copying a lexical concept without borrowing the words themselves.) My unconcern is due to my theorization that borrowed and calqued words both culturally evolve in the same niche as words independently invented. They must all be subject to approximately the same cultural selection factors. That is, like locally invented words, borrowed and calqued words for authority ranking survive, reproduce, and diffuse to the extent that they resonate with the iconic dimensional conformation niche. And why would anyone borrow or calque a word incongruent with the niche in the first place? The second-language learner would need a certain amount of experience with authority ranking relations in the culture they were visiting before they would even recognize that an incongruent word in the second language did conform authority ranking. When the person visiting a culture realized that people were using a niche-incongruent word to conform authority ranking, the word would not feel "natural" – it would not seem intuitively apt. So, if anyone did borrow or calque a word that did not resonate with the conformation niche in which it must function, that word generally would not take root. Even if it survived for a while, a word that did not resonate with the authority ranking iconic dimension conformation niche would not be as social-relationally effective as words that resonated well. The more a person relied on the incongruent word, the weaker, less reliable, less smoothly coordinated, and less stable their authority ranking relationships would be. And the more a person relied on the incongruent word, the more relational confusion would occur because of misperception and memory errors.

By the same logic, the longer a language community retains the conformational use of a dimension, the stronger the inference that the conformational use is due to the dimension's iconic resonance with the niche in which it flourishes. Word usage is subject to many influences. Hence, despite the effects of convention, the use of a word is likely to change over time, or cease to be used. Thus, the longer a language community and its successors continue to use a dimensional word to conform authority ranking, the stronger the evidence that its conformational use is fostered by its resonance with the iconic dimensional niche. Convention alone cannot make a word immortal. Convention combined with conformation-niche resonance can make a word endure and spread for millennia.

Hence, for each dimension word, when adding up the evidence that the conformational use of the word supports conformation systems theory, we should count every language community that uses that dimension word to conform authority ranking – regardless of whether that language community independently invented the word to conform authority ranking, borrowed or calqued that conformational use from another language community, or inherited the conformational use from the same ancestral language community that passed it on to other language communities in our sample.

For discussion of some related issues regarding when a "culture" can be statistically treated as an independent case, see Mace and Pagel 1994, as well as Korotayev and de Munck 2003.

Ancient Chinese

We are exploring iconic conformations, so it is especially interesting to look into a language written in characters that, in many or most cases, developed out of iconic pictographs. Chinese is a Sino-Tibetan language whose speakers had relatively limited early contact with speakers of Indo-European languages. What iconic dimensions – if any – does Chinese use to lexically metaconform authority ranking, and how early did they emerge as authority ranking metaconformations?

It is not the earliest source we will examine, but let us begin with intriguing Verse 66 from the Daodejing, or Laozi, from the third century BCE, possibly earlier.

What enables the great rivers and seas to be king over all
 the valley streams
Is that they are good at staying below them,
And thus can be kings over the valley streams.
Therefore if one wants to be above the people,
One must, in using words, remain below them.
If one wants to be ahead of the people,
One must, in using one's person, remain behind them.
Therefore when the sage places himself above,
The people do not feel it a burden [do not feel oppressed/
 crushed by the weight]
When he places himself ahead,
The people are not hurt [obstructed, offended].
Therefore the world finds joy in praising [supporting,
 advancing] him, without wearying of it,
And because he contends with no one,
No one can contend with him.[2]

江海所以能為百谷王者
以其善下之
故能為百谷王。
是以聖人欲上人
必以言下之。 欲先人
必以身後之。
是以聖人處上 而人不重
處前 而人不害。
是以天下樂推而不厭
以其不爭
故天下莫能與之爭。

[2] Translation by de Barry & Bloom 1999. Bracketed additions are mine, based on comparisons with several other translations and dictionaries.

The verse above shows that more than 2,200 years ago, literate Chinese conformed authority ranking as ABOVE–BELOW, IN FRONT–BEHIND, and as MASSIVE/CRUSHING–SUPPORTING/CARRYING.

Similarly, in the *Liji*, from the Warring States Period (475–221 BCE), the Summary of the Rules of Propriety, Part I, Section 27, says:

曲禮上

凡與客入者,每門讓於客。客至於寢門,則主人請入為席,然後出迎客。客固辭,主人肅客而入。主人入門而右,客入門而左。主人就東階,客就西階,客若降等,則就主人之階。主人固辭,然後客復就西階。主人與客讓登,主人先登,客從之,拾級聚足,連步以上。上於東階則先右足,上於西階則先左足。

Qu Li I

> Whenever (a host has received and) is entering with a guest, at every door he should give place to him. When the guest arrives at the innermost door (or that leading to the feast-room), the host will ask to be allowed to enter first and arrange the mats. Having done this, he will come out to receive the guest, who will refuse firmly (to enter first). The host having made a low bow to him, they will enter (together). When they have entered the door, the host moves to the right, and the guest to the left, the former going to the steps on the east, and the latter to those on the west. If the guest be of the lower rank, he goes to the steps of the host (as if to follow him up them). The host firmly declines this, and he returns to the other steps on the west. They then offer to each other the precedence in going up, but the host commences first, followed (immediately) by the other. They bring their feet together on every step, thus ascending by successive paces. He who ascends by the steps on the cast should move his right foot first, and the other at the western steps his left foot. (Chinese Text Project 2011)

Still more intriguing is the fact that the iconic physics of authority ranking is built into many Chinese characters. The characters of Chinese have been remarkably stable over the nearly 4,000-year history of the language, changing only slowly, until the modern character simplification. Using the well-established etymology of the Chinese characters themselves, we can discover how the people in the early second millennium BCE who first invented and used Chinese writing iconically conformed authority ranking. What we find is that the components of characters denoting sociopolitical rank or authority include a great many radicals representing physical position, magnitude, or time. That is, social relationships of rank or authority are represented with radicals or characters whose original, primary, or alternate reference is to the material physical dimensions of ABOVE–BELOW, BIGGER–SMALLER, IN FRONT–BEHIND, STRONG FORCE–WEAK FORCE, TEMPORALLY PRECEDING–TEMPORALLY FOLLOWING, and BRIGHTER.

For example, the use of spatial position to indicate social position is clear in the conceptualization of 位, *wèi*, "position, location, place," which combines with many other characters to indicate social "position" in a rank order: for example, 位列, *wèi liè*, "to rank"; 地位, *dì wèi*, "social status"; 位次, *wèi cì*, "order of precedence, level on employment scale"; 即位, *jí wèi*, "succeed to the throne"; 纂位, *cuàn wèi*, "to seize the throne";遜位, *xùn wèi*, "to abdicate, resign a position"; 上位, *shàng wèi*, "first/top seat, leader"; 居位, *jū wèi*, "to occupy a high administrative position"; 名位, *míng wèi*, "fame and position; official rank"; 帝位, *dì wèi*, "the title of Emperor"; and many more (Chinese.gratis: https://chinese.gratis/; YellowBridge).[3]

Above–Below

A radical showing a vertical line rising above the level surface, ⊥, signifying "above," combines with 巾, "turban, kerchief, bonnet" to make the word 帝, *dì*, "supreme ruler, emperor, god, ancestor" (Wieger 1965: 698, YellowBridge). Cognates in related languages denote celestial or sky gods (Schuessler 2007). A radical derived from ⊥ is 上, *shàng*, "on; up; on top; upon; first (of two parts); upper part; previous or last (week, etc.); upper; higher; above; previous; to climb; to mount; to go up, rise" (YellowBridge, Schuessler 2007; see Daodejing verse 66, quoted earlier). Apparently under the influence of Western ideas about an anthropomorphic supreme deity, 上, *shàng* was added again to 帝, *dì*, to compose 上帝, *shàngdì*, "god" [above the emperor]. 上, *shàng*, also combines with 級, *ji*, "level, grade, step," to form 上級, *shàngjí*, "higher authorities, superiors." With 層, *céng*, "layer, level," it forms 上層, *shàngcéng*, "upper social strata." With 階, *jiē*, "rank or step; stairs," it forms 階層, "hierarchy, rank, social strata."

高, *gâo*, which has meant "high, tall" since Old Chinese, is derived from a pictograph of a high tower or pavilion on a lofty substructure (Wieger 1965: 191, Shi 1997: 505, Peng 2005: 176, Schuessler 2007, YellowBridge).

[3] I use the classic characters throughout, rather than the simplified ones. Where no other references are indicated, character compositions and translations are from YellowBridge (www.yellowbridge.com). Where Schuessler 2007 is cited, the character and its meaning have been traced back to Old Chinese (i.e., before 200 BCE and generally before 600 BCE).

Indeed, in Shang oracle bone inscriptions it probably represents a temple on a raised mound, at which only the Emperor himself could make offerings to a deity or deities superior to others' ancestors, thus conforming himself as superior to all others (Hwang 1996: 372–382). 高, *gâo*, combines with 層, *céng*, to form 高層, *gāocéng*, "high level (in society, bureaucracy, or politics); high class"; it combines with 貴, "expensive, noble, precious," to form 高貴, *gāoguì*, "grandeur, noble, elitist," and it is also a component of 高傲, *gāo'ào*, "arrogant, supercilious" (Peng 2005: 177, Fazzioli 1986: 234, YellowBridge). 高, *gâo*, also combines with 級, *ji*, "level, grade," to form 高級, *gāojí*, "high level; high grade; advanced; high-ranking." A similar character, 喬, *qiáo*, "be tall," is combined with a character for "horse" to make the word 驕, *jiāo*, "proud, arrogant, haughty" (YellowBridge, Schuessler 2007). 升, *shēng*, "raise, hoist," also means "promote, advance."

Other characters representing objects "above" are also used to conform social superiority. For example, 崇, *chóng*, "high; dignified; lofty; eminent; to honor, esteem, revere, venerate," is based on 山, *shān*, "mountain, hill, peak" (Wieger 1965: 697, YellowBridge). Likewise, 霄, *xiāo*, "sky, clouds, heaven," combines with 漢, Hàn (dynasty), to form 霄漢, *xiāohàn*, which literally also means "sky, heavens above" but is used to denote the royal court.

We also see magnitude used to conform social status in 嘏, *jiǎ*, which, since Old Chinese, has meant "be great" in reference to heaven or rulers, and also "abundance." Today it also means "far; large, and strong; prosperity, felicity"; it seems to be related to other Chinese words meaning "be large, increase, wide, broad" (YellowBridge; Schuessler 2007).

Upward motion as social movement is evident in the usage for more than two millennia of 舉, *jǔ*, "rise, lift up, raise, promote, choose, elect, recommend" (YellowBridge, Schuessler 2007).

The iconic spatial positions used in Chinese characters include not only "above" and "below," but also at least one character that means "in the middle." This is 中, *zhōng*, "central, center, middle, in the midst of"; it may be derived from a pictograph of an arrow piercing the center of a target. Pronounced *zhòng*, 中 still means today to "hit the mark" (Wieger 1965: 260, Shi 1997: 351, Peng 2005: 19, YellowBridge; another possibility is that the pictograph originally represented an image of a flag). It is a component of 中學, *zhōngxué*, "middle school," and, combines with 等, *děng*, "class; rank; grade; equal to; same as," to form 中等, *zhōngděng*, "middle class." Another character, 平, *píng*, "flat, level, equal," combines with 等, *děng*, to make 平等, *píngděng*, "social equality."

Social inferiority is represented in many compound characters based on characters meaning low, below, or small. A common one is 下, *xià*, which derives from a pictograph that originally seems to have represented a small object underneath a larger upwardly convex object covering it (Katô 1952: 219). 下, *xià*, means "under; second (of two parts); next (week, etc.); lower; below; inferior; underneath; down(wards); to decline; to go down, bring down; latter" (YellowBridge, Shi 1997: 332, Schuessler 2007; see Daodejing verse 66). It is a component of several words meaning socially inferior, such as 部下, *buxia*, "troops under one's command; subordinate." In addressing or referring to the emperor, one says, 陛下, *bìxià*, "Your Majesty; His/Her Majesty"; this character is composed of two characters, 下, *xià*, and 陛, *bì*, meaning "steps to the throne." The word 低下, *dīxià*, "low status, lowly," combines 下, *xià* with a word for a deferential posture, 低, *dī*, "to lower (one's head); to let droop; to hang down; low; to incline; beneath; low." Also, 低, *dī*, is a component of 降低, *jiàngdī*, "to reduce, to lower, to bring down"; a component of 贬低, *biǎndī*, "belittle, depreciate, play down"; and a component of 低級, *dījí*, "low (social) level." Another word, 卑, *bēi*, has meant both spatially "low" and socially "humble" since Old Chinese (1250–600 BCE, Schuessler 2007). A character based on an image depicting a dog lying next to a person, 伏, *fú*, since Old Chinese has meant "to lie face down on the ground, put down, submit, yield" (YellowBridge, Schuessler 2007).

Bigger–Smaller and Postural Abasement–Elevation

Two etymologies have been proposed for 尊, *zūn*, "respect, revere, venerate, honor." It may derive from a pictograph of two hands raising a ceremonial wine jug in offering (Shi 1997: 374). Alternatively, it may be composed of 酋, *qiú*, "chief of tribe, chieftain," together with 寸, *cùn*, "small, tiny" (YellowBridge). At any rate, 寸, *cùn*, "tiny," is a component of 尅, *kè*, "subdue, overcome, dominate" (Wieger 1965: 695; Yellowbridge). Another character meaning "small, tiny; few; young," 小, *xiǎo*, is a constituent of 小人, *xiǎorén*, "small/inferior person" – that is, a person of ordinary low virtue. Confucius often contrasts 小人, *xiǎorén*, with 君子, *jūnzi*, "the noble/superior man of virtue." In Old Chinese, 小, *xiǎo*, was also used to mean "belittle" (Schuessler 2007).

The body positions involved in vertical differentiation give rise to interesting words. One classic example is 仰, *yǎng*, "to lift the face, look up, raise the head to look; look up to, rely on, admire," which is a component of敬仰, *jìngyǎng*, "revere, highly admire," and is part of 瞻仰, *zhānyǎng*, "revere, admire," as well as 仰慕, "adoration" (YellowBridge, Schuessler 2007). Conversely, a pictograph of a person with an "angry" eye standing or stamping on an enemy weapon evolved into 蔑, *miè*, "contempt, disdain, disregard, slight, nothing," a component of 蔑視, *mìeshi*, "loathe, despise," 侮蔑, *wǔmiè*, "contempt, despise," 誣蔑, *wūmiè*, "slander, smear, vilify," and 輕蔑, *qīngmiè*, "disdain" (Shi 1997: 347; YellowBridge).

The subordination of women is evident in the character 女, *nǚ*, "woman," derived from a pictograph depicting a person bowing and, in a later form, kneeling in respect (Fazzioli 1986: 26; Peng 2005: 1). Likewise, the character, 臣, *chén*, "vassal, slave, subject, courtier, minister, official," is probably based on a pictograph representing the vertically oriented eye of a person bowing – before the emperor. An alternative etymology derives 臣 from a pictograph of a person kneeling, head down and hands on the floor (Wieger 1965: 211, 214, Katô 1954: 196, Fazzioli 1986: 31, Wang 1993: 159, Shi 1997: 62). A pictograph representing a mouth [giving orders] above a kneeling person became 令, *lìng*, "to command, order, decree; to cause to be; honorable, commandant, magistrate." Further, 令, *lìng* combines with other words to form various honorific terms. And with 下, *xià*, "under, inferior," it makes 下令, *xiàlìng*, "to give an order" (Shi 1997: 78; YellowBridge).

Postural abasement is also used to depict social abasement and reverence in religious words. A pictograph representing a kneeling or bowing person at an altar to a deity is the source of the character, 祀, *sì*, "to sacrifice, worship," and a representation of a person kneeling in front of an ancestor altar became the character, 祝, *zhù*, "pray, invoke, wish, express good wishes for happiness or blessings" (Shi 1997: 360, 365; Xie 1997: 305, YellowBridge).

In contrast, the character, 大, *dà*, which originally depicted a man in an expansive pose, since Old Chinese has meant "big, huge, large, great, wide; high; major; deep; exceed, be greater than; oldest; eldest"; it has long been a respectful term of address (YellowBridge, Wieger 1965: 156, Katô 1952: 229, Fazzioli 1986: 243, Wang 1993: 3, Shi 1997: 23, Schuessler 2007, Chinese Text Project 2011). It is the basis for 大家, *dàjiā*, "authority." When 大 combines with another word meaning "big, large, great, robust; extraordinary," 偉, *wěi*, it forms 偉大, *wěidà*, "great (in social status), mighty, huge." In addition, 偉, *wěi*, combines with 人, rén, "person, man," to make 偉人, *wěirén*, "great person." Since Old Chinese it has been a component of titles meaning "grand-" (Schuessler 2007). A pictograph in which 大, *dà*, is placed over another man (who, tellingly, was ultimately reduced to a tiny stroke) became 太, *tài*, "greatest, highest, biggest, extremely, too much" (YellowBridge, Wang 1993: 3).

The pictographic depiction of person's head developed into the representation of a leadership role in the character 首, *shǒu*, "head, chief, leader, first, foremost, highest," which is used in a number of words for social authority, such as 首相, *shǒuxiàng*, "prime minister," and 首長, *shǒuzhǎng*, "senior official." 長 can be pronounced *zhǎng*, "senior, elder, authoritative, chief, leader," or *cháng*, "long, length" (YellowBridge, Wang 1993: 11, Shi 1997: 52, Peng 2005: 151). A similar pictographic of a head evolved into 頁, *yè*, *xié*, which, when written alone, now means "page, leaf, sheet," but as a radical in combination with other elements retains its original sense of "head" in various words such as 順, *shùn*, "obey, submit, follow, go along with, docile, reasonable" (Wieger 1965: 803; Yellowbridge). An icon indicating "above the head of a man" is the pictographic origin of 元, *yuán*, which meant "head" in Old Chinese, and from that developed to mean "to be at the head, first, eldest, principal, great." It has cognates in Tibetan meaning "head, summit, beginning," as well as "protector, master, lord" (Schuessler 2007). In modern Chinese 元, *yuán*, means "primary, first, in first place," and is used in the word 元首, *yuánshǒu*, "head of state" (Wieger 1965, YellowBridge, Shi 1997: 16, Wang 1993: 2). In conforming authority ranking, 巨, *jù*, "very large, huge, tremendous, gigantic," combines with 頭, *tóu*, head, to make 巨頭, *jùtóu*, "tycoon, magnate": literally, "giant head."

Three pictographic sources have been proposed for another character, 亢, *kàng*, "high, proud, haughty, overbearing, extreme, excessive, skilled." This may be based on a pictograph of a person stretching his head high on a long neck; it could be derived from 大, *dà*, standing with something between his legs; or, perhaps more likely, it developed from 亠, *tóu*, head, over 几, *jǐ*, "small table" (YellowBridge, Shi 1997: 33, Wang 1993: 4).

Strong Force–Weak Force and Heavy Mass

There are at least five Chinese words that encompass force and authority ranking. One is 強 or 彊, *qiáng*, "strong, strength; force; power; powerful; better, superior." It is used for political power as well as the strength of an animal or the intensity of a sensation (Yellowbridge, Schuessler 2007). The same character, 彊, pronounced *qiǎng*, can also mean "to compel." Another character, 力, *lì*, originally represented a [strong] forearm or sinew, but in Old Chinese it had already come to denote the physical strength of a person or the power of natural forces, and also to refer to social influence and capability, including governmental power (Schuessler 2007). This radical is also a component of 勢, *shì*, "force, power, influence, authority" (Wieger 1965: 678; Yellowbridge). The primary sense of another character, 壮, *zhuàng*, is "strong, robust, to strengthen," but it also means "impressive, magnificent, eminent" (Peng 2005: 151). Conversely, 衰,

shuāi, means "weak, feeble; decline, wane," with regard to both the health and strength of a person and of a nation or empire. Likewise, 弱, *ruò*, means "weak, feeble, young," and also "social inferior." The word 嬬, *rú* or *xū*, "weak," also means "mistress, concubine."

Weight pressing down is also iconic for authority ranking in Chinese. 壓, *yā*, means "to press, to push down, to keep under (control)." It is also the root of 高壓, *gāoyā*, "high-handed," and of 壓迫, *yāpò*, oppress, oppression (just as English *press* is the root of *oppression*). Conversely, 撐, *chēng*, "to support," can be used in either the physical sense of a brace or prop, or in the social sense of loyal political support. Similarly, a character 推, *tuī*, "push, shove" (which incorporates the radical 扌, hand) is used in the Daodejing verse quoted above to mean "support, advance" in a sociopolitical sense. An old Chinese word which was originally a pictograph of a hand pressing down on a kneeling person became 服, *fú*, "to submit." It is the basis of the words 屈服, *qūfú*, "to surrender, yield"; 征服, *zhēngfú*, "to conquer, subdue, vanquish"; 服務, *fúwù*, "to serve, to service"; and 服從, *fúcóng*, "obey" (Shi 1997: 98, Schuessler 2007).

The character 龍, *lóng*, "dragon," has been used since the oracle bones to metaconform the powerful, awesome emperor (Xie 1997: 482).

In Front–Behind

As can be seen in the verse from the Daodejing quote given earlier, 後, *hòu*, means "back, behind, rear, afterwards, after, later." It can be used for spatial position, such as "back" wall; it also is used temporally, in the sense of "subsequent," and to mean social inferiority, as in "fall behind" someone who is progressing in rank (YellowBridge). It is a close cognate to an Old Chinese word written with the same character that meant "be behind [be a backer], support, attend" (Schuessler 2007). The earliest source of this character is a pictograph of a woman giving birth, and from very early times it was used in the titles of emperors. So it is not clear whether its eventual use for "empress" derives from one of those earlier sources, or from its later meaning of "behind, after" (Wang 1993: 25, Shi 1997: 49).

Anteriority in space and in social position is also denoted by 踔, which can be pronounced *zhuó*, *chuō*, *diào*, *zhuō*, or *tiào*; it means "to stride, to get ahead, to excel." Similarly, from the earliest oracle bone inscriptions though the early bronze inscriptions and later seals, two men running composed the character 競, *jìng*, "to compete, to strive to get ahead of someone," as in 競選, "to run for office" (Xie 1997: 17, YellowBridge).

Chinese, like English, uses a word meaning "lead, command," 率, *shuài*, to signify being socially "in front" and bringing others along behind; it is used alone, or in combination with 領, *lǐng*, "neck, collar, to lead; to receive," forming 率領, *shuàilǐng*, "lead, command, head." Likewise, 前, *qián*, "before, front, in front; ago, former, previous, earlier," is also used for social position of leadership, as in the Daodejing verse 66.[4]

As can be seen in the sixty-sixth verse of the Daodejing, 先, *xiān*, means "first, before, ahead, early, in advance, prior, former, to go in front, to walk in front in order to protect]." It is based on a pictograph of a foot or ascending footprint on top of a man, meaning "preceding man" or "ancestor" (Wang 1993: 30, Shi 1997: 120). It combines with 生, *shēng*, "to be born; to give birth; life; to grow," to form the respectful title or term of address, 先生, *xiānsheng*, "sir, mister, teacher" (Peng 2005: 160, YellowBridge, Schuessler 2007). The same iconic principle is the basis of 從, *cóng*, which is derived from a pictograph of a person walking behind another person, the leader (Wieger 1965: 79, Fazzioli 1986: 15, Shi 1997: 4). (The simplified character, 从, captures the icon.) It means "from, by, whence; obey, follow," and is part of words such as 隨從, *suícóng*, "entourage, attendants."

Confucius originally set down, and in the first century BCE his disciples re-created based on memory, the *Lǐj*, 禮記, "Book of Rites," in which a crucial ceremony in the Míng Tang aligned the king, courtiers, lords, and chieftains in *wei*, 位, linear honorific anteriority positions (Hung 2007: 193).

Another pictograph that represents feet ascending stairs evolved into one of the components of 陟, *zhì*, "climb, scale, ascend; merit, advance, promote" (Wieger 1965: 266, Schuessler 2007). Conversely, a pictograph of two footprints going down (descending a ladder or stairs) evolved into 降, a character with two related senses: *jiàng*, "to drop, to fall, to come down, to descend, to get down, to send down," or, pronounced *xiáng*, "to surrender, to submit, to vanquish" (YellowBridge, Wang 1993: 30, Shi 1997: 220, Schuessler 2007).

Brilliant Luminance

An ancient Chinese legend, probably composed 2300–2100 BCE, begins by extolling the virtues of the (probably mythical) preeminent sage Yao, stating that his 光, *guāng*, "light, brightness," covered his entire realm from

[4] I thank Yunxiang Yan and Hung-hsiang Chou for graciously checking an earlier, partial draft of this section, and Xiaolei Wu and Ming Xue for carefully checking and correcting the penultimate draft.

corner to corner and from heaven above to the earth below. The text then declares that his virtue was 明, *míng*, "clear, bright" (de Barry & Bloom 1999: 29). The charter 光 also combines with 明 to form 光明, *guāngming*, "light, illumination, radiance," a term commonly used to express the glory of Buddha, as well as being a component of 光榮, *guāngróng*, "honor and glory"; a component of 光辉, *guānghuī*, "radiance, glory; brilliant, magnificent"; and a component of 光临, *guānglín*, the honorific expression "welcome, you honor us with your presence" (Yellowbridge).

Ode 235 of the Wenwang to the twelfth-century BCE founder of the Zhou dynasty, King Wen, in verses 1, 4, 6, and 7 contains lexical LUMINOSITY conformations to the king:

> King Wen is on high (上, *shàng*),
> Oh, he shines / is bright (昭, zhāo) in Heaven
> . . .
> August was King Wen,
> continuously bright (熙, *xī* or *yí*) and reverent.
> . . .
> Look to Yin as a beacon / mirror / reflection (鑒, *jiàn*)
> . . .
> Display and make bright (昭, *zhāo*) your good fame
> (de Barry & Bloom 1999: 38; verse 6: Chinese Text Project [Legge translation]).

Furthermore, in inscriptions from this early Zhou period, dedications by various lineages refer to the "brilliant" ancestors to whom they make sacrifices (Hung 1995: 92–94). Moreover, during the Western Zhou dynasty (1046–771 BCE), the 明 堂, Míng Tang, "Bright/Luminous Hall," was a focal structure of the royal temple where major state ceremonies were conducted. By the end of the Eastern Zhou dynasty (254 BCE), the conception of the Bright Hall had become salient as "a supreme embodiment of sovereignty and political order" (Hung 2007: 194). During the following Han Dynasty and afterwards, although the architectural configurations were reimagined, the ideal of legitimate rule was to build a Míng Tang and receive vassals in its luminance.

A Qin Dynasty (221–206 BCE) inscription legitimating an heir's accession to office credits the first three "brilliant patriarchs" (where brilliant = "golden yellow," *huáng*, 黃) of Qin uniting with the will of "brilliant heaven," *huáng tian*, to conquer their enemies. The inscription declares that the heir's "illumination," 明, *míng*, allowed him to form an alliance that defeated his enemies (Cook 2009: 256–258; Cook's translation of *huáng*). Authors of other Qin and Jin inscriptions also legitimate a ruler's authority with reference to a "brilliant (*huáng*) ancestor," and credit the ruler's own "luminous inner power," *míng de*, and radiance.

Like his predecessor, Zhu Yuanzhang, the Ming Dynasty founder, claimed to have been born in luminance (Li Min, personal communication). Indeed, naming itself 明, ming, "brilliance," the Míng Dynasty (1368–1644) began a tradition of displaying in their office court in the Forbidden Palace a plaque expressing the ideal of rulership. The plague proclaimed 明光大正 (read right to left) *zhèng dà guāng míng*, literally "just, huge, bright/hot, bright/luminous/clever" (Nu He, personal communication).

An ancient tradition of divination based on facial features includes the idea that a glowing spot between the eyebrows augers health, prosperity, and, specifically, social advancement to high rank. Such a spot is 印堂发亮, *yìn ang fā liàng*, which roughly translates as "bright shining mark issuing in greatness" (Li Min, personal communication). Today people also use this phrase as a compliment, meaning "you are doing awesome," "you will have great luck or prosperity" (Ming Xue, personal communication).

****

A philologist with thorough knowledge of Chinese or an epigrapher who comprehensively searched the oracle bones and early bronze inscriptions could certainly expand, improve, and correct my naïve exposition. But it seems safe to conclude that since its inception, iconic dimensional conformations of authority ranking have been extensive and prominent in Chinese writing. It is also apparent that often, for centuries, the same radical or character was used to represent more than one of these physical dimensions. For example. the radical might mean either above or bigger, smaller or below or support, in front or before, strong or heavy. Furthermore, the etymologies of numerous characters show that these dimensions were embodied as social actions conforming authority ranking, such as looking down, lowering the head or body, and standing below versus above. These postures in turn were incorporated into Chinese writing as conformations of authority ranking. So, in Chinese characters we find iconic dimensions metaconforming authority ranking, while also demonstrating that thousands of years ago, Chinese postures of respect iconically conformed authority ranking in these dimensions: BELOW, BEHIND, AFTER, MASS, EXERTING (GREATER) FORCE, and, one conformation we have not seen elsewhere, PRESSING DOWN ON. Did Chinese construe that as a dimension of DOWNWARD FORCE? Being ABOVE?

It is striking that the Chinese lexical metaconformations of authority ranking employ the same dimensions as English lexemes. Given the infrequency of contact between these two language communities, it seems unlikely that many of these numerous iconic dimensional conformations of authority ranking are calques. That is, it seems unlikely that speakers of either language borrowed from the other language the idea of conforming authority ranking with iconic dimensions.

When scholars fully explore some languages from other language families, especially those maximally isolated from contact with Indo-European and Sino-Tibetan languages, we will see if these same dimensions are manifest in them, too: ELEVATION, ANTERIORITY, MASS, VOLUME, SURFACE AREA, FORCE, TEMPORAL PRECEDENCE, and LUMINANCE. At present it is a mystery whether and why NUMEROSITY and LOUDNESS are prominently and widely manifest in physical conformations of authority ranking, but seemingly absent from its lexical conformations, despite NUMEROSITY being such a common linguistic metaconformation in respectful plural pronouns.

Do Other Languages Also Use the Canonical Conformations for Communal Sharing, for Authority Ranking, and for Equality Matching?

What holds for Mooré, Chinese, English, and Proto-Indo-European may not hold true for the other 7,000 languages currently spoken, or for languages now extinct. However, cursory examinations of a few other languages suggest that iconic dimensional conformations of authority ranking may be widespread. Turkish colleagues and American friends who are fluent in Turkish have kindly given me several examples of the canonical iconic dimensional and magnitude conformations in Turkish.[5] There are several Turkish lexical conformations using ELEVATION, several using FORCE, and several using LUMINOSITY; there are also some using ANTERIORITY and some using MASS. Turkish ELEVATION lexemes include *alt*, *ast*, *baş*, *birinin altýnda çalýþmak*, *birinin üstünde çalýþmak*, *üst*, *ulu*, *yüce*, *zatı-ali*, and *ayak takımıt.* The FORCE lexemes include *baskin*, *erk(li)*, *ezilen*, *güçlü*, *güçsüz*, *and iktidar(li).* LUMINOSITY lexical conformations include *debdebe*, *güneş*, *parlak*, *parlamak*, *şaşaa*, and *yildiz.* The MASS lexemes include *ağırlık (koymak)*, *büyük adam*, *büyük ortak/*

[5] My grateful thanks to Diane Sunar (a distinguished social psychologist who speaks Turkish fluently) for generously and carefully researching this for me, and to Murat Yasavul, Aret Karademir, and John Bolendermeta for coming up with additional Turkish lexical conformations of authority ranking.

küçük ortak, and *aile büyükleri*. Turkish ANTERIORITY lexical conformations include *öncelik* and *ileri gelen*.

None of the Turkish linguistic conformations of authority ranking seem to me obvious cognates of Indo-European conformations of authority ranking, but we need expert analyses to be sure. Turkish is in the Turkic language family, but for many centuries there have been at least modest levels of contact between speakers of Turkish and some Indo-European languages, so there could have been calquing in one direction or the other.

In the chapters on postural, architectural, artifactual, and artistic conformations, we touched on some Sumerian LUMINOSITY and LOUDNESS lexical conformations from almost 5,000 years ago. The Sumerian LOUDNESS lexical conformations are intriguing, since LOUDNESS, though prominent for centuries in artifactual conformations across the English-speaking world (trumpet fanfares and drum ruffles and flourishes, cannot salutes, and so forth), does not seem to be a common lexical conformation in Mooré, English, or Chinese. Nor is it in Turkish, apparently. In English, we address a monarch as, "Your highness," but not "Your loudness."

American Sign Language is a natural language, with its own syntax and lexicon. In ASL, when signing about someone of high rank, one holds one's hands high, and conversely, holds one's hands low when signing about someone of low status (Margaret Compton, personal communication, July 2023). Likewise, ASL denotes increasing social "power" or promotion with upward movement of the hands, while decreasing social status or demotion is denoted by downward movement of the signing hands (Taub 2001: 149–153). Of course, ASL signers have extensive contact with English speakers, so these signs could be calqued from English.

Bedouin sign language began in the late twentieth century. Bedouins are polygamous, and the status of cowives depends on the order in which they married their husband. The sign for "first wife" is the sign for "spouse" followed by a raised hand sign indicating above, the sign for second wife is "spouse" with a sign indicating middle elevation, and the sign for third wife is "spouse" plus a lowered hand indicating "below" (Carol Padden, personal communication). Similarly, the sign for a high-status person, such as a community leader or imam, is made with raised hands signing "person" (a thumb sticking up), with the other hand signing "top level" (a flat hand, palm down). To sign "peers of equal status," the two hands are held level, palms down, and brought together – an indication of even level. Signers of Bedouin sign language may have calqued these signs from Arabic, assuming that standard Arabic, or some dialects, conform authority ranking with iconic dimensions. I do not know.

In a number of languages, including English and French, the word for the highest part of the body, the head, is also used to conform the highest-ranking person. For example, Mayan script uses the glyph *ba*, "head," as an exaltive epithet for "first, highest ranking, principal" lord, ruler, sculptor (Houston et al. 2006: 62).

Apart from conformations systems theory, it is hard to imagine any other explanations for the extensive use of iconic dimensional and magnitude lexemes for authority ranking in languages as isolated from each other as Mooré, English, and Chinese. To be sure, it would be illuminating to investigate languages from other families, especially languages that must have had little or no contact with speakers of Chinese, English, Mooré, or Proto-Indo-European. Nicaraguan Sign Language would be an interesting case to study, since many of its signs were invented by deaf children signers, so there may not be much, if any, calquing from Spanish.

Language is much, much more than words. Beyond words, are there other aspects of language that iconically conform authority ranking with dimensions?

Box 11.1

In English it is difficult to talk about authority ranking without using words that also refer to dimensions, or that once did. My impression is that the same may be true of Mooré, but we need to check that with native speakers. What about Chinese? Are nearly all Chinese words for authority ranking based on dimensional iconicity? It is important to find out whether this is true of Mooré, Chinese, and other languages unconnected to them.

If so, that would confirm that iconic dimensional words for authority ranking are its primary lexical metaconformations, not metaphors in the usual sense. The usual conceptualization of metaphor is that it consists of using a simpler, well understood reference to represent something that is complex or difficult to grasp (e.g. Lakoff & Johnson 1980, Lakoff 1993). Hence a metaphor consists of the bracketed substitution of a fictive but simpler representation, understood "not to be taken literally," for the fundamental, true, but opaque and excessively complex representation of the real thing. Neither the person who utters the metaphor nor the listener believes that the simpler representation is real. But in linguistic metaconformations of authority ranking, one does not find two juxtaposed representations; there is only dimensional iconicity. There is no more literal, more real, more true representation of authority ranking. That's all there is.

Which makes sense, since iconic dimensionality is the primary mode of conforming authority ranking in postures, positions, dress and headgear, architecture, art, artifacts, and practices.

Polarity and Conforming Distinctions at the Top

In the iconicity of magnitudes and dimensions of the conformation of authority ranking, there is a polarity so intuitively obvious that it easily escapes attention. I mentioned it earlier, but let's come back to it. On each dimension, there is one pole that invariably conforms "higher rank," while the other pole never does. Most of the dimensions of authority ranking conformations have an intrinsic zero at one pole, and an infinite maximum at the opposite pole: ELEVATION, MASS, VOLUME, SURFACE AREA, NUMEROSITY, FORCE, DURATION AND DURABILITY, LUMINANCE, AND LOUDNESS. For all of these, the conformation of lower status is toward the pole with an intrinsic zero, while higher status is toward the pole with an infinite maximum. Superior rank is rarely, if ever, conformed by BELOW, LESSER MASS, SMALLER SURFACE AREA, LESSER FORCE, etcetera.

Another fact so obvious that it is easy to miss is that the rank of the supreme being – emperor and/or prime deity – is conformed more prominently than the ranks of other elites, while the ranks of most of the population are conformed far less conspicuously, though nevertheless consistently, in many societies. Recall that the fewest guns in a salute is five, for a vice-consul. Below that rank, no one gets any cannon salute at all when they arrive or depart. (Maybe you do, but I don't.) Similarly, in ancient Egypt, the pharaoh had a giant pyramid build for himself, and sometimes a distinctly smaller one for his wife. Important officials built elaborate tombs, often mostly underground, but not pyramids. Most people had no pyramid, and no tomb as such. Likewise, when eating, the most common conformation is that everyone waits for the highest-ranking person to begin, and then everyone starts eating, without any further temporal distinctions. This is surely because distinctions at the top are crucial, while differentiation among lower ranks is much less important. It matters a lot to everyone who is the king, but to most people it matters much less, if it matters at all, just who is ninety-fourth in the hierarchy and who is ninety-fifth. And, of course, most people do not have the wealth to build a pyramid – and would likely be mocked for pretentiousness if they did build some sort of pyramid.

The result in many dimensional conformations is that the superiority of the superior is directly and constantly or repeatedly conformed, but the inferiority of the inferior may not be conformed on the same dimension. Persons looking up at an Egyptian pyramid feel its enormity relative to themselves, not to small pyramids of theirs. A Mayan ruler does not have a bigger pyramid than his subjects, he has the only pyramid. In some cases, what may be intended is an implicit comparison with the pyramid of a previous ruler, or with the pyramids of rulers of neighboring states. But in other cases, there seems not to be any implicit comparison. At key moments in his life, the Buddha does not outshine everyone else, he is the only one who shines. No one else is mentioned as less luminous or as lacking luminosity. Sumerian relief carvings show the king as much bigger and above everyone else. But when a Sumerian relief carving depicts the king killing a fierce animal, the relief does not show a lesser person killing a less fierce animal. The same is true of ancient Egyptian murals: bigger than their subjects, but no representation of inferior hunters appear. In other words, certain iconic dimensional conformations do not patently conform the highest-ranking person or deity's relative rank, they simply conform the ruler's or the god's "awesomeness" on certain dimensions. Such conformations use dimensions iconically, but not relatively. The ruler is incomparable.

In Sum: The Magnitudes and Dimensions of the Iconic Conformations of Authority Ranking

- Elevation
- Mass
- Volume
- Surface area and personal space (entitlement to approach)
- Numerosity (sensorially comparative, without necessity of enumerating)
- Anteriority
- Temporal precedence
- Temporal duration (apparently uncommon)
- Force (embodied as strength)
- Luminance
- Loudness

Vision is the primary sensory mode of all of the conformations of authority ranking, except for LOUDNESS and TEMPORAL PRECEDENCE. Generally, because it is not visible, FORCE is not depicted but is implied by apparent muscular exertion.

CHAPTER 12

Experimental Research on Western Adults' and Infants' Cognitive Representations of Rank

Implicit Cognitive Conformations: Evidence from Experiments

We began with material from my participant observation in a tiny West African village; then we explored ethnographies; archeological artifacts, ancient architecture, and humanly sculpted landscapes; sculptures, reliefs, and other visual depictions; narratives from ancient and classical texts; lexemes and etymologies; and a smattering of other materials. Our perusal has been guided by a theory that itself was inductively derived, initially from my participant observation and lexical discoveries in the Moosé language, then further developed and revised using the other materials presented in this book. All of this can be loosely described as description, inductively used to identify patterns that we can fairly call a theory: the theory of conformation systems. Throughout my career, I have found induction from observations and descriptions to be fruitful and enlightening. But this epistemological approach does have limitations and drawbacks. This approach does not permit strong inferences about proximal causation, and it is potentially vulnerable to selection bias: of necessity, researchers using this approach must examine only what they believe to be "relevant." One cannot look at everything that humans do; one must reflectively or intuitively choose where to look and what to examine. The necessity of selectivity can readily result in examination of materials that mostly match the researcher's prior expectations and the expectations that subsequently emerge from the research. Without intending to, the researcher may ignore or set aside materials that are inconsistent with their emerging theory.

To counterbalance potential confirmation bias of this sort, let us bring experimental evidence into the picture. Well-designed, rigorously analyzed, and scrupulously reported experiments allow examination of one or more "independent variables" at a time, ideally isolated from all the other factors that may be operating in "real life." That permits much stronger inferences about causation than are possible with only naturalistic observation, and offers data that is relatively free of selection bias.

Of course, even when beautifully replicated in preregistered large-sample experiments by multiple independent laboratories drawing on diverse samples, even the best experiments have limitations, and are vulnerable to biases, too. One huge limitation is that experiments are artificial situations that differ from everyday situations in many crucial but unidentified respects. Another limitation is that experiments nearly always rely on more or less artificial stimuli, highly artificial modes of presenting stimuli, and highly artificial response modes. So, experiments are always at risk of lacking external validity; what happens in the lab is not a mirror of what happens in "real life."

Fortunately, the limitations and potential biases of experimentation tend to be distinct from the limitations and potential biases of induction from observation and description. Compared to experiential and observational reports, experimental findings are much less liable to the researcher's biased attention, biased memory, biased recording, and biased reporting. Indeed, the new Open Science (osf.io) standards virtually eliminate such biases in experimental research.

For present purposes, perhaps the greatest merit of experimental research is that it provides evidence about certain responses to conformations. That fills a crucial gap in the sorts of material we have covered up to this point in the book, which reveal too little about how people are affected by conformations. Do iconic conformations shape how people cognitively represent authority ranking relationships, along with emotions, motives, and moral sentiments that support the relationship? Do indexical conformations motivate people to care about others in communal sharing relationships? Do concrete operations comprise the basic moral templates for equality matching relationships? Do symbolic conformations induce commitment to market pricing relationships? Experiments alone are not sufficient to provide clear and deep elucidation of such questions, but experiments are invaluable complements to the ethnographic and ethnological comparison methods used and the sources compiled in this book.

Although there is no deception in the experiments that we will review, participants are not aware of just what it is about their responses that is being measured. They do not know and are unlikely to guess, for example, that the purpose of the experiment is to determine whether there is a difference between reactions times in condition X and reactions times in condition Y, and, indeed, are unlikely to recognize that these conditions are distinct. Modern cognitive and social psychological experiments are designed to reflect cognitive processing that is maximally free of most conceivable cultural and social effects due to participants' own feelings about what they should do in the experiment. In particular, in well-designed experiments, the results are largely independent of participants' beliefs or concerns about what they suppose that experimenters wish them to do. And the results are mostly independent of what participants suppose that other participants are doing in response to the same conditions, or suppose that anyone judges that participants should do. And, for that matter, few people have any concerns about their own or others' reaction times, let alone differences between reaction times in different conditions, which is the dependent variable in many of these studies. Or, at any rate, these are crucial criteria that reviewers and editors consider, and that peers critique.

Beginning around 2005, cognitive social psychologists began doing relevant experiments, at first unaware of conformation systems theory. But soon, some studies were specifically designed to test conformations systems theory, as initially and sketchily set forth in Fiske 2004, after being presaged in Fiske 1991 and 1992. Most of this experimental cognitive research has focused on iconic conformations of authority ranking, especially ELEVATION, along with some studies relevant to SURFACE AREA, FORCE, MASS, and/or VOLUME.

The studies of adult cognition that we now look at were designed to show how people mentally represent what the researchers conceptualized as *power* or, for the German researchers and participants, *Macht.* Note that there is ambiguity in the folk lexeme *Macht*, which may reference pure coercive force and control, or legitimate authority ranking relations. However, the stimuli that these researchers typically present are words that I would call "role terms," denoting social positions that participants in fact perceive as mostly or entirely legitimate, not as positions derived from pure coercive force. The typical stimuli in these studies are words such as *lawyer*, *captain*, *mayor*, *chief editor*, *minister*, *pope*, *secretary*, *sailor*, *citizen*, *worshipper*, *chambermaid*, or similar role terms in German (examples of the stimuli of Zanolie et al. 2012). The experimenters intuitively selected pairs of role terms that they judge to contrast in "power" or "*Machet*," but that, for the most part, relational models theory would characterize as implementations of authority ranking.

Thomas Schubert (2005) did the very first of these studies. German participants were asked to judge which of two role terms displayed on a screen was the most "powerful" (*Machtig* is the word that participants read in the instructions). Participants were instructed to respond as fast as possible, pressing the "up" cursor key if the most *Macht* word [always a role term] was the upper of the two words, and the "down" cursor key if the most *Machet* word [role] was the lower of the two words. Participants responded significantly more slowly when the powerful role was displayed on the screen BELOW the less powerful, compared to when the powerful role was displayed ABOVE the less powerful (Schubert 2005). To illustrate, the equivalent in English would be asking participants to quickly press the up or down key to select the more *powerful* person, showing this on the monitor:

servant
master

compared to other trials, showing this on the monitor;

master
servant

Many previous experiments on many phenomena by many researchers have found that participants take longer to respond, and/or make more errors, when they see stimuli whose relations are discordant with the participants' prior representations of those relations. So, in this case one can conclude that when participants see *servant* above *master*, more cognitive processing (and hence longer reaction time) is required because what they see is not what they expect, and/or is not what they evaluate that it "should be."

Replicating and extending Schubert's (2005) results, von Hecker et al. (2013) found the same effects when participants read about pair-wise

Box 12.1

There is an interesting story behind Schubert's (2005) article that reported these results. When Schubert submitted his manuscript to the *Journal of Personality and Social Psychology* (the premier journal in social psychology), in their comments on the manuscript, a reviewer (not I) and the editor, Jeff Greenberg, responded to tell Schubert that these studies fortuitously tested Alan Fiske's theory of the modes of representation of authority ranking (Fiske 1991, 1992, 2004). Surprised and intrigued to hear this, Schubert had a look at my work. Then he emailed me to ask if I planned to attend the upcoming annual social psychology meetings. I did, so we met there. Thomas quickly became a close research collaborator and a close friend, along with his partner and research collaborator, Beate Seibt. The three of us continue to collaborate and socialize extensively.

rankings among four fictional persons, and then responded to probes about pairs that they had not read about but could infer if they assumed transitivity of rank. Participants responded more slowly when they saw on the monitor the higher-ranking person's name BELOW the lower-ranking person's name, compared to quicker response times when the higher-ranking person's name appeared ABOVE the lower-ranking person's name. Furthermore, von Hecker et al. found that participants responded more rapidly the greater the "distance" between the fictional persons' ranks. For example, using inequality symbols to represent rank, when A > B > C > D, participants were able to judge more quickly who ranked higher, A or D, compared to slower responses when asked who ranked higher, B or C. Many studies have established that this distance effect is characteristic of judgments comparing all sorts of physical and numerical magnitudes; it is part of what is called Weber's Law.

With a more rigorous design and finer-grained analyses, in three studies, Holmgren, Isager, and Schubert (2018) replicated this Weber distance effect for ranks that Norwegian participants learned from accounts of interactions among fictional persons; and the same distance effect appeared when participants chose the more powerful in pairs of Catholic religious ranks, feudal political ranks, and military ranks (all systems that were familiar to participants). Concordant with these results are the findings from a study in which fifteen Chinese participants saw only one role term in each experimental trial; they were asked to strike a key if and only if the term denoted a "powerful" category of persons. Participants took longer to identify a role term as powerful when the role term was displayed low on the screen, compared to when it was displayed high on the screen (Wu et al. 2016; they do not indicate which Chinese lexeme they translated as "powerful"). Evidently these participants, too, implicitly expected that powerful persons should be HIGH while nonpowerful persons should be LOW – and the participants extended that expectation about persons to implicit expectations about the spatial position of Chinese characters for these role terms.

Giessner and Schubert (2007) looked at how Western European students depicted power in organization charts and how they inferred "power" from such charts. They had participants read a description of a manager that included either the statement that the manager was very powerful, or a statement that the manager had very little power. When then asked to place a box labeled "Manager A" into position on an organization chart, participants placed the manager box HIGHER if they had read that the manager was very powerful, compared to when the participant had read that the manager had very little power. Giessner and Schubert obtained the same results when Dutch participants were asked to move a small drawing of a leader to represent the leader's social relationship with their followers, who were also represented by small drawings: they placed powerful leaders HIGHER than leaders with little power.

In the same paper, Giessner and Schubert (2007) also found that their participants inferred a manager's power in the organization from the vertical distance between the manager's box and his subordinates boxes in organization charts: the longer the line, the more power participants attributed to the manager. However, this finding did not hold up in a large-scale replication attempt by Klein et al. (2018). Giessner and Schubert (2019) ran follow-up studies and confirmed that their 2007 results had been a false positive. Instead, they found that putting Manager A's box ABOVE Manager B's box in an organization chart leads people to assume Manager A has more power, but increasing the distance doesn't matter. (This is exactly what relational models theory and conformation systems theory predict: social ranks are ordinally compared, such that asymmetrical difference is meaningful, but not interval or ratio distance between adjacent ranks.) The 2019 paper also successfully replicated the result related above that participants placing a manager on a chart depicted more powerful leaders with more vertical distance above subordinates. In other words: When viewing and interpreting organization charts, Dutch students only interpreted the ranking, not the distance between the boxes. However, when they produced an organization chart, the Dutch students apparently visualized information about greater or lesser power as greater or lesser vertical distance.[1]

The results of these four sets of studies, taken together, show that the slowing of cognitive processing, and/or slower generation of responses, does not depend on the language of the participants and stimuli, nor do the results depend on whether participants see isolated words, or read narratives.

There are similar results for SURFACE AREA and/or MASS. In two studies by Schubert, Waldzus, and Giessner (2009), German and Dutch participants were asked to rapidly pick the more powerful (*Mächtig*) group from two role terms or social categories named on the screen. Participants made fewer errors when the font size fit the magnitude conformation, and more errors when the name of the powerful group was presented in 12pt font and the name of the less powerful group was shown in 26pt font. In English, that might be, for example, seeing on the screen

[1] My thanks to Thomas Schubert for drafting these two paragraphs, which I then edited.

lawyers **janitors**

Concordantly, participants who were asked to pick the "powerless" group made more errors when the name of the powerless group was shown in a larger font and the powerful group in a smaller font. Response latencies in trials where font size did not fit the conformation of power were likewise greater for the German participants in their first study, but not for their Dutch participants in their second study. Some features of the two experiments differed. Prior warnings to expect these effects reversed them. We cannot be certain what magnitude or dimension is operating in font size; it could be SURFACE AREA, but my subjective sense is that the 26 pt font looks MASSIVE. And, of course, it is taller, so it may evoke responses via the UP–DOWN dimension.

Something similar occurs when people think about real persons. Studies have shown that relative social rank distorts North American participants' perceptions of their own and others' heights: people perceive higher-ranking persons to be taller than they really are, and judge lower-ranking persons to be shorter than they are (Dannenmaier & Thumin 1964, Higham & Carment 1992).

Zanolie at al. (2012) hypothesized that, if people represent authority ranking as vertical spatial position on the UP–DOWN dimension, thinking about a "high" ranking person should immediately direct their visual attention UP, while thinking about a "low" ranking person should direct their immediate attention DOWN. To test this hypothesis, they showed Dutch participants words, one at a time, representing powerful (*machtig*) people (e.g., king, director, general), or powerless (*onmachtig*) people (e.g., baby, prisoner, slave). On each trial, the participants judged whether the word denoted a powerful or powerless person; then, 200 milliseconds later, the letter *p* or the letter *q* appeared and the participant had to indicate, as quickly as possible, which letter it was. After reading and classifying a word denoting a powerful person, participants responded more rapidly when the *p* or *q* appeared high on the screen, and conversely, after reading and classifying a word denoting a powerless person, participants responded more rapidly when the letter appeared low on the screen. This suggests that participants' attention is focused higher on the screen immediately after reading a single word denoting a high-ranking role, and vice versa. Error rates did not show this pattern, however. Increasing the lag between word and letter to 500–700 milliseconds eliminated this effect.

Taken together, these studies show that these German, Dutch, and Chinese participants in one way or another "think" that persons in higher-status roles are HIGH, and/or perhaps in some sense, ideally ought to be, HIGH, while thinking that persons in lower-status roles are, or should be, LOW. This understanding that spatial positions of persons conform social ranks is not limited to actual persons, but extends to words on a screen. This HIGH–LOW conformation directs spatial attention, as well as perception and/or memory of living persons. Participants rely on this HIGH–LOW conformation when considering hierarchies they have often encountered or heard of, and also hierarchies of fictitious persons whose relationships the participants have just learned. The conformation is strong enough to interfere with reading comprehension, slowing reading comprehension down and sometimes causing errors. There are similar affects for font size, which presumably concerns SURFACE AREA, and/or possibly MASS or HIGH–LOW.

The stimuli in these studies are not conformational acts as such. But there are experimental studies of one iconic magnitude: the VOLUME that persons occupy by configuring their bodies. Witkower et al.'s (2020) review of psychological studies, together with seven experiments of their own, show that high-ranking persons adopt expansive poses that expand the VOLUME occupied by their bodies, and, conversely, others perceive expansive poses to conform high rank:

> First, high-ranking individuals tend to show open and expansive bodily displays, including chest expansion, arm movements extended outward, open leg positions, wide stances, hands behind the head with elbows out, and other physically enlarging behaviors ... These same behaviors are perceived as indicative of high rank by signal receivers, and result in rank conferral ... Furthermore, expansive nonverbal behaviors have been shown to communicate high rank across diverse populations ... These findings suggest that, at a broad level, bodily expansion may be an evolved signal of high rank ... Second, individuals who have increased in rank also tend to display the emotion expression of pride, which features arms extended out from the body, with hands either on hips or raised above the head with clenched fists, chest expanded, head tilted slightly upward, and a small smile. (Witkower et al. 2020: 90)

In short, experimental and other controlled, statistically analyzed psychological studies of adults (mostly European) confirm that at least some magnitudes and dimensions do iconically conform authority ranking relations.

Studies of Infant Core Cognition of Authority Ranking

Children (and other cultural novices) cannot learn who has what kind of social relationship with whom unless they somehow know *what* are

> basic kinds of relationships to look for between people, as well as *how* to recognize them in the world . . .
>
> We suggest that humans have evolved an innate, finite set of conceptual primitives that specify relational models for communal sharing, social hierarchy, and equality and are coupled with innate input analyzers that automatically identify some instances of each in the social world. Such a universal vocabulary of basic kinds of relational models would make it possible to *learn* the relational makeup of their particular culture by means of specifying the kinds of social relationships they should be looking for and at least some initial ways of recognizing them.
>
> (Thomsen & Carey 2013, pp. 20 & 21 [italics in the original]).

Relational models theory posits that just four relational models structure most human cooperation: communal sharing, authority ranking, equality matching, and market pricing (Fiske 1991, 1992, Fiske & Haslam 2004). The theory posits that infants innately know the structures of each relational model. Additionally, relational models theory posits that, while the coordination structure is innately "known," it is not sufficient to enable coordinated social relationships. An infant – or any person – needs to understand the social interactions that they observe or want to join. An infant, or any person, needs to be able to effectively initiate and participate in social action. And an infant – or any other prospective participant – needs to evaluate social action while understanding how others evaluate social action. To do any of that, the infant or other prospective participant must reliably recognize the relational model that is operating to coordinate any given aspect of any given interaction in any given context in their particular community. Extending more primitive concepts in earlier versions of relational models theory, conformation systems theory posits that infants quickly develop the capacity to do all of this because infants innately recognize the conformation systems, are innately motivated by them, innately use them to initiate social relations and motivate others, and innately use them as moral frameworks for evaluating social relations. This innate foundation is the chief explanation for why people everywhere, throughout history and prehistory, rely on the conformation systems.

Relational models theory was quickly supported by all sorts of experimental evidence and interpretive insights regarding adult social relations. But almost all developmental psychologists have long assumed that infants could not possibly understand social relationships. So it was only fairly recently that any researcher investigated the theory that infants know the relational models, together with their respective conformation systems.

The first such investigation was a pathbreaking series of experiments in which Thomsen, Frankenhuis, Ingold-Smith, and Carey (2011) showed for the first time that preverbal infants have definite expectations about social relationships, in particular authority ranking relationships. During a Fulbright year at UCLA and then during her PhD study at UCLA, Thomsen worked closely with me. When she moved to Harvard, she specially designed a series of studies to test infants' understanding of relational models theory, specifically, authority ranking, together with its iconic conformations of physical magnitudes and dimensions. Thomsen et al. showed infants videos of two blocks with simple eyes and a mouth line; one block was much larger than the other. The two blocks repeatedly moved across a surface from opposite sides until they gently "ran into each other," backed up a little bit, and stopped. Infants evidently interpreted this to indicate that the depicted agents could proceed no further, apparently blocking each other's way forward. In test trials, at this point, one of the blocks then turned face down on the surface and moved sideways out of the way of the other, which then proceeded on its way. Ten-month old US infants, as well as infants aged twelve and thirteen months, looked longer when the larger block prostrated itself and moved out of the way of the smaller block than when the smaller block did so.

What this shows is that infants expect three different physical dimensions to be joint icons of authority ranking: First, VOLUME (and/or MASS or SURFACE AREA) of the agentic blocks; second, prostrating-lowering to make the self BELOW; and third, TEMPORAL PRECEDENCE in crossing the surface to go on their way. That is, the infants expected the SMALLER block to LOWER itself so that the LARGER block could go FIRST. We can assume that these infants in Cambridge, Massachusetts have never seen anyone bow, let alone prostrate themselves on the floor or slide sideways. Probably none of the infants, who are barely beginning to sit up on their own, have ever seen two persons proceeding in opposite directions on a narrow path, such that neither person can continue where they intend to go. Yet at ten months they already have expectations about such interactions. At eight months their looking times in the two conditions do not differ, but there is a steady increase in the difference between their looking times, such that, even with the very small samples feasible in infant studies, the difference becomes statistically significant at ten months. It is logically conceivable that this developmental process could result from some kind of experience that most of these infants share, but it is difficult to imagine what experiences would lead them to expect smaller agents to bow and move out of a larger agent's path in order to allow the larger agent to proceed first. More likely, this expectation results from brain maturation in a normal social environment realizing an evolved adaptation–maturation that occurs without the infant ever observing anything like the interaction they observe in the lab.

A subsequent study, with sixteen-month-old human infants, showed the infants two puppets and two objects that afford sitting: one beige cube, and one shiny bright purple high-backed chair with a slightly higher seat than the cube (Enright, Gweon & Sommerville 2017; they do not report the infants' nationality, but apparently they were in the US). The two puppets "compete" for the taller chair, and then one puppet sits in it; the other puppet bows to the seated puppet and then sits on the lower cube. A male experimenter then distributes four Legos either equally, or unequally (3:1), giving either the "dominant" or nondominant puppet three Legos. The infants expect the experimenter to give more Legos to the puppet who "won" the higher, shiny chair and sat in it. This expectation can be inferred because the infants look longer if the experimenter either divides the Legos equally or gives more to the nondominant puppet. It is not clear whether the infants expectations are determined solely by one puppet's obtaining the seat that it sought, with the other puppet "losing." And/or the infants could expect the experimenter to give more Legos to puppet who sat in the higher, high-backed, shiny chair. And/or the infants may expect that the puppet who bowed will receive fewer Legos. Enright and colleagues studies did not test those factors separately. But the studies do show that the infants expect a third-party to distribute more to a higher agent, not to distribute equally.

Margoni et al. (2018) conducted another set of studies, again in considerable part motivated by conformations systems theory's concept of the iconic physics of magnitudes and dimensions that conform legitimate authority ranking. One sample of Italian twenty-one-month-olds repeatedly watched an animated scene in which a "bully" appears while three red oval figures are playing with a ball. The bully is a yellow oval figure with face and arms, wearing a small cap. The bully hits each of the red figures with a long stick, takes the red figures' ball, and leaves with it. Then the toddlers saw a scene in which the bully appears and tells the ball players to go to bed, and the ball players obey, going into a house and (still visible through a large window) close their eyes. Another sample of twenty-one-month-olds repeatedly watched the three red figures playing with the ball. A yellow "leader" appears, wearing a very tall headdress. The players cease playing, and bow low, saying "ohhhh." The leader taps his stick on the ground, inclines slightly, and the three red figures again bow low. In the following scene, the infants see this same sequence of events again, but this time the leader taps his stick and one of the red figures brings the ball to the leader, who then departs, leaving the ball with the three red figures. Then, the toddlers see the leader reappear and tell the ball players to go to bed, which they do, as they did when sent to bed by the bully.

Using the usual measure of looking time, Margoni et al. measured what infants expected to happen. If the Italian toddlers watched the bully scene, when the bully sends the red figures to bed and then leaves, the Italian toddlers evidently are not surprised to see the ball players get up from their beds, go outside, and play ball. But they are surprised (i.e., they look longer) if the ball players stay in bed when the bully leaves!

In contrast, if the toddlers watched the leader send the ball players to bed, the toddlers are not surprised when the ball players stay in bed after the leader leaves. They are surprised if, when the leader leaves, the ball players get out of bed, go out and play ball!

In short, at twenty-one months, Italian toddlers expect the red animated agents to stay in bed after a leader tells them to do so and departs, but the toddlers expect the agents to get up, leave their beds, go out and play when a bully has told them to go to bed and then leaves them alone.[2] That is, the Italian infants apparently understand the iconic meaning of a tall headdress (making an agent TALLER), and/or bowing (LOWERING themselves) – although surely they have never seen either, and notwithstanding the fact that the very simple figures performing these actions do not look anything like humans. Obviously, these results are consistent with conformation systems theory: for these Italian toddlers, wearing a tall headdress and being bowed to "legitimate" the agent's authority, so the ball players obey the agent. Unfortunately, in this study Margoni et al. did not run experiments testing these two ABOVE–BELOW conformations separately (tall hat and bowing). Nor did they test the effect of the big agent returning the ball versus keeping it, or the infants' expectations based on whether the big agent hit or did not hit the smaller ones, so we cannot draw inferences about which one (or combination) of the four factors produced the result.

Margoni and Thomsen (2024) then conducted eight preregistered experiments in which 128 Norwegian twenty-one-month-old infants viewed animations. They found that when the infants observe a set of agents bow before a character, who then gives them an order and departs,

[2] Of course, using the looking-time measure, the infants' expectations can only be compared in one condition relative to another, not assessed in any absolute terms, so my use of the terms "surprised" and "not especially surprised" are purely relative.

the infants expect that the leader will be obeyed, even in her absence. In contrast, the infants do not expect obedience to the departed character if the infants have observed that character conferring benefits on the other agents, or, conversely, if the agents had given items of tribute to the departed character. Nor did the infants expect continued obedience to a character in her absence if the character had imposed costs on the other or was bigger than the others. In short, bowing has an especially powerful effect on expectations of twenty-one-month old Norwegian toddlers, though surely these toddlers have never seen anyone bowing.

Meng et al. (2019) showed 12–16-month-old Japanese infants two agents, one of whom is in a spatially higher position than the other. The two agents are not shown touching each other, and no conflict is depicted. In a subsequent scene, both agents are on the same level and one object is presented to them. They do not fight over it; one of them simply takes possession of the ball. The infants expect that the agent who was higher in the previous scene will be the one who takes the ball.

Stavans and Baillargeon (2019) conducted what was, in effect, another test of the ELEVATION dimension. They performed an experiment in which half of a sample of US seventeen-month-old infants observed three bear puppets, two of whom are similar and one of whom, a red bear, is taller than the others and wears a tall hat. The other half of the infants observed three bears all of the same size, similarly dressed, except that one wears red. After the infants were familiarized with the puppets, the red bear brought out two cubes, announced "Toys," and the other two bears shouted "Yay!" The red bear placed the cubes in the middle, and then one of the other bears took both toys. The infants looked for about an equal length of time when the same-sized red bear intervened to give one of the toys to the bear who had none, compared to how long they looked when the red bear failed to intervene. But the infants looked longer if the tall bear in the tall hat does not intervene, compared to their shorter looking time when the tall bear in the tall hat does intervene to give one of the toys to the bear who had none. In other words, the infants have no definite expectation about whether a nonleader resembling the other two bears will intervene or not, but expect a tall bear in a tall hat to intervene to even the allocation of cubes between two shorter agents.

Note that these experiments do not clearly distinguish between two possibilities: whether infants perceive social power as the property of the individual agent, or whether infants perceive social rank to be a property of a social relationship. Moscaro and Csibra (2012) did some studies designed to make that distinction. They found that when twelve- and fifteen-month-olds viewed an agent ceding a resource to another, they inferred a stable relationship between two agents, rather than a property of the individuals.

Putting all of these studies together, and especially considering Margoni and Thomsen's (2024) systematic comparison, it has now been conclusively demonstrated that infants use the iconic ABOVE–BELOW conformation to understand and predict authority ranking behavior that they observe. We do not yet know at what age infants or toddlers use the iconic conformation of the ABOVE–BELOW dimension to understand, predict, evaluate, or motivate their own relationships. At what age, and in what circumstances, does it matter to an infant or toddler whether she herself is ABOVE or BELOW another person? When elevation does begin to matter, how does being ABOVE or BELOW affect the infant or toddler's social relational emotions, motives, and evaluations of their relationship?

Developmental psychologists have hardly begun to explore the other iconic dimensions that, for adults, conform authority ranking. There is one study that investigated what may be a precursor to, or even the basis of, the MULTIPLICITY dimension conformation. In many species of primates, dominance ranks are determined in large part by the relative number (and ranks) of allies who will support each animal in a confrontation (Gilby et al. 2013, Bissonnette et al. 2015, Kajokaite et al. 2019, Feldblum et al. 2021). In these species, for any two animals, the dominant animal is the one with the larger number of allies expected to support it. Note that the allies need not be present in any given interaction between the individuals whose dominance rank is determined by the relative number of their expected allies. Do human infants have expectations about whether the number of allies will affect positions in legitimate authority ranking relations? To find out, Pun et al. (2016) showed Canadian infants as young as 6–9-months-old animations of two groups of squares with faces. The squares move up and down together in synchrony, side by side. One group is composed of three of these agents, the other of two agents. After observing this, the infants see an agent from one group encounter an agent from the other group, each finding their way blocked by the other, as in the original Thomsen, Frankenhuis, Ingold-Smith, and Carey (2011) study. The infants expect an agent associated with the group of two agents to "bow" (rotate 90°) and move back out of the way of the agent from the group of three agents, allowing the latter to proceed on its way first. They look longer when, unexpectedly, the agent from the group of three bows and moves out of the way of the agent from the group of two. This can be interpreted as infants understanding one instantiation of the multiplicity conformation.

In sum, even preverbal infants implicitly make the attribution that LOWER agents are subordinate, and have something like deferential emotions, or motives to obey. Or, what amounts to the same thing, infants judge that HIGHER agents are legitimately entitled to command and will be obeyed. Infants in these studies understand these ELEVATION conformations when they themselves are still too young to be able to stand, let alone bow or prostrate themselves, and have never observed bowing or prostrating.

Already, after the first few of these studies, in a chapter on core cognition of social relationships, Thomsen and Carey (2013) put it this way:

> This chapter examines how children figure out how to behave in the social world. It is argued that humans have evolved an innate, finite set of conceptual primitives that specify relational models for communal sharing, social hierarchy, and equality, and are coupled with innate input analyzers that automatically identify some instances of each in the social world. Such a universal vocabulary of basic kinds of relational models would make it possible for young children to learn the relational makeup of their particular culture by specifying the kinds of social relationships they should be looking for and at least some initial ways of recognizing them.

For a thorough review of the research on infants' core understanding of communal sharing, authority ranking, and equality matching relationships, see Thomas's (2024) outstanding, comprehensive review, as well as Thomsen and Carey's (2013) review of the early findings. She discusses more studies than I have room to consider here. In most of the studies considered herein or reviewed by Thomas, researchers were primarily or exclusively aiming to determine if infants understood social relationships, as such. It seems that for many infant researchers, editors, reviewers, and readers, the manner of conforming the relationship never arose at all. Some researchers do not even explain, for example, why they chose iconic dimensional conformations to present authority ranking relationships to infants, apparently relying on what the researchers assumed to be the obvious means to conform authority ranking relationships. In any case, virtually every study of infant understanding of authority ranking actually tests whether infants recognize the iconic dimensional conformation that identifies authority ranking relations, and know what kind of interactions to expect in an authority ranking relationship.

The researchers who did these studies were focused on discovering whether infants know about hierarchical social relationships, and whether they distinguish between legitimate authority, and power based on coercive force and violence. Their paper titles, introductory reviews, hypotheses, and discussions do not mention the conformation system that infants must recognize in order to know what to expect in an authority ranking interaction. Unless infants recognize iconic dimensional conformations, they would not know what sort of interaction to expect. Yet, to my knowledge, every published study showing infant understanding of authority ranking has one thing in common: researchers represented authority ranking with iconic dimensions. Of course, it makes perfect sense for researchers to take for granted that iconic dimensions are the right media for representing authority ranking to nonverbal infants: researchers, just like infants and everyone else, implicitly know the conformation system. People naturally think about authority ranking as relative positions on dimensions, and that is the "natural" manner to communicate about authority ranking – to anyone, adult or infant.

Studies showing that infants have core knowledge about authority ranking demonstrate something else, too. Infants expect that, after engaging in an iconic dimensional conformation, subordinates will do what the superior tells them to do, and also will cede an attractive resource to the superior. Infants expect the superior to intervene to even out an uneven distribution among subordinates. Infants expect a subordinate to "bow" to their superior, and move aside, ceding the right of way to their superior, waiting while the superior proceeds first. The experiments do not reveal whether the infant expects the agents to have emotions, or motives, or moral sentiments that induce the agents' social actions in the authority ranking relationship. But the results definitely show that infants know that authority ranking is more than a linear ordering in the purely mathematical sense. Infants expect that, after engaging in an iconic dimensional conformation, in subsequent interactions the animated figures or puppets will act in accord with their respective social positions in the authority ranking relationship that results from that conformation.

Likewise, the infant studies of communal sharing show that infants expect people who engage in consubstantial assimilation to have emotions or motives or moral sentiments that induce kindness and care in a communal sharing relationship. Infants readily recognize that consubstantial assimilation creates or reaffirms communal sharing relationships. In short, infant core knowledge about consubstantial assimilation conformation, and infant knowledge about iconic dimensional conformation, consist of far more than recognition that consubstantial assimilation makes a set of persons socially equivalent in a purely mathematical sense, while iconic dimensional conformations establish much more than the formal structure that mathematicians describe as a linear order. Infants know that each type of conformation impels participants to perform social actions corresponding to the kind of relationship the conformation created or displayed. Infants perceive the agents to be engaging in, respectively, communal sharing and authority ranking relationships. A theory of mind cannot explain what infants in these experiments are expecting; infants must have a theory of relationships – actually, four theories of relationships, incorporating theories of their respective conformation systems (Fiske & Haslam 1996, Haslam & Fiske 2004).

There is no reason to suppose that infants' "theories" of the relational models and their conformation systems are conscious. Infants' and adults' theories of relational models and conformation systems are probably not readily accessible to reflection, any more than are people's "theories" of phonemes and syntax, of depth perception, color vision, or hand–eye coordination (for some cogent thoughts on such matters, see Carruthers 2011). (If adults had valid, explicit, articulable theories of relational models and their conformation systems, there would be no point in my writing this book.)

To understand what other people are up to when interacting with them, preverbal infants and toddlers presumably use the same implicit theories of relational models and conformation systems that they use to make sense of social interactions they observe among puppets and among animated agents. And it seems likely that preverbal infants and toddlers use those same implicit theories to generate their own social initiatives, and their own responses to others. But that remains to be studied experimentally.

In any case, infants clearly do have definite expectations about the behaviors of people who have engaged in iconic dimensional conformations. Infants', older children's, and adults' implicit confidence in those expectations likely increases when they observe the persons repeatedly engaging in the same conformation together, over a period of hours, days, and weeks. If, for the most part, that confidence is warranted, it would go a long way toward solving the coordination problem that people face when each person's benefit depends on the other(s)' cooperation, and there are substantial costs to cooperating while others defect. As we considered with regard to communal sharing relationships in Chapter 4, mutually beneficial coordination in authority ranking relationships would be enabled if engaging in iconic dimensional conformations actually does reliably generate representations, emotions, motives, and moral sentiments that dispose participants to cooperate rather than defect. That is, if engagement in iconic dimensional conformations reliably makes people committed to cooperation in authority ranking relationships, and if that fact is common knowledge, then a great many social dilemmas can be solved: people can trust each other, enabling cooperation that would be too risky without each participant's trust in every other participant's commitment.

In all likelihood, people would build that trust in small increments, initially testing each other's commitment in cooperations with relatively little at stake, then, if everyone adheres to their commitments, testing commitments with a bit more at stake, and so on. However, a person's cooperation with stakes of a given magnitude does not assure their

Box 12.2

There is a far-reaching implication of these two adaptations: infants' innate preconception that consubstantial assimilation conformations generate communal sharing relationships, and infants' innate preconception that iconic dimensional conformations generate authority ranking relationships. These innate preconceptions can only have evolved to enable infants to quickly understand and successfully begin participating in the human social worlds they find themselves in. That is, infants' innate preconceptions about these conformations strongly imply that in fact these conformations universally do have the effects that infants expect – and have had those effects for at least several hundred years, and likely many tens of thousands of years or more. That is precisely why innate knowledge of conformation systems evolved, along with the supporting emotional, motivational, and moral affect. These adaptations each include all of these aspects.

Let me put this another way. Infant knowledge of the respective conformation systems of communal sharing and authority ranking, conjoined with knowledge of the respective relational models, are adaptations tailored to the social environments that infants have been born into for many, many generations. These two psychosocial adaptations must have evolved because they enhanced infant fitness by enabling infants to function well in the vital social relations of every human community. These adaptations provide infants with a huge and crucial head start. Without them, it would be exceedingly difficult, if not impossible, to discover the coordination structures that others have in mind in any given potential interaction. There is no other plausible explanation for this innate knowledge. Consequently, these two adaptations show that for a great many generations, humans have usually conformed communal sharing with consubstantial assimilation, and conformed authority ranking with iconic dimensions. That is what infants innately know, because that is what infants have always found, wherever they were born. That is, these two adaptations are the evolutionary distillate of the social relations of all the human communities that have existed for thousands of years. This is a unique and unprecedented window into the social relations of prehistoric humans.

cooperation with larger stakes; every increment requires some trust in everyone's commitment. People who have repeatedly engaged in iconic dimensional conformations with one another thereby successively develop more trust in each other, at the same time as they become more and more committed, and therefore trustworthy. In their game-theoretic analyses of social dilemmas, Schelling (2006), Hirshleifer (1987), Frank (1988), and Nesse (2001) have shown that mutual commitment magnificently resolves those dilemmas, enabling mutually beneficial cooperation. What is not known is how people can come to trust each other's commitments, and have their trust vindicated. Schelling, Hirshleifer, Frank, and Nesse have come up with some ways that this might be achieved, but the sticking point is that it seems impossible to know whether others truly are committed. Engaging together in the appropriate conformations helps create commitment, so that knowing that everyone has engaged in the conformation engenders a degree of justified trust in each other's commitments. Infants' expectations about the effects of consubstantial assimilation conformations and the effects of iconic dimensional conformations show that infants start life with the belief that when people have engaged in a conformation together, they will do what the relationship requires of them. That is, infants innately know that a person who has engaged in the appropriate conformation is worthy of some degree of trust. That is a good start.

CHAPTER 13

The Biology of Iconic Dimensions and Magnitudes

> There is now a broad consensus that the perception of numerosity and elementary numerical computation (the application of the ordering operation, ≥, for example) to number percepts are found even in arthropods. The arthropods diverged from the chordata (hence from the later evolving vertebrata and mammalia) in the early Cambrian. (Butterworth, Gallistel, & Vallortigara 2017: 2)

To fully understand the iconic conformations of authority ranking, we need to know as much as possible about the neurocognitive system that supports these conformations; that is what this chapter begins with. We also need to know the phylogeny of these iconic conformations. Do other species use any of these dimensions to mediate whatever dominance ranking they engage in? If so, that might suggest something about how humans evolved the disposition to use and respond to this conformation systems, beginning with the psychosocial adaptation that enables nearly all vertebrates to function in dominance hierarchies. From there, ancestral humans must have evolved the moral sentiments that are absent in dominance hierarchies, but crucial to authority ranking. The disposition to form, sustain, and commit to authority ranking relations evolved so as to encompass superiors' moral commitment to lead, wisely guide, protect, and stand up for their subordinates. This sense of superiors' moral responsibility for subordinates has not been identified in the dominance relations of other animals, including chimpanzees and bonobos. As it evolved in human ancestors, it greatly increased the fitness benefits of subordinating oneself to superiors, enabling radically new forms of hierarchical social organization.

Here I shall admonish readers to keep in mind the fact that the biological systems involved in iconic dimensional conformations do not make this conformation system manifest itself in one invariant manner for each dimension. This adaptation consists of psychosocial capacities, dispositions, and proclivities that cannot be realized without the cultural complements that, in each community, specify how, when, and where each dimension shall be used to conform authority ranking. In some cultures rulers receive cannon salutes, in other cultures they do not. In some cultures, no one may harvest until the chief begins to harvest; in other cultures people do no such thing. Rulers in many cultures build pyramids and great temples, but in other cultures they do not. None of these iconic dimensional conformations would exist without the conformational adaptation that motivates rulers to build such things, and that generates deference and allegiance in those who encounter monumental structures. Bonobos and chimpanzees are not impressed by pyramids, or are not impressed in a manner that transfers to reverential awe of the rulers who had them built.

The Analog Magnitude System and the Lateral Segment of the Intraparietal Sulcus

As mentioned at the end of Chapter 8, human adults and children in a number of cultures, as well as adults of at least some species of primates, have an analog magnitude system (AMS) that is crucial to the representation and processing of comparisons of approximate cardinality of numbers, volume or mass, temporal duration, temporal and spatial order, height, muscular force, loudness, and brightness (Walsh 2003, Cohen et al. 2008). On each dimension, the AMS functions to compare "amounts": BIGGER–SMALLER AREA, MORE–LESS SUBSTANCE, MORE NUMEROUS–FEWER, LOUDER–SOFTER, BRIGHTER–LESS BRIGHT, LONGER–SHORTER DURATION, GREATER VELOCITY–LESSER VELOCITY, STRONGER–WEAKER. The system does not enumerate or otherwise quantify the stimuli, it just assesses which one is more. That is, it ordinally ranks the perceived entities or stimuli. The cognitive representations and/or processing of magnitudes on each of these dimensions appear to employ shared or overlapping cognitive and neural systems. The evidence for this – and its apparent consequences – includes priming and interference effects, such as Stroop-like effects. For example, relative font size affects adults' judgments of the relative magnitude of numerals. There are similar cross-magnitude effects between judgments of relative numeral magnitude and luminance, and interference between judgments of size and speed, size and duration, number and duration, and duration and brightness (Cohen Kadosh et al. 2008, Bueti & Walsh 2009). Further evidence includes unconscious and occasionally conscious mapping of one magnitude onto the another, including the ability to judge and report the magnitude of a stimulus in terms of magnitude on another dimension (Tang et al. 2008, Cantlon et al. 2008). For example, people find it easy to report brightness by mapping it onto numerals, line length, loudness, and grip pressure. Across species, an identifying signature of the AMS is that comparisons obey Weber's Law: the greater the ratio between the values, the faster the discrimination and the lower the error rate (Gallistel & Gelman 2000). What matters for cognitive processing is the ratio of the values, not the absolute difference obtained by subtracting one value from the other. The analog magnitude system notes and compares approximate amounts or intensities, judging which is more, but does not enumerate; it is not a symbolic numeral system that counts things.

Functional imagining (fMRI) studies, clinical studies of brain lesions, a few transcranial magnetic stimulation studies, and single-unit recordings have converged to localize the focal substrate for the AMS in the posterior parietal lobe. Deficits in temporal, spatial, numerical, and velocity perception tend to co-occur in parietal lesion patients (Bueti & Walsh 2009). More specifically, the magnitude comparisons characterized cognitively in the AMS depend on neural systems that crucially involve the human intraparietal sulcus (IPS) bilaterally, and the homologous ventral intraparietal area in the species of monkeys that have been studied (Walsh 2003, Stevens et al. 2007, Franklin & Jonides 2008, Tang, Ward & Butterworth 2008, Cantlon et al. 2008, Boeken & Markett 2023).

The IPS representation and/or processing of magnitudes encompasses information from diverse sensory systems and modes. For example, acoustically based inferences about the size of a person or object activate the IPS (von Kriegesten et al. 2007) and tactile spatial discriminations activate the IPS in proportion to acuity (Stilla et al. 2007). The IPS is involved in perception of one's own body size: a manipulation that creates the illusion that one's waist and hips are shrinking activates the anterior segment of the IPS in proportion to the perceived shrinkage (Ehrsson et al. 2005). It is also involved in the serial organization of both cognitive tasks and motor sequences (Jubault et al. 2007) and in making judgments about the ordinal position of letters in the alphabet (Fias et al. 2007). The IPS is involved in translations among magnitude representations from different sensory modalities and is fundamental to the organization of action based on perception, such as reaching and grasping (Walsh 2003). In some studies, the lateral segment of the IPS appears to be the crucial substrate of the AMS.

Recall that authority ranking has the structure of a linear ordering, which is also the structure of an ordinal scale of measurement (Fiske

1991, 1992). So, one might expect the IPS to be focally involved in assessing and cognizing human ranks. Indeed, in a pioneering study, Chiao and colleagues showed activation in the bilateral IPS when naval ROTC midshipmen compared the social ranks of uniform insignia, the ranks of their officers photographed in uniform, the status of Toyota car models, and, of course, the magnitudes of numerals (Chiao et al. 2009). As in studies of other dimensions and magnitudes focally cognized in the AMS, when Chiao et al.'s participants compared closer pairs of social ranks their reactions times were slower and their IPS was more activated, compared to when they compared more distant ranks. In other studies, human comparisons of social ranks have also been found to fit Weber's Law, which implies a common representation of physical magnitudes and of social ranks (see Holmgren, Isager, & Schubert 2018 and sources reviewed therein). Subsequent studies have confirmed that the IPS is highly activated when people think about social ranking (Mason, Magee, & Fiske 2013; see also Cloutier et al. 2012, 2016).

In sum, fMRI studies demonstrate the colocation of cognizing authority ranking and cognizing material, physical dimensions, and magnitudes. Experiments have established that cognition to identify the greater of two social relational ranks exhibits Weber's Law, which is the distinctive experimental signature of cognition to identify the greater of two material, physical dimensions and magnitudes. This is very strong evidence that iconic dimensions and magnitudes conformations are the fundamental conformations of authority ranking. These iconic conformations are not conceptual metaphors on top of any deeper conformations of authority ranking. In authority ranking, ranks are represented as relative positions on dimensions. There is no deeper or more fundamental cognitive representation. (There certainly is some kind of encoding at the cellular level, and/or in the system of connections among neurons and their propensity to send signals, but how that works is still mysterious. For recent revolutionary possibilities, see Langille & Gallistel 2020 and Gallistel 2021.)

Phylogeny and Ontogeny of the Iconic Conformation of Authority Ranking

> A chimpanzee likely to attack is silent, and increases his apparent size by hair erection, hunching of the shoulders, approach, bipedalism, and other conspicuous display patterns. A chimpanzee unlikely to attack vocalizes loudly (pant-grunting or screaming), keeps hair flat, tends to crouch, and may orient away from the other individual (by

presenting or avoiding), thus keeping his apparent size to a minimum. (Bygott 1979: 421)

African antelopes and buffalo: Dominance displays are designed to make the performer looks as impressive as possible, especially taller and often more massive and powerful. Associated movements . . . are highly ritualized. The message is, "I am the greatest," or "I am superior to you." . . . There are two types of submissive display: a) postures that are the opposite of threat or intimidation, especially lowering the head with chin raised (head-low/chin-out posture) so that the horns blend into the body silhouette . . . ; b) infantile behavior, including bleating or crying like a calf in distress . . ., and kneeling and lying-out with head outstretched like a calf in concealment [alone, hidden from predators]. (Estes 1991: 24–25)

Hoofed animals: One common principle in dominance displays is to make the animal appear as long and broad as possible. This is verified by broadside displays and related behavior patterns. Another widespread principle is to make the animal appear as tall as possible. This is mainly achieved by the erect, nose-up, and head-and-neck-forward/upward postures. (Walther 1984: 245)

Elephant bulls: Dominance is usually determined and acknowledged the moment 2 bulls meet, simply on the basis of which stands taller. When the size difference is obvious, the smaller animal flattens its ears, keeps its head lowered, moves backward and sideways, and makes writhing trunk movements . . . When 2 equal-size bulls meet, they take each other's measure by coming together with head's raised until their trunk bases and/or tusks are firmly engaged . . . This is also the position during combat. Each tries to be taller, or press downward on the other's trunk. Or, if contact is made on the underside of their raised trunks, they may grapple for a hold. Tusk length is important, but so are height and weight, for these determine who can push whom around. The elephant that holds his head higher, whether because he is bigger or more confident, usually wins. Aggressive interactions between mature bulls are rare and usually low key, although serious and even fatal fights sometimes occur when 2 bulls of each size compete over a cow in heat and/or are simultaneously in musth (Estes 1991: 264–265; see also Moss 2000).

African monkeys: The postures and movements of monkeys often reflect their social status. A confident animal appears relaxed, walks with its limbs extended and back level, looks around casually, and appears equally at ease when resting. A subordinate walks with back hunched, limbs somewhat bent, and tail low or curved downward, and sits hunched over, lowers its head, and peers around nervously. . . . When trying to intimidate a rival, a monkey stands as tall as possible and bristles, which can make species with capes and face ruffs of long hair (especially baboons) appear much bigger. Adult

> males of species with colorful genitals display them. . . . Dominant animals . . . sit apart on high vantage points away from the troop and scan . . . Dominant animals of various forest monkeys, especially mangabeys, elevate their tails in a conspicuous and species-specific manner. The crested mangabey stands with tail arched over its back and touching its head, the gray-cheeked mangabey brings its tail to the vertical. (Estes 1991: 480)

The great majority of social mammals and birds have approximately linear dominance hierarchies, as do many relatively solitary mammals who regularly encounter a limited number of conspecifics (e.g., among lizards, see Alberts 1994). In an encounter between animals who have not yet abolished their dominance relation, the obviously smaller will almost always defer. If they are approximately matched in size, each adopts a posture that makes it appear massive and high, which will make the other animal defer if it cannot match that mass and height. To establish dominance, animals with horns or antlers run at each other and crash together, and/or push their antlers, horns, or heads against each other; the stronger animal thereby establishes dominance. Yet in establishing dominance, very few species of animals commonly engage in injurious all-out fights. This is usually maladaptive, it seems, because, in establishing dominance, each animal benefits from anticipating who would win a brutal contest to the death and then avoiding such a fight. For the subordinated animal, being subordinate is preferable to being seriously injured or killed. For the dominant animal, once its dominance is acknowledged by the subordinate, killing the subordinate is very rarely worth risking the injuries it may suffer in a fight to the death. Once dominance is established, on that initial occasion and subsequent encounters, the subordinate acknowledges subordination by keeping out of the way of the dominant, and, in an encounter, making itself appear small, while lowering itself so that it is vulnerable to attack. For some details, see Estes (1991); he concisely describes the precise dominance and subordination postures and actions of a great many African mammals. For a concise recent review of the enormous literature on dominance, see Tibbetts et al. (2022). These patterns are so pervasive across mammals, birds, and other classes of animals that it is no wonder that humans iconically conform authority ranking with ELEVATION, MASS, and FORCE.

LOUDNESS is an indicator of volume that, in some species, males use to attract mates, and, to a lesser extent, to deter other males from infringing on the social space sonically "claimed" by the vocalizing animal. It is less obvious why humans conform authority ranking with other dimensions and magnitudes. That is likely due in some way to their sharing the AMS cognitive system and the IPS neural system with ELEVATION, MASS, and FORCE. But the integrated evolutionary, ontogenetic, cognitive, and cultural processes remain to be worked out.

However, in thinking about how the iconic dimensional and magnitude conformations of authority ranking grow out of nonhuman dominance hierarchies, it is crucial to definitively distinguish authority ranking from dominance. In nonhuman animals, the entailments of dominance rank consists of just one thing: priority of access to resources that are not yet in the possession of any of the animals in the hierarchy. Dominance over a given animal means first choice of where to forage, where to drink, where to nest, and so forth. For males, a key benefit of high rank is being free to mate with any receptive female, without interference from males of lower rank. For females, dominance also means that subordinates will not threaten offspring, or will back off when the dominant animal appears on the scene. In most species, dominant animals are more or less circumspect about attempting to displace a subordinate who is already eating something, who has established a territory, or has denned somewhere; possessors are likely to defend what they have, even against a dominant interloper (e.g., for wolves, Mech 1970: 71–73; for certain primates, Kummer et al. 1974; de Waal 1989). Perhaps tolerant acceptance of rights of priority is fertile ground for the emergence of TEMPORAL conformations of authority ranking.

Certainly, the main phylogenetic basis for conformation on the temporal dimension is the ubiquity of dominance hierarchies. It seems that vertebrates have had many tens of millions of years to evolve adaptive representational, emotional, and motivational neurocognitive adaptations that enable "smart" functioning in social relations consisting of linear ordering. It would be astonishing if those adaptations, hugely affecting fitness across innumerable species, were not firmly entrenched in human psychology. Nevertheless, those phenomena do not imply that human sociality is essentially hierarchical, much less inevitably hierarchical. Those inferences are completely fallacious. The ethnographic facts contradict that conclusion. From many ethnographies, we know how social relations are organized among the hunter-gather societies in which people do not store food, nor commonly engage in market pricing or equality matching with people from other tribes, and never do so within their community. In every place where they have been studied, hunter-gatherers who subsist this way organize most of their relations through communal sharing. They abhor dominance relations. If anyone begins to attempt to assert dominance, these communities fiercely resist, and, if necessarily, harshly sanction the person (Boehm 2009). More generally, we know for certain that culture can almost completely overcome even the most basic and ancient psychological adaptations that are essential to reproductive success. Today, billions of humans routinely use contraception and limit their fertility in other ways.

An intriguing question arises from a point discussed in multiple chapters. Though both authority ranking and dominance are ordinal rankings, they are fundamentally different. Animal dominance is essentially "power" – successful bullying. In contrast, a higher-ranking human in an authority ranking relationship is expected to make decisions on behalf of the group, to wisely guide subordinates, to stand up for them, to look out for them, and to provide for subordinates when needed (e.g., giving out food). In many settings, the highest-ranking person plays a central redistributive role, receiving tribute and subsequently giving it out to those in need – and to those who support him (Polanyi 1971). In nonhuman animals, dominance entails little or none of that, although in some species the most dominant animal will intercede to stop fights between subordinates. So, the question is this: do these differences between dominance hierarchy and authority ranking affect the conformational use of dimensions ? Or are iconic conformations inherently an assertion of legitimate authority ranking? In particular, it seems that when persons acquire dominance by force, they then typically attempt to transform their dominant position into rightful rank in authority ranking relations, as Weber (2019) argued so persuasively. As I understand Weber, he observed that even when people establish dominance by pure coercive force – or especially in those cases – those who dominate want to legitimize their power as moral, natural, inevitable, and salutary – that is, as authority ranking. The iconic conformation system of magnitudes and dimensions may be the typical mode used by the merely powerful, seeking to become acknowledged as legitimate rulers. In most respects, "legitimation of authority" is simply another way of describing the evocation of moral sentiments supporting authority ranking, where "legitimation" emphasizes the naturalness and inevitability aspect of the moral sentiments.

Finally, concluding this brief discussion of the biology of iconic dimensional and magnitude conformations, we need to note an obvious biological fact. In conjunction with phylogenetically ancient psychological adaptations for participating in dominance hierarchies, ontogenetic experience may contribute to the human proclivity to iconically conform authority ranking – along certain dimensions, at least. Every mammal starts out BELOW, LESS

MASSIVE, having less VOLUME and LESS SURFACE AREA, and being WEAKER than its parents, siblings, and other conspecifics. But it is not obvious how ontogenetic experience contributes to conformations consisting of NUMEROSITY, ANTERIORITY, LUMINANCE, or LOUDNESS. The newborn finds its mother already in existence, and, in some species, finds other kin there, too. But, phenomenologically, in order for infants to experience that discovery as TEMPORAL PRECEDENCE, they would have to perceive their own birth as occurring at a moment in time, relative to others' existence. In what sense, if any, does the newborn know that its mother and others existed before it was born? In any case, ontogenetic experience affects not only individual learning but also natural selection, because it is beneficial to have the head start of being born knowing what every human needs to know.

Coda

In exploring the phylogeny, neurobiology, and cognitive organization of dimensional and magnitudinal conformations of authority ranking – and of the other conformation systems – my aims are not reductionist. I certainly do not aim to suggest that iconic conformation, or any of the other three conformation systems, is "nothing but" phylogeny, neurobiology, and evolved cognitive systems. That is certainly not true. What I hope to begin to illuminate is how human phylogeny, neurobiology, and cognition enable, afford, and shape this and other conformation systems in conjunction with cultural evolution and local cultural practice. Or, stated the other way around, I hope to begin to illuminate how conformations, as human cultural practices, utilize the materials and opportunities provided by our phylogeny, evolved cognitive adaptations, and neurobiology. Stated another way, the phylogenetically deep neurocognitive systems of the iconic magnitudes and dimensions conformation system provide a fecund niche for the cultural evolution of practices, artifacts, and narratives of authority ranking.

Specifically, we may ask, for example, what are the phylogenetic, neurobiological, and cognitive media that inspire halos, giant Buddha statues, and cannon salutes? What are the media with which humans compose narratives of mighty divinities in the sky, or sculptures of a divinity with a thousand arms and eleven heads? Why did rulers of newly stratified empires in Egypt, Mesopotamia, and Central America all conceive of massive pyramids, and what were the sources of the motivation to mobilize the vast amounts of labor and materials to actually build them? Why did it make sense for President Lincoln to wear a stove pipe hat, and for Chinese emperors to build vast courtyards – in both cases to conform their superiority? How did it happen that in both the Old World and the New World, rulers energetically pushed the technologies of mining, smelting, and metallurgy in order to be able to make themselves brilliantly reflect the sun? This book is an attempt to begin to figure out how these things might fit together.

Finally, it is crucial to recognize that, precisely because iconic conformations establish legitimacy, evoke commitments to authority ranking relations, and induce supporting emotions and motives, iconic conformations are essential in transforming, resisting, or rejecting any system of authority ranking relations. Social movements, and certainly revolutionaries, must transmute existing iconic conformations of the operative authority relations, or else destroy the old ones and replace them. Without transmuting or replacing existing conformations, without redirecting them toward the relations one seeks, one cannot transform the perceptions of legitimacy, nor the emotions, motivations, and moral commitments that support the existing authority ranking relationships. More radically, to replace the existing authority ranking with a new relational model, people must dislocate the conformation system of iconic dimensions, replacing that with one of the other conformation systems. Adopting a different relational model results in new standards of evaluating social action, new perceptions of the relations, new conceptions of what the relations could be, and should be, and that adoption evokes new motives and commitments. Adoption of a new relational model requires mobilization of the corresponding conformation system.

Every human action, and, a fortiori, every social practice, has multiple causes, and multiple factors that potentiate, impede, orient, and shape it. So, conformation systems theory does not posit that a conformation system is the only cause of anything, nor that conformation, as such, is a person's only purpose in performing a conformational action. Nor does conformation systems theory posit that a conformation system is ever the only system generating responses to a conformational action. A pharaoh's primary purpose in having a pyramid built may be to conform his paramountcy, but the pharaoh also wants to build a tomb that is secure against grave robbers. Perceiving the pyramid conforms an Egyptian citizen's subordination to the pharaoh, but may also make the citizen curious about how the pyramid's sheathing was polished so perfectly. A child's primary purpose cuddling up with a parent may be to conform their communal sharing relationship, but the child may also be cold and want to get warm. Conversely, getting warm may be the child's only intention, though cuddling to get warm may still have effects on the child's or the parent's representations of their relationship, effects on their emotions regarding the relationship, effects on their subsequent communal sharing motives, or effects on their moral sentiments about their communal sharing. For the parent, too, the child's cuddling conforms the communal sharing relationship than joins them, but the parent may also be frustrated by how hard it is to type on their laptop while the child is curled up in their lap, and wiggling.

The aim of this book is to articulate conformation systems theory, primarily inductively, by considering instances of conformation, and juxtaposing them to reveal patterns. In a single volume, it would be impossible to unpack everything that goes into a pyramid, or informs a snuggle, or everything that goes on around them. But even if it were possible, it would be distracting to stop to consider all of the influences on each of the myriad conformational acts and practices set out in the book. And it is entirely unnecessary to do so, given the aim of articulating conformation systems.

Presumably, gene activation and hormones modulate performance and response to iconic conformations of authority ranking, while conformations of authority ranking in turn modulate gene activation and hormones. Among humans, rising in rank – for example, by winning a sports contest – raises levels of circulating testosterone, while falling in rank – for example, by losing a sports contest – lowers levels of circulating testosterone (Jiménez et al. 2012). Likewise, in nonhuman primates, rising and falling in dominance rank, respectively raises and lowers circulating testosterone, in both males and females. In humans, the most plausible adaptive function of this is theorized to be modulating the trade-off between focusing efforts on competing for dominance rank versus focusing on nurturing offspring, depending on which is most likely to yield greater fitness (Gray et al. 2017). Different phases of the life cycle require different motivations.

PART IV

Concrete Operations of One-to-One Correspondence for Equality Matching, Arbitrary Symbolism for Market Pricing, Combinations of Conformations, and What Children Discover

CHAPTER 14

Conforming Equality Matching by One-to-One Correspondence

Equality matching consists of using equality as the standard for what the social relations ought to be: being even, or keeping track of how many units need to be added or subtracted by whom in order to make things even. Examples include taking turns, tit-for-tat, owing and then returning a favor, voting, even distribution, matching contributions, fair lotteries and coin flips, and most of the rules of most of the world's games and sports. The social relational structure of equality matching corresponds to the measurement structure of an interval scale. That is, addition and its inverse, subtraction, are meaningful, but there is no defined zero; ratios and proportions have no meaning. Taking turns buying coffee, the two participants may not have any idea who began (they do not have a zero), but they perpetually know whose turn it is today.

In equality matching, everyone has to get or give or do the same thing – however "same thing" is culturally defined. If it is Y's turn to get coffee, Y cannot get muffins instead. However, if the understanding is that the participants take turns bringing the "snack" for both, then whatever people perceive as "a snack" is suitable. In the same way, when a person has done a favor for someone, people generally have a sense of what counts as an appropriately matching return favor that counts as counterbalancing the original favor.

To conform equality matching, people generally perform concrete operations of one-to-one matching. "Concrete operations" is a construct originally formulated by Piaget (1952, 1941–1951) to characterize how, at one particular "stage" of cognitive development, children think about equality, inequality, and other basic concepts of physics and mathematics. Piaget's concept of developmental stages has been supplanted, and in any case his theories of cognition were entirely individualistic, with no role for social relations or learning from others. That is, Piaget construed concrete operations, like other stages, as a mode of thought of an individual, figuring out the world on their own.

I encountered concrete operations in high school, as a research assistant in a huge project on young children's interaction with their mothers and how this prepared them for kindergarten and beyond. I was sort of intrigued by the researchers' methods of testing the children's cognitive development by asking them to compare quantities of water in different glass vessels, compare number of objects in two aligned sets, and so forth. But I gave it no further thought until college, when I took Jerome Bruner's cognitive science class and I again encountered the concept of concrete operations as a stage in cognitive development. I shrugged my shoulders. About eight years later, my classmates and I wrestled with the concept in Richard Shweder's graduate seminar in the Committee on Human Development at the University of Chicago. Then I left concrete operations in the far back of my mind for several more years. But, doing my PhD fieldwork in 1980–1982, I observed Moosé adults consistently using a set of hands-on operations to partition kola nuts and suchlike into even shares – the matching procedures I described in Chapter 2. These matching procedures looked familiar; I realized that in this context and many others, they were performing concrete operations to constitute their equality!

Concrete operations of one-to-one matching are the most intuitive, most "natural," most evocative conformations of equality matching; and they are the most widespread conformation of equality matching across the world's cultures. The meaning of concrete operations is most easily recognized, and resonates most strongly with the innate cognitive relational model of equality matching, thereby having a uniquely powerful effect on implicit and explicit understandings of the social relationship. Concrete operations most effectively make the equality matching morally binding, and conversely are the standard against which people judge the relationship. That is, concrete operations of one-to-one matching are the benchmark for evaluating the rightness or wrongness of action in equality matching. Such evaluations are most typically sentiments, not logical reasons, not reflective analysis or even conscious awareness of the evaluative process, unless the evaluation has to be articulated and defended. In conjunction with those moral sentiments, concrete operations are most liable to evoke the emotions that regulate equality matching, such as a certain kind of "anger" if the other person takes two turns in a row, and a certain kind of "shame-embarrassment" if a person discovers that she has taken more than an equal share. Furthermore, suppose people are creating a new equality matching relationship for which they do not see a clear and familiar model or an analogue they can use to come up with a conformation for their new relationship. Then the "natural," pleasingly suitable conformation for it – the one that the people come up with most readily and that feels most apt, and the one they are most likely to stick with for a long time – will be some form of concrete operations of one-to-one matching.

Box 14.1

The Mandarin character 平, *píng*, is derived from a pictograph that depicts a level balance scale, and means "flat, level, equal," in reference to flat land and even tones. When used in a social sense, what kind of relationship is meant? Is it just a coincidence that the English word "equal," which of course we use to refer to a particular kind of social relationship, comes from the Latin ***aequus***, level, even – related to ***aequor***, level surface, sea, from an Indo-European or sub-Proto-Indo-European root meaning water (Onions et al. 1965: 321, Watkins 2000: 2, Mallory & Adams 2006)? When we assure or restore a certain kind of relationship, why do we say that we have made things "even"?

****

We had eight chapters to dig deeply in order to properly delineate the conformations of authority ranking by iconic magnitudes and dimensions. For equality matching, we will comfortably make do with just one chapter. We can do so because we do not need to address again the general issues about conformations that we already considered when they arose with regard to consubstantial assimilation or iconic dimensions. Moreover, this chapter can be comparatively brief simply because, so far as I have been able to find, compared to the first two conformation systems we explored, there are far fewer ethnographic and historical accounts, fewer relevant narratives with sufficient elaboration about concrete operations, few ancient visual depictions – if any – that definitely show concrete operations, let alone just how such a conformation was performed. There are some seemingly relevant archeological artifacts, especially what appear to be games, as well as some items patently for determining outcomes by "chance," but hardly any evidence about just how they were used. We very rarely know the rules of ancient games (if they are games), nor the exact systems of divination or selection in which people used dice-like and dreidel-like artifacts. There is a bit of nice linguistic material, but I have not found a whole lot that is particularly illuminating. Altogether, concrete operations of one-to-one matching, conforming equality matching, are much less conspicuous, ethnologically speaking, than iconic dimensions conforming authority ranking – less conspicuous in the world, and less conspicuous in descriptions of the world.

But what can be found is intriguing and illuminating.

Tokens and Notches

Tokens and tally marks have long been used as concrete operations[1] for keeping track and attesting what two parties have done, while showing how much needs to be added to one side in order to make things even. Tokens and tally marks provide mnemonic support for equality matching, while assuring that both sides agree on where they stand. In early fifteenth-century England, the men ordered by Henry V to requisition supplies for a military expedition to France, unable to pay immediately, gave each supplier a wooden tally: a stick scored with transverse notches to indicate the number of items taken. After making the notches, the stick was split longitudinally, with each party taking half the stick, showing all tally marks (Barker 2005: 99). Along the Volga River in the eighteenth century, people in Tcheremiss and Tchouvach communities used exactly the same concrete operation when one person lent money to another (Ifrah 1981: 94). In some nineteenth-century Swiss villages, marks corresponding to family names were inscribed to indicate the order of turn-taking for responsibilities or privileges such as night-watchman, village policeman, flag carrier, sexton, and other roles (Ifrah 1981: 97).

Place-holding tokens are almost essential when the balancing is indirect rather than bilateral. Thus, in a babysitting cooperative with many participants, chits can serve as concrete tokens for turns: it is not feasible, and not necessary, for anyone to mentally keep track of everyone's hours. If someone babysits for X for two hours, X gives them two chits. Chits have no meaning or value outside the co-op, nor can members exchange them for anything other than hours of babysitting. Similarly, Bascom (1952) reports that among the Yoruba, each member of a rotating credit association (*esusu*) kept track of their own contributions by making marks on the wall of their house, which they could then match with the sum they received when it was their turn to take the whole pot.

In the ethnographic literature, bride wealth is the best-studied example of placeholders. In a great many traditional cultures, kin groups give their daughters in marriage to other groups, expecting to receive brides in return. Sometimes the reciprocation is immediate, but when it is not, the delays can be substantial: sometimes more than a generation passes. Moreover, in what Lévi-Strauss (1949) called "generalized" exchange, group A gives brides to group B, but receives brides from group C: the

[1] For brevity, writing about conformations of equality matching from this point on, I will generally shorten this to "concrete operations." In every case of this shortening, "concrete operations of one-to-one matching" should be understood.

reciprocation is indirect and cyclical. (The loops can be closed in a variety of network paths.) When the reciprocation of brides is indirect or long delayed, cultures almost invariably make use of placeholders: as a condition for the bestowal of the bride, and/or in a process drawn out over some months or years, the recipients transfer to the bride's kin group certain special valuables such as cattle, ritual tools or weapons, or other major objects used for this purpose. Typically the bride-wealth items are used only, or primarily, within a very restricted sphere of exchange, limited to the transfer of brides, and sometimes also as compensation for homicides. The place-holding items rarely, if ever, enter into market transactions (Firth 1938: 340–344, Evans-Pritchard 1940, Bohannan 1955, Douglas 1963, Meillassoux 1975, Fiske 1991).

Equating Devices

There are many devices and concrete operations for dividing up material objects into equal shares. One operation is aligning the objects to be distributed in adjacent rows, so their evenness is apparent by visual inspection. Mechanical devices such as a balance scale may be used; level balance between the two pans defines equality. Hence, blindfolded Justice holding a pan balance is a symbol of equal treatment under the law. Drinking equal rounds of alcoholic beverages is an old Anglo-European custom. In England, equality was assured by peg tankards (Hackwook 1909: 146). Attributed to the Saxon Saint Dunstan (909–988, Archbishop of Canterbury), the two-quart peg tankard (or pin cup) had eight pegs marking equal portions (Hackwook 1909: 343–344). D'Israeli (1791) describes how each person in turn was to drink down to the next peg, apparently in one draught – for if they drank short or drank past the peg, they had to drink another draught. D'Israeli cites an ecclesiastical rule attesting peg tankards in 1102. He also describes Elizabethan tankards with hoops inside to mark off even quantities of drink, so that, as the tankard was passed around, each person in turn would drink the same quantity. He cites a source attributing hoop tankards to King Edgard (c. 942–975). D'Israeli (1791) also describes other Elizabethan concrete operations for conforming equality of draughts in each round of drinking. In one, each drinker in turn shows that his tankard is full, drains it, and then inverts it up on his thumb; the drinker then quaffs the last drop from his thumb – but if enough remains so that the ale drips off his thumb, he must drink another tankard. He also describes another contemporaneous device: a bottle or glass with a hemispherical bottom, so that it cannot stand upright. Each participant drinks in turn from the same vessel. The even matching of the amount of ale that each drinks is concretely demonstrated by the requirement that each drinker must drain the vessel before setting it down, or else it tips over, spilling to reveal his shirking. These practices are a clear instance of combining consubstantial assimilation (commensalism) with concrete operations of one-to-one correspondence.

As I described in Chapter 2, Moosé sometimes make even-quantity exchanges of different goods, where a unit container serves as the standard of equality. Moosé call this *tekre*, distinguishing it from gift giving, purchase, appropriation, and other forms of exchange and transfer. To recall: A woman who needs cotton goes to her neighbor with a basket full of, say, peanuts. If the neighbor is willing, they empty the peanuts onto a mat and fill the basket to the same level with, say, cotton, which the first woman takes back with her. In the Bolivian Andes, the Laymis in the Likina region sometimes exchange an item for the quantity of another substance that fills up that item: "For example, empty earthenware pots are exchanged against the amount of grain or *ch'unu* (dehydrated potato) which they contain. When quality cloth is sought by Likina households they offer in exchange the cloth's capacity in maize grain" (Harris 1982: 77).

Procedures for equality matching may be borrowed from other contexts, and people create ad hoc inventions shaped by the natural proclivity for concrete operational conformation of equality matching. At the barber shop that I used to go to, the available barbers take turns cutting the hair of walk-in customers. However, since barbers may be on break, going out for coffee, or at various stages of cutting other customers' hair, there would often be ambiguity about who should take the next turn; simple errors of memory might also lead to disagreements. The mechanism they use is a clothespin labeled with the name of each barber, clipped to a wire. A barber coming on duty puts his or her clothespin at the left end of the row. The available barber whose clothes pin is furthest to the right is entitled to cut the hair of the next customer who arrives; when the customer sits down in that barber's chair, the barber moves his or her clothespin to the left end of the wire.

An undergraduate informant reported a device that she and her three roommates had once used to organize house cleaning. It was a "chore wheel," consisting of a circular piece of laminated paper divided into quarters, respectively labeled: "toilet," "floor," "shower," and "sink and mirror." In the center of this chore wheel rotated a smaller circle with the names of the four roommates. Every month, they turned the inner circle 90°, indicating the task for each person that month.

Turn-Taking

Turn-taking is one of the most pervasive concrete operations for conforming equality matching because it works well to evenly balance an indivisible entity among people. This is the conformation for the rotating Chairship of the United Nations Security Council, standing alternate watches on a ship, and, in some families, siblings getting the favored seat in the car. The number of participants is limited by the feasibility of keeping track of participation and the delay that is acceptable before the relationship is balanced.

The reciprocated, matching acts need not be benevolent. Consider tit-for-tat operating to conform violent equality matching, where harm is matched to harm, life for life, eye for eye, tooth for tooth, hand for hand, foot for foot, burn for burn, bruise for bruise, wound for wound (Exodus 21: 23–26).

Distribution of a set of equal material entities can be classified as turn-taking in allocation, or classified as one-to-one alignment. The conformation consists of the distributor giving "One for you [person A], one for you [person B], and one for me. One for you [A], one for you [B], and one for me . . ." In such a concrete operation, again people may not know how many they have, or how many anyone else has, but participants all know they are even, and know that everyone else knows they are all even, and knows that everyone knows that everyone knows that everyone knows that they are all even.

In this kind of concrete operation, when there are multiple kinds of entities to distribute, each kind must be allocated in a separate round. Thus, in my experience, when young American children split the proceeds from a lemonade stand, they do not know the relative values of pennies, nickels, dimes, and quarters, and, even if they did, they could not do the arithmetic to make a monetarily even distribution. So, typically they set out pennies, one for each participant, going around as many complete rounds as needed; then they do rounds of nickels, one to each; then cycles of distributing dimes; then quarters: one for you, and one for you, and one for me. When coins remain after a complete round, but there are too few coins to complete another full round, those left coins over may be given to mom, or set aside for the next occasion, or used to buy gum which can be evenly divided. Moosé, and also Yakut (northern Russia), use a similar procedure when dividing a slaughtered cow or bullock into equal shares: they butcher the animal, separating it into distinct types of tissue (e.g., leg meat, neck meat, ribs, intestines, fat, etcetera); then they divide each respective type of meat into equal-sized piles, side by side. If they have eight kinds of meat, there are eight separate concrete matching operations. They never compare two different kinds of meat, and never substitute or combine two kinds in one concrete operation (Sieroszewski 1896; compare with Hunting & Sharpley 1988, Hunting 1991).

As I mentioned, a one-to-one correspondence operation does not depend on – or indicate – the cardinal quantity; performing or observing such an operation, participants may be unaware of how many items they received, yet know that the distribution is equal by virtue of the process of one-to-one allocation. Interestingly, mathematicians do the same thing to determine whether two infinities are equal or not. Infinities cannot be enumerated, but it is possible to prove that two infinite sets are equal by demonstrating that there is an operation for putting them in one-to-one correspondence, so they evenly match.

Simultaneous Starting and Simultaneous Ending

Simultaneity of starting an action, or simultaneous starting and subsequent simultaneous stopping, are concrete operations to conform equality matching. Like the Moosé at reciprocally attended cultivating bees (described in Chapter 2), Tiv farmers convene weeding bees at which they line up and start together, hoeing across the field side by side to the rhythm of a drum or song (Bohannan 1968: 72).

Starting a race at the same moment, evenly lined up along a line, makes it "fair," and not only in sports. For example, in 1893 the Cherokee Strip Land Run conformed equal chances for white settlers to stake claims for free homesteads on 6 million acres of Oklahoma that the Federal Government had purchased from the Cherokee. On September 16, 1893, an estimated 100,000 participants assembled at one or another of four starting lines that the army had laid out. At noon they were released and galloped off to choose their new homestead, mark its perimeter with stakes, and then register it (Turner 2023). (There were three other Oklahoma land runs, using the same concrete operation.) When the Cherokee and other nations were driven from Georgia, the state distributed the vacated land in seven lotteries from 1805 to 1832 (Wikipedia, Georgia Land Lotteries: https://en.wikipedia.org/wiki/Georgia_Land_Lotteries). Each adult white male had one lot, except for veterans of the Revolutionary War (and beginning in 1820, veterans of the War of 1812), who had two lots, as did widows and orphans of veterans. A man who had won land in a previous lottery was excluded from participating in later Georgia land lotteries, unless he was a veteran, in which case he had one lot in the current lottery. Tickets for each person were drawn from a barrel.

Eight-year-old children in my own California community use a rhyme and alternation procedure to synchronize the start of a "thumb war," in which the contestants grasp each other's fingers and try to pin each other's thumb. While swinging thumbs left and right of each other, the two contestants recite "One, two, three, four, I declare a thumb war. Five, six, seven, eight, try to keep your thumb straight" – at that moment, the contest begins. The contest is made fair by concrete operation of simultaneously starting at the end of the ditty.

Matches

Around the world and throughout history, people have organized sports and games with concrete operations that conform the equality of the contest. The objective and outcome of a game or sporting contest is a difference on some magnitude or dimension: being ahead at the finish, high-jumping higher, or having more game chips. That difference conforms the ranking of the contestants. An election is like that, too: an equality matching contest conformed by concrete operations, resulting in an authority ranking relationship determined by positions on a dimension.

Any one game or sport is constituted by a whole set of concrete operations conforming the equality of the conditions. The same number of players come out to each side of the board or playing field, each player receives the same number pieces or cards; if there are several types of pieces, as in chess, the opponents have equal numbers of each type, and start with their pieces arrayed opposite each other, one-to-one, in matching positions on the board. The pieces are in one-to-one correspondence in mirror symmetry. The two sides take turns playing or making a move, or take turns playing offense and defense (e.g., batting and fielding), with turns defined by some concrete operation such as serving the ball, or getting outs. The court or board is bilaterally symmetrical, and the two sides further conform the equality matching of the set up by taking turns on each side. When play requires taking turns or choosing up sides, there is typically a quick equality matching game or random process for deciding who starts, such as a coin flip. If the participants have multiple matches, the opponents may also take turns starting play, or dealing the cards, or playing on each side's home field. If there is a time limit for a side to make their play, they have the same amount of time, matched by something such as the 24-second clock in professional basketball. A race typically requires a starting line on which contestants line up side-by-side on a starting line, a course of equal length for all contestants, a finish line orthogonal to the course, and a signal or mechanisms for a simultaneous start.

Board games, in particular, are composed of equality matching concrete matching operations and arrays that manifestly display equality[2] (Murray 1952, Bell 1979, Bell & Cornelius 1988). There may be an initial shuffle, cut, and dealing of cards; or there may be a spinner or dice that give each player equal chances. In short, in the vast majority of games everywhere, players conform the game with concrete matching operations that make it a game, or make a sport a sport. The exception is the category of hunt, hiding, and tag games which start with one player who is opposed by all the others together (see Murray 1952, Bell 1979). But even in those games, players often take turns being "it" when they play repeatedly.

Children and adults played board games as far back as we can see into the archeological record. Egyptians played three men's Morris, nine men's Morris, alquerque (related to chess), and mankala games by approximately 1400 BCE; they played senat (a race game distantly related to parchisi) by about 2650 BCE (Murray 1952, Bell & Cornelius 1988, Lhôte 1994: 606). For senet, each player had seven pawns which they advanced according to the throw of one or two dice or small marked batons (Decker 1987: 124–129, Lhôte 1994: 606). In Ur (present-day Iraq) and Egypt, boards and pieces for other games date to about 3000 BCE. These were race games for two players with matching numbers of pawns for each player; these games are associated with dice which players presumably tossed to move their pieces along a course of successive positions to reach the winning point. Race game boards for *mehen*, in the form of a snake-like spiral of quadrilateral positions, appear in Egypt from around 3000 BCE; only about fifteen have been found, varying in the number of positions (Decker 1987: 131–133, Lhôte 1994: 552). Ancient Egyptians also played a game with pegs placed in holes; there were twenty-nine holes on each side of the board, presumably for each player, coming together at the end in a (winning?) hole at the top (Lhôte 1994: 630). In Egypt there is widespread evidence of this game during the eighteenth dynasty (1550–1292 BCE), often appearing on the reverse of the same boards used for senat (Lhôte 1994: 638). Ancient Egyptian balls have been found, and there are several images of juggling and ball games, and tug-of-war, including games with women players. Their rules are still unknown, but the images show teams with even numbers of players (Decker 1987: 117). Children's sports and games with

[2] Certain war and hunting games are exceptions to this, although they have most of the other features.

two opponents are depicted in ancient Egypt, as well as wrestling matches and a number of individual or cooperative agility, dexterity, strength, fighting, and other contests, and also guessing games. Game boards and pieces for "twenty houses" have been found from as early as 1800 BCE in Mesopotamia. A game board resembling parchisi with symmetrical sides, eight dark playing pieces, and eight light ones, was found in a tomb at Ur, dated to Early Dynastic IIIa, 2600–2500 BC (Saggs 1995: 64, pl. 38).

A Chinese game, *wei-k'I* (similar to Japanese go), may have been invented around 2300 BCE. In the Warring States Period (fifth–third century BCE) of China, people played *liubio* (six sticks), using a doubly bilaterally symmetric board; the two players tossed six bamboo sticks or two eighteen-sided dice to move twelve cubical pawns (Scarpari 2000: 130–131). Knucklebones used as dice appear in eastern Europe by the fifth millennium BCE (Lhôte 1994: 125).

Inuit, Australian aboriginals, and natives of New Guinea are not known to have had board games before Europeans arrived, but they played string games (Murray 1952) conformed by concrete operations.

In precontact South and Central America and Southern North America, people played various related team games with a rubber ball (Stern 1948). Although most accounts provide few details, there are many descriptions of even numbers of players on opposing teams, with a dividing line separating the two teams; the two halves of the court were symmetrical. Apparently each team usually stayed at their own end. Play in all variants consisted of striking the ball back and forth between the two sides without using hands. Points were scored for the other team when a player touched the ball with an improper part of the body (such as an arm), when the ball passed the end of the court, or when it stopped in the opponents' end of the court. Players or spectators often placed bets. The Choquito kept track of the score by collecting corn cob tokens (Stern 1948: 18). Amniapä players laid wagers of two arrows per player and used corn kernel counters to keep score, beginning with six for each side and moving the kernels as each team scored until one side had none. Then if the winning side scores again, it is the victor and wins the arrows (Stern 1948: 21).

> The games of chance [played by American Indian adults] fall into one of two categories: First, games in which implements, like dice, are thrown at random to determine a number or numbers, the sum of the counts being kept with sticks, pebbles, etc., or upon an abacus or counting board or circuit; second, games in which one or more of the players guess in which of two or more places an odd or particularly marked lot is concealed, success or failure resulting in the gain or loss of counters. (Culin 1902: 58)

Culin points out that in some American Indian cultures, games are "played" in religious ritual contexts, for example to secure good fortune or avert misfortune. At least some games of chance seem to be derived from divination performed at altars, Culin posits. Throwing a javelin or shooting an arrow through a hoop is an important part of fertility rituals and courtship play in a number of Indian tribes. Horse racing and games of chance using dice and other mechanisms were extremely popular and widespread among native North Americans. Players sometimes wagered all of their "possessions," including wives, and sometimes included their own enslavement (Gabriel 1996). Gambling is prominent in North American Indian myths that depict the temptations and costs of gambling, which are faced and overcome by a culture hero (Gabriel 1996: 17–21).

As this illustrates, there is a continuum from games involving skill, with no element of chance, through games combining skill and chance, to pure "gambling" with no element of skill. All have multiple concrete operational conformations of equality matching.

Lotteries

When there is one indivisible role or entity to be allocated on a unique occasion, a common procedure is a fair lottery. Children have many traditions to manage this, including counting-out (or choosing up) rhymes to pick who is "it," such as the English "Eenie, meenie, miney, mo, catch a tiger by the toe, if he hollers, let him go, eenie, meenie, miney, mo." Folklorists have compiled several collections of counting-out rhymes: Bolton (1888) cites counting-out rhymes from 22 cultures; Abrams & Rankin (1980) list 582 English counting-out rhymes with many variants. As children, forming teams for softball games, my friends and I in Chicago used another widespread procedure to "choose up" which captain got first pick of the assembled players. One captain tossed a baseball bat to the other, nearby, who caught and held on; the tosser then grasped the bat immediately above the catcher's hand; then the catcher grasped it above the tosser; and so on, until the last person who could hold the bat by his finger tips was entitled to the first pick from among those who wanted to play. Then the two captains would alternate picking players. (See Chase 1976 for a description of this procedure in New York City stickball.) For similar allocations, my children used "pick a number": a third person secretly selects a number, say, between 1 and 20. Each of the others declares a number, and the one who comes closest wins. Chess players pick between playing white, with first move, and playing black, by having one person hold a white pawn concealed in one fist, a black pawn in the other. The opponent chooses a fist and thereby plays whatever color pawn is revealed to be in that fist. Card players may use six or more concrete operations for evenly balancing the chances of each player: they shuffle, cut the deck, deal cards in cycles around the table, bid in cycles around the table, and rotate as dealer. They may also take turns hosting their meetings or supplying new decks.

Between two parties, such as sports teams, a coin flip is common. A larger group needing to select one person fairly – perhaps to undertake a dangerous task – may draw straws. One person holds a set of straws whose tops are aligned but whose ends are concealed, while the others choose; the person drawing the short straw is selected.

If there is only one item, or if the issue is who gets the first turn, it may also be allocated by equal opportunity to stake a claim according to a recognized procedure. In American preadolescent culture of my youth, for example, the first person to call out "shotgun!" claimed the right to sit in the front passenger seat, which was regarded as the best seat.[3] Ostensive equality of opportunity is manifest when people form a queue to buy scarce tickets, or to get into a store holding a remarkable sale: the distribution is in order of the person's order of arrival to line up in the queue.

The concept of lottery as fair in an equality matching sense is evident in Indo-European mythology. The Akkadian Atrahasis epic poem, and later Homer in the *Iliad* (15.187–93), both represent the gods as dividing the sky, the sea, and the earth by lot; the sky becomes the realm of Anu or Zeus, the sea the realm of Enki or Poseidon, and the earth the realm of Enlil or Hades (Morris 1997: 602).

The Celts and Teutons practiced divinatory decision making and allocation by lots (Ewen 1932: 22–23). When something could not appropriately be divided, such as a body for ritual burial, or risking one's life to obtain food, early northern European Christians did likewise. Roman emperors distributed presents by lottery at banquets, sometimes requiring each guest to purchase (at the same price) tickets and take an equal chance at very unequal prizes (Ewen 1932: 21). By 1411 in Bruges, the office of *scrooder*, a controller of wines, had long been allocated by lottery. In the domain of the Duke of Burgandy in the Low Countries, records show lotteries in wide use by the early fifteenth century, evidently to raise funds for parish or city treasuries (Ewen 1932: 25). Subsequently, state-run lotteries for fund raising became widespread in Europe, Britain, and the

[3] Michael Sean Smith reminded me about these practices.

American colonies. Each such lottery offered opportunities to win several prizes, including suits of armor, gilt or silver plate, linen, or cash. Subscribers often wrote a short verse on the tickets that were to be drawn, enabling them to prove their ownership of a winning ticket, while also, if they wished, maintaining their anonymity (Ewen 1932). By the eighteenth century, at least, many Western lotteries seem to have involved double randomization, with one enormous "wheel" filled with tickets bearing the names or numbers of lottery ticket purchasers, and another enormous wheel holding tickets inscribed with each prize, together with blank tickets exactly sufficient to add up to the number of tickets purchased. Thus, the drawing involved simultaneously picking one ticket from the wheel of purchaser names and matching it with one ticket from the wheel of results, and then yelling out the results. For a lottery that sold tens or hundreds of thousands of tickets, this drawing process lasted for weeks, even up to four months! In Britain, at least, individuals who could not afford the price of a ticket could purchase $^1/_2$, $^1/_4$, $^1/_8$, $^1/_{16}$, $^1/_{32}$, or $^1/_{64}$ of a ticket. Brokers took commissions when they divided tickets, a practice which public sentiment often resented and public edicts often forbade (Ewen 1932). Betting on the results was widespread – for example, betting that someone would win on a given day. Apparently because the commissions on such bets were regarded as illegitimate or exploitive, in Britain such betting and insurance were officially censured, then made illegal, then ultimately legalized.

In medical trials, random assignment lotteries are regarded as the fair mechanism for "allotting" unknown risks and benefits of new treatments compared to standard treatments (Silverman & Chalmers 2001). Random assignment is also the only valid method for making scientific inferences from any differences in response rates between patients receiving the new treatment and the control group, because given an adequate sample size, a lottery results, in fact, in each group being statistically representative of the population from which both were drawn. The Flemish physician John Baptiste Van Helmet was one of the first who is known to have conceptualized this procedure, in 1662. He proposed dividing a large sample by lots into one group who would receive traditional bloodletting and purging, while the other group – that he would treat – would not. Then, Van Helmet challenged, they could count the number of funerals of patients in each group. However, this method of randomized assignment trials was not actually adopted for two hundred years, and did not become the standard until 1948. In that year, in an early trial of antibiotics, random numbers were used to divide a sample of tuberculosis patients into two groups: one receiving streptomycin, the other not (Silverman & Chalmers 2001). Streptomycin worked and has been among the drugs used to treat tuberculosis ever since.

A lottery is also regarded as a fair way to distribute resources that cannot be made universally available, or when resources are differentially preferable, such as dormitory rooms at many universities. University dorm-room lotteries are often stratified, so that seniors draw lots and choose, then juniors draw lots and choose among the remaining rooms, then sophomores and freshmen. This, of course, is a combination of iconic dimensional precedence conforming authority ranking between class years, then, in the next step, a concrete operation conforming equality matching among members of the same class year.

Conversely, when burdens, hardships, or dangers have to be borne by some but not by all, authorities may impose a lottery to select among those deemed to have the responsibility to serve if called. Military conscription in the United States in World War I and the Vietnam War was based on lotteries.

Just as we noted for consubstantial assimilation conformations of communal sharing, and for iconic dimensional and magnitude conformations of market pricing, concrete operations that conform equality matching are often combined or concatenated. Combinations of concrete operations enable people in traditional societies to divide arable land according to equality matching, despite the fact that land is never uniform in quality or in suitability for particular crops, and farmers may need to grow multiple crops. To conform equality matching in such complex circumstances, people may begin by delineating sections of land that, so far as possible, are each homogenous with respect to quality and crop suitability. Then the participants measure each of these sections into equal parcels, and assign one parcel in each plot to each household or kin group, often by a lottery or rotation, or both (parts of sixteenth-century England: Gray 1915: 208–209, Beresford 1943, Ernle 1961: 26; Ethiopia: Hoben 1963: 48–49; Taiwan: Barnett 1971: 109; Andes: Harris 1982: 74; premodern Denmark: Andersen 1989). In many communities in medieval England and Europe, everyone had to plant and harvest the same crop at the same time in each block of adjacent fields. Then they switched to communal sharing, opening the entire block to gleaning by all comers. After this, fences were removed and all the fields in the block were open to the conjoined village herds of cattle, sheep, or swine (for an example, see Ernle 1961: 25). This system was associated with a mandatory, coordinated two- or three-year crop rotation, so that each participant had, for example, one field in a specific barley block, one in particular rye block, one in another rye block, one in the block of spring crops, one in hay, etcetera, up to a dozen or more separate fields, and one in the fallow block where livestock were grazed during the summer (Bloch 1955). In short, they conformed equality matching separately for each kind of field. Concrete operations of one-to-one matching do not work to conform equality matching if people are matching, say, barley blocks to rye blocks or matching spring-crop blocks to hay blocks. Equality matching does not allow for trade-offs between, say, the area of a field and the value of the field's crop per unit area.

Greeks in the Classical period regarded selection of administrative officials by lot as essential to democracy (Headlam 1891: 12ff). In the democratic era of classical Athens, each year administrators were selected by lot to a one-year, nonrenewable term. Administrative posts assigned this way included collectors of fines, sellers of confiscated property, sellers of state mining rights, sellers of indirect tax collection rights, receivers of city taxes, jury paymasters, treasurers of the temple of Athena, treasurers of the other gods, treasurers who collected tribute from tribute allies, regulators of the markets, port officials, prison wardens and executioners, and religious officials with continuous duties (Headlam 1891, Roberts 1982). Of course, they held a separate lottery for each kind of office. Apparently Athenians employed this combination of lottery with annual turn-taking rotations to prevent the development of an oligarchic political elite or a professional administrative class with a distinct identity or will, especially an administrative class that might oppose the decisions of the Assembly. In each office, at the end of his year of service, a board examined each incumbent's accounts. The Athenians wanted to minimize the possibility that an incumbent, having embezzled, could bribe the board to certify his accounts. So, the board was chose by lot at the last minute.

Similarly, the democratic Athenians designed brilliant sets of concrete operations to assure that they truly conformed equality matching. Athenians devised a machine, the *klērōtērion*, to assure the fairness of such lotteries and preclude any tampering. The *klērōtēria* assured that all demes were equally represented in juries, and that members of each deme were equally likely to be chosen for each office (Taylor 2007, Kosmetatou 2013). The integrity of Athenian allocations to office was assured by a system of double lotteries: one to select the person, the other to select the office; each lottery was held at about the same time in different locations, so those conducting either lottery could not know the result of the other lottery. Likewise, the procedure for assigning jurors made bribing them improbable. From among a large pool of awaiting volunteers seeking jury pay, jurors were selected by lot, and then assigned to cases by lot. In

Box 14.2

There is inherent, inextricable temporal order when taking turns, when flipping a coin to see who kicks off in American football, when distributing cookies by "one-for-you, one-for-you, one-for-you, one-for-me," and in some other concrete operations of one-to-one matching. As I mentioned, where going first matters, there may be a random procedure or other concrete operation to determine who goes first. But even in those cases and certainly in many others, there may be little or no authority ranking conformed by who goes first, nor any conformational aspect of the subsequent temporal order among more than two persons. This is another example of the principle we considered at the end of Chapter 2, with regard to the absence of any conformational function of most of the ever-present, unavoidable positions of persons on every one of the ten dimensions. At every moment, every person occupies a position on every dimension relative to every other person, but only a few of these function as conformations. We will return to this issue in Chapter 16's section on Felicity.

the court, the accuser spoke until the water clock ran out; then the accused took his turn speaking until the same water clock, refilled to the same level, ran out. That was it; the jury (often hundreds of persons) did not discuss the case, but immediately voted by secret ballot.

A common concrete operation for continuous entities is for person X to divide things up in even allotments to their own satisfaction, and then the other person or persons choose what they each want, leaving person X with the last allotment. As boys, every Saturday my father and his brother had to mow the grass: front lawn, back lawn, and the irregular strips beside the house. This week, say, my father would carefully divide the lawn into two parts that he judged were equal, then his brother chose which part he would mow. The following week, my father's brother would meticulously divide the grass into two parts, and then my father chose which half he would mow. And so on, alternating who divided and who chose. Looking back on it, my father was amused that each week it took far longer for the divider to divide the lawn evenly than it took for the two of them to mow it once they started.

Human Infants Have Adapted to Thousands of Years of Equality Matching, Conformed by Concrete Operations

Many mammals and birds, as well as bees and apparently at least some spiders, have been shown to "count" up to three or four, and do "subtraction" within sets of up to three or four (Skorupski et al. 2018, Howard et al. 2019). For example, suppose an animal with this capacity sees an empty box, and then the box is turned so they can no longer see inside. Seeing three squirrels go into a box, then one came out, the animal knows that there must be exactly two squirrels in the box still. Then if two more squirrels come out, animals with this capacity know that there are none remaining. If an animal with this capacity observes four flashes of light, and then hears three "boom" sounds, it expects to hear one more boom. Likewise, by five months of age, and likely earlier, human infants are able to detect, remember, and compare the numerosity of sets, even across sensory modalities (Féron et al. 2006 & sources cited therein). This system functions only for sets of four or fewer items or events, and in some cases only functions well for sets less than or equal to three. Depending on the research paradigm and species studied, the cognitive system for this is referred to as "subitizing," "object files," or "individual object tracking" – though the system operates on events and momentary sensations, as well as objects. In some primate species, researchers have identified individual neurons that respond specifically to a distinct small number of items or events (Nieder 2016).

It is not known what adaptive functions this system has, nor what evolutionary and neurocognitive factors limit it to sets less than or equal to four (or three). But this subitizing system that naturally performs one-to-one mapping is ideally suited for utilization as the substrate for the concrete operations of one-to-one correspondence that comprise the conformation system of equality matching. It would enable a person to encode, track, and compute the balance of turns performed and turns owed in return, so long as no one took more than four turns on any given occasion. The subitizing system would enable a person to represent whether people received the same number of apples, and if not, how many more apples a person needs to match the number that the other one got – so long as that was no more than four. This subitizing system is cognitively distinct from the AMS; they are completely different neurocognitive systems, doing different things.

Using well-established looking-time methods, it has been shown in several experiments that when infants observe a person distribute a small number of crackers to two puppets, the infants expect the person to divide them equally (Buyukozer Dawkins et al. 2019, Meristo et al. 2016, Somerville et al. 2013). For example, at nineteen months, at nine months, and at four months, US infants expect an experimenter to divide two cookies equally (1:1) between two similar animated puppets. The infant looks longer if the experimenter distributes the cookies unequally: two cookies to one puppet, none to the other (Sloane at al. 2012, Ziv & Sommerville 2017, Surian &

Margoni 2020). Furthermore, at four months, and also at nine months, infants not only prefer an agent who distributes apples evenly, they take into account distributors' intentions, preferring agents who tried but failed to distribute items evenly (Geraci & Surian 2023a, Strid & Meristo 2020). By sixteen months, Italian infants prefer (i.e., choose when offered a photo) a puppet distributor who gives each of two other puppets one disk, compared to a distributor who gives both disks to one and none to the other (Geraci & Surian 2011). By twenty-five months, Italian toddlers are more likely to help a person who has distributed a resource equally to two agents than to help a person who distributed the resource unequally (Surian & Franchin 2017).

Beyond simply expecting even distributions, preverbal infants expect a third party to enforce and reward even distribution. Geraci and Surian found that nine-month-old infants

> looked longer when they saw a bystander delivering a corporal punishment to a "fair distributor," who distributed some windfall resources equally to the possible recipients, rather than to an "unfair distributor," who distributed the resources unequally. This pattern of looking times was reversed when, in Experiment 2, punishments were replaced with rewards. (Geraci and Surian 2023b: 1)

What happens when an infant herself can reward or punish a distributor? Ziv et al. (2021) taught sixteen-month-old infants that pressing one side of the screen resulted in a voice uttering praise, with positive intonation; pressing the other side of the screen resulted in a voice uttering disapproval, with negative intonation. Then the infants observed a videotaped human distribute either crackers or Lego blocks to two other humans. The sixteen-month-old infants learned that pressing one side of the screen gave the distributor a cracker; pressing the other side of the screen resulted in a cracker being taken away from the distributor. After observing a video of a human distributing crackers equally between two other humans, the infants choose to award the distributor a cracker much more frequently than they choose to have a cracker taken away from the distributor. When the infants saw an unequal distribution, they were equally likely to give a cracker to the distributor or take a cracker away.

These are just a few examples of many studies with similar results. As Sommerville at al. (2013: 44) indicate, many studies have shown that by early in "the second year of life infants expect goods and resources to be allocated equally to recipients, prefer agents that perform fair (equal) distributions, and expect other agents to affiliate with or approach fair over unfair distributors." However, in those studies, in the condition where infants see a pre-existing situation, or recognize that a distribution is occurring, but the action is screened so that the infants cannot see the process, infants typically do not expect an equal distribution, compared to an unequal distribution. Neither seems "surprising." This strongly suggests that infants only expect equal distributions when they observe the concrete operation of one-to-one matching, but not otherwise. Their reward and punishment choices are driven by observation of the concrete one-to-one operation, not by viewing who has how much. That "makes sense," since there are infinitely many processes that could lead to any given distribution of resources.

Australian children aged three years ten months to four years ten months are unable to divide continuous substances into "even" shares, and show little awareness of what the experimenter's request to do so means (Hunting & Sharpley 1988). Yet many of these toddlers can distribute evenly matched sets of discrete crackers among three dolls by allocating one to each doll in a cyclical procedure. That is, toddlers can conform equality matching with concrete operations of one-to-one matching.

In their review of the literature on infants' expectations about distributions of resources, McAuliffe and colleagues (2017: 1) noted that even before they can speak, infants expect an agent distributing resources to make an even distribution, with the same number of items for each recipient: Several recent studies have found that infants are surprised when witnessing resources distributed unequally for no apparent reason. Thomas (2024) reviews the same studies along with more recent ones, studies with varying displays and agents of several sorts, validating that infants expect agents to make even distributions among agents, and in some sense or other "prefer" an agent who does so. This is expectation is specific to distributions to agents; infants have no such expectation that a distributor will put equal sets of resources next to inanimate objects.

Reading this with the idea that concrete operations of one-to-one correspondence conform equality matching, the crucial finding is that infants do not expect that a set of agents will or will not each have the same number of cookies; they are not surprised when they see agents with unequal resources. Rather, infants expect that distributors will perform concrete operations of one-to-one matching, unless there is an indication that the agents are conforming a relationship other than equality matching.

Two components of equality matching emerge after infancy. Toddlers first become willing to give up an item to make participants equal, and, a bit later, develop motivation to punish others who take more than their equal share (McAuliffe and colleagues 2017).

Although most of the studies have been focused on infant expectations about distributions, infants understand equality matching in other contexts as well. Studying sixteen-month old infants, Jin et al. (2024: 2) found that

> after agent1 acts positively toward agent2, infants are surprised if agent2 chooses to act negatively toward agent1 in a new context. Similarly, after agent1 acts negatively toward agent2, infants are surprised if agent2 chooses to act positively toward agent1 in a new context. Both responses are eliminated when agent2's actions are not knowingly directed at agent1 (because they are directed at a new agent, or because agent2 does not know she is acting on agent1's possessions).

In most of the studies, researchers were primarily or exclusively aiming to determine if infants understood social relationships, as such. It seems that for many infant researchers, editors, reviewers, and readers, the manner of conforming the relationship never arose at all. Some researchers do not even explain why they chose the conformations they present in their experiments, apparently relying on what the researchers assume to be the

Box 14.3

Infants innately expect concrete operations of one-to-one correspondence to conform equality matching relationships – because that is, in fact, the way people everywhere do conform equality matching, and have done for many thousands of years. This psychosocial adaptation enables infants to immediately recognize this conformation and its equality matching consequences, which infants must understand in order to make sense of many of the social interactions they observe. Moreover, this adaptation enables the maturing child to proficiently participate in equality matching relationships, one of the forms of cooperation essential to social relations, wherever the infant happens to be born. That adaptation can only have evolved because for thousands of years it has been beneficial for human infants and toddlers, utterly dependent as we are on trustful egalitarian cooperation. Conversely, as scholars, we can confidently make an important inference based on the discovery that infants are adaptively prepared for concrete operations of one-to -one correspondence that conform equality matching. That adaptation absolutely implies that for many thousands of years, *Homo sapiens* have, indeed, ordinarily employed concrete operations of one-to-one correspondence to conform their equality matching relations. In short, infants' evolved innate knowledge of equality matching conformations consisting of concrete operations of one-to-one correspondence. That adaptation gives us a window into the social relations prevalent around the world throughout the last millennium, at least.

obvious way to conform equality matching relationships. In any case, we see the same epistemological result in virtually every study that I have located and/or that Thomas reviews: Whenever researchers have aimed to study infant understanding of communal relations, de facto, their studies necessarily also test whether infants recognize the conformation system of equality matching.

So, it seems clear that infants have two kinds of social relational core knowledge: they know how to recognize communal sharing, authority ranking, and equality matching; and they know in each of these three kinds of relationships, respectively, how people are likely to interact. Infants have definite and distinct expectations about social interaction in equality matching relationships, specifically; infants have quite different expectations about social interaction specific to authority ranking relationships; and they expect yet another pattern of interactions specific to communal sharing relationships.

Nonhuman Animals

There are few, if any, studies of nonhuman animals that find social interaction clearly homologous to equality matching. In species that recognize individuals and remember their behavior, every animal's behavior toward other individuals is affected by their past experience of that animal's behavior. But contingency and correlation do not imply one-to-one matching.

There is some apparently nonquantitative tendency of quid pro quo reciprocity in some primates' grooming (de Waal 1996). Correlations either within or across grooming bouts indicate modest tendencies to reciprocate grooming among bonded females of white-faced capuchins, chacma baboons, and bonnet macaques (see analyses and review in Manson et al. 2004). Similarly, in the gentle herb-field mouse, the grooming that each mouse receives from another male or female mouse is correlated with the grooming it provides to it; within each sex, the amounts given and received tend to be equal, but females return less grooming to males than they receive from them (Stopka & Graciasová 2001). Experiments also show some degree of reciprocity among captive brown capuchins' toleration for others taking some of what they are eating (de Waal 2000). Toothed whales sometimes forage cooperatively by spreading out in a long rank abreast, which increases their chances of finding food (Connor 2000: 210–211). This coordination consists of swimming parallel at more or less equal-spaced intervals.

There is also evidence suggesting that sperm whales more or less "take turns" babysitting calves at the surface (Whitehead 2003). Sperm whales dive deep, often 300 to 1,000 meters or more, commonly staying down for 30–45 minutes as they seek squid, then coming back to the surface, where they rest and breath for 8–10 minutes. When only adults are present, they tend to keep each other company, diving and surfacing in close synchrony – their respective dives are separated by a median time of about 6 seconds, compared to the 123 second interval that would result from randomly distributed diving. But the sperm whales do just the opposite when caring for any of the calves in the cluster. Calves cannot dive as deep or remain submerged as long as adults, and unprotected calves are exposed to the risk of predation by killer whales. When a cluster of sperm whales has one or more calves, the adults spread out their diving so that, most of the time, there is at least one adult on the surface "baby-sitting." But this pattern does not imply one-to-one turn-taking, as such. On the move, many different sperm whale adults and immatures in a group "escort" calves, so that one or more large sperm whale is nearly always close to each calf, in a pattern that Whitehead (2003: 262) calls "serial accompaniment." When one adult companion dives, a calf will swim to another nearby adult, or go to the spot where an adult is about to surface (Whitehead & Weilgart 2000: 165).

Many bird species and some mammals respond to some predators by mobbing: gathering to jointly, overwhelmingly attack the predator in order to drive it away. If many animals quickly join in the mobbing, these attacks are much more likely to be successful, and much less dangerous to the attackers. Field studies of breeding pied flycatchers in Latvia show that neighboring pairs nearly always (30/32) responded to calls and help their neighbors mob a stuffed owl if the calling neighbor recently helped them (Krams et al. 2008). But when the calling neighbor had been experimentally prevented from helping the last time the owl appeared, other flycatchers never (0/32) came out to mob the owl.

Vampire bats need to feed every night; if they do not eat for two consecutive nights, they are likely to become too weak to go out and forage. So how do they survive? Vampire bats, especially females, may regurgitate blood to feed hungry associates who have been roosting with them. They are much more likely to regurgitate to a roost-mate who has previously given them blood (Wilkinson 1984, 1985, DeNault & McFarlane 1995). The amounts of blood regurgitated would be extremely difficult to measure, so it is not known whether vampire bats match the amount received to the amount given to a roost-mate.

There are many other observations of nonhuman animals' correlation and approximate contingency of giving and getting among conspecifics, but among the nonhuman animals that have been carefully studied so far there is no definite evidence of exact one-to-one correspondence between the amount of some benefit that an individual gives to an associate and the amount of the same benefit the associate returns to that individual. In some species, there is evidence of a correlation between how much (or how many) benefits of a certain kind an animal bestows to a given associate and how much (or how many) of that particular benefit the animal tends to receive from that associate. But a correlation way below 1.0 is not an indication of equality matching. And, so far as I am aware, nonhuman animals have never been observed engaged in a social process of dividing up a resource into even shares, nor returning harm for the same harm, matched one-to-one, an-eye-for-an-eye.

A recent meta-analysis finds that no nonhuman primate, nor any other mammal, is averse to any sort of unequal distribution (Ritov et al. 2024). All animals can visually compare two quantities and reliably judge which is greater; if the substance is a desirable food, animals prefer the larger of two quantities. Animals may display frustration when they see that their portion is smaller than another "portion," but that is true regardless of whether that larger portion goes to another animal or is merely visible but not accessible to the observer, with no other apparent recipient

Limitations of Concrete Operations of One-to-One Matching: Why They Are Not Always Workable

Concrete operations to conform equality matching have at least two major limitations. First, some concrete operations are difficult to scale up to conform equality matching among a large number of persons. For example it does not seem feasible for the 5,000 inhabitants of my community to take turns at, say, collecting the whole town's garbage. Technological means may be devised to scale up concrete operations to conform equality matching in large populations, but these means may not be fully effective, particularly if they are not in the mode of concrete operations of one-to-one correspondence, and it is not feasible for everyone to observe their operation. When people vote by a show of hands, or by casting physical ballots that they can observe others casting, and observe being compared or counted, people generally judge the outcome to be legitimate, feel morally committed to it, and are motivated to support it. However, when digital voting machines record and computers compile the results of 159,000,000 votes, some people question the legitimacy of the outcome, and many people feel no moral obligation to adhere to it nor have any motivation to make it work. For some people, voting on digital machines and tallying on computers are not trustworthy because the operations are not concrete – or not observably concrete – and there is no palpable one-to-one correspondence between persons and votes, so one does not know whether some people voted twice, or votes were counted that were not cast by eligible living voters, so digital voting and tallying may be ineffective for conforming the equality matching of one-person, one-vote.

The second partial constraint on concrete operations for conforming equality matching is that whatever it is that people are coordinating in this manner, it must naturally occur in acceptably equal units, or else there must be a concrete operation that people can legitimately use for making equal units ahead of time. It is not enough that a concrete operation of one-to-one matching be performed. To conform effectively, people must observe that concrete operation or trust that it was performed, and performed properly.

A day's work, a vote, a kola nut, or a goat make obvious units, although of course they differ in various respects. But a concrete operation matches units in just one respect, ignoring all else. Culture typically has a large role in determining what aspect of the units people equalize in concrete operations of conformation, and what aspects of the units people conventionally deem irrelevant for such operations.

Even so, for concrete operations to operate smoothly, participants cannot be too strict about what counts as a unit. In innumerable respects, A's day of work to help B differs from B's subsequent day of work to help A, but if all that can be put aside, then A and B, and observers, can construe what occurred as concrete one-to-one matching, so A and B are even. If the units are egregiously, manifestly unequal in ways that matter a lot to the participants, the concrete operation fails, and, along with it, the equality matching relationship. If X gave a goat to Y last year, and now Y returns a goat, that operationally matches the exchange, concretely bringing Y back to even with X. Unless the "goat" that Y returns is just a skin and skeleton. In that case, Y's putative reciprocation is an insult, or a joke.

For conforming equality matching, different concrete operations are feasible, and suitable, for equalizing different things. This is especially clear with regard to material stuff. Many entities do not naturally occur in discrete and equal chunks. In such cases, to conform equality matching people must initially use a culturally established concrete operation that creates equal units – that is, units that are equal with respect to the manner in which the conformation then puts them in one-to-one correspondence. Or else participants must devise their own concrete operation – an operation not only mutually satisfactory, but also recognized by all to be binding. Suppose person Z has an excess of peaches, which will spoil before they can be consumed. Person H has an excess of blueberries, which will spoil before they can be consumed. Peaches are so different from blueberries that the peach picker may not be satisfied with the concrete operation of exchanging each peach for a blueberry. But perhaps they would both be pleased with an exchange conformed by the concrete operation of one-for-one correspondence between buckets of fruit given and buckets of fruit received. Z fills up the bucket with peaches, passes it to H, who empties the peaches onto her mat, fills up the bucket with blueberries, and passes it over to Z, who empties the blueberries onto her mat. That is workable. In Chapter 2, I described this operation, *tekre*, as performed between Moosé neighbors.

While humans have had thousands of years to devise concrete operational conformations for equality matching, new aspects of social life, and new technologies, may make possible new concrete conformations, and/or require new ones. As is the case for each of the four conformation systems, new developments motivate people to invent and collectively, cumulatively perfect newly needed conformations concordant with the system.

Cultural practices for conforming equality matching do not just fortuitously arise and flourish. The adaptation for concrete operational one-to-one conforming of equality matching potentiates concordant conventions, while letting discordant equality matching-conforming conventions languish and fade away. Also, people want to conform equality matching effectively and reliably, so they seek and foster conformations concordant with the adaptation, when they intuit and then experience that those conformations are the most effective and reliable ones.

Symmetry

There is another way to conceptualize concrete operations, borrowing a core concept of physics. Concrete operations of one-to-one correspondence establish "symmetry." Symmetry under a given transformation means that the properties remain unchanged. So, for a geometric example, a square is rotationally symmetric with regard to both shape and orientation when rotated 90° on the plane, 180°, 270°, 360°, or any integer multiple of 90°. It is not rotationally symmetric with respect to orientation if rotated to any other degree, though rotation does not affect symmetry of shape or size. A square is shape- and size-symmetric under reflection on any line going through its center, or any line that does not intersect the square. For mathematical structures, symmetry is defined as unchanged relations between values under a given transformation.

Conformations of one-to-one correspondence create symmetry among the participants, and symmetry among the things that participants do or get. That is, these conformations are not affected by participants replacing what they got with what another participant got. If all of the cookies are pretty much the same and, after the distribution, I give you my cookie and you give me your cookie, the conformation is unchanged. Distributing a set of virtually identical cookies, if a distributor had given out different cookies to the participants, that alternate conformation would be symmetrical with the original conformation, in the sense that it would do exactly the same thing, and the transformation would not matter.[4]

Consider symmetry in the *sisoaaga* that I briefly described earlier, in which a group of people take positions side by side along one edge of a field, and at a signal each begins to cultivate the strip in front of him or her; everyone continues in alignment as they work to the opposite edge of the field, then stop. The concrete operation of participants all starting work simultaneously on a strip parallel to all the others' strips, working across the field in a line, and ceasing simultaneously when they all reach the far edge, has translational symmetry across participants. That is, a person's moving to a different starting position in the line at the edge of the field does not affect the equality between the work that the person does and the work that everyone else in the line does.

Now imagine a number of persons seated in a circle, with their allocations of, say, kola nuts, in front of them. The allocations were made by going around the circle – "one for you, one for you, one for you," etcetera – until the cycle is completed, and then, if kolas remain, beginning the cycle again. There is rotational symmetry: it does not change the equality of any persons' allocation if everyone moves any number of places around the circle either clockwise or counter clockwise, and takes possession of the kola nuts in front of them in place of the kola nuts that were in front of them before the rotation. Likewise, there is temporal symmetry when a distributor gives one item to each person in succession, repeating the one-to-each allocation in one or more complete rounds. In essence, this is

[4] Physicists have discovered, theoretically posited, or avidly search for symmetries that structure all matter, energy, and forces. Likewise, Bolender (2010) shows that the relational models are structured according to a specific set of symmetries, while the four relational models together comprise a natural symmetry-breaking sequence.

translational symmetry over time. Similarly, turn-taking and tit-for-tat are concrete operations that exhibit reflectional symmetry over time: if I take your turn and you take my turn, that does not affect the equality of the turns. An indefinitely continuing sequence of turn-taking or tit-for-tat also exhibits translational temporal symmetry, which we can suitably call serial symmetry.

In sum, concrete operations of one-to-one correspondence establish the translational, serial, rotational, and reflectional symmetries that constitute equality matching. In messy reality, of course the symmetries are not perfect. In reality, it may matter when you take your turn. Your turn inevitably differs a bit from my turn; my four kolas differ a bit from your four kolas. Even with a micrometer and stop watch we cannot possibly make them exactly equal. So, to make equality matching function in practice we must implicitly accept that what you get is sufficiently similar to what I get. Sufficient symmetry is what the concrete operations establish.

In Chapter 10 I raised eleven questions with regard to the ten dimensions that iconically conform authority ranking. Scholars should ask more or less corresponding questions with regard to the different kinds of concrete operations of one-to-one matching. Most important, are all kinds interchangeable? Or do some concrete operations more effectively evoke equality matching emotions, say, while other concrete operations more effectively evoke the moral sentiments of equality matching? Are different one-to-one conformations differently memorable?

Recursion is important for concrete operations conforming equality matching. In dyadic turn-taking without a known end point, I take a turn because I expect you to take the next turn because you expect me to take the next turn because I expect you to take the next turn, ad infinitum. (I use "expect" as shorthand for the integral combination of all aspects of a conformation.) In an even distribution, or when making even contributions, or when voting, common conformation is crucial: each person feels that it is fair (in the sense of being even) because they can see that it is fair, and believes that everyone else feels that it is fair because they, too, can see that it is fair. A concrete one-to-one correspondence conforms effectively if it makes each participant committed, and makes each participant judge that everyone else must be committed. And that should be recursive, up to the limits of cognitive resources with any supporting devices: each participant judges that every other participant ought to be morally committed, while judging that every other participant ought to judge that every other participant ought to be morally committed to the judgment that every participant should judge that they are committed, and everyone else should be committed. Thus, we should have a vital adjunct to common knowledge: common moral commitment.

For example, to accept the legitimacy of the outcome of a vote, each participant must recognize that the concrete one-to-one correspondence conformation of casting ballots commits oneself to the outcome of the vote, because one knows and feels and judges that, because everyone saw for themselves that there was one-person, one-vote, everyone ought to feel a binding commitment to the results, everyone ought to feel that everyone else ought to feel a binding commitment, and so on.

Now We Should Adopt a New Paradigm of What Makes People Social

It seems to me that there is a scientifically revolutionary result of the discovery of infants' knowledge of the conformation systems of communal sharing, authority ranking, and equality matching, together with infants' knowledge of each of the three relational models. All existing theories of child "socialization" and "internalization" are now obsolete and ought to be abandoned forthwith. The experimental evidence conclusively shows that infants and children do not need to "internalize" communal norms, authority ranking norms, or equality matching norms – infants already know what each of the three types of relationships are, and recognize their respective conformation systems. So, it seems that norms as such may not be all that important; knowing and abiding by relational models does not depend on propositional or prescriptive semantic norms. Instead of "internalizing" norms imparted to and imposed on them by adults, infants must be actively on the lookout for consubstantial assimilation, and know how people (or puppets and animated agents) interact in the ensuing communal sharing relationship. Infants want to engage in equality matching, so they need to discover how equality matching is implemented in their community. They have to figure that out, they are assiduously looking to see who does equality matching with whom with regard to what sorts of coordination. Infants know how to recognize equality matching, no matter what community on earth they happen to be born into. They are on the lookout for concrete operations of one-to-one correspondence, and, when they observe that, they know they are looking at an equality matching relationship. Infants also know communal sharing and authority ranking, along with their respective conformation systems, and have the same eagerness to find those conformations. The infant knows that when it finds an iconic dimensional conformation, it has detected an instance of authority ranking. The infant observes who is ranked above whom, and what they are coordinating with authority ranking. Also, from multiple observations, the infant can see precisely how people conformationally implement each of the ten dimensions. To show respect, lowering the head? Kneeling and putting the forehead on the ground? Bowing? Curtseying? Prostrating 30 feet away while raising and lowering the forearms?

This prior knowledge of three relational models and their conformation systems, plus assiduous infant-initiated search for instances of each of the three conformation systems – that's virtually the opposite of "socialization" and "internalization" of prescriptive norms. It is, if you like, the "externalization" of relational models and endogenous affective engagement with them. That is the paradigm we need to adopt in further study of what makes people mostly cooperative and moral.

CHAPTER 15

Symbolic Conformation of Market Pricing

The conformation system of market pricing is symbolism, in Peirce's sense that the meaning of a symbol is purely the result of people using the symbol to mean that. Peirce is primarily concerned with how symbols and his two other types of signs refer to things. In adopting his taxonomy for conformation systems theory, recall that we adapt and extend Peirce's conceptions of indexes, icons, and symbols to encompass not only reference, but all of the social relational things that signs do. Thus, a conformation symbol, in particular, refers to market pricing relations that exist, or that the symbolizers imagine, but also market pricing that the symbolizer offers, seeks, or asserts. So, for example, one can imagine the price, a numeric symbol, at which one might be able to sell one's house, in the event that one put it on the market. Or conform the price that one wishes one could obtain, or feels one is entitled to, even if one knows that in reality it will never sell at that price. Numeric symbols may serve as a binding offer to sell at the specified price, whether the offer is a real estate listing or the price tag on a peach. In a final signed contract for a house, people use numeric symbols to commit to pay the specified amount. The contract consists entirely of linguistic and numeric symbols, as does the check that completes the purchase. Such symbols may elicit motivation, for example, to hurry and make an offer on a house. And, by the same token, symbols evoke emotions, as when the buyer and/or the seller are overjoyed at the deal that they struck, or distraught that it fell through. The numeric symbols for the price of a completed purchase become a standard against which people evaluate the value of other houses, or the same house at a later date. Those sale price symbols inform the tax accessor, as well as insurance assessors.

In very simple interactions, coordinating very few entities or actions, entities, or actions that are present at hand, and coordinating in a short time frame around the current moment, market pricing can be done without symbolism, albeit awkwardly, within narrow limitations. But even in simple bartering, market pricing without symbolism is cumbersome; it is prone to confusion, misunderstanding, and disagreement about what commitments were made; and it is vulnerable to breakdown and conflict. Imagine attempting to conduct your market pricing relations without symbolism. There would be no currency, no checks, no digital transactions, no numerals, no convenient way to store and yet quickly utilize wealth, and, of course, no market pricing among persons not presently face-to-face with each other and not in view of whatever they aimed to coordinate. When, for example, as a lumberjack, you work at a location distant from your employer's place of work, how would you and your employer come to agreement with you about how much work you did, and then how would they compensate you for your labor? All that would be barely possible, but clumsy, slow, inflexible, and unreliable, with frequent misunderstandings or differing recollections.

Despite its name, the market pricing model is by no means limited to "economic" interactions, and symbolic conformation is vital to any market pricing relations, "economic" or not, consisting of material transactions or not. For example, course grades are usually determined by a market pricing scheme. Grades for each assignment should be, are intended to be, and are announced to be proportional to students' performance. That is, on a syllabus and verbally in class, professors symbolically conform their commitment to market pricing grading. Each assignment is valued as a proportion of the final grade. In a class with several assignments, it is hard to imagine how grades could be assigned without manipulating symbols to perform the addition and multiplication needed for the computations. In any case, the resultant letter or numeric grades themselves are symbols, as are grade point averages.

Every kind of utilitarian moral or pragmatic decision depends on manipulating symbols for ratio-scale values. Consider how the US Food and Drug Administration and the Centers for Disease Control and Prevention decide whether to approve vaccines. From experimental trials conducted through linguistic symbols and numeric records, they compare rates of immunity of vaccinated and unvaccinated trail participants, set against the rates of each side effect, weighted by its severity. That process is prototypical market pricing. It definitely requires symbolism to record and report beneficial and deleterious effects, weight them, make the computations of net benefits or costs, discuss the decision, and compose and disseminate a report explaining and justifying the decision.

People use symbols to conform even fairly simple market pricing. Suppose backpacker X and backpacker Y are planning to set out from opposite ends of a fairly long trail, whose ends are near their respective homes. They are planning to set off at dawn, and want to figure out where to meet up. Backpacker X says to Y "You hike literally twice as fast as I do, so let's meet at that lake that's two-thirds of the way along the trail from your end, and one-third of the way from my end. Are you good with getting there around 3:00 pm, so we can set up camp and go for a swim before dark?" That symbolic conformation commits and motivates them to hike fast enough to get there by approximately 3:00 pm. Those numerals – 3:00 – symbolically represent a future time, symbolically coordinate the hikers' interaction, and symbolically indicate a goal that is also a standard for evaluating each other's performance. If either hiker is egregiously late, the person who is late will be embarrassed-ashamed, and the person who sat there waiting may be irritated-angry – justifiably so, because each of them made a commitment that the slowpoke failed to adhere to.

Like the other three conformation systems, people use symbols communicatively, but also to cognize market pricing without making the symbols available to others' senses. That is, symbolic conformations of market pricing may be materially "externalized," but before and after being "externalized," or without ever being externalized, the symbols function in the mind. For example, people symbolically think over possible courses of action, symbolically compute utilities, and symbolically evaluate the morality of alternatives.

Conformation systems of each of the four kinds offer relationships, claim and declare relationships, demand relationships, and provide ideal models of social relationships. For both participants and third parties, conformation systems convey crucial information about the relationship. Conformations are standards against which people morally evaluate the relationship. Conformations initiate and modulate relationships. Furthermore, conformations are mode of relating – ways to coordinate so that participants' actions fit together as complementary constituents of the whole. Within the conformation system of a given relational model, specific conformations may perform any of these functions well, or not so well. In order to enhance social relationships, people sometimes seek ways to conform a given sort of relationship better. That is, people devise techniques of conforming that enhance some or all of the effects they seek. Let us call such devised techniques "technologies," without meaning to imply that conformational technologies necessarily consist of material engineering or abstruse processes; "technologies" may be any means of making conformations more effective. In Part III, we surveyed a great many technologies of the iconic conformations of authority ranking. In this chapter, we will take a look at five technologies originally devised to conform market pricing more effectively and to enable the reliable conduct of market pricing relations across large populations and between geographically and socially distant persons. Subsequently, each of these technologies culturally evolved far beyond their original function of conforming market pricing. These cultural-evolutionary expansions transformed human life. The technologies are weights and measures, money, calendars, numerals, and writing. Today, all five of these symbolic technologies are so ubiquitous, and so essential in contemporary life, that people ordinarily take them for granted. Hardly anyone knows that humans originally devised and perfected weights and measures, numerals, and writing in order to conform market pricing more effectively.

Metrology

When people use market pricing to transact material things, they do so proportionally. If the coordination consists of a court sentencing a person to X years in jail, moral sentiments and the law require that the length of the sentence be proportion to the magnitude of the wrong the person did. To conform such transactions mentally and to coordinate interaction, the fastest, clearest, and most precise mode is conventional symbols. Numeric symbols, in particular, greatly facilitate making offers and counteroffers, negotiating, and making commitments. To award symbolic grades, it helps a lot to have symbols for the quality and number of assignments completed. Symbolism is almost essential for coordinating transactions in which X gives something now, or performs work now, at a proportionate rate for something to be received subsequently.

Later in this chapter we will look into the historical origins and early uses of written numeric symbols, so far as is presently known. But first let us consider another requirement for many market pricing transactions: standard measures of weight and volume.

To cognize, offer, negotiate, commit to, perform, and evaluate a market pricing transaction, one must have a way of measuring amounts of substances, or units of work, or whatever is transacted. If the relevant units of work naturally and consistently occur in definite, unambiguously delineated units (days of harvesting potatoes), then numeric symbols enable neat proportionality, with comparatively little ambiguity – though even in that case, some conventions are necessary to a market pricing transaction, such as when the "day" begins and ends, what to do about damaged tools or ruined potatoes, and how many breaks of what length the laborer is entitled to take for water, food, rest, or recovery from injury. The spoken lexemes "day's work" symbolically conform all that, and more.

If the substances do not occur in definite units, or if the parties decide to coordinate in terms of "bushels of apples" or "sacks of potatoes," the parties need agreed-upon measures, including conventions for measurement processes (can one shake the bag before determining whether it is a full bag?). To make a market pricing transaction of rice for cider, one must have measurement technologies that are replicable, accurate with respect to some standard, and resistant to cheating. That is, one needs conventional measures of weight or volume. Those measures are symbols: it is purely a matter of convention how much a kilogram is, and how much a liter is.

Systems of standards for measurement of distances, surface areas, and weights appear early in the archeological record, with units and their relations symbolically recorded. In particular, scales and weights were used in Mesopotamia and Egypt by around 3000 BCE, and were in use in precontact Peru (Kisch 1965). In fourteenth- and thirteenth-century BCE Ugarit, for example, documents indicate silver-weight prices for gold, copper, tin, minerals, gems, donkeys, horses, raw and tinted wool, clothing, naval equipment, and various crops and produce, including olives, olive oil, and wine (Courtois 1990). In contrast, only a very small number of documents indicate direct rates of exchange between commodities such as oil, copper, or tin. That suggests that people typically used silver weight as the symbolic medium for market pricing transactions. Other documents give customs duties, tax assessments, and salaries, and some specify huge payments of tribute, all denominated in silver weight. Land sales are recorded priced in silver weight; so are fines. Early Mesopotamian weights have been found weighing $^1/_4$, $^1/_3$, $^2/_5$, $^3/_4$, 1, 2, 5, 10, 20, 50, and 1,000 *sicles*, enabling easy computation of proportions. In Sumer and in Egypt there were official calibration weights with symbolic inscriptions, or in the shape of a lion, in the shape of a duck with its head over its back, or any other arbitrary, conventional form whose meaning was established and known through its use, and perhaps also by a ruler's fiat (Dilke 1987: 46, Ascalone 2005: 237–238).[1]

[1] Peirce cogently defines symbolism as consisting of signs whose meaning utterly and entirely depends on convention – including, one might add, common knowledge of the convention. But there is another common basis for symbolism, a basis that is often temporally prior to convention: fiat by authority. For example, the meaning and moral weight of currency often initially consists of a ruler, government, or designated bureaucracy declaring its meaning and validity. E.g., this coin has such and such a value because a legitimate authority proclaims that it has that value, and 'stands behind'

Similarly, most ancient Egyptian commodities were valued in terms of their exchange equivalent in copper/bronze weight, silver, or even gold, or valued in terms of the volume of grains or sesame oil they were worth (Kemp 1989: 248–251). Many documents from the New Kingdom community of Deir el-Medina show transactions in which diverse sets of commodities are traded for something else, according to the sums of their respective values (Kemp 1989: 258). In other words, people were combining multiplication and addition, using the distributive law to compute the symbolic conformation of a combination of symbols.

Three types of devices for weighing were used in the ancient eastern Mediterranean world, all using a beam suspended from a fulcrum (Dilke 1987: 48–50). Pan balances are depicted in Egyptian tomb images (e.g., at Sakkara, tomb of Meruru-ka; Pritchard 1954, fig. 133, evidently showing a scribe recording the weighing of gold). Egyptians also believed that after death their heart would be weighed on a balance against the *shu* feather of the Goddess of truth, justice, order, and morality, determining whether the deceased should remain in the underworld or go on to paradise (represented in many versions of the Book of the Dead and related wall paintings; see Pritchard 1954, fig. 639).

Two other devices were used to measure very heavy quantities in the ancient eastern Mediterranean. The *bismar*, or what is now called the "Danish steelyard," was in use by the fourth century BCE. It had a fixed counterpoise (counterweight) and a movable fulcrum suspended from a hook (Kisch 1965). The beam was marked so that the weight of the substance to be measured could be determined by the suspension point at which the beam reaches level equilibrium. The more accurate and reliable steelyard, independently invented around 200 BCE by the Chinese and the Romans (*statera*; many were found at Pompeii; Kisch 1965), is suspended

that value, as guarantor. Scores on tests such as the U.S. SAT, GRE, and TOEFL have value and meaning in the first place because the Educational Testing Service certifies them. Similarly, in the United Kingdom, the Ministry of Education establishes the meaning and uses of GCSE and A-Level scores, which then take on conventional value backed by the official declaration of their value.

On a more micro-sociological level, for the purposes of exams and essays in a university course, the validity of what a professor says in her lectures follows from the fact that she stated it (and it is common knowledge among the students and teaching assistants that she stated it). Similarly, when a social science theorist publishes a theory, it is exactly the fact that this theorist published the theory that endows it with the meaning it starts off with, as well as shaping its subsequent meanings.

Symbolic meaning by fiat often has other sources beyond authority ranking relations. If the faculty at a university take up and vote to create a new professorial rank, "Super-duper Professor Until the End of Time," equality matching is the source of the meaning and effects of that title.

I am not aware of previous discussions of symbolic meaning and symbolic efficacy based on fiat. In any case, it is not immediately clear to me what implications, if any, meaning by fiat may have for conformation systems theory. Perhaps implications may occur to the reader.

from a fixed fulcrum. The entity to be weighed is hung from a hook affixed to the short end, while the movable counterpoise is suspended from the long end of the graduated beam. The counterpoise is moved along the beam until the beam is level. Both the bismar and steelyard are mechanisms whose weighing procedures and visual displays are proportional representations of weights: the weight of the substance is proportional to the distance along the beam of the suspension point of the beam (*bismar*), or the suspension point of the counterpoise (steelyard). Steelyards with multiple fulcrums (and/or multiple counterweights) offer ratios with multiple denominators. In 2007 I found steelyards of various sizes commonly used to weigh commodities in and around Xian, Chengdu, and Shanghai, China.

Throughout history, systems of measurement, whether of length, area, volume, weight, or time, invariably have been structured on the basis of ratios: smaller units are integer fractions of larger units, while larger units are integer multiples of smaller ones (Kisch 1965). By around 2500 BCE weights and balances appear to have been used in India. Found at several sites, they were initially used for weighing gold dust, and only later for other commodities. The weights were in proportions of 1:2:4:8:16:32:64:160:320:640:800 :1,600:3,200:6,400:8,000. Another system of Indian weights described in Sanskrit literature includes a system with steps in ratios that included 2, 3, 4, 5, 6, 8, 10, and 16 (Kisch 1965: 222–234). In ancient India, Srinivasan (1979) describes more than eleven systems of length and even systems each of volumes, of weights, and of time and date, each system composed of several levels of units that were fractions of the next higher level.

> Systems of grouping and division are a more basic and durable feature of a given metrological system than are the absolute values of its measures. It would be more feasible to alter the latter than to effect changes in the ways of dividing and multiplying that have been used for generations in the mental arithmetic practiced by the common people . . . The system of divisions and multiples is the fundamental property of every metrological system. (Kula 1986: 84)

Historically, measures start out concrete and become abstract, conventional, and eventually based on explicit formal agreement (Kula 1986: 120ff.). Since there is a natural zero weight and a natural zero volume, metrological systems invariably become ratio scales.

All of these mechanisms for weighing are good examples of the development of technologies in order to enable better conformations. Originally arising, fostered, and culturally evolved to augment the conformation of market pricing, conventionally standardized weights and measures turned out to have myriad additional uses, and far-reaching social and scientific effects. Imagine the world as it was 5,000 years ago, without any symbolism to conform market pricing.

Money

> [Money is] a pure symbol, an abstract expression of abstract relationships. (Durkheim 1901: 142, characterizing Simmel's 1900 conception; my translation from Durkheim's French)

Money is the quintessential symbol, since money only has meaning by convention – the value of any unit of money depends on people's past, present, expected, and imperative use of it in conformations to mediate certain types of relationships, especially (though not exclusively) market pricing. Modern forms of money have no intrinsic value. As Einzig (1966), Polanyi (1957), Melitz (1974), and Grierson (1978) each point out, money acquires its meaning by virtue of its use in payment of obligations, as a standard of value, or as a means of indirect exchange. Historically and ethnologically, different monies have often been used in each of these respective three domains. That is, in certain cultures, people had special-purpose monies, each of which they used for just one of these functions, without being usable in the other domains and without being exchangeable for either of the other two kinds of money. Conventional use was the basis for the value-validity of each of the monies. Furthermore, in certain cases, convention was the basis for the restriction of the domain of value-validity of one money to payment of obligations, another money to use as a standard of value, and a third money as a means of exchange. Note again, however, that convention is not the only foundation for money; in many cases the value-validity of currency is established by a ruler's fiat, and guaranteed by the state's regulatory apparatus. The image of the ruler's face on a coin or bill is an iconic representation of the ruler's fiat and his standing behind the currency.

Money has no iconic or concrete operational relation to the infinitude of ratios that it conforms. Indeed, money has no necessary, intrinsic features of its own, even within any one culture (Simmel 1900). Currency in diverse denominations, demand deposits, credit card balances and debt limits, lines of credit, electronic funds transfers, bank ledgers, and digitally encoded accounts have no common attributes except that they are forms of money. The conformational value of any form of money is a purely symbolic link mediating an indefinite number of heterogeneous commodities, persons, and transactions that are otherwise remote from each other.

In Parsons' (1967) terms, money is a generalized symbolic mode of social interaction, simultaneously a form of communication, and a form of influence or inducement.[2]

Money Functions Through Common Knowledge and Recursion

Money can only do all this so long as people use it in these ways at these rates, and everyone expects others to continue to use it in these ways at these rates, and everyone believes that everyone believes that the money will continue to be used in these ways at these rates, and so forth, in indefinite recursion. In other words, money is recursively symbolic. For another example, consider the explicit ratio symbolizing conformation of a market pricing relationship by a salary of, say, $3,000/month. That has no meaning separable from the unstated ratios of dollars/pound of potatoes, dollars/membership in a gym, dollars/fine for driving 20 mph over the speed limit, and so on, ad infinitum. Thus, a price is an abstract representation of the ratio of the market pricing value of a given quantity of a commodity (or, for course grades, wages, interest, and rents, taxes, fines, and so forth) in proportion to all other commodities in the system – an infinite recursion on infinite paths through the web of entities that are priced.

But it is not just knowledge recursions that monetary symbols depend on. Consider another example. The bank lends a person a lot of money to buy a house because the bankers believe that it is very likely that the borrower will make her mortgage payments, but the bankers would not make the loan based only on a statistical prediction as such. The bankers judge that the person ought to have a moral and legal commitment to make the mortgage payments, the bankers judge that the borrower should feel morally committed to do so, and the bankers believe that indeed the borrower is morally committed to do so. Furthermore, of course, the bankers know that, if need be, the courts will enforce that commitment, because the courts are legally and morally bound to do so, and feel obligated to do so. Furthermore, everyone in the jurisdiction believes that everyone believes the courts feel legally and morally bound to enforce

[2] By "generalized," Parsons did not mean that money is the medium of all social interaction, but rather that money is impersonal, without intrinsic connection to any person, event, or thing, so that the meaning of money derives from its mediation of diverse market exchanges and its omnipotent relation to all commodities. Zelizer's (1994) first chapter provides a nice overview of theories of money. In counterpoint to Parsons, she shows that in many circumstances people do imbue money with circumscribed meanings that restrict its intended use to specific social functions. For other discourses on the symbolism of money, see Ganßmann's 1988 review of modern German social theorists.

such commitments, and, consequently, the courts can be counted on to enforce the commitments. This is not just recursive knowledge. Beyond knowledge (or belief), there are recursive emotions, recursive motives, and recursive moral sentiments. For example, in the process of purchasing a house in the US, everyone feels that, at the event called *closing*, in order to take possession of a house, it is morally essential for the buyer to pay a specified amount, everyone feels that everyone ought to feel that payment of that amount of is morally essential, and everyone feels that everyone ought to feel that everyone ought to feel that everyone ought to feel that this payment is morally essential.

This illustrates again how monetary symbolism functions through recursion. In action, a certain money is money because person A uses that money to buy things (including labor, rent, interest on loans, payment of fines, and so forth) from persons B. A can count on B accepting that money in payment because B has used and expects to use that money for purchases and for savings for eventual payments. B can make purchases, or save money for future uses, because other persons, C, accept the money in payment because they can count on other persons, D, to accept the money in payment, because they count on persons, E, to accept the money, and so on, ad infinitum. If E declines to accept this money, D will decline payments from C, so C will decline payments from B, so B will decline payments from A, so A's money has no value. For clarity of exposition, this is a linear simplification; real money functions in networks of recursions that ramify, branch, and loop.

Obviously, cognitive representation is a crucial aspect of each recursive step. However, let me emphasize that each representation represents much more than others' belief-knowledge. In each recursion, each mind represents others' knowledge integrally combined with the others' emotions, motives, and moral sentiments, including the others' commitment. In other words, each mind conforms others' conformations.

The Origins of Money

In general, metrology appears in the archeological record long before money. The intermediate step between metrology and money is often the use of precious metals as the media of exchange, with values denominated in terms of the weight in silver or gold, as was common in premonetary Mesopotamia, Egypt, and the Aegean (Michailidou 2005). In fact, in this region, weights of precious metals were used as standards of value and accounting, even outside the immediate context of exchange: a person might owe a certain weight of silver without the implication that the debt would be paid in silver per se.

Archeology, history, and ethnography show that extensive market pricing transactions in large networks ineluctably give rise to measurement symbolism and monetary symbolism (Einzig 1966, Dalton 1965). Documents from the New Kingdom period (about sixteenth century BCE to eleventh century BCE) show that Egyptians exchanged commodities extensively; values were denominated in terms of *deben* and *kite* weights of silver or of copper/bronze, or *khar* and *oipe* volumes of grain, or *hin* volumes of sesame oil (Kemp 2006: 319). Thus, rather than having a single currency, they used two weight units of two metals, two volume units of grain, and one volume unit of oil, despite the fact that exchange rates varied among these. Hence, a man could buy an ox worth 50 *deben* of copper/bronze in exchange for a combination of a jar of fat worth 30 *deben*, 2 pieces of linen together worth 10 *deben*, 10 *hin* of vegetable oil worth 5 *deben*, and scraps of copper and bronze weighing 5 *deben*. Labor and rents were also priced in *deben*. Thus, these commodities were doing double duty as substances valued in their own right, and as proto-currency.

Later, coins were invented in Lydia, and quickly spread throughout the eastern Mediterranean, as a form of official, authoritative marking of the weight of bits of valuable metals used as media of exchange. That is, rather than having to weigh bits of silver or gold each time they were transacted in an exchange, and rather than the customer having to trust that the merchant's weights had been or could be calibrated to the reference weights, a polity or person could place a distinctive stamp on a bit of metal to certify its weight. This value-by-fiat obviated the problem of standard weights, avoiding the complications when two parties to a transaction had different systems of weights.

Money needs to be durable and difficult to counterfeit, or otherwise limited in supply. Generally it is also useful for it to be readily transportable, and divisible into halves, thirds, quarters, or such. Within these constraints, a tremendous variety of things have functioned as media of transactions, for storage or display of wealth, as standards of value, or as means for settling obligations. The most widespread forms of money have included cowrie shells (*Cypraea* species), and various other whole or processed marine, terrestrial, turtle, and other shells (Quiggin 1949). Beads and disks made of shell, stone, or ceramics have functioned as money in many cultures. So have gold, silver, copper, tin, and alloys of these, either directly by weight or as standardized ingots or pieces of wire, rods, rings, semicircular manillas, spear points, axe heads, knives, hoe blades, and occasionally bells or gongs – all often fabricated in conventional forms rather than being functional artifacts. Other moneys have included bolts of fabric, mats, many kinds of animal teeth, coils of feathers, and occasionally beeswax. In Yap, stone disks with a hole through the middle functioned as money; these varied from around 5 centimeters up to 4 meters in diameter (Quiggin 1949). Comestible substances such as salt, tobacco, grain, or bricks of tea have also been used as money. Livestock have been used in diverse cultures for settling large accounts, and as a mode for storing wealth.

In 2025, in many places, most money has no palpable material instantiation, and no definite location. *In the cloud* somewhere, there are digital memory chips on which money is arbitrarily encoded as the magnetization of tiny loci. But the addresses of those loci can change, and any particular memory chip or digital drive can fail, with no effect, because the same encoded information is redundantly stored in several locations. To make a payment, of course, one simply enters a sequence of number and letter symbols onto a keyboard or keypad, and those numbers and letters are transduced into strings of binary digits, encrypted, and transmitted into the cloud. That is symbolism taken to several recursions.

People originally conceived, and then improved, and still continue to perfect money, in order to better conform market pricing relations. Subsequently, and in large part as a result of the extensive cultural evolution of monetary symbolism, people have found innumerable additional uses for sophisticated symbol systems, beyond their ever-greater efficacy in conforming market pricing. Among other things, science and media depend on these sophisticated symbol systems.

I have not extensively addressed the emotional, motivational, or moral aspects of monetary symbolism. For readers of this book, it hardly seems necessary to do so, because every day they experience and see these emotions, motives, and moral sentiments. But I have found it worthwhile to alert the undergraduates in my classes to these aspects of money and other symbols. I wanted to make sure that the students paid attention to my points about these aspects of symbols, and remembered them. So, in the relevant lecture I used to ask if any student had a $20 bill, and ask the first person to raise a hand to kindly let me have their $20 bill. Then I took out a lighter and burned the bill to ashes. Many students displayed affective responses to my burning it, and generally someone would point out that what I had done was illegal. The student who gave me the $20 always had an emotional and moral response to the fire. They responded this way despite being quite aware that my incendiary act had a pedagogical purpose that bracketed my burning the bill as somehow less real, and perhaps exempt from the usual moral sentiments and consequences. But I judged it real enough to reimburse the helpful student at the end of class.

Calendars

Humans use astronomically based cycles to coordinate innumerable social activities, including regional gatherings, ritual and religious activities and assemblies, life-cycle rites, hunting, fishing, gathering, pastoralism, transhumance, agriculture, every kind of work, gift exchange, markets, tribute, rents, salaries, taxes, sports, sex, warfare, and just about everything else. A calendar greatly facilitates reliable temporal coordination, and is essential for complex scheduling among people who are not otherwise in frequent communication with each other. Symbolism is essential to do the calculations necessary to construct a calendar, to record and disseminate it, and to read and use it. The configurations for visual display of calendars are symbolic.

In the archeological record, the earliest records of express calculations of ratios or rates are calendric. Calendars link cycles of days, months, seasons, and years into a system. Thus, a calendar enables prediction of day length, phases of the moon (and hence nocturnal illumination), tides, eclipses, annual meteor showers, and the positions on the horizon at which the sun, moon, and each star rises and sets at different dates and times – including, in particular, the solstices and equinoxes. Agricultural seasons and foraging opportunities vary as functions of these cycles, so there is great value in being able to predict them. A calendar represents the ratio relations between the phase and period of each of the cycles that compose the calendar. However, the periods of the earth's rotation, the moon's orbit, and the earth's orbit are not integer multiples of each other; their ratios are about 1:29.53:365.256. The position of each of the five visible planets has its own period, out of phase with each other and out of phase with the day, month, and year. Calculating and comparing the ratios of these cycles is impossible without abstract symbolic notation for numbers, along with the operations of addition and subtraction, multiplication and division (see Kelley & Milone 2005 for the math of ancient astronomy, and Dilke 1987 for the combinations of cycles used in ancient calendars).

If a person used this system simply to predict the phases of the moon, the length of day, and so forth, it would not be a conformation. When calendars mediate payments of rent, wages, interest, or taxes, then clearly the relationship is market pricing and the calendar is conforming it. But in fact calendars in Mesoamerica and elsewhere were originally devised to coordinate planning and performing of rituals, most of which one would define as religious, not involving market pricing. People looked at the calendar to determine when to worship the sun, or another deity. And, to this day, calendars mediate worship, such as the convention to worship every seventh day, or to begin fasting when the new moon is sighted on the ninth lunar month of the calendar.

However, recall the definition of market pricing: it consists of constituting, modulating, coordinating, motivating, and evaluating social interaction with reference to ratios. Calendars consist of ratios of celestial cycles. That means that when people calendrically conform social relations, the social relations are market pricing relationships. The original definition of market pricing unreflectively assumed that its ratios were among persons – for example, 2:7, where the first person gives two pineapples to the other, who returns seven figs. Nevertheless, let us provisionally consider market pricing to encompass social coordination among a set of persons who act in concert according to a ratio they all observe, such as a calendar. But whether or not we categorize calendrical conformations as market pricing, they are the third case, along with metrology and money, in which, for thousands of years, people have been devising technologies to facilitate and extend ratio-based social relationships.

Christopher Pool (2007) points out that Aztecs, Mayans, and Zapotecs conceived of events as cyclical, so they expected past events to recur at calendrically determined intervals. They also believed that certain calendrically defined days were auspicious for certain activities, while others were inauspicious not only for agricultural activities, but also for accession to rule, for initiating battle, and for making sacrifices. They believed that the date of an individual's birth shaped his or her destiny, and people were often named for the day they were born (Pool 2007: 258–260). This made calendrical calculations politically and socially important, and was associated with the calculation and recoding in abstract symbols of legitimating and prognosticative dates.

Calendars subsequently found a great many other uses, or course. Calendars organize labor and lending, commerce and contracts, schools and sports, travel, taxation, terms of office, social events, and a whole lot more. By virtue of using the symbolism of the ratios that comprise a calendar, these are market pricing relations.

Writing

Let us define "writing" as the recording of a set of symbols in systematic material form. (Allowing that this must be updated to encompass quasi-material digital writing.) One might imagine that writing is simply the material instantiation of language, and that people invented writing in order to record speech. But that is not the case. It turns out that writing was invented for commerce and bookkeeping (Nemat-Nejat 1993: 1).

Mesopotamia

Writing was independently invented only a few times in history, although in several additional instances people who had encountered a system of writing then invented new systems for writing their own languages. Far more is known about the precursors and development of writing in Mesopotamia than is known about the emergence of writing anywhere else, so we will focus on Mesopotamia. The most striking feature of the precursors and earliest forms of Mesopotamian writing is that they represented quantities of goods, together with information about their owners or their transaction (Nissen et al. 1993). It appears that hundreds of years passed before writing was developed from a system of bookkeeping into a system that could also represent speech: "In summary ... before the appearance of the first true ideograms, numerical notations were already known. In other words the first written signs were therefore exclusively 'numerical'" (Nissen et al. 1993: 130). That is, the first writing represented cardinal numbers, with distinct sign systems for counting different classes of things (Nissen et al. 1993: 25–30, 124–155). That is, they represented the number "120" cows with signs that differed from the number "120" days, and yet other symbols for "120" baskets of barley groats. One system was used to count generally discrete objects, such as humans, animals, dairy and textile products, wooden and stone implements, and containers. Another was used to count such things as animals in a herd that had died, and jars of certain liquids. Another was used for foods that were distributed to workers as rations: grain products, cheeses, and fresh fish. Mesopotamians used another system for measuring the areas of fields, and another for time and calendar units. They had distinct systems for counting capacity units of barley and other grains, another for capacity units of malt (germinated barley used for brewing beer), a third for capacity units of another grain (probably emmer), and a forth for another grain, probably barley groats (hulled and crushed). Two other sign systems represented quantities of different milk products. Also, a solid circle represented ten of the next smaller units when enumerating discrete objects, but six of the next smaller unit when enumerating dry measures of cereal, and eighteen of the next smaller unit when measuring land area (Nissen et al. 1993: 131).

By the Old Babylonian period, along with this system there developed a place value system of numerical representation (Nissen 1993: 124–151; Nemat-Nejat 1993: 3). This place value system was somewhat difficult to read and use reliably because zero had not been invented, so there was no null placeholder to eliminate ambiguity in place value notation. Thus, the symbols for 1 10 5 could indicate $60 + 10 + 5$, or $60^2 + 10 + 5$, or $1 + (10+5)/60$. Old Babylonian texts also contain specific symbols for $^1/_3$, $^1/_2$, $^2/_3$, $^5/_6$, together with a notation for the reciprocals of a number. Some texts show calculations of powers of a number, with examples going up to 5^{10} and 100^{10}. This place value notation may have developed in some way from the creation of tokens of distinct sizes and shapes to represent different number values (Lieberman 1980).

These Old Babylonian symbol systems incorporated a sign for multiplication. Sumerian and Babylonian scribes did not do division, as such; rather, they multiplied by the reciprocal (Nemat-Nejat 1993: 11). Thus, most fractions were calculated as multiplication of the numerator by the reciprocal of the denominator.

Clay models, enclosed in clay balls, were the precursors to Mesopotamian writing that represented words other than numbers. These were *bullae*, hollow clay balls enclosing tokens that iconically represented goods. These bullae could have been designed to compare tribute collected by tax collectors with tribute the collectors delivered to central authorities. The bullae could have been used to compare goods put into storage with goods brought out, compare goods entrusted to a shipper with goods actually delivered, or compare goods lent with goods repaid. In a few instances, people marked the outside of these bullae with impressions of the tokens they enclosed, presumably to permit intermediate inspection without breaking open the bullae. Evidently, people soon realized that the impressions were sufficient on their own; the impressions did not need to be accompanied by any tokens. Mesopotamians soon began to make noniconic, conventional round or oblong depressions on rectangular clay tablets, evidently to indicate numbers, together with other signs that probably signify names. Some of these were sealed in clay containers. Merchants used this system to record and convey information about the shipment of commodities (i.e., bills of lading). The obverse of some of these tablets are divided into columns and cases, with marks seeming to represent the sum of the entries on the obverse. After this sum are signs that appear to indicate a person or institution, presumably the owner (Nissen et al. 1993: 21). For example, at Kahesh about 20,000 cuneiform tablets from around 1900 BCE, some sealed in clay envelopes, consist mostly of contracts between merchants and forwarders, and letters between merchants and their representatives in other cities.

Then Mesopotamians must have found that such records could easily be counterfeited; they needed a way for the persons concerned to attest to the validity of the marks on the clay. For this purpose, before the invention of writing, ancient Mesopotamians used cylinder seals that they rolled on soft clay "tags." They were placed so that a jar, sack, or storeroom could not be opened without breaking the clay tag. Thus, the distinctive images of each unique seal served as a combination signature and lock, attesting to the ownership and inviolate status of the contents (Nissen et al. 1993: 19–21). These imprinted tags are indexical because their placement on a container or door indicates that the imprinter attests to the contents of this particular container or door, and, unbroken, attests that the container or door has not been opened. If seal-owners did not delegate authority to use his seals, the tags are also indexical proof that the seal-owner imprinted the tag. Such an imprint is iconic because its conformational validity depends on its resembling a known image. But the signs that apparently indicate the name of the seal-owners are sufficiently arbitrary and dependent on convention that their meanings are still conjectural – that is, the names on the seals are symbols.

By the Uruk III.2 phase, the tablets are mostly lists, apparently records of animals, textiles, metal or wooden objects, textiles, vessels, and the like (Nissen et al. 1993: 21–24). None of the early Mesopotamian texts are narratives or religious documents.

Once the Mesopotamians invented writing for market pricing conformations, they discovered all sorts of things that writing enables or facilitates.

Egypt

Egyptian hieroglyphics were invented in the predynastic period, around 3150 BCE, probably inspired by knowledge of Mesopotamian cuneiform (Ray 1986). Short but detailed notes about the delivery of goods were recorded several generations before the first dynasty – that is, soon after the establishment of a large, centralized state (Baines 1989: 472). Writing was used for some administrative purposes, including tax records (Baines 1989: 473) Early in the history of Egyptian writing, two scripts diverged:

hieroglyphics, for public display and especially for tomb inscriptions, and a cursive script that developed into hieratic, used entirely for administration (Baines 1989).

Around 2400 BCE, in the fifth dynasty, a series of papyri from the pyramid temple of King Negerirkara include detailed inventories of items categorized according to whether they were made of hematite, crystalline stone, flint, iron, or silver, and subcategorized by their functional form: bowls, jars, knives, blades, silver items, and small and large offering tables (Kemp 2006: 168–169, fig. 60). Daily accounts of inventory and income, well organized in tabular form, list the delivery porter; the number of jars of various drinks and types of flour and their place of origin; the loaves of bread and containers of beer brought from the palace; consignments of bread on hand, due, and delivered for the solar temple; and the balance of delicacies delivered and the number due (Kemp 2006: 164–165, fig. 58). Other documents include duty rosters, inspection reports, and land records. Scribes recorded numbers of cattle branded and numbers slaughtered, beer inventories, weapons issued to troops, and proceedings of trials (Casson 1975: 39–40, 50–51). Scribes recorded numbers of scoops of threshed grain, shipments loaded on board boats, shipments unloaded, and grain delivered to the granaries. They calculated the capacity of each grain silo. Scribes recorded the grain delivered to bakeries and breweries, and the loaves and jars produced. They then compared this with the standard ratios, *pesu* or *pefsu*, of hekats of grain input to loaves of molded bread or jars of beer. Different ratios were used for different types of loaves and jars, and scribes were taught how to convert from one to another by dividing and multiplying (Kemp 2006: 174–175). This was not very easy to do: While Egyptian hieroglyphics included a sign for $^2/_3$, all other fractions had numerator 1 (Kemp 2006: 170). Thus, to write or do a calculation, $^3/_4$ was written $^1/_2 + ^1/_4$; $^6/_7$ was written $^1/_2 + ^1/_4 + ^1/_{14} + ^1/_{28}$. So, to aid in calculations and conversions, Egyptians had manuals in which they could look up results.

Scribes kept track of daily rations of ten loaves of bread and from $^1/_3$ to one or even two jugs of beer issued to laborers and soldiers. Officials received multiples of these base amounts – up to fifty times this base. Scribes learned how to divide a fixed total allotment for a crew into amounts for each man and each official. They also calculated shares of temple allotments; at a provincial Middle Kingdom temple allotments were based on a year of 360 days, with each staff member due $^2/_{360}$, except the chief priest, who received $^4/_{360}$. This meant that as allocations came into the temple they must have had to keep track of receipts, disbursements, and amounts due, on a proportional basis, since presumably each shipment did not arrive in 360 parts.

Scribes also made plans, functioned as quartermasters, and kept records for building projects. For any structure, they calculated the necessary numbers of blocks of cut stone or mud bricks, and the amounts of earth and straw for making the mud bricks, together with amounts of sand or rubble fill (Kemp 2006: 179). From this, they calculated total volumes of materials, and from that, based on standard production ratios, the number of required labor units and, in turn, the amount of rations needed to feed the laborers. They marked out the rock to be cut in quarries, supervised the rates of work there, and the transportation of materials and construction. Scribes also recorded royal edicts, such as the one that prescribed a punishment for any fortress commander who took gold, leopard, or giraffe skins or giraffe tails from boats coming down the Nile from Kush (Nubia) to the Temple at Abydos: the punishment was 100 blows and a fine of 80 times the value of the goods stolen (Kemp 2006: 308).

By the New Kingdom there are many records of rates of exchange of numerous commodities against *hekats* of grain or weights of bronze or other metals: "A feeling for relative values seems from this material to have been part of the basic mental equipment for living that Egyptians possessed from an early age" (Kemp 2006: 178). A text from the second half of the nineteenth century BCE, copied about two centuries later onto what is now known as the Rhind Mathematical Papyrus, shows that, by then, Egyptian scribes were quite proficient with fractions, including calculations of dilutions (Robins & Schute 1987, Wikipedia Rhind Mathematical Papyrus: https://en.wikipedia.org/wiki/Rhind_Mathematical_Papyrus).

Once writing was invented for conforming market pricing, it turned out to be quite handy for representing speech, and hence for recording and disseminating just about anything. Early civilizations quickly adopted writing to commemorate rulers, rulers' military triumphs, and other accomplishments, and to record prayers, rituals, and the results of divination (Trigger 2003: 587–588).

Elsewhere

Three different writing systems developed in Crete, beginning with hieroglyphics in the second millennium BCE. At the time of the first Cretan palaces (1900–1625 BCE), the Minoans developed Linear A, a script representing syllables, but also numerical ideas, together with pictographs of objects (some similar to the depictions in Cretan hieroglyphic). "It seems more than likely that the Minoans developed their system of writing in response to economic needs," and all three systems were used predominantly to record economic activities (Oliver 1986: 379, 386). Linear B, representing archaic Greek, appeared later; it is the only Cretan script that has been deciphered, and it "seems to have been used solely for economic purposes" (Oliver 1986: 386). All three scripts used much the same system of decimal numeric representation, and they represented fractions, weights, and measures, but each with a different system.

The first preserved Chinese writing consist of records of the results of divination performed for the king, scratched on ox scapulae (shoulder blades) or plastrons (the lower shells of tortoise shells) in the late Shang period, about 1200 BCE (Boltz 1986). This writing is a fully developed logographic system, apparently in existence for some time; earlier writing must have been on materials that have not survived, or have not yet been discovered, so the invention of Chinese writing remains obscure.

Mesoamerican writing is an exception to the general rule that writing emerged as a technology specifically designed for conforming economic forms of market pricing. Mesoamerican writing, beginning with numerical and mathematical symbols, was developed for the preservation and manipulation of calendrical information that could only be remembered and manipulated in the mode of a symbolic system (Sharer 1996: 176). The first preserved Mesoamerican writing, among the Olmec beginning around 650 BCE, concerns dates associated with rulers (Pohl et al. 2002). The first preserved writing of the Mayans was used primarily to record a calendrical system, representing numerical ratios values as cycles of component values. Early Mesoamerican inscriptions often connect events, rulers, and astronomy. "The key ingredient in the development of these early Mesoamerican writing systems was the encoding of abstract calendrical information not readily represented by iconic images" (Pool 2007: 266). Over the centuries, Mesoamerican calendars and writing diffused together.

Nonhuman Animals and Human Infants

When dealing with nonsocial entities, human infants and nonhuman animals are sensitive to ratios of set numerosity, and ratios of dimensions (McCrink & Wynn 2007, Tecwyn et al. 2017, Denison & Xu 2014, Drucker et al. 2016, Eckert et al. 2018, Park et al. 2021). But there is scant evidence for whether any nonhuman animal uses ratios in the coordination of social relationships.

Even animals with very simple nervous systems calculate ratios of numbers and reward/time rates in the context of foraging, predator avoidance and evasion, dead-reckoning navigation, and other learning (Gallistel 1990). Some ant species have been shown to compute distances by multiplying the number of steps they have taken by the mean length of their step. This would only be possible if the ants were manipulating "symbols" (Gallistel 1990).

Honeybees have an innate dance that unambiguously and accurately communicates to other bees that it has found food, at a specified distance in a specified direction relative to the solar ephemeral time. In addition, the bee's rate of dancing communicates how much food it saw; the communication is based on ratios. When other bees go to find the food that the first bee signaled by its dance, they necessarily use the position of the sun to compute the direction where the food will be found. But the follow-up bees may not go out for the food for some time, and of course the sun moves constantly. So, when later responding to the dance, the bees use internal clocks, and compute the angular correction to use, based on the difference between the time of the dance and the present time. So, the bees are assessing and remembering quantities of food communicated by a rate of dancing; are computing and communicating time, angles, and distance; are remembering the observed communication; and are making foraging decisions accordingly. Every component of this rests on representations of proportions. As Gallistel (1990) shows, the bees have to be using symbols to compute and remember this; associative mentation could not do such computations or store such memories. All of the bees have to use the same symbols in the same way, or else they could not communicate and understand each other's communications. There is no other way to do any of this. That is, the bees are certainly using a shared symbol system that represents distance, time, angles, direction, and quantity; for the bee that found the food, the system must transduce those mental symbols into a dance; for the observing bees, the system must transduce dance symbolism into mental symbolism, and then transduce those mental systems into motor control resulting in successful navigation. Whatever this symbol system is in the bees' brains and their dances, presumably it is mostly or entirely innate. However, I do not know whether bee researchers have made the observations and experiments necessary to identify any differences between hives, or to identify any process of social transmission of the symbolism, if any social transmission takes place. Thus, there is no evidence that bee-dance symbolism is based on convention.

Many plants, and probably all animals, rely on internal biological clocks and responses to geophysical phenomena with which they organize tidal, circadian, lunar, or annual behavioral cycles; predict environmental cycles; measure intervals; and remember event times (Gallistel 1990, 2001, Kumar 2002, Stillman et al. 2007). Endogenous clocks synchronized through social interaction, together with conspecifics' parallel responses to temporal cues such as the position of the sun or day length, are crucial to social coordination in many species (Helm et al. 2006, Sharma & Chandrasekharan 2005). Courtship and breeding, communal nest building, care of young, flocking or group reunion, and migration are temporally coordinated in many species.

It is meaningful to call such systems of social coordination "market pricing" if we put aside two defining features of relational models: generativity, and moral sentiments regarding adherence to or violation of the relational model. Honey-bee dancing is the coordination system closest to human market pricing. If we could discover the evolutionary steps resulting in honey-bee dancing, that might possibly shed light on the human evolution of symbolically conformed market pricing. But, as honey bees are so different from humans in so many ways, the evolutionary path to bee market pricing was probably quite different from the evolutionary path to human generative market pricing with moral sentiments.

This very brief overview should make clear that humans, like most other animals, cognize ratios all the time, for all sorts of adaptive purposes. Bonobos and chimpanzees must do so, too. All animals evidently use innate symbol systems. So the question is: How did human evolution borrow and develop these capacities into morally informed, generative market pricing, and why did no other animal (except honey bees) do so? Surely all of the conformation systems are exaptations that reuse older neurocognitive systems (Anderson 2014, 2016, Parkinson & Wheatley 2015), so just how did this occur to give rise to the symbolic conformation of market pricing relationships?

Human Infants

Infant researchers have not yet designed studies to see whether human infants have core knowledge of market pricing and its symbolic conformation. Any animal can learn that any arbitrary stimulus "means" any sort of punishment or reward, and humans readily learn the symbolics of language. Every animal cognizes many kinds of proportionality. So, there is no reason to believe that symbolically conformed market pricing is beyond the cognitive capacities of infants.

Human infants expect an agent who contributed more to a task to then take more of a resource than an agent who contributed less (see Wang &

Henderson 2018 and other studies they cite). But just any amount more? To my knowledge, infant researchers have not yet published experiments testing whether preverbal infants conform strict proportionality in any social relationship.

Piaget claimed that children (even when schooled) do not attain mastery of formal operations, including declarative proficiency with proportions, until late-middle childhood (Piaget 1945, 1952). However, so far as I have read, Piaget never explored formal operations mediating children's social relationships'. Later research has revealed that some initial explicit understanding of formal operations with symbols, including fractions, emerges in social contexts around age seven (Empson 1999, Mix et al. 1999, Watson, Campbell, & Collis 1999). But core "knowledge" of every kind starts out as implicit. And even among adults, "knowledge" and proficient use of the four relational models and their conformation systems is implicit, just like the knowledge of language. So, while it is interesting to study explicit cognition of all sorts, such research is not informative about infant core knowledge of market pricing and its symbolic conformation.

CHAPTER 16

Contemplations

Simultaneous and Sequential Combinations of Conformations of Different Types?

Practices that combine multiple conformations are common. For example, there might be a huge (great volume or mass) hill-top temple, next to a giant gilded sculpture of a deity, along with a thousand smaller sculptures of the deity, with a great gong that sounds in worship. Or think of the ordinary combination of suckling a baby while holding and rocking it. In a sports contest, there are symmetrical halves of a playing field, with teams taking turns defending each end, in an order determined by a coin toss, along with matching numbers of players, and, if regulation time ends in a draw, an equal number of attempts at free kicks. Or note what we are up to right now: using lots of linguistic symbols combined in sentences. In each case, the linked conformations all conform the same relational model. Probably the multiplicity of the linked conformations increases the efficacy of their combined effect beyond the effects of any of them individually. Using multiple conformations in the same system helps to remove ambiguity, failures of attention, and memory errors, if any.

Are there simultaneous or sequential combinations of conformations of different types, conforming multiple relational models among the same persons (and/or other beings)? When there are co-occurring conformations of two or more different types modulating two or more types of relationship, do they interact, affecting each other in some way?

Each Mode of Conforming Requires a Little Support from Secondary Sign Types

In most cases I have presented the instances of each of the four types as if each instance conformed in one pure sign type alone: indexicality, or iconicity, or concrete one-to-one operations, or symbolism. Just one type in each instance. For the exposition of conformation systems theory, this is the clearest rhetorical perspective, and is a good initial analytic heuristic for empirical research. However, for some purposes in some research or applications, one may choose to "dig deeper," for greater precision and better validity, at the cost of greater complexity in theories, and/or the cost of formulating multiple independent theories that each account for a narrower range of phenomena, tolerating the loss of any theory that articulates how the various phenomena affect each other. One may make either choice because of some need for greater scope, greater precision or better validity, or esthetic preference. Semioticians have long been aware that many signs – perhaps even all signs – are not purely indexical, not purely iconic, and not purely symbolic. Indeed, to function as signs, a sign of any type typically needs a bit of help from the other sign types. For example, the word "Exit" is symbolic, but it is of no use unless – indexically – it is located at a portal that permits leaving. Conversely, iconicity is needed to support the symbolism of such a sign: the "E" in the sign must resemble the "E" in other fonts and handwritten block letters.

The same thing is true in conformations: a conformation in one mode – say, indexicality – may require the support of one or more other sign systems. For example, a specific form of body modification, such as a style of filing teeth, is indexical because it shapes a part of the body of the social person, marking that specific body. But it only functions indexically when the configuration of a person's filed teeth iconically resembles the configuration of the filed teeth of others in the group that is conformed by this dental modification.

Similarly, a signature is a symbol, but it is a valid commitment by virtue of its indexicality; it is binding if and only if the signature was written by the signatory. That is, the indicated person must have directly caused the symbol, and, through their pen, been in contact with the document. That causal relation is the indexicality of the symbol. Likewise, a teacher's symbolic email communications to students about the grading system conform the market pricing governing that particular facet of the relationship between the teacher and their students. But for that symbolically encoded message to have its intended effect, students must perceive its true indexicality, believing that the email was created by the professor in charge of the course, not just anyone. Similarly, in the classroom, students tend to believe, and take notes on, statements uttered by the professor, but are less confident of the truth of statements made by their fellow students, and take fewer notes on those statements. The verbal statements are symbolic, but their uptake depends on their indexicality. Whenever the uptake of symbols depends in part, at least, on who produced them, that is dependence on indexicality. The indexicality is the "who said that," or, with regard to this book, for example, "who wrote that."

In short, a conformation of any of the four types may require, or benefit from, the support of a sign system other than the canonical sign system of the conformation. That does not mean that there are two or conformation systems operating simultaneously; rather, it is multiple sign systems that are functioning together – for example, iconicity supported by indexicality, or concrete operations of one-to-one correspondence supported by symbolic conventions.

There are innumerable forms of indexicality, but only one form of indexicality composes consubstantial assimilation: the bodies of persons indexing the social selves of the respective persons, with bodily equivalence thereby indexing social relational equivalence. Innumerable other forms of indexicality support iconicity, concrete operations, or conventional symbolism.

Likewise, there are innumerable forms of iconicity, as we considered when first reviewing C. S. Peirce's semiotics, but only dimensions and magnitudes universally and intuitively conform authority ranking relationships, by relative positions on a polarized dimension or magnitude iconically conforming social relational rank. Innumerable other forms of iconicity support the indexicality of consubstantial assimilation conforming communal sharing, or may support the concrete operations of one-to-one correspondence conforming equality matching, or may be essential to the symbolic conforming market pricing.

Similarly, there are innumerable forms of concrete operations, but only concrete operations of one-to-one correspondence conform equality matching. Many other concrete operations may support the indexicality of consubstantial assimilation conforming communal sharing, iconic dimensions and magnitudes conforming equality matching, or symbols conforming market pricing.

Let us reconsider a few of the conformations presented in this book to see how any sign type may be enabled by another sign type that the primary sign type of the conformation partially or completely depends on. We began with me prostrate in the dirt in front of the village chief, later analyzing that as an instance of being BELOW him in an iconic conformation of my subordination to the chief in an authority ranking relationship. Recall that I noted that, of course, had I prostrated a few kilometers away, my prostration would not have been an iconic conformation of authority ranking; to be that conformation, I needed to prostrate myself just a few meters away, and facing the chief, at a point in time when he, too, was there, making it evident that I was conforming my being BELOW him. That dependence of the sign on proximity is one very common sort of indexicality in conformational iconicity. A similar one is the knowledge that the pyramid was built by the ruler. In Peirce's semiotics, one of the basic types of indexicality consists of a sign Y representing X because X caused Y. The hugest pyramid does nothing to conform a pharaoh's supremacy if viewers do not know that the pharaoh caused it to be built.

There are at least ten dimensions that can iconically conform authority ranking, each implemented in innumerable ways. As we saw in Chapter 6, to posturally conform BELOW, a person can bow, courtesy, kneel, or prostrate themselves, and, if kneeling, put their head to the ground, or, as Moosé women do, curl up in a ball, combining BELOW and SMALLER. That illustrates what is generally the case: symbolism enables iconic conformations in the sense that the manner in which a person conforms authority ranking on each dimension is conventionally used and common knowledge in the community at the time. Thus, had I sat cross-legged, bending way over backward, in a physics-geometry sense I would have been lower than the chief, but I would not have been conformationally BELOW; I would not have been conformationally BELOW because I failed to symbolize being BELOW according to Moosé conformational convention.

Likewise, conformational concrete operations of one-to-one correspondence often rely on indexicality, iconicity, or symbolism. In a distribution, when matching what each person gets, iconicity consists of the necessity for each share to look like every other share, for them to have the same heft, or it being apparent that the two sides of the pan balance are mirror reflections of each other. A concrete operational distribution depends on indexicality when the concrete operation consists of handing items to respective recipients, or placing the items in front of their respective recipients. In a game on a board or a sport on a playing field, the two halves must be mirror images of each other, iconically congruent. When voting by casting ballots, each ballot should be indistinguishable from every other, except for the marks indicating choices; the ballots are icons of each other, and that configuration of the ballots for this particular election is valid because it is conventional. When people vote by secret ballot, placing a ballot in a container corresponding to their choice, iconicity is crucial in that the ballots must be totally indistinguishable.

Symbolism enables conformational concrete operations by defining what counts as one-to-one correspondence. What counts as a turn on the swing? In the equality matching reciprocity of dinner invitations, when one was invited to a dinner of lobster, cornbread made from scratch, and Brussel sprouts grown in the host's garden, what counts as an even return? That's a rather arbitrary convention. Matching too precisely would be rude, absurd, weird, or humorous. There are conventions about, say, matching the wine the first host served, and how long it is appropriate to wait before inviting the other family to dinner, to implicitly match the dinner that they fed you. To get that delay right, you must be familiar with the practices in the particular community and social circles that you and your hosts belong to. Inviting one's host back immediately, the same evening, is a crude, awkward faux pas. Waiting too long to reciprocate suggests that the relationship is not important. But the proper duration of the delay is a convention.

So, conformations functioning in any sign type often, perhaps always, need to be supported by the signs simultaneously functioning as one or more other sign types. That is not specific to signs employed in conformations; signs of any type, whatever people use them for, typically require support from one or more of the other sign types.

Conformation Systems Are the Means by Which Children Become Competent Participants in the Social Systems of Their Particular Community

It is possible for people to use any relational model to coordinate any domain of social life, though in each domain people are more likely to implement some relational models than others. Further, there are indefinitely many ways that people can implement any relational model in any domain, though some are more common than others. Without innate knowledge of the respective conformation systems of each of the four relational models, it would be extremely difficult for a child, or any newcomer, to figure out which relational models people are using to coordinate each domain of social life, and how people are implementing whatever relational models they are using. Without this innate knowledge, infants and other learners would constantly be baffled by social interactions, they would often make incorrect guesses about what was happening, and it would take many years to figure out what was going on in each and every social interaction – if they ever did figure that out. This is not merely a problem of grasping what others are up: not just learning how other people are coordinating, how they are motivated, what emotions and motives others are likely to have, what moral framework others are probably using to evaluate action and intentions, and what commitments they are making. Without innate capacities to recognize each conformation system and know what relational model it conforms, infants and newcomers would not understand how people were attempting to relate to them. Also, with that innate adaptation, infants are able to initiate social relationships. Seeking, say, a communal sharing relationship, infants need to know what to do in order to be understood, and in order to evoke in prospective relational partners the emotions, motives, and moral sentiments essential to communal sharing. Furthermore, to create, sustain, modulate, resist, or terminate social relationships, infants need the supporting emotions, motives, and moral sentiments that respectively inform each of the four fundamental types of relationships. Dispassionate knowledge is insufficient (Fiske 2002, 2010).

Human infants and children need social relationships to survive and prosper. So, for at least tens of thousands of years much more, and likely, there must have been strong natural selection for innate knowledge of the relational models, together with their respective conformation systems. Let us consider this point in each relational model in turn. Like any newcomer, the infant expects that the conformation system for communal sharing will be consubstantial assimilation. In every culture this implicit attunement is sufficient, and necessary, to discover how to culturally complete innately structured and motivated but indeterminate relational mods. (For the general theory of that, see Fiske 2000.) "The child has to learn through the carrying out of the daily routines of mealtimes the structure and unity of the family group, and its relations to the other households" of the community (Richards 1948: 62). By observing with whom and in what manner people share food, and participating in food sharing, children discover the core solidarities: "It is by lessons such as these that the whole kinship structure is felt rather than explained. Family sentiment is imprinted by a series of daily [food] habits rather than taught by any definite lesson or rule" (Richards 1948: 66; see also 212). Likewise, "In just such a concrete fashion, the segregation of different groups at mealtimes makes [the child] aware of the interrelation of the various households comprising the village or clan" (68); "The food routine teaches the child his place in a complicated social structure" (72). In wider ritual contexts, food preparation and shared consumption also evoke and reflect sentiments of solidarity linking humans with their ancestors (Richards 1948: 79, 173, 186, 190).

Children innately desire to relate to others, and they need to form relationships. In particular, children expect to belong to communal sharing groups and actively seek to form close communal sharing relationships. But at birth, infants cannot know what primary or secondary groups operate in their own community. So, infants and older children are looking for consubstantial assimilation conformations enabling them to translate their relational proclivity for communal sharing into actual, solid, functioning communal sharing relationships. Consubstantial assimilation is the mode that connects this innate relational proclivity to culturally informed practices in definite communal sharing relationships. Infants and children need this link. What they must do – what they in fact do – is attend to the conformations that permit them to connect with people. For communal sharing, this is consubstantial assimilation.

To discover the cultural complements that specify how to realize indeterminate relational models, a child needs to attend to, and have an intuitive incipient understanding of, others' conformations of social relationships. The infant needs to know that snuggling, grooming, feeding, commensalism, and synchronous rhythmic motions are conformations of communal sharing. The infant also needs to readily and accurately map what she perceives and feels onto a mental conformation that enables her to encode, categorize, process, store, and retrieve social memories. In turn, from birth, her conformations selectively filter the social acts she notices and experiences, and how she interprets them. In Chapter 5, we considered some of the many studies that show that preverbal infants in fact recognize consubstantial assimilation, and know how people interact in communal sharing relationships. In Chapter 12 we sampled illustrative examples of the many studies that show that preverbal infants recognize iconic dimensional conformations, and know how people will interact in the authority ranking relationships conformed that way. In Chapter 14, we Considered a few of many studies that demonstrate that preverbal infants recognize concrete operational one-to-one conformations, and have definite expectations about how people interact in the ensuing equality matching relationships.

If humans innately "expect" and "want" certain kinds of relationships conformed in certain media, and are especially attentive, and especially sensitive emotionally, motivationally, and morally to those media, then human culture will be informed accordingly. People will sometimes invent and perform conformations that do not conform to these expectations, but, compared to innovations that resonate with the conformation system for the type of relationship, such incompatible inventions will have weaker effects, be comparatively rare, will not be culturally reproduced as well, and will not often diffuse to new communities.

There is a crucial converse to young children's highly tuned sensitivity to the mode of communicative representation and constitution of each specific type of relationship. For example, consider an infant attuned to the iconic physical dimensional conformations of authority ranking. The infant and then toddler attends to this mode of conformation in order to discover and participate in the culturally informed implementations of authority ranking in the child's community, and will have the necessary emotions, motives, and moral sentiments to support those authority ranking relationships. By that means, this iconic-dimensional mode becomes the channel for cultural reproduction of local cultural implementations of authority ranking. That is, cultural instantiations of authority ranking are reproduced and diffuse primarily by iconic dimensions. To reproduce each culturally particular set of authority ranking practices, one uses this iconic mode. You want to be the next king? To do so you have to use ABOVE–BELOW, GREATER–LESSER VOLUME, GREATER–LESSER MASS, MORE FORCE–LESS FORCE, IN FRONT–BEHIND, GOING FIRST–FOLLOWING LATER. Use these iconic dimensions in the manner they were previously used, and the culture is thereby transmitted.

Likewise, to transform or resist the existing authority ranking structures in a culture, people have to transform or reject the existing uses of these dimensions. Whether and how this iconic physics is reproduced determines whether and how the culture reproduces or changes. This is another way of describing the iconic dimensions conformational niche, in which myriad specific and fortuitous cultural practices thrive, to the extent that a practice is congruent with that conformational mode. That is, the iconic magnitudes and dimensions niche potentiates the cultural reproduction of congruent authority ranking conformations, while inhibiting the cultural reproduction of incongruent conformations. The other three conformations function in the same manner as channels for the cultural reproduction and transformation of their respective relational models.

Intentional or Not, By Choice or Not, Aware or Unaware

People often intentionally engage in a conformation, at their own initiative, or given the opportunity to engage, or when they have to do so. But a person also may engage in a conformation without intending to conform any relationship, or without choosing to engage in the conformation at all. Yet the person's engagement in the conformation may still have the usual relational effects. A person may not be aware that what they are about to do will affect their relational emotions, motives, moral sentiments, or representations of any relationship. A person may engage in conformations as a routine, a habit, a taken-for-granted practice that they never reflect on. Yet the person's engagement in the conformation may still have the usual relational effects. A person may engage in a conformation for reasons that have nothing to do with the social relationship that is conformed, though the person is aware of the relational effects of engaging in the conformation. A person may engage in a conformation despite knowing that engagement will foster a social relationship that the person does not want. Yet the person's engagement in the conformation may still have the usual relational effects. I do not know how often such things happen, nor do I know whether or how any of them mediate the effects of engaging in the conformation. But we should keep these possibilities in mind. Let us consider a couple of examples.

On an expedition in the desert, a person may constantly be extremely thirsty, so every time others pass around a canteen, the person drinks from it, without regard for any social relational effects of doing so. In another case, a person inducted into an army may be forced to perform military drill, manipulating weapons in synchrony with the group, and then march in time with them, while having to sing a chant with them. This may have the usual effects of consubstantial assimilation, though the person did not intend or even anticipate that, and abhors any feeling of belonging to the communal sharing group that results. In a third case, every year, at several events, an African woman joins kinswomen and neighbors to pound each other's courtyards in unison. Every day, at the big circular grinding platform, in rhythmic synchrony with fifteen other women, she grinds her grain into flour for the daily meals, often while singing in unison. When she pounds other foods in the great mortar, with her heavy two-meter pestle, she typically pounds in rhythmic alternating stokes with a co-wife, the two of them singing together. All this is simply what women do. It is what every Moosé woman has always seen and heard since she was an infant; she takes it as given. It is pleasant to participate this way, though often she is tired or her muscles are sore. She never gives any thought to doing or not doing any of it. These are unarticulated, unreflective practices (Bourdieu 1977, 1990). These routine performances of rhythmic synchronous motion constantly renew and sustain her communal sharing bonds every day, although she did not engage in them with any conscious intention to reinforce her communal sharing relationships with the other wives, let alone in order to sustain and reproduce her culture.

Not Doing a Routine Conformation Is More Striking than Doing It Again

Consider a series of repeated conformations, each conforming the same relationship of the same dyad or set of persons, in more or less the same way. For example, day after day, the same set of persons share meals commensally, eating directly out of the same bowl. Presumably these daily conformations combine to have greater conformational effect than just one commensal meal. But surely the meals combine asymptotically, with each successive meal increasing the total conformational effect a bit less than the last one. The people sitting around the bowl are doing so out of habit and courtesy. Perhaps, anyway, the family has only two bowls: one for the staple *sagabo* and one for the boiled vegetables. They are reaching their hands into the same bowls, commensally eating the same food because that is what there is. It is the only way that one can eat, under the circumstances. Without intending to do so, or realizing that they are doing so, their daily engagement together in this communal sharing-conforming consubstantial assimilation sustains and affirms their relationship.

Within any one conformation system such as this consubstantial assimilation, do different subtypes combine in their effects on any aspect of conformation? Suppose a set of persons have been eating commensally for years. If, one day, they also perform a blood brotherhood rite, or row a boat in rhythmic synchrony, what is the impact of adding those new and different forms of consubstantial assimilation?

The absence of an habitual conformation may be quite salient, evoking strong emotions, motives, and moral sentiments, even putting commitment to the relationship in doubt. For example, kissing is not simply kissing; there are important nuances in how one kisses. Moreover, suppose your partner always kisses you when you come home at the end of the day, and, a fortiori, when you return from a trip. Now suppose that you return from a trip, and your partner pointedly does not kiss you? That draws your attention, has a pronounced emotional and moral impact, and gets you wondering about your relationship: "Hey, what's going on here?" The not-kissing may indicate that the relationship is over. At least, it has the potential to begin to change the relationship. The absence of the kiss certainly gets your attention, though you would hardly have noticed if your partner kissed you as usual.

A similar asymmetry exists in the conformation impact of artifacts. Every day, walking to work, you pass under a massive statue of Stalin, high on a pedestal. If the statue once mildly conformed your subordination to the current ruler of Russia, after passing it again and again, it ceases to have much effect. But pulling the statue down and removing it! That has an effect. For quite a while, every time you walk by where it is not, you may intensely feel that you, collectively, have overcome your former subordination to Stalin's successors. In sum, refraining from an habitual, anticipated, or desired conformation modulates the relationship as much or more than docilly engaging in the conformation.

Conformational Disdain and Punishment

Unless there are plausible excuses, refraining from an habitual, anticipated, or desired conformation constitutes and communicates the refrainer's diminished relational emotions, motives, and moral commitment to the relationship, together with the refrainer's representation of the relationship as presently attenuated, and perhaps the refrainer's representation of the relationship as waning. Or refraining may communicate something like "I don't need this relationship," or "You can't make me participate in this relationship." Think of a teenager who declines to be home for dinner with their family, or a person who declines to sign a contract. Refraining from engaging in a conformation may be intended to "hurt the feelings" of the others who participate in the relationship, to evoke the others' moral outrage, or to motivate the others to tailor the relationship so it better accords with the refrainer's representation of what the relationship ought to be. It may be a protest against the relationship or something that occurred in it. It may be a warning: "You are not living up to my expectations. If you don't start doing what I feel that you should, I may cease doing what you want me to do in this relationship, and I might even end the relationship."

In these and similar ways, except in extenuating circumstances, there is a range of meanings and effects of ceasing to engage in conformations that others expect. Toward one end of this range, such cessation approaches punishing them. If I usually shop and cook for you, and serve you dinner, but then I don't, you may take my not-doing this as a punishment, which may be what I intended it to be. More upsetting to you, perhaps, would be my not preparing your meal because I couldn't be bothered, or simply forgot, because others things mattered more to me. That means that my affectionate emotions toward you, along with my sentiment of moral obligation to care for you, have diminished to the point of having little effect on my motivation to cook your dinner.

There are extreme consubstantial assimilation punishments, such as making the transgressor's body differ from others' bodies by branding or amputation. In several cultures, people formerly were punished for sexual transgressions by having their noses cut off (Skinner 2014). If a maharaja offended the Viceroy, the Viceroy, using an iconic dimension, might decrease the number of guns fired in canon salutes to the maharaja, so henceforth the maharaja receives eleven-gun salutes, instead of the thirteen-gun salutes he was formerly entitled to.

Using concrete operations of one-to-one matching, people punish by having the culprit's allocation not match one-to-one. A person can be deprived of their turn, or deprived of their right to vote. A team can be penalized by removing one of their players from the field or rink, so the two sides are uneven. Using arbitrary conventional symbolism, people can punish by imposing a monetary fine, and nations may punish a transgressing nation by refusing to accept their currency in payment for goods or debts. If a student cheats or plagiarizes, the professor can lower the student's grade, or disallow transcript credit for the course. If a professor does not meet their teaching obligations for a given semester, the department chair and the dean might subtract that semester from the seven years of "teaching credit" – a symbolic quantity – that the professor must earn in order to be entitled to sabbatical.

As may be apparent from my use of imagined examples, the sources that I used to research this book said hardly anything about the strategic uses of conformations, whether to create, sustain, transform, resist, or reject social relationships. But I bring up these possibilities because I do not want to leave the impression that people always use conformations rotely, let alone without will. I would be intrigued to see instances of strategizing about conformations, instances of strategizing about resistance to conformations, and instances of struggles for and against conformations. Those might be good stories in their own right, and might well reveal aspects of conformation systems that we do not readily see otherwise.

Felicity Conditions

Conformations are conformations only when people take them to be so, which depends on the conditions in which they occur. This concept of contingency of conforming corresponds to John Austin's (1962) "felicity" conditions that make a speech act valid. Strawson (1969) argued that a key condition is that the person(s) performing the action intend to be recognized as intending to perform the action. While this tends to be important for many conformation system practices, it does not universally obtain. For example, a person who inadvertently turns his back on the monarch has committed an offense regardless of his intention; the person's respect for the monarch should have manifested in full attention to the conformation.

The crucial subtlety of conformation systems is that the persons involved must somehow be disposed to be receptive, and have no objection to anyone else seeing it. Illegitimate or unwelcome conformational acts, or ones that observers will condemn or ridicule, may have effects opposite to their felicitous deployments. If a person is romantically attracted to you, kissing them just right may intensify the relationship. But you cannot create or intensify a communal sharing relationship with just anyone at any time by simply walking up and kissing them on the mouth. The person you kiss may find that disgusting, feel that it is morally wrong, get angry, distance themselves from you, or ridicule you (Fiske & Schubert 2012, Schubert, Schubert, & Topolinski 2012). Pretty much the same thing is true of all conformational acts and perceptions: they modulate relationships under felicitous conditions, but otherwise have untoward effects, are seen as laughable, or have no impact at all.

Although I cannot offer anything like a complete or systematic account of the felicity conditions for conformation acts, it is helpful to sketch some examples of the issue. In certain traditional Moosé ritual processions, men proceed in order of rank precedence, with the chief leading – except that a boy walks ahead of him to absorb any poison that may have been put in the path to kill the chief. This is just like a king's taster eating some of his food first. In both cases, everyone "just knows" that the boy or the taster is not being accorded social precedence by going first – he has not been made paramount chief. Likewise, if it's a very dark night and no one has a lamp, then it's possible that someone – a literal interloper – happens to be walking on the same path ahead of the ritual procession, without knowing or without intending to assert superiority to the chief and the elders who follow him. If the moon comes out and this is discovered, there are a number of possibilities. The interloper could simply be ignored; his walking ahead is treated as simply "not counting" as a manifestation of or claim to superiority. This might be the way people would treat a person with schizophrenia who, for unknown reasons, walked ahead of the ritual procession – his "crazy" action does not have the social relational meaning that it would have if he were "sane." A second possibility is that the interloper's literal "faux pas" is perceived as offensive, but pardonable, provided that he beg forgiveness. A third possibility is that in this culture the act of walking in front is lèse-majesté regardless of the intent or even knowledge of the interloper. (Among the Moosé, in fact, there are certain acts that are grave moral transgressions regardless of knowledge or intent, and lead to immanent death.) This example illustrates another issue. If an interloper is walking two kilometers ahead of the procession, or walked along the path the day before the ritual, that probably will not be construed as an offense.

In the consubstantial assimilation conformation system, gentle touch is often an invitation to communal sharing, or a mild affirmation of an existing relationship. (For a scientific exploration of who may touch whom where on the body, in Japan and in the United Kingdom, see Suvilehto et al. 2019.) But of course your barber, doctor, makeup artist, or fellow passenger in an elevator may gently touch you without thereby conforming any relationship with you. It does not mean anything special unless they touch you more than necessary, put their hand on an inappropriate part of your body, or touch you in a manner more like an overt caress. But ambiguity of intent makes flirtation possible. A person may touch you in an intentionally ambiguous manner, inviting a conformational interpretation and response, while facilitating a rejection that isn't awkward for either party. The very ambiguity of the meaning of the touch may grab the attention of the recipient, and motivate the recipient to explore the possibilities.

Felicity factors need not be binary; situational factors and interactional history may amplify or attenuate the effects of conformation systems, or may provide desired ambiguity or deniability. There are degrees of "counting as a conformation," along with a variety of senses in which a nominal conformation does not count: misfires, corrections, learning, play, and pretense.

The felicity of conformations is often contingent on having previously engaged in conformations with less impact, and sometimes on having performed those lesser conformations many times. That is, there is a felicitous sequence of conformations. For example, once upon a time in some US subcultures, a teenage boy and girl tentatively developing a romantic communal sharing relationship should follow the following temporal sequence of conformations, spread out over some days. First, a few possibly accidental, deniable, brief touches. Then hand holding. Then resting against each other while seated. Then kissing. Then a series of steps of sexual contact that used to be called *getting to first base*, *getting to second base*, *getting to third base*, and *going all the way*. In this subculture, in general, it was infelicitous to skip a step. Synchronically viewed, this ordering of conformational steps results in a Guttman scale; Guttman scales have been reported in conformations of authority ranking in Pacific Island cultures (Goodenough 1944, 1965; also Firth 1970, Keating 2000), and probably occur in many societies. In a Guttman structure of conformations, at any point in time, if people engage in conformation #4, they also engage in conformation #3, #2, and #1; if they engage in conformation #3, they also engage in conformations #2 and #1; if they engage in #2, they also engage in #1. But just engaging in #1 and #2 does not imply and does not make it felicitous to engage in #4. Before they do #4, they should do #3, if that is also felicitous in other respects.

From felicity conditions for conformation systems it is a small step to their strategic deployment – another topic that this book does not address. I imagine that it will be intriguing to explore conformation systems strategies and tactics, and that doing so will illuminate many aspects of everyday life. Perhaps learning about strategic utilization of conformation systems will shed additional light on the nature of conformation systems. But I doubt that one could shed much light on conformational strategies or tactics before we have a thorough, sure understanding of what conformation systems are. In linguistic terms, researchers need to have a solid grasp of *langue* before they can get very far studying *parole* (Saussure 1971).

The distinction between felicity and infelicity is a close cousin of the distinction between "real" and "pretend." If a person bows satirically, as a joke, or with a serious mien but in a play, or when practicing for a presentation to the monarch, everyone understands that the conformation act is "not real" (see Bateson 1972).

In many African and other societies, people in certain relations of kinship, citizens of certain pairs of communities, and members of certain pairs of ethnic groups or cultures engage in prescribed joking relations. On both sides of a joking relationship, the participants should tease, insult, and make mock sexual advances. In funerals, the deceased's joking partner(s) mockingly imitate the roles of the serious participants, for example, by making ridiculous offerings to the deceased. In some ways joking partners' performances resemble those of Medieval European court jesters.

Targets of all such "pretend" actions are not supposed to take them "seriously." However, because in these contexts the actors have license to communicate and perform without being held accountable for what they say or do, they have the opportunity to say and do things that, in one sense, they actually mean, but would not say or do if they were to be held accountable. They can playfully critique without the consequences that would have if they "actually" critiqued. Pretend conformations are illuminating for the researcher if they reduce "real" conformations to their essence, or exaggerate them.

A conformation may be oriented toward a past, present, planned, or conceived relationship. That is, the conformation may be a blueprint for future construction of relations, a model for considering relational alternatives and strategies, or a model of the relationship one seeks. Conformation systems theory posits that most conformations are all of these, to varying degrees. This points to an epistemological ambiguity. Suppose that, 3,000 years ago, a stone carver cut a relief image of a king interacting with others. Did the carver intend the image to metaconform the king as he actually was, or did the carver intend the image to be an ideal model of what kings ought to be? Was the carver intending to make a metaconformation of what the king believed or hoped to be his authority ranking relationship with his people? How are we to know whether the carver intended "true" metaconformation of the actual authority ranking, or intended an idealization that the carver knew was not a realistic conformation? How are we to know to what degree various contemporaries perceived the image as realistically valid, or as an unfulfilled ideal?

Can We Help?

Can conformation systems theory provide new ways to help people who tend not to have satisfying, strong, or enduring social relationships? The better we understand how humans typically conform social relationships, the better we should be able to help people who have severe difficulties with social relations, such as people on the autism spectrum, people with schizophrenia, people who are near the high end of dimensions of personality disorders, and people who have had traumatic social experiences. People use conformations to initiate, sustain, and repair social relationships, to reflect on them, and to discuss them. But what happens when a person's conformations of their relationships are discrepant with other people's conformations of the relationships? What happens if a person does not intuitively use, or recognize, or affectively and morally respond to one or more of the conformation systems the same ways that others typically do?

Are conformation systems teachable to people for whom they are neither intuitive nor intrinsically evocative? Would people on the autism spectrum benefit from treatment that included explaining and practicing conformation systems? Would they benefit from learning the conformation systems by guided observation of videos, skits, or puppet shows? Would they benefit from performing skits or puppet shows in which they practiced doing conformations, and appropriately responding to them? Would such interventions help people with personality disorders or schizophrenia? (See Haslam, Reichert, & Fiske 2002; Caralis & Haslam 2004; Sergi et al 2009; Green et al 2011; Horan et al 2011; Lee et al 2018.)

L'Envoi

As I described in Chapter 2, an idea occurred to me in 1980, in the course of my participation and observation in a West African village. That idea developed, languished, developed, and languished over the next forty-four years. The original idea was fostered and shaped by my searches through hundreds of ethnographies, histories, archeological books, translations of ancient texts, and sources on the etymology of Chinese characters, together with reports of field studies of primates and other mammals. Colleagues' experiments helped to support some aspects of the theory, and to eliminate misconceptions. As I write this book, the idea is still developing.

In each of my three previous books and in this book, my aim has always been to formulate theories of the social relations of *Homo sapiens* – theories that could account for what is universal and what is particular to specific cultures in particular eras. I have always believed that a theory of human sociality could not be valid unless it plausibly accounted for how deep universals inherently gave rise to variability across cultures and time. Such a theory cannot be constructed without extensive and detailed knowledge about social relations in a great many places and times. In the research resulting in each book, the instigating idea was rather simple, primitive, and ill-specified. In each case, the theory gradually grew more complete, better specified, and more valid as I read and read and read, inductively modifying and extending my theory to fit my own observations and others' observations everywhere. That epistemology has been very fruitful, confirming my conviction that, to understand human sociality, an inductive epistemology is necessary though not sufficient. I hope that you, the reader, have been intrigued by the inductive conceptualization opportunity this book provides, and I hope you will find that it continues to be illuminating after you put it down.

References

Abegg, Martin G., Jr. 1997. 1540 Gdl. In Willem A. VanGemeron, Ed., *New International Dictionary of Old Testament Theology and Exegesis* (Vol. 1, pp. 823–827). Grand Rapids: Zondervan.

Abusharaf, Rogia Mustafa 2001. Virtuous Cuts: Female Genital Circumcision in an African Ontology. *Differences: A Journal of Feminist Cultural Studies* 12(1):112–140.

Ackerley, Rochelle 2022. C-Tactile (CT) Afferents: Evidence of their Function from Microneurography Studies in Humans. *Current Opinion in Behavioral Sciences* 43:95–100.

Adams, Douglas Q. 1997a. Bright. In James Mallory and Douglas Q. Adams, *Encyclopedia of Indo-European Culture* (p. 83). Chicago: Fitzroy Dearborn.

Adams, Douglas Q. 1997b. Shine. In James Mallory and Douglas Q. Adams, *Encyclopedia of Indo-European Culture* (pp. 513–514). Chicago: Fitzroy Dearborn.

Adams, Douglas Q., & James Mallory 1997. Comparative Mythology. In James Mallory and D. Q. Adams, *Encyclopedia of Indo-European Culture* (pp. 116–123). Chicago: Fitzroy Dearborn.

Adams, Laurie Schneider 2004. *World Views: Topics in Non-Western Art*. Boston: McGraw Hill.

Adams, Laurie Schneider 2008. *A History of Western Art*. Revised 4th ed. Boston: McGraw Hill.

Adegbite, Ademola 1988. The Drum and Its Role in Yoruba Religion. *Journal of Religion in Africa* 18:15–26.

Adler, Mariana 1991. From Symbolic Exchange to Commodity Consumption: Anthropological Notes on Drinking as Symbolic Practice. In Susan Barrows and Robin Room, Eds., *Drinking: Behavior and Belief in Modern History* (pp. 376–398). Berkeley: University of California Press.

Ahlberg, Beth Maina, Wangui Njau, Karanja Kiiru, & Ingela Krantz 2000. Gender Masked or Self-Inflicted Pain: Female Circumcision, Eradication and Persistence in Central Kenya. *African Sociological Review/Revue Africaine de Sociologie* 4(1):35–53.

Alberts, Allison C. 1994. Dominance Hierarchies in Male Lizards: Implications for Zoo Management Programs. *Zoo Biology* 13:479–490.

Aldenerfer, Mark, Nathan M. Craig, Robert J. Speakman, & Rachel Popelka-Filcoff 2008. Four-Thousand-Year-Old Gold Artifacts from the Lake Titicaca Basin, Southern Peru. *Proceedings of the National Academy of Sciences* 105:5002–5005.

Alexander, André, Yutaka Hirako, Lundrup Dorje, & Pimpim de Azeved, n.d. Beijing Historic City Study. www.achr.net/UAC%20Web%20DLs/Beijing02a.doc. Accessed April 18, 2008.

Alexandre, Gustave 1953. *La Langue Mõré*. Two volumes. Dakar: Mémoires de L'Institut Français d'Afrique Noire.

Algaze, Guillermo 2001. Initial Social Complexity in Southwestern Asia. *Current Anthropology* 42.2:199–233.

Allen, Charles, & Sharada Dwivedi 1984. *Lives of the Indian Princes*. London: Century.

Allen, Leslie C. 1997. 8123 Rwm. In Willem A. VanGemeron, Ed., *New International Dictionary of Old Testament Theology and Exegesis* (Vol. 3, pp. 1078–1081). Grand Rapids: Zondervan.

Alley, Thomas R. 2012. Contaminated and Uncontaminated Feeding Influence Perceived Intimacy in Mixed-Sex Dyads. *Appetite* 58:1041–1045.

Alley, Thomas R., Lauren W. Brubaker, & Olivia M. Fox 2013. Courtship Feeding in Humans? *Human Nature* 24:430–443.

Allman, Jean. Ed. 2004. *Fashioning Power: Clothing, Politics and African Identities*. Bloomington: Indiana University Press.

Allsen, Thomas D. 2001. Robing in the Mongolian Empire. In Steward Gordon , Ed., *Robes and Honor: The Medieval World of Investiture* (pp. 305–313). New York: Palgrave.

Alster, Bendt 1974. *The Instructions of Suruppak: A Sumerian Proverb Collection*. Mesopotamia; Copenhagen Studies in Assyriology, Vol. 2. Copenhagen: Akademisk Forlag.

Altorki, Soraya 1980. Milk-Kinship in Arab Society: An Unexplored Problem in the Ethnography of Marriage. *Ethnology* 19:283–244.

Amin, Mohamed, Duncan Willetts, & John Eames 1987. *The Last of the Maasai*. London: Bodley Head.

Andersen, Bent Schiermer 1989. *Plov og Køl: Danskernes Virkelighed 1720–1814* (Plough and Keel: The Danes' Reality 1720–1814). Copenhagen: Gyldendal.

Anderson, Michael L. 2010. Neural Reuse: A Fundamental Organizational Principle of the Brain. *Behavioral and Brain Sciences* 33:245–266. https://doi.org/10.1017/s0140525x10000853.

Anderson, Michael L. 2014. *After Phrenology: Neural Reuse and the Interactive Brain*. Cambridge, MA: MIT Press.

Anderson, Michael L. 2016. Précis of After Phrenology: Neural Reuse and the Interactive Brain. *Behavioral and Brain Sciences* 39:e120. https://doi.org/10.1017/s0140525x15000631.

Anthony, David W. 2007. *The Horse, the Wheel, and Language: How Bronze-Age Riders from the Eurasian Steppes Shaped the Modern World*. Princeton: Princeton University Press.

Arnold, Kate, & Filippo Aureli, 2007. Postconflict Reconciliation. In Christina J. Campbell , Agustín Fuentes, Katherine C. MacKinnon, & Melissa Panger (Eds.), *Primates in Perspective* (pp. 592–608). Oxford: Oxford University Press.

Aron, Arthur, Elaine N. Aron, & Danny Smollan 1992. Inclusion of Other in the Self Scale and the Structure of Interpersonal Closeness. *Journal of Personality and Social Psychology* 63:596–612. https://doi.org/10.1037/0022-3514.63.4.596.

Ascalone, Enrico 2005. *Mesopotamia: Assyrians, Sumerians, Babylonians.* Berkeley: University of California Press.

Asher, Catherine B. 2004. A Ray from the Sun: Mughal Ideology and the Visual Construction of the Divine. In Matthew T. Kapstein, Ed., *The Presence of Light: Divine Radiance and Religious Experience* (pp. 161–194). Chicago: University of Chicago Press.

Ashok, Ranjitha 2000. Salutations! The Reading Lounge. Chennai, India: The Horizons. www.thehorizons.com/story/art04.htm. Accessed April 28, 2025.

Ashton-James, Claire, Rick B. van Baaren, Tanya L. Chartrand, Jean Decety, & Johan Karremans 2007. Mimicry and Me: The Impact of Mimicry on Self–Construal. *Social Cogntion* 25:518–535.

Atiya, Nayra N. 1982. *Khul-khaal, Five Egyptian Women Tell Their Stories.* Syracuse: Syracuse University Press.

Austin, John L. 1961. Performative Utterances. In John L. Austin, *Philosophical Papers,* edited by J. O. Urmson and G. J. Warnock (pp. 220–239). Oxford: Clarendon Press.

Austin, John L. 1962. *How to Do Things with Words.* Oxford: Oxford University Press.

Ayer, Alfred Jules 1968. *The Origins of Pragmatism: Studies in the Philosophy of Charles Sanders Peirce and William James.* San Francisco: Freeman, Cooper. [I am grateful for access to this book through the Hathi Trust Digital Library.]

Badawy, Alexander 1956. The Ideology of the Superstructure of the Mastaba-Tomb in Egypt. *Journal of Near Eastern Studies* 15:180–183.

Badrian, Alison, & Noel Badrian 1984. Social Organization of Pan Paniscus in the Lomako Forest, Zaire. In Randall L. Susman, Ed., *The Pygmy Chimpanzee: Evolutionary Biology and Behavior* (pp. 325–346). New York: Plenum.

Baines, John 1989. Communication and Display: The Integration of Early Egyptian Art and Writing. *Antiquity* 63(240):471–482.

Barker, Juliet 2005. *Agincourt: Henry V and the Battle that Made England.* New York: Little Brown.

Barnett, William Kester, 1971. An Ethnographic Description of Sanlei Ts'un, Taiwan, With Emphasis on Women's Roles: Overcoming Research Problems Caused by the Presence of a Great Tradition. PhD thesis, Michigan State University.

Barnhart, Robert K. 1988. *The Barnhart Dictionary of Etymology.* New York: H. W. Wilson.

Barteson, Gregory 1974. Observations of a Cetacean Community. In Joan McIntyre, Ed., *Mind in the Waters: A Book to Celebrate the Consciousness of Whales and Dolphins* (pp. 146–165). New York: Charles Scribner's Sons; Sierra Club Books.

Barth, Fredrik 1975. *Ritual and Knowledge among the Baktaman of New Guinea.* Oslo: Universitetsforlaget/New Haven: Yale University Press.

Bascom, William R. 1952. The Esusu: A Credit Institution of the Yoruba. *Journal of the Royal Anthropological Institute of Great Britain and Ireland* 82:63–69.

Bass-Krueger, Maude n.d. The High-Life: A History of Men in Heels. *Google Arts and Culture.* http://bit.ly/4lQubH7. Accessed June 23, 2024.

Bata Shoe Museum Foundation 2015. Standing Tall: The Curious History of Men in Heels. Toronto. *Google Arts and Culture* https://artsandculture.google.com/story/AgVRZR_j5AhtLA. Accessed June 23, 2024.

Bateson, Gregory 1972. *A Theory of Play and Fantasy.* Boston: MIT Press.

Bateson, Gregory, &Margaret Mead 1942. *Balinese Character: A Photographic Analysis.* New York: New York Academy of Sciences.

Baxter, P. T. W., & Uri Almagor, Eds. 1978. *Age, Generation and Time: Some Features of East African Age Organizations.* New York: St. Martin's Press.

Beck, Jacob 2015. Analogue Magnitude Representations: A Philosophical Introduction. *The British Journal for the Philosophy of Science* 66:829–855.

Beidelman, T. O. 1963. The Blood Covenant and the Concept of Blood in Ukaguru. *Africa* 33(321):342.

Beidelman, T. O. 1973. Kaguru Symbolic Classification. In Rodney Needham, Ed., *Right and Left: Essays on Dual Symbolic Classification* (pp. 128–166). Chicago: University of Chicago Press.

Bell, Robert C. 1979. *Board and Table Games from Many Civilizations.* Rev. ed., two vols bound as one. New York: Dover.

Bell, Robbie, & Michael Cornelius, 1988. *Board Games Round the World: A Resource Book for Mathematical Investigations.* Cambridge: Cambridge University Press.

Bennett, John 1966. Pyramid Names. *The Journal of Egyptian Archaeology* 52:174–176.

Beresford, M. W. 1943. Lot Acres. *Economic History Review* 13:74–79.

Berjonneau, Gerard & Jean-Louis Sonnery, Eds. 1985. *Rediscovered Masterpieces of Mesoamerica: Mexico-Guatemala-Honduras.* Boulogne: Editions Arts.

Bian, Lin, & Renée Baillargeon 2022. When are Similar Individuals a Group? Early Reasoning About Similarity and In-Group Support. *Psychological Science* 33:752–764.

Biebuyck, Daniel, & Kahombo C. Mateene 1969. *The Mwindo Epic.* Berkeley: University of California Press.

Birnbaum, Raoul 2004. Light in the Wutai Mountains. In Matthew T. Kapstein, Ed., *The Presence of Light: Divine Radiance and Religious Experience* (pp. 195–226). Chicago: University of Chicago Press.

Bissonnette, Annie, Susan Perry, Louise Barrett, John C. Mitani, Mark Flinn, Sergey Gavrilets, & Frans B. M. de Waal 2015. Coalitions in Theory and Reality: A Review of Pertinent Variables and Processes. *Behaviour* 152(1):1–56.

Black Elk 1971 [originally published 1953]. *The Sacred Pipe: Black Elk's Account of the Seven Rites of the Oglala Sioux.* Recorded and edited by Joseph Epes Brown. Baltimore: Penguin.

Black, J. A., G. Cunningham, E. Fluckiger-Hawker, E. Robson, & G. Zólyomi 1998–2007. *The Electronic Text Corpus of Sumerian Literature*. https://etcsl.orinst.ox.ac.uk/.

Blades, James 1970. *Percussion Instruments and Their History*. London: Faber & Faber

Blakeslee, Donald J. 1981. The Origin and Spread of the Calumet Ceremony. *American Antiquity* 46:759–768.

Blitz, John H., & Patrick Livingood, 2004. Sociopolitical Implications of Mississippian Mound Volume. *American Antiquity* 69:291–301. www.jstor.org/stable/4128421.

Bloch, Marc 1955. *Les Caractères Originaux de L'Histoire Rurale Française*. New Edition. Paris: Librairie Armand Colin.

Bloch, Marc 1989. *Feudal Society*. L. A. Manyon, Trans. London: Routledge. [Originally published 1940.]

Boehm, Christopher 2009. *Hierarchy in the Forest: The Evolution of Egalitarian Behavior*. Cambridge, MA: Harvard University Press.

Boeken, Ole Jonas, & Sebastian Markett 2023. Systems-Level Decoding Reveals the Cognitive and Behavioral Profile of the Human Intraparietal Sulcus. *Frontiers in Neuroimaging* 1: 1074674.

Bogucka, Maria 1991. Gesture, Ritual, and Social Order in Sixteenth- to Eighteenth-Century Poland. In Jan Bremmer & Herman Roodenburg , Eds. *A Cultural History of Gesture: From Antiquity to the Present Day* (pp. 190–209). Cambridge: Polity.

Bohannan, Paul 1955. Some Principles of Exchange and Investment among the Tiv. *American Anthropologist* 57:60–70.

Bohannan, Paul 1968. *Tiv Economy*. Evanston: Northwestern University Press.

Bohl, Vivian 2015. We Read Minds to Shape Relationships. *Philosophical Psychology* 28:674–694.

Bolender, John 2010. *The Self-Organizing Social Mind*. Cambridge, MA: MIT Press.

Bolton, Henry Carrington 1888. *The Counting-Out Rhymes of Children: Their Antiquity, Origin, and Wide Distribution*. New York: D. Appleton. [Re-issued 1969 by Singing Tree Press, Book Tower.]

Boltz, William G. 1986. Early Chinese Writing. *World Archaeology* 17:420–436.

Botterweck, G. Johannes, Helmer Ringgren, & Heinz-Joesph Favry 1995. *Theological Dictionary of the Old Testament* Vol. 7. Translated by David E. Green. Grand Rapids: Eerdmann.

Boturini Codex: Copia heliográfica de la Tira de la peregrinación, interpretada por José Fernando Ramírez. 1958. [Created between 1530 and 1541.] México: Vargas Rea

Boulboullé, Jenny & Sven Dupré 2022. Introduction. In *Burgundian Black: Reworking Early Modern Colour Technologies*. Santa Barbara: EMC Imprint. https://burgundianblack.tome.press/.

Bourdieu, Pierre 1977 [1972]. *Outline of a Theory of Practice*. Cambridge: Cambridge University Press.

Bourdieu, Pierre 1990 [1980]. *The Logic of Practice*. Stanford: Stanford University Press.
Bowles, Edmund A. 1958. La Hiérarchie des Instruments de Musique dans l'Europe Féodale. *Revue de Musicologie* 42(118):155–169.
Boyce, Mary, Ed. & Trans. 1984. *Textual Sources for the Study of Zoroastrianism*. Chicago: University of Chicago Press.
Brain, Robert 1976. *Friends and Lovers*. New York: Basic Books.
Brandes, Mark A. 1980. Modelage et Imprimerie aux Débuts de L'Écriture en Mésopotamia. *Akkadica* 18 (May–August):1–30.
Brennan, Thomas 1991. Social Drinking in Old Regime Paris. In Susan Barrows and Robin Room, Eds., *Drinking: Behavior and Belief in Modern History* (pp. 61–86). Berkeley: University of California Press.
Brewer, Douglas J., & Emily Teeter 1999. *Egypt and the Egyptians*. Cambridge: Cambridge University Press.
British Museum London B 226. www.perseus.tufts.edu/hopper/artifact?name=London+B+226&object=Vase.
Brito, Rodrigo, Sven Waldzus, Thomas Wolfgang Schubert, Maciej Sekerdej, Ana Louceiro, & Cláudia Simão 2023. Commensality Constitutes Communalism: Producing Emergent Bonds in Experimental Small Groups by Sharing Food and Drink. *European Journal of Social Psychology* 53:1128–1143.
Bromiley, Geoffrey W. 1982. Glory. In Geoffrey W. Bromiley, Ed., *International Standard Bible Encyclopedia: E–J* (pp. 477–482). Grand Rapids: William B. Eerdmans.
Brooks, Lisa 2008. *The Common Pot: The Recovery of Native Space in the Northeast*. Minneapolis: University of Minnesota Press.
Brown, Daniel James 2013. *The Boys in the Boat*. New York: Macmillan.
Brown, Linda Keller, and Mussell, Kay, Eds. 1984. *Ethnic and Regional Foodways in the United States*. Knoxville: University of Tennessee Press.
Brown, Robert L. 1984. The Śrāvastī Miracles in the Art of India and Dvāravatī. *Archives of Asian Art* 37:79–95.
Bueti, Domenica, & Vincent Walsh 2009. The Parietal Cortex and the Representation of Time, Space, Number and Other Magnitudes. *Philosophical Transactions of the Royal Society B* 364:1831–1840.
Burkert, Walter 1996. *Creation of the Sacred: Tracks of Biology in Early Religions*. Cambridge: Harvard University Press.
Butterworth, Brian, Charles R. Gallistel & Giorgio Vallortigara 2017. Introduction: The Origins of Numerical Abilities. *Philosophical Transactions of the Royal Society B* 373:20160507. http://dx.doi.org/10.1098/rstb.2016.0507.
Buyukozer Dawkins, Melody, Stephanie Margaris Sloane, & Renée Baillargeon 2019. Do Infants in the First Year of Life Expect Equal Resource Allocations? *Frontiers in Psychology* 10:116.
Bygott, David J. 1979. Agonistic Behavior, Dominance, and Social Structure in Wild Chimpanzees of the Gombe National Park. In David A. Hamburg and Elizabeth R. McGowan, Eds., *The Great Apes* (pp. 405–427). Perspectives on Human Evolution, Vol. V. San Francisco: Benjamin/Cummings.

Cameron, Averil, Ed. 1876. *Flavius Cresconius Corippus. In Laudem Iustini Augustus Minoris, Libri IV*. London: Athlone.

Cameron, Averil 1987. *The Construction of Court Ritual: The Byzantine Book of Ceremonies*. In David Canandine & Simon Price, Eds., *Rituals of Royalty: Power and Ceremonial in Traditional Societies* (pp. 106–135). Cambridge: Cambridge University Press.

Cantlon, Jessica F., Michael L. Platt, & Elizabeth M. Brannon 2008. Beyond the Number Domain. *Trends in Cognitive Science* 13:83–91.

Carlson, John B. 1981. Olmec Concave Iron-Ore Mirrors: The Aesthetics of a Lithic Technology and the Lord of the Mirror. In Michael Coe, Matthew Williams Stirling, Michael D. Coe, & David C. Grove, Eds., *The Olmec and Their Neighbors: Essays in Memory of Matthew W. Stirling* (pp. 117–147). Washington, DC: Dumbarton Oaks.

Carr, Gillian 2005. Woad, Tattooing and Identity in Later Iron Age and Early Roman Britain. *Oxford Journal of Archaeology* 24:273–292.

Caralis, Dionyssios, & Nick Haslam 2004. Relational tendencies associated with broad personality dimensions. *Psychology and Psychotherapy: Theory, Research and Practice* 77:397–402.

Carruthers, Peter 2011. *The Opacity of Mind: An Integrative Theory of Self-Knowledge*. Oxford: Oxford University Press.

Carsten, Janet 1992. The Process of Childbirth and Becoming Related among Malays in Pulau Langkawi. In Göran Aijmer, Ed., *Coming into Existence: Birth and Metaphors of Birth* (pp. 19–46). Gothenberg: Institute for Advanced Studies in Social Anthropology at the University of Gothenberg.

Carsten, Janet 1995. The Substance of Kinship and the Heat of the Hearth: Feeding, Personhood, and Relatedness among Malays in Pulau Langkawi. *American Ethnologist* 22:223–241.

Cartier, Ginette 1984. Musique et Pouvoir à l'Aube de la Renaissance: Le Metier du Musicien à la Cour des Grand Ducs Valois de Bourgogne. *Renaissance and Reformation* 20(3):157–175. (New Series Vol. 8.)

Cartmill, Erica A., Sian Beilock, & Susan Goldin-Meadow 2012. A Word in the Hand: Action, Gesture and Mental Representation in Humans and Non-Human Primates. *Philosophical Transactions of the Royal Society B: Biological Sciences* 367(1585):129–143.

Cassin, Elena 1968. *Le Splendeur Devine: Introdution a L'Étude del a Mentalité Mésopotamienne*. Paris: Mouton.

Casson, Lionel 1975. *Everyday Life in Ancient Egypt*. Revised & expanded edition. Baltimore: Johns Hopkins Press.

Cavan, Sherri 1966. *Liquor License: An Ethnography of Bar Behavior*. Chicago: Aldine.

Chan, Chiu Ming 1982. *Ancient Chinese Architecture. Compiles by Chinese Academy of Architecture*. Hong Kong: Joint Publishing Co./Beijing: China Building Industry Press.

Chandra, Lokesh 1988. *The Thousand-Armed Avalokitesvara*. New Delhi: Abhinav, and Indira Ghandhi National Center for the Arts.

Charney, E. Joseph 1966. Psychosomatic Manifestations of Rapport in Psychotherapy. *Psychosomatic Medicine* 28:305–315.

Chase, John H. 1976. Street Games of New York City. In Brian Sutton Smith, Ed., *A Children's Games Anthology*. New York: Arno Press.

Chelkowski, Peter J. (Ed.) 2010. *Eternal Performance: Ta'ziyeh and Other Shiite Rituals*. London: Seagull.

Chen, T. M. 2003. Proletarian White and Working Bodies in Mao's China. *Positions* 1:361–93.

Chiao, Joan Y., Tokiko Harada, Emily R. Oby, Zhang Li, Todd Parrish, & Donna J. Bridge 2009. Neural Representations of Social Status Hierarchy in Human Inferior Parietal Cortex. *Neuropsychologia* 47:354–363.

Chinese Text Project. 2011. Liji, The Classic of Rites. Translated by James Legge. https://ctext.org/liji.

Christenson, Allen J. 2005. *You Are What You Speak: Maya Creation Ceremonies and the Language of Maize*. Lecture at Cotsen Institute of Archeology, UCLA, on October 28.

Cirelli, Laura K., Kathleen M. Einarson, & Laurel J. Trainor 2014. Interpersonal Synchrony Increases Prosocial Behavior in Infants. *Developmental Science* 17:1003–1011.

Cirelli, Laura K., Stephanie J. Wan, & Laurel J. Trainor 2014. Fourteen-Month-Old Infants Use Interpersonal Synchrony as a Cue to Direct Helpfulness. *Philosophical Transactions of the Royal Society B: Biological Sciences* 369: 20130400.

Cirelli, Laura K., Stephanie J. Wan, & Laurel J. Trainor 2016. Social Effects of Movement Synchrony: Increased Infant Helpfulness Only Transfers to Affiliates of Synchronously Moving Partners. *Infancy* 21:807–821.

Cirelli, Laura K., Stephanie J. Wan, Christina Spinelli, & Laurel J. Trainor 2017. Effects Of Interpersonal Movement Synchrony on Infant Helping Behaviors: Is Music Necessary? *Music Perception: An Interdisciplinary Journal* 34:319–326.

Cloutier, J., N. Ambady, T. Meagher, & J. D. E. Gabrieli 2012. The Neural Substrates of Person Perception: Spontaneous Use of Financial and Moral Status Knowledge. *Neuropsychologia* 50:2371–2376. https://doi.org/10.1016/j.neuropsychologia.2012.06.010.

Cloutier, Jasmin, Carlos Cardenas-Iniguez, Ivo Gyurovski, Anam Barakzai, & Tianyi Li 2016. Neuroimaging investigations of social status and social hierarchies. In *Neuroimaging Personality, Social Cognition, and Character* (187–203). New York: Academic Press.

Cobo, Bernabe. 1990. Inca Religion and Customs. Translated & edited by Roland Hamilton. [Originally completed in 1653.] Austin: University of Texas Press.

Cohen, David 1991. *The Circle of Life: Rituals from the Human Family Album*. San Francisco: Harper.

Cohen, Kadosh, Jan Lammertyn Roi, & Veronique Izard 2008. Are Numbers Special? An Overview of Chronometric, Neuroimaging, Developmental and Comparative Studies of Magnitude Representation. *Progress in Neurobiology* 84:132–147.

Collins, C. John 1997b. 3877 Kbd. In Willem A. VanGemeron, Ed., *New International Dictionary of Old Testament Theology and Exegesis* (Vol. 2, pp. 577–587). Grand Rapids: Zondervan.
Connor, Richard C., Randall S. Wells, Janet Mann , & Andrew J. Read 2000. The Bottlenose Dolphin: Social Relationships in a Fission-Fusion Society. In Janet Mann, Janet Mann, Richard C. Connor, Peter L. Tyack, & Hal Whitehead, Eds., *Cetacean Societies: Field Studies of Dolphins and Whales* (pp. 91–126). Chicago: University of Chicago Press.
Conroy, David W. 1995. *In Public Houses: Drink and the Revolution of Authority in Colonial Massachusetts. Published for the Institute of Early American History.* Chapel Hill: University of North Carolina Press.
Cook, Arthur Bernard 1902. The Gong at Dodona. *The Journal of Hellenic Studies* 22:5–28.
Cook, Constance A. 2009. Ancestor Worship during the Eastern Zhou. In John Lagerwey & Marc Kalinowski, Eds., *Early Chinese Religion: Shang Through Han (1250 BC–220 AD)* (pp. 237–280). Leiden: Brill.
Cooler, Richard M. 1986. The Use of Karen Bronze Drums in the Royal Courts and Buddhist Temples of Burma and Thailand: A Continuing Mon Tradition? In Robert J. Bickner, Thomas J. Hudak, and Patcharin Peyasantiwong, Eds., *Papers from a Conference on Thai Studies in Honor of William J. Gedney.* Michigan Papers on South and Southeast Asia Number 25 (pp. 107–120). Ann Arbor: Center for South and Southeast Asian Studies, University of Michigan.
Cooper, Jerrold S. 1984. *The Curse of Agade.* Baltimore: Johns Hopkins University Press.
Cooper, Jerrold S. 2004. Babylonian Beginnings: The Origin of the Cuneiform Writing System in Comparative Perspective. In Stephen D. Houston, Ed., *The First Writing: Script Invention as History and Process* (pp. 71–99). Cambridge: Cambridge University Press.
Cordoza, Carmen Rosa 1990. La Domestication des Animaux au Perou. In Sergio Purin, Ed., *Inca-Perú: 3000 Ans D'Histoire* (pp. 64–77). Brussels: Musées Royaux d'Art et d'Histoire.
Cotter, Holland 2008. Artists, Toe the Party Line. Review of exhibition, "Art and China's Revolution" at the Asia Society, *New York Times*, September 5, 2008, pp. B21 and 28, and at www.nytimes.com/2008/09/05/arts/design/05revo.html.
Courtois, Jacques-Claude 1990. Poids, Prix, Taxes et Salaires, Á Ougaret (Syrie) at IIE Millénaire. In Rika Gyselen, Ed., *Prix, Salaires, Poids et Mesures* (pp. 119–127). Res Orientales Vol. 2. Paris: Groupe pour l'Étude de la Civilzation du Moyen-Orient.
Crawley, Alfred Ernest 1902 [1965]. *The Mystic Rose: A Study of Primitive Marriage and of Primitive Thought in Its Bearings on Marriage.* Revised and enlarged edition, 1927, reprinted in 1965. London: Spring Books.
Creighton, Oliver. H. 2002. *Castles and Landscapes.* London: Continuum.
Culin, Stewart 1902. American Indian Games. *American Anthropologist* 5:58–64.

Cyphers, Ann 1999. From Stone to Symbols: Olmec Art in Social Context at San Lorenzo Tenochtitlán. In David C. Grove & Rosemary A. Joyce, Eds., *Social Patterns in Pre-Classic Mesoamerica* (pp. 155–181). Washington, DC: Dumbarton Oaks.

D'Andrade, Roy G. 1984. Cultural Meaning Systems. In Richard A. Shweder and Robert A. LeVine, Eds., *Culture Theory: Essays on Mind, Self, and Emotion* (pp. 88–119). Cambridge: Cambridge University Press.

D'Andrade, Roy G., & Claudia Strauss 1992. *Human Motives and Cultural Models.* Cambridge: Cambridge University Press.

D'Errico, Francesco 2008. Le Rouge et le Noir: Implications of Early Pigment Use in Africa, the Near East and Europe for the Origin of Cultural Modernity. *Goodwin Series: Current Themes in Middle Stone Age Research,* 10: 68–174. http://www.jstor.org/stable/40650028.

D'Israeli, Isaac 1791. *Curiosities of Literature.* London. Passage on "Drinking-Customs in England." www.gutenberg.org/files/16350/16350-h/16350-h.htm#DRINKING_CUSTOMS_IN_ENGLAND.

Dalton, George 1965. Primitive Money. *American Anthropologist* 67:44–65.

Dampierre, Éric de 1967. *Un Ancien Royaume Bandia du Haut-Oubangui. Recherches en Sciences Humains #24.* Paris: Librairie Plon.

Dannenmaier, W. D., & F. J. Thumin 1964. Authority Status as a Factor in Perceptual Distortion of Size. *Journal of Social Psychology* 63:361–365.

Darwin, Charles 1872 [1965]. *The Expression of the Emotions in Man and Animals.* Chicago: University of Chicago Press.

Davies, Norman de G. 1908. *The Rock Toms of El Amarna: Part VI – Tombs of Parennefer, Tutu, and Aÿ.* London: Egyptian Exploration Fund.

Davis, John H. R. 1977. *People of the Mediterranean: An Essay in Comparative Social Anthropology.* London: Routledge & Kegan Paul.

de Barry, William Theodore, and Irene Bloom 1999. *Sources of Chinese Tradition, Second Edition, Volume I: From Earliest Times to 1600.* New York: Columbia University Press.

de la Vallée, Poussin 1910. Avalokiteshvara. In James Hastings, John Alexander Selbie, & Louis Herbert Gray , Eds., *Encyclopædia of Religion and Ethics,* Vol. 2 (pp. 256–261). New York: Charles Scribner's Sons.

de la Vega, Garcilasco 1961. *The Incas: The Royal Commentaries of the Inca.* Translated by Maria Jolas from the French translation by Alain Gheerbrant. New York: Orion.

de Waal, Frans B. M. 1988. The Communicative Repertoire of Captive Bonobos *(Pan Paniscus)* Compared to that of Chimpanzees. *Behaviour* 106:183–251.

de Waal, Frans B. M. 1989. *Peace Making among Primates.* Harvard: Harvard University Press.

de Waal, Frans B. M. 1996. *Good Natured: The Origins of Right and Wrong in Humans and Other Animals.* Harvard: Harvard University Press.

de Waal, Frans B. M. 2000. Attitudinal Reciprocity in Food Sharing among Brown Capuchins. *Animal Behaviour* 60:253–261.

de Waal, Frans B. M. 2001. Apes from Venus; Bonobos and Human Sexual Evolution. In Frans B. M. de Waal, Ed., *Tree of Origin: What Primate Behavior Can Tell Us about Human Social Evolution* (pp. 41–68). Harvard: Harvard University Press.

Deacon, Terrence William 1997. *The Symbolic Species: The Co-Evolution of Language and the Brain.* New York: W.W. Norton.

Dean, Larry M., Frank N. Willis, & Jay Hewitt 1975. Initial Interaction Distance among Individuals Equal and Unequal in Military Rank. *Journal of Personality and Social Psychology* 32:294–299.

Dean, Trevor, Ed. 2000. *The Towns of Italy in the Later Middle Ages.* Manchester: Manchester University Press.

Debarbieux, Berhard 1998. The Mountain in the City: Social Uses and Transformations of a Natural Landform in Urban Space. *Ecumene* 5(4):399–431.

Decker, Wolfgang 1987. *Sports and Games of Ancient Egypt.* New Haven: Yale University Press.

DeMarrais, E., L. J. Castillo, & T. Earle 1996. Ideology, Materialization and Power Strategies. *Current Anthropology* 37:15–32.

Denault, Lisa K. & Donald A. McFarlane 1995. Reciprocal Altruism between Male Vampire Bats, *Desmodus rotundus. Animal Behaviour* 49:855–856.

Denison, Stephanie, and Fei Xu. 2014. The Origins of Probabilistic Inference in Human Infants. *Cognition* 130(3):335–347.

Dettwyler, Katherine A. 1988. More Than Nutrition: Breastfeeding in Urban Mali. *Medical Anthropology Quarterly* 2:172–183.

Dietler, Michael. 2001. Theorizing the Feast: Rituals of Consumption, Commensal Politics, and Power in African Contexts. In Michael Dietler & Brian Hayden, Eds., *Feasts: Archeological and Ethnographic Perspectives on Food, Politics, and Power* (pp. 65–114). Washington, DC: Smithsonian Institution.

Dietrich, B. C. 1983. Divine Epiphanies in Homer. *Numen* 30:53–79.

Dilke, Oswald A. W. 1987. *Mathematics and Measurement.* Berkeley: University of California Press.

Dim Delobsom, A. A. 1932. *L'empire du Mogho-Naba. Coutumes des Mossi de la Haute-Volta. Études de sociologie et d'ethnologie juridiques de l'Institut de droit comparé.* Paris: F. Lovition et Cie.

Donnan, Christopher B. 2011. Dressing the Body in Splendor: Expression of Value by the Moche of Ancient Peru. In Gary Urton & John Papadopoulos, Eds., *The Construction of Value in the Ancient World* (pp. 186–196). Los Angeles: Cotsen Institute of Archaeology Press, UCLA.

Douglas, M. 1963. *The Lele of the Kasai.* London: Published for the International African Institute by Oxford University Press.

Douglas, Mary 1966 [1985]. *Purity and Danger: An Analysis of the Concepts of Pollution and Taboo.* London: Routledge & Kegan Paul.

Dresden Codex 1975. *Codex Dresdensis, Sächsische Landesbibliothek Dresden* (Mscr. Dresd. R 310). Graz: Akadem. Druck- u. Verlagsanst.

Drucker, Caroline B., Marley A. Rossa, and Elizabeth M. Brannon 2016. Comparison of Discrete Ratios by Rhesus Macaques (Macaca mulatta). *Animal Cognition*19:75–89.

Duarte, Carlos M., 2014. Red Ochre and Shells: Clues to Human Evolution. *Trends in Ecology & Evolution* 29: 560–565. https://doi.org/10.1016/j.tree.2014.08.002.
Dulaney, Siri, & Alan P. Fiske 1994. Cultural Rituals and Obsessive-Compulsive Disorder: Is There a Common Psychological Mechanism? *Ethos* 22:243–283.
Dumézil, Georges 1958. *L'Idéologie Triparte des Indo-Européens*, Vol. 31. Brussels: Collections Latomus.
Dumézil, Georges 1983. *La Courtisane et les Signeurs Colorés et Autres Essais*. Paris: Gallimard.
Durkheim, Émile 1893 [1933]. *The Division of Labour in Society*. George Simpson, Trans. New York: Free Press.
Durkheim, Émile 1897. La prohibition de l'inceste et ses origines. *L'Année sociologique* 1897:1-70. www.jstor.org/stable/27880584. Accessed August 23, 2021.
Durkheim, Émile 1901. Philosophie des Geldes. [Review of Simmel 1900.] *L'Anneé Sociologique* 5:140–145.
Durkheim, Émile 1912 [1965]. *The Elementary Forms of the Religious Life*. Joseph Ward Swain, Trans. New York: Free Press.
Durkheim, Émile 1919. *Les règles de la méthode sociologique. Septième edition*. Paris: Librarie Félix Alcan. https://archive.org/details/lesrglesdelamoodurkuoft/page/n3/mode/2up, accessed August 23, 2021.
Dutton, Arthur H. 1893. *Customs of the Service: A Handbook of Naval Etiquette*. Boston: Nathan Sawyer & Sons. http://bit.ly/46stn7d. Accessed April 28, 2025.
Eckert, Johanna, Josep Call, Jonas Hermes, Esther Herrmann, & Hannes Rakoczy 2018. Intuitive Statistical Inferences in Chimpanzees and Humans Follow Weber's Law. *Cognition* 180:99–107.
Ehrsson, H. Henrik, Tomonori Kito, Norihiro Sadato, Richard E. Passingham & Eiichi Naito 2005. Neural Substrate of Body Size: Illusory Feeling of Shrinking of the Waist. *PLoS Biology* 3, e412. https://doi.org/10.1371/journal.pbio.0030412.
Eibl-Eibesfeldt, Irenäus 1989. *Human Ethology*. New York: Aldine de Gruyter.
Eibl-Eibesfeldt, Irenäus 1996. The Evolution of Nurturant Dominance. In Polly Wiessner & Wulf Schiefenhövel, Eds., *Food and the Status Quest: An Interdisciplinary Perspective* (pp. 33–38). Providence: Berghahn Books.
Eicher, Joanne B., Ed. 1995. *Dress and Ethnicity: Change across Space and Time*. Oxford: Berg.
Einzig, Paul 1966. *Primitive Money in Its Ethnological, Historical and Economic Aspects*, 2nd ed. Oxford: Pergamon. [First published 1948.]
Eisenstadt, S. N. 1956. Ritualized Personal Relations – Blood Brotherhood, Best Friends, Compadre, Etc.: Some Comparative Hypotheses and Suggestions. *Man* 56:90–95.
Eliade, Mircea 1971. Spirit, Light, and Seed. *History of Religions* 11:1–30.
Eller, Jack David 2010. *Cruel Creeds, Virtuous Violence: Religious Violence across Culture and History*. Amherst: Prometheus.
Ellis, Lee 1994. The Hight and the Mighty among Man and Beast: How Universal Is the Relationship between Height (or Body Size) and Social Status? In Lee Ellis, Ed., *Social Stratification and Socioeconomic Inequality, Volume 2:*

Reproductive and Interpersonal Aspects of Dominance and Status (pp. 93–111). Westport: Praeger.
Emelianov, Vladimir 2010. On the Early History of Melammu. *Proceedings of the RAI* 53, Language in the Ancient Near East. 1109–1119. Winona Lake: Eisenbrauns.
Emmerich, André 1965. *Sweat of the Sun and Tears of the Moon: Gold and Silver in Pre-Columbian Art*. Seattle: University of Washington Press.
Empson, Susan B. 1999. Equal Sharing and Shared Meaning: The Development of Fraction Concepts in a First-Grade Classroom. *Cognition & Instruction* 17:283–342.
Enright, Elizabeth A., Hyowon Gweon, & Jessica A. Sommerville 2017. "To the Victor go the Spoils": Infants Expect Resources to Align with Dominance Structures. *Cognition* 164:8–21.
Ernle, Lord [Rowland Edmund Prothero] 1961. *English Farming Past and Present*, 6th ed. Chicago: Quadrangle Books.
Erwin, Philip G., Annie Burke, & David G. Purves 2002. Food Sharing and Perceptions of the Status of a Relationship. *Perceptual And Motor Skills* 94: 506–508.
Estes, Richard Despard 1991. *The Behavior Guide to African Mammals, Including Hoofed Mammals, Carnivores, Primates*. Los Angeles: University of California Press.
Evans-Pritchard, Edward E. 1933. Zande Blood-Brotherhood. *Africa* 6:369–401.
Evans-Pritchard, Edward E. 1937. *Witchcraft, Oracles and Magic Among the Azande*. Oxford: Oxford University Press.
Evans-Pritchard, Edward E. 1940 [1967]. *The Nuer: A Description of the Modes of Livelihood and Political Institutions of a Nilotic People*. Oxford: Clarendon Press.
Evans-Pritchard, Edward E. 1951. *Kinship and Marriage among the Nuer*. Oxford: Clarendon Press.
Ewen, C. L'Estrange 1932. *Lotteries and Sweepstakes: An Historical, Legal, and Ethical Survey of their Introduction, Suppression and Re-establishment in the British Isles*. London: Heath Cranton.
Fagan, Brian M. 2005. *Ancient North America: The Archaeology of a Continent*. 4th ed. New York: Thames and Hudson.
Fajens, Jane 1985. The Person in Social Context: The Social Character of Banning "Psychology." In Geoffrey M. White & John Kirkpatrick, Eds., *Person, Self, and Experience: Exploring Pacific Ethnopsychologies* (pp. 367–397). Berkeley: University of California Press.
Farmer, George Henry 1939. *Studies in Oriental Musical Instruments*, 2nd series. Glasgow: Civic Press.
Fauconnier, Gilles, & Mark Turner 2002. *The Way We Think: Conceptual Blending and the Mind's Hidden Complexities*. New York: Basic Books.
Fawcett, Christine, & Bahar Tunçgenç 2017. Infants' Use of Movement Synchrony to Infer Social Affiliation in Others. *Journal of Experimental Child Psychology* 160:127–136.
Fazzioli, Edoardo 1986. *Chinese Calligraphy: From Pictograph to Ideogram: The History of 214 Essential Chinese/Japanese Characters*. New York: Abbeville Press.

Feeley-Harnik, Gillian 1994. *The Lord's Table: The Meaning of Food in Early Judaism and Christianity*. Washington: Smithsonian Institution Press.

Feldblum, Joseph T., Christopher Krupenye, Joel Bray, Anne E. Pusey, & Ian C. Gilby 2021. Social Bonds Provide Multiple Pathways to Reproductive Success in Wild Male Chimpanzees. *Iscience* 24(8). www.cell.com/iscience/fulltext/S2589-0042(21)00832-4.

Femenìas, B. 2004. "Why do Gringos Like Black?": Mourning, Tourism, and Changing Fashions in Peru. In R. A. Root, Ed., *The Latin American Fashion Reader* (pp. 93–113). Oxford: Berg.

Ferhat, Halima 2010. Le Saint et Son Corps: Une Lutte Constante. *Al-Qanṭara: Revista de Estudios Árabes* 21(2):456–469.

Féron, Julie, Edouard Gentaz, & Arlette Streri 2006. Evidence of Amodal Representation of Small Numbers Across Visuo-Tactile Modalities in 5-Month-Old Infants. *Cognitive Development* 21:81–92.

Fias, Wim, Jan Lammertyn, Bernie Caessens, & Guy A. Orban 2007. Processing of Abstract Ordinal Knowledge in the Horizontal Segment of the Intraparietal Sulcus. *Journal of Neuroscience* 27:8952–8956.

Fildes, Valerie 1988. *Wet Nursing: A History from Antiquity to the Present*. New York: Basil Blackwell.

Firth, Raymond 1938 [1965]. *Primitive Polynesian Economy*, 2nd ed. New York: Norton.

Firth, Raymond 1970. Postures and Gestures of Respect. In Jean Pouillon and Pierre Maranda, Eds., *Échanges et Communications: Mélanges Offerts à Claude Lévi-Strauss à l'Occasion de son 60ème Anniversaire* (pp. 188–209). The Hague: Mouton. Reprinted in Ted Polhemus, Ed., 1978, *The Body Reader: Social Aspects of the Human Body*. New York: Pantheon [in association with the Institute of Contemporary Arts, London].

Firth, Raymond 1973. *Symbols, Public and Private*. Ithaca: Cornell University Press.

Fischler, Claude 2011. Commensality, Society and Culture. *Social Science Information* 50:528–548.

Fisher, Michael H. 1990. The Resident in Court Ritual, 1764–1858. *Modern Asian Studies* 24:419–458.

Fisher, Robert E. 1993. *Buddhist Art and Architecture*. London: Thames & Hudson.

Fishler, Claude 1988. Food, Self, and Identity. *Social Science Information* 27:275–292.

Fiske, Alan Page 1991. *Structures of Social Life: The Four Elementary Forms of Human Relations*. New York: Free Press (Macmillan).

Fiske, Alan. P. 1992. The Four Elementary Forms of Sociality: Framework for a Unified Theory of Social Relations. *Psychological Review 99*:689–723.

Fiske, Alan. P. 2000. Complementarity Theory: Why Human Social Capacities Evolved to Require Cultural Complements. *Personality and Social Psychology Review* 4:76–94.

Fiske, Alan P. 2002. Socio-Moral Emotions Motivate Action to Sustain Social Relationships. *Self and Identity* 1:169–175.
Fiske, Alan P. 2004. Relational Models Theory 2.0. In Nick Haslam , Ed., *Relational Models Theory: A Contemporary Overview* (pp. 3–25). Mahwah: Erlbaum.
Fiske, Alan P. 2010. Dispassionate Heuristic Rationality Fails to Sustain Social Relationships. In Andrea W. Mates, Lisa Mikesell, & Michael Sean Smith , Eds., *Language, Interaction and Frontotemporal Dementia: Reverse Engineering the Social Brain* (pp. 199–241). Oakville: Equinox.
Fiske, Alan P. 2011. Metarelational Models: Configurations of Social Relationships. *European Journal of Social Psychology* 42:2–18. https://doi.org/10.1002/ejsp.847.
Fiske, Alan P. 2019. *Kama Muta: Discovering the Connecting Emotion*. London: Routledge.
Fiske, Alan P. 2020a. The Lexical Fallacy in Emotion Research: Mistaking Vernacular Words for Psychological Entities. *Psychological Review* 127:95–113.
Fiske, Alan P. 2020b. Ways of Knowing Emotion, and What You Don't Know about Your Own Emotions: The Case of Kama Muta. *Social Research: An International Quarterly* 87:171–195.
Fiske, Alan P. 2023a. *An Emotion Niche for the Cultural Evolution of Social Practices*. In Joseph P, Forgas, Bill Crano & Klaus Fiedler. Eds., *The Psychology of Sociability*. London: Routledge.
Fiske, Alan P. 2023b. Seeking Moral Meaning in Misfortune: Assigning Blame, Without Regard for Causation. In Joseph P. Forgas, William D. Crano, & Klaus Fiedler, Eds. *The Psychology of Insecurity* (pp. 170–184). Sydney Symposium of Social Psychology. Routledge.
Fiske, Alan P. n.d. Learning Culture the Way Informants Do: Observing, Imitating, and Gradually Participating. Unpublished manuscript.
Fiske, Alan P. & Nick Haslam 1996. Social Cognition Is Thinking About Relationships. *Current Directions in Psychological Science* 5:143–148.
Fiske, Alan P. & Nick Haslam 1997. Is Obsessive-Compulsive Disorder a Pathology of the Human Disposition to Perform Socially Meaningful Rituals? Evidence of Similar Content. *Journal of Nervous and Mental Disease* 185:211–222.
Fiske, Alan P. & Lisa Schubert 2012. How to Relate to People: The Extra-Terrestrial's Guide to Homo Sapiens. In Omri Gillath, Glenn Adams, & Adrianne D. Kunkel (Eds.), *Relationship Science: Integrating Evolutionary, Neuroscience, and Sociocultural Approaches* (pp. 169–195). American Psychological Association.
Fiske, Alan P., Thomas Schubert, & Beate Seibt 2025. Seeking Communal Emotions in Culturally Evolved Social Practices: Worship, Kitten Videos, Marriage Proposals, Memorials, and More. *Annual Review of Psychology* 76 (1):607–633.

Fiske, Alan P., Beate Seibt, & Thomas Schubert 2019. The Sudden Devotion Emotion: Kama Muta and the Cultural Practices Whose Function is to Evoke it. *Emotion Review* 11:74–86.

Fiske, Alan P. & Tage Shakti Rai 2014. *Virtuous Violence*. Cambridge: Cambridge University Press.

Fletcher, Alice C. 1996. *The Hako: Song, Pipe and Unity in a Pawnee Calumet Ceremony*. Lincoln: University of Nebraska Press.

Ford, John K. B., & Graeme M. Ellis 1999. *Transients: Mammal-Hinting Killer Whales of British Columbia, Washington, and Southeastern Alaska*. Vancouver: UBC Press.

Ford, John K. B., Graeme M. Ellis, & Kenneth C. Balcomb 1994. *Killer Whales: The Natural History and Genealogy of Orcinus orca in British Columbia and Washington State*. Vancouver: UBC Press.

Foreign Service Institute US Department of State 2013. Protocol for the Modern Diplomat. https://2009-2017.state.gov/documents/organization/176174.pdf. Accessed August 11, 2023.

Fortes, Meyer 1945. *The Dynamics of Clanship among the Tallensi: Being the First Part of an Analysis of the Social Structure of a Trans-Volta Tribe*. London: Oxford University Press.

Fortes, Meyer 1969. *Kinship and the Social Order. Lewis Henry Morgan Lectures*. Chicago: Aldine.

Fossey, Dian 1983. *Gorillas in the Mist*. Boston: Houghton Mifflin.

Fossum, John E. 1999. Glory. In Karel van der Toorn, Bob Becking, & Pieter W. van der Horst, Eds., *Dictionary of Deities and Demons in the Bible*, 2nd Ed. (pp. 348–352). Leiden: Brill.

Frank, Robert H. 1988. *Passions Within Reason*. New York: Norton.

Frankfort, Henri 1948. *Kingship and the Gods: A Study of Ancient Near Eastern Religion as the Integration of Society and Nature*. Chicago: University of Chicago Press.

Franklin, Michael S., & John Jonides 2008. Order and Magnitude Share a Common Representation in Parietal Cortex. *Journal of Cognitive Neuroscience 21*:2114–2120.

Frazer, James George 1890 [1987]. *The Golden Bough: A Study in Magic and Religion*. Abridged ed. New York: Collier Books.

Freud, Sigmund 1913. Totem and Taboo. In *The Standard Edition of the Complete Works of Sigmund Freud*, Vol. 13 (pp. 1–255). James Strachey, Ed. London: Hogarth Press.

Freud, Sigmund 1939. *Moses and Monotheism*. Katherine Jones, transl. New York: Vantage (Random House).

Freund, Paul J. 1985. Polish-American Drinking: Continuity and Change. In Linda A. Bennett & Genevieve M. Ames, Eds., *The American Experience with Alcohol: Contrasting Cultural Perspectives* (pp. 77–92). New York: Plenum Press.

Freyer, John 1909–1915 [originally published 1698]. *A New Account of East India and Persia: Being Nine Years' Travels, 1672–1681*. William Crooke, Ed.

London: Hakluyt Society. http://nrs.harvard.edu/urn-3:FHCL:2766645. Accessed April 28, 2025.
Frijhoff, Willem 1991. The Kiss Sacred and Profane: Reflections on a Cross-Cultural Confrontation. In Jan Bremmer & Herman Roodenburg, Eds., *A Cultural History of Gesture: From Antiquity to the Present Day* (pp. 210–236). Cambridge: Polity.
Gabriel, Kathryn 1996. *Gambler Way: Indian Gaming in Mythology, History, and Archeology in North America*. Boulder: Johnson Books.
Gallese, Vittorio 2003. The Manifold Nature of Interpersonal Relations: The Quest for a Common Mechanism. *Philosophical Transactions of the Royal Society of London: Biological Sciences* 358:517–528.
Gallistel, Charles R. 1990. *The Organization of Learning*. Cambridge, MA: MIT Press.
Gallistel, Charles R. 2001. Mental Representations, Psychology of. In *International Encyclopedia of the Social and Behavioral Sciences* (pp. 9691–9695). Amsterdam: Elsevier.
Gallistel, Charles R. 2021. The Physical Basis of Memory. *Cognition* 213:104533.
Gallistel, Charles R., & Rochel Gelman 2000. Non-Verbal Numerical Cognition: From Reals to Integers. *Trends in Cognitive Science* 4:59–65.
Gamkrelidze, Thomas V., & Vjaceslav V. Ivanov 1995. Indo-European and the Indo-Europeans: A Reconstruction and Historical Analysis of a Proto-Language and a Proto-Culture. Part I, The Text. English version by Johanna Nichols, edited by Werner Winter. Berlin: Mouton de Gruyter.
Ganßmann, Heiner 1988. Money: A Symbolically Generalized Means of Communication? On the Concept of Money in Recent Sociology. *Economy and Society* 17:285–316.
Gardiner, Juliet 2010. *The Blitz: The British Under Attack*. London: HarperCollins.
Garnier, François 1982. *Le Langage de L'Image au Moyen Âge: Signification et Symbolique, vol. 1* [no location indicated]: Le Léopard D'Or.
Garnier, François 1989. *Le Langage de L'Image au Moyen Âge: Signification et Symbolique, vol. 2* [no location indicated]: Le Léopard D'Or.
Garvin, Paul L., & S. H. Riesenberg, 1952. Respect Behavior on Ponape: An Ethnolinguistic Study. *American Anthropologist* 54:201–220.
Gaubatz, Piper 1995. Changing Beijing. *Geographical Review* 85:79–96.
Geertz, Clifford 1966. Religion as a Cultural System. In M. Banton (ed.), *Anthropological Approaches to the Study of Religion* (pp. 1–46). London: Tavistock Publications.
George, A. R. 2003. *The Babylon Gilgamesh Epic. Volume 1: Introduction, Critical Edition and Cuneiform Texts*. Oxford: Oxford University Press.
Geraci, Alessandra, & Luca Surian 2011. The Developmental Roots of Fairness: Infants' Reactions to Equal and Unequal Distributions of Resources. *Developmental Science* 14:1012–1020.

Geraci, Alessandra, & Luca Surian 2023a. Intention-Based Evaluations of Distributive Actions by 4-Month-Olds. *Infant Behavior and Development* 70:101797. www.sciencedirect.com/science/article/pii/S0163638322001114.

Geraci, Alessandra, & Luca Surian 2023b. Preverbal Infants' Reactions to Third-Party Punishments and Rewards Delivered Toward Fair and Unfair Agents. *Journal of Experimental Child Psychology* 226:105574. https://doi.org/10.1016/j.jecp.2022.105574.

Gerszten, Peter C., and Enrique Gerszten 1995. Intentional Cranial Deformation: A Disappearing Form of Self-Mutilation. *Neurosurgery* 37:374–382.

Giesey, Ralph E. 1985. Models of Rulership in French Royal Ceremonial. In Sean Wilentz, Ed., *Rites of Power: Symbolism, Ritual, and Politics since the Middle Ages* (pp. 41–64). Philadelphia: University of Pennsylvania Press.

Giessner, Stephen R., & Thomas W. Schubert 2007. High in the Hierarchy: How Vertical Location and Judgments of Leaders' Power Are Interrelated. *Organizational Behavior and Human Decision Processes* 104:30–44.

Giessner, Stephen R., & Thomas W. Schubert 2019. Power and Vertical Positions in an Organization Chart: A Pre-Registered Replication Report of Study 3a and a Modification of Study 1a, Giessner & Schubert (2007). *Collabra: Psychology* 5(1):25. https://doi.org/10.1525/collabra.216.

Gilbert, M. Jean 1985. Mexican-Americans in California: Intracultural Variation in Attitudes and Behavior Related to Alcohol. In Linda A. Bennett & Genevieve M. Ames, Eds., *The American Experience with Alcohol: Contrasting Cultural Perspectives* (pp. 255–277). New York: Plenum Press.

Gilby, Ian C., Lauren JN Brent, Emily E. Wroblewski, Rebecca S. Rudicell, Beatrice H. Hahn, Jane Goodall, & Anne E. Pusey 2013. Fitness Benefits of Coalitionary Aggression in Male Chimpanzees. *Behavioral Ecology and Sociobiology* 67:373–381.

Gildersleeve, Basil L., Ed. 1885. *Pindar, The Olympian and Pythian Odes.* New York: American Book Company.

Gillison, Gillian 1983. Cannibalism among Women in the Eastern Highlands of Papua New Guinea. In P. Brown & D. Tuzin, Eds., *The Ethnography of Cannibalism* (pp. 33–50). Washington, DC: Society for Psychological Anthropology.

Gippert, Jost 2002. The Avestan Language and Its Problems. In Nicholas Sims-Williams (Ed.), *Indo-Iranian Languages and Peoples* (pp. 165–187). Oxford: Oxford University Press.

Girard, Rene 1977. *Violence and the Sacred.* Baltimore: Johns Hopkins Press.

Goffman, Erving 1971. *Relations in Public: Microstudies of the Public Order.* New York: Basic Books.

Goffman, Erving 1976. *Gender Advertisements.* New York: Harper Colophon.

Goldin-Meadow, Susan, & Martha Wagner Alibali 2013. Gesture's Role in Speaking, Learning, and Creating Language. *Annual Review of Psychology* 64:257–283.

Goldman, Alvin, and Frederique de Vignemont 2009. Is Social Cognition Embodied? *Trends in Cognitive Sciences* 13(4):154–159.

Gollaher, David L. 2000. *Circumcision: A History of the World's Most Controversial Surgery*. New York: Basic Books.
Gombrich, Ernst H. 1972. Action and Expression in Western Art. In Robert A. Hinde, Ed., *Non-Verbal Communication* (pp. 373–393). Cambridge: Cambridge University Press.
Gonda, Jan 1954. *Aspects of Early Viṣṇsnuism*. Utrecht: Oosthoek.
Gonda, Jan 1956. Ancient Indian Kingship from the Religious Point of View. *Numen* 3:36–71.
Goodall, Jane 1986. *The Chimpanzees of Gombe: Patterns of Behavior*. Cambridge: Harvard (Belknap).
Goodenough, Ward 1944. A Technique for Scale Analysis. *Educational and Psychological Measurement* 4:179–190.
Goodenough, Ward 1965. Rethinking "Status" and "Role": Toward a General Model of the Cultural Organization of Social Relationships. In Michael Banton, ed., *The Relevance of Models to Social Anthropology* (pp. 1–14). Association of Social Anthropologists Monograph 1. London: Tavistock.
Goosen, C. 1987. Social Grooming in Primates. In G. Mitchell & J. Erwin , Eds., *Comparative Primate Biology, Volume 2, Part B: Behavior, Cognition, and Motivation* (pp. 107–131). New York: Alan Liss.
Gordon, Andrew W. 1984. Alcohol Use in the Perspective of Cultural Ecology. In Marc Galanter, Ed., *Recent Developments in in Alcoholism, Volume 2: Learning and Social Models, Alcohol and the Liver, Aging and Alcoholism, Anthropology* (pp. 355–375). New York: Plenum Press.
Gordon, Jonathon 1998. *Sperm Whales*. Stillwater: Voyager.
Gordon, Stewart 2001. A World of Investiture. In Steward Gordon, Ed., *Robes and Honor: The Medieval World of Investiture* (pp. 1–19). New York: Palgrave.
Gottstein, Alon Goshen 1994. The Body as Image of God in Rabbinic Literature. *The Harvard Theological Review* 87:171–195.
Gourlay, K. A. 1982. Long Trumpets of Northern Nigeria: Yesterday and Today. *Journal of International Library of African Music* 6:48–72.
Grabar, André 1936. *L'Empereur dans L'Art Byzantin: Recherches sur L'Art Officiel de L'Empire D'Orient*. Paris: Les Belles Lettres.
Green, Michael F., Carrie E. Bearden, Tyrone D. Cannon, Alan P. Fiske, Gerhard S. Hellemann, William P. Horan, Kimmy Kee, Robert S. Kern, Junghee Lee, Mark J. Sergi, Kenneth L. Subotnik, Catherine A. Sugar, Joseph Ventura, Cindy M. Yee, Keith H. Nuechterlein 2012. Social cognition in schizophrenia, part 1: performance across phase of illness. *Schizophrenia Bulletin* 38:854–864.
Gray, Howard Levi 1915. *English Field Systems*. Cambridge: Harvard University Press.
Gray, Peter B., Timothy S. McHale, & Justin M. Carré 2017. A Review of Human Male Field Studies of Hormones and Behavioral Reproductive Effort. *Hormones and Behavior* 91:52–67.
Greenfield, Michael D., & Bjorn Merker 2023. Coordinated Rhythms in Animal Species, including Humans: Entrainment from Bushcricket Chorusing to the Philharmonic Orchestra. *Neuroscience & Biobehavioral Reviews* 153: 105382.

Grewenig, Meinrad Maria 2004. *Inka Gold: 3000 Years of Advanced Civilisations: Masterpieces from Peru's Larco Museum*. Heidelberg: Kehrer.
Grierson, Philip 1978. The Origins of Money. *Research in Economic Anthropology* 1:1–35.
Guernsey, Julia & Michael Love 2005. Late Preclassic Expressions of Authority on the Pacific Slope. In Virginia M. Fields & Dorie Reents-Budget, Eds., *Lords of Creation: The Origins of Sacred Maya Kinship* (pp. 37–43). Los Angeles: Los Angeles County Museum & Scala Publishers.
Gummere, Francis 1910. *The Oldest English Epic: Beowulf, Finsbury, Waldere, Deor, Widsith, and the German Hildebrand*. New York: Macmillan. www.fordham.edu/halsall/basis/beowulf.html. Accessed April 22, 2025.
Gutierrez, C. Paige 1984. The Social and Symbolic Uses of Ethnic/Regional Foodways: Cajuns and Crawfish in South Louisiana. In Linda Keller Brown, & Kay Mussell, Eds., *Ethnic and Regional Foodways in the United States* (pp. 169–182). Knoxville: University of Tennessee Press.
Guttman, Louis 1944. A Basis for Scaling Qualitative Data. *American Sociological Review* 9:139–150.
Guttman, Louis 1950. The Basis for Scalogram Analysis. In Samuel A. Stouffer, Ed., *Measurement and Prediction: Studies in Social Psychology in World War II*, Vol. 4 (pp. 60–90). Princeton: Princeton University Press.
Hackwood, Frederick W. 1909. *Inns, Ales, and Drinking Customs of Old England*. London: T. Fisher Unwin.
Hall, Judith A., Erik J. Coats, & Lavonia Smith LeBeau 2005. Nonverbal Behavior and the Vertical Dimension of Social Relations: A Meta-Analysis. *Psychological Bulletin* 131:898–924.
Hall, Robert L. 1997. *An Archeology of the Soul: North American Indian Belief and Ritual*. Urbana: University of Illinois Press.
Halloran, John A. 2006. *Sumerian Lexicon: A Dictionary Guide to the Ancient Sumerian Language*. Los Angeles: Logogram Publishing.
Hambly, Gavin R. G. 2001. From Baghdad to Bukhara, from Ghanza to Delhi: The Khil'a Ceremony in the Transmission of Kingly Pomp and Circumstance. In Steward Gordon, Ed., *Robes and Honor: The Medieval World of Investiture* (pp. 193–222). New York: Palgrave.
Hamlin 2022. Simplicity and Validity in Infant Research. *Cognitive Development* 63:101213. https://doi.org/10.1016/j.cogdev.2022.101213.
Hammond, Peter B. 1966. *Yatenga: Technology in the Culture of a West African Kingdom*. New York: Free Press.
Hanley, Sarah 1985. Legend, Ritual, and Discourse in the Lit de Justice Assembly: French Constitutional Ideology, 1527–1641. In Sean Wilentz, Ed., *Rites of Power: Symbolism, Ritual, and Politics Since the Middle Ages* (pp. 65–106). Philadelphia: University of Pennsylvania Press.
Hansen, Karen Tranberg 2004. The World in Dress: Anthropological Perspectives on Clothing, Fashion, and Culture. *Annual Review of Anthropology* 33:369–392.
Harper, Douglas 2025. *Online Etymological Dictionary*. www.etymonline.com/.

Harris, Olivia 1982. Labor and Produce in an Ethnic Community. In David Lehmann, Ed., *Ecology and Exchange in the Andes* (pp. 77–96). Cambridge: Cambridge University Press.

Hartland, Edwin Sidney 1895. *The Legend of Perseus; A Study of Tradition in Story, Custom and Belief*, Vol. 2. London: David Nutt.

Haslam, Nick & Alan Page Fiske 2004. Social Expertise: Theory of Mind or Theory of Relationships? In N. Haslam, Ed., *Relational Models Theory: A Contemporary Overview* (pp. 147–163). Mahwah: Erlbaum.

Haslam, Nick, Therese Reichert, & Alan Page Fiske 2002. Aberrant Social Relations in the Personality Disorders. *Psychology and Psychotherapy: Theory, Research and Practice* 75:19–31.

Hawkes, Kristen, James F. O'Connell, & Nicholas G. Blurton Jones 2001. Hunting and Nuclear Families: Some Lessons from the Hadza about Men's Work. *Current Anthropology* 42: 681–709.

Haynes, Douglas 1990. Imperial Ritual in a Local Setting: The Ceremonial Order in Surat, 1890–1939. *Modern Asian Studies* 24:493–527.

Haynes, Edward S. 1990. Rajput Ceremonial Interactions as a Mirror of a Dying Indian State System, 1820–1947. *Modern Asian Studies* 24:459–492.

Head, Brian F. 1978. Respect Degrees in Pronominal Reference. In Joseph H. Greenberg, Ed., *Universals of Human Language, Volume 3: Word Structure* (pp. 151–212). Stanford: Stanford University Press.

Headlam, James Wycliffe 1891. *Election by Lot at Athens*. Cambridge: Cambridge University Press.

Heaney, Seamus 2000. *Beowulf: A New Verse Translation*. New York: Farrar, Straus and Giroux.

Heath, Dwight B. 1991a Drinking Patterns of the Bolivian Camba. In David J. Pittman & Helene Raskin White, Eds., *Society, Culture, and Drinking Patterns Reexamined* (pp. 62–77). New Brunswick: Rutgers Center of Alcohol Studies [first published 1958].

Heath, Dwight B. 1991b. Continuity and Change in Drinking Patterns of the Bolivian Camba. In David J. Pittman & Helene Raskin White, Eds., *Society, Culture, and Drinking Patterns Reexamined* (pp. 78–108). New Brunswick: Rutgers Center of Alcohol Studies.

Heizer, Robert F., & Gullberg, Jonas E. 1981. Concave Mirrors from the Site of Le Venta, Tabasco: Their Occurrence, Mineralogy, Optical Description, and Function. In Michael Coe, Matthew Williams Stirling, Michael D. Coe, & David C. Grove, Eds., *The Olmec and Their Neighbors: Essays in Memory of Matthew W. Stirling* (pp. 109–116). Washington, DC: Dumbarton Oaks.

Helm, Barbara, Theunis Piersma, & Henck van den Jeugd 2006. Sociable Schedules: Interplay between Avian Seasonal and Social Behavior. *Animal Behavior* 72:245–262.

Helms, Mary W. 1981. Precious Metals and Politics: Style and Ideology in the Intermediate Area and Peru. *Journal of Latin American Lore* 7:215–238.

Hendon, Julia A. 1999. The Pre-Classic Maya Compound as the Focus of Social Identity. In David C. Grove & Rosemary A. Joyce, Eds., *Social Patterns in Pre-Classic Mesoamerica* (pp. 97–125). Washington, DC: Dumbarton Oaks.

Hendrickson C. 1995. *Weaving Identities: Construction of Dress and Self in a Highland Guatemalan Town*. Austin: University of Texas Press.

Hendrie, Colin, & Isolde Shirley 2019. Courtship-Feeding in the "First Dates" Restaurant is Highly Predictive of a Second Date. *Appetite* 141:104329.

Henry, Stuart 1988. Rules, Rulers, and Ruled in Egalitarian Collectives: Deviance and Social Control in Cooperatives. In James G. Flanagan and Steve Rayner, Eds., *Rules, Decisions and Inequality in Egalitarian Societies*. Aldershot: Avebury.

Hensley, W. E., & R. Cooper 1987. Height and Occupational Success: A Review and Critique. *Psychological Reports* 60: 843–849.

Herdt, Gilbert, Ed. 1982. *Rituals of Manhood: Male Initiation in Papua New Guinea*. Berkeley: University of California Press.

Herman, Gabriel 1987. *Ritualised Friendship and the Greek City*. Cambridge: Cambridge University Press.

Hertz, Robert 1909. La Prééminence de la Main Droite: Étude sur la Polarité Religieuse. *Revue Philosophique de la France et de l'Étranger* 68:553–580. [Translated by Rodney and Claudia Needham (2013), The Pre-Eminence of the Right Hand: A Study in Religious Polarity, *HAU: Journal of Ethnographic Theory* 3:335–357.]

Hettwer, Mike 2008. Photographs appearing in *University of Chicago Magazine* Sept.–Oct. 2008. http://magazine.uchicago.edu/0810/investigations/original_source.shtml.

Higham Philip A., & D. William Carment 1992. The Rise and Fall of Politicians: The Judged Heights of Broadbent, Mulroney and Turner before and after the 1988 Canadian Federal-Election. *Canadian Journal of Behavioural Science-Revue Canadienne Des Sciences Du Comportement* 24:404–409.

Hirshleifer, Jack 1987. On the Emotions as Guarantors of Threats and Promises. In John Dupré , Ed., *The Latest and the Best: Essays in Evolution and Optimality* (pp. 307–326). Cambridge, MA: MIT Press.

Hiuen, Tsiang 1908. *Buddhist Records of the Western World Volume 1*. Samuel Beal, transl. London: Kegan Paul, Trench, Trübner.

Hoben, Allan 1963. The Role of Ambilineal Descent Groups in Gojjam Amhara Social Organization. Anthropology PhD thesis, University of California, Berkeley.

Hocart, A. M. 1927. *Kingship*. Oxford: Oxford University Press.

Hodges, Frederick M. 2001. The Ideal Prepuce in Ancient Greece and Rome: Male Genital Aesthetics and Their Relation to *Lipodermos*, Circumcision, Foreskin Restoration, and the *Kynodesme*. *Bulletin of the History of Medicine* 75:375–405.

Hodgskiss, Tammy 2018. Ochre Use in the Middle Stone Age. *Anthropology. Oxford Research Encyclopedias*. https://doi.org/10.1093/acrefore/9780190854584.013.51.

Hohti, Paula 2022. Power, Black Clothing, and the Chromatic Politics of Textiles in Renaissance Europe. In Jenny Boulboullé & Sven Dupré, Eds., *Burgundian Black: Reworking Early Modern Colour Technologies*. Santa Barbara: EMC Imprint. Online only: http://bit.ly/4lptwww

Hollis, Alfred C. 1905. *The Masai: Their Language and Folklore*. Oxford: Clarendon Press.

Holmgren, Jostein, Peder M. Isager, & Thomas W. Schubert 2018. Evidence for Magnitude Representations of Social Hierarchies: Size and Distance Effects. *PLoS ONE* 13(9). e0203263. https://doi.org/10.1371/journal.pone.0203263.

Horan, William P., Michael F. Green, Michael DeGroot, Alan Fiske, Gerhard Hellemann, Kimmy Kee, Robert S. Kern, Junghee Lee, Mark J. Sergi, Kenneth L. Subotnik, Catherine A. Sugar, Joseph Ventura, & Keith H. Nuechterlein 2011. Social Cognition in Schizophrenia, Part 2: 12-Month Stability and Prediction of Functional Outcome in First Episode Patients. *Schizophrenia Bulletin* 38:865–872.

Hornung, Erik 1982. *Conceptions of God in Ancient Egypt: The One and The Many*. John Baines, transl. Ithaca: Cornell University Press.

Hosler, Dorothy 1994. *The Sounds and Colors of Power: The Sacred Metallurgical Technology of Ancient West Mexico*. Cambridge: MIT Press.

Hosler, Dorothy 2009. West Mexican Metallurgy: Revisited and Revised. *Journal of World Prehistory* 22:185–212.

Houston, Stephen, & Karl Taube, 2000. An Archeology of the Senses: Perception and Cultural Expression in Ancient Mesoamerica. *Cambridge Archeological Journal* 10:261–294.

Houston Stephen, David Stuart, & Karl Taube 2006., *The Memory of Bones: Body, Being, and Experience among the Classic Maya*. Austin: University of Texas Press.

Howard, Angela Falco, Song Li, Hung Wu & Hong Yang 2006. *Chinese Sculpture*. New Haven: Yale University Press.

Howard, Scarlett R., Aurore Avarguès-Weber, Jair E. Garcia, Andrew D. Greentree, & Adrian G. Dyer 2019. Numerical Cognition in Honeybees Enables Addition and Subtraction. *Science Advances* 5:eaav0961.

Hua, Hsüan 2003. *The Shurangama Sutra with Commentary, Volume 5*. Burlingame: Buddhist Text Translation Society.

Hung, Wu 1995. *Monumentality in Early Chinese Art and Architecture*. Stanford: Stanford University Press.

Hung, Wu 2007. Picturing or Diagramming the Universe. In Georges Métailié, Vera Dorofeeva-Lichtmann, & Francesca Bray, Eds., *Graphics and Text in the Production of Technical Knowledge in China: The Warp and the Weft* (pp. 191–201). Leiden: Brill.

Hunting, Robert P. 1991. The Social Origins of Pre-Fraction Knowledge in Three Year Olds. In Robert P. Hunting & Gary Davis, *Early Fraction Learning* (pp. 55–72). New York: Springer.

Hunting, Robert P., & Sharpley, Christopher F. 1988. Fraction Knowledge in Preschool Children. *Journal for Research in Mathematics Education* 19:175–180.

Hwang, Ming-Chorng 1996. Ming-Tang: *Cosmology, Political Order and Monuments in Early China*. PhD dissertation, Department of East African Languages and Civilizations, Harvard University.

Ifrah, George 1981. *Histoires Universelle des Chifres*. Paris: Seghers.

Iseminger, William 2010. *Cahokia Mounds: American's First City*. Charleston: History Press.
Izard, Michel 1985. *Gens Du Pouvoir, Gens De La Terre: Les Institutions Politiques De L'ancien Royaume Du Yatenga*. Paris: Editions de la Maison des Sciences de L'Homme.
Izard-Heritier Françoise, & Michel Izard 1959. *Les Mossi Du Yatenga*. Bordeaux: Institiut des Sciences Humaines Appliquees de l'Université de Bordeaux.
James, Peter, & Marinus Anthony van der Sluijs, 2008. Ziggurats, Colors, and Planets: Rawlinson Revisited. *Journal of Cuneiform Studies* 60:57–79.
Jameson, Michael H. 1988. Sacrifice and Ritual: Greece. In Michael Grant & Rachel Kitzinger, Eds., *Civilization of the Ancient Mediterranean: Greece and Rome, Volume II* (pp. 959–979). New York: Charles Scribner's Sons.
Jansen, Maarten, & Gabina Aurora Pérez Jiménez, Eds. 2005. *Codex Bodley: A Painted Chronicle from the Mixtex Highlands, Mexico*. Oxford: Bodleian Library.
Jaymous, Raymond 1981. *Honneur et Baraka: Les Structures Sociales Traditionelles dans le Rif.* Paris: Editions de la Maison des Sciences de L'Homme.
Jiménez, Manuel, Raúl Aguilar, & José R. Alvero-Cruz 2012. Effects of Victory and Defeat on Testosterone and Cortisol Response to Competition: Evidence for Same Response Patterns in Men and Women. *Psychoneuroendocrinology* 37:1577–1581.
Jin, Kyong-sun, Fransisca Ting, Zijing He, & Renée Baillargeon 2024. Infants Expect Some Degree of Positive and Negative Reciprocity between Strangers. *Nature Communications* 15:7742.
Joannès, Francis 2007. Le Rituel de L'Audience en Mésopotamie au 1er Millénaire avant Notre Ère. In Jean-Pierre Caillet & Michel Sot, Eds., *L'Audience Rituels et Cadres Spatiaux dans L'Antiquité et le Haut Moyen Age* (pp. 33–48). Paris: Picard.
Johnson, Christine M., & Norris, Kenneth S. 1994 Social Behavior. In Kenneth S. Norris, Bernd Würsig, Randall S. Wells, & Melanie Würsig, Eds., *The Hawaiian Spinner Dolphin* (pp. 243–286). Berkeley: University of California Press.
Johnson, Norris R. 1987. Panic and the Breakdown of Social Order: Popular Myth, Social Theory, Empirical Evidence. *Sociological Focus* 20:171–183.
Johnson, Norris R. 1988. Fire in a Crowded Theater: A Descriptive Investigation of the Emergence of Panic. *International Journal of Mass Emergencies and Disasters* 6:7–26.
Jones, H. Stuart 1916. Mithraism. In James Hastings, John A. Selbie, & Louis Gray, Eds., *Encyclopedia of Religion and Ethics, Part 16* (pp. 752–758). New York: Charles Scribner's Sons.
Jouravlev, Olessia, David Zheng, Zuzanna Balewski, Alvince Le Arnz Pongos, Zena Levan, Susan Goldin-Meadow, & Evelina Fedorenko 2019. Speech-Accompanying Gestures Are Not Processed by the Language-Processing Mechanisms. *Neuropsychologia* 132:107132.
Joyce, Rosemary J. 2000. High Culture, Mesoamerican Civilization, and the Classic Maya Tradition. In Janet Richards & Mary Van Buren, Eds., *Order,*

Legitimacy, and Wealth in Ancient States (pp. 64–76). Cambridge: Cambridge University Press.

Joye, Yannick, & Jan Verpooten 2013. An Exploration of the Functions of Religious Monumental Architecture from a Darwinian Perspective. *Review of General Psychology* 17:53–68.

Jubault, Thomas , Chrystele Ody, & Etienne Koechlin 2007. Serial Organization of Human Behavior in the Inferior Parietal Cortex. *Journal of Neuroscience 41*:11028–11036.

Judge, Timothy A., & Daniel M. Cable 2004. The Effect of Physical Height on Workplace Success and Income: Preliminary Test of a Theoretical Model. *Journal of Applied Psychology* 89:428–441.

Juliano, Annette 1981. *Treasures of China*. New York: Richard Marek Publishers.

Kaeuper, Richard W. 1999. *Chivalry and Violence in Medieval Europe*. Oxford: Oxford University Press.

Kaiser, Patricia L. 1984. The Lakota Sacred Pipe: Its Tribal Use and Religious Philosophy. *American Indian Culture and Research Journal* 8:1–26.

Kajokaite, Kotrina, Andrew Whalen, Karthik Panchanathan, & Susan Perry. 2019. White-Faced Capuchin Monkeys Use Both Rank and Relationship Quality to Recruit Allies. *Animal Behaviour* 154:161–169.

Kakridis, Hélène J. 1963. *La Notion de L'Amitié et le L'Hospitalité chez Homère. H Bibliothke tou Philologou, ar 9*. Thessaloniki: [n.p.].

Kapstein, Matthew T., Ed., 2004a. *The Presence of Light: Divine Radiance and Religious Experience*. Chicago: University of Chicago Press.

Kapstein, Matthew 2004b. The Strange Death of the Demon Tamer. In Matthew T. Kapstein, Ed., *The Presence of Light: Divine Radiance and Religious Experience* (pp. 118–156). Chicago: University of Chicago Press.

Kapstein, Matthew 2004c. Rethinking the Religious Experience: Seeing the Light in the History of Religions. In Matthew T. Kapstein, Ed., *The Presence of Light: Divine Radiance and Religious Experience* (pp. 265–299). Chicago: University of Chicago Press.

Katô, Jôken 1952. Chinese Characters. *Monumenta Nipponica* 9:193–229.

Katô, Jôken 1954. Chinese Characters III. *Monumenta Nipponica* 10:193–202.

Keating, Elizabeth 1995. Spatial Conceptualizations of Social Hierarchy in Pohnpei, Micronesia. In Anrew Frank & Werner Kuhn, Eds., *Spatial Information Theory: A Theoretical Basis for GIS* (pp. 463–474). Berlin: Springer.

Keating, Elizabeth 2000. Moments of Hierarchy: Constituting Social Stratification by Means of Language, Food, Space and the Body in Pohnpei, Micronesia. *American Anthropologist* 102:303–320.

Keating, Elizabeth, & Alessandro Duranti 2006. Honorific Resources for the Construction of Hierarchy in Samoan and Pohnpeia. *Journal of the Polynesian Society* 115:145–172.

Keen, Mauise 1962. Brotherhood in Arms. *History: Journal of the Historical Association* 47:1–17.

Kelley, David H., & Eugene F. Milone 2005. *Exploring Ancient Skies: An Encyclopedic Survey of Archeoastronomy*. New York: Springer.

Kelley, Katie, 2006. In This Mayor's Race, Heads or Tails May Be Deciding Factor. *New York Times* Final National Edition, 26 November, p. 20.

Kemp, Barry J. 1989. *Ancient Egypt: Anatomy of a Civilization*. London: Routledge.

Kemp, Barry J. 2006. *Ancient Egypt: Anatomy of a Civilization*. 2nd ed. London: Routledge.

Kertzer, David L. 1988. *Ritual, Politics, and Power*. New Haven: Yale University Press.

Khatib-Chahidi, Jane 1992. Milk Kinship in Shi'ite Islamic Iran. In Vanessa Maher, Ed., *The Anthropology of Breast Feeding: Natural Law or Social Construct*. Cross-Cultural Perspectives on Women. Oxford: Berg (distributed by St. Martin's Press, New York).

King James Bible. (2017). *King James Bible Online*. www.kingjamesbibleonline .org/ [original work published 1769].

Kingdon, J. 1979. *East African Mammals*. Chicago: The University of Chicago Press.

Kirch, Patrick V. 1990. Monumental Architecture and Power in Polynesian Kingdoms: A Comparison of Tonga and Hawaii. *World Architecture* 22(2: Monuments and the Monumental):206–222.

Kirch, Patrick V. 2001. Polynesian Feasting in Ethnohistorical, Ethnographic, and Archeological Contexts. In Michael Dietler & Brian Hayden, Eds., *Feasts: Archeological and Ethnographic Perspectives on Food, Politics, and Power* (pp. 243–286). Berkeley: University of California Press.

Kisch, Bruno 1965. *Scales and Weights: A Historical Outline*. New Haven: Yale University Press.

Klam, Mathew 2001. Experiencing Ecstasy. *New York Times Magazine*, January 21, 38–43, 64, 68, 72, 78–79.

Klein, Jacob 1981. *Three Šulgi Hymns: Sumerian Royal Hymns Glorifying King Šulgi of Ur*. Ramta-Gan: Bar-Ilan University Press.

Klein, Richard A., Michelangelo Vianello, Fred Hasselman, et al. 2018. Many Labs 2: Investigating variation in replicability across samples and settings. *Advances in Methods and Practices in Psychological Science* 1:443–490. https://doi.org/10.1177/2515245918810225.

Kolata, Alan L. 2004. The Flow of Cosmic Power: Religion, Ritual, and People of Tiwanaku. In Margaret Upimg-Sánchez, Ed., *Tiwanaku: Ancestors of the Inca* (pp. 96–113, 120–124). Lincoln: Denver Art Museum & University of Nebraska Press.

Kolb, Michael J. 2011. The Genesis of Monuments in Island Societies. In Michael E. Smith, Ed., *The Comparative Archaeology of Complex Societies* (pp. 138–164). Cambridge: Cambridge University Press.

Kominsky, Jonathan F., Kelsey Lucca, Ashley J. Thomas, Michael C. Frank, and J. Kiley Korotayev, Andrey & Victor de Munck 2003. Galton's Asset and Flower's Problem: Cultural Networks and Cultural Units in Cross-Cultural Research. *American Anthropologist* 105:353–358. https://doi.org/10.1525/aa.2003.105.2.353.

Kosmetatou, Elizabeth 2013. Tyche's Force: Lottery and Chance in Greek Government. In Hans Beck, ed., *A Companion to Ancient Greek Government* (pp. 235–251). Wiley Online Library. https://doi.org/10.1002/9781118303214.ch16.

Kövecses, Zoltán 2010. *Metaphor: A Practical Introduction*, 2nd ed. Oxford: Oxford University Press.

Kramer, Samuel Noah 1963. *The Sumerians: Their History, Culture, and Character*. Chicago: University of Chicago Press (Phoenix Books).

Kramrisch, Stella 1981. *The Presence of Śhiva*. Princeton: Princeton University Press.

Krams, Indrikis, Tatjana Krama, Kristine Igaune, & Raivo Mänd 2008. Experimental Evidence of Reciprocal Altruism in the Pied Flycatcher. *Behavioral Ecology and Sociobiology* 62:599–605.

Kristiansen, Kristian, & Thomas B. Larsson 2005. *The Rise of Bronze Age Society: Travels, Transmissions and Transformations*. New York: Cambridge University Press.

Kross, Jessica 1997. "If You Will Not Drink with Me, You Must Fight with Me": The Sociology of Drinking in the Middle Colonies. *Pennsylvania History* 64:28–55.

Kula, Witold 1986. *Measures and Men*. R. Szreter, Trans. Princeton: Princeton University Press.

Kumar, Vinod (Ed.) 2002. *Biological Rhythms*. New York: Springer.

Kummer, Hans, W. Götz, & W. Angst 1974. Triadic Differentiation: An Inhibitory Process Protecting Pair Bonds in Baboons. *Behavior* 49:62–87.

Kuroda, Suehisa 1984. Interactions over Food among Pygmy Chimpanzees. In Randall L. Susman, Ed., *The Pygmy Chimpanzee: Evolutionary Biology and Behavior* (pp. 201–324). New York: Plenum.

Kurtzman, Jeffrey, & Koldau, Linda Maria 2002. Trombe, Trombe d'argento, Trombe squarciate, Tromboni, and Pifferi in Venetian Processions and Ceremonies of the Sixteenth and Seventeenth Centuries, II. Trumpets, Pifferi and Other Instruments in Venetian Processions and Ceremonies. *Journal of Seventeenth-Century Music* 8(1). https://sscm-jscm.org/v8/no1/kurtzman.html.

Lakoff, George, & Johnson, Mark 1980. *Metaphors We Live By*. Chicago: University of Chicago Press.

Langdon, S. 1916. New Inscriptions of Nabuna'id. *The American Journal of Semitic Languages and Literatures* 32:102–117.

Langille, Jesse J., & Charles R. Gallistel 2020. Locating the Engram: Should we Look for Plastic Synapses or Information-Storing Molecules? *Neurobiology of Learning and Memory* 169:107164.

Laponce, J. A. 1981. *Left and Right: The Topography of Political Perceptions*. Toronto: University of Toronto Press.

Latta, R. Michael 1978. Relation of Status Incongruence to Personal Space. *Personality and Social Psychology Bulletin* 4:143–146.

Lattimore, Richard 1951. *The Iliad of Homer*. Chicago: University of Chicago Press. https://homer.library.northwestern.edu.

Laye, Camara 1966. *L'Enfant Noir*. Ed. Joyce A. Hutchinson. Cambridge: Cambridge University Press.

Leach, Edmund 1972. The Influence of Cultural Context on Non-Verbal Communication in Man. In Robert A. Hinde, Ed., *Non-Verbal Communication* (pp. 315–344). Cambridge: Cambridge University Press.
Leakey. Louis S. B. 1966. *White African: An Early Autobiography.* Cambridge, MA: Schenkman.
Lechtman, Heather 1984. Andean Systems and the Development of Prehistoric Metallurgy. *Technology and Culture* 25:1–36.
Lechtman, Heather 2007. The Inka, and Andean Metallurgical Tradition. In Richard Berger, Craig Morris, & Ramiro Matos Medieta, Eds., *Variations in the Expression of Inka Power: A Symposium at Dumbarton Oaks, 18 and 19 October 1997* (pp. 314–355). Washington, DC: Dumbarton Oaks (distributed by Harvard University Press).
Leclerc Jean, & Claude Masset 2006. L'évolution de la pratique funéraire dans la sépulture collective néolithique de La Chaussée-Tirancourt (Somme). *Bulletin de la Société Préhistorique Française.* 103:87–116.
Lee, Junghee, Keith H. Nuechterlein, Barbara J. Knowlton, Carrie E. Bearden, Tyrone D. Cannon, Alan P. Fiske, Livon Ghermezi, Jacqueline N Hayata, Gerhard S Hellemann, William P Horan, Kimmy Kee, Robert S Kern, Kenneth L Subotnik, Catherine A Sugar, Joseph Ventura, Cindy M Yee, & Michael F Green 2018. Episodic memory for dynamic social interaction across phase of illness in schizophrenia. *Schizophrenia Bulletin* 44:620–630.
Lee, Sandra Soon-Jin 2000. Dys-Appearing Tongues and Bodily Memories: The Aging of First-Generation Resident Koreans in Japan. *Ethos* 28:198–223.
Lee, Won-bok 1998. Largest Buddhist Temple Bell: The Divine Bell, Emille. *Koreana* 12(4):70–71.
Lehner, Mark 1998. *The Complete Pyramids: Solving the Ancient Mysteries.* London: Thames & Hudson.
Leidy, Denise Patry 2008. *The Art of Buddhism: An Introduction to Its History and Meaning.* Boston: Shambhala.
Lender, Mark Edward, & James Kirby Martin 1982. *Drinking in America: A History.* New York: Free Press.
Leroi-Gourhan, André 1967. *Treasures of Prehistoric Art.* New York: Harry N. Abrams.
Levinson, Stephen C. 2003. *Space in Language And Cognition: Explorations in Cognitive Diversity.* Cambridge: Cambridge University Press.
Levinson, Stephen C. 2006. On the Human "Interaction System." In Nicholas J. Enfield & Stephen C. Levinson (Eds.). *Roots Of Human Sociality: Culture, Cognition and Interaction* (pp. 30–69). Oxford: Berg.
Lévi-Strauss, Claude 1949 [1961]. *The Elementary Structures of Kinship*, revised ed. James H. Bell, John R. von Sturmer, & Rodney Needham, Trans. Boston: Beacon.
Lewis, David Levering 2008. *God's Crucible: Islam and the Making of Europe, 570 to 1215.* New York: Norton.
Lewis, Mark Edward 1990. *Sanctioned Violence in Early China.* Albany: State University of New York Press.

Lhôte, Jean-Marie 1994. *Historie des Jeux de Société: Géométries du Désir*. Paris: Flammarion.

Li, Eric P. H., Min, Hyun Jeong, Blek, Russell W., Kimura, Junko, & Bahl, Shalini 2008. Skin Lightening and Beauty in Four Asian Cultures. *Advances in Consumer Research* 34:444–449.

Li, Zhang 2011. Long-Distance Interactions as Reflected in the Earliest Chinese Bronze Mirrors. In Lothar von Falkenhausen, Ed., *Beyond the Surface: The Lloyd Cotsen Study Collection of Chinese Bronze Mirrors, Volume II: Studies* (pp. 34–49). Los Angeles: UCLA Cotsen Institute of Archaeology Press.

Lichtenberger, Elisabeth 2001. Wem Gehört die Dritte Dimension der Stadt? *Mitteilungen der Österreichischen Geographischen Gesellschaft* 143:7–34.

Lindauer, Owen, & Blitz, John H. 1997. Higher Ground: The Archeology of North American Platform Mounds. *Journal of Archeological Research* 5:169–207.

Lindblom, Gerhard 1920. *The Akamba in British East Africa: An Ethnological Monograph*, Vol. 17. 2nd ed. Upsala: Archives d'Études Orientales.

Lindenbaum, Shirley 1979. *Kuru Sorcery: Disease and Danger in the New Guinea Highlands*. Palo Alto: Mayfield.

Lindon, Thomas 1990. Oríkì Òrìsà: The Yoruba Prayer of Praise. *Journal of Religion in Africa* 29:205–224.

Linduff, Kathryn M., & Yan, Sun 2004. *Gender and Chinese Archeology*. Lanham: Rowman Altamira.

Linke, Uli 1999. *Blood and Nation: The European Esthetics of Race*. Philadelphia: University of Pennsylvania Press.

Linrothe, Robert N., Jeff Watt, Marylin M. Rhie, & Carly Busta 2004. *Demonic Divine: Himalayan Art and Beyond*. Chicago: Serindia.

Liu, Lawrence 1989. *Chinese Architecture*. New York: Rizzoli.

Liu, Shari, Tomer D. Ullman, Joshua B. Tenenbaum, & Elizabeth S. Spelke 2017. Ten-month-old infants infer the value of goals from the costs of actions. *Science* 358:1038–1041.

Locke, Harvey 2006. The Spiritual Dimension of Moving to the Mountains. In Laurence A. G. Moss, Ed., *The Amenity Migrants: Seeking and Sustaining Mountains and Their Cultures* (pp. 26–33). Wallingford: CAB International.

Loerke, William C. 1981. Observations on the Representation of Doxa in the Mosaics of S. Maria Maggiore, Rome, and St. Catherine's, Sinai. *Gesta* 20:15–22.

Loofs-Wissowa, Helmut 1991. Dongson Drums: Instruments of Shamanism or Regalia? *Arts Asiatiques* 46:39–49.

Louth, Andrew 2004. Light, Vision, and Religious Experience in Byzantium. In Matthew T. Kapstein, Ed., *The Presence of Light: Divine Radiance and Religious Experience* (pp. 85–103). Chicago: University of Chicago Press.

Love, Michael 1999. Ideology, Material Culture, and Daily Practice in Pre-Classic Mesoamerica: A Pacific Coast Perspective. In David C. Grove & Rosemary A. Joyce, Eds., *Social Patterns in Pre-Classic Mesoamerica* (pp. 127–153). Washington, DC: Dumbarton Oaks.

Lutz, Catherine 1988. *Unnatural Emotions: Everyday Sentiments on a Micronesian Atoll and Their Challenge to Western Theory*. Chicago: University of Chicago Press.
Lyle, Emily B. 1982. Dumézil's Three Functions and the Indo-European Cosmic Structure. *History of Religions* 22:25–44.
Lytwyn, Victor P. 1997. A Dish with One Spoon: The Shared Hunting Grounds Agreement in the Great Lakes and St. Lawrence Valley Region. In David H. Pentland, Ed., *Papers of the Twenty-Eighth Algonquin Conference* (pp. 210–227). Winnipeg: University of Manitoba.
Mace, Ruth, & Mark Pagel 1994. The Comparative Method in Anthropology. *Current Anthropology* 35:549–564. https://doi.org/10.1086/204317.
Maestripieri, Dario, & Josep Call 1996. Mother-Infant Communication in Primates. *Advances in the Study of Behavior* 25:613–642.
Magnone, Paolo 1992. The Development of "Tejas" from the Vedas to the Purāṇas. *Wiener Zeitschrift für die Kunde Südasiens/Vienna Journal of South Asian Studies*. 1993 Supplement Band:137–147.
Maida, Carl A. 1984. Social-Network Considerations in the Alcohol Field. In Marc Galanter, Ed., *Recent Developments in in Alcoholism, Volume 2: Learning and Social Models, Alcohol and the Liver, Aging and Alcoholism, Anthropology* (pp. 339–353). New York: Plenum Press.
Malinowski, Bronislaw 1935 [1978]. *Coral Gardens and Their Magic: A Study of the Methods of Tilling the Soil and of Agricultural Rites in the Trobriand Islands*. New York: Dover.
Mallory, J. P. 1989. *In Search of the Indo-Europeans: Language, Archeology, and Myth*. New York: Thames & Hudson.
Mallory, J. P. & D. Q. Adams 1997. *Encyclopedia of Indo-European Culture*. Oxford: Taylor and Frances.
Mallory, J. P., & D. Q. Adams 2006. *The Oxford Introduction to Proto-Indo-European and Proto-Indo-European World*. Oxford: Oxford University Press.
Mangin, P. Eugène 1916. Essai sur les us et coûtumes du people Mossi au Soudan Occidental, Vienna. *Anthropos* Bd. 10/11, H. 3./4. (May–Aug., 1915/1916), pp. 323–331. www.jstor.org/stable/40442823.
Mann, Janet, & Smuts, Barbara 1999. Behavioral Development in Wild Bottlenose Dolphin Newborns (*Tursiops Sp.*). *Behaviour* 136: 529–566.
Manson, Joseph H., Carlos D. Navarette, Joan B. Silk, and Susan Perry 2004. Time-Matched Grooming in Female Primates? New Analyses from Two Species. *Animal Behaviour* 67:493–500.
Marett, R. R. 1929 [1909]. *The Threshold of Religion*. London: Methuen and Company.
Margoni, Francesco, Renée Baillargeon, & Luca Surian 2018. Infants Distinguish between Leaders and Bullies. *Proceedings of the National Academy of Sciences* 115: E8835–E8843.
Margoni, Francesco, Luca Surian, & Renée Baillargeon 2023, The Violation-of-Expectation Paradigm: A Conceptual Overview. *Psychological Review* 131:716–748.

Margoni, Francesco, & Lotte Thomsen 2024. How Infants Predict Respect-Based Power. *Cognitive Psychology* 152: 101671. https://osf.io/preprints/psyarxiv/m426d.

Marx, Patricia Ann 1988. *The Attributes of Athena in Athenian Narrative Art, circa 675 to 530 BC.* University of Maryland, College Park.

Mason, Kathryn F. 1988. Co-Wife Relationships can be Amicable as well as Conflictual: The Case of the Moosé of Burkina Faso. *Canadian Journal of African Studies/Revue canadienne des études africaines* 22:615–624.

Mason, M., J. C. Magee, S. T. Fiske 2013. Neural substrates of social status inference: Roles of medial and prefrontal cortex and superior temporal sulcus. *Journal of Cognitive Neuroscience* 26:1131–1140. https://doi.org/10.1162/jocn_a_00553.

Matusky, Patricia 2008. Borneo: Sabah, Sarawak, Brunei, Kalimantin. In Terry E. Miller & Sean Williams, Eds., *The Garland Handbook of Southeast Asian Music* (pp. 406–414). New York: Routledge.

Maynard Smith, J. 1991. Must reliable signals always be costly? *Animal Behavior* 47:1115–11120.

McAuliffe, Katherine, Peter R. Blake, Nikolaus Steinbeis, & Felix Warneken 2017. The developmental foundations of human fairness. *Nature Human Behaviour* 1(2):0042.

McCrink, Koleen, & Karen Wynn 2007. Ratio Abstraction by 6-month-old Infants. *Psychological Science* 18(8):740–745.

McDermott, Joesph P. 1999. Emperor, Élites, and Commoners: The Community Pact Ritual of the Late Ming. In Joseph P. McDermott, Ed., *State and Court Ritual in China* (pp. 299–351). Cambridge: Cambridge University Press.

McGuire, Joseph D. 1899. Pipes and Pipe-Smoking Customs of the American Aborigines, Based on Material in the US National Museum. Annual Report of the Smithsonian Institution, 1897 I:351–645.

McNeill, William H. 1995. *Keeping Together in Time: Dance and Drill in Human History.* Cambridge: Harvard University Press.

Mech, L. David 1970. *The Wolf: The Ecology and Behavior of an Endangered Species.* Garden City: American Museum of Natural History, Natural History Press.

Mehrabia, Albert 1981. *Silent Messages: Implicit Communication of Emotions and Attitudes.* 2nd ed. Belmont: Wadsworth.

Mehta, Deepak 1986. Circumcision, Body, Masculinity: The Ritual Wound and Collective Violence. In Veena Das, Arthur Kleinman, Mamphela Ramphele, & Pameal Reynolds, Eds., *Violence and Subjectivity* (pp. 79–101). Berkeley: University of California Press.

Meillassoux, Claude 1975 [1981]. *Maidens, Meal and Money: Capitalism and the Domestic Economy.* Cambridge: Cambridge University Press.

Meisch Lynn A. 2002. *Andean Entrepreneurs: Otavalo Merchants and Musicians in the Global Arena.* Austin: University of Texas Press.

Melamed, Tuvia, & Nicholas Bozionelos, 1992. Managerial Promotion and Height. *Psychological Reports* 71:587–593.

Melitz, Jacques 1974. *Primitive and Modern Money: An Interdisciplinary Approach*. Reading, MA: Addison-Wesley.

Meng, Xianwei, Yo Nakawake, Hiroshi Nitta, Kazuhide Hashiya, & Yusuke Moriguchi 2019. Space and Rank: Infants Expect Agents in Higher Position to be Socially Dominant. *Proceedings of the Royal Society B* 286:20191674. https://doi.org/10.1098/rspb.2019.1674.

Menuhin, Yehudi 1984. Preface. In Arthur Wills, *Organ: Yehudi Menuhin Music Guides*. London: Macdonald.

Meristo, Marek, Karin Strid, & Luca Surian 2016. Preverbal Infants' Ability to Encode the Outcome of Distributive Actions. *Infancy* 21(3):353–72.

Mettinger, Tryggve N. D. 1982. The Dethronement of Saboath: Studies in Shem and Kabod Theologies. Translated by Frederick H. Cryer. *Coniectanea Biblia, Old Testament Series* 19. Lund: CWK Gleerup.

Meyer C., R. Ganslmeier, & K. W. Alt (2008) The Human Skeletal Remains from the Neolithic Burial Chamber of Benzingerode. Anthropological Analyses of the Inhumations in a Collective Grave of the Bernburg Culture. *Archäologie in Sachsen-Anhalt Sonderband* 7:107–151.

Meyer, William B. 1994. Bringing Hypsography Back In: Altitude and Residence in American Cities. *Urban Geography* 15:505–513.

Meyer, William B. 2005. *The Poor on the Hilltops? The Vertical Fringe of a Late Nineteenth-Century American City. Annals of the Association of American Geographers* 95(4):773–788.

Michailidou, Anna 2005. *Weight and Value in Pre-Coinage Societies: An Introduction*. Research Center for Greek and Roman Antiquity; Melethmata, 42. Athens. Paris: Diffusion de Boccard.

Michalowski, Piotr 1989. *The Lamentation over the Destruction of Sumer and Ur*. Winona Lake: Eisenbraums.

Michalski, Sergiusz 1998. *Public Monuments: Art in Political Bondage 1870–1997*. London: Reaktion.

Miller, Lisa F., Paul Rozin, & Alan P. Fiske 1998. Food Sharing and Feeding Another Person Suggest Intimacy: A Study of American College Students. *European Journal for Social Psychology* 28:423–436.

Miller, Mary Ellen 1986. *The Murals of Bonampak*. Princeton: Princeton University Press.

Mix, Kelly S., Susan Cohen Levine, & Janellen Huttenlocher 1999. Early Fraction Calculation Ability. *Developmental Psychology* 35:164–174.

Monier-Williams Sanskrit-English Dictionary 2003. www.sanskrit-lexicon.uni-koeln.de/scans/MWScan/2020/web/webtc2/index.php; www.sanskrit-lexicon.uni-koeln.de/scans/MWScan/2020/web/webtc/indexcaller.php. [Based on the IITS – Cologne Digital Sanskrit Lexicon: www.sanskrit-lexicon.uni-koeln.de/scans/MWScan/tamil/index.html]. Accessed April 22, 2025.

Montagu, Ashley 1979, The Skin, Touch, and Human Development. In Shirley Weitz, Ed., *Nonverbal Communication: Readings with Commentary* (pp. 328–337). 2nd ed. New York: Oxford.

Montagu, Ashley 1986. *Touching: The Human Significance of the Skin*. 3rd ed. New York: Harper & Row.
Morinis, Alan 1985. The Ritual Experience: Pain and the Transformation of Consciousness in Ordeals of Initiation. *Ethos* 13:150–174. https://doi.org/10.1525/eth.1985.13.2.02a00040.
Morris, Desmond 1973. *Intimate Behavior*. New York: Bantam.
Morris, Desmond 1977. *Man Watching: A Field Guide to Human Behavior*. New York: Harry Abrams.
Morris, Friedell 1969. On the Structure of Shared Awareness. *Behavioral Science* 14:28–39.
Morris, Sarah 1997. Homer and the Near East. In Ian Morris & Barry B. Powell, Eds., *A New Companion to Homer* (pp. 599–623). Brill.
Morrison, India 2012. CT Afferents. *Current Biology* 22(3):R77–R78.
Moss, Cynthia 2000. *Elephant Memories*. Chicago: University of Chicago Press.
Muir, Edward 1981. *Civic Ritual in Renaissance Venice*. Princeton: Princeton University Press.
Muir, Edward 2005: *Ritual in Early Modern Europe: New Approaches to European History*. 2nd ed. Cambridge: Cambridge University Press.
Muroyama, Yasuyuki, & Yukimaru Sugiyama 1994. Grooming Relationships in Two Species of Chimpanzees. In Richard W. Wrangham, W. C. McGrew, Frans B. M. de Waal, & Paul G. Heltne, Eds., *Chimpanzee Politics* (pp. 169–180). Cambridge: Harvard University Press.
Murphey, Robert M., Mateus J. R. Paranhos da Costa, Roberto Gomes da Silva, & Roberto C. de Souza 1995. Allonursing in River Buffalo, *Bubalus bubalis*: Nepotism, Incompetence, or Thievery? *Animal Behaviour* 49:1611–1616.
Murray, H. J. R. 1952. *A History of Board Games Other than Chess*. Oxford: Oxford University Press (Clarendon).
Needham, Rodney Ed. 1973. *Right and Left: Essays on Dual Symbolic Classification*. Chicago: University of Chicago Press.
Neihardt, John Gneisenau 1979. *Black Elk Speaks: Being the Life Story of a Holy Man of the Oglala Sioux*. Lincoln: University of Nebraska Press.
Nemat-Nejat, Karen Rhea 1993. *Cuneiform Mathematical Texts as a Reflection of Everyday Life in Mesopotamia*. New Haven: American Oriental Society.
Nesse, Randolph M., Ed. 2001. *Evolution and the Capacity for Commitment*. New York: Russell Sage Foundation.
Newman, Cathy 2001. *National Geographic Fashion*. Washington: National Geographic Society.
Nguyễn, Phong T. 2008. Vietnam. In Terry E. Miller & Sean Williams, Eds., *The Garland Handbook of Southeast Asian Music* (pp. 247–290). New York: Routledge.
Nieder, Andreas 2016. The Neuronal Code for Number. *Nature Reviews Neuroscience* 17:366–382.
Nissen, Hans J. 1988. *The Early History of the Ancient Near East 9000–2000 BC*. Elizabeth Lutzeier, Trans. Chicago: University of Chicago Press.

Nissen, Hans J., Peter Damerow, & Robert K. Englund 1993. *Archaic Bookkeeping: Early Writing and Techniques of Economic Administration in the Ancient Near East.* Paul Larsen, transl. Chicago: University of Chicago Press.

Nuckolls, Charles W. 1990. The Durbar Incident. *Modern Asian Studies* 24:529–559.

Nyrop, Kristoffer 1901. The Kiss and Its History. William Frederick Harvey, Trans. London: Sands. [The English translation is from the Danish 2nd edition, 1897.]

Olausson, Håkan, Johan Wessberg, Francis McGlone, & Åke Vallbo 2010. The Neurophysiology of Unmyelinated Tactile Afferents. *Neuroscience & Biobehavioral Reviews* 34(2):185–191.

Olaveson, Tim 2003. "Connectedness" and the Rave Experience: Rave as New Religious Movement? In Graham St. John, Ed., *Rave Culture and Religion* (pp. 85–106). London: Routledge.

Olivova, Vera 1984. *Sports and Games in the Ancient World.* London: Orbis.

Onions, Charles Talbut, George Washington Salisbury Friedrichsen, & Robert William Burchfield 1965. *The Oxford Dictionary of English Etymology.* Oxford: Clarendon Press.

Oppenheim, A. Leo 1949. The Golden Garments of the Gods. *Journal of Near Eastern Studies* 8:172–219.

Oschema, Klaus 2006. Blood-Brothers: A Ritual of Friendship and the Construction of the Imagined Barbarian in the Middle Ages. *Journal of Medieval History* 32:275–301.

Ottenberg, Simon 1994. Initiations. In Philip K. Bock, Ed., *Psychological Anthropology* (pp. 351–377). Westport: Praeger.

Oxford English Dictionary 2022. Online. www.oed.com.

Panaino, Antonio 2002. The Lists of Names of Ahura Mazdā (Yašt 1) and Vayu (Yašt XV). https://bit.ly/40R6aaQ. See also https://ahuramazda.com/pages/101_names_of_ahuramazda_.html. Accessed June 7, 2025.

Panouillé, Jean-Pierre 2003. *Les Châteaux Forts dans la France du Moyen Âge.* Rennes, France: Éditions Ouest-France.

Paper, Jordan 1988. *Offering Smoke: The Sacred Pipe and Native American Religion.* Moscow, Idaho: University of Idaho Press.

Paper, Jordan 2005. Sacred Pipe. In Suzanne J. Crawford & Dennis F. Kelley, Eds., *American Indian Religious Traditions* Vol. 3 (pp. 935–941). Santa Barbara: ABC-Clio.

Park, Yunji, Alexandria A. Viegut, & Percival G. Matthews 2021. More than the Sum of its Parts: Exploring the Development of Ratio Magnitude versus Simple Magnitude Perception. *Developmental Science* 24(3):e13043.

Parkinson, Carolyn, & Thalia Wheatley 2015. The Repurposed Social Brain. *Trends in Cognitive Sciences* 19(3):133–141.

Parsons, Talcott 1967. On the Concept of Influence. In Talcott Parsons, *Sociological Theory and Modern Society* (pp. 355–382). New York: Free Press.

Partridge, Eric 1958. *Origins: A Short Etymological Dictionary of Modern English.* New York: Macmillan.

Pauketat, Timothy R., & Susan M. Alt 2003. Mounds, Memory, and Contested Missipian History. In Ruth M. Van Dyke & Susan E. Alcock, Eds., *Archeologies of Memory* (pp. 151–179). Malden: Blackwell.

Peirce, Charles S. 1931–1958. *The Collected Papers of C. S. Peirce*. Edited by Charles Hartshorne, Paul Weiss, & A. W. Burks. Cambridge: Harvard University Press.

Peng, Tan Huay 2005. *What's in a Chinese Character*. Middle Island: New World Press.

Perrot, Jean 1965. *L'Orgue: De se Ses Origines Hellénistiques à la Fin du XIIIe Siècle*. Paris: Picard.

Peters, John P. 1921. The Tower of Babel at Borsippa. *Journal of the American Oriental Society* 41:157–159.

Piaget, Jean 1932a. *The Language and Thought of the Child*. 2nd ed. New York: Harcourt, Brace.

Piaget, Jean 1932b [1973]. *Le Jugement Moral Chez L'Enfant*. Bibliothèque de Philosophie Contemporaine. Paris: Presses Universitaries de France. [Translated by Marjorie Gabain 1965 as *The Moral Judgment of the Child*. New York: Free Press].

Piaget, Jean 1941–1951 [1965]. *Études Sociologiques*. Geneva: Librarie Droz.

Piaget, Jean 1945. *La Formation du Symbole Chez L'enfant: Imitation, Jeu et Rêve, Image et Représentation*. Neuchâtel, France: Delachaux & Niestlé.

Piaget, Jean 1952. *The Child's Conception of Number*. New York: Humanities Press.

Piaget, Jean 1962. *Play, Dreams and Imitation in Childhood* NewYork: Norton.

Pinault, David 1992. *The Shiites: Ritual and Popular Piety in a Muslim Community*. New York: St. Martin's.

Pirazzoli-T'Serstevens, Michelle 1979. The Bornze Drums of Shizhai shan, their Social and Ritual Significance. In Ralph B. Smith & William Watson, *Early South East Asia: Essays in Archeology, History and Historical Geography* (pp. 125–136). Oxford: Oxford University Press.

Pitt-Rivers, Julian 1968. Pseudo-Kinship. In David L. Sills, Ed. *International Encyclopedia of the Social Sciences*, Vol. 7 (pp. 408–413). New York: Macmillan and Free Press.

Pitt-Rivers, Julian 1973. The Kith and the Kin. In Jack Goody, Ed., *The Character of Kinship* (pp. 89–105). Cambridge: Cambridge University Press.

Pohl, Mary E. D., Kevin O. Pope, & Christopher von Nagy 2002. Olmec Origins of Mesoamerican Writing. *Science* 298:1984–1987.

Polanyi, Karl 1957. The Semantics of Money Uses. *Explorations* 8:19–29. Reprinted in George Dalton, Ed., 1968, *Primitive, Archaic and Modern Economies: Essays of Karl Polanyi* (pp. 175–190). Garden City: Doubleday (Anchor Books).

Polanyi, Karl 1971. *Primitive, Archaic, and Modern Economies: Essays of Karl Polanyi*. George Dalton, Ed. Boston: Beacon

Pollock, Susan 1999. *Ancient Mesopotamia: The Eden that Never Was*. Cambridge: Cambridge University Press.

Pool, Christopher A. 2007. *Olmec Archeology and Early Mesoamerica*. Cambridge: Cambridge University Press.

Poole, Fitz John Porter 1985. Coming Into Social Being: Cultural Images of Infants in Bimin-Kuskusmin Folk Psychology. In Geoffrey M. White & John Kirkpatrick, Eds., *Person, Self, and Experience: Exploring Pacific Ethnopsychologies* (pp. 183–242). Berkeley: University of California Press.

Powell, Lindsey J., & Elizabeth S. Spelke 2013. Preverbal Infants Expect Members of Social Groups to Act Alike. *Proceedings of the National Academy of Sciences* 110:E3965–E3972.

Powers, Medelon 1991. Decay from Within: The Inevitable Doom of the American Saloon. In Susan Barrows & Robin Room, Eds., *Drinking: Behavior and Belief in Modern History* (pp. 112–131). Berkeley: University of California Press.

Price, Percival 1983. *Bells and Man*. Oxford: Oxford University Press.

Price, Percival 2004. Japanese Bells. In Calvin L. French, Ed., *Studies in Japanese Culture* 2 (pp. 35–66). Center for Japanese Studies Publications, Ann Arbor, Michigan: University of Michigan University Library, Scholarly Publishing Office. http://hdl.handle.net/2027/spo.bby8150.0001.001.

Pritchard, James B. 1954. *The Ancient Near East in Pictures Relating to the Old Testament*. Princeton: Princeton University Press.

Pritchard, James B. 1969. *The Ancient Near East; Supplementary Text and Pictures Relating to the Old Testament*. Princeton: Princeton University Press.

Proferes, Theodore N. 2007. *Vedic Ideals of Sovereignty and the Poetics of Power*. American Oriental Series Vol. 90. New Haven: American Oriental Society.

Prudhommeau, Germanine 1965. *La Danse Greque Antique, Vol 2*. Paris: Editions CNRS. Plate 229 reproduced from Louvre Museum 1936–38, *Encyclopedie Photographique de L'Art*. Paris: Edition Tel. Vol 2, 277, A. Figure 171. Plate 303 reproduced from Ernst Pfuhl 1923, *Maelrei und Zeichnung der Greichen*. Munich: Bruckmann. Plate 536 from Scheurleer Museum, The Hague. Corpus VII 1 III H b 1, 1. Bronze "bracelet" of 7 women from Olympia, 12th century BC. Plate 835 from Louis Sechan 1926, *Etudes sur la Tragedie Grecque dans ses rapports avec la Ceramique*. Thesis, Paris. p. 2.

Pun, Anthea, Susan A. J. Birch, & Andrew Scott Baron 2016. Infants Use Relative Numerical Group Size to Infer Social Dominance. *Proceedings of the National Academy of Sciences* 113:2376–2381.

Pun, Anthea, Susan A. J. Birch, & Andrew Scott Baron 2021. The Power of Allies: Infants' Expectations of Social Obligations During Intergroup Conflict. *Cognition* 211:104630.

Quiggin, A. Hingston 1949. *A Survey of Primitive Money: The Beginnings of Currency*. London: Methuen.

Quilter, Jeffrey 2005. *Treasures of the Andes: The Glories of Inca and Pre-Columbian South America*. London: Duncan Baird.

Quinones Kebber, Eloise 1985. *Codex Telleriano-Remensis: Ritual, Divination, and History in A Pictorial Aztec Manuscript*. Austin: University of Texas Press.

Rabain, Jacqueline 1979 *L'Enfant du Lignage: Du Sevrage à la Class d'Âge chez les Wolof du Sénégal*. Paris: Payot.

Rai, Tage, & Alan Page Fiske 2011. Moral Psychology is Relationship Regulation: Moral Motives for Unity, Hierarchy, Equality, and Proportionality. *Psychological Review* 118:57–75.

Ramsey, William 2007. *Representation Reconsidered.* New York: Cambridge University Press.

Ramsey, William 2018. Maps, Models and Computational Simulations in the Mind. In Mark Sprevak & Matteo Colombo, Eds., *The Routledge Handbook of the Computational Mind*, pp. 259–271. London: Routledge.

Ravines, Rogger 1990. Garagay: Un Centre Cérémonial du Formatif. In Sergio Purin, Ed., *Inca-Perú: 3000 Ans D'Histoire* (pp. 132–143). Brussels: Musées Royaux d'Art et d'Histoire.

Rawls, John 1955. Two Concepts of Rules. *The Philosophical Review* 64:3–32.

Ray, John D. 1986. The Emergence of Writing in Egypt. *World Archaeology* 17:307–316.

Redford, Paul, & Aaron Sorkin 2001 [February 28]. Somebody's Going to Emergency, Somebody's Going to Jail. *The West Wing* (season 2, episode 16). Directed by Jessica Yu. Warner Brothers.

Reece, Steve 1993. *The Stranger's Welcome: Oral Theory and the Aesthetics of the Homeric Hospitality Scene.* Ann Arbor: University of Michigan Press.

Rees, Charlotte E., Knight, Lynn V., & Wilkinson, Clare E. 2007. Doctors Being Up There and We Being Down Here: A Metaphorical Analysis of Talk About Student/Doctor–Patient Relationships. *Social Science & Medicine* 65:725–737.

Renfrew, Colin. 1978. Varna and the Social Context of Early Metallurgy. *Antiquity* 52:199–203.

Revencu, Barbu, & Gergely Csibra 2024. Puppets as Symbols in Early Development: From Whether to How in the Theory of Puppets Debate. *Cognitive Development* 71:101487. https://doi.org/10.1016/j.cogdev.2024.101487.

Reynolds, Valrae 1990. Myriad Buddhas: A Group of Mysterious Textiles from Tibet. *Orientations* 21(4):39–50.

Rice, Kym S. 1983. *Early American Taverns: For the Entertainment of Friends and Strangers.* Chicago: Regenery Gateway, for the Frances Tavern Museum, New York.

Richards, Audrey I. 1948 [1932]. *Hunger and Work in a Savage Tribe: A Functional Study of Nutrition among the Southern Bantu.* Glencoe: Free Press.

Ricks, Stephen D. 2006. *Dexiosis* and *Dextrarum Iunctio*: The Sacred Handclasp in the Classical and Early Christian World. *The Fauthority Ranking MS Review* 18(1):431–436.

Ringle, William M. 1999. Per-Classic Cityscapes: Ritual Politics among the Early Lowland Maya. In David C. Grove & Rosemary A. Joyce, Eds., *Social Patterns in Pre-Classic Mesoamerica* (pp. 183–223). Washington, DC: Dumbarton Oaks.

Ritov, Oded, Christoph J. Völter, Nichola J. Raihani, & Jan M. Engelmann 2024. No Evidence for Inequity Aversion in Non-Human Animals: A Meta-Analysis of Accept/Reject Paradigms. *Proceedings B* 291(2035):20241452.

Rivers, Victoria Z. 1999. *The Shining Cloth: Dress and Adornment that Glitters.* London: Thames and Hudson.

Robbins, Philip, & Murat Aydede, Eds. 2008. *The Cambridge Handbook of Situated Cognition*. Cambridge: Cambridge University Press.

Roberts, Jennifer Tolbert 1982. *Accountability in Athenian Government*. Wisconsin Studies in Classics. Madison: University of Wisconsin Press.

Roberts, Julian V., & Herman, C. Peter 1986. The Psychology of Height: An Empirical Review. In C. Peter Herman, Mark Zanna, & E. Tory Higgins, Eds., *Physical Appearance, Stigma, and Social Behavior* (pp. 113–140). Hillsdale: Lawrence Erlbaum.

Robins, Gay 1993. *Proportion and Style in Ancient Egyptian Art*. New York: University of Texas Press.

Robins, Gay 1994. Some Principles of Compositional Dominance and Gender Hierarchy in Egyptian Art. *Journal of the American Research Center in Egypt* 31:33–40. www.jstor.org/stable/40000664.

Roesler, Ulrike 1997. *Licht und Leuchten im Ṛgveda: Untersuchungen zum Wortfeld des Leuchtens und zer Bedeutung des Lichts*. Swisttal-Odendorf: Indica et Tibetica-Verlag.

Róheim, Géza 1945. *War, Crime and the Covenant*. Journal of Clinical Psychopathology Monograph Series No. I. Monticello: Medical Journal Press.

Rolle, Renate 1989. *The World of the Sythians*. F. G. Wells, transl. Berkeley: University of California Press.

Roodenburg, Herman 1991. The "Hand of Friendship": Shaking Hands and Other Gestures in the Dutch Republic. In Jan Bremmer & Herman Roodenburg, Eds., *A Cultural History of Gesture: From Antiquity to the Present Day* (pp. 152–189). Cambridge: Polity.

Rose, Naomi Anne 1992. The Social Dynamics of Male Killer Whales, *Orcinus orca*, in Johnstone Strait, British Columbia. PhD dissertation, Department of Biology, University of California, Santa Cruz.

Rosenblatt, J. S. 1994. Psychobiology Of Maternal-Behavior: Contribution to the Clinical Understanding of Maternal-Behavior Among Humans. *Acta Paediatrica* 83:3–8.

Rosenfeld, Paul, Giacalone, Robert A., & Kennedy, John G. 1987. Of Status and Suits: Personal Space Invasions in an Administrative Setting. *Social Behavior and Personality* 15:97–99.

Rossing, Thomas D. 2000. *Science of Percussion Instruments*. Singapore: World Scientific.

Roth, Martha T. (Editor-in-Charge) 1977. *The Assyrian Dictionary of the Oriental*. Institute of the University Of Chicago.

Rothschild-Whitt, Joyce 1979. The Collectivist Organization: An Alternative to Rational-Bureaucratic Models. *American Sociological Review* 44:509–527.

Rotman, Andy (Transl.) 2008. *Divine Stories: Divyāvadāna Part 1*. Boston: Wisdom Publications.

Rowe, Ann Pollard 1984. *Costumes and Featherwork of the Lords of Chimor: Textiles from Peru's North Coast*. Washington, DC: Textile Museum.

Rozin, Paul, Carol Nemeroff, Marcia Wane, & Amy Sherrod 1989. Operation of the Sympathetic Magical Law of Contagion in Interpersonal Attitudes among Americans. *Bulletin of the Psychonomic Society* 27:367–370.

Ruiz, Teofilo 2009. The Symbolic Meaning of Sword and Palio in Late Medieval and Early Modern Ritual Entries: The Case of Seville. *Memoria y Civilzation* 12:13–48.

Saffire, William 2008. Is This the End of the High-Five? *New York Times*, July 6. www.nytimes.com/2008/07/06/magazine/06wwln-safire-t.html?ref=magazine. Accessed April 28, 2025.

Saggs, H. W. F. 1995. *Babylonians. Peoples of the Past.* London: British Museum Press.

Sahlins, Marshall 1965. On the Sociology of Primitive Exchange. In Michael Banton, ed., *The Relevance of Models for Social Anthropology.* Association of Social Anthropologists, Monograph 1. London: Tavistock.

Samuels, A., Sevenich, M., Gifford, T., Sullivan, T., & Sustman, J. 1989. Gentle Rubbing Among Bottlenose Dolphins. *Eighth Biennial Conference on the Biology of Marine Mammals*, Pacific Grove, CA, Abstracts.

Sanchez, Julia L. J. 2007. Procession and Performance: Recreating Ritual Soundscapes among the Ancient Maya. *The World of Music* 49(2):35–44.

Sánchez-Moreno, Eduardo 2001. Cross-Cultural Links in Ancient Iberia: Socio-Economic Anatomy of Hospitality. *Oxford Journal of Archaeology* 20:391–414.

Sanders, Paula 2001. Robes of Honor in Fatamid Egypt. In Steward Gordon, Ed., *Robes and Honor: The Medieval World of Investiture* (pp. 225–239). New York: Palgrave.

Sapir, Edward 1949 [1927]. The Unconscious Patterning of Behavior in Society. In *Selected Writings of Edward Sapir in Language, Culture, and Personality* (pp. 544–559). David G. Mandelbaum, Ed. Berkeley: University of California Press.

Saunders, Nicholas J. 1998. Stealers of Light, Traders in Brilliance: Amerindian Metaphysics in the Mirror of Conquest. *RES: Anthropology and Aesthetics* 33(1):225–252.

Saunders, Nicholas J. 1999. Biographies of Brilliance: Pearls, Transformations of Matter and Being, c. AD 1492. *World Archeology* 31:243–257.

Saunders, Nicholas J. 2003. "Catching the Light": Technologies of Power and Enchantment in Pre-Columbian Goldworking. In Jeffrey Quilter & John W. Hoopes, Eds., *Gold and Power in Ancient Costa Rica, Panama, and Columbia: A Symposium at Dumbarton Oaks, 9 and 10 October 1999* (pp. 15–47). Washington, DC: Dumbarton Oaks.

Scarpari, Maurizio 2000. *Splendors of Ancient China.* London: Thames & Hudson.

Schäfer, Heinrich 1974. *Principles of Egyptian Art.* Emma Brunner-Traut, Ed.; John Baines, Transl. Oxford: Clarendon Press.

Scharfe, Hartmut 1985. The Vedic Word for "King." *Journal of the American Oriental Society* 105:543–548

Schele, Linda 1997. *Hidden Faces of the Maya.* Photography by Jorge Pérez de Lara. [no city given]: Impetus Comunicación.

Schelling, Thomas C., 2006. *Strategies of Commitment and Other Essays.* Cambridge, MA: Harvard University Press.

Schieffelin, Edward L. 1976. *The Sorrow of the Lonely and the Burning of the Dancers.* New York: St. Martin's.

Schiffrin, Deborah 1974. Handwork as Ceremony: The Case of the Handshake. *Semiotica* 12:189–202.

Schirmer, Annett, Ilona Croy, & Rochelle Ackerley 2023. What Are C-Tactile Afferents and How Do They Relate to "Affective Touch." *Neuroscience & Biobehavioral Reviews* 151:10523610–1016.

Schneider, David M. 1980. *American Kinship: A Cultural Account*, 2nd ed. Chicago: University of Chicago Press.

Schneider, Jane 1978. Peacocks and Penguins: The Political Economy of European Cloth and Colors. *American Ethnologist* 5:413–447.

Schubel, Vernon James 1993. *Religious Performance in Contemporary Islam: Shi'a Devotional Rituals in South Asia.* Columbia: University of South Carolina Press.

Schubert, Lisa, Thomas W. Schubert, & Sascha Topolinski 2012. The Effect of Spatial Elevation on Respect Depends on Merit and Medium. *Social Psychology* 44(2):147–159.

Schubert, Thomas 2005. Your Highness: Vertical Positions as Perceptual Symbols of Power. *Journal of Personality and Social Psychology* 89:1–21.

Schubert, Thomas W., Sven Waldzus, & Beate Seibt 2011. More than a Metaphor: How the Understanding of Power is Grounded in Experience. In Thomas W. Schubert & Anne Maass, Eds., *Spatial Dimensions of Social Thought* (pp. 153–186). Berlin: De Gruyter Mouton.

Schubert, Thomas, Sven Waldzus, & Steffen Giessner 2009. Control Over the Association of Power and Size. *Social Cognition* 27:1–19

Schuberth, D. 1968. *Kaiserliche Liturgie: Die Einbeziehung von Musikinstrumente, Insbesondere del Orgel, in den Frühchristlichen Gottesdienst. Veröffentlichungen der Evangelischen Gesellschaft für Liturgieforschung 17.* Göttingen: Vandenhoeck & Ruprecht.

Schuessler, Axel 2007. *ABC Etymological Dictionary of Old Chinese.* Honolulu: University of Hawai'i Press.

Schuster, Carl 1986. Materials for the Study of Social Symbolism in Ancient and Tribal Art: A Record of Tradition and Continuity. *Volume 1 in 4 books. Edited and written by Edmund Carpenter, assisted by Lorraine Spiess.* Rock Foundation.

Schuster, Carl, & Carpenter, Edmund 1996. *Patterns that Connect: Social Symbolism in Ancient and Tribal Art.* New York: Harry N. Abrams.

Schutz, Alfred 1977/1951 Making Music Together; A Study in Social Relationship. *Social Research* 18:76–97. Reprinted in Janet L. Dolgin, David S. Kemnitzer, & David M. Schneider (Eds.) *Symbolic Anthropology; A Reader in the Study of Symbols and Meanings.* New York: Columbia University Press.

Schwartz, Barry 1981. *Vertical Classification: A Study in Structuralism and the Sociology of Knowledge.* Chicago: University of Chicago Press.

Seabrook, John 2012. The Geek of Chic: How Federico Marchetti Brought E-commerce to Fashion. *New Yorker* September 10, pp. 50–56.
Searle, John R. 1989. How Performatives Work. *Linguistics and Philosophy* 12:535–558.
Sefati, Yitschak 1998. *Love Songs in Sumerian Literature: Critical Edition of the Dumuzi–Inanna Songs.* Ramat Gan: Bar-Ilan University Press.
Selman. Martin J. 1997a. 239 ʽWr. In Willem A. VanGemeron, Ed., *New International Dictionary of Old Testament Theology and Exegesis* (Vol. 1, pp. 324–329). Grand Rapids: Zondervan.
Selman. Martin J. 1997b. 3649 Ypʽ. In Willem A. VanGemeron, Ed., *New International Dictionary of Old Testament Theology and Exegesis* (Vol. 2, pp. 44–46). Grand Rapids: Zondervan.
Selman. Martin J. 1997c. 5585 Ngh. In Willem A. VanGemeron, Ed., *New International Dictionary of Old Testament Theology and Exegesis* (Vol. 3, pp. 18–19). Grand Rapids: Zondervan.
Selman. Martin J. 1997d. 5642 Nhr II. In Willem A. VanGemeron, Ed., *New International Dictionary of Old Testament Theology and Exegesis* (Vol. 3, pp. 497–8). Grand Rapids: Zondervan.
Selman. Martin J. 1997e. 7966 Qrn. In Willem A. VanGemeron, Ed., *New International Dictionary of Old Testament Theology and Exegesis* (Vol. 3, pp. 989–990). Grand Rapids: Zondervan.
Sengupta, Padmini 1951. *Everyday Life in Ancient India.* London: Oxford University Press.
Sereno, Paul C., Garcea, Elena A. A., Jousse, Helene, et al. 2008. Lakeside Cemeteries in the Sahara: 5000 Years of Holocene Population and Environmental Change. *PLoS ONE* 3(8): e2995. https://doi.org/10.1371/journal.pone.0002995.
Sergi, Mark, Alan Page Fiske, William Horan, Robert Kern, Kimmy S. Kee, Kenneth L. Subotnik, Keith H. Nuechterlein, & Michael F. Green 2009. Development of a Measure of Relationship Perception in Schizophrenia. *Psychiatry Research* 166:54–62.
Sharer, Robert J. 1996. *Daily Life in Maya Civilization.* Westport: Greenwood.
Sharma, Vijay Kumar, & M. K. Chandrashekaran 2005. Zeitgebers (*Time Cues*) for Biological Clocks. *Current Science* 89:1136–1146.
Shaw, Miranda 2006. *Buddhist Goddesses of India.* Princeton: Princeton University Press.
Shi, Zhengyu 1997. *Picture Within a Picture: An Illustrated Guide to the Origins of Chinese Characters. Illustrations by Fan-ling Meng.* Beijing: New World Press.
Shih, Hsio-yen 1990. Bronze Drums. *Orientations* 21(1):33–39.
Shubert, Thomas W. 2019. Grounding of Rank: Embodiment, Space, and Magnitude. *Current Opinion in Psychology* 33:222–226.
Shweder, Richard A. 2002. "What about Female Genital Mutilation?" and Why Understanding Culture Matters in the First Place. In Richard A. Shweder, Martha Minow, & Hazel Rose Markus, Eds., *Engaging Cultural Differences: The*

Multicultural Challenge in Liberal Democracies (pp. 216–251). New York: Russell Sage Foundation.

Sidéris, Georges 2002. "Eunuchs of Light": Power, Imperial Ceremonial and Positive Representations of Eunuchs in Byzantium (4th–12th Centuries AD). In Shaun Tougher, Ed., *Eunuchs in Antiquity and Beyond* (pp. 161–175). London: Duckworth.

Sieroszewski, Waclaw 1896 [1993]. *The Yakut: an Experiment in Ethnographic Research. Moskva: Assotsiatsiia "Rossiiskaia polit. entsiklopediia."* Human Relations Area Files translation, HRAF Computer File Ms.: 1044. New Haven: HRAF.

Silverman, William A., & Iain Chalmers 2001. Casting and Drawing Lots: A Time-Honoured Way of Dealing with Uncertainty and Ensuring Fairness. *BMJ* 323(7327):1467–1468.

Simmel, Georg 1900 [1990]. *The Philosophy of Money*. Edited by David Frisby, translated by Tom Bottomore & David Frisby. 2nd enl. ed. London: Routledge.

Simpson, Leanne 2007. Looking after Gdoo-naaganinaa: Precolonial Nishnaabeg Diplomatic and Treaty Relationships. *Wicazo Sa Review* 23, 2:29–42. https://doi.org/10.1353/wic.0.0001.

Singer, Itamar 2002. *Hittite Prayers*. Harry A. Hoffner, Ed. Leiden: Brill.

Singh, Yagyendra Bahadur 1981. *Social Life in Ancient India*. New Delhi: Light and Life.

Sinha, Chitta Ranjan Prasad 1980. *Early Sculpture of Bihar*. Rajendra Nagar, Patna, India: Indological Book Corporation.

Skinner, Elliott Percival 1964. *The Mossi of the Upper Volta: The Political Development of a Sudanese People*. Stanford: Stanford University Press.

Skinner, Patricia 2014. The Gendered Nose and Its Lack: "Medieval" Nose-Cutting and Its Modern Manifestations. *Journal of Women's History* 26(1):45–67. https://doi.org/10.1353/jowh.2014.0008.

Skorupski, Peter, HaDi MaBouDi, Hiruni Samadi Galpayage Dona, & Lars Chittka 2018. Counting Insects. *Philosophical Transactions of the Royal Society B: Biological Sciences* 373:20160513.

Sloane, Stephanie, Renée Baillargeon, & David Premack 2012. Do Infants Have a Sense of Fairness? *Psychological Science* 23:196–204.

Smith, David E., Frank N. Willis, & Joseph Gier 1980. Success and Interpersonal Touch in a Competitive Setting. *Journal of Nonverbal Behavior* 5:26–34.

Smith, Michael E. 2003. *The Aztecs*. 2nd Ed. Malden: Blackwell.

Smith, W. Robertson 1885 [1903]. *Kinship and Marriage in Early Arabia*. London: Adam & Charles Black.

Smith, William Robertson 1889 [1927]. *Lectures on the Religion of the Semites: The Fundamental Institutions*. Edinburgh: Adam and Charles Black. [3rd ed. reprinted in New York by KTAV.]

Smuts, R. Malcolm 1989. Public Ceremony and Royal Charisma: The English Royal Entry in London, 1485–1642. In A. L. Beier, David Cannadine , & James

M. Rosenheim, Eds., *The First Modern Society: Essays in Honor of Lawrence Stone* (pp. 65–93). Cambridge: Cambridge University Press.

Sobal, Jeffrey 2000. Sociability and Meals: Facilitation, Commensality, and Interaction. In Herbert L. Leiselman, Ed., *Dimensions of the Meal: The Science, Culture, Business and Art of Eating* (pp. 119–133). Gaithersburg: Aspen.

Sommerville, Jessica A., Marco F. H. Schmidt, Jung-eun Yun, & Monica Burns 2013. The Development of Fairness Expectations and Prosocial Behavior in the Second Year of Life. *Infancy* 18:40–66.

Soper, Alexander C. 1950. Aspects of Light Symbolism in Gandharan Sculpture (part 3). *Artibus Asiae* 13:63–85.

Soudavar, Abolala 2009. The Vocabulary and Syntax of Iconography in Sasanian Iran. *Iranica Antiqua* 44:417–447.

Spencer, Herbert 1896. *The Principles of Sociology* (2nd ed.). Vol. 2, Part 1. New York: D. Appleton.

Spencer, Paul 1985. *The Maasai of Matapato: A Study of Rituals of Rebellion. International African Library*. Bloomington: Indiana University Press.

Sperber, Dan 1985. Anthropology and Psychology: Towards an Epidemiology of Representations. *Man* [new series] 20: 73–89.

Spiegel, John, & Pavel Machotka 1974. *Messages of the Body*. New York: Free Press.

Spokes, Annie C., & Elizabeth S. Spelke 2017. The Cradle of Social Knowledge: Infants' Reasoning about Caregiving and Affiliation. *Cognition* 159:102–116.

Srinivasan, Doris Meth 1997. *Many Heads, Arms, and Eyes: Origin, Meaning, and Form of Multiplicity in Indian Art*. Leiden: Brill.

Srinivasan, Mahesh, & Susan Carey 2010. The Long and the Short of It: On the Nature and Origin of Functional Overlap between Representations of Space and Time. *Cognition* 116(2):217–241.

Srinivasan, Saradha 1979. *Mensuration in Ancient India*. Delhi: Ajanti Publications.

Stacy, Pam J. 1997. Birth of a "Resident" Killer Whale off Victoria, British Columbia, Canada. *Marine Mammal Science* 13:504–508.

Stallman, Robert C. 1997. 787 `arî, In Willem A. VanGemeron, Ed., *New International Dictionary of Old Testament Theology and Exegesis* (Vol. 1, pp. 513–517). Grand Rapids: Zondervan.

Stausberg, Michael 2008. *Zarathustra and Zoroastrianism*. Margret Preisler-Weller, transl. Munich: Beck.

Stavans, Maayan, and Renée Baillargeon 2019. Infants Expect Leaders to Right Wrongs. *Proceedings of the National Academy of Sciences* 11:16292–16301.

Steele, Christina, Megan Richardson, Azwayla Taylor, Denis Tatone, & Ashley J. Thomas. 2024. Early Threads of Connection: Probing Infants' Early Understandings of Caregiving Relationships. In *Proceedings of the Annual Meeting of the Cognitive Science Society*, 6. https://escholarship.org/content/qt6vo8d2h2/qt6vo8d2h2.pdf.

Stephey, M. J. 2008. A Brief History of the Fist Bump. *Time*, June 5. www.time.com/time/nation/article/0,8599,1812102,00.html. Accessed April 22, 2025.

Stern, Theodore 1948. *The Rubber-Ball Games of the Americas. Monographs of the American Ethnological Society 17*. New York: Augustin.
Stevens, Jeffrey R., Justin N. Wood, & Marc D. Hauser 2007. When Quantity Trumps Number: Discrimination Experiments in Cotton-Top Tamarins (*Saguinus oedipus*) and Common Marmosets (*Calithrix jacchus*). *Animal Cognition 10*:429–437.
Stevenson, Mark 2009. Have It Your Way: Burger King to Change Mexican Ad. Associated Press, April 14. https://abc13.com/archive/6761185/.
Stevenson, Robert 1959. Ancient Peruvian Instruments. *The Galpin Society Journal* 12:17–43.
Stevenson, Robert 1968. *Mustic in Aztec and Inca Territory*. Berkeley: University of California Press.
Stierlin, Henri 1984. *Art of the Incas and Its Origins*. Betty & Peter Ross, Trans. New York: Rizzoli.
Stilla, Randall, Gopikrishna Deshpande, Stephen LaConte, Xiaoping Hu, & K. Sathian 2007. Posteromedial Parietal Cortical Activity and Inputs Predict Tactile Spatial Acuity. *Journal of Neuroscience* 27:11091–11102.
Stillman, Bruce, David Stewart, & Terri Grodzicker, Eds. 2007. *Clocks and Rhythms*. (Cold Spring Harbor Symposia on Quantitative Biology LXXII). Cold Spring Harbor Laboratory Press.
Stopka, Pavel & Romana Graciasová, 2001. Conditional Allogrooming in the Herb-Field Mouse. *Behavioral Ecology* 12:584–589.
Strathern, Andrew 1973. Kinship, Descent and Locality: Some New Guinea Examples. In Jack Goody, Ed., *The Character of Kinship* (pp. 21–33). Cambridge: Cambridge University Press.
Strathern, Andrew, & Marilyn Strathern 1971. *Self Decoration in Mount Hagen*. Toronto: University of Toronto Press.
Strathern, Andrew, & Marilyn Strathern 1981. *Self-Decoration on Mount Hagen*. Toronto: University of Toronto Press.
Strawson, P. F. 1969. Intention and Convention in Speech Acts. In K. T. Fann, Ed., *Symposium on J. L. Austin* (pp. 380–400). London: Routledge & Kegan Paul.
Strid, Karin, & Marek Meristo 2020. Infants Consider the Distributor's Intentions in Resource Allocation. *Frontiers in Psychology* 11:596213.
Strommenger, Eva 1964. *5000 Years of the Art of Mesopotamia*. New York: Abrams.
Strong, Roy 1973. *Splendor at Court: Renaissance Spectacle and the Theater of Power*. Boston: Houghton Mifflin.
Surian, Luca, & Francesco Margoni 2020. First Steps Towards an Understanding of Procedural Fairness. *Developmental Science* 23(5):e12939. https://doi.org/10.1111/desc.12939.
Surian, Luca, & Laura Franchin 2017. Toddlers Selectively Help Fair Agents. *Frontiers in Psychology* 8:944.
Suvilehto. Juulia T., Lauri Nummenmaa, Tokiko Harada, Robin I. M. Dunbar, Riitta Hari, Robert Turner, Norihiro Sadato, & Ryo Kitada 2019. Cross-

Cultural Similarity in Relationship-Specific Social Touching 2019. *Proceedings of the Royal Society B*. 286 0467. http://doi.org/10.1098/rspb.2019.0467.
Sword, George 1896. The Pipe. Bruce Means, interpreter. In James Walker 1980, *Lakota Belief and Ritual* (pp. 82–83). Edited by Raymond J. DeMallie & Elaine A. Jahner. Lincoln, Nebraska: University of Nebraska Press.
Tajfel, Henri, Ed. 1978. *Differentiation between Social Groups: Studies in the Social Psychology of Intergroup Relations*. London: Academic Press.
Tang, Joey, Jamie Ward, & Brian Butterworth 2008. Number Forms in the Brain. *Journal of Cognitive Neuroscience*, *20*, 1547–1556.
Taub, Sarah F. 2001. *Language from the Body: Iconicity and Metaphor in American Sign Language*. Cambridge: Cambridge University Press.
Taube, Karl A. 1992. The Iconography of Mirrors in Teotihuacan. In Janet Catherine Berlo, Ed., *Art, Ideology, and the City of Teotihuacan. A Symposium at Dumbarton Oaks 8th and 9th October 1988* (pp. 169–204). Washington DC: Dumbarton Oaks.
Taylor, Claire 2007. From the Whole Citizen Body? The Sociology of Election and Lot in the Athenian Democracy. *Hesperia: The Journal of the American School of Classical Studies at Athens* 76:323–345.
Tecwyn, Emma C., Stephanie Denison, Emily J. E. Messer, & Daphna Buchsbaum 2017. Intuitive Probabilistic Inference in Capuchin Monkeys. *Animal Cognition* 243–256.
Tegnaeus, Harry 1952. *Blood Brothers: An Ethno-Sociological Study of the Institutions of Blood-Brotherhood with Special Reference to Africa*. New York: Philosophical Library.
Testart, Alain 1987. Game Sharing Systems and Kinship Systems among Hunter-Gatherers. *Man* [new series] 22: 287–304.
Thayer, Stephen 1982. Social Touching. In William Schiff & Emerson Foulke, Eds., *Tactual Perception: A Sourcebook* (pp. 263–304). Cambridge: Cambridge University Press.
Thomas, Ashley J. 2024. Cognitive Representations of Social Relationships and their Developmental Origins. *Behavioral and Brain Sciences*, 1–53.
Thomas, Ashley J., Brandon Woo, Daniel Nettle, Elizabeth Spelke, & Rebecca Saxe 2022. Early Concepts of Intimacy: Young Humans Use Saliva Sharing to Infer Close Relationships. *Science* 375:311–315.
Thompson, Stith 1989. *Motif-Index of Folk-Literature*. Rev. & enlarged ed. Bloomington: Indiana University Press.
Thomsen, Lotte 2020. The Developmental Origins of Social Hierarchy: How Infants and Young Children Mentally Represent and Respond to Power and Status. *Current Opinion in Psychology* 33:201–208.
Thomsen, Lotte, & Susan Carey 2013. Core Cognition of Social Relations. In Mahzarin Banaji & Susan A. Gelman, Eds., *Navigating the Social World: What Infants, Children, and Other Species Can Teach Us* (pp. 17–22). Oxford: Oxford University Press.
Thomsen, Lotte, Willem E. Frankenhuis, McCaila Ingold-Smith, & Susan Carey 2011. Big and Mighty: Preverbal Infants Mentally Represent Social Dominance. *Science* 331:477–480.

Thomson, Karen, & Jonathon Slocum 2011. Ancient Sanskrit Online. Series Introduction. https://lrc.la.utexas.edu/eieol_toc/vedol. Accessed June 7, 2025.

Thueux, Ernest n.d. (possibly 1978). *Langue Möre: Classification des Mots.* Guilongou, Oubri Tenga, Burkina Faso: Centre d'Étude de Langue Guilongou.

Tibbetts, Elizabeth A., Juanita Pardo-Sanchez, & Chloe Weise 2022. The Establishment and Maintenance of Dominance Hierarchies. *Philosophical Transactions of the Royal Society B* 377:20200450.

Ting, Francisca, Zijing He, & Renée Baillargeon 2019. Toddlers and Infants Expect Individuals to Refrain from Helping an Ingroup Victim's Aggressor. *Proceedings of the National Academy of Sciences* 116:6025–6034.

Tingey, Carol 1992. Sacred Kettledrums in the Temples of Central Nepal. *Asian Music* 23:97–103. http://www.jstor.org/stable/834175.

Tlusty, B. Ann 2001. *Bachus and Civic Order: The Culture of Drink in Early Modern Germany.* Charlottesville: University Press of Virginia.

Tolaas, Jon 1991. Notes on the Origin of Some Spatialization Metaphors. *Metaphor and Symbol* 6:203–218. https://doi.org/10.1207/s15327868ms0603_4.

Tolstoy, Paul 1989. Caopexco and Tlatilco: Sites with Olmec Materials in the Basin of Mexico. In Robert J. Sharer & David C. Grove, Eds., *Regional Perspectives on the Olmec* (pp. 85–121). Cambridge: Cambridge University Press.

Toren, Christina 1990 *Making Sense of Hierarchy: Cognition as Social Process in Fiji.* London School of Economics Monographs on Social Anthropology No. 61. London: Athlone Press.

Travis, William 1999. Representing "Christ as Giant" in Early Medieval Art. *Zeitschrift für Kunstgeschichte* 62. Bd., H. (2):167–189. www.jstor.org/stable/1482979.

Trigger, Bruce G. 1990. Monumental Architecture: A Thermodynamic Explanation of Symbolic Behavior. *World Architecture* 22(2):119–132.

Trigger, Bruce G. 2003. *Understanding Early Civilizations: A Comparative Study.* Cambridge: Cambridge University Press.

Trumbell, H. Clay 1885. *The Blood Covenant: A Primitive Rite and Its Bearing on Scripture.* New York: Scribner's.

Tuan, Yi-Fu 1977. *Space and Place: The Perspective of Experience.* Minneapolis: University of Minnesota Press.

Tunçgenç, Bahar, & Emma Cohen 2016. Movement Synchrony Forges Social Bonds Across Group Divides. *Frontiers in Psychology* 7:782. http://dx.doi.org/10.3389/fpsyg.2016.00782.

Tunçgenç, Bahar, Emma Cohen, & Christine Fawcett 2015. Rock with Me: The Role of Movement Synchrony in Infants' Social and Nonsocial Choices. *Child Development* 86:976–984.

Turner, Alvin O. 2023. Cherokee Outlet Opening. Encyclopedia of Oklahoma History and Culture. www.okhistory.org/publications/enc/entry.php?entry=CHo21. Accessed September 14, 2023.

Turner, Terence S. 1980. The Social Skin. In *Not Work Alone: A Cross-Cultural View of Activities Superfluous to Survival* (pp. 112–140). Jeremy Cherfas & Roger Lewin, Eds. Beverly Hills: Sage.

Turner, Victor 1967. *The Forest of Symbols: Aspects of Ndembu Ritual.* Ithaca: Cornell University Press.

Turner, Victor 1969. *The Ritual Process: Structure and Anti-Structure.* London: Routledge and Kegan Paul.

Turner, Victor 1973. The Center Out There: Pilgrim's Goal. *History of Religions* 12:191–230.

Turner, Victor 1975. *Revelation and Divination in Ndembu Ritual.* Ithaca and London: Cornell University Press.

Twain, Mark 1876 [2004]. *The Adventures of Tom Sawyer.* [no place given]: Borders Classics Editions.

Tylor, Edward B. 1871. *Primitive Culture: Researches into the Development of Mythology, Philosophy, Religion, Art, and Custom.* London: J. Murray.

Tylor, Edward B. 1878. *Researches into the Early History of Mankind and Development of Civilization.* 3rd ed., rev. London: John Murray.

Ubbelohde-Doering, Heinrich 1954. *The Art of Ancient Peru.* 2nd ed. New York: Praeger.

Ueland, Jeff, & Barney Warf 2006. Racialized Topographies: Altitude and Race in Southern Cities. *The Geographical Review* 96:50–78.

Urbanus, Jason 2008. Eternal Embrace. *Archaeology* 61(1). https://archive.archaeology.org/0801/abstracts/valdaro.html.

Van Beek, Walter E. A 1991. Dogon Restudied: A Field Evaluation of the Work of Marcel Griaule. *Current Anthropology* 32(2):139–167.

van de Mieroop, Marc 2003. Reading Babylon. *American Journal of Archaeology* 107:257–275.

van Gennep, Arnold 1908 [1960]. *The Rites of Passage.* Monika B. Vizedom & Gabrielle L. Caffe, Trans. Chicago: University of Chicago Press.

VanGemeren, Willem A. 1997. Index of Semantic Fields. In Willem A. VanGemeron, Ed., *New International Dictionary of Old Testament Theology and Exegesis* (Vol. 5, pp. 1–216). Grand Rapids: Zondervan.

Vansina, Jan 1969. The Bells of Kings. *The Journal of African History* 10:187–197.

Vansina, Jan 1989. Deep-Down Time: Political Tradition in Central Africa. *History in Africa* 16:341–362.

Vansina, Jan 1994. *Living with Africa.* Madison: University of Wisconsin Press.

Vanstiphout, H. 1984. On the Sumerian Disputation between the Hoe and the Plough. *Aula Orientalis* 2:239.

Vermeulen, A. J. 1956. *The Semantic Development of Gloria in Early-Christian Latin. Latinitas Christianormum Primaeva*, Vol. 12. Nijmegen: Dekker & van de Vegt.

Vienna Convention on Diplomatic Relations and Optional Protocols 1961. From the web site of the Organization of American States, Department of Legal Services. www.oas.org/legal/english/docs/viennaconvdiplomrelat..htm. Accessed August 12, 2023.

Voget, Fred W. 1984. *The Shoshoni-Crow Sun Dance.* Norman: University of Oklahoma Press.

Von Falkenhausen, Lothar 1993. *Suspended Music: Chime-bells in the Culture of Bronze Age China.* Berkeley: University of California Press.

von Gernet, Alexander 2000. North American Indigenous Nicotania Use and Tobacco Shamanism: The Early Documentary Record, 1520–1660. In Joseph C. Winter, Ed., *Tobacco Use by Native North Americans: Sacred Smoke and Silent Killer* (pp. 59–78). Norman: University of Oklahoma Press.

von Hecker, Ulrich, Karl Christoph Klauer, & Sindhuja Sankaran 2013. Embodiment of Social Status: Verticality Effects in Multilevel Rank-Orders. *Social Cognition* 31:374–389.

von Sicard, Harald V. 1942. The Ancient East African Bantu Drum. *Ethnos* 1:49–54.

Waldman, Nahum M. 1984. A Note on Ezekiel 1:18. *Journal of Biblical Literature* 103:614–618.

Walker, Barbara 1969. It's All the Fault of Adam. In Barbara Walker, Ed., *The Dancing Palm Tree and Other Nigerian Folktales* (pp. 55–62). New York: Four Winds Press (Macmillan).

Walker, Iain 2012. *Ntsambu*, the Foul Smell of Home: Food, Commensality and Identity in the Comoros and in the Diaspora. *Food and Foodways* 20:187–210.

Walker, J. D. 1917. The Sun Dance and other Ceremonies of the Oglala Division of the Teton Dakota. *Anthropological Papers of the American Museum of Natural History*, Vol. 16, Part II. New York.

Wallace-Hadrill, Andrew 2003. Domus and Insulae in Rome: Families and Households. In David L. Balch & Carolyn Osiek, Eds., *Early Christian Families in Context: An Interdisciplinary Dialogue* (pp. 13–14). Grand Rapids: Eerdmans.

Wallis, Neill J. 2008. Networks of History and Memory: Creating a Nexus of Social Identities in Woodland Period Mounds on the Lower St Johns River, Florida. *Journal of Social Archaeology* 8:236–271. https://doi.org/10.1177/1469605308089972.

Walsh, Vincent 2003. A Theory of Magnitude: Common Cortical Indices of Time, Space and Quantity. *Trends in Cognitive Science* 11, 483–488.

Walther, Fritz R. 1984. *Communication and Expression in Hoofed Mammals*. Bloomington: Indiana University Press.

Wang, Honyuan 1993. *The Origins of Chinese Characters*. Beijing: Sinolingua.

Wang, Ying, & Annette M. E. Henderson 2018. Just Rewards: 17-month-Old Infants Expect Agents to Take Resources According to the Principles Of Distributive Justice. *Journal of Experimental Child Psychology* 172:25–40.

Wason, Paul K. 1994. *The Archeology of Rank*. Cambridge: Cambridge University Press.

Watkins, Calvert 2000. *The American Heritage Dictionary of Indo-European Roots*, 2nd ed. Boston: Houghton Mifflin.

Watson, James L. 1987. From the Common Pot: Feasting with Equals in Chinese Society. *Anthropos* 82:389–401.

Watson, Jane M., K. Jennifer Campbell, & Kevin F. Collis 1999. The Structural Development of the Concept of Fraction by Young Children. *Journal of Structural Learning & Intelligent Systems* 13:171–193.

Watson, William 1975. *Realistic Style in the Art of Han and T'ang China*. Hull: University of Hull.

Watson, William 2000. *The Arts of China 900–1620*. New Haven: Yale University Press.

Watts, Ian 2018. Ochre and Human Evolution. *International Encyclopedia of Anthropology*. Wiley Online Library. https://doi.org/10.1002/9781118924396.wbiea1811.

Weber, Max. *Economy and Society: A New Translation 2019*. Keith Tribe, Ed. & Transl. Harvard University Press, 2019.

Weinfeld, M. 1995. Kabod. In G. Johannes Botterweck, Helmer Ringgren, & Heinz-Zosef Fabry, Eds., *Theological Dictionary of the Old Testament*, Vol. 7 (pp. 22–38). Translated by David E. Green. Grand Rapids: William B. Eerdmans.

Weissman, Ronald E. 1982. *Ritual Brotherhood in Renaissance Florence*. New York: Academic Press.

Wells, Rebecca 1996. *Divine Secrets of the Ya-Ya Sisterhood: A Novel*. New York: Harper Collins.

Wen, Wu, & Sun Shuming 2002, *Ancient Sculpture*. Beijing: Foreign Language Press.

West, George A. 1934. *Tobacco, Pipes and Smoking Customs of the American Indians. Bulletin of the Public Museum of the City of Milwaukee* 17:1–994 [reprinted 1970]. Westport: Greenwood.

West, Martin L. 2007. *Indo-European Poetry and Myth*. Oxford: Oxford University Press.

Westermarck, Edward 1926. *Ritual and Belief in Morocco*. London: Macmillan

Western, John 1996 [1981]. *Outcast Cape Town*. Berkeley: University of California Press.

Wetzel, Patricia J. 1993. The Language of Vertical Relationships and Linguistic Analysis. *Multilingua* 12:387–406.

Whitaker, Jarrod L. 2000. Divine Weapons and *Tejas* in the Two Indian Epics. *Indo-Iranian Journal* 43: 87–113.

White, David Gordon 2003. *Kiss of the Yoginī: "Tantric Sex" in Its South Asian Context*. Chicago: University of Chicago Press.

White, Geoffrey M. 1985 Premises and Purposes in a Solomon Islands Ethnopsychology. In Geoffrey M. White and John Kirkpatrick (Eds.), *Person, Self and Experience: Exploring Pacific Ethnopsychologies* (pp. 328–366). Los Angeles: University of California Press.

White, Peter A. 2009. Perception of Forces Exerted by Objects in Collision Events. *Psychological Review* 116:580–601.

White, Theodore 1961. *The Making of the President, 1960*. New York : Atheneum.

Whitehead, Hal 2003. *Sperm Whales: Social Evolution in the Ocean*. Chicago: University of Chicago Press.

Whitehead, Hal, & Linda Weilgart 2000. The Sperm Whale: Social Females and Roving Males. In Janet Mann, Richard C. Connor, Peter L. Tyack, & Hal Whitehead, Eds., *Cetacean Societies: Field Studies of Dolphins and Whales* (pp. 154–172). Chicago: University of Chicago Press.

Whitehead, Harriet 2000. *Food Rules: Hunting, Sharing, and Tabooing Game in Papua New Guinea*. Ann Arbor: University of Michigan Press.

Whiting, John W. M. 1941. *Becoming a Kwoma: Teaching and Learning in a New Guinea Tribe.* New Haven: Published for the Institute of Human Relations by Yale University Press.

Whiting, John W. M. 1961 Socialization Process and Personality. In Francis L. K. Hsu, Ed., *Psychological Anthropology*. Dorsey Press.

Wieger, L. 1965 [1927]. *Chinese Characters: Their Origin, Etymology, History, Classification and Significance; A Thorough Study from Chinese Documents*, 2nd ed. L. Davrout, transl. New York: Paragon and Dover.

Wiessner, Polly 2001. Of Feasting and Value: Enga Feasts in a Historical Perspective (Papua New Guinea). In Michael Dietler & Brian Hayden, Eds., *Feasts: Archeological and Ethnographic Perspectives on Food, Politics, and Power* (pp. 115–143). Washington, DC: Smithsonian Institution.

Wilkinson, Gerald S. 1984. Reciprocal Food Sharing in the Vampire Bat. *Nature* 308:181–184.

Wilkinson, Gerald S. 1985. The Social Organization of the Common Vampire Bat I. Pattern and Cause of Association. *Behavioral Ecology and Sociobiology* 17:111–121.

Williams, Edward V. 1985. *The Bells of Russia.* Princeton: Princeton University Press.

Williams, Peter 1993. *The Organ in Western Culture 750–1250*. Cambridge Studies in Medieval and Renaissance Music. Cambridge: Cambridge University Press.

Williams, Robert A. 1997. *Linking Arms Together: American Indian Treaty Visions of Law and Peace, 1600–1800*. New York: Oxford University Press.

Wilson V. 1999. Dress and the Cultural Revolution. In V. Steele & J. Major, Eds., *China Chic: East Meets West* (pp. 167–186). New Haven: Yale University Press.

Wilson, Ben 1998. *Dolphins of the World.* Stillwater: Voyager.

Wilson, Peter J. 1988. *The Domestication of the Human Species.* New Haven: Yale University Press.

Winter, Irene J. 1987. Women in Public: The Disk of Enheduanna, the Beginning of the Office of En-Priestess, and the Weight of Visual Evidence. In Jean-Marie Durand, Ed., *La Femme dans le Proche-Orient Antique* (pp. 189–201). Compte Rendu de la XXXIIIe Rencontre Assyrologique Internationale. Paris: Editions Recherche sur les Civilisations.

Witkower, Zachary, Jessica L. Tracy, Joey T. Cheng, & Joseph Henrich 2020. Two Signals of Social Rank: Prestige and Dominance are Associated with Distinct Nonverbal Displays. *Journal of Personality and Social Psychology* 118:89–120.

Wolf, Sibylle, Nicholas J. Conard, Harald Floss, Rimtautas Dapschauskas, Elizabeth Velliky, & Andrew W. Kandel 2018. The Use of Ochre and Painting During the Upper Paleolithic of the Swabian Jura in the Context of the Development of Ochre Use in Africa and Europe. *Open Archaeology* 4:185–205. https://doi.org/10.1515/opar-2018-0012.

Wolfson, Elliot R. 2004. Hermeneutics of Light in Medieval Kabbalah. In Matthew T. Kapstein, Ed., *The Presence of Light: Divine Radiance and Religious Experience* (pp. 105–118). Chicago: University of Chicago Press.

Woolley, Kaitlin, & Ayelet Fishbach 2019. Shared Plates, Shared Minds: Consuming from a shared Plate Promotes Cooperation. *Psychological Science* 30:541–552.

Wu, Xiangci, Huibin Jia, Enguo Wang, Chenguang Du, Xianghua Wu, & Caiping Dang 2016. Vertical Position of Chinese Power Words Influences Power Judgments: Evidence from Spatial Compatibility Task and Event-Related Potentials. *International Journal of Psychophysiology* 102:55–61.

Xie, Guanghui G. 1997. *The Composition of Common Chinese Characters: An Illustrated Account.* Beijing: Beijing da xue chu ban she.

Yamagata, Naoko 1994. *Homeric Morality.* Leiden: E. J. Brill.

Yamamoto, Kosho. 2007. *The Mahayana Mahaparinirvana Sutra.* Edited, revised, and copyright by Tony Page, Taisho Tripitaka Vol. 12, No. 374. [Translated into English from Dharmakshema's Chinese version, 1973.] http://bodhimarga .org/docs/Mahaparinirvana_Sutra_Yamamoto_Page_2007.pdf.

Yearsley, David 2002. An Ideal Organ and Its Experts Across the Seventeenth Century. In Kerala J. Snyder, Ed., *The Organ as a Mirror of Its Time: North European Reflections, 1610–2000* (pp. 93–111). Oxford: Oxford University Press.

YellowBridge. [n.d.] Chinese Language Center [website]. www.yellowbridge.co m/chinese/character-dictionary.php.

Young, Frank W. 1965. *Initiation Ceremonies: A Cross-Cultural Study of Status Dramatization.* Indianapolis: Bobbs-Merrill.

Yü, Chün-Fang 2001. *Kuan-yin: The Chinese Transformation of Avalokiteśvara.* New York: Columbia University Press.

Zahavi, Amotz., Zahavi, Avishag 1999. *The Handicap Principle: A Missing Piece of Darwin's Puzzle.* Oxford: Oxford University Press.

Zanolie, Kiki, Saskia van Dantzig, Inge Boot, Jasper Wijnen, Thomas W. Schubert, Steffen R. Giessner, & Diane Pecher 2012. Mighty Metaphors: Behavioral and ERP Evidence that Power Shifts Attention on a Vertical Dimension. *Brain and Cognition* 78:50–58.

Zee, A. 1986. *Fearful Symmetry: The Search for Beauty in Modern Ohysics.* Princeton: Princeton University Press.

Zelizer, Viviana A. 1994. *The Social Meaning of Money: Pin Money, Paychecks, Poor Relief, and Other Currencies.* New York: Basic Books.

Zemplini-Rabain, Jacqueline 1973 Food and the Strategy Involved in Learning Fraternal Exchange among Wolof Children. In Pierre Alexandre, Ed., *French Perspectives in African Studies* (pp. 221–233). London: Oxford University Press.

Zickfeld, Janis H., Thomas W. Schubert, Beate Seibt, et al. 2019. Kama Muta: Conceptualizing and Measuring the Experience Often Labelled Being Moved Across 19 Nations and 15 Languages. *Emotion* 19:402–424.

Ziv, Talee, & Jessica A. Sommerville 2017. Developmental Differences In Infants' Fairness Expectations from 6 to 15 Months of Age. *Child Development* 88:1930–1951.

ZivE, Talee, Jesse D. Whiteman, & Jessica A. Sommerville 2021. Toddlers' Interventions Toward Fair and Unfair Individuals. *Cognition* 214:104781 https:// doi.org/10.1016/j.cognition.2021.104781.

Index

For EU product safety concerns, contact us at Calle de José Abascal, 56–1°, 28003 Madrid, Spain or eugpsr@cambridge.org.

www.ingramcontent.com/pod-product-compliance
Ingram Content Group UK Ltd.
Pitfield, Milton Keynes, MK11 3LW, UK
UKHW021912141225
465965UK00009B/370

* 9 7 8 1 1 0 8 9 3 1 6 2 5 *